A LAWYER
LOOKS AT THE
GOSPELS

A LAWYER
LOOKS AT THE
GOSPELS

NORMAN GRIFFITH

WINEPRESS WP PUBLISHING

Packaged by WinePress Publishing, PO Box 428, Enumclaw, WA 98022. The views expressed or implied in this work do not necessarily reflect those of WinePress Publishing. Ultimate design, content, and editorial accuracy of this work are the responsibilities of the author.

ISBN 1-57921-089-9
Library of Congress Catalog Card Number: 97-62532

CONTENTS

CHAPTER 1: A LAWYER LOOKS AT THE GOSPELS

CHAPTER 2: JESUS' LIFE AND MINISTRY

Contents

CHAPTER 3: JESUS IN AND AROUND JERUSALEM

CHAPTER 4: JESUS' RESURRECTION AND ASCENSION

CHAPTER 5: JESUS' MOVEMENT AND ITS ORGANIZATION

CHAPTER 6: THE BACKGROUND FOR UNDERSTANDING
JESUS' TEACHINGS

Contents

CHAPTER 7: KINGDOM TOPICS

CHAPTER 8: JESUS' TEACHINGS ON RICHES

Chapter 9: Church Topics

Chapter 10: Spiritual Laws

Contents

CHAPTER 11: SOCIAL TOPICS

CHAPTER 12: JESUS AND GOD

CHAPTER 13: JESUS' MISSION AND AUTHORITY

CHAPTER 14: THE HOLY SPIRIT / GOD / THE DEVIL

CHAPTER 15: SIN / SALVATION

CHAPTER 16: PRAYER

Contents

CHAPTER 17: FASTING / BAPTISM / PIOUS ACTS / CHARITY

CHAPTER 18: THE HEALINGS

CHAPTER 19: MISCELLANEOUS MIRACLES

CHAPTER 1

A LAWYER LOOKS AT
THE GOSPELS

THE RECORD

J esus Christ was either a man, or some unique being. The issue
is what he was, not what either his followers or his enemies say.
The record must be examined.

If, as Christians affirm, he is the only Son of God, great and
particular attention must be paid to what he said and did. If, as
others claim, Jesus was just a man, he is entitled to the respect that
is paid any other man; and what he said and did must be examined
with care before an opinion is formed as to his life and work.

The record of what Jesus said and did is found in the four New
Testament Gospels—Matthew, Mark, Luke and John—plus a few
words in the New Testament outside those Gospels. Scholars have
examined many other writings, including the apocryphal gospels,
but the primary historical sources for Jesus' life and work remain
the four Gospels.

That is not to say that those Gospels contain all Jesus said and
did. We know that they do not since the Gospels themselves state
to the contrary. John's Gospel states:

> And many other signs truly did Jesus in the presence of his dis-
> ciples, which are not written in this book. *J 20:30*

It is also certain that other early books about Jesus once existed. Luke's Gospel begins with these words:

> Forasmuch as *many* have taken in hand to set forth in order a declaration of those things which are most surely believed among us, even as they delivered them unto us, which from the beginning were eyewitnesses, and ministers of the word; it seemed good *to me also*, having had perfect understanding of all things from the very first, to write unto thee in order, most excellent Theophilus, that thou mightest know the certainty of those things, wherein thou has been instructed. *L 1:1–4*

These other books have for the most part perished; and what has survived is useful mainly as background material to illuminate our primary sources, the four Gospels.

It must be stated immediately that Jesus himself did not write those Gospels. In fact, it is common scholarly opinion that it was at least about twenty-five years after Jesus' crucifixion before they began to be written. However, they do contain in detail many conversations of and statements made by Jesus, as well as his actions.

It may be true, at least in part, that the Gospels were written by Christians, for Christians. Allowance must be made for that fact; but after that allowance is made, the Gospels remain valid historical sources, in fact, historical sources technically superior to other sources routinely accepted for the history of the Greek and Roman world. In any movement, particularly in its beginning phases, the available source documents are likely to have been written by adherents to the movement. It was no different with Christianity.

When Christianity began, it seemed an obscure Jewish sect. One of the Jewish charges against Paul was that he was "a ringleader of the sect of the Nazarenes." *Acts 24:5* Porcius Festus, the Roman procurator of Judea, summarized these charges against Paul as involving "certain questions against him of their own superstition, and of one Jesus, which was dead, whom Paul affirmed to be alive." *Acts 25:19* When Paul appealed to Caesar and was sent to Rome around A.D. 59, the chief Jews of Rome told him:

> But we desire to hear of thee what thou thinkest: for as concerning *this sect*, we know that every where it is spoken against. *Acts 28:22*

This obscure sect left only brief, obscure and disputed traces in Roman history books and in the books of Josephus, the first-century Jewish historian. Accordingly, the historical evidence of earliest Christianity is found in its own documents, the various writings that were later collected as the New Testament. This is precisely what would be expected since no one else would care about chronicling this obscure group.

The Gospels are not records of the early church, but they were written to meet the need of that church to have a written record of the acts and words of Jesus for those who never saw him in the flesh. It is likely that all of the Gospels were written for the purpose expressly stated in John's Gospel:

> But these [signs] are written, that ye might believe that Jesus is the Christ, the Son of God; and that believing ye might have life through his name. *J 20:31*

This persuasive purpose must, of course, be considered in weighing what the Gospels say but does not destroy their historical value. Many scholars concede the historical value of the first three Gospels—Matthew, Mark and Luke—although they may challenge parts thereof. These three Gospels are called the synoptic Gospels since they follow a common outline of events in the life of Jesus.

Some scholars challenge John's Gospel as a record of Jesus' own statements. This seems unscientific for the following reasons. We are, historically speaking, investigating a first-century Jew, and there are essentially only four historical sources of his life and works: the four Gospels. The question is whether we can deduce from the synoptic Gospels that the sayings of Jesus as recorded in John's Gospel are not Jesus' own sayings. All that can be said is that many of these sayings are different, and the sayings in John's Gospel, if authentic, present a different aspect of Jesus. That is, however, quite different from claiming that Jesus' sayings in John's Gospel are not, in fact, sayings of Jesus. We are investigating an unknown, and we cannot reject one of our sources by assuming it is untrue simply because it is different.

Some scholars go further and contend that many of the statements attributed to Jesus by the first three Gospels are not, in fact, his. These scholars, either consciously or unconsciously, have selected as "authentic" certain statements by Jesus in the Gospels from the whole stock of Gospel statements attributed to him. They then proceed to test all of the Gospel statements attributed to Jesus against those statements of his that they have selected as "authentic."

If it is assumed (as it must for historical investigation) that we do not know which of Jesus' statements in the Gospels are authentic, there is no objective basis for selecting the "authentic" test statements, and each scholar is actually using his own *a priori* beliefs as to what Jesus is likely to have said in order to pick the "authentic" test statements.

Those scholars discarding statements attributed to Jesus by the Gospels may claim that they are simply applying rules of evidence. Their "rules" are not the rules of evidence used in courts of law, but are instead summary statements of scholars' lore for construing the Gospels as documents. These summary statements of scholars' lore are not, however, accepted by all scholars.

Now it is true that the Gospels, like all documents, may have problems of construction and analysis, but the only acceptable rules of construction and analysis are those that apply to all documents, not just Gospel documents. Universal and objective rules of construction and analysis must be distinguished from summary statements of assumptions about what Jesus was like, what he said, and how he said it. These are the very questions under investigation.

If the "rules" relied upon are really simply those assumptions, then no matter how learned and laborious is the "rule" analysis, its results cannot rise any higher than the initial assumptions. That is why scholars using this "rule" analysis often do not agree whether or not a given statement attributed to Jesus by the Gospels is his.

All we have are the texts of the Gospels as best generations of scholars have been able to restore and translate them. They are the record, and we should rely upon the whole record, and not just bits and pieces thereof. Our duty is to respect the integrity of the Gospels as historical documents and not arbitrarily exclude parts thereof not congenial to us. The only appropriate investigatory assumption is that Jesus, like anyone else, may have said many different things in many different ways.

Everyone can read and compare the words of Jesus as we have them in the Gospels. The ultimate question is simply whether the words of Jesus, as reported, seem to ring true. This is basically a question of human experience on which scholars, despite their massive learning, have no particular competence. That competence ends when they have restored and translated the Gospel texts as best they can.

It should be noted that the historical value of the four Gospels is not destroyed by the possibility that other earlier documents were used to assist their authors. The most famous example is the hypothetical document "Q", from the German word *quelle*, meaning "source." That hypothetical document is supposed to have consisted of material common to the Gospels of Matthew and Luke, but not appearing in Mark. If such a document existed and was used as a convenient source of Jesus' sayings, it does not destroy the Gospels as historically reliable documents—although such a source history may be helpful in interpreting the texts of the Gospels as we now have them.

The introduction to the Gospel of Luke may refer to just such sources:

> Forasmuch as *many* have taken in hand *to set forth in order* a declara-
> tion of those things which are most surely believed among us, even
> as they delivered them unto us, which from the beginning were eye-
> witnesses, and ministers of the word; it seemed good to me also,
> having had perfect understanding of all things from the very first, to
> write unto them *in order*, most excellent Theophilus . . . L 1:1–3

In substance, Luke states that "many" had written accounts and he had received such accounts and that "it seemed good" to him to write his own account. That account is the Gospel of Luke.

19

Luke expressly claims that these accounts and his account were based upon the statements of persons who "from the beginning were eyewitnesses and ministers of the word." L 1:2

The claim that the Gospels are eyewitness accounts is disputed in many and elaborate ways by various scholars. Here I have chosen to regard what is written in the Gospels as "the record" in the sense that that term is used by an appellate lawyer preparing an appeal. Just as an appellate lawyer must take the trial court record as a given, so I have taken the words and deeds of Jesus as recorded in the Gospels as a given.

As "the record" it must and will be meticulously and impartially quoted and analyzed. It will be examined with care and, I hope, some sophistication. The insights of generations of scholars will not be ignored. The inescapable fact remains, however, that if we are to know anything much of Jesus and his works, we must assume that "the record", so far as it goes, is generally accurate and reliable. Indeed, it is hard to see why much time should be spent on the Gospel record unless it is generally accurate and reliable.

The Gospel record seems to be a record of episodes and summaries of conversations, and that is the only way it is understandable to me and, I assume, the bulk of my readers. Scholars and others who wish to assume that this or that saying is or is not a saying of Jesus, or that this or that episode is a later construct and not a part of "the record", will no doubt continue in their assumptions, which are essentially no more than arguments. I have, however, considered such arguments in deciding whether the Gospel writers meant a particular section to be a part of "the record" or editorial material, which may be interspersed in even as bare a record as a stenographic transcript of testimony. Now, the Gospel writers were not stenographers but men compiling large blocks of material into books; and so there are inevitably additions in the form of introductions, transitions and conclusions.

Basically, my position is that these parts of "the record" do not require esoteric analysis to recognize and allow for, once it is remembered that Jesus spoke Aramaic, the Gospels were written in Greek, broken into chapters in the thirteenth century, split into numbered verses in 1551, and punctuated and paragraphed in various ways as the various translators have tried to render the Greek manuscripts into English.

The problem of what Greek manuscripts are to be used as the basis of the Greek text of the Gospels has involved generations of scholars, and their work continues; but essentially the Greek text is a composite based on fitting many manuscript versions together.

The Greek text then has to be translated into English, and these translations vary with the scholar or group of scholars producing them. Like expert witnesses at a trial, they do not always agree on how to render into English what Jesus said in Aramaic, as later written down in the Greek manuscripts, even with the help of manuscripts written in other ancient tongues like Syriac and Coptic.

I have used the King James Version as "the record" of Jesus' acts and words, for the simple reasons that its text is in the public domain, and its wordings are most familiar to most people. However, as will be seen from the detailed quotations of the Gospel record, the use of the King James Version does not usually involve a substantial meaning problem; and when it does, as when the wording in the King James is so archaic as to be obscure, I have, by a noted insertion in the quotation, supplied some currently understandable wording. In addition, for the same reasons, I have uniformly changed "Holy Ghost" to "Holy *Spirit*". That change is not otherwise noted but all of the other insertions are specifically noted, usually by inserting the modern word in brackets after the King James word. Otherwise I have attempted to quote meticulously the King James text.

Although I have quoted meticulously the King James text, I have felt free to drop the verse numbers (except at the end of quotations); to modernize spelling and names; to capitalize, paragraph and punctuate in the current fashion, in accordance with the apparent meaning of the text. Modern translations do this with their versions, and it is also helpful in understanding the meaning of the King James text. The capitalization, paragraphing and punctuation found in the English translations are not in the Greek text.

For these reasons, I have felt free to capitalize the English phrases "Kingdom of God" and "Kingdom of Heaven", to emphasize this important concept of Jesus, even though he may not have been speaking of a kingdom or realm in the ordinary earthly sense.

To break through the familiar King James words to their meanings, I have sometimes, for emphasis, italicized a word or phrase. Accordingly, I have not followed the established King James tradition of italicizing English words that are not based on equivalent Greek words in the Greek manuscripts.

The point is this: The acts and words of Jesus come to us across two thousand years and through a three-language lens—an Aramaic-Greek-English lens—from a first-century Jewish culture and society to the modern world. The Aramaic words spoken by Jesus come to us in manuscripts of ancient colloquial, not classical, Greek, which have been translated into English—a language then unknown and that did not exist for another thousand years and which continues to change. Accordingly, the acts and words of Jesus as stated in the Gospels are not to be read as if they were meticulously worded legal documents or systematic theological treatises.

Instead, the Gospel record resembles and is best understood as testimony of witnesses, interspersed here and there with notes and background material. It is, therefore, illuminating to compare in detail how the various Gospels report in parallel many sayings and incidents. It is often like reading different accounts by several witnesses of the same incident. These parallel accounts add a stereoscopic depth to "the record".

My intent is quite simple: to analyze every bit of "the record" to see what Jesus actually taught and did. Accordingly, I have attempted to quote every statement of Jesus' own words in full. I have not always quoted verbatim all parallel Gospel accounts of other matters if the differences between the accounts seemed insignificant or trivial. In such cases, I have put parentheses around the reference to the Gospel or Gospels not quoted verbatim. When such parallel accounts are found in the synoptic Gospels, I have usually quoted only Mark's account verbatim. I have done so because Mark's account is usually shorter; and I do not enter into the scholastic controversies over whether or not Matthew and Luke had Mark's Gospel to work from in writing their Gospels.

To make this outline as objective and factual as possible, I have attempted to give a specific source for each statement made when I have such a source. Each such source is listed immediately after the end of the sentence making the statement. This avoids the scholarly impedimenta of footnotes, but ties the statement to its source. Since my sources—Matthew, Mark, Luke and John—must each be referred to hundreds of times, I have used special short forms of abbreviations, without periods, which fit well at the end of sentences: *Mt* for Matthew, *Mk* for Mark, *L* for Luke and *J* for John. If there are several sources for a quotation or a statement, I cite them all but put last and in parenthesis those sources that are not precisely identical.

I have either quoted or cited every verse in each of the four Gospels, but I have not discussed in detail two blocks of material.

First, I have not discussed in detail the accounts of Jesus' genealogy, birth and infancy, which are found only in Matthew and Luke. *Mt 1 and 2:1–23; L 1:26–56, 2:1–20, 2:23–38.* I have, however, summarized from the Gospel sources the bare human facts as to Jesus' birth, family, and village boyhood.

Second, I have not discussed in detail the account of the birth of John the Baptist, which is found only in Luke. *L 1:5–25, 57–80* This seemed appropriate since the accounts of the birth of Jesus himself are not discussed.

The reason for this treatment of these two blocks of material is not my disbelief, but because I have accepted the judgment of Mark's and John's Gospels which omit them and focused like they do, on Jesus' ministry and teaching when he was an adult.

So far as I am concerned, the Gospels are "the record". My function is to take that record as I find it and summarize it into an outline of the acts and words of Jesus. I have tried to focus on Jesus' own words and let them speak for themselves. My goal, in which I have not often succeeded, was to make my commentary shorter than his words.

When Jesus' words are examined with care, it is evident that his teachings are subtle and intricate and the popular emphasis on a few familiar texts produces gross distortions of his claims and teachings. To the conservative, I say that if Jesus is truly Lord and did truly rise from the dead, his teachings in his lifetime cannot be ignored as a mere prelude to his death and resurrection. To the liberal, I say that Jesus' teachings show that he claimed more than being simply a great teacher and a noble man and that his causes were not limited to turning the other cheek and helping the poor and afflicted.

The basic premise of this outline is that Christianity is what Jesus said and did. Protestants, generally, and Evangelicals, especially, tend to see Jesus mainly through the words of Paul. My point is that Jesus' own words ought not to be neglected. Jesus' own words, as recorded in the Gospels, are not simply a prologue to Paul's Epistles. In a sense, the words of Jesus himself are text, while the writings of Paul are commentary.

The question is not whether Paul's Epistles are Christian scripture. They are. They have been from the earliest days of the Christian church:

> And account that the long suffering of our Lord is salvation; even as our beloved brother Paul also according to the wisdom given unto him hath written unto you; as also in *all his epistles*, speaking in them of these things; in which are some things hard to be understood, which they that are unlearned and unstable wrest, as they do also the *other scriptures*, unto their own destruction. *2 Peter 3:15*

But the Christian church is Jesus' church, and Paul was a convert to that church, a great convert but still a convert. Paul himself wrote:

> For we preach not ourselves, but Christ Jesus the Lord; and ourselves your servants for Jesus' sake. *2 Corinthians 4:5*

Paul also wrote that, "Every tongue should confess that 'Jesus Christ is Lord.'" *Philippians 2:11* If "Jesus is Lord," Jesus' own words must be primary; and I am sure that Paul would say, "Of course, how could it be otherwise?"

In Acts, Paul is quoted as saying:

> I have showed you all things, how that so laboring ye ought to support the weak, and to remember *the words of the Lord Jesus*, how he said, "It is more blessed to give than to receive." *Acts 20:35*

Paul looked back to the "words of our Lord Jesus Christ," writing:

> If any man teach otherwise, and the consent not to wholesome words, *even the words of our Lord Jesus Christ*, and to the doctrine which is according to godliness, he is proud, knowing nothing, but doting about questions and strifes of words, whereof cometh envy, strife, railings, evil surmisings. *1 Timothy 6:3–4*

Paul clearly distinguished his own words from Jesus' words and deferred to Jesus' words. Paul wrote:

> And unto the married I command, yet not I, *but the Lord,* let not the wife depart from her husband; but and if she depart, let her remain unmarried, or be reconciled to her husband, and let not the husband put away his wife. But to the rest speak I, *not the Lord.* If any brother hath a wife that believeth not, and she be pleased to dwell with him, let him not put her away. *1 Corinthians 7:10–12*

> Now concerning virgins I have *no commandment of the Lord;* yet I give my judgment, as one that hath obtained mercy of the Lord to be faithful. *1 Corinthians 7:25*

The test for Paul, as it should be for us, was what did Jesus say? This takes nothing from Paul; and his Epistles are illuminated by remembering that he wrote looking back to the words of Jesus whom he regarded as "the image of God"—"the image of the invisible God." *2 Corinthians 4:4; Colossians 1:15*

All persons who claim God as their Father will want to consider carefully one of Jesus' own statements directed to some Jews:

> If God were your Father, you would love me; for I proceeded forth and came from God; neither came I of myself, but he sent me.
>
> Why do ye not understand *my speech*? Even because ye can not hear *my word.*" J 8:42–43

This outline examines Jesus' own word and speech. Christians affirm that "Jesus Christ is Lord" and therefore will want to examine Jesus' own words with care. For others, Jesus is the founder of a great religion or an important historical figure whose words must be examined with care before judgment is passed upon either him or his religion.

We turn now to an examination of the record. A helpful introduction to the evidence is a brief summary of Jesus' life and works dating from around A.D. 41.

CAPSULE OVERVIEW OF JESUS' LIFE AND WORK SPOKEN IN A.D. 41

Humanly speaking, Jesus was a Jew. His key disciple, Peter, explained Jesus' life and mission to a Roman centurion in approximately A.D. 41 as follows:

> The word which God sent unto the children of Israel, preaching peace by Jesus Christ (he is Lord of all). That word, I say, ye know, which was published throughout all Judea, and began from Galilee, after the baptism which John preached; how God anointed Jesus of Nazareth with the Holy Spirit and with power, who went about doing good, and healing all that were oppressed of the devil; for God was with him.
>
> And *we were witnesses of all things which he did* both in the land of the Jews, and in Jerusalem; whom they slew and hanged on a tree: him God raised up the third day, *and shewed [showed] him openly; not to all people, but unto witnesses chosen before of God, even to us, who did eat and drink with him after he rose from the dead.* And he commanded us to preach unto the people, and to testify that it is he which was ordained of God to be the Judge of quick and dead. To him gave all the prophets witness, that through his name whosoever believeth in him shall receive remission of sins. *Acts 10:36–43*

Peter began his explanation to this Roman officer by stating that "God anointed Jesus *of Nazareth* with the Holy Spirit and power . . . for God was with him." *Acts 10:38* Shortly after Jesus' resurrection when preaching to his fellow Jews, Peter described Jesus as, "Jesus *of Nazareth*, a man approved of God among you by miracles and wonders and signs, which God did by him in the midst of you, as ye yourselves also know." *Acts 2:22*

Jesus grew up and lived in Nazareth, a town in Galilee, one of the northern provinces of Israel. He conducted a ministry both in Galilee and in Judea. The precise year of his birth is disputed, but it was around 4 to 6 B.C. Herod the Great, who was king at the time of Jesus' birth, died in 4 B.C., and this establishes the latest possible year for this birth. *Mt 2:1* Jesus' life was short, and he was crucified in Jerusalem around A.D. 29 or 30.

Jesus was baptized by John the Baptist, and shortly thereafter began his own ministry at about the age of thirty. *L 3:23* There is a statement in John's Gospel quoting some bystanders as taunting Jesus with this question:

> Thou art *not yet* fifty years old, and hast thou seen Abraham? *J 8:57*

This statement made by bystanders in the course of an argumentative dispute with Jesus does not establish that Jesus was then fifty. A careful analysis of all the evidence shows instead that Jesus was then in his early thirties.

Jesus' ministry is traditionally assumed to have lasted about three years, but detailed analyses of the Gospel sources produce various results ranging from one year to about three years.

Eyewitness Impressions of Jesus

Matthew concludes his account of the Sermon on the Mount with this statement:

> And it came to pass, when Jesus had ended these sayings, the people *were astonished* at his doctrine: for he taught them as one having authority, and not as the scribes. When he was come down from the mountain, great multitudes followed him. *Mt 7:28–29, 8:1*

The Mount was in Galilee near the Sea of Galilee. Sometime later Jesus was back in his own part of Galilee, in Nazareth, his home town. Both Matthew and Mark have accounts of this episode:

Mark	Matthew
And he went out from thence,	And when
and he came into	he was come into
his own country;	his own country,
and his disciples	
follow him.	
And when the Sabbath day	
was come,	
he began to teach	he taught them
in the synagogue:	in their synagogue,
and many hearing him	insomuch that they
were astonished,	*were astonished*,
saying,	and said,
"From whence hath	"Whence hath
this man these things?	this man
And what wisdom	this wisdom,
is this which is given	
unto him,	
that even such mighty works	and these mighty works?
are wrought by his hands?	
Is not this	Is not this
the carpenter	the carpenter's son?
the son of Mary,	Is not his mother called Mary?
the brother of James,	And his brethren James

MARK (cont.)	**MATTHEW** (cont.)
and Joses,	and Joses,
and of Judas, and Simon?	and Simon, and Judas?
And are not his sisters	And his sisters,
here with us?"	are they not all with us?
	Whence then hath this man
	all these things?"
And they *were offended*	And they *were offended*
at him.	*in him.*
But Jesus said	But Jesus said
unto them:	unto them:
"A prophet is not	"A prophet is not
without honor,	without honor,
but in his own country,	save in his own country,
and among his own kin,	
and in his own house."	and in his own house."
And he could there do no	And he did not
mighty work,	many mighty works there
save that he laid his hands	
upon a few sick folk,	
and healed them,	
And he marvelled	
because of their unbelief.	because of their unbelief.
And he went round about	*Mt 13:54–58*
the villages, teaching.	
Mk 6:1–6	

The crowds were "astonished" at a man who taught on his own authority rather than as an expositor of the Scripture and the traditions, like the scribes.

Much later at the Feast of the Tabernacles in Jerusalem when Jesus was teaching in the Temple, his listeners had the same reaction as the crowds in Galilee:

And the Jews *marvelled*, saying, "How knoweth this man letters, having never learned?" *J 7:15*

Jesus answered:

> My doctrine is not mine, but his that sent me. *J 7:16*

The synagogue congregation in Nazareth were also "astonished" at Jesus' wisdom and works, but in a negative way, bred of superficial familiarity. Actually they were offended at him. *Mk 6:3; Mt 13:57* They knew Jesus and his family, and that he was not a scribe, only a local layman.

Jesus' answer to their offended pride was to quote what was probably a common proverb:

> A prophet is not without honor, but in his own country, and among his own kin, and in his own house. *Mk 6:4 (Mt 13:57)*

His own synagogue doubted the wisdom of his teaching and questioned his mighty works. The necessary condition of belief was absent, and he could not do any miracles there, save heal a few sick. *Mk 6:5; Mt 13:58*

Jesus marvelled at their unbelief and continued to teach in the villages near Nazareth. *Mk 6:6* Perhaps Jesus had the members of the Nazareth synagogue in mind when he later told the story of the shut door and the Lord who answers the knock, saying:

> I know you not whence [who] ye are: Then shall ye begin to say, "We have eaten and drunk in thy presence, and thou hast taught in our streets." *L 13:25–26*

It is ironic that the crowds in Jerusalem at Jesus' final Passover answered the question, "Who is this?" by saying "This is Jesus, the prophet of *Nazareth* of Galilee." *Mt 21:10–11*

Despite the doubts of his own synagogue in Nazareth, the rumor in Galilee generally was:

> That a great prophet is risen up among us; and that God hath visited his people. *L 7:16*

> This is of a truth that prophet that should come into the world.
> *J 6:14*

The dominant impression Jesus made on people was that he was a prophet: for example, so thought the Samaritan woman at the well in Sychar; the blind man whose sight he restored; and the Jerusalem crowd who "took him for a prophet." *J 4:19, 9:7; Mt 21:46* Despite the dominant impression, there were skeptics who quibbled "for out of Galilee arises no prophet," and "This man, if he were a prophet, would have known who and what manner of woman this is that toucheth him." *J 7:52; L 7:39*

Jesus repeatedly made statements which implied that he was a prophet: *Mk 6:4; Mt 13:57; L 4:24, 13:33; J 4:44.* It is sufficient to quote just two of those statements:

> Verily I say unto you, no prophet is accepted in his own country.
> *L 4:24*

> Nevertheless I must walk today, and tomorrow, and the day following: for it can not be that a prophet perish out of Jerusalem. *L 13:33*

While Jesus accepted the label of "prophet," his own view of his mission was much more complex and transcended that label. For details, see especially "Jesus' Own View Of His Mission," pp. 765–769, and generally chapter 12, "Jesus and God," and chapter 13, "Jesus' Mission and Authority," pp. 725–784.

In Jesus' lifetime, up to the very end, his closest disciples considered him to be a prophet. Immediately after his death two of them spoke to a stranger:

> Concerning Jesus of Nazareth, which was a prophet mighty in deed and word before God and all the people. *L 24:19*

JESUS OF NAZARETH

Two of the four Gospel sources for the life of Jesus, Mark and John, begin their story of his life with his baptism by John the Baptist just before he began his ministry at about the age of thirty. *L 3:23* The other two Gospel sources, Matthew and Luke, have the familiar accounts of Jesus' birth and genealogies. *Mt 1, 2:1–23; L 1:5–80, 2:1–20, 3:23–38* Only one of the four Gospel sources, Luke, mentions any episode of Jesus' boyhood: a pilgrimage to Jerusalem when he was twelve years old. *L 2:41–50*

Jesus was born in Bethlehem, a small town in southern Judea, located about six miles south of Jerusalem. *Mt 2:1; L 2:6* Jesus' mother, Mary, and Joseph, her betrothed husband, were residents of Nazareth, a small hill town in Galilee in the northern reaches of the land of Israel. *L 2:39* After Jesus' birth Mary and Joseph returned to Nazareth and brought up Jesus in that town where Joseph, and later Jesus, were carpenters. *L 2:39; Mt 2:23, 13:55; Mk 6:3*

Nazareth itself was a byword in Galilee. When Philip reported to Nathanael that "we have found him, of whom Moses in The Law and The Prophets did write, Jesus of Nazareth, the son of Joseph", Nathanael's reply was, "Can any good thing come out of Nazareth?" *J 1:45–56*

Nathanael referred to Jesus as "Jesus of Nazareth." That is how he was known in his own times. That is the name by which the Jewish authorities knew him. *J 18:5–7; Acts 6:14* This was the name under which the Romans crucified him. *J 19:19* This was the name by which the people knew him. *Mk 10:47; L 18:37; Mk 14:67; Mt 26:71* This was the name by which his disciples knew him and preached his resurrection. *J 1:45; L 24:19; Acts 2:22, 10:38*

In his lifetime Jesus was a public figure in the land of the Jews. At his trial before Pilate the chief priests charged that "he stirreth up the people, teaching throughout all Jewry, beginning from Galilee to this place." *L 23:5* When Pilate remanded Jesus to Herod's jurisdiction, Herod "was exceeding glad: for he was desirous to see him of a long season, because he had heard many things of him; and he hoped to have seen some miracle done by him." *L 23:8*

After Jesus' death Peter could explain Jesus' mission to either Jews or Gentiles by referring to this man who was known as "Jesus of Nazareth":

A. In a sermon to Jews, Peter said:

Ye men of Israel, hear these words; *Jesus of Nazareth*, a man approved of God among you by miracles and wonders and signs, which God did by him in the midst of you, *as ye yourselves also know*: . . . *Acts 2:22*

B. In an interview with a Roman centurion, Peter noted:

How God anointed *Jesus of Nazareth* with the Holy Spirit and with power: who went about doing good, and healing all that were oppressed of the devil; for God was with him. *Acts 10:38*

The name "Jesus" is the Greek transliteration of the Hebrew name "Joshua" ("Yahweh is salvation" or "Yahweh shall save"). In our time and culture the name "Jesus" has become a sort of religious icon, but in his time it was just a common Jewish name. Colossians 4:11 refers to a Jewish convert as "Jesus, which is called Justus." Josephus, a Jewish historian born in A.D. 37, a few years after Jesus' death, repeatedly mentions in his own autobiography various men called Jesus: "Jesus, the son of Sapphias"; "Jesus, the captain of those robbers who were in the confines of Ptolemais"; and "Jesus, the son of Gamala." *The Life of Flavius Josephus, Sec. 12, 27, 22, 38, 41*

Nazareth was Jesus' home village. Therefore, Peter could identify Jesus to his Palestinian contemporaries by referring to him as "Jesus of Nazareth," but for others Peter used the title "Jesus Christ." *I Peter 1:1–3*

"Christ" is the English transliteration of *Christos*, the Greek word used to translate the Hebrew religious title *Messiah* (the anointed one). Jesus was known in his own time as Jesus of Nazareth, but his church and history have come to know him as Jesus Christ.

CHAPTER 2

JESUS' LIFE AND MINISTRY

A VILLAGE BOYHOOD

F rom the time Jesus came to Nazareth until his baptism at about the age of thirty years we have only a few sentences from Luke's Gospel to describe his life:

> And the child grew, and waxed strong in spirit, filled with wisdom: and the grace of God was upon him.
>
> Now his parents went to Jerusalem every year at the Feast of the Passover. And when he was twelve years old, they went up to Jerusalem after the custom of the feast.
>
> And when they had fulfilled the days, as they returned, the child Jesus tarried behind in Jerusalem; and Joseph and his mother knew not of it. But they, supposing him to have been in the company, went a day's journey; and they sought him among their kinsfolk and acquaintance. And when they found him not, they turned back again to Jerusalem, seeking him.
>
> And it came to pass, that after three days they found him in the Temple, sitting in the midst of the doctors, both hearing them, and asking them questions. And all that heard him were astonished at his understanding and answers.

And when they saw him, they were amazed: and his mother said unto him, "Son, why hast though thus dealt with us? Behold, thy father and I have sought thee sorrowing."

And he said unto them, "How is it that ye sought me? Wist [know] ye not that I must be about my Father's business?"

And they understood not the saying which he spake unto them.
And he went down with them, and came to Nazareth, and was subject unto them: *but his mother kept all these sayings in her heart.*"

And Jesus increased in wisdom and stature, and in favor with God and man. *L 2:40–52*

Luke writes that Mary and Joseph did not understand the saying which Jesus spoke unto them: "Wist [know] ye not that I must be about my Father's business?" *L 2:49* Modern translations render "about my Father's business" as "in my Father's house."

What Jesus had to say interested the doctors of the Jewish law at the national shrine, but he was learning too. He was found in the Temple "sitting in the midst of the doctors, both hearing them, and asking questions." *L 2:46*

To participate in such a dialogue, it is obvious that Jesus had had some schooling. We do know that he could read and write. *L 4:16; J 8:6, 8:8* The only schooling which would have been available to him as a village boy was the synagogue school. None of our sources directly state that Jesus as a boy attended synagogue school where he would have been taught the Jewish Law and the Prophets, most of the Old Testament. However, we do know that there was a synagogue in Nazareth and the synagogues usually had schools, and the reasonable supposition is that the Nazareth synagogue had a school which Jesus attended. *L 4:16*

When Jesus was a man he would on occasion read the lesson in the Nazareth synagogue on the Sabbath and expound on it. *L 4:16–19; Mk 6:2; Mt 13:54* Although Jesus was not a technically trained scribe, he was able to interpret Israel's religious traditions in an impressive way. When he taught, bystanders in the Temple in Jerusalem, "marvelled, saying, 'How knoweth this man letters, having never learned?'" *J 7:15*

Joseph was a carpenter, and Jesus himself also followed that trade. *Mk 6:3; Mt 13:55* When Jesus began his ministry he was "about thirty years of age." *L 3:23*

This is what we know of Jesus as a boy and young man. It is tempting to add to Luke's bare record, but the rest is speculation or based on documents that both the church and scholars have rejected.

What the Home Town Folks Thought

It came as a surprise to the home town folks of Nazareth that Jesus had any special mission or was any different from them. The fact that Jesus had amazed and astonished the Jewish religious teachers in the Great Temple of Jerusalem when he was twelve was a matter which his mother kept "in her heart." *L 2:51*

According to the local folk, he was "as was supposed" the son of Joseph and Mary. *L 3:23; Mk 6:13; Mt 13:55* More colloquially they simply called him "the carpenter's son." *Mt 13:55* Since Jesus followed Joseph's trade, Jesus was also known as "the carpenter." *Mk 6:3*

After Jesus' baptism and his forty days of spiritual testing in the wilderness, he returned to Galilee, "and there went out a fame of him through all the region round about." *L 4:14* Luke adds:

And he taught in their synagogues, being glorified of all. *L 4:15*

He then made a visit back to Nazareth:

And he came to Nazareth, *where he had been brought up*: and, as his custom was, he went into the synagogue on the Sabbath day, and stood up for to read. And there was delivered unto him the book of the prophet Isaiah. And when he had opened the book, he found the place where it was written.

"The Spirit of the Lord is upon me, because he hath anointed me to preach the gospel to the poor; he hath sent me to heal the broken hearted, to preach deliverance to the captives, and recovering of sight to the blind, to set at liberty them that are bruised, to preach the acceptable year of the Lord." *[Isaiah 61:1–2]*

And he closed the book, and he gave it again to the minister, and sat down. And the eyes of all them that were in the synagogue were fastened on him. And he began to say unto them:

"This day is this Scripture fulfilled in your ears."

And all bare him witness, and wondered at the gracious words which proceeded out of his mouth. And they said: "Is not this Joseph's son?" *L 4:16–22*

Jesus then said:

Ye will surely say unto me this proverb, 'Physician, heal thyself'. Whatsoever we have heard done in Capernaum, do also here in thy country. *L 4:23*

Jesus continued:

Verily I say unto you, no prophet is accepted in *his own country.* *L 4:24*

Despite Jesus' fame throughout Galilee, he was just a local boy to the Nazareth synagogue members:

Is not this Joseph's son? *L 4:22*

Both Matthew and Mark record the following incident in Nazareth. Jesus had returned to Nazareth with his disciples:

MARK	MATTHEW
And when	And when
the Sabbath day	he was come into
was come,	his own country,
he began to teach	he taught them
in the synagogue:	in their synagogue,
and many hearing him	insomuch that they
were astonished,	*were astonished,*
saying,	and said, . . .
"From whence	["Whence then
hath this man	hath this man
these things?	all these things?" *Mt 13:56*]*
And	"Whence hath this man

MARK (cont.)	**MATTHEW** (cont.)
what wisdom	this wisdom,
is this which is given unto him,	
that even	and
such mighty works	these mighty works?
are wrought	
by his hands?	
Is not this the carpenter,	Is not this the carpenter's son?
	Is not his mother
the son of Mary,	called Mary?
the brother of	And his brethren,
James, and Joses,	James and Joses,
and of	and
Judas, and Simon?	Simon, and Judas?
And are not	And
his sisters	his sisters,
here with us?"	are they not all with us?"
And they were offended	And they were offended
at him.	in him.
But Jesus said	But Jesus said
unto them,	unto them,
"A prophet	"A prophet
is not	is not
without honor,	without honor,
but in *his own* country,	save in *his own* country,
and among *his own* kin,	
and in *his own* house."	and in *his own* house."
Mk 6:2–4	*Mt 13:54–57*
	* Conformed to Mark's order

The result of the scornful skepticism of the home town folk was predictable:

MARK	**MATTHEW**
And he could	And he did not
there do	

MARK (cont.)	MATTHEW (cont.)
no mighty work,	many mighty works there
save that he laid	
his hands upon	
a few sick folk,	
and healed them.	
And he marvelled	
because of	because of
their unbelief.	their unbelief.
Mk 6:5–6	*Mt 13:58*

Later on at Capernaum, Galilee which was about twenty miles from Nazareth, the Jews murmured at Jesus because he had said:

I am the bread which came down from heaven. *J 6:41*

The Jews continued:

Is not this Jesus, the son of Joseph, whose father and mother we know? How is it then that he saith, "I came down from heaven"? *J 6:42*

To the home town folks Jesus was just a local boy, the son of Joseph and Mary. They knew his brothers and sisters. They doubted that he could do what it was said that he had done elsewhere. They were astonished at his wisdom and his mighty works and were offended by his claim that he was "the bread" which had come down from heaven to do his Father's will.

JESUS' FAMILY

Jesus grew up in a devout Jewish family. His parents had Jesus circumcised on the eighth day of his life in conformity to Jewish religious law. *L 2:21; Leviticus 12:3* At that time and as part of that rite, he was named Jesus. *L 2:21*

Under Jewish religious law, Mary had to "then continue in the blood of her purifying three and thirty days." *Leviticus 12:4* At the end of those thirty-three days, Mary and Joseph brought Jesus to Jerusalem, and Mary completed her purification by offering, as required, either "a pair of turtledoves, or two young pigeons." *L 2:22– 24; Leviticus 12:6–8*

One bird was for the burnt offering; the other bird was for the sin offering. This was the minimum offering required by Jewish law for the mother's atonement so that she should "be clean." *Leviticus 12:8* This offering was sufficient if the mother was not financially able to bring a yearling lamb for the burnt offering and either a young pigeon or a turtledove for the sin offering.

Mary was not financially able to afford a yearling lamb for the burnt offering, but she did present her son "to the Lord." *L 2:22* This also was a requirement of Jewish religious law. Luke freely summarizes *Exodus 13:2, 12* as follows:

> Every male that openeth the womb shall be called holy to the Lord. *L 2:23*

Exodus 13:2, 12 states:

> Sanctify unto me all the *firstborn*, whatsoever openeth the womb among the children of Israel, both of man and of beast, it is mine . . .

> That thou shalt set apart to the Lord all that openeth the matrix . . .

Jesus was Mary's firstborn child. *L 2:7* He was dedicated to the Lord like any other Jewish firstborn son, as the Jewish law required. Jesus' parents brought him to the great Jewish national shrine, the Temple in Jerusalem, to do this:

To do for him after the custom of the Law. *L 2:27*

Simeon, a just and devout man who waited "for the consolation of Israel" happened to appear at this rite of dedication. According to Luke, Simeon's appearance was impelled by the Holy Spirit. *L 2:25, 27* Luke also states that the Holy Spirit had revealed to Simeon "that he should not see death, before he had seen the Lord's Christ [the Anointed One]." *L 2:26*

Simeon took up Jesus in his arms, and blessed God, and said in phrases drawn mostly from Isaiah:

Lord, now lettest thou thy servant depart in peace, according to thy word.

For mine eyes have *seen thy salvation [Isa. 52:10]*, which thou hast prepared before the face of all people; *a light to lighten the Gentiles [Isa. 42:6, 49:6]* and the glory of thy people Israel. *L 2:29–32*

Simeon then blessed Mary and Joseph and said to Mary:

Behold, this child is set for the fall and rising again of many in Israel; and for a sign which shall be spoken against; (Yea, a sword shall pierce through thy own soul also) that the thoughts of many hearts may be revealed. *L 2:34–35*

Luke notes:

And Joseph and his mother marvelled at those things which were spoken of him. *L 2:33*

At that very moment also appeared an aged widow prophetess, Anna, who stayed at the Temple and "served God with fastings and prayer night and day." *L 2:36–37* She gave thanks to the Lord and spoke of the child Jesus "to all them that looked for redemption in Jerusalem." *L 2:38*

The circumcision of Jesus, Mary's purification and offering, and the bringing of Jesus to the Temple to present him, as a first-born child, to the Lord of Israel attest the devout Jewishness of Jesus' family. Luke, writing a gospel for Gentiles, recognizes that Jewishness when he sums up that first visit to Jerusalem:

> And when they had performed all things *according to the Law of the Lord*, they returned to Galilee, to their own city Nazareth. L 2:39

Jesus' parents kept the key Jewish religious festival, the Feast of the Passover, in Jerusalem each year. *L 2:41* They probably stayed for the entire seven days of the Feast of the Unleavened Bread, ("fulfilled the days") even though technically the Feast of the Passover was only the first of the seven days. *L 2:43; Deuteronomy 16:1–8* This meant a journey of several days on each way on foot since even the airline distance from Nazareth to Jerusalem is about 65 miles. They went with "their kinsfolk and acquaintance." *L 2:44*

This implies that Mary and Joseph had relatives in or near Nazareth. Jesus himself was the eldest of a large family. When he began his ministry he had four brothers: James, Joseph, Judas, and Simon. *Mk 6:3; Mt 13:55* He also had some sisters but they are not named in our sources. *Mk 6:3; Mt 13:56*

Our sources do not state that Joseph died before Jesus entered his ministry, but such is a reasonable inference from Joseph's omission when our sources refer to the mother, brothers, and sisters of Jesus. We do know that Joseph still lived when Jesus was twelve and was taken by "his parents" to Jerusalem for the Passover. *L 2:41–42*

At the beginning of his ministry Jesus' relations with his family were happy. Jesus and his mother attended a wedding in Cana, a town a few miles north of Nazareth. Jesus' mother told him that there was no wine at the wedding and directed the servants to obey Jesus: "Whatsoever he saith unto you, do it." *J 2:5* The servants obeyed, and Jesus performed his first miracle: transformation of six waterpots of water into wine.

John then states that "his disciples believed on him" and then adds:

> After this he went down to Capernaum, he, and his mother, and his brethren, and his disciples: and they continued there not many days. *J 2:12*

John omits to say his family believed upon him. A little later in the ministry Mark suggests that Jesus' family were concerned for him. After he had called the twelve disciples and the crowd pressed them so much "that they could not so much as eat bread," Jesus' friends went out to lay hold on him, saying: "He is beside himself." *Mk 3:21*

To add to the turmoil some Jerusalem scribes had come down to Galilee to investigate Jesus, and they were saying that Jesus was demon-possessed: "He hath Beelzebub"; "He hath an unclean spirit." *Mk 3:22, 30*

Jesus' concerned family came to his side:

> There came then his brethren and his mother, and, standing without, sent unto him, calling him. And the multitude sat about him, and they said unto him, "Behold, thy mother and thy brethren without seek for thee." *Mk 3:31–32 (Mt 12:46–47; L 8:19–20)*

There was, however, an undercurrent of doubt in his family. Jesus recognized this in his famous saying about a prophet being without honor in his own country. The full saying is as follows:

MARK	MATTHEW
A prophet is not	A prophet is not
without honor, but	without honor, save
in his own country,	in his own country,
and *among his own kin*,	
and *in his own house*.	and *in his own house*.
Mk 6:4	Mt 13:57

Jesus' mother was just that—his mother. He was unacquainted with the Blessed Virgin which later piety has constructed. His own attitude towards his mother is shown by the following incident.

As he was teaching, a woman lifted up her voice, and said unto him:

Blessed is the womb that bare thee, and the paps which thou hast sucked. *L 11:27*

But Jesus said:

Yea rather, blessed are they that hear the word of God, and keep it. *L 11:28*

Mary stood by her son at his cross:

Now there stood by the cross of Jesus his mother, and his mother's sister, Mary the wife of Cleophas, and Mary Magdalene. When Jesus therefore saw his mother, and the disciple standing by, whom he loved, he saith unto his mother, "Woman, behold thy son!"

Then saith he to the disciple, "Behold thy mother!" And from that hour that disciple took her unto his own home. *J 19:25–27*

Mary vanishes from our sight in the first chapter of Acts as a member of the new church of her son. *Acts 1:14*

In Jesus' lifetime Jesus' brothers were not believers in him. In the middle of his ministry he was staying in Galilee because in Judea "the Jews sought to kill him." *J 7:1* Jerusalem was in Judea. The Feast of Tabernacles was approaching and was celebrated in Jerusalem. At that time Jesus' brothers sneered at him:

Depart hence, and go into Judea, that thy disciples also may see *the works that though doest*. For there is no man that doeth any thing in secret, and he himself seeketh to be known openly.

If thou do *these things*, shew thyself to the world. *J 7:3–4*

John then adds:

For neither did his brethren believe in him. *J 7:5*

This seems, to put it mildly, an understatement. Jesus' brothers had urged him to go to Judea even though he might get killed during the visit, arguing that he owed it to his disciples there and to the world not to secret himself in Galilee. The hostility of Jesus' brothers to "the works that thou doest . . . these things" is obvious. *J 7:3–4*

As observant Jews, Jesus' brothers did keep the Feast in Jerusalem that year. *J 7:10* After Jesus' resurrection his brothers became believers. Acts states:

> These all [the disciples] continued with one accord in prayer and supplication, with the women, and Mary the mother of Jesus, *and with his brethren. Acts 1:14*

The brothers of Jesus became leaders in the church, apparently traveling about with their wives. Paul asks:

> Have we not power to lead about a sister, a wife, as well as other apostles, and as *the brethren of the Lord*, and Cephas? *1 Corinthians 9:5*

James, Jesus' eldest brother, was one of the few persons who saw Jesus alone after his resurrection. In a letter (*1 Corinthians*) Paul repeats what he had been taught as a convert about Jesus' appearances after his resurrection:

> And that he was seen of Cephas, then of the twelve: after that, he was seen of above five hundred brethren at once; of whom the greater part remain unto this present, but some are fallen asleep. *After that, he was seen of James*; then of all the apostles. *1 Corinthians 15:5–7*

James became the leader of the church in Jerusalem. *Acts 12:17, 15:13–21, 21:18* Paul described James as a "pillar" of the church, along with John and Cephas. *Galatians 2:9*

Paul states that three years after his conversion:

I went up to Jerusalem to see Peter, and abode with him fifteen days. But other of the apostles saw I none, save James the Lord's brother. *Galatians 1:18–19*

James was executed in A.D. 62. Josephus, the Jewish historian, writes that Ananus, the high priest "assembled the sanhedrim of the judges, and brought before them the brother of Jesus, who was called Christ, whose name was James, and some others, (or some of his companions;) and when he had formed an accusation against them as breakers of the law, he delivered them to be stoned: . . ." *Josephus, Antiquities, Book XX, Ch. IX, Sec. 1*

Eusebius, the early Christian historian writing in A.D. 303, has a different account of James's death:

> But the Jews, after Paul had appealed to Caesar, and had been sent by Festus to Rome, frustrated in their hope of entrapping him by the snares they had laid, turn themselves against James, the brother of the Lord, to whom the episcopal seat at Jerusalem was committed by the apostles. The following were their nefarious measures also against him. Conducting him into a public place, they demanded that he should renounce the faith of Christ before all the people; but contrary to the sentiments of all, with a firm voice, and much beyond their expectation, he declared himself fully before the whole multitude, and confessed that Jesus Christ was the Son of God, our Savior and Lord. Unable to bear any longer the testimony of the man, who, on account of his elevated virtue and piety was deemed the most just of men, they seized the opportunity of licentiousness afforded by the prevailing anarchy, and slew him. For as Festus died about this time in Judea, the province was without a governor and head. But, as to the manner of James's death, it has been already stated in the words of Clement, that he was thrown from a wing of the temple, and beaten to death with a club. *Eusebius, Ecclesiastical History, Book II, Ch. XXIII*

Eusebius also quotes Hegesippus, a Christian writer who lived from A.D. 110 to 180, as to James' character and personality:

> But James, the brother of the Lord, who, as there were many of this name, was surnamed the Just by all, from the days of our Lord until

now, received the government of the church with the apostles. This apostle was consecrated from his mother's womb. He drank neither wine nor fermented liquors, and abstained from animal food. A razor never came upon his head, he never anointed with oil, and never used a bath. He alone was allowed to enter the sanctuary. He never wore woolen, but linen garments. He was in the habit of entering the temple alone, and was often found upon his bended knees, and interceding for the forgiveness of the people; so that his knees became as hard as camel's, in consequence of his habitual supplication and kneeling before God. And indeed, on account of his exceeding great piety, he was called the Just, and Oblias (or Zaddick and Ozleam) which signifies justice and protection of the people; as the prophets declare concerning him. *Op. cit., Book II, Ch. XXIII*

Some years later in the reign of the Roman emperor Domitian A.D. 81–96, the grandchildren of Jesus' brother, Judas, "ruled the churches, both as witnesses and relatives of the Lord." *Op. cit., Book III, Ch. XX* Eusebius quotes Hegesippus as follows:

There were yet living in the family of our Lord, the grandchildren of Judas, called the brother of our Lord, according to the flesh. These were reported as being of the family of David, and were brought to Domitian by the Evocatus. For this emperor was as much alarmed at the appearance of Christ as Herod. He put the question, whether they were of David's race, and they confessed that they were. He then asked them what property they had, or how much money they owned. And both of them answered, that they had between them only nine thousand denarii, and this they had not in silver, but in the value of a piece of land, containing only thirty-nine acres; from which they raised their taxes and supported themselves by their own labour. Then they also began to show their hands, exhibiting the hardness of their bodies, and the callosity formed by incessant labour on their hands, as evidence of their labour. When asked also, respecting Christ and his kingdom, what was its nature and when and where it was to appear, they replied "that it was not a temporal nor an earthly kingdom, but celestial and angelic; that it would appear at the end of the world, when coming in glory he would judge the quick and the dead, and give to every one according to his works." Upon which Domitian despising them, made no reply; but treating them with contempt, as simpletons, commanded them to be dismissed, and by a decree ordered the persecution to cease. This delivered, *they ruled the churches, both as witnesses and relatives of the Lord. When peace was established, they continued living even to the times of Trajan. Op. cit., Book III, Ch. XX*

Trajan reigned as Roman emperor from A.D. 98–117. It was in his reign that the family of Jesus vanished into the mists of history.

John the Baptist

Humanly speaking, Jesus' ministry grew out of that of his second cousin, John the Baptist. Jesus' mother, Mary, was the cousin of John's mother, Elisabeth. L 1:36 John's father was Zacharias, a priest. L 1:5, 3:2 Luke describes John's parents as follows:

> And they were both righteous before God, walking in all the commandments and ordinances of the Lord blameless. L 1:6

John was born about six months before Jesus. L 1:26, 31, 56; L 2:1–5 Three months before John's birth, Mary fled to Zacharias' house in a city of the hill country of Judea. L 1:36, 39–40 Mary stayed there three months, returning to her own home shortly before John's birth. L 1:56–57

Elisabeth had been "called barren" but she bore John in her old age. L 1:36 For this and other reasons, John's birth was "noised abroad throughout all the hill country of Judea." L 1:65

Both John and Jesus were circumcised on the eighth day of their lives in Jewish religious practice required. L 1:59, 2:21 As in the case of Jesus, the Gospels have little to say of John's youth:

> And the child grew, and waxed strong in spirit, and was in the deserts till the day of his shewing [showing] unto Israel. L 1:80

Luke, with ancient precision, states that "in the fifteenth year of the reign of Tiberius Caesar, Pontius Pilate being Governor of Judea and Herod being Tetrarch of Galilee, and his brother, Philip, Tetrarch of Ituraea and the region of Trachonitis, and Lysanias the Tetrarch of Abilene, Annas and Caiaphas being the High Priests, the word of God came unto John the son of Zacharias in the wilderness." L 3:1–2 Despite the precision of Luke's wording, computation problems make the exact year uncertain.

That year was around A.D. 28. In that year John the Baptist came preaching in the wilderness of Judea near the Jordan River. Mk 1:4–5; Mt 3:1,6; L 3:3 This wilderness lies immediately west of the Dead Sea and is a desolate, dry, rugged wasteland. It is near Jerusalem; and the people of Jerusalem, the rest of Judea and the region around the Jordan River came out to be baptized by John "confessing their sins." *Mk 1:5; Mt 3:5* John baptized them in the Jordan. *Mk 1:5; Mt 3:6*

John apparently baptized at a number of locations. Jesus, himself, was baptized by John in the Jordan, apparently at a place called "Bethabara beyond Jordan," i.e., on the east bank of the Jordan. *J 1:28 (Mk 1:9; Mt 3:13)* Modern translations follow the manuscripts that have this name as "Bethany." This is not the Bethany near Jerusalem, but another Bethany whose location is uncertain except that it was on the east bank of the Jordan.

Another place where John baptized was at "Aenon near to Salim." *J 3:23* The location of Aenon is disputed. It was probably in Samaria or a few miles from Scythopolis, both sites being many miles north of the probable location of Bethabara.

John wore garments of camel's hair and a leather belt; John ate locusts and wild honey. *Mk 1:6; Mt 3:4*

John's mission was immensely popular and became a landmark in the history of Israel. The Gospels repeatedly refer to John's popularity. *Mt 3:7, 14:5, 21:26; L 3:7, 3:12, 7:29–30, 20:6; Mk 11:32*

Matthew states that "many" Pharisees and Sadducees came to be baptized by John. *Mt 3:7* Luke states that publicans came to be baptized by John. *L 3:12* Luke sums up the response of Israel to John's baptism as follows:

> And all of the people that heard him, and the publicans, justified God, *being baptized* with the baptism of John. But the Pharisees and lawyers rejected the counsel of God against themselves, being *not baptized* of him." *L 7:29–30*

The Pharisees and legalists generally refused John's baptism, but the people received John's baptism. The popular acceptance of John's baptism was so great that Jesus used it to turn away a hostile question directed at himself:

CHIEF PRIESTS, SCRIBES, ELDERS: By what authority doest thou these things? And who gave thee this authority to do these things?

JESUS: I will also ask of you one question, and answer me, and I will tell you by what authority I do these things. The baptism of John, was it from heaven, or of men? Answer me.

CHIEF PRIESTS, SCRIBES, ELDERS: We cannot tell.

JESUS: Neither do I tell you by what authority I do these things. *Mk 11:28–38 (Mt 21:23–27; L 20:1–8)*

These Jewish religious leaders reasoned:

If we shall say, "From heaven"; he will say, "What then did ye not believe him?" But if we shall say, "Of men"; they feared the people: for all men counted John, that he was a prophet indeed. *Mk 11:31–32 (Mt 21:25–26; L 20:5–7)*

The "baptism of John" was only part of his ministry. He preached many other things. *L 3:18* He preached:

MARK	MATTHEW	LUKE
There cometh one mightier than I after me, the latchet of whose shoes I am not worthy to stoop down and unloose.		
I indeed have baptized you with water:	I indeed baptize you with water *unto repentance*: but he that cometh after me is mightier than I,	I indeed baptize you with water; but one mightier than I cometh, the latchet of whose shoes I am not worthy to unloose:
	whose shoes I am not worthy to bear:	
but		

MARK (cont.)	MATTHEW (cont.)	LUKE (cont.)
he shall baptize	he shall baptize	he shall baptize
you	you	you
with the Holy Spirit.	with the Holy Spirit	with the Holy Spirit
Mk 1:7–8	and with fire.	and with fire.
	Mt 3:11	*L 3:16*

He also preached:

Repent ye: for the Kingdom of Heaven is at hand. *Mt 3:2*

Mark and Luke summarize the ministry of John as follows:

MARK	LUKE
John did baptize	And he came into
in the wilderness,	all the country
	about Jordan,
and preach	preaching
the baptism of repentance	the baptism of repentance
for the remission of sins.	for the remission of sins.
Mk 1:4	*L 3:3*

John's three key points were:

1. A water baptism
2. Of repentance
3. For remission, that is, the forgiveness, of sins.

This was how Paul understood John's baptism. Acts quotes Paul as saying John had preached "the baptism of repentance to all the people of Israel" and that "John verily baptized with the baptism of repentance." *Acts 13:24; 19:4*

That is why John's disciples confessed their sins as they were baptized. *Mk 1:5; Mt 3:6* Our sources do not state whether confession was done orally or just symbolically by receiving the rite.

It is a historical fact that Jesus sought baptism by John and was baptized by John in the Jordan River. *Mk 1:9–11; Mt 3:13–17; L 3:21–22*

The details as to Jesus' baptism are analyzed in the section entitled "Jesus' Baptism." pp. 79–82

The power and popularity of the ministry of John the Baptist inevitably raised the question whether or not he himself was, in fact, the Christ (the Anointed One):

> And as the people were in expectation, and all men mused in their hearts of John, whether he were the Christ or not. *L 3:15*

John rejected that surmise:

Mark	Matthew	Luke
There cometh	But he that cometh after me	But one mightier than I
one mightier than I after me,	is mightier than I,	cometh,
the latchet of whose shoes I am not worthy to stoop down and unloose	whose shoes I am not worthy to bear: . . ."	the latchet of whose shoes I am not worthy to unloose: . . ."
Mk 1:7	*Mt 3:11*	*L 3:16*

Acts reports a similar statement by John the Baptist in Paul's outline of gospel to the synagogue congregation at Antioch near Pisidia in Asia Minor. After Paul had stated that "God raised unto Israel a Savior, Jesus," he referred to the preaching by John the Baptist prior to Jesus' coming and concluded:

> And as John fulfilled his course, he said, "Whom think ye that I am? I am not he. But, behold, there cometh one after me, whose shoes of his feet I am not worthy to loose." *Acts 13:25*

The Jews sent a committee of priests and Levites from Jerusalem to investigate John who was then baptizing at Bethabara [Bethany] beyond Jordan. *J 1:19, 28* The committee was to ask John:

Who art thou? *J 1:19*

John's answer was terse:

I am not the Christ. *J 1:20*

The interrogation continued:

PRIESTS AND LEVITES: What then? Art thou Elijah?
JOHN: I am not.
PRIESTS AND LEVITES: Art thou that prophet?
JOHN: No.
PRIESTS AND LEVITES: Who art thou? That we may give an answer to
them that sent us. What sayest thou of thyself?
JOHN: I am the voice of one crying in the wilderness, "Make straight
the way of the Lord," as said the prophet Isaiah.
PRIESTS AND LEVITES: Why baptize thou then, if thou be not that
Christ, nor Elijah, neither that Prophet?
JOHN: I baptize with water: *but there standeth one among you*, whom
ye know not; he it is, who coming after me is preferred before
me, whose shoe's latchet I am not worthy to unloose. *J 1:21–27*

Jesus was then standing in the crowd: "standeth one among
you." *J 1:26* The next day John pointed Jesus out and said:

Behold the Lamb of God, which taketh away the sin of the world.
This is he of whom I said, "After me cometh a man which is preferred before me: for he was before me. And I knew him not: but
that he should be made manifest to Israel, therefore am I come
baptizing with water." *J 1:29–31*

John continued:

I saw the Spirit descending from Heaven like a dove, and it abode
upon him. And I knew him not: but he that sent me to baptize with
water, the same said unto me, "Upon whom thou shalt see the Spirit
descending, and remaining on him, the same is he which baptizeth

with the Holy Spirit." And I saw, and bare record that this is the Son of God. *J 1:32–34*

After Jesus' baptism by John and before John's imprisonment, Jesus and John conducted parallel but not identical ministries.

Jesus' first disciples were disciples of John the Baptist. This certainly included Andrew, and probably included Peter, Philip and Nathanael. John's Gospel states:

> Again the next day after John stood, and *two of his disciples*; and looked upon Jesus as he walked, he saith, "Behold the Lamb of God!"
>
> And *the two disciples* heard him speak, and they followed Jesus . . . *One of the two* which heard John speak, and followed him, was Andrew, Simon Peter's brother. *J 1:35–37, 40*

Later on, but at different locations, Jesus' disciples and John personally were baptizing. *J 3:22–23, 26; 4:1–2* Jesus' disciples were baptizing more people than John. *J 4:1–2*

The parallel ministries of Jesus and John inevitably raised questions. One question was about purifying (ceremonial washing):

> Then there arose a question between some of John's disciples and the Jews about purifying. And they came unto John, and said unto him, "Rabbi, *he that was with thee beyond Jordan*, to whom thou barest witness, behold, the same baptizeth, and all men come to him." *J 3:25–26*

John answered:

> A man can receive nothing, except it be given him from heaven. Ye yourselves bear me witness, that I said, "I am not the Christ, but that I am sent before him."
>
> He that hath the bride is the bridegroom: but the *friend of the bridegroom* which standeth and heareth him, rejoiceth greatly because of the bridegroom's voice: this my joy therefore is fulfilled. He must increase, but I must decrease. *J 3:27–30*

John characterized himself as simply the "friend of the bride-groom" who in that culture was not simply the best man but also the marriage arranger.

Before John was imprisoned, Jesus had been conducting a ministry in Judea at the same time John was baptizing at another place called "Aenon near to Salim." *J 3:22–24* When Jesus heard that John was imprisoned, Jesus withdrew into Galilee. *Mt 4:12 (Mk 1:14; J 4:3)*

John was imprisoned by Herod Antipas, Tetrarch of Galilee and Perea, in a prison in his palace at Machaerus on the east side of the Dead Sea. *Mk 6:17; Mt 14:3* John's imprisonment was instigated by Herodias, Herod's wife, for the following reasons. Herodias had formerly been the wife of Herod's brother, Philip, and John had admonished Herod:

> It is not lawful for thee to have thy brother's wife. *Mk 6:18 (Mt 14:4)*

Herodias was able to get John imprisoned, but Herod was reluctant to execute him. The Gospels give two versions of Herod's reasons:

MARK	MATTHEW
For Herod feared John,	And when
knowing that	he would have
he was a just man,	put him to death
and an holy,	he feared the multitude,
and observed him;	because
and when he heard him,	they counted him
he did many things,	a prophet.
and heard him gladly.	*Mt 14:5*
Mk 6:20	

The story is well known how Herodias finally got her way, quite unexpectedly. *Mk 6:21–28; Mt 14:6–11* Herod had a birthday, and at a banquet to celebrate the event, Herodias' daughter, Salome, danced and greatly pleased Herod. He vowed to give her whatever she desired, and she went out to consult her mother who told her to ask for the head of John the Baptist. She did, and Herod, who was bound by his oath, complied. John was then beheaded, and his head was brought in a charger and Salome gave it to her mother.

The Gospels continue:

MARK	MATTHEW
And when his disciples heard of it,	And his disciples
they came	came,
and took up his corpse,	and took up the body,
and laid it in a tomb.	and buried it,
Mk 6:29	*and went*
	and told Jesus.
	Mt 14:12

Josephus, the first century Jewish historian, summarized John the Baptist's life as follows:

2.   Now, some of the Jews thought that the destruction of Herod's army came from God, and that very justly, as a punishment of what he did against *John, that was called the Baptist*; for Herod slew him, who was a good man, and commanded the Jews to exercise virtue, both as to righteousness towards one another, and piety towards God, and so to come to baptism; for that the washing (with water) would be acceptable to him, if they made use of it, not in order to the putting away, (or the remission) of some sins (only,) but for the purification of the body: supposing still that the soul was thoroughly purified beforehand by righteousness. Now, when (many) others came to crowd about him, for they were greatly moved (pleased) by hearing his words, Herod, who feared lest the great influence John had over the people might put it into his power and inclination to raise a rebellion, (for they seemed ready to do anything he should advise,) thought it best, by putting him to death, to prevent any mischief he might cause, and not bring himself into difficulties, by sparing a man who might make him repent of it when it should be too late. Accordingly he was sent a prisoner, out of Herod's suspicious temper, to Macherus, the castle I before mentioned, and was there put to death." *Josephus, Antiquities, Book XVIII, Ch. V, Sec. 2*

The impact of John's ministry continued for many years. The natural result of that ministry was the presence in Israel both in the homeland and among the Jews dispersed abroad, of persons who had received John's baptism of repentance. Acts states that Apollos, a Jew from Alexandria who was "mighty" in the Jewish scriptures, had come to Ephesus, a town in what is now Turkey, and that:

> This man was instructed in the way of the Lord; and being fervent in the spirit, he spake and taught diligently the things of the Lord [Jesus], *knowing only the baptism of John. Acts 18:25*

Modern translations prefer the manuscripts which state "the things of Jesus" rather than "the things of the Lord." The point is that a Jew who "was instructed in the way of the Lord" knew "only the baptism of John."

Later on Paul found certain other disciples in Ephesus who had never received any baptism except John's baptism. *Acts 19:1–4* The baptism of John was so well known that Peter, in about A.D. 41, while summarizing the gospel to a Roman centurion at Caesaria in Palestine, used it as a historical reference point:

> That word, I say, ye know, which was published throughout all Judea, and began from Galilee, *after the baptism which John preached*; how God anointed Jesus of Nazareth with the Holy Spirit and with power: . . . *Acts 10:37–38*

In about A.D. 45, Paul, while preaching in a synagogue at Antioch, Pisidia in present day Turkey, referred to this same historical reference point, stating that John had preached before Jesus' coming "the baptism of repentance to all the people of Israel." *Acts 13:24*

John had begun his preaching of the baptism of repentance for the remission of sins in about A.D. 28. For a substantial period of time, beginning shortly after John's baptism of Jesus and ending with John's imprisonment, Jesus and John conducted parallel, but not identical, ministries. We turn now to a comparison of those two ministries.

JESUS AND JOHN

John the Baptist had, from the beginning of his ministry, preached:

Repent ye: for the Kingdom of Heaven is at hand. *Mt 3:2*

After John's imprisonment and Jesus' withdrawal to Galilee, Jesus began to preach the same thing:

MARK	MATTHEW
Now after that	Now when
	Jesus had heard that
John was put in prison,	John was cast into prison,
Jesus came into Galilee,	he departed into Galilee;
	. . .
	From that time
preaching the gospel	Jesus began to preach,
of the Kingdom of God,	
and saying,	and to say,
"The time is fulfilled,	
	"Repent:
and the Kingdom of God	for the Kingdom of Heaven
is at hand:	is at hand."
repent ye,	*Mt 4:12, 17*
and believe	
the gospel."	
Mk 1:14–15	

According to Mark Jesus sent his twelve core disciples out in pairs and they "preached that men should repent." *Mk 6:7, 12*

Both Jesus and John preached repentance and, in addition, that a new spiritual era was about to begin. The new era of the Kingdom was "at hand." *Mk 1:15; Mt 3:2, 4:17, 10:7* Jesus was very specific on this point. He specifically instructed his twelve disciples:

And as ye go, preach, saying, "The Kingdom of God is at hand." *Mt 10:7*

Jesus' and John's teaching overlapped as follows:

A. O generation of vipers, how can ye being evil, speak good things? *Mt 12:34* (Jesus)

Ye serpents, ye generation of vipers how can ye escape the damnation of hell? *Mt. 23:33* (Jesus)

Oh generation of vipers, who hath warned you to flee from the wrath to come? *Mt 3:7; L 3:7* (John)

B. Except ye repent, ye shall all likewise perish. *L 13:3, 5* (Jesus)

Bring forth therefore fruits meet for repentance. *Mt 3:8 (L 3:8)* (John)

C. Every tree that bringeth not forth good fruit is hewn down, and cast into the fire. *Mt 7:19* (Jesus)

And now also the axe is laid out unto the root of the trees: therefore every tree which bringeth not forth good fruit is hewn down, and cast into the fire. *Mt 3:10 (L 3:9)* (John)

D. Give to him that asketh thee, and from him that would borrow of thee turn not thou away. *Mt 5:42 (L 6:30)* (Jesus)

(In answer to questions, "What shall we do then?" *L 3:10*)

He that hath two coats, let him impart to him that hath none; and he that hath meat, let him do likewise. *L 3:11* (John)

Both Jesus and John rejected arguments based on the premise that "Abraham is our father." John taught:

And think not to say within yourselves, "We have Abraham to [as] our father": for I say unto you that God is able of these stones to raise up children unto Abraham. *Mt 3:9 (L 3:8)*

When the Jews argued with Jesus that "Abraham is our father," Jesus replied:

> If ye were Abraham's children, ye would do the works of Abraham.
> J 8:39

Jesus' and John's attitudes toward the Roman occupation were similar. The Romans collected taxes through publicans. These men purchased the right to collect the taxes and were allowed to keep all that they could collect. This was an open invitation to greed and oppression, and in addition, these men were despised as collaborators with the heathen Romans.

Both Jesus and John had a large response from the publicans and harlots.

"Publicans and harlots" believed John, and he baptized publicans. Mt 21:32; L 3:12, 7:29 The publicans asked John:

> Master, what shall we do? L 3:12

John replied:

> Exact no more than that which is appointed to you. L 3:13

Jesus' attitude was essentially similar although Matthew quotes him as saying, in passing, when discussing discipline of a brother believer:

> Let him be unto thee as an heathen man and a publican. Mt 18:17

However, Jesus did tell the chief priests and elders:

> Verily I say unto you, that the publicans and harlots go into the Kingdom of God before you. Mt 21:31

Luke reports:

> Then drew near unto him all the publicans and sinners for to hear him. And the Pharisees and scribes murmured, saying, "This man receiveth sinners, and eateth with them." L 15:1–2

Jesus did eat with publicans. *Mk 2:17; Mt 9:10; L 5:29* A publican named Levi had a great banquet for Jesus, and Jesus attended along with "a great company of publicans." *L 5:29* Jesus requested an invitation from Zacchaeus, a chief publican, and was a guest in his house. *L 19:5–7*

Jesus refused to counsel that the Roman tribute money not be paid, saying instead:

> Render to Caesar, the things that are Caesar's, . . . *Mk 12:17 (Mt 22:21; L 20:25)*

John gave a similar answer to native soldiers recruited by the Roman occupation, who asked him:

> And what shall we do? *L 3:14*

John did not tell these soldiers to leave the Roman service, but he did tell them:

> Do violence to no man, neither accuse any falsely; and be content with your wages. *L 3:14*

With this similarity between the preaching of John and the teaching of Jesus, Herod Antipas' bewilderment when he heard the fame of Jesus after he had beheaded John the Baptist is understandable:

> And King Herod heard of him (for his name was spread abroad:) and he said, that "John the Baptist was risen from the dead, and therefore mighty works do shew forth themselves in him."
>
> Others said, that "It is Elijah."
>
> And others said, that "It is a prophet, or as one of the prophets."
>
> But when Herod heard thereof, he said, "It is John, whom I beheaded: he is risen from the dead." *Mk 6:14–16 (Mt 14:1–2)*

Luke's account is generally similar *(Luke 9:7–8)* but ends differently, quoting Herod as saying:

> "John have I beheaded: but who is this, of whom I hear such things? And he desired to see him." *L 9:9*

There were other aspects to the ministries of Jesus and John that would probably have seemed indistinguishable to a man like Herod Antipas. For example, both Jesus and John taught their disciples to pray. We do not know what John taught his disciples about prayer, but we do know that Jesus once instructed his disciples how to pray because of the example of John:

> And it came to pass, that, as he [Jesus] was praying in a certain place, when he ceased, one of his disciples said unto him, "Lord, teach us to pray, *as John also taught his disciples.*" *L 11:1*

Jesus then did teach his disciples to pray by giving a model prayer we now know as the Lord's Prayer. *L 11:2–4*

There were, of course, important differences between the ministries of Jesus and John. For their contemporaries the most important difference was that Jesus did miracles and John did not. The popular opinion then, said:

> John did no miracle; but all things that John spake of this man [Jesus] were true. *J 10:41*

For us looking with the hindsight of history their best known difference is the nature of their baptisms. Everyone knows that Jesus himself, after his resurrection, said:

> For John truly baptized with water; but ye shall be baptized with the Holy Spirit not many days hence. *Acts 1:5 (Acts 11:16)*

The first three gospels quote John as saying:

MARK	MATTHEW	LUKE
I indeed	I indeed	I indeed
have baptized you	baptize you	baptize you
with water:	with water	with water;
	unto repentance:	
	. . .	. . .
but he shall	he shall	he shall
baptize you	baptize you	baptize you
with the Holy Spirit.	with the Holy Spirit	with the Holy Spirit
Mk 1:8	and with fire.	and with fire.
	Mt 3:11	*L 3:16*

The difference between the baptism which Jesus predicted and John's baptism was the difference between fire and water. That is not to say that there were not certain similarities between Jesus and John as to water baptism.

Jesus himself did not baptize with water, but his disciples did. *J 3:22–23, 26; 4:1–2* John did baptize with water. *Mk 1:8; Mt 3:11; L 3:16* This was a baptism "unto repentance." ("the baptism of repentance") *Mt 3:11; Acts 13:24, 19:4*

MARK	LUKE
John did baptize	And he came into
in the wilderness,	all the country about Jordan,
and preach	preaching
the baptism of repentance	the baptism of repentance
for the remission of sins.	for the remission of sins.
Mk 1:4	*L 3:3*

John did not preach simply "the baptism of repentance" but a "baptism of repentance for the remission of sins." This was similar to what Peter preached after Jesus' resurrection:

Repent, and be baptized every one of you in the name of Jesus Christ for the remission of sins, . . . *Acts 2:38*

The water baptisms performed by John and preached by Peter were both "for the remission of sins"; but these two water baptisms differed in that Peter preached baptism "in the name of Jesus Christ." *Acts 2:38* This difference distinguished John's baptism from Christian water baptism.

Some years after Jesus' resurrection Paul found some disciples at Ephesus who had received John's baptism. *Acts 19:1–3* Acts then continues:

> Then said Paul, John verily baptized with the baptism of repentance, saying unto the people, that they should believe on him which should come after him, that is, on Christ Jesus. When they heard this, they were baptized *in the name of the Lord Jesus. Act 19:4–5*

Some years earlier at Caesarea, Peter summarized the gospel of Jesus Christ to a Roman centurion, his kinsmen and near friends. *Acts 10:24–43* The Holy Spirit fell on all who listened. *Acts 10:44* Acts then quotes Peter as saying:

> Can any man forbid water, that these should not be baptized, which have received the Holy Spirit as well as we? *Acts 10:47*

Acts continues:

> And he commanded them to be baptized *in the name of the Lord. Acts 10:48*

Even earlier Philip, one of seven deacons, had preached Christ in Samaria. *Acts 8:5–12* These Christian converts were then "baptized in the name of the Lord Jesus." *Acts 8:12–13, 16*

This crucial difference between John's baptism and Christian water baptism should not obscure their similarities:

John's Baptism		Christian Baptism
MARK	LUKE	ACTS
John did	And he came . . .	Peter
. . . preach	preaching	said, . . .
the baptism	the baptism	"Repent, and
of repentance	of repentance	be baptized"

MARK (cont.)	LUKE (cont.)	ACTS (cont.)
		every one of you
		in the name
for the remission	for the remission	of Jesus Christ
of sins.	of sins.	for the remission
Mk 1:4	*L 3:3*	of sins."
		Acts 2:38

John seems to have had a greater appeal to Pharisees and Sadducees than Jesus. According to Matthew, John "saw many of the Pharisees and Sadducees come to his baptism." *Mt 3:7* However, it is probable that most Pharisees and scribes rejected John's baptism. *L 7:30*

Jesus' differences with the Pharisees are well known. See the section "Jesus and the Pharisees," pp 444–456 for details. There were some Pharisees who were friendly. *L 13:31* On three occasions Jesus was asked to dine at a Pharisee's house, and he went. *L 7:36, 11:37, 14:1* There were probably a few Pharisees who were secret disciples of Jesus. Nicodemus is our only sure example. *J 3:1–2, 7:50, 19:39*

Despite the fact that some Pharisees were friendly to Jesus, it seems clear that usually they were hostile, either overtly or covertly. On the other hand, "many" Pharisees accepted John's baptism. *Mt 3:7* Although the evidence is scanty, it seems likely that the Pharisees preferred John to Jesus.

Jesus and John differed on fasting:

MARK	MATTHEW	LUKE
And the disciples		
of John		
and of the Pharisees		
used to fast:		
and they come	Then came him	And they
	the disciples of John,	
and say unto him,	saying,	said unto him,
"Why do	"Why do	"Why do
the disciples of John	we	the disciples of John
and of the Pharisees	and the Pharisees	
fast,	fast oft,	fast often,

68

MARK (cont.)	MATTHEW (cont.)	LUKE (cont.)
		and make prayers,
		and likewise
		the disciples of
		the Pharisees;
but thy disciples	but thy disciples	but thine
fast not?"	fast not?"	eat and drink?"
Mk 2:18	*Mt 9:14*	*L 5:33*

This difference between Jesus and John on fasting was to be expected since John was an ascetic, and Jesus was not.

John was an ascetic. He preached in the desert wilderness clothed in camel's hair garments and lived on locust and wild honey. *Mk 1:4, 6; Mt 3:1, 4* He came, according to Jesus, "neither eating bread nor drinking wine." *L 7:33 (Mt 11:18)*

Jesus was not an ascetic. By his own testimony he came "eating and drinking." *L 7:34, Mt 11:19* He was accused of being "a gluttonous man and a winebibber, a friend of publicans and sinners." *L 7:34 (Mt 11:19)*

While he was in prison John heard what Jesus was doing and sent two of his disciples to ask Jesus:

Art thou he that should come, or do we look for another? *Mt 11:2–3 (L 7:19)*

Jesus replied:

MATTHEW	LUKE
Go and show John	Go your way, and tell John
again those things	what things
which ye do hear and see:	ye have seen and heard;
the blind receive their sight,	how that the blind see,
and the lame walk,	the lame walk,
the lepers are cleansed,	the lepers are cleansed,
and the deaf hear,	the deaf hear,
the dead are raised up,	the dead are raised,
and the poor have	to the poor
the gospel preached	the gospel is preached.

MATTHEW (cont.)
to them.
And blessed is he,
whosoever shall not
be offended in me.
Mt 11:4–6

LUKE (cont.)

And blessed is he,
whosoever shall not
be offended in me.
L 7:22–23

After John's disciples left, Jesus told the crowd about John:

MATTHEW
What went ye out
into the wilderness
to see?
a reed shaken
with the wind?

But what went ye out
for to see?
A man clothed
in soft raiment?
Behold, they that
wear soft clothing

are in kings' houses.

But what went ye out
for to see?
A prophet?
Yea, I say unto you,
and much more than
a prophet.
For this is he, of whom
it is written,
"Behold, I send
my messenger
before thy face,
which shall
prepare thy way
before thee."
[*Malachi 3:1*]

LUKE
What went ye out
into the wilderness
for to see?
A reed shaken
with the wind?

But what went ye out
for to see?
A man clothed
in soft raiment?
Behold, they which
are gorgeously apparelled,
and live delicately,
are in kings' courts.

But what went ye out
for to see?
A prophet?
Yea, I say unto you,
and much more than
a prophet.
This is he, of whom
it is written,
"Behold, I send
my messenger
before thy face,
which shall
prepare thy way
before thee."
[*Malachi 3:1*]

MATTHEW (cont.)
Verily I say unto you,
among them that are
born of women
there hath not risen
a greater than
John the Baptist:
notwithstanding
he that is least in
the Kingdom of Heaven
is greater than he.

And from the days
of John the Baptist
until now
the Kingdom of Heaven
suffereth violence,
and the violent take it
by force.

For all
the Prophets and the Law
prophesied until John.
And if ye
will receive it,
this is Elijah,
which was
for to come.

He that hath ears
to hear,
let him hear.

But whereunto
shall I liken
this generation?

It is like
unto children

LUKE (cont.)
For I say unto you,
among those that are
born of women
there is not
a greater prophet than
John the Baptist:
but
he that is least in
the Kingdom of God
is greater than he."
L 7:24–28

Whereunto then
shall I liken
the men of this generation?
And to what are they like?

They are like
unto children

71

MATTHEW (cont.)
sitting in the markets,
and calling
unto their fellows,
and saying,
"We have piped
unto you,
and ye have
not danced;
we have mourned
unto you,
and ye have
not lamented."

For John came
neither eating
nor drinking,
and they say,
"He hath a devil."

The Son of man came
eating and drinking,
and they say,
"Behold a man gluttonous,
and a winebibber,
a friend of publicans
and sinners."

But Wisdom is justified
of her children.
Mt 11:7–19

LUKE (cont.)
sitting in the marketplace,
and calling
one to another,
and saying,
"We have piped
unto you,
and ye have
not danced;
we have mourned
to you,
and ye have
not wept."

For John the Baptist came
neither eating bread
nor drinking wine;
and ye say,
"He hath a devil."

The Son of man is come
eating and drinking;
and ye say,
"Behold a gluttonous man,
and a winebibber,
a friend of publicans
and sinners."

But Wisdom is justified
of all her children.
L 7:31–35

John the Baptist had previously told an investigating committee of priests and Levites at Bethany beyond the Jordan River that he was not Elijah:

Q: Art thou Elijah?
A: I am not.
Q: Art thou that prophet?
A: No. *J 1:21*

The last book of the Old Testament, Malachi, had prophesied over 400 years before:

Behold, I will send you Elijah the prophet, before the coming of the great and dreadful day of the Lord; and he shall turn the heart of the fathers to the children, and the heart of the children to their fathers, lest I come and smite the earth with a curse. *Malachi 4:5–6*

Despite John's denial that he was the returned Elijah, Jesus regarded John as the fulfillment of Malachi's prophecy. John's answers to his priestly questioners at Bethany were literally true: he was not Elijah. The truth was, as his father, Zacharias, had heard from the angel of the Lord, John came "in the spirit and power of Elijah":

And many of the children of Israel shall he [John] turn to the Lord their God. And he [John] shall go before him *in the spirit and power of Elijah*, to turn the hearts of the fathers to the children, and the disobedient to the wisdom of the just; to make ready a people prepared for the Lord. *L 1:16–17*

Jesus was asked by his disciples:

Why say the scribes that Elijah must first come? *Mk 9:11 (Mt 17:10)*

Jesus answered:

MARK	MATTHEW
Elijah verily cometh first,	Elijah truly shall come first,
and restoreth all things;	and restore all things.
and how it is written	[Likewise shall also
of the Son of man,	of the Son of man
that he must suffer many things	suffer of them.] *
and be set at nought.	
But I say unto you,	But I say unto you,
that Elijah	that Elijah
is indeed come.	is come already,
	and they knew him not,
and they have done	but have done

73

MARK (cont.)	MATTHEW (cont.)
unto him	unto him
whatsoever they listed,	whatsoever they listed.
as it is *written* of him.	
Mk 9:12–13	
	Mt 17:11–12
	*Conformed to Mark's order

Matthew then adds the comment:

Then the disciples understood that he spake unto them of John the Baptist. *Mt 17:13*

The Elijah "condition" of the scribes had been met in the form of John the Baptist. The birth prophecy of John's father, Zacharias, had been met:

And thou, child, shall be called the prophet of the Highest [Jesus]: for thou shalt go before the face of the Lord [Jesus] to prepare *his* ways; to give knowledge of salvation unto *his* people by [preaching] the remission of their sins, through the tender mercy of our God, whereby the dayspring from on high hath visited us, to give light to them that sit in darkness and in the shadow of death, to guide our feet into the way of peace. *L 1:76–79*

Jesus' own statement was that John was unsurpassed as a prophet, but that his status was inferior to the lowest ranking subject in the Kingdom of God:

MATTHEW	LUKE
Verily I say unto you,	For I say unto you,
among them that are	among those that are
born of women	born of women
there hath not risen	there is not
a greater than	*a greater prophet* than
John the Baptist:	John the Baptist:
notwithstanding	but
he that is least	he that is least
in the Kingdom of Heaven	in the Kingdom of God
is greater than he.	is greater than he.
Mt 11:1	*L 7:28*

If Jesus' statement is read carefully and without presuppositions, it does not give any information as to whether the Kingdom was then present, or still in the future; and whether John was, or was not, included in that Kingdom. Jesus' simple point was that being in that Kingdom was the supremely important thing. Jesus made this point by using an obvious rhetorical device: John is the greatest prophet, but even the lowest subject of the Kingdom has greater status.

Jesus did not say that John's mission was a part of the Kingdom of God; he did say that John came "in the way of righteous":

> For John came unto you *in the way of righteousness*, and ye believed him not: but the publicans and harlots believed him: and ye, when ye had seen it, repented not afterward, that ye might believe him.
> Mt 21:32

This really says no more than that John came preaching righteousness and repentance. That is what prophets did; but John was more than an austere Old Testament prophet born out of due time. We have Jesus' own word that John was "much more than a prophet." Mt 11:9; L 7:26

Jesus proclaimed that John was the messenger described in *Malachi 3:1*

MATTHEW	LUKE
For this is he,	This is he,
of whom it is written,	of whom it is written,
"Behold, I send	"Behold, I send
my messenger	*my messenger*
before thy face,	before thy face,
and which shall prepare	and which shall prepare
thy way before thee."	thy way before thee."
Mt 11:10	L 7:27

The word *messenger* is a technically correct translation of Malachi 3:1, but is inadequate to convey in modern English the majesty of John's mission as the divinely appointed herald of Jesus himself.

Mark chose this "messenger" passage from Malachi to introduce his description of the mission of John the Baptist (Mk 1:2), but he adds to it a quotation of Isaiah 40:3. The other two synoptic Gospels quote only Isaiah 40:3 as their introduction of the mission of John the Baptist:

MARK	MATTHEW	LUKE
As it is written		As it is written
	For this is he	
in	that was spoken of	in the book of the words
the Prophets,	by the Prophet Isaiah,	of Isaiah, the Prophet,
	saying	saying
"Behold I send		
my messenger		
before thy face		
which shall prepare		
thy way		
before thee."		
[Malachi 3:1]		
"The voice of	"The voice of	"The voice of
one crying	*one crying*	*one crying*
in the wilderness,	*in the wilderness,*	*in the wilderness,*
Prepare ye	Prepare ye	Prepare ye
the way of the Lord,	the way of the Lord	the way of the Lord,
make his paths	make his paths	make his paths
straight."	straight."	straight."
Mk 1:2–3 (Isaiah 40:3)	*Mt 3:3 (Isaiah 40:3)*	*L 3:4 (Isaiah 40:3)*

Luke alone continues his quotation of Isaiah beyond 40:3 through 40:4–5:

> Every valley shall be filled and every mountain and hill shall be brought low; and the crooked shall be made straight, and the rough ways shall be made smooth; and all flesh shall see the salvation of God. *L 3:5–6*

The quotation by all three synoptic Gospels of Isaiah 40:3 has created an indelible image of John the Baptist as "one crying in the wilderness." Our sources tell us that John did, in fact, come preaching "in the wilderness of Judea." *Mt 3:1* Mark adds that "John did baptize in the wilderness." *Mk 1:4* Luke simply says that "the word of God came unto John the son of Zacharias *in the wilderness.*" *L 3:2*

Jesus himself regarded John's ministry as a crucial turning point in divine history:

MATTHEW	LUKE
For all the Prophets	The Law
and the Law	and the Prophets
prophesied until John.	were until John:
Mt 11:13	since that time
	the Kingdom of God
	is preached . . .
	L 16:16

This great turning point created confusion so when John (the gospel writer, not John the Baptist) came to write his Gospel he is careful to state in its introduction that John was a "man sent from God" and that he was sent to bear witness to the Light, but he was not himself, the Light:

There was a man sent from God, whose name was John. The same came for a witness, to bear witness to the Light [Jesus], that all men through him might believe. He was *not* that Light, but was sent to bear witness of that Light . . .

John bare witness of him, and cried, saying, "This was he of whom I spake, He that cometh after me is preferred before me: for he was before me." *J 1:6–8, 15*

Jesus himself also recognized that John was a witness to him, but Jesus bluntly stated that he had "a greater witness than that of John":

If I bear witness of myself, my witness is not true.

There is another that beareth witness of me; and I know that witness which he witnesseth of me is true.

Ye sent unto John, and he bear witness unto the truth. But I receive not testimony from man: but these things I say, that ye might be saved. He was a burning and a shining light: and ye were willing for a season to rejoice in his light.

But *I have greater witness than that of John:* for the works which the Father hath given me to finish, the same works that I do, bear witness of me, that the Father hath sent me. *J 5:31–36*

Jesus' decisive proof was not John's testimony but "the works which the Father hath given me to finish, the same works that I do." *J 5:36* Jesus' judgment on John, as it must be for us, was that:

He was a burning and a shining light: and ye were willing *for a season* to rejoice in his light. *J 5:35*

Jesus' own claims were broader:

I am the light of the world. He that followeth me shall not walk in the darkness, but shall have the light of life. *J 8:12*

Jesus' Baptism

Jesus' own ministry began with his baptism by John the Baptist in the Jordan River. *Mk 1:9; Mt 3:13; L 3:21* Jesus was about thirty years old at the time. *L 3:23* The place where Jesus was baptized in the Jordan River is unknown. *Compare J 10:40* The traditional site is southeast of Jericho a few miles north of where the Jordan flows into the Dead Sea. It is usually assumed that this place was named Bethabara beyond Jordan. ("Bethany beyond Jordan" in modern translations) *J 1:28*

Jesus had come from his home at Nazareth in Galilee for the specific purpose of being baptized by John. *Mk 1:9; Mt 3:13* Jesus' baptism was an awesome experience for him:

And straightway coming up out of the water, he saw the heavens opened, and the Spirit like a dove descending upon him: and there came a voice from Heaven, saying, "Thou art my beloved Son, in whom I am well pleased." *Mk 1:10–11*

This awesome experience is reported by all of the first three gospels:

MARK	MATTHEW	LUKE
		Now when all the people were baptized, it came to pass,
And	And Jesus, when he	that Jesus also
	was baptized,	being baptized,
straightway coming up out of the water,	went up straightway out of the water: and, lo,	and praying,
	the heavens were opened unto him,	the heaven was opened,
he saw the heavens opened,	and *he saw*	and

79

MARK (cont.)	MATTHEW (cont.)	LUKE (cont.)
and the Spirit	the Spirit of God descending	the Holy Spirit descended in a bodily shape
like a dove descending	like a dove, and	like a dove
upon him:	lighting upon him:	upon him,
and there came	and lo	and
a voice	a voice	a voice came
from heaven,	from heaven,	from heaven,
saying,	saying,	which said,
"Thou art	"This is	"Thou art
my beloved Son,	my beloved Son,	my beloved Son;
in whom I am	in whom I am	in thee I am
well pleased."	well pleased."	well pleased."
Mk 1:10–11	*Mt 3:16–17*	*L 3:21–22*

According to Luke, the Holy Spirit "descended in a bodily shape like a dove upon him." *L 3:21* The wording in Matthew and Mark is easier for us to understand. They write that Jesus "saw" the Spirit:

MARK	MATTHEW
. . .	. . .descending
like a dove	like a dove
descending	and lighting
upon him.	upon him.
Mk 1:10	*Mt 3:16*

This probably means that Jesus "saw" with inner sight the heavens open and the Spirit descend upon him "like a dove" with celestial beauty and gentleness.

The accounts probably also mean that Jesus heard with inner hearing the "voice from heaven." This traditional Jewish wording "a voice from heaven" literally means a daughter (echo) of the voice of God. The point is not the literal linguistics but the awesome announcement Jesus heard that day:

Thou art my beloved Son, in whom I am well pleased. *Mk 1:11 (Mt 3:17; L 3:22)*

John's Gospel does not record Jesus' baptism. It simply assumes that it has already occurred prior to the arrival of priests and Levites from Jerusalem to interrogate John the Baptist about John's own status. J 1:19–34

On the day after the priests and Levites interrogated John, he saw Jesus "coming unto him" *J 1:29*, and this seems to mean that Jesus was coming to John *again*, i.e., after some earlier occasion when John had baptized Jesus.

What we do know is that on that day John said, apparently referring to Jesus' baptism:

> I saw the Spirit descending from heaven like a dove, and it abode upon him. *And I knew him not*: but he that sent me to baptize with water, the same said unto me, "Upon whom thou shalt see the Spirit descending, and remaining on him, the same is he which baptizeth with the Holy Spirit." And I saw, and bare record that this is the Son of God. *J 1:32–34*

This statement implies that John had not recognized Jesus as the Son of God at the time of Jesus' baptism, but that God had soon revealed this fact to John.

The only record we have of a conversation between Jesus and John at the time of Jesus' baptism is found in Matthew's Gospel:

> Then cometh Jesus from Galilee to Jordan unto John, to be baptized of him. But John forbade him, saying,
>
> "I have need to be baptized of thee, and comest thou to me?"
>
> And Jesus answering said unto him,
>
> "Suffer it to be so now: for thus it becometh us to fulfill all righteousness."
>
> Then he suffered him. *Mt 3:13–15*

This conversation does not necessarily imply that John then knew of Jesus' special status. It may only state that Jesus (as, say,

John's holy second cousin) had just as much right as John to administer John's baptism of repentance.

Jesus, however, insisted that he should be baptized that day like all the people who were being baptized. *L 3:21* He thereby endorsed, although he did not need, John's baptism of repentance.

The crucial point is not what John the Baptist thought or why Jesus wanted to be baptized by John. The crucial point is that at the time Jesus was baptized he received powerful and specific heavenly assurance that he was, indeed, divinely commissioned:

> Thou art my beloved Son, in whom I am well pleased. *Mk 1:11 (Mt 3:17; 1 3:22)*

Jesus' Temptation

Matthew, Mark and Luke agree that following his baptism Jesus spent forty days in the wilderness. *Mk 1:12–13; Mt 4:1–2; L 4:1–2* John omits any account of Jesus' temptation in the wilderness.

The word translated *wilderness* in the Gospel accounts primarily means an uninhabited, lonely place, not necessarily desert or waste land. The location is unknown, but tradition has placed it in the desert hills west of Jericho. We do know that Jesus' temptation was a lonely struggle with Satan himself.

Mark gives us only a bare summary of that struggle:

> And immediately the Spirit driveth him into the wilderness. And he was there in the wilderness forty days, tempted of Satan; and was with the wild beasts; and the angels ministered unto him. *Mk 1:12–13*

Both Matthew and Luke give us detailed accounts of that struggle and add that Jesus fasted those forty days. *Mt 4:1–11; L 4:1–13.* There were no witnesses to Jesus' temptation, except the Devil. Accordingly, what Matthew and Luke have written must have its source in Jesus himself, either directly or indirectly.

Their accounts are as follows:

INTRODUCTION

MATTHEW	LUKE
Then was Jesus	And Jesus being full of the Holy Spirit returned from Jordan,
led up	and was led
to the Spirit	by the Spirit
into the wilderness	into the wilderness,
to be	being forty days
tempted of the Devil.	tempted of the Devil.
And when	And in those days
he had fasted forty days	he did eat nothing:
and forty nights,	

MATTHEW (cont.)	LUKE (cont.)
	And when they were ended,
he was afterward an hungered.	he afterward hungered.
Mt 4:1–2	*L 4:1–2*

CHALLENGE: COMMAND STONES BE MADE BREAD

And when the tempter	And the Devil
came to him,	said unto him,
he said,	
"If thou be the Son of God,	"If thou be the Son of God,
command that these stones	command this stone
be made bread."	that it be made bread"
But he answered and said,	And Jesus answered him, saying
"It is written *[Deut. 8:3],*	"It is written *[Deut. 8:3],* that
man shall not live	man shall not live
by bread alone,	by bread alone,
but by every word	but by every word
that proceedeth out	
of the mouth	
of God."	of God."
Mt 4:3–4	*L 4:3–4*

CHALLENGE: CAST THYSELF DOWN FROM THE TEMPLE

Then the Devil	And he
taketh him up	brought him up
unto the Holy City,	to Jerusalem,
and setteth him on	and set him on
a pinnacle of the Temple,	a pinnacle of the Temple,
and saith unto him,	and said unto him,
"If thou be	"If thou be
the Son of God,	the Son of God,
cast thyself down:	cast thyself down from hence:
for it is written,	for it is written,
[Psalm 91:11–12]	*[Psalm 91:11–12]*
'He shall give	'He shall give
his angels charge	his angels charge
concerning thee;	over thee,

MATTHEW (cont.)

and in their hands
they shall bear thee up,
lest at any time
thou dash thy foot
against a stone.'"

Jesus said unto him,

"It is written again
[*Deut. 6:1*],
'Thou shalt not tempt
the Lord thy God.'"
Mt 4:5–7

LUKE (cont.)
to keep thee,
and in their hands
they shall bear thee up,
lest at any time
thou dash thy foot
against a stone.'"

And Jesus answering said
unto him,
"It is said
[*Deut. 6:16*],
'Thou shalt not tempt
the Lord thy God.'"
L 4:9–12

OFFER: ALL KINGDOMS OF THE WORLD

Again, the Devil
taketh him up into
an exceeding high mountain,
and sheweth him
all the kingdoms of the world,
and the glory of them;

and he saith unto him,
"All these things
will I give thee

if thou
wilt fall down and worship me."

Then
saith Jesus unto him,
"Get thee hence, Satan;
for it is written

And the Devil,
taking him up into
an high mountain,
shewed unto him
all the kingdoms of the world

in a moment of time.
And the Devil said unto him,
"All this power
will I give thee,
and the glory of them:
for that is delivered unto me;
and to whomsoever I will
I give it.
If thou therefore
wilt worship me,
all shall be thine."
And Jesus answered
and said unto him,
"Get thee behind me, Satan;
for it is written

MATTHEW (cont.)	LUKE (cont.)
[*Deut. 6:13*],	[*Deut. 6:13*],
'Thou shalt worship	'Thou shalt worship
the Lord thy God,	the Lord thy God,
and him only shalt thou serve.'"	and him only shalt thou serve.'"
Mt 4:8–10	*L 4:5–8*

CONCLUSION

Then the Devil	And when the Devil
	had ended all the temptation,
leaveth him,	he departed
	from him for a season.
and behold, angels came	*L 4:13*
and ministered unto him.	
Mt 4:11	

It has often been noted that Matthew's and Luke's accounts do not have the second and third temptation in the same sequence. The reason for the variation is not known. Here, I have followed Matthew's order and rearranged the sequence of Luke's verses to match. Accordingly, my reference to the second temptation refers to a jumping from a pinnacle of the Temple; and my reference to the third temptation refers to the vision from a high mountain.

The first and second temptation each begin with the same challenge: "If thou be the Son of God," do some act to prove it. *Mt 4:3, 6; L 4:3, 9* The first challenge was to change stones into bread: a challenge to Jesus to prove his divine status by doing some wonder-working breadmaking. *Mt 4:3; L 4:3* The second challenge was to cast himself off of a height, from literally, a wing (pinnacle) of the Temple: a challenge to Jesus to prove his divine status by superseding the ordinary physical law of gravity.

The accounts of the second challenge state that the Devil either took or brought Jesus up to Jerusalem and set him on a pinnacle of the Temple. This probably does not mean that Jesus was physically transported to that place, just as the third temptation probably does not mean that Jesus was physically taken up on a high mountain.

The question really is this: were the words "brought" and "took up" meant by Jesus to be understood literally (physical movement) or figuratively (as in a vision)? *Mt 4:5, 8; L 4:5, 9* Luke states that from a high mountain the Devil showed Jesus "all the kingdoms of the world *in a moment of time.*" *L 4:5* The Devil used his pervasive powers to disregard time-space limitations to give Jesus this mountain top showing, as well as to give Jesus the view from the pinnacle of the Temple; but Jesus himself remained in the wilderness where his temptation took place. His journeys were spiritual, not physical journeys.

The crucial point of the first two temptations is that Jesus rejected the challenges by the Devil to deny his human limitations and to make stones into bread and to jump harmlessly from the pinnacle of the Temple and thereby nullify Jesus' special mission in the long war between God and the Devil. As the early church put it:

> For we have not an high priest which can not be touched with the feeling of our infirmities; but was in all points tempted like as we are, yet without sin. *Hebrews 4:15*

Essentially, the challenges of Jesus' first two temptations are the same as the challenge by the railing passersby at his cross:

> If thou be the Son of God, come down from the cross. *Mt 27:40*

Jesus rejected those challenges, both in the wilderness and at the cross. The Devil, having failed in his two temptation challenges ("If thou be the Son of God"), was reduced to making his final gambit in the form of a crude offer of all kingdoms of the world if Jesus would defect from God:

> All these things will I give thee, if thou wilt fall down and worship me. *Mt 4:9 (L 4:6–7)*

Jesus did not dispute the Devil's ability to deliver the kingdoms of the world. He did not question the Devil's statement that the power over all kingdoms of the world had been "delivered" unto the Devil. *L 4:6*

The Devil's offer was real, but Jesus flatly rejected it. Jesus rejected the offer because he would not fall down and worship the Devil. That would have been an abandonment of his mission on which God his Father had sent him.

Humanly speaking, Jesus was a devout Jew who customarily attended synagogue on the Sabbath. *L 4:16* As such, he was familiar with the Law and the Prophets and, in fact, used them as the reference point for his own teaching. *Mt 5:17, 7:12, 11:13, 22:40; L 16:16*

It was then to be expected that at the time of his temptation he would turn to the Law and Prophets for his answers. And he did. Each temptation was answered with a quotation from the Law and the Prophets: first temptation, *Deuteronomy 8:3*; second temptation, *Psalm 91:12* and *Deuteronomy 6:16*; and third temptation, *Deuteronomy 6:13.*

Jesus had undertaken a forty-day fast in the wilderness. As his hunger grew and he was tempted to turn stones into bread, it was natural that his thoughts should turn to the manna which had fed his people in the wilderness and to the portion of the Law which stated:

> And thou shalt remember all the way which the Lord thy God led thee these forty years in the wilderness, to humble thee, and to prove thee, to know what was in thine heart, whether thou wouldest keep his commandments, or no. And he humbled thee, and suffered thee, to hunger, and fed thee with manna, which thou knowest not, neither did thy fathers know; that he might make thee know that *man doth not live by bread only, but by every word that proceedeth out of the mouth of the Lord* doth man live." *Deuteronomy 8:2–3*

The Law supplied Jesus' answer to the first temptation:

> It is written, "Man shall not live by bread alone, but by every word that proceedeth out of the mouth of God." *Mt 4:5 (L 4:4)*

While the word of God was reliable and angels would protect Jesus, it was not right to try God by requiring him to do wonder-working miracles on cue. *Deuteronomy 6:16; Psalm 91:11–12* Finally, Jesus quoted the plain statement of Deuteronomy 6:13 that God requires the undivided allegiance of all men, including Jesus his Son.

The temptation of Jesus was not a battle of words, but a titanic battle of wills. Finally, the Devil broke off the combat and withdrew. Angels then ministered to Jesus to soothe the exhaustion of that battle. *Mt 4:11; L 4:13*

JESUS' TRANSFIGURATION

The first three gospels report Jesus' transfiguration. This occurred on a high mountain probably in Galilee some time before Jesus went to Jerusalem for the last time. Unlike the temptation, Jesus was not alone; the inner circle of his disciples, Peter, James, and John, accompanied him. *Mk 9:2; Mt 17:1; L 9:28*

Jesus went to the mountain to pray. *L 9:28* The others slept while he prayed. *L 9:32* They were then startled awake from a heavy sleep and saw Jesus in "his glory," i.e., transfigured. *L 9:33* Matthew and Mark simply say that Jesus "was transfigured before them." *Mk 9:2; Mt 17:2*

The Greek word translated *transfigured* simply means a change in form. We do not have the Aramaic word or phrase these three disciples later used to describe what they saw. For us, the Transfiguration has become a technical theological event; for them, the word translated *transfigured* is simply the opening summary of the dazzling and overwhelming detail of how Jesus looked:

MARK	MATTHEW	LUKE
	And his face did shine as the sun,	The fashion of his countenance was altered,
And his raiment became shining,	and his raiment	and his raiment
exceeding white as snow;	was white as the light.	was white and glistering.
so as no fuller on earth can white them.	*Mt 17:2*	*L 9:29*
Mk 9:3		

When the three disciples were startled awake, they not only were overwhelmed with the glory of Jesus' transfiguration they saw two men standing talking with him: Moses and Elijah. *L 9:32* *(Mk 9:4; Mt 17:3)* In Luke's phrase, they, like Jesus, "appeared in glory." *L 9:31* This "glory" recalls Moses' appearance when he came down off of Mt. Sinai with the second tables of the Law and the skin of his face "shone." *Exodus 34:29–30, 35*

The disciples heard the conversation between the two men and Jesus. *Mk 9:4; Mt 17:3; L 9:30* They spoke of his death, literally his exodus, "which he should accomplish at Jerusalem." *L 9:31* As the two men left (*L 9:33*), Peter said to Jesus:

MARK	MATTHEW	LUKE
Master,	Lord,	Master,
it is good	it is good	it is good
for us to be here;	for us to be here;	for us to be here;
	if thou wilt,	
and let us make	let us make here	and let us make
three tabernacles;	three tabernacles;	three tabernacles;
one for thee,	one for thee,	one for thee,
one for Moses, and	one for Moses, and	one for Moses, and
one for Elijah.	one for Elijah.	one for Elijah.
Mk 9:5	*Mt 17:4*	*L 9:33*

The disciples were overwhelmed with fear, and Peter did not know what he had said. *Mk 9:6; L 9:33* While Peter was still speaking, a bright cloud overshadowed them. We have three accounts:

MARK	MATTHEW	LUKE
And	And while he yet	While he thus
there was	spake, behold,	spake, there came
a cloud that	a bright cloud	a cloud, and
overshadowed them;	overshadowed them:	overshadowed them:
		and they feared
		as they entered
		into the cloud,
and a voice	and behold a voice	and there came a voice
came out of the cloud,	out of the cloud,	out of the cloud,
saying	which said,	saying,
"This is	"This is	"This is
my beloved Son:	my beloved Son,	my beloved Son:
	in whom	
	I am well pleased;	
hear him."	hear ye him."	hear him."
Mk 9:7	*Mt 17:5*	*L 9:34–35*

When Peter came later to write about this incident, he stressed that when they heard the voice, it authenticated that Jesus had "received from God the Father honor and glory." *2 Peter 1:17* That voice which Peter flatly states "we heard," repeated words that probably only Jesus himself heard at his baptism. *2 Peter 1:18*

The words spoken by the voice at Jesus' baptism and at his transfiguration were very similar.

BAPTISM:

MARK	MATTHEW	LUKE
Thou art	This is	Thou art
my beloved Son,	my beloved Son,	my beloved Son;
in whom	in whom	in thee
I am	I am	I am
well pleased.	well pleased.	well pleased.
Mk 1:11	*Mt 3:17*	*L 3:22*

TRANSFIGURATION:

MARK	MATTHEW	LUKE
This is	This is	This is
my beloved Son:	my beloved Son,	my beloved Son:
	in whom	
	I am	
	well pleased;	
hear him.	hear ye him.	hear him.
Mk 9:7	*Mt 17:5*	*L 9:35*

Peter's full written statement made years later is as follows:

For we have not followed cunningly devised fables, when we made known unto you the power and coming of our Lord Jesus Christ, but *were eyewitnesses of his majesty*. For he received from God the Father honor and glory, when there came such voice to him from the excellent glory, "This is my beloved Son, in whom I am well pleased." And this voice which came from heaven *we heard, when we were with him in the holy mount*. *2 Peter 1:16–18*

Towards the end of Jesus' ministry, a voice from heaven came again. Some Greek-speaking proselytes to Judaism were in Jerusalem for the Passover Festival. They approached Philip to arrange an interview with Jesus, saying:

Sir, we would see Jesus. *J 12:21*

Jesus answered them directly:

The hour is come that the Son of man should be glorified. *J 12:23*

Jesus continued:

Now is my soul troubled; and what shall I say? Father, save me from this hour; but for this cause came I unto this hour. Father glorify thy name. *J 12:27–28*

At this point John writes:

Then came there a voice from heaven, saying, "I have both glorified it, and will glorify it again." The people, therefore, that stood by, and heard it, said that it thundered; others said, "An angel spake to him." *J 12:28–29*

Jesus then said:

This voice came not because of me, but for your sakes. *J 12:30*

The voice came to authenticate to the crowd Jesus' glory. The crowd obviously heard the voice, but differed, as one would expect, as to just how to describe it. Peter, James, and John heard the voice on the mountain and agreed on what it said. The voice was, in fact, specifically directed to them, saying, in part: "Hear him." *Mk 9:7; L 9:35 (Mt 17:5)*

That voice and the awesome vision on that mountain were etched in their minds forever:

1. Jesus' face "was altered" and "did shine as the sun." *L 9:29; Mt 17:2*
2. Jesus' clothing became "white as the light" and "as no fuller on earth can white them." *Mt 17:2; Mk 9:3*
3. The white was "glistering" and "shining, exceeding white as snow." *L 9:29; Mk 9:3*

When Peter later wrote of this sight, he simply said that we "were eye witnesses to his majesty." *2 Peter 1:16* It was an observed fact just like Jesus' "power and coming." *2 Peter 1:16*

There is no record that the disciples did, in fact, construct any tabernacles or shrines on this high mountain. The only materials which would have been on hand would have been brush and branches, but the Jews did use branches to construct tabernacles [ritual huts] for the Feast of Tabernacles.

The incident ended as abruptly as it had begun. When the disciples heard the awesome voice out of the cloud, they had fallen on their faces, prostrate with fear. *Mt 17:6* Jesus came and touched them, saying:

Arise, and be not afraid. *Mt 17:7*

The gospel accounts continue:

MARK	MATTHEW	LUKE
And suddenly, when they had looked round about,	And when they had lifted up their eyes,	And when the voice was past,
they saw no man any more,	they saw no man,	
save Jesus only with themselves. *Mk 9:8*	save Jesus only. *Mt 17:8*	Jesus was found alone. *L 9:36*

Luke closes his account with this statement:

And they kept it close, and told no man *in those days* any of the things which they had seen. *L 9:36*

This was in accordance with Jesus' instruction as they came down the mountain:

MARK	MATTHEW
And as they came down from the mountain, he charged them	And as they came down from the mountain, Jesus charged them, saying,
that they should tell no man what things they had seen, *till* the Son of man were risen from the dead. And they kept that saying with themselves, questioning one with another what the rising from the dead should mean. *Mk 9:9–10*	*"Tell the vision to no man,* *until* the Son of man be risen again from the dead." *Mt 17:9*

The disciples were puzzled by his instruction because their Jewish popular theology held that Elijah must return first. The following dialogue then ensued:

	MARK	MATTHEW
DISCIPLES:	Why say the scribes that Elijah must first come?	Why then say the scribes that Elijah must first come?
JESUS:	Elijah verily cometh first, and restoreth all things;	Elijah truly shall first come, and restore all things.

MARK (cont.)	**MATTHEW** (cont.)
and how it is written	[Likewise shall also
of the Son of man,	the Son of man
that he must suffer	suffer
many things,	of them.
and be set at nought.	
But I say unto you,	But I say unto you,
that Elijah is indeed come,	that Elijah is come already,
	and they knew him not,
and they have done	but have done
unto him	unto him
whatsoever they listed,	whatsoever they listed.]*
as it is written of him."	*Mt 17:10–12*
Mk 9:11–13	*Conformed to Mark's order

Matthew only adds:

Then the disciples understood that he spake unto them of John the Baptist. *Mt 17:13*

(See "Jesus and John," pp. 72–74 for a discussion of the Elijah "condition.")

THE VOICE FROM THE EXCELLENT GLORY

All we know is that Jesus took his key disciples up on a high mountain, not necessarily to the top, but to a place where they were alone so he could pray. He prayed; they slept. *L 9:32* It was no different than Gethsemane. *Mk 14:37; Mt 26:40; L 22:45*

The disciples were startled awake from heavy sleep and saw Jesus' face and clothes were dazzlingly different and he was standing, talking with two men, Moses and Elijah, about his coming death in Jerusalem. *L 9:31–32*

Peter made a bumbling remark about building three tabernacles, and while he was still speaking, a cloud engulfed "them." *Mk 9:7; Mt 17:5; L 9:34* Luke adds that "they feared as they entered the cloud." *L 9:34* Translations differ as to whether the cloud engulfed the disciples as well as the others.

Whether the disciples themselves were engulfed in the cloud or not, it is clear that they heard the voice which rang "out of the cloud":

This is my beloved Son: hear ye him. *Mk 9:7; Mt 17:5; L 9:35*

Then there was nothing, just Jesus alone; but his Father had claimed Jesus as his own Son in a way that the disciples could never forget, nor did they. *2 Peter 1:18* But, Jesus expressly instructed them to keep their experience confidential until "the Son of man were risen from the dead." *Mk 9:9 (Mt 17:9)*

Jesus' own word was that their experience was a "vision." *Mt 17:9* The Greek word used in Matthew for Jesus' word is the same Greek word used in Acts to describe the "sight" of the angel of the Lord in a flame of fire in a bush, the vision of Ananias, the vision of Cornelius, the vision of Peter as to unclean beasts and fowls, the vision of Peter upon being released from prison, the vision of Paul as to the man of Macedonia, and the vision of Paul in Corinth. *Acts 7:31, 9:10, 10:3, 10:17, 19, 11:5, 12:9, 16:9, 18:9*

We cannot penetrate beyond the words used. Matthew has the word "vision" while Mark has simply, "things they had seen":

MARK	MATTHEW
And as they came down	And as they came down
from the mountain,	from the mountain,
he charged them that	Jesus charged them,
they should tell no man	saying, "Tell
what things they had seen,	*the vision* to no man
till the Son of man	until the Son of man
were risen from the dead.	be risen again from the dead."
Mk 9:9	*Mt 17:9*

The things which they had seen and heard were real. And, Jesus did rise from the dead, and the disciples did then tell of their awesome experience. Peter wrote of that experience:

For he received from God the Father honor and glory, when there came *such a voice to him from the excellent glory*, "This is my beloved Son, in whom I am well pleased." *2 Peter 1:17*

THE BEGINNINGS OF JESUS' MINISTRY

Jesus' transfiguration occurred late in his ministry; his baptism and temptation occurred just before it began. After his temptation, he went to a place where John was engaged in a confrontation with some priests and Levites sent from Jerusalem to investigate John's status. *J 1:19–27* Jesus was there as a bystander. *J 1:26*

This place is described in John's gospel as "Bethabara beyond Jordan, where John was baptizing." *J 1:28* ("Bethany beyond Jordan" in modern translations) This place is usually assumed to be the place where John baptized Jesus. *Mk 1:9; Mt 3:16; L 3:21*

This assumption may not be correct for several reasons. First, John baptized at a number of places. For example, "Aenon near to Salim," *J 3:23,* and "the place where John at *first* baptized." *J 10:40* Second, it was then over forty days since Jesus' baptism and, in the meantime, John may have moved north from the site of Jesus' baptism somewhere east of Jericho to the place, Bethany beyond Jordan, where John was being interrogated by the investigating priests and Levites. *J 1:19–28* The site of Bethany beyond Jordan is unknown, but the apparent fact that Jesus walked from that place to Cana in Galilee in two days strongly suggests that it must have been in the Jordan valley north towards the Sea of Galilee rather than in the southern valley east of Jericho. The apparent fact that Bethany beyond Jordan was a two-day walk from Cana is based upon an analysis of the rather vague chronology in John's Gospel. *J 1:29, 35, 43, 2:1*

What is important is that Jesus called his first disciples at Bethany beyond Jordan the next day after he had been a bystander to the confrontation between John and the investigating priests and Levites. *J 1:37–42* It is also important that these first four disciples were apparently already disciples of John. It is certain that this was the case with Andrew and is likely with Peter, Philip and Nathanael since, at the very least, they were present at a site where John was baptizing and they were a long way from their homes in Galilee. *J 1:35, 37, 40, 42, 43*

At Bethany beyond Jordan John the Baptist saw Jesus walk by and said:

Behold the Lamb of God! *J 1:38*

Two disciples of John were standing with him and heard what John had said. They started to follow Jesus. He turned around, saw them following him and said to them:

What seek ye? *J 1:38*

They answered:

Rabbi, where dwellest thou? *J 1:38*

Jesus replied:

Come and see. *J 1:39*

It was then about 4:00 P.M., and the two men came to Jesus' lodgings and stayed with him the rest of the day. *J 1:39* One of the two men was Andrew, Simon Peter's brother. *J 1:40* Afterward Andrew went to his brother and told him:

We have found the Messiah. *J 1:41*

Andrew brought Peter to Jesus, and Jesus said:

Thou art Simon the son of Jona: thou shalt be called Cephas. *J 1:42*

The following day, Jesus decided to return to Galilee and found a man named Philip and said to him:

Follow me. *J 1:43*

Philip, Peter, and Andrew were all from the same town, Bethsaida, on the north side of the Sea of Galilee. *J 1:44* Nathanael

was also a Galilean, and his home town, Cana, was near Nazareth.
J 21:2

Philip then told Nathanael:

We have found him, of whom Moses in the Law, and the Prophets,
did write, Jesus of Nazareth, the son of Joseph. J 1:45

Nathanael was skeptical and retorted:

Can any good thing come out of Nazareth? J 1:46

Philip replied:

Come and see. J 1:46

When Nathanael went to meet Jesus, the conversation went
like this:

JESUS: Behold an Israelite indeed, in whom is no guile! J 1:47
NATHANAEL: Whence knowest thou me? J 1:48
JESUS: Before that Philip called thee, when thou wast under the fig
tree, I saw thee. J 1:48
NATHANAEL: Rabbi, thou art the Son of God; thou art the King of
Israel. J 1:49
JESUS: Because I said unto thee, I saw thee under the fig tree, believest
thou? Thou shalt see greater things than these. Verily, verily, I
say unto you, hereafter you shall see heaven open, and the an-
gels of God ascending and descending upon the Son of Man.
J 1:50–51

Jesus then left Bethany and went to Cana in Galilee, arriving
two days later. J 2:1 He was apparently accompanied by his new
disciples since he "and his disciples" were guests at a wedding in
Cana that day. J 2:2 Cana is only about eight miles from Nazareth,
and Jesus' mother was also a guest at the wedding. J 2:1
She told Jesus:

They have no wine. *J 2:3*

Jesus replied:

Woman, what have I to do with thee? Mine hour is not yet come.
J 2:4

His mother told the servants:

Whatsoever he saith unto you, do it. *J 2:5*

They had six waterpots of stone, each with a capacity of two or
three *firkins. J 2:6* A firkin is about 8 3/4 gallons. These pots were
used to hold water for the ritual washings required by the tradition of the elders before eating. *J 2:6; Mk 7:3–5*
Jesus told the servants:

Fill the waterpots with water. *J 2:7*

They did so, and Jesus instructed them:

Draw out now, and bear unto the governor of the feast. *J 2:8*

They did so. The governor tasted "the water that was made
wine" and was impressed with the quality of the wine. *J 2:9–11*
This was Jesus' first miracle, and it is discussed in detail in the
section, "The Miracle Of Water Into Wine," pp 1021–1022. Here
the point is that it was an impressive sign to his first disciples.
John writes:

This beginning of miracles did Jesus in Cana of Galilee, and manifested forth his glory, *and his disciples believed on him. J 2:11*

After attending the wedding at Cana, Jesus went to Capernaum,
a town on the northwest shore of the Sea of Galilee a short distance west of Bethsaida. *J 2:21* John's own words are:

After this he went down to Capernaum, he, and his mother, and his brethren [brothers], and his disciples; and they continued there not many days. J 2:12

The next sentence in John's Gospel abruptly shifts to a visit by Jesus to Jerusalem at the time of Passover:

And the Jews' Passover was at hand, and Jesus went up to Jerusalem. J 2:13

John reports that while Jesus was in Jerusalem he cleansed the Temple. J 2:14–22 Scholars argue whether Jesus cleansed the Temple only once, or twice: once as stated in John and again late in his ministry as stated in the synoptic gospels. Mk 11:15–18; Mt 21:12–16; L 19:45–48 Here we assume that there were two cleansings of the Temple and that the first cleansing is described in John's Gospel in chapter 2:14–22. This cleansing was the first incident in Jesus' First Judean Ministry, which is outlined next.

THE FIRST JUDEAN MINISTRY

The Passover occurred on the 14th day of Nisan, the Jewish lunar month of March-April, and was followed by other religious observances lasting about a week, all commemorating the divine deliverance of the Jews from Egypt some 1,300 years before.

In the Temple in Jerusalem there were dealers who sold oxen, sheep and doves for religious sacrifice and money changers who changed pilgrims' money so that they could pay, in coins without heathen inscriptions, the temple tax laid on all Jews. *J 2:14* Jesus made a scourge of small cords and drove out the dealers and money changers: ". . .he drove them all out of the Temple, and the sheep, and the oxen; and poured out the changers' money and overthrew the tables." *J 2:15*

He then told the dove-sellers:

Take these things hence; make not my Father's house an house of merchandise. *J 2:16*

The Jews then said:

What sign shewest thou unto us that thou doest these things? *J 2:18*

Jesus replied:

Destroy this temple, and in three days I will raise it up. *J 2:19*

The Jews then said:

Forty and six years was this Temple in building, and wilt thou rear it up in three days? *J 2:20*

Jesus' statement not only puzzled the Jews but it also was not understood even by his disciples until after his resurrection several years later when they "remembered that he had said this unto them" and they then understood that he had spoken of "the temple of his body." *J 2:21–22*

Jesus' action in cleansing the Temple did, however, remind his disciples of Psalm 69:9 which states:

The zeal of thine house hath eaten me up. *J 2:17 (Psalm 69:9)*

Jesus had indeed struck at the corruption of the holy Temple of the Jews like an Old Testament prophet consumed with the fire of righteousness, but he was known as "a teacher come from God" who had been doing miracles. *J 3:2*

This, even a leading member of the Jewish religious establishment, Nicodemus, was ostensibly prepared to concede. The King James Version simply calls Nicodemus "a ruler of the Jews." *J 3:1* More specifically, he was a member of the Jewish ruling council known as the Sanhedrin and a Pharisee as well. *J 3:1, 7:50–51*

He said to Jesus:

Rabbi, we know that thou art a teacher come from God, for no man can do these miracles, . . . *except* God be with him. *J 3:2*

Jesus retorted with a hint of irony:

Verily, verily I say unto thee, *except* a man be born again, he can not see the Kingdom of God. *J 3:3*

This was a sardonic thrust at a man who dared to interview him only secretly: he came "by night." *J 3:2* Actually, Nicodemus did not then believe that Jesus was "a teacher come from God." Jesus bluntly told him, "Ye receive not our witness," and "I have told you earthly things, and ye believe not, how shall ye believe, if I tell you of heavenly things?" *J 3:11–12*

The dialogue of Jesus and Nicodemus had gone like this:

NICODEMUS: How can a man be born when he is old? Can he enter the second time into his mother's womb, and be born?
JESUS: Verily, verily, I say unto thee, except a man be born of water and of the Spirit, he cannot enter the Kingdom of God. That

which is born of the flesh is flesh; that which is born of the
Spirit is spirit. Marvel not that I said unto thee, "Ye must be
born again."
The wind bloweth where it listeth, and thou hearest the sound
thereof, but canst not tell whence it cometh, and whither it
goeth: so is every one that is born of the Spirit.

NICODEMUS: How can these things be?

JESUS: Art thou a master of Israel, and knowest not these things?
Verily, verily, I say unto thee, we speak that we do know, and
testify that we have seen; *and ye receive not our witness.* If I
have told you earthly things, *and ye believe not,* how shall ye
believe, if I tell you of heavenly things? *J 3:4–12*

Despite Nicodemus' rejection of Jesus' witness, he was impressed enough by Jesus' miracles to have come to inquire. *J 3:2*
Many others were impressed with Jesus' miracles and believed:

Now when he was in Jerusalem at the Passover, in the feast day,
many believed in his name, when they saw the miracles which he
did. *J 2:23*

Despite this popularity Jesus reserved judgment:

But Jesus did not commit himself unto them, because he knew all
men, and needed not that any should testify of man: for he knew
what was in man. *J 2:24–25*

Jesus then left Jerusalem and ministered in Judea, its surround-
ing province:

After these things came Jesus and his disciples into the land of Judea;
and there he tarried with them, and baptized. *J 3:22*

John is careful to add that it was not Jesus but his disciples
who did the baptizing. *J 4:2* In fact, they were baptizing more persons than John the Baptist, who was continuing his own ministry
"in Aenon near to Salim." *J 3:23, 4:1* The location of this place is

unknown but was probably in Decapolis and not in Judea. While John ministered there, Jesus conducted his own ministry in Judea, making more disciples than John. *J 4:1*

The success of this Judean ministry is probably back of Jesus' statement after he got back to Galilee that "a prophet hath no honor in his own country." *J 4:44* Jesus' return to his native Galilee was apparently induced by the arrest of John the Baptist:

MARK	MATTHEW
Now after that	Now when
	Jesus had heard
John was	that John was
put in prison,	cast into prison,
Jesus came	he departed
into Galilee, . . .	into Galilee.
Mk 1:14	*Mt 4:12*

John, in a guarded way, perhaps suggests the same thing, although he states that Jesus was concerned that the Pharisees knew that he was making more disciples than John the Baptist:

When therefore the Lord [Jesus] knew how the Pharisees had heard that Jesus made and baptized more disciples than John, . . . he left Judea, and departed again into Galilee." *J 4:1, 3*

Jesus then returned to Galilee by way of Samaria. *J 4:3–4*

The Journey Home Through Samaria

While crossing Samaria on the way to Galilee, Jesus became weary and stopped to rest about noon at Jacob's Well outside the town of Sychar. *J 4:5–6* His disciples continued on into Sychar to buy meat. *J 4:8*

As Jesus waited, a Samaritan woman came to the well to draw water, and Jesus asked her for a drink. *J 4:7*

The woman replied:

How is it that thou, being a Jew, askest drink of me, which am a woman of Samaria? *J 4:9*

Jesus answered:

If thou knewest the gift of God, and who it is that saith to thee, "Give me to drink"; thou wouldest have asked of him, and he would have given thee living water. *J 4:10*

The woman replied:

Sir, thou hast nothing to draw with, and the well is deep; from whence then hast thou that living water? Art thou greater than our father Jacob, which gave us the well, and drank thereof himself, and his children, and his cattle? *J 4:11–12*

Jesus then said to her:

Whosoever drinketh of this water shall thirst again. But whosoever drinketh of the water that I shall give him shall never thirst; but the water that I shall give him shall be in him a well of water springing up into everlasting life. *J 4:13–14*

The woman replied:

Sir, give me this water, that I thirst not, neither come hither to draw. *J 4:15*

The conversation then turned to the woman's marital status. *J 4:16–18* The woman ultimately said:

> Sir, I perceive that thou art a prophet. Our [Samaritan] fathers worshipped in [on] this mountain [Mt. Gerizim]; and ye say [as a Jew], that in Jerusalem [at the Temple] is the place where men ought to worship. *J 4:19–20*

The Samaritans had had their own temple on nearby Mt. Gerizim, but the Jews had destroyed that temple in the course of the Maccabean Wars about 150 years earlier, in 128 B.C. The Temple of the Jews was, of course, in Jerusalem.

Jesus said to the woman:

> Woman, believe in me, the hour cometh, when ye shall neither in [on] this mountain, nor yet at Jerusalem, worship the Father. Ye worship ye know not what; we [Jews] know what we worship: for salvation is of the Jews.

> But the hour cometh, and now is, when the true worshippers shall worship the Father in spirit and in truth: for the Father seeketh such to worship him. God is a spirit: and they that worship him must worship him in spirit and in truth.

The woman replied:

> I know that Messias [the Messiah] cometh, which is called Christ [the Anointed One]. When he is come, he will tell us all things. *J 4:25*

Jesus then said:

> I that speak unto thee am he. *J 4:25*

In the meantime Jesus' disciples, who had been in town purchasing meat, had come up and they said:

> Master, eat. *J 4:31*

Jesus replied cryptically:

I have meat to eat that ye know not of. *J 4:32*

This puzzled his literal-minded disciples who asked each other:

Hath any man brought him ought to eat? *J 4:33*

Jesus then made his point:

My meat is to do the will of him that sent me, and to finish his work. *J 4:34*

The Samaritan woman was so impressed with Jesus that she left her waterpot at the well and went about town telling the men of the town *J 4:28*:

Come, see a man, which told me all things that ever I did: is not this the Christ? *J 4:29*

Many of the townspeople believed on Jesus by reason of what the woman said. *J 4:39* Accordingly, they requested Jesus to stay at Sychar, and he did stay there two days, adding many more converts "because of his own word." *J 4:40–41, 43*
They told the woman:

Now we believe, not because of thy saying; for we have heard him ourselves, and know that this is indeed the Christ, the Savior of the world. *J 4:42*

JESUS' RECEPTION IN GALILEE

After two days in Sychar, Samaria, Jesus went on to Galilee. *J 4:43* He apparently went first to Cana, where he had done his first miracle before he had gone to Jerusalem for Passover. *J 2:1–13, 4:46* A royal official who had a sick son in Capernaum was in Cana. *J 4:46* The official contacted Jesus "and besought him that he would come down, and heal his son: for he was at the point of death." *J 4:47* Jesus' response was guarded:

Except ye see signs and wonders, ye will not believe. *J 4:48*

The official pleaded:

Sir, come down ere my child die. *J 4:49*

Jesus replied:

Go thy way; thy son liveth. *J 4:50*

The Gospel then states that "the man believed the word that Jesus had spoken unto him, and he went his way." *J 4:50* On his way down to Capernaum, the official was met by his servants, who told him, "Thy son liveth." *J 4:51*

The official asked when the change came and was told, "Yesterday at the seventh hour the fever left him." *J 4:52*

This was the hour when Jesus had spoken. *J 4:53* The official "believed, and his whole house." *J 4:53*

John's Gospel then summarizes:

This is again the second miracle that Jesus did, when he was come out of Judea into Galilee. *J 4:54*

This statement is ambiguous. John introduces the report of this healing with a reference to the miracle of water into wine, which he had previously stated was Jesus' first miracle. *J 2:11, 4:46* It is likely that John 4:54, which states that "This is again the second miracle that Jesus did" is saying that this was his second miracle *in Cana* and took place *after* Jesus had returned from Judea, not that it was his second miracle after he had returned from Judea.

What is certain is that this healing took place in the glow of reports by his fellow Galileans who had seen his miracles in Jerusalem when they were also there for the Passover feast:

> Then when he was come into Galilee, the Galileans received him, having seen all the things that he did at Jerusalem at the feast: for they also went unto the feast. *J 4:45*

Matthew states that Jesus' ministry in Galilee was fulfillment of a prophecy of Isaiah:

> That it might be fulfilled which was spoken by Isaiah the prophet, saying, "The land of Zabulon, and the land of Nephthalim, by the way of the sea, beyond Jordan, Galilee of the Gentiles; the people which sat in darkness saw great light; and to them which sat in the region and the shadow of death, light is sprung up." *Mt 4:14–16 (Isaiah 9:1–2)*

Zabulon, now spelled *Zebulun* and Nephthalim, now spelled *Nephtali*, were the areas occupied by those two tribes of Israel after the conquest of Canaan. These areas lay generally west of the Sea of Galilee. "By way of the sea" refers to the trade route from Damascus, Syria, that passed northwest of the Sea of Galilee and then turned south and west towards the Mediterranean Sea. Isaiah called Galilee, "Galilee of the Gentiles," or "Galilee of the nations," because it was ringed, except in the south, by various Gentile nations. *Isaiah 9:1*

At the time of Jesus, this was still true, and Galilee was also crossed by major trade routes, which encouraged Gentile infiltration. Galilee was then prosperous and thickly populated, with agriculture thriving due to the richness of its soil and its well-watered northern location. *Josephus, Wars of the Jews, Book III, Ch. III, Sec. 2*

The Judean Jews looked down upon Galilee and its Jews. *J 4:41, 51–52; Acts 5:37* Galileans had their own local dialect. *Mk 14:70; Mt 26:73; L 22:59* Galilee was the site of most of Jesus' ministry.

Jesus was known in Judea as "Jesus of Galilee" or as "Jesus the prophet of Nazareth of Galilee." *Mt 26:69; Mt 21:11* However, when Jesus returned from Judea to Galilee, he did not return to Nazareth where he had been brought up, but instead established his residence in Capernaum. *Mt 4:13; L 4:16, 31*

Thus Capernaum became "his own city." *Mt 9:1* Matthew describes Capernaum's location as "upon the sea coast, in the borders of Zabulon and Nephthalim." *Mt 4:13* In plain English, Capernaum was on the northwest shore of the Sea of Galilee within the historic boundaries of Galilee.

THE DISCIPLES

Shortly after Jesus' return to Galilee from Judea, the synoptic gospels, Matthew, Mark, and Luke, report what has come to be known as the "call" of four fishermen to be "fishers of men": Andrew, Peter and two Zebedee brothers, James and John. *Mk 1:16–20; Mt 4:18–22; L 5:1–11* This call is discussed in detail in the section "Jesus' Recruitment Of His Disciples," pp. 342–347.

Here it is sufficient to note that the casual impression from reading the synoptic gospels that this was Jesus' first contact with these four disciples is not correct. He already knew Peter and Andrew from Bethany beyond Jordan. *J 1:40–42* We tend to assume that the disciples immediately upon recruitment became full-time "professional" disciples. It is more likely that they returned to their jobs, fishing, since they would have to make a living, and only gradually over time did they accompany Jesus about full time. In short, Jesus' call to two of these four fishermen, Andrew and Peter at the Sea of Galilee was a call to further commitment, not their initial recruitment.

This analysis is reinforced when the accounts of the four gospels are closely compared chronologically. John reports that Jesus met Andrew, Peter, Philip and Nathanael at Bethany beyond Jordan. *J 1:35–51* The synoptic gospels omit this incident, Jesus' return to Galilee shortly thereafter, his journey to Jerusalem for Passover, his first ministry in Judea and his return to Galilee by way of Samaria. Instead, the synoptic gospels go directly from Jesus' temptation to his return to Galilee after his first Judean ministry. *Mk 1:14; Mt 4:12; L 4:14*

After Jesus called these four fishermen by the Sea of Galilee, they accompanied him back to Capernaum. *Mk 1:21* He and the four fishermen apparently stayed in the house of Peter and Andrew there and on the Sabbath went to the synagogue together. *Mk 1:21, 29* On that Sabbath, Jesus taught in the synagogue, and a man with unclean spirit was healed. *Mk 1:23–27; L 4:33–36* Later that day Jesus healed Peter's mother-in-law and numerous others. *Mk 1:29–34; Mt 8:14–16; L 4:38–41*

114

Shortly thereafter Jesus recruited Matthew, called Levi in Mark's and Luke's gospels. *Mk 2:14; Mt 9:9; L 5:27–28* He was manning an internal tariff collection booth near the Sea of Galilee. The accounts are laconic. Jesus passed by and said, "Follow me," and Matthew got up and did so. *Mk 2:14; Mt 9:9; L 5:27–28*

Some time later Jesus decided to appoint twelve special disciples from all the men who were following him. We have three accounts:

MARK	MATTHEW	LUKE
		And it came to pass in those days,
And he goeth up into a mountain,		that he went out into a mountain to pray, and continued all night in prayer to God.
	And when	And when it was day,
and calleth	he had called	he called
unto him	unto him	unto him
whom he would:	his twelve disciples,	his disciples:
and they came unto him.		
And he		And of them he
ordained twelve,		chose twelve,
that they should be		whom also
with him,		he named apostles.
and that he might		*L 6:12–13*
send them forth		
to preach,	he gave them	
and to have power	power against unclean spirits, to cast them out,	
to heal	and to heal	
sicknesses,	all manner of sickness	
and to cast out	and all manner	
devils.	of disease.	
Mk 3:13–15	*Mt 10:1*	

Each of the three accounts then gives a list of the names of the twelve disciples. *Mk 3:16–19; Mt 10:2–4; L 6:14–16* For further details see "Jesus' Recruitment of His Disciples," pp. 342–347, and "The Mission of the Twelve," pp. 399–404. Some time later Jesus sent out either seventy or seventy-two disciples with specific instructions as to preaching and procedures to be followed. See "The Mission of the Seventy," pp. 405–411.

Our looking backward focus on the Twelve, whose names we know, and the Seventy, whose instructions we have, ought not to obscure the fact that Jesus had a large number of disciples, not just great crowds of onlookers. Luke states that when Jesus came down from a mountain after a night of prayer, that he called unto him "his disciples; and *of them* he chose twelve." *L 6:13* Luke continues:

> And he came down with them, and stood in the plain, and the company of his disciples, *and* a great multitude of people out of all Judea and Jerusalem, and from the sea coast of Tyre and Sidon, . . . *L 6:17*

Modern translations make it clear that King James' phrase, "the company of disciples," is more accurately translated by a phrase like a *big crowd of disciples.*

Although Jesus had crowds of disciples, some of those defected. John reports one instance. *J 6:59–67* Jesus had taught in the synagogue at Capernaum that "Whoso eateth my flesh and drinketh my blood, hath eternal life" *(J 6:54)* and this had offended many disciples. John reports:

> Many therefore of his disciples, when they had heard this, said, "This is an hard saying; who can hear it?"

> When Jesus knew in himself that his disciples murmured at it, he said unto them, "Doth this offend you?" . . .

> From that time many of his disciples went back, and walked no more with him. *J 6:60–61, 66*

When this defection occurred, Jesus turned to his inner core of disciples, the Twelve:

Then said Jesus unto the Twelve, "Will ye also go away?" *J 6:67*

The Twelve did not leave Jesus; instead they accompanied him to Jerusalem, and to his death. *Mk 10:32–34; Mt 20:17–19; L 18:31–34*

Jesus' Ministry in the Galilean Synagogues

Luke writes:

And Jesus returned in the power of the Spirit into Galilee: and there went out a fame of him through all the region round about. And he *taught in their synagogues*, being glorified of all. *L 4:14–15*

The flavor of this early synagogue ministry is caught by three summary statements, one in Mark and two in Matthew:

Mark	Matthew	Matthew
And he	And Jesus went about all Galilee,	And Jesus went about all the cities and villages,
preached in their synagogues throughout all Galilee, and cast out devils. *Mk 1:39*	*teaching in their synagogues,* and preaching the gospel of the Kingdom, and healing	*teaching in their synagogues,* and preaching the gospel of the Kingdom, and healing every sickness
	all manner of disease among the people. *Mt 4:23*	and every disease among the people. *Mt 9:35*

Specifically we know that Jesus taught on the Sabbath in synagogues in Capernaum and Nazareth: *Mk 1:21; J 6:59 (Capernaum); Mk 6:1–2; Mt 13:54; L 4:16 (Nazareth)* Some time after he had established his residence in Capernaum, he went "as his custom was" to the synagogue in Nazareth, the town "where he had been brought up." *L 4:16, 23*

When he stood up to read the Scripture, the synagogue attendant handed him the book of the prophet Isaiah and he opened to the place where it is written:

The Spirit of the Lord is upon me, because he hath anointed me to preach the gospel to the poor; he hath sent me to heal the broken-hearted, to preach deliverance to the captives, and recovering of

118

sight to the blind, to set at liberty them that are bruised, to preach the acceptable year of the Lord." *L 4:18–19 [Isaiah 61:1–2]*

Jesus then closed the book and gave it to the attendant and sat down:

And the eyes of all them that were in the synagogue were fastened on him. *L 4:20*

Then Jesus said:

This day is this scripture fulfilled in your ears. *L 4:21*

The congregation was stunned and said:

Is not this Joseph's son? *L 4:22*

Jesus then spoke:

Ye will surely say unto me this proverb, "Physician, heal thyself": whatsoever we have heard done in Capernaum, do also here in *thy country*.

Verily I say unto you, no prophet is accepted in *his own country*.

But I tell you of a truth, many widows were in Israel in the days of Elijah, when the heaven was shut up three years and six months, when great famine was throughout all the land; but unto none of them was Elijah sent, save unto Sarepta, a city of Sidon, unto a woman that was a widow.

And many lepers were in Israel in the time of Elisha the prophet; and none of them was cleansed, saving Naaman the Syrian." *L 4:23–27*

This blunt indictment enraged the entire congregation. *L 4:28* They immediately seized him and forced him to the brow of the hill on which this hill town was built and tried to throw him "down headlong." *L 4:29* Jesus, however, managed to elude them and returned to Capernaum. *L 4:30–31*

At Capernaum Jesus resumed his teaching. *L 4:23, 31* This was done on the Sabbath days. *L 4:31* This was done in the synagogue there as Mark expressly states. *Mk 1:21; (J 6:59)* Jesus' teaching astonished the people, because he taught on his own authority and not simply as an expositor of the traditions:

MARK	LUKE
And they were astonished	And they were astonished
at his doctrine:	at his doctrine:
for he taught them	for his word
as one that had authority,	was with power.
and not as the scribes.	*L 4:32*
Mk 1:22	

Later on after his miracles became known, Jesus returned with his disciples on another Sabbath to the synagogue at Nazareth. *Mk 6:1–2; Mt 13:54* The mood of the congregation had changed from wrath to astonishment. *L 4:28; Mk 6:2; Mt 13:54* The congregation was saying:

MARK	MATTHEW
From whence hath	Whence hath
this man these things?	this man
And what wisdom is this	this wisdom,
which is given unto him,	
that even such mighty works	and these mighty works?
are wrought by his hands?	
Is not this the carpenter,	Is not this the carpenter's son?
the son of Mary,	Is not his mother called Mary?
the brother of James,	And his brethren, James,
and Joses,	and Joses,
and of Judas, and Simon?	and Simon, and Judas?
And are not his sisters	And his sisters,
here with us?	are they not all with us?
	Whence then
	hath this man
	all these things?
And they were	And they were
offended at him.	offended in him.
Mk 6:2–3	*Mt 13:54–57*

120

Jesus' reply is now one of his best known statements:

MARK	MATTHEW
A prophet	A prophet
is not without honor,	is not without honor,
but in his own country,	save in his own country,
and among his own kin,	
and in his own house.	and in his own house.
Mk 6:4	*Mt 13:57*

The gospel accounts of this visit to the Nazareth synagogue close with these statements:

MARK	MATTHEW
And he could there	And he
do no mighty work	did not many mighty works
save that	there
he laid his hands	
upon a few sick folk,	
and healed them.	
And he marvelled	
because of their unbelief.	because of their unbelief.
And he went	*Mt 13:58*
round about the villages,	
teaching.	
Mk 6:5–6	

The negative reception of Jesus at the Nazareth synagogue was atypical. Generally he was enthusiastically received, both in Galilee generally and elsewhere.

After he had healed a man of an unclean spirit in the synagogue at Capernaum, the gospels report:

MARK	LUKE
And immediately	And
his fame	the fame of him
spread abroad	went out
throughout all the region	into every place

MARK (cont.)

round about Galilee.
Mk 1:28

LUKE (cont.)
of the country
round about.
L 4:37

Jesus' Healing Ministry in Galilee

In Capernaum after sunset on a Sabbath, a crowd gathered at the house of Peter and Andrew. *Mk 1:30; L 4:38* The synoptic gospels have this report:

MARK	MATTHEW	LUKE
And at even,	When the even	Now when
when the sun did set,	was come,	the sun was setting,
they brought unto him	they brought unto him	
all that were diseased,	many	all they
and them that were	that were	
possessed with devils.	possessed with devils:	
And all the city		
was gathered together		
at the door.		
And he healed many		
that were sick		that had any sick
of divers diseases,		with divers diseases
and cast out	and he cast out	brought them
many devils;	the spirits	unto him;
	with his word,	and he laid
		his hands on
	and healed all that	every one of them,
	were sick:	and healed them.
and suffered not		And devils
the devils to speak,		also came out
because		of many,
they knew him.	that it might be	crying out,
Mk 1:32–34	fulfilled	and saying,
	which was spoken by	"Thou art Christ
	Isaiah the prophet,	the Son of God."
	saying,	And he
	"Himself took	rebuking them
	our infirmities,	suffered them
	and bare	not to speak:
		for they knew

MARK (cont.)	MATTHEW (cont.)	LUKE (cont.)
	our sicknesses."	that he was Christ.
	Mt 8:16–17	*L 4:40–41*

Earlier on that Sabbath in the synagogue as Jesus was teaching, a man with an unclean spirit cried out:

Let us alone; what have we to do with thee, thou Jesus of Nazareth? Art thou come to destroy us? I know thee who thou art, the Holy One of God. *Mk 1:24; L 4:34*

Jesus rebuked him:

Hold thy peace, and come out of him. *Mk 1:25; L 4:35*

Mark and Luke state what then happened as follows:

MARK	LUKE
And when the unclean spirit had torn him, and cried with a loud voice, he came out of him.	And when the devil had thrown him in the midst, he came out of him, and hurt him not.
And they were all amazed, insomuch that they questioned among themselves, saying, "What thing is this? What new doctrine is this? For with authority commandeth he even the unclean spirits, and they do obey him."	And they were all amazed, and spake among themselves, saying, "What a word is this! For with authority and power he commandeth the unclean spirits, and they come out."
And immediately his fame spread abroad throughout all the region round about Galilee. *Mk 1:26–28*	And the fame of him went out into every place of the country round about. *L 4:35–37*

The second healing that Sabbath, which is reported in detail, was that of Peter's wife's mother at the house of Peter and Andrew. She was in bed with a fever. Jesus came to her directly from the synagogue with Peter, Andrew, James, and John:

MARK	MATTHEW	LUKE
And he came and took her by the hand and lifted her up; and immediately the fever left her. *Mk 1:31*	And he touched her hand, and the fever left her; and she arose, and ministered unto them. *Mt 8:15*	And he stood over her and rebuked the fever; and it left her; and immediately she arose and ministered unto them. *L 4:39*

All of the first three gospels tell in detail the story of two healings. The first healing involved a leper who knelt down or prostrated himself before Jesus and said, "If thou wilt, thou canst make me clean." *Mk 1:40 (Mt 8:2; L 5:12)*

The three accounts continue:

MARK	MATTHEW	LUKE
And Jesus, moved with compassion, put forth his hand, and touched him, and saith unto him, "I will; be thou clean."	And Jesus put forth his hand, and touched him, saying, "I will; be thou clean."	And he put forth his hand, and touched him, saying, "I will; be thou clean."
And as soon as he had spoken, immediately the leprosy departed from him, and he was cleansed.	And immediately his leprosy was cleansed.	And immediately the leprosy departed from him.

MARK (cont.)	MATTHEW (cont.)	LUKE (cont.)
And he	And Jesus	And he
straightly charged		charged him
him,		
and forthwith		
sent him away;		to,
and saith unto him,	saith unto him,	
"See thou	"See thou	
say nothing	tell	"Tell
to any man;	no man,	no man;
but go thy way,	but go thy way,	but go and
shew thyself	shew thyself	shew thyself
to the priest	to the priest,	to the priest,
and offer	and offer	and offer
for thy cleansing		for thy cleansing,
those things which	the gift that	according as
Moses commanded,	Moses commanded,	Moses commanded,
for a testimony	for a testimony unto	for a testimony
unto them."	them."	unto them."
	Mt 8:3–4	
But he went out,		But
and began		
to publish it much,		so much the more
and to blaze		went there a fame
abroad		abroad
the matter,		of him;
insomuch that		
Jesus could no more		
openly enter		
into the city		
but was without		
in desert places;		and great multitudes
and they came to him		came together
from every quarter.		to hear,
Mk 1:41–45		and to be healed
		by him
		of their infirmities.
		L 5:13–15

Despite Jesus' strict admonition, the leper "blazed abroad" his cleansing. Jesus did not desire the publicity, and when it came he had to stay out of the towns in remote places. It is to be noted that Jesus also strictly charged the leper to obey the Law of Moses as evidence that there had indeed been a cleansing.

A few days later, Jesus tried to slip into Capernaum, his own city, unnoticed, but the word got about that he was home. *Mk 2:1; Mt 9:1* All of the first three gospels have the story:

MARK	MATTHEW	LUKE
And straightway many were gathered together, insomuch that there was no room to receive them, no, not so much as about the door; and he preached the word unto them.		
And they come unto him,	And, behold, they	And, behold, men
bringing one sick of the palsy,	brought to him a man sick of the palsy, lying on a bed.	brought in a bed a man which was taken with a palsy:
which was borne of four.		
And when they could not		and they sought means to bring him in, and to lay
come nigh unto him, for the press, they uncovered the roof where he was; and then they had broken it up,		him before him. And when they could not find by that way they might bring him in because of the multitude, they went upon

MARK (cont.)	MATTHEW (cont.)	LUKE (cont.)
		the housetop, and
they let down		let him down through
		the tiling
the bed		with his couch
wherein the sick		
of the palsy lay.		into the midst
		before Jesus.
When Jesus	And Jesus	And when he
saw their faith,	seeing their faith,	saw their faith,
he said unto	said unto	he said unto
the sick of the palsy,	the sick of the palsy,	him,
"Son,	"Son,	"Man,
	be of good cheer;	
thy sins	thy sins	thy sins
be forgiven thee."	be forgiven thee."	are forgiven thee."
But there were	And, behold,	And the scribes
certain of the scribes	certain of the scribes	and the Pharisees
sitting there,		
and reasoning	said	began to reason,
in their hearts,	within themselves,	saying,
"Why doth this man	"This man	"Who is this which
thus speak		speaketh
blasphemies?	blasphemeth."	blasphemies?
Who can forgive sins		Who can forgive sins,
but God only?"		but God alone?"
And immediately	And	But
when Jesus perceived	Jesus knowing	when Jesus perceived
in his spirit		
that they so reasoned		
within themselves,	their thoughts	their thoughts,
		he answering
he said unto them,	said,	said unto them,
"Why reason you	"Wherefore think ye	"What reason ye
these things	evil	
in your hearts?	in your hearts?	in your hearts?
Whether it is	For whether is	Whether is
easier to say	easier, to say,	easier, to say,
to the sick		

MARK (cont.)	MATTHEW (cont.)	LUKE (cont.)
of the palsy,		
'Thy sins	'Thy sins	'Thy sins
be forgiven thee';	be forgiven thee';	be forgiven thee';
or to say, 'Arise,	or to say, 'Arise,	or to say, 'Rise up
and take up thy bed,		
and walk?'"	and walk'?	and walk'?
But that ye may know	But that ye may know	But that ye may know
that the Son of man	that the Son of man	that the Son of man
hath power	hath power	hath power
on earth	on earth	upon earth
to forgive sins, . . .	to forgive sins, . . .	to forgive sins, ***
I say unto thee,		I say unto thee,
"Arise,	'Arise,	'Arise,
and take up thy bed,	take up thy bed,	and take up thy couch,
and go thy way	and go	and go
into thine house."	into thine house.'"	into thine house.'"
And immediately		And immediately
he arose,	And he arose,	he rose up
		before them,
took up		and took up
the bed,		that whereon he lay,
and went forth	and departed	and departed
before them all;	to his house.	to his own house,
		glorifying God.
insomuch that	But when	And
	the multitudes saw it,	
they were all amazed	they marvelled,	they were all amazed,
and	and	and they
glorified God,	glorified God,	glorified God,
		and were filled
		with fear,
saying,		saying,
"We never saw it	which had given	"We have seen
on this fashion.'"	such power unto men.	strange things today."
Mk 2:2–12	*Mt 9:2–8*	*L 5:18–26*

Among those present were Pharisees and doctors of the Law who "were come out of every town of Galilee, and Judea, and Jerusalem." L 5:17 These men had apparently been waiting for Jesus to come out of hiding so that they could verify the rumors of his miraculous healings. Jesus healed the paralytic man in front of them to show that he had "power upon earth to forgive sins." L 5:24 Even these religious intellectuals were impressed: ". . .they were <u>all</u> amazed, and they glorified God." L 5:26 With scholarly caution they conceded, "We have seen strange things today." L 5:26 Perhaps they even concluded, as Luke says, "the power of the Lord was present to do the healings." L 5:17

Shortly thereafter on a Sabbath in the Capernaum synagogue, it just happened that a man with a withered hand was present. Mk 3:!; Mt 12:9; L 6:6 This was apparently no accident since the Pharisees and teachers of the Law wanted evidence that Jesus broke the Sabbath rules. Mk 3:2; Mt 12:!0; L 6:7 A full account of the incident is set out in the section, "Jesus and the Sabbath," pp. 692–703. Here it is sufficient to quote only part of the accounts:

MARK	MATTHEW	LUKE
And they	And they	And the scribes
	asked him,	and Pharisees
watched him,	saying,	watched him,
	"Is it lawful	
whether he would		whether he would
heal him	to heal	heal
on the Sabbath day,	on the Sabbath days?",	on the Sabbath day,
that they	that they	that they
might	might	might find an
accuse	accuse	accusation
him."	him."	against him."
Mk 3:2	Mt 12:10	L 6:7

Jesus healed the man, restoring his hand. Mk 3:5; Mt 12:13; L 6:10 The various aspects of this healing are analyzed in the sections, "Jesus' Modalities of Healing," pp. 977–983, and "Were Jesus' Modalities of Healing Sufficient Themselves To Heal?", p. 984–989, and "Jesus' Doctrine of Healing Summarized," p. 997–1004.

Here we note the effect of this healing on the Pharisees:

MARK	MATTHEW	LUKE
And the Pharisees went forth,	Then the Pharisees went out,	And they were filled with madness;
and straightway took counsel with the Herodians against him, how they might destroy him. *Mk 3:6*	and held a council against him, how they might destroy him. *Mt 12:14*	and communed one with another what they might do to Jesus. *L 6:11*

The rage of the Pharisees over Jesus' healing on a Sabbath was more than matched by his surging popularity based on his healing ministry, which was not restricted to Sabbaths or synagogues. He was healing in Galilee but "his fame went throughout all Syria." *Mt 4:24* People came from around Tyre and Sidon as well as from Jerusalem, Judea, Idumea, Decapolis and the east bank of Jordan. *Mk 3:7–8; Mt 4:25; L 6:17* Great multitudes followed Jesus and they pressed to touch him and brought him sick persons to heal. *Mk 3:7–8, 10; Mt 4:25; L 6:17, 19* In addition to those vexed with unclean spirits and possessed with devils and those who were "lunatic, and those that had the palsy," he healed many who had "divers diseases and torments." *Mt 4:24 (Mk 3:10–11; L 6:18)* He healed "every sickness and every disease among the people." *Mt 9:35*

A little later the gospels state:

MARK	MATTHEW
And [they] ran through that whole region round about, and began to carry about in beds those that were sick, where they heard	They sent out into all the country round about, and brought unto him all that were diseased;

MARK (cont.)	**MATTHEW** (cont.)
he was.	
And whithersoever	
he entered,	
into villages,	
or cities,	
or countries,	
they laid the sick	
in the streets	
and besought him	and besought him
that they might touch	that they might only touch
if it were	
but the border	the hem
of his garment;	of his garment;
and as many	and as many
as touched him	as touched
were made whole.	were made perfectly whole.
Mk 6:55–56	*Mt 14:35–36*

All of Jesus' healings, both in Galilee and elsewhere, are analyzed in detail under the general heading "The Healings," pp.935–1004, but this brief account summarizes the impact of his healing ministry in Galilee.

The essence of this healing ministry is caught by Matthew in two sentences:

And great multitudes came unto him, having with them those that were lame, blind, dumb, maimed, and many others, and cast them down at Jesus' feet; and he healed them. Insomuch that the multitude wondered, when they saw the dumb to speak, the maimed to be whole, the lame to walk, and the blind to see; and they glorified the God of Israel. *Mt 15:30–31*

Jesus' Ministry in Galilee
AN OVERVIEW

Jesus' ministry in Galilee was not confined to healing or to synagogues. The popular picture that Jesus ministered to crowds in the open air is correct. It is also correct that Jesus was often hard pressed to get away from the crowds he attracted.

Very early in his ministry in Galilee, Jesus, on one occasion, got up "a great while before day" and went out to "a solitary place, and there prayed." *Mk 1:35 (L 4:42)* His followers sought him out and said to him:

All men seek for thee. *Mk 1:37*

Jesus replied:

MARK	LUKE
Let us go into the next towns, that I may preach	I must preach the Kingdom of God to other cities also:
there also: for therefore came I forth. *Mk 1:38*	for therefore am I sent. *L 4:43*

After some days Jesus was back in Capernaum and the word got out that he was in the house where he lived. *Mk 2:1 (Mt 9:1)* Mark continues:

"And straightway many were gathered together, insomuch that there was no room to receive them, no, not so much as about the door: and he preached the word unto them." Mk 2:2

At about the same time Luke reports:

And it came to pass on a certain day, as he was teaching, that there were Pharisees and doctors of the Law sitting by, which were come out of every town of Galilee, and Judea, and Jerusalem: . . . L 5:17

Matthew summarizes Jesus' Galilean ministry:

And there followed him great multitudes of people from Galilee, and from Decapolis, and from Jerusalem, and from Judea, and from beyond Jordan. *Mt 4:25*

Mark and Luke's accounts are similar:

MARK	LUKE
But Jesus withdrew himself with his disciples to the sea [of Galilee]:	And he came down with them, and stood in the plain, and the company of his disciples
and a great multitude from Galilee followed him, and from Judea, and from Jerusalem, and from Idumea, and from beyond Jordan; and they about Tyre and Sidon, a great multitude, when they had heard what great things he did, came unto him. And he spake to his disciples, that a small ship should wait on him because of the multitude, lest they should throng him. Mk 3:7–9	and a great multitude of people out of all Judea and Jerusalem, and from the seacoast of Tyre and Sidon, which came to hear him, and to be healed of their diseases. L 6:17

Jesus felt the pressure of the crowds, and he withdrew to a mountain near the Sea of Galilee to give his disciples intensive instructions by what has come to be known as "the Sermon on the Mount":

> And seeing the multitudes, he went up into a mountain: and when he was set, his disciples came unto him; and he opened his mouth and taught them, saying, . . ." Mt 5:1–2

Despite Jesus' withdrawal, the crowds apparently followed him since Matthew concludes his account of the Sermon on the Mount with these words:

> And it came to pass, when Jesus had ended these sayings, *the people* were astonished at his doctrine: for he taught them as one having authority, and not as the scribes. When he was come down from the mountain, *great multitudes* followed him. Mt 7:28–29, 8:1

Jesus taught in crowd contexts. When he heard the centurion's faith, he turned to the ever-present crowd:

> When Jesus heard these things, he marvelled at him, and turned him about, and said unto *the people* that followed him, "I say unto you, I have not found so great faith, no, not in Israel." L 7:9

The crowd was present when he approached the gate of the city of Nain. L 7:11–12 As Luke has it, "many of his disciples went with him, and much people." L 7:11 This was the pattern of Jesus' ministry in Galilee, immersed in crowds, "he went throughout every city and village, preaching and shewing the glad tidings of the Kingdom of God: and the Twelve were with him." L 8:1

Even the Twelve suffered. Mark reports that they (Jesus and the Twelve) went into a house:

> And the multitude cometh together again, so that they could not so much as eat bread. Mk 3:20

Even his mother and his brothers could not penetrate the perpetual crowd:

Mark	Matthew	Luke
	While he yet	
There came then	talked to the people, behold,	Then came to him
his brethren	his mother	his mother
and his mother, and,	and his brethren	and his brethren, and
standing without,	stood without,	could not
sent unto him,	desiring to speak	come at him
calling him,	with him.	
and the multitude		for the press.
sat about him,		And it was told him
and they said	Then one said	by certain which said,
unto him,	unto him,	
"Behold,	"Behold,	
thy mother	thy mother	"Thy mother
and thy brethren	and thy brethren	and thy brethren
without	stand without,	stand without,
	desiring	desiring
seek for thee."	to speak with thee."	to see thee."
Mk 3:31–32	Mt 12:46–47	L 8:19–20

The gospels are studded with references to the "multitudes" or "great multitudes" who surrounded Jesus on many occasions during his ministry in Galilee. For example, when he taught in parables by the side of the Sea of Galilee, Mark reports "a great multitude"; Matthew, "great multitudes," and Luke, "much people." *Mk 4:1; Mt 13:2; L 8:4* The crowd was so great he had to teach from a boat which stood off from the shore. *Mk 4:1; Mt 13:2* Sometimes Jesus took ship to escape the multitude. *Mk 8:10, 13; Mt 15:3*

On another occasion when Jesus returned across the Sea of Galilee from the country of Gadarenes, Mark reports that "much people gathered unto him" while Luke states that "the people gladly received him: for they were all waiting for him." *Mk 5:21; L 8:40* The people "thronged him." *Mk 5:24*

136

The crowds actually pressed Jesus physically. On one occasion Jesus asked who touched him. *Mk 5:30; L 8:45* The reply of his disciples was instructive:

MARK	LUKE
Thou seest	Master,
the multitude	the multitude
thronging thee,	throng thee
	and press thee,
and sayest thou,	and sayest thou,
"Who touched me"?	"Who touched me"?
Mk 5:31	*L 8:45*

Although the crowds thronged Jesus, he was moved with compassion for them:

> But when he saw the multitudes, he was moved with compassion on them, because they fainted, and were scattered abroad, as sheep having no shepherd. *Mt 9:36*

Sometimes his crowds were very large. On one occasion Jesus and his disciples fed about five thousand persons at a remote location. *Mk 6:44; Mt 14:21; L 9:14* John contents himself with reporting that "a great company" were fed. *J 6:5* On another occasion Jesus and his disciples fed about four thousand persons. *Mk 8:9; Mt 15:38* (". . .four thousand men, besides women and children.")

Jesus' ministry was not confined to synagogues, the open country or the shore of the Sea of Galilee. He also "went round about the villages, teaching"; or as Luke has it, "he went throughout every city and village, preaching." *Mk 6:6; L 8:1*

While the multitudes were not always present with Jesus, they seem to have been easily available to him. After a dialogue between Jesus and some Pharisees and scribes from Jerusalem, Matthew and Mark report:

MARK	MATTHEW
And when	And
he had called	he called
all the people	the multitude,
unto him,	
he said unto them,	and said unto them,
"Hearken unto me	"Hear,
every one of you,	
and understand: . . ."	and understand: . . ."
Mk 7:14	*Mt 15:10*

Sometimes Jesus would withdraw, either to be alone or to be with his disciples. One such occasion was when Jesus took his three key disciples, Peter, James and John, and went up "into an high mountain apart by themselves." *Mk 9:2 (Mt 17:1; L 9:28)* But the multitudes were still there with the disciples Jesus left behind. When Jesus came down the mountain the next day, the gospels state:

MARK	LUKE
	And it came to pass,
And when	that on the next day, when
he came	they were come down
to his disciples,	from the hill,
he saw	
a great multitude	*much people*
about them,	met him.
and the scribes	*L 9:37*
questioning	
with them.	
And straightway	
all the people,	
when they	
beheld him,	
were greatly amazed,	
and running	
to him saluted him.	
Mk 9:14–15	

Shortly thereafter Jesus taught his disciples as follows:

MARK	MATTHEW	LUKE
		Let these sayings
		sink down
		into your ears:
The Son of man	Son of man	for the Son of man
is delivered	shall be betrayed	shall be delivered
into the hands	into the hands	into the hands
of men,	of men:	of men.
and they shall	and they shall	L 9:44
kill him;	kill him,	
and after that	and	
he is killed,		
he shall rise	the third day	
the third day.	he shall be	
Mk 9:31	raised again.	
	Mt 17:23	

The gospels then state the reaction of the disciples:

MARK	MATTHEW	LUKE
But they	And they	But they
understood not	were exceedingly	understood not
that saying,	sorry.	this saying,
	Mt 17:23	and it was hid
		from them,
		that they
		perceived it not;
and were afraid		and they feared
to ask him.		to ask him
Mk 9:32		of that saying.
		L 9:45

Jesus had sensed the gathering storm and had tried to warn his disciples. His Galilean ministry soon ended when he left Galilee for Jerusalem for the last time. The die was cast:

And it came to pass, when the time was come that he should be received up, he stedfastly set his face to go to Jerusalem. *L 9:51*

A Brief Summary of Jesus' Ministries

Jesus' ministry in Galilee was, of course, not restricted to a healing ministry. He had become a great popular figure, replacing and sometimes confused with John the Baptist. The popular opinion of Jesus varied. Some said:

MARK	LUKE
	That John was risen from the dead. And of some,
That it is Elijah. And others said, that it is a prophet, or as one of his prophets. *Mk 6:15*	that Elijah had appeared; and of others, that one of the old prophets was risen again. *L 9:7–8*

Jesus' disciples repeated those opinions when Jesus asked them:

MARK	MATTHEW	LUKE
Whom do men say that I am? *Mk 8:27*	Whom do men say that I the Son of man am? *Mt 16:13*	Whom say the people that I am?" *L 9:18*

The disciples answered:

MARK	MATTHEW	LUKE
	Some say that thou art	
John the Baptist: but some say Elijah; and others,	John the Baptist: some, Elijah; and others, Jeremiah,	John the Baptist; but some say, Elijah; and others say, that
one of the prophets. *Mk 8:28*	or one of the prophets. *Mt 16:14*	one of the old prophets is risen again. *L 9:19*

It is helpful to use the history of John the Baptist as time reference marks for the various phases of Jesus' own ministry. After John the Baptist was imprisoned by Herod Antipas, Jesus "came into Galilee, preaching the gospel of the Kingdom of God." *Mk 1:14* Jesus then had a spectacular ministry in Galilee, teaching, healing, and doing exorcisms and miracles.

While John was imprisoned, he sent two of his disciples to ask Jesus:

Art thou he that should come, or do we look for another? *Mt 11:3*
(*L 7:19–20*)

Herod Antipas ultimately had John the Baptist beheaded. *Mk 6:16–28; Mt 14:3–11; L 9:9* John's disciples buried him. *Mk 6:29; Mt 14:12* They then "went and told Jesus." *Mt 14:12* Hearing this, Jesus immediately left for a place where he could be alone. *Mt 14:13*

Jesus' own ministry in Galilee continued with its spectacular successes, and Herod Antipas "was perplexed" (*L 9:7*) and is reported to have said:

MARK	MATTHEW	LUKE
That John	This is John	
the Baptist	the Baptist;	
was risen	he is risen	
from the dead,	from the dead;	
and therefore	and therefore	
mighty works	mighty works	
do shew forth	do shew forth	
themselves	themselves	
in him. . .	in him.	
	Mt 14:2	
It is John,		John
whom I beheaded:		have I beheaded:
he is risen		but who is this,
from the dead.		of whom
Mk 6:14, 16		I hear such things?
		L 9:9

Luke records a warning by some Pharisees to Jesus some time later, "Get thee out, and depart hence: for Herod will kill thee." *L 13:31*

Jesus replied:

> Go ye, and tell that fox, behold, I cast out devils, and I do cures today and tomorrow, and the third day I shall be perfected. Nevertheless I must walk today, and tomorrow, and the day following: for it cannot be that a prophet perish out of Jerusalem. *L 13:32–33*

This warning occurred at a time when Jesus was already "journeying toward Jerusalem." *L 13:22* Jerusalem was, of course, in Judea and out of Herod's domain since he was only Tetrarch of Perea and Galilee. Before Jesus made his final journey to Jerusalem from Galilee, he made a brief trip to "the borders" or "the coasts" of Tyre and Sidon. *Mk 7:24; Mt 15:21* These were Gentile towns on the Mediterranean Sea: Tyre being about thirty-five airline miles northwest of the Sea of Galilee and Sidon being about twenty-three miles north of Tyre.

In Tyre, Jesus "entered into a house, and would have no man know it: but he could not be hid." *Mk 7:24* We infer from this that Jesus' fame followed him even this far out of Galilee "for his name was spread abroad." *Mk 6:14*

In any case, Jesus apparently did not stay long and left Tyre and proceeded north to Sidon and from there returned to the area around the Sea of Galilee through Decapolis, an administrative area of ten Greek cities lying generally southeast of the Sea of Galilee. *Mk 7:31; Mt 15:29*

Matthew states:

> And Jesus departed from thence, and came nigh unto the Sea of Galilee; and went up into a mountain, and sat down there. And great multitudes came unto him, having with them those that were lame, blind, dumb, maimed, and many others, and cast them down at Jesus' feet; and he healed them. Insomuch that the multitude wondered, when they saw the dumb to speak, the maimed to be

whole, the lame to walk, and the blind to see: they followed the God of Israel. *Mt 15:29–31*

After a stay around the Sea of Galilee, Jesus and his disciples again went out of Galilee. This time he went north to "the towns" or "the coasts" of Caesarea Philippi. *Mk 8:17; Mt 16:13* This area near the slopes of Mt. Hermon was part of the territory administered by Philip as tetrarch and was the site of a large spring, the main source of the Jordan River. Philip had rebuilt an existing town and re-named it "Caesarea" for the Roman emperor, and it had come to be known as Caesarea Philippi to distinguish it from the town of Caesarea on the Mediterranean coast.

After six or eight days at Caesarea Philippi, Jesus took Peter, James, and John with him up into a high mountain, where he was transfigured before them. *Mk 9:2–13; Mt 17:1–13; L 9:29–36* For details, see "Jesus' Transfiguration," pp. 90–98.

On his way back through Galilee to Capernaum with his disciples, Jesus "would not that any man should know it." *Mk 9:30, 33* It is not clear from the text whether Jesus simply wanted to be undisturbed while indoctrinating his disciples or whether he did not wish Herod to know that he was back in Galilee. Whatever was the case, he almost immediately left Galilee and proceeded south on the east bank of the Jordan:

MARK	MATTHEW
And he . . .	He departed from Galilee,
cometh into	and came into
the coasts of Judea	the coasts of Judea
by the farther side of Jordan:	beyond Jordan;
and the people	and great multitudes
resort unto him again;	followed him;
and, as he was wont,	
he taught them again.	and he healed them there.
Mk 10:1	*Mt 19:1–2*

"Coasts" is used in the obsolete sense of *frontiers*, so we are left with a statement that Jesus came into (or near) the frontiers of Judea and went into the area east of the Jordan, "the farther side of Jordan." His destination was Jerusalem. *Mk 10:32; Mt 20:17; L 18:31* As he went, great multitudes followed him, and he healed and taught them. *Mk 10:1; Mt 19:2* He proceeded south along the east bank of the Jordan, ultimately crossing the river and arriving in Jericho. *Mk 10:46; Mt 20:29; L 18:35* From there it was a short, perhaps about twelve miles, journey uphill, up over 3,000 feet, through the wilderness of Judea to Bethany, a village on the outskirts of Jerusalem. Jesus entered Jerusalem from Bethany. *Mk 11:2–22; Mt 21:1–11; L 19:28–44*

When he entered Jerusalem, Matthew reports:

> All the city was moved, saying, "Who is this?" And the multitude said, "This is Jesus the prophet of Nazareth of Galilee." *Mt 21:10–11*

Jesus' ministry was about to end, but the popular opinion that he was a prophet had not changed. Early in his ministry at Nain in Galilee he had revived a boy by touching his burial bier and speaking to him. *L 7:11–15* Luke continues:

> And there came a fear on all: and they glorified God, saying, "That a great prophet is risen up among us"; and "That God hath visited his people." And this rumor of him went forth throughout all Judea, and throughout all the region round about." *L 7:16–17*

JESUS IN AND AROUND JERUSALEM

JESUS AT THE FEAST OF TABERNACLES

The Feast of Tabernacles is one of the three great Jewish feasts along with Passover and Pentecost. The book of Leviticus laid down its manner of observance:

The fifteenth day of this seventh month shall be the Feast of Tabernacles for seven days unto the Lord. On the first day shall be a holy convocation: ye shall do no servile work therein. Seven days ye shall offer an offering made by fire unto the Lord: it is a solemn assembly; and he shall do no servile work therein. . . .

Also in the fifteenth day of the seventh month, when ye have gathered in the fruit of the land, ye shall keep a feast unto the Lord seven days. On the first day shall be a sabbath, and on the eighth day shall be a sabbath.

And ye shall take you on the first day the boughs of goodly trees, branches of palm trees and boughs of thick trees, and willows of the brook; and ye shall rejoice before the Lord your God seven days.

And ye shall keep it a feast unto the Lord seven days in the year. It shall be a statute for ever in your generations: ye shall celebrate it in the seventh month. *Ye shall dwell in booths seven days*; all that are Israelites born shall *dwell in booths*: that your generations may know that I made the children of Israel *to dwell in booths*, when I brought them out of the land of Egypt: I am the Lord your God. Leviticus *23:34–36, 39–43*

The Feast of Tabernacles (or Feast of Booths) was an eight-day harvest festival in the early fall of the year. Jesus went up to Jerusalem to attend this feast in the fall of the year before he was crucified. However, at first he thought he would stay in Galilee despite the feast because his life was in danger any place in Judea, and Jerusalem was the capital of Judea. *J 7:1, 2, 8, 9*

While he was still in Galilee, he told his brothers:

My time is not yet come; but your time is alway ready.

The world cannot hate you; but me it hateth, because I testify of it, that the works thereof are evil.

Go ye up unto this feast. I go not up yet unto this feast; for my time is not yet full come. *J 7:6–8*

John then writes:

But when his brethren were gone up, then went he also up unto the feast, not openly, but as it were in secret. Then the Jews sought him at the feast, and said, "Where is he?"

And there was much murmuring among the people concerning him; for some said, "He is a good man"; others said, "Nay, but he deceiveth the people." Howbeit no man spake openly of him for fear of the Jews." *J 7:10–13*

In the middle of the festival Jesus taught in the Temple itself. *J 7:14* His teaching amazed his listeners since he was not a formally trained religious teacher; and they asked, "How knoweth this man letters having never learned?" *J 7:15*

Jesus' reply was:

My doctrine is not mine, but his that sent me. If any man will do his will, he shall know of the doctrine, whether it be of God, or whether I speak of myself.

He that speaketh of himself seeketh his own glory; but he that seeketh his glory [the glory of him] that sent him, the same is true, and no unrighteousness is in him.

Did not Moses give you the Law, and yet none of you keepeth the Law? Why go ye about to kill me? *J 7:16–20*

The crowd scoffed:

Thou hast a devil; who goeth about to kill thee? *J 7:20*

Jesus answered:

I have done one work, and ye all marvel.

Moses therefore gave unto you circumcision; (not because it is of Moses, but of the fathers;) and ye on the Sabbath Day circumcise a man. If a man on the Sabbath Day receive circumcision, that the Law of Moses should not be broken, are ye angry at me, because I have made a man every whit whole on the Sabbath Day?

Judge not according to the appearance, but judge righteous judgment. *J 7:21–24*

Some of the crowd wondered:

Is not this he, whom they seek to kill? But, lo, he speaketh boldly, and they say nothing unto him. Do the rulers know indeed that this is the very Christ?

Howbeit we know this man whence he is; but when Christ cometh, no man knoweth whence he is. *J 7:25–27*

Jesus cried out his answer:

Ye both know me, and ye know whence I am; and I am not come of myself, but he that sent me is true, whom ye know not.

But I know him: for I am from him, and he hath sent me. *J 7:28–29*

The Jews Were Divided

Many of the people believed on him, and argued, "When Christ cometh, will he do more miracles than these which this man hath done?" *J 7:31*

This undercurrent of acceptance alarmed the Jewish religious establishment, and the Pharisees and chief priests sent officers to arrest Jesus. *J 7:32*

Jesus then made a cryptic remark:

Yet a little while am I with you, and then I go unto him that sent me.

Ye shall seek me, and ye shall not find me; and where I am, thither ye cannot come. *J 7:33–34*

This puzzled his hearers, and some of them speculated that this meant Jesus would leave Judea and go to Greek lands to teach the Jews who were dispersed among the Greeks and teach the Greeks themselves. *J 7:35–36*

On the last great day of the Festival, its final Sabbath, Jesus stood, probably in the Temple, and cried out:

If any man thirst, let him come unto me, and drink.

He that believeth on me, as the [Jewish] Scripture hath said, out of his belly [heart] shall flow rivers of living water. *J 7:37–38*

Again Jesus' sayings produced a division in the people, *J 7:43*
Some said, "Of a truth, this is the prophet"; others said, "This is
the Christ." *J 7:40–41*

Others argued:

Shall Christ come out of Galilee. Hath not the [Jewish] Scripture
said that Christ cometh of the seed of David, and out of the town of
Bethlehem, where David was? *J 7:41–42*

This division among the people was so violent that some sought
to seize him. *J 7:43–44* This had happened before when Jesus was
teaching in the Temple. *J 7:30* Again no one laid hands on him.
J 7:30, 44

The police whom the Pharisees and chief priests had sent apparently stood by uncertain what they should do, but they did
have to report back. When they reported back, their reception was
icy: "Why have ye not brought him?" *J 7:45*

The officers replied, "Never man spake like this man." *J 7:46*
The reaction of the Pharisees was acid:

Are ye also deceived? Have any of the rulers or of the Pharisees
believed on him?

But this people [the common people] who knoweth not the Law
are cursed [because they are so deceived]. *J 7:47–49*

This vindictiveness split even the Pharisees. A prominent Pharisee named Nicodemus objected:

Doth our Law judge any man, before it hear him, and know what
he doeth? *J 7:50–51*

The other Pharisees turned on Nicodemus personally:

Art thou also of Galilee? Search and look, for out of Galilee ariseth
no prophet. *J 7:52*

The episode closes with everyone going to "his own house" except for Jesus, who went to the Mount of Olives. *J 7:53; 8:1* Early the next morning, he returned again to the Temple and sat down to teach the people. *J 8:2* However, the Jewish religious establishment wished to continue their confrontation with Jesus.

THE WOMAN TAKEN IN ADULTERY

That same morning the scribes and Pharisees brought a woman who they claimed had been taken in adultery and then asked Jesus this artful test question:

Master, this woman was taken in adultery, in the very act. Now Moses in the Law commanded us, that such should be stoned; but what sayest thou? *J 8:4*

John's account continues:

But Jesus stooped down, and with his finger wrote on the ground, as though he heard them not. So when they continued asking him, he lifted up himself, and said unto them, "He that is without sin among you, let him first cast a stone at her."

And again he stooped down, and wrote on the ground. And they which heard it, being convicted by their own conscience, went out one by one, beginning at the eldest, even unto the last; and Jesus was left alone, and the woman standing in the midst.

When Jesus had lifted up himself, and saw none but the woman, he said unto her, "Woman, where are those thine accusers? Hath no man condemned thee?"

She said, "No man, Lord [Sir]."

And Jesus said unto her, "Neither do I condemn thee. Go, and sin no more." *J 8:6–11*

Jesus had rejected the transparent invitation of the scribes and Pharisees to say, "Do not stone her" — do not obey what Moses in the Law commanded. See John 8:6. Jesus did not, however, reject the reality of her sin. Her sin was adultery. She was not to commit adultery anymore.

WHO ART THOU?

Jesus continued to teach in the Temple. *J 8:20* The controversy with the Pharisees continued. *J 8:13* Jesus taught:

I am the light of the world; he that followeth me shall not walk in darkness but shall have the light of life. *J 8:12*

The Pharisees challenged his credentials, "Thou bearest record of thyself; thy record is not true." *J 8:13*
Jesus answered this challenge as follows:

Though I bear record of myself, yet my record is true: for I know whence I came, and whither I go; but ye cannot tell whence I come, and whither I go.

Ye judge after the flesh; I judge no man. And yet if I judge, my judgment is true: for I am not alone, but I and *the Father* that sent me.

It is also written in your law, that the testimony of two men is true. I am one that bear witness of myself, and *the Father* that sent me bearest witness of me. *J 8:14–18*

Their answer was a sneering, "Where is *thy* Father?" *J 8:19* Everyone knows you are an illegitimate child.
Jesus calmly answered:

Ye neither know me, nor my Father: if ye had known me, ye should have known my Father also . . .

I go my way, and ye shall seek me, and shall die in your sins: whither I go, ye cannot come. *J 8:19, 21*

The Jews murmured, "Will he kill himself?" because he had said, "Whither I go, ye cannot come." *J 8:22*
Jesus heard and answered:

Ye are from beneath; I am from above; ye are of this world; I am not of this world.

I said therefore unto you, that ye shall die in your sins: for if ye believe not that I am he, ye shall die in your sins. *J 8:23–24*

The Jews then asked "Who art thou?" *J 8:25*
Jesus answered:

Even the same that I said unto you from the beginning. I have many things to say and to judge of you, but *he* that sent me is true; and I speak to the world those things which I have heard of *him*. *J 8:25–26*

At this point Jesus sensed that the crowd did not understand that when Jesus was talking of "he" and "him" Jesus was speaking of the Father. *J 8:27* So Jesus said:

When ye have lifted up the Son of man, then shall ye know that I am he, and that I do nothing of myself; but as *my Father* hath taught me, I speak these things. And *he* that sent me is with me: *the Father* hath not left me alone; for I do always these things that please *him*. *J 8:28–29*

The controversy continued and Jesus, after a digression, said:

I know that ye are Abraham's seed; but ye seek to kill me, because my word hath no place in you. I speak that which I have seen with my Father; and ye do that which ye have seen with your father. *J 8:37–38*

The Jews' answer was: "Abraham is our father." *J 8:39*

152

Jesus rejected this contention:

> If ye were Abraham's children, ye would do the works of Abraham.
> But now ye seek to kill me, a man that hath told you the truth,
> which I have heard of God. This did not Abraham. Ye do the deeds
> of your father. *J 8:39–41*

Again, the answer was a slur, "*We* [unlike you] be not born of
fornication; we have one Father, even God." *J 8:41*

Jesus replied:

> If God were your Father, ye would love me: for I proceeded forth
> and came from God, neither came I of myself, but he sent me.
>
> Why do ye not understand my speech? Even because ye cannot
> hear my word.
>
> Ye are of your father the Devil, and the lusts of your father ye will
> do. He was a murderer from the beginning, and abode not in the
> truth, because there is no truth in him. When he speaketh a lie, he
> speaketh of his own: for he is a liar, and the father of it.
>
> And because I tell you the truth, ye believe me not. Which of you
> convinceth me of sin? And if I say the truth, why do ye not believe
> me?
>
> He that is of God heareth God's words; ye therefore hear them not,
> because ye are not of God." *J 8:42–47*

The Jews' answer was abusive, "Say we not well that thou art a
Samaritan [a half-Jewish heretic], and hast a devil?" *J 8:48*

Jesus' answer was serene:

> I have not a devil; but I honor my Father, and ye do dishonor me.
> And I seek not mine own glory: there is one that seeketh and judgeth.
>
> Verily, verily, I say unto you, if a man shall keep my saying, he shall
> never see death. *J 8:49–51*

The Jews felt that they had Jesus. He had claimed too much. They said:

> Now we know that thou hast a devil. Abraham is dead, and the prophets; and thou sayest, "If a man keep my saying, he shall never taste of death." Are thou greater than our father Abraham, which is dead? And the prophets are dead. Whom makest thou thyself? *J 8:52–53*

Jesus was glad to tell them:

> If I honor myself, my honor is nothing. It is my Father that honoreth me: of whom ye say, that he is your God.

> Yet ye have not known him; but I know him. And if I should say, I know him not, I shall be a liar like unto you. But I know him and keep his saying.

> Your father Abraham rejoiced to see my day: and he saw it, and was glad. *J 8:54–56*

The Jews answered sarcastically, "Thou art not yet fifty years old, and hast thou seen Abraham?: *J 8:57*
Jesus then made his ultimate claim:

> Verily, verily I say unto you, before Abraham was, I AM. *J 8:58*

The Jews then picked up stones to stone Jesus, but he succeeded in slipping out of the Temple. *J 8:59*

THE MAN BORN BLIND

That fall, while Jesus still remained in Jerusalem, he healed a man born blind, and this triggered an investigation by the Pharisees. The situation was already tense because the authorities had decided "that if any man did confess that he was the Christ, he should be put out of the synagogue." *J 9:22*

To make matters worse, this healing had been done on a Sabbath. *J 9:14* It all began innocuously enough. Jesus walked past a blind beggar. *J:1, 8* It was his disciples, not the Pharisees, who asked, "Master, who did sin, this man, or his parents, that he was born blind?" *J 9:2*

Jesus replied:

Neither hath this man sinned, nor his parents; but that the works of God should be made manifest in him.

I [we*] must work the works of him that sent me, while it is day. The night cometh, when no man can work. As long as I am in the world, I am the light of the world. *J 9:3–5* *Modern versions follow the manuscripts reading "we" rather than "I".

Then Jesus spat upon the ground, made clay with the spittle, and anointed the eyes of the blind man with the clay and said to him, "Go, wash in the Pool of Siloam." *J 9:6–7*

The Pool of Siloam was located in the southeast corner of Jerusalem, about 850 yards south of the south wall of the Temple. This pool had been constructed for city defense purposes in Hezekiah's reign 725–697 B.C.

The beggar did go and wash and came back with his sight. *J 9:7* His neighbors and passersby who had seen him blind were astounded, and said, "Is not this he that sat and begged?" *J 9:8*

Some said, "This is he." *J 9:9*

But the man said, "I am he." *J 9:9*

They then asked him, "How were thine eyes opened?: *J 9:10*

The man said:

A man that is called Jesus made clay, and anointed mine eyes, and said unto me, "Go to the Pool of Siloam, and wash." And I went and washed, and I received sight. *J 9:11*

They said, "Where is he?" *J 9:12*

The man said, "I know not." *J 9:12*

The man was brought to the Pharisees, and their investigation began. *J 9:13* They repeated the question how he had received his sight. *J 9:15*

The man said, "He put clay upon mine eyes, I washed and do see." *J 9:15*

The Pharisees were split. Some of them said, "This man is not of God, because he keepeth not the Sabbath day"; others of them said, "How can a man that is a sinner do such miracles?" *J 9:16*

The Pharisees continued their investigation, asking:

Q: What sayest thou of him, that he hath opened thine eyes?
A. He is a prophet. *J 9:17*

This was as awkward situation for the Pharisees. The obvious solution was that the man had not, in fact, been born blind. His parents were interrogated and they stated that he had been born blind. *J 9:18–19* The interrogation continued:

Q. Is this your son, who ye say was born blind? How then doth he now see?
A. We know that this is our son, and that he was born blind. But by what means he now seeth, we know not; or who hath opened his eyes, we know not. He is of age; ask him. He shall speak for himself. *J 9:19–21*

The situation was so threatening that even the man's parents were afraid to antagonize the Pharisees. There was nothing for the Pharisees to do but call the man to testify again:

Q. Give God the praise. We know that this man is a sinner.
A. Whether he be a sinner or no, I know not. One thing I know, that, whereas I was blind, now I see.
Q. What did he to thee? How opened he thine eyes?
A. I have told you already, and ye did not hear. Wherefore would ye hear it again? Will ye also be his disciples?

Q. [With fury] Thou art his disciple; but we are Moses' disciples. We know that God spake unto Moses. As for this fellow, we know not from whence he is.

A. Why herein is a marvellous thing, that ye know not from whence he is, and yet he hath opened mine eyes. Now we know that God heareth not sinners, but if any man be a worshipper of God, and doeth his will, him he heareth. Since the world began was it not heard that any man opened the eyes of one that was born blind. If this man were not of God, he could do nothing. *J 9:24–33*

The Pharisees were outraged:

Thou wast altogether born in sins, and dost thou teach us? *J 9:34*

The Pharisees' investigation had been a disaster, so they abruptly ended it by throwing the man out. *J 9:34*

Jesus heard of this and sought out the man and asked him:

JESUS: Dost thou believe on the Son of God? [Some manuscripts have "Son of man"]

MAN: Who is he, Lord [Sir], that I might believe on him?

JESUS: Thou hast both seen him, and it is he that talketh with thee.

MAN: Lord, I believe. *J 9:35–37*

Some Pharisees were watching. The man worshipped Jesus, and Jesus taught his watchers an object lesson, saying:

For judgment I am come into this world, that they which see not might see; and that they which see might be made blind. *J 9:39*

The Pharisees then have to ask, "Are we blind also?" *J 9:40* Jesus replied:

If ye were blind, ye should have no sins; but now ye say, "We see"; therefore your sin remaineth.

Verily, verily, I say unto you, he that entereth not by the door into the sheepfold, but climbeth up some other way, the same is a thief and a robber. But he that entereth in by the door is the shepherd of the sheep. To him the porter openeth; and the sheep [like this ex-blind man] hear his voice; and he calleth his own sheep by name, and leadeth them out.

And when he putteth forth his own sheep, he goeth before them, and the sheep follow him for they know his voice. And a stranger will they not follow, but will flee from him for they know not the voice of strangers." *J 9:41–10:5*

The parable escaped them, so Jesus explained it as follows:

Verily, verily, I say unto you I am the door of the sheep [fold]. All that ever came before me are thieves and robbers; but the sheep did not hear them. I am the door [of the sheep-fold]. By me if any man enter in, he shall be saved, and shall go in and out, and find pasture.

The thief cometh not, but for to steal, and to kill, and to destroy. I am come that they might have life, and that they might have it more abundantly.

I am the good shepherd. The good shepherd giveth his life for the sheep.

But he that is an hireling, and not the shepherd, whose own the sheep are not, seeth the wolf coming, and leaveth the sheep, and fleeth; and the wolf catcheth them, and scattereth the sheep. The hireling fleeth, because he is an hireling, and careth not for the sheep.

I am the good shepherd, and know my sheep, and am known of mine. As the Father knoweth me, even so know I the Father; and I lay down my life for the sheep.

And other sheep I have, which are not of this fold: them also must I bring, and they shall hear my voice; and there shall be one fold, and one shepherd.

Therefore doth my Father love me, because I lay down my life, that I might take it again. No man taketh it from me, but I lay it down of myself. I have power to lay it down, and I have power to take it again. This commandment have I received of my Father. *J 10:7–18*

Jesus used a dual metaphor; he is both the door of the sheepfold and the shepherd himself. His explanation of his role did not, however, satisfy many of the Jews, who split. *J 10:19*
Some said:

He hath a devil, and is mad. Why hear ye him? *J 10:20*

Others remembered his healing of the blind beggar and said:

These are not the words of him that hath a devil. Can a devil open the eyes of the blind? *J 10:21*

After the good shepherd incident, John's account abruptly shifts at verse 22 to the Feast of Dedication which occurred in early winter. *J 10:22* It is not clear from John's account whether Jesus remained continuously in Jerusalem from the time of the Feast of Tabernacles in early fall until the Feast of Dedication. See John 7:37 (last day of the feast) to John 10:22 (the Feast of Dedication).
We do know that in that interval Jesus did teach in Jerusalem in the Temple. For example, he taught in the Temple treasury. *J 8:20* He was not arrested, even though as early as the Feast of Tabernacles some Jews were saying that he was the Messiah. *J 7:30, 41, 44, 8:20*
Later on that fall Jesus said:

And he that sent me is with me; the Father hath not left me alone; for I do always those things that please him. *J 8:29*

John then notes:

As he spake these words, many believed on him. *J 8:30*

FESTIVAL OF LIGHTS

John begins a new period in his account with the Feast of Dedication. *J 10:22* He writes:

> And it was at Jerusalem the Feast of the Dedication, and it was winter. And Jesus walked in the Temple in Solomon's Porch. *J 10:22–23*

The Feast of the Dedication or Festival of Lights is now called Hanukkah (*Renewal*) and falls on the twenty-fifth day of the Jewish month of Chislev (November-December). It was in Jesus' time a comparatively new festival since it had been instituted in 164 B.C., about 190 years before when the Temple had been purified and rededicated after three years of Gentile occupation by the forces under Antiochus IV Epiphanes.

This Jewish revolt was led by Judas Maccabeus. Josephus, a Jewish historian who was born a few years after Jesus' death, describes the festival as it must have seemed to the Jews of Jesus' time:

> Now Judas celebrated the festival of the restoration of the sacrifices of the Temple for eight days; and omitted no sort of pleasures thereon: but he feasted them upon very rich and splendid sacrifices; and he honoured God, and delighted them, by hymns and psalms. Nay, they were so very glad at the revival of their customs, when after a long period of intermission, they unexpectedly had regained the freedom of their worship, that they made it law for their posterity, that they should keep a festival, on account of the restoration of their temple worship, for eight days. And from that time to this we celebrate this festival, and call it Lights. *Josephus, Antiquities, Book XII, Ch. VII, Sec. 7.*

During this festival, since it was winter, Jesus walked and taught in Solomon's Porch, a covered area on the east side of the Temple. *J 10:23* John reports that the Jews came round him, and asked:

> How long dost thou make us to doubt? If thou be the Christ, tell us plainly. *J 10:24*

Jesus answered:

I told you, and ye believed not. The works that I do in my Father's name, they bear witness of me. But ye believe not, because ye are not of my sheep, as I said unto you.

My sheep hear my voice, and I know them, and they follow me. And I give unto them eternal life; and they shall never perish, neither shall any man pluck them out of my hand.

My Father, which gave them me, is greater than all; and no man is able to pluck them out of my Father's hand. *I and my Father are one." J 10:25–30*

Again, the Jews took up stones to stone him, but Jesus said:

Many good works have I shewed you from my Father; for which of those good works do ye stone me? *J 10:32*

The Jews replied:

For a good work we stone thee not: but for blasphemy, and because that thou, being a man, maketh thyself God. *J 10:33*

Jesus' answer was:

Is it not written in your Law, "I said, Ye are gods"? *J 10:34 (Psalm 82:6)*

Jesus continued his argument:

If he called them gods, unto whom the word of God came, and the Scripture can not be broken, say ye of him, whom the Father hath sanctified, and sent into the world, "Thou blasphemest"; because I said, "I am the Son of God"?

If I do not the works of my Father, believe me not. But if I do, though ye believe not me, believe the works: that ye may know, and believe, that the Father is in me and I in him." *J 10:34–38*

Here Jesus succinctly states really all that can be known of his relation to God the Father: I and my Father are one, because I am his Son and I am in Him and He is in me and He sanctified me and sent me into the world. The proof of these facts, according to Jesus, are the works which Jesus did.

This was lost on the Jews and they again sought to take him, but again he escaped. *J 10:39* This time he escaped beyond the Jordan River to Bethabara, the place where John the Baptist had begun his baptisms. *J 10:40* Many came to him there and believed, saying:

John did no miracle, but all things that John spake of this man were true. *J 10:41*

John then adds:

And many believed on him there. *J 10:42*

THE LAZARUS INCIDENT

Despite Jesus' favorable reception in Perea, the region beyond the Jordan River, he was still in danger of being stoned if he crossed over into Judea. *J 10:31–39; 11:8*

While Jesus was staying in Perea, a man named Lazarus, who lived in Bethany, a village in Judea near Jerusalem, became ill. *J 11:2, 18* Lazarus was known to Jesus through his two sisters, Mary and Martha. Jesus and his group had, in fact, been guests in Martha's house in Bethany on a prior occasion. *L 10:38* On that occasion, Mary had stayed at Jesus' feet, listening to him teach, while her sister was left with all the serving. *L 10:39–40*

Martha complained to Jesus:

Lord dost thou not care that my sister hath left me to serve alone? Bid her therefore that she help me. *L 10:40*

Jesus replied:

Martha, Martha, thou are careful [full of care] and troubled about many things. But one thing is needful; and Mary hath chosen that good part, which shall not be taken away from her. *L 10:41–42*

The manuscripts vary and it is not certain exactly what was said, but its probable thrust was that Mary was properly concerned with Jesus' teaching — the "one thing needful" — rather than the mechanics of food service.

Be that as it may, later on, when Lazarus became sick, his sisters sent a message to Jesus where he was staying beyond Jordan, saying:

Lord, behold, he whom thou lovest is sick. *J 11:3*

The paradoxical thing is that Jesus did not respond to this message, even though John states that "Jesus loved Martha, and her sister, and Lazarus." *J 11:5* Jesus merely said, cryptically:

This sickness is not unto death, but for the glory of God, that the Son of God might be glorified thereby. *J 11:4*

163

Jesus then stayed two days *(J 11:6)* before he said to his disciples:

Let us go into Judea again. *J 11:7*

His disciples objected:

Master, the Jews of late sought to stone thee; and thou goest thither again? *J 11:8*

Jesus answered with a proverb:

Are there not twelve hours in the day? If any man walk in the day, he stumbleth not, because he seeth the light of this world. But if a man walk in the night, he stumbleth, because there is no light in him. *J 11:9–10*

Jesus meant by the proverb that he was safe until his appointed time to die should come; in the meantime, "I must work the works of him that sent me, while it is day." *J 9:4*

Jesus continued:

Our friend Lazarus sleepeth; but I go, that I may awake him out of sleep. *J 11:11*

The disciples said:

Lord, if he sleep, he shall do well. *J 11:12*

By this, the disciples meant that he will get well without us. The disciples were reluctant to go and construed sleep as a coma from which Lazarus would recover, not the sleep of death which Jesus meant. *J 11:13*

So Jesus then told them plainly:

Lazarus is dead. And I am glad for your sakes that I was not there, to the intent that ye may believe; nevertheless let us go unto him. *J 11:14–15*

The Twin (Thomas) then said to his fellow disciples:

Let us also go, that we may die with him. *J 11:16*

This was not exactly a full-hearted response, but Thomas, like the rest of the disciples, anticipated being stoned to death if they returned to Judea.

By the time Jesus and his party arrived near Bethany, Lazarus had been buried four days and many Jews had gathered to comfort Lazarus' sisters, Mary and Martha. *J 11:17, 19* Mary sat home. *J 11:20* Martha came out of Bethany to meet Jesus and said:

Lord, if thou hadst been here, my brother had not died. But I know, that even now, whatsoever thou wilt ask of God, God will give it thee. *J 11:21–22*

Jesus said:

Thy brother shall rise again. *J 11:23*

Martha replied:

I know that he shall rise again in the resurrection at the last day. *J 11:24*

Jesus then said:

I am the resurrection, and the life: he that believeth in me, though he were dead, yet shall he live. And whosoever liveth and believeth in me shall never die.

Believest thou this? *J 11:25–26*

Martha replied:

Yea, Lord: I believe that thou art the Christ, the Son of God, which should come into the world. *J 11:27*

Martha then went home and privately told her sister, Mary:

The Master is come, and calleth for thee. *J 11:28*

Mary immediately left for the place where Jesus had stopped. *J 11:29–30* When she left the house, the assembled mourners in the house followed her, supposing and saying, "She goeth unto the grave to weep there." *J 11:31*

When Mary reached Jesus, she fell down at his feet and said, just as her sister had said:

Lord, if thou hadst been here, my brother had not died. *J 11:32*

Mary and the mourners were weeping and Jesus "groaned in the spirit, and was troubled" *(J 11:33)* and asked:

Where have ye laid him? *J 11:34*

Jesus joined in the weeping and the mourners said, "Behold how he loved him!" And some of them added, "Could not this man, which opened the eyes of the blind, have caused that even this man should not have died?" *J 11:35–37*

Jesus "again groaning in himself" came to the grave which was a cave whose entrance was blocked with a stone. *J 11:38* He then said:

Take ye away the stone. *J 11:39*

Martha protested:

Lord, by this time he stinketh; for he hath been dead four days. *J 11:39*

Jesus said:

Said I not unto thee, that, if thou wouldest believe, thou shouldest see the glory of God? *J 11:40*

When they took away the stone, Jesus lifted up his eyes, and said:

> Father, I thank thee that thou hast heard me. And I know that thou hearest me always: but because of the people which stand by I said it, that they may believe that thou hast sent me. *J 11:41–42*

And when he thus had spoken, he cried with a loud voice:

> Lazarus, come forth. *J 11:43*

Lazarus came forth bound hand and foot with the grave clothes and his face bound with a cloth. Jesus said:

> Loose him, and let him go. *J 11:44*

Many of the Jewish mourners who saw what Jesus did, believed upon him, but others merely reported to the Pharisees what Jesus had done. *J 11:45–46*

It was now clear why Jesus had chosen to take the great risk of going into Judea. The resurrection of Lazarus was needed by Jesus to show the people that "they may believe that thou [The Father] hast sent me." *J 11:42*

Jesus had known from the beginning that Lazarus' sickness "was not unto death" by which he meant irreversible death. *J 11:4* It was for the glory of God that Lazarus was resurrected even after his decaying body had begun to stink. *J 11:4, 40, 39* For this Jesus was grateful and thanked God that Lazarus came out of the burial cave bound though he was with graveclothes. *J 11:41*

But the point of the whole episode was that his followers should know, and indeed the whole world, that he is "the resurrection, and the life" and he that liveth and believes in Jesus like Lazarus did "shall never die." *J 11:25–26* The resurrection of Lazarus did announce the new age wherein death is swallowed up in victory. The last enemy to be destroyed in that age is death, but Lazarus was a man raised up out of his own time to be the occasion for

Jesus' announcement of the new age when "whosoever liveth and believeth in me shall never die." *J 11:25* That age began with the resurrection of Jesus himself a few weeks later and still continues.

At the time, the resurrection of Lazarus was a problem that the Jewish religious establishment could not ignore, so the chief priests and the Pharisees called the council (the Sanhedrin) together. The discussion there was as follows:

> What do we? For this man doeth many miracles. If we let him thus alone, all men will believe on him; and the Romans shall come and take away both our place and nation. *J 11:47–48*

One of them, Caiaphas, the high priest that year, said:

> Ye know nothing at all, nor consider that it is expedient for us, that one man should die for the people, and that the whole nation perish not. *J 11:49–50*

The consensus was, death:

> Then from that day forth they took counsel together for to put him to death. *J 11:53*

Accordingly, both the chief priests and the Pharisees ordered that "if any man knew where he were, he should shew it, that they might take him." *J 11:57*

As John later reflected on the words of Caiaphas, it seemed to him that Caiaphas, by virtue of his office as High Priest, had been unknowingly inspired to prophesy "that Jesus should die for that nation," and that by so dying, Jesus also "should gather together in one the children of God that were scattered abroad," meaning even the Gentiles, the sheep of the other fold. *J 11:51–52*

Since there was a consensus in the Sanhedrin that Jesus should be put to death and accordingly orders had been given to arrest him (*J 11:53, 57*) Jesus had to go into hiding:

Jesus therefore walked no more openly among the Jews; but went thence unto a country near to the wilderness, into a city called Ephraim, and there continued with his disciples. *J 11:54*

Ephraim is usually assumed to be a town some ten miles north and east of Jerusalem near where the Jordan valley breaks away to the east ("the wilderness").

It was then the custom for up-country Jews to come to Jerusalem before the Feast of the Passover to purify themselves by the prescribed ritual. *J 11:55* It was then nearly Passover time, and as the members of the Jewish religious establishment stood in the Temple from time to time, they speculated, "What think ye, that he will not come to the Feast?" *J 11:56*

JESUS RETURNS TO BETHANY

Six days before Passover, Jesus and his disciples returned to Bethany. *J 12:1* This was Lazarus' village and was about two miles southeast of Jerusalem. *J 11:1, 18*

Lazarus and his sisters, Mary and Martha, gave Jesus and his disciples a supper. *J 12:2* This is the same Mary who had let her sister, Martha, do all the serving the last time Jesus had been their guest. *L 10:38–42* This time she anointed Jesus' feet and wiped them with her hair. *J 11:2, 12:3*

Lazarus sat with guests, and as usual, Martha served. *J 12:2* John's account continues:

> Then took Mary a pound of ointment of spikenard, very costly, and anointed the feet of Jesus, and wiped his feet with her hair: and the house was filled with the odour of the ointment. *J 12:3*

Judas Iscariot was one of the disciples present, and he objected that this costly ointment (worth 300 pence) could have been sold and given to the poor. *J 12:4–5*

Jesus rebuked him:

> Let her alone: against the day of my burying hath she kept this. For the poor always ye have with you; but me ye have not always. *J 12:7*

Matthew and Mark have the story a little differently. They are specific that the supper was in the house of Simon the Leper. *Mk 14:3; Mt 26:6* This is not necessarily inconsistent with Lazarus and his sisters giving the supper. *J 12:2* In their accounts an unidentified woman emptied an alabaster box of very precious ointment (Mark says spikenard) on Jesus' head as he sat at meat. *Mk 14:3; Mt 26:6–7* The disciples generally, rather than Judas alone, were indignant, and murmured against her:

> Why was this waste of the ointment made? For it might have been sold for more than three hundred pence [denarii], and have been given to the poor. *Mk 14:4–5*

To what purpose is this waste? For this ointment might have been sold for much, and given to the poor. *Mt 26:8–9*

Jesus said:

Let her alone; why trouble ye her? She hath wrought a good work on me. For ye have the poor with you always, and whensoever ye will ye may do them good: but me ye have not always. She hath done what she could: she is come aforehand to anoint my body to the burying. *Mk 14:6–8*

Why trouble ye the woman: For she hath wrought a good work upon me. For ye have the poor always with you; but me ye have not always. For in that she hath poured this ointment on my body, she did it for my burial. *Mt 26:10–12*

Both Matthew and Mark note that Jesus also said:

Verily I say unto you, wheresoever this gospel shall be preached throughout the whole world, this also that she hath done shall be spoken of for a memorial of her. *Mk 14:9*

Verily I say unto you, wheresoever this gospel shall be preached in the whole world, there shall also this, that this woman hath done, be told for a memorial of her. *Mt 26:13*

Actually Jesus was not the sole attraction at the supper. Many people came to see "Lazarus also, whom he had raised from the dead." *J 12:9*

The persons who had been present when Jesus had called Lazarus out of his grave and raised him from the dead, were convinced, and they had been talking. *J 12:17*

Many Jews thus had come to believe on Jesus. *J 11:45* They saw that Lazarus was alive and went away believing on Jesus. *J 12:11* For this reason the Chief Priests considered putting Lazarus also to death. *J 12:10*

A large crowd had come to Bethany not only to see Jesus, but also to see Lazarus. *J 12:9* Bethany is only a short distance from Jerusalem, and the next day Jesus made a triumphal entry into the holy city. *J 12:12–19*

Jesus' Entry into Jerusalem

The great Jewish national holiday of Passover was to begin in a few days. Jerusalem was crowded with visitors who had come for the holiday. *J 12:12* People who had been present when Jesus had raised Lazarus from the dead at Bethany, just outside Jerusalem, had been talking, and the holiday crowd had heard about this miracle. *J 12:17–18* The popular excitement was so great that his enemies, the Pharisees, concluded, "Behold, the world is gone after him." *J 12:19*

The crowd's mood was exuberant as it surged forth to meet Jesus on his way to Jerusalem, cutting palm tree branches to wave a tumultuous welcome and to throw on the road, along with items of clothing. *Mk 11:8; Mt 21:8, L 19:36; J 12:13*

The crowd shouted:

Hosanna! *Mk 11:9; Mt 21:9; J 12:13*

"Hosanna" means literally, *Save, we pray.* Here it was the key word in a victory shout:

MARK	MATTHEW	LUKE	JOHN
Hosanna:	Hosanna to the son of David:		Hosanna:
Blessed is he	Blessed is he	Blessed be the King	Blessed is the King of Israel
that cometh in the name of the Lord: Blessed be the kingdom of our father David, that cometh in the name	that cometh in the name of the Lord;	that cometh in the name of the Lord:	that cometh in the name of the Lord. *J 12:13*

MARK (cont.)	MATTHEW (cont.)	LUKE (cont.)	JOHN (cont.)
of the Lord:		peace in heaven,	
Hosanna	Hosanna	glory	
in the highest.	to the highest.	in the highest.	
Mk 11:9–10	*Mt 21:9*	*L 19:38*	

The crowd was both ahead and behind him. *Mk 11:9; Mt 21:9* According to Luke, as he came along the road as it descends the Mount of Olives, the crowd "began to rejoice and praise God with a loud voice for all the mighty works that they had seen, saying, 'Blessed be the King that cometh in the name of the Lord, peace in heaven, and glory in the highest.'" *L 19:37–38*

This triumphal procession was observed discreetly by certain Pharisees, who groused among themselves:

Perceive ye how ye prevail nothing? Behold, the world is gone after him. *J 12:19*

Other Pharisees were in the procession itself and said to Jesus:

Master, rebuke thy disciples. *L 19:39*

Jesus answered:

I tell you that, if these should hold their peace, the stones would immediately cry out. *L 19:40*

Just before this, he had sent two of his disciples to go into a nearby village to find an ass with her unbroken colt and to bring the colt. *Mk 11:1–4; Mt 21:1–3; L 19:29–31* They found the colt and started to loose him, when his owners objected, and the two disciples said, as Jesus had instructed them, "The Lord hath need of him." *Mk 11:3–6; Mt 21:3–6; L 19:31–34*

The two disciples brought the colt to Jesus and threw their garments on the colt for a saddle, and Jesus mounted up. *Mk 11:7; Mt 21:7; L 19:35 (J 12:14)* At the time, it just seemed a practical thing to do, but later on, after Jesus' resurrection, the disciples realized that there was more to it than that. *J 12:16* It was a fulfillment of Zechariah's prophecy (*Mt 21:4*), which John and Matthew quote:

> Fear not, daughter of Zion: behold, thy King cometh sitting upon an ass's colt. *J 12:15* (*Zechariah 9:9*)

> Tell ye the daughter of Zion, "Behold, thy King cometh unto thee, meek, and sitting upon an ass, and a colt the foal of an ass." *Mt 21:5* (*Zechariah 9:9*)

As Jesus rode and saw the City of Jerusalem loom up before him, he wept and said:

> If thou hadst known, even thou, at least in this thy day, the things which belong unto thy peace!

> But now they are hid from thine eyes.

> For the days shall come upon thee, that thine enemies shall cast a trench about thee, and compass thee round, and keep thee in on every side, and shall lay thee even with the ground, and thy children within thee; and they shall not leave in thee one stone upon another; because thou knewest not the time of thy visitation. *L 19:42–44*

Jesus and his procession then entered the city and proceeded to the Temple itself. *Mk 11:11; Mt 21:10* This caused a tremendous stir in the city, and everyone was saying, "Who is this?" *Mt 21:10* The procession chanted, "This is Jesus, the prophet from Nazareth of Galilee." *Mt 21:11*

After Jesus had looked upon all things in the Holy City he withdrew at dusk back to Bethany, a nearby village. *Mk 11:11*

The next morning, as Jesus and his disciples walked back into Jerusalem, Jesus was hungry and noticed by the roadside a fig tree in leaf. *Mk 11:12–13; Mt 21:18–19* Jesus examined the tree but found that it had no figs. We have two accounts of what Jesus said:

MARK	MATTHEW
No man eat fruit	Let no fruit grow
of thee	on thee
hereafter for ever.	henceforth for ever.
Mk 11:14	*Mt 21:19*

At this point the accounts diverge. Matthew states that "presently the fig tree withered away." *Mt 21:19* Mark states that on their trip into Jerusalem the next morning the disciples "saw the fig tree dried up from the roots." *Mk 11:20* Matthew's statement as to when the withering occurred is ambiguous. Mark's account is clear that it was *noticed* the next morning by Peter.

The text of the two accounts state:

MARK	MATTHEW
And Peter	And when
calling to remembrance	the disciples saw it,
saith unto him,	they marveled, saying,
"Master, behold,	"How soon is
the fig tree	the fig tree
which thou cursedst	
is withered away."	withered away!"
Mk 11:21	*Mt 21:20*

Jesus' answer (*Mk 11:22–23; Mt 21:21*) is treated in detail elsewhere. See page 1032. Here it is sufficient to quote part of Matthew's account of Jesus' answer:

Verily I say unto you, if ye have faith, and doubt not, ye shall not only do this which is done to the fig tree, but also if ye shall say unto this mountain, "Be thou removed, and be thou cast into the sea,' it shall be done." *Mt 21:21*

Perhaps later the same day some Greek converts to Judaism who had come to Jerusalem to worship at the feast of the Passover discreetly approached Jesus through Philip, a disciple with a Greek name, saying, "Sir, we would see Jesus." *J 12:20–21* Philip consulted

Andrew, the other disciple with a Greek name, and together they approached Jesus. *J 12:22* It is not certain that Jesus actually talked to the Greeks, but he apparently did consider the inquiry of the Greeks to mean that his mission was approaching its culmination, and said:

The hour is come, that the Son of man should be glorified. *J 12:23*

Jesus continued:

Verily, verily, I say unto you, except a corn [kernel] of wheat fall into the ground and die, it abideth alone; but if it die, it bringeth forth much fruit . . .

Now is my soul troubled; and what shall I say? 'Father, save me from this hour': but for this cause came I unto this hour.

Father, glorify thy name. *J 12:23–24, 27–28*

John continues:

Then came there a voice from heaven, saying "I have both glorified it, and will glorify it again." *J 12:28*

The bystanders heard something, but their accounts of what happened varied: some said, "It thundered"; others said, "An angel spake to him." *J 12:29*

Jesus then said:

This voice came not because of me, but for your sakes. Now is the judgment of this world; now shall the prince of this world be cast out.

And I, if I be lifted up from the earth, will draw all men unto me." *J 12:30–32*

The bystanders had heard something but they did not associate Jesus with the "Son of man" who was to be glorified, because they then asked Jesus why he said:

The Son of man must be lifted up? Who is this Son of man? *J 12:34*

Jesus answered cryptically:

Yet a little while is the light with you. Walk while ye have the light, lest darkness come upon you; for he that walketh in darkness knoweth not whither he goeth. While ye have light, believe in the light, that ye may be the children of light. *J 12:35–36*

Jesus then left and resumed hiding, probably in Bethany. *J 11:54, 12:36*

As John looked back at Jesus' statement that "I, if I be lifted up from the earth, will draw all men unto me" (*J 12:32*), John understood Jesus' statement as "signifying what death he should die." *J 12:33; 18:32* John also reflected on the paradox that Jesus "had done so many miracles before them [the people], yet they believed not on him." *J 12:37*

It seemed to John that this situation fulfilled certain prophecies of Isaiah which he then quotes:

Lord, who hath believed our report? And to whom hath the arm of the Lord been revealed? *J 12:38 (Isaiah 53:1)*

In fact, John concluded that "they could not believe" (*J 12:39*), quoting another prophecy of Isaiah:

He hath blinded their eyes, and hardened their heart; that they should not see with their eyes, nor understand with their heart, and be converted, and I should heal them. *J 12:40 (Isaiah 6:10)*

Finally, John wrote that when Isaiah had so prophesied he had seen Jesus in his glory:

These things said Isaiah, when he saw his glory, and spake of him. *J 12:41*

Although many did not believe on Jesus, many others did. *J 12:19* This included many of Israel's religious elite:

> Nevertheless *among the chief rulers also many believed on him*; but because of the Pharisees they did not confess him, lest they should be put out of the synagogue: for they loved the praise of men more than the praise of God. *J 12:42–43*

One of the days in this week before Passover, Jesus cleansed the Temple by casting out the money changers and the dove sellers. *Mk 11:15–17; Mt 21:12–13; L 19:45–46* Every day that week Jesus was in the Temple teaching, and healing the blind and lame. *Mt 21:14; L 19:47* Every evening he would go out of the city to the village of Bethany where he lodged. *Mk 11:11, 19; Mt 21:17*

Matthew sums up the Passover Week's ministry as follows:

> And when the chief priests and scribes saw the wonderful things that he did, and the *children* crying in the Temple, and saying, "Hosanna to the son of David," they were sore displeased and said unto him, "Hearest thou what these say?" *Mt 21:15*

Jesus replied:

> Yea; have ye never read, "Out of the mouth of babes and sucklings thou hast perfected praise"? *Mt 21:16*

Both Mark and Luke assert that the chief priests and scribes in that week sought how they might destroy him, but they feared the great following he had among the people. *Mk 11:18; L 19:47* Mark has it that "all the people were astonished [enthralled by] at his doctrine"; while Luke states "all the people were very attentive to hear him." *Mk 11:18; L 19:48*

The chief priests, scribes and elders decided that they had to confront him and approached him in the Temple as he walked, teaching the people. *Mk 11:27; Mt 21:23; L 20:1* They bluntly asked him:

> By what authority doest thou these things? And who gave thee this authority to do these things? *Mk 11:28 (Mt 21:23; L 20:2)*

Jesus did not assert the authority of his Father but instead temporized:

> I will also ask of you one question, and answer me, and I will tell you by what authority I do these things. The baptism of John, was it from heaven, or of men? Answer me. *Mk 11:20–30*

This question they did not dare answer either way. *Mk 11:29–30 (Mt 21:25–26; L 20:5–6)* So they said, "We cannot tell." *Mk 11:33 (Mt 21:27; L 20:7)*

Jesus then said:

> Neither do I tell you by what authority I do these things. *Mk 11:33 (Mt 21:27; L 20:8)*

Was Jesus "The Son of David"?

One day in that Passover Week, Jesus was teaching in the Temple
and he challenged some Pharisees:

JESUS: "What think ye of Christ? Whose son is he?"

PHARISEES: "The son of David." *Mt 22:41–42*

What did Jesus want to teach by starting this dialogue? The
other two synoptic gospels have only Jesus' question and the answer of the bystanders is omitted:

MARK	LUKE
How say the scribes	How say they
that Christ	that Christ
is the son of David?	is David's son?
Mk 12:35	*L 20:41*

All three synoptic gospels then continue with Jesus' point:

MARK	MATTHEW	LUKE
For David	How then	And David
himself said	doth David	himself saith
by the Holy Spirit,	in spirit	in the book of Psalm
	call him Lord,	
	saying,	
"The Lord said	"The Lord said	"The Lord said
to my Lord,	unto my Lord,	unto my Lord,
sit thou on	sit thou on	sit thou on
my right hand,	my right hand,	my right hand,
till I make	till I make	till I make
thine enemies	thine enemies	thine enemies
thy footstool."	thy footstool?"	thy footstool."
David therefore	If David	David therefore
himself calleth him	then call him	calleth him

181

MARK (cont.)	MATTHEW (cont.)	LUKE (cont.)
"Lord";	"Lord",	"Lord",
and whence		
is he then	how is he	how is he then
his son?	his son?	his son?
Mk 12:36–37	Mt 22:43–45	L 20:42–44

Jesus' point is that the scribal notion that Christ (the Messiah) was the son of David was wrong: the Messiah transcended such categories. Jesus proved his point to these scribes and Pharisees by applying Psalm 110:1 with their own narrow scribal logic. In terms of that logic, Jesus' final question, "if David then call him 'Lord', how is he his son?" was unanswerable, and his listeners did not even try:

> And no man was able to answer him a word, neither durst any man from that day forth ask him any more questions. Mt 22:46

The crowd enjoyed the embarrassment of the scribes and Pharisees:

> And the common people heard him gladly. Mk 12:37 (Mt 23:1; L 20:45)

The more important point is that Jesus did not believe that Christ was the Son of David; otherwise there was no reason for him to have challenged the Pharisees with his question which would end in discrediting their narrow, traditional scribal title, Son of David.

The Gospels record many statements in which the crowds, or individuals, apply this scribal title, Son of David, to Jesus. Mt 9:27, 12:23, 15:22, 20:30, 21:9, 15; Mk 10:47–48, 11:10; L 18:37 For example, Bartimaeus, a blind beggar, cried out:

> Jesus, thou Son of David, have mercy upon me. Mk 10:47

Another example is the crowd's reaction after Jesus had healed a man "possessed with a devil, blind and dumb.":

And all the people were amazed, and said, "Is not this the Son of David?" *Mt 12:23*

In none of these cases does Jesus himself endorse this title as applied to himself. Just before Jesus' pointed challenge to the Pharisees about the relation of the Messiah to the Son of David (*Mt 22:42*), Jesus had incurred the displeasure of the chief priests and scribes because the children were crying in the Temple:

Hosanna to the Son of David. *Mt 21:15*

The chief priests and scribes objected to Jesus:

Hear thou what these say? *Mt 21:16*

Jesus noncommittally turned aside their objections by quoting a line from Psalm 8:2:

Yea; have ye not read, "Out of the mouth of babes and sucklings thou hast perfected praise"? *Mt 21:16*

To sum up, Jesus claimed to be Christ, the Son of the Blessed. *Mk 14:61–62* He did not claim to be the Son of David, the traditional Jewish title. In fact, as interchange with the Pharisees showed, he rejected the concept that Christ, the Messiah, was the Son of David.

The question whether Jesus was in fact "of the seed of David, according to the flesh" is a different one. *Romans 1:3; 2 Timothy 2:8; Acts 2:30, 13:23* It was then a popular opinion in Israel that the Jewish scriptures taught that "Christ cometh of the seed of David, and out of the town of Bethlehem where David was." *J 7:42* Therefore Matthew, writing the most Jewish of the Gospels, is at pains to begin his gospel with a genealogy attempting to demonstrate that Jesus was indeed the Son of David according to the flesh. The first sentence in his gospel accordingly reads:

The book of the generation [genealogy] of Jesus Christ, the son of David, the son of Abraham. *Mt 1:1*

The genealogy then proceeds from Abraham down to Jacob. Its last sentence reads:

> And Jacob begat Joseph the husband of Mary of whom was born Jesus, who is called Christ. *Mt 1:16*

The inference from Matthew's genealogy is clear that Joseph was Mary's husband, not Jesus' father. It follows that the genealogy Matthew used proves a Davidic descent for *Joseph*, but not for Jesus.

Luke also asserts that *Joseph*, not Jesus, "was of the house and lineage of David." *L 2:4* This seems irrelevant because Luke later writes that Jesus was only "(as was supposed) the son of Joseph." *L 3:23*

Both Matthew's and Luke's genealogies trace Joseph's descent from David. *Matthew 1:1–17; L 3:23–38* Both genealogies recognize the absence of the final "begat" link between Joseph and Jesus. *Mt 1:16; L 3:23* If Jesus was descended from David in the ordinary biological sense, he was descended through his mother, Mary, and we do not have her genealogy.

It is sometimes said that the genealogy of Luke (*L 3:23–38*) is Mary's genealogy. A simple reading of these verses in Luke will show that Luke's genealogy, like Matthew's, is a genealogy of Joseph.

Luke writes that Mary was "a virgin espoused to a man whose name was Joseph, of the house of David." *L 1:27* Since Jesus' supposed father was Joseph who was "of the house of David," Jesus himself in that sense could be considered to have been of the house of David.

Luke writes that this virgin was told by the angel Gabriel:

> Fear not, Mary, for thou hast found favor with God. And, behold, thou shalt conceive in thy womb, and bring forth a son, and shalt call his name, JESUS. He shall be great and shall be called the Son of the Highest; and the Lord God shall give unto him the throne of his father David, and he shall reign over the house of Jacob for ever; and of his kingdom there shall be no end. *L 1:30–33*

Mary replied:

How shall this be, seeing that I know not a man? *L 1:34*

The angel answered:

The Holy Spirit shall come upon thee, and the power of the Highest shall overshadow thee; therefore also that holy thing which shall be born of thee shall be called Son of God. *L 1:35*

We know that Jesus claimed to be the Son of God. John quotes Jesus as saying, "I am the Son of God." *J 10:36* (For a full statement of the relevant quotations, see section "There Is But One God and Jesus Is His Only Son," pp. 729–734.)

We also know that Jesus did not think that being the Christ expected by the Jews was limited to being the son of David. We have no quotation from Jesus where he affirms that biologically speaking he was of the seed of David, although Matthew and Luke state that Joseph, Mary's husband, was of Davidic descent.

We have the clear statement of Paul, in Romans, that Jesus "was made of the seed of David, according to the flesh." *Romans 1:3; 2 Timothy 2:8 Cf. Acts 2:30, 13:23* This descent from David according to the flesh was through Mary, his mother.

More important than Jesus' fleshly descent is the fact, as Paul wrote, that Jesus was:

Declared to be the Son of God with power, according to the spirit of holiness, by the resurrection from the dead. *Romans 1:4*

KILLING THE PROPHETS

In the last week of his life, Jesus inveighed against his own people, Israel, referring to them by the figurative name, Jerusalem:

MATTHEW	LUKE
O Jerusalem, Jerusalem,	O Jerusalem, Jerusalem,
thou that killest the prophets,	which killest the prophets,
and stonest them	and stonest them
which are sent unto thee,	that are sent unto thee;
how often	how often
would I have gathered	would I have gathered
thy children together,	thy children together,
even as a hen	as a hen
gathereth her chickens	doth gather her brood
under her wings,	under her wings,
and ye would not!	and ye would not!
Behold,	Behold,
your house is left	your house is left
unto you desolate.	unto you desolate;
For I say unto you,	and verily I say unto you,
Ye shall not see me	Ye shall not see me,
henceforth,	until the time come
till	when
ye shall say,	ye shall say,
"Blessed is he	"Blessed is he
that cometh	that cometh
in the name of the Lord."	in the name of the Lord."
[Psalm 118:26]	*[Psalm 118:26]*
Mt 23:37–39	*L 13:34–35*

Luke does not place this saying in the last week of Jesus' life but instead detaches it and inserts it in his account of Jesus' "journeying toward Jerusalem." *L 13:22, 31–35* Luke does this because he considered that Jesus' later lament over Jerusalem should be in mind when Jesus said on that journey, referring to himself:

It can not be that a prophet perish out of Jerusalem. *L 13:33*

Jesus implies that it was he who had sent the prophets in ages past because he would have gathered Jerusalem's children, the people of Israel, as a hen protects its chicks, but "ye would not!" Jerusalem's rejections, past and about to happen, would leave her desolate and unable to see Jesus until his ultimate triumphant return in an age yet to come.

Both Matthew and Luke couple Jesus' lament over Jerusalem with a prediction that prophets and other divine messengers will be sent, only to be slain and persecuted in their turn, just as had suffered the prophets of old:

MATTHEW	LUKE
Wherefore, behold,	Therefore also said
	the wisdom of God,
I send unto you prophets,	I will send them prophets
and wise men,	and apostles,
and scribes:	
and some of them	and some of them
ye shall kill and crucify;	they shall slay
and some of them	
shall ye scourge	and persecute:
in your synagogues	that the blood
and persecute them	of all the prophets,
from city to city:	which was shed
that upon you may come	from the foundation of
all the righteous blood	the world
shed upon the earth,	may be required of
	this generation;
from the blood of	from the blood of
righteous Abel	Abel
unto the blood of Zacharias	unto the blood of Zacharias,
son of Barachias,	
whom ye slew	which perished
between the temple	between the altar
and the altar.	and the temple:
Verily I say unto you,	verily I say unto you,
All these things	It shall be

MATTHEW (cont.)
shall come upon
this generation."
Mt 23:34–36

LUKE (cont.)
required of
this generation.
L 11:49–51

This tradition of bloody persecution of the prophets was to come upon "this generation," Jesus' generation. In fact, this tradition of bloody persecution would apply to Jesus himself. He stated this in the course of a statement he made when he received a warning that Herod Antipas, Tetrarch of Galilee and Perea, was about to seize and kill him:

> Go ye, and tell that fox, Behold, I cast out devils, and I do cures today and tomorrow, and the third day I shall be perfected. Nevertheless I must walk today, and tomorrow, and the day following: *for it can not be that a prophet perish out of Jerusalem. L 13:32–33*

It is clear that Jesus was not to be deterred from his mission by a warning, whether or not these Pharisees were in fact acting for Herod Antipas, particularly since he did not believe that he, as a prophet, was fated to perish out of Jerusalem. What is not clear is whether Jesus simply meant he had three days' work to do before leaving Herod's territory, or whether he referred, in addition, in an oblique way, to his future resurrection on "the third day." L 13:32 Later piety sees such a reference, but it seems more likely that Jesus simply meant that his work at that place would be finished in three days.

More importantly, Jesus had set his face toward Jerusalem, and he anticipated that he, like the prophets before him, would perish in Jerusalem. That is why he lamented:

> O Jerusalem, Jerusalem, thou that killest the prophets! Mt 23:37; (L 13:34)

He even anticipated that he would perish by crucifixion. He told his disciples a couple of days before it happened:

> Ye know that after two days is the Feast of the Passover, and the Son of man is betrayed to be crucified. Mt 26:1–2

THE LAST DAYS OF JESUS

At this time Jesus was teaching in the Temple, the national shrine, each day, and then withdrawing out of the city each night to the Mount of Olives:

> And in the day time he was teaching in the Temple; and at night he went out, and abode in the mount that is called the Mount of Olives. And all the people came early in the morning to him in the Temple, for to hear him. *L 21:37–38*

The Feast of the Passover was to begin in a couple of days. *Mt 26:2* The Feast of the Passover was a great Jewish national religious festival commemorating the Jews' release from bondage in Egypt by God's deliverance. The book of Exodus in the Old Testament gives this brief explanation of what the Passover Feast meant to the Jews:

> And it shall come to pass, when your children shall say unto you, "What mean ye by this service?"
>
> That ye shall say, "It is a sacrifice of the Lord's Passover, who passed over the houses of the children of Israel in Egypt, when he smote the Egyptians, and delivered our houses." *Exodus 12:26–27*

The Feast of the Passover and the Feast of Unleavened Bread together constituted a single holiday season which lasted seven days. Josephus, the first century Jewish historian, described the Feast of Unleavened Bread as follows:

> The Feast of Unleavened Bread succeeds that of the Passover, and falls on the fifteenth day of the month, continues seven days, wherein they feed on unleavened bread, on every one of which days two bulls are killed, and one ram, and seven lambs. *Josephus, Antiquities, Book III, Ch. X, Sec. 5*

In Jesus' time, Jerusalem filled with pilgrims who came to celebrate the holidays from the remote places of the country and from the foreign lands where Jews were dispersed. Josephus writes that at Passover "An innumerable multitude came thither out of the country, nay, from beyond its limits also." *Josephus, Antiquities, Book XVII, Ch. IX, Sec. 3.* We get glimpses of the scale of these pilgrimages from John's Gospel which mentions "certain Greeks . . . that came up to worship at the Feast [Passover]." *J 12:20* We do not know whether these Greeks were full converts to Judaism, or simply, "God-fearers."

Many Jews, like Jesus' parents, "went to Jerusalem every year at the Feast of the Passover" as was "the custom" and there "fulfilled the Days." *L 2:41–43*

Passover began on the fifteenth day of Nisan, the Jewish lunar month falling in the period covered by our months of March-April. By Jewish reckoning, days began and ended at sundown. Passover holiday preparations began the day before. On Nisan 14, work stopped at noon, and lambs were sacrificed that afternoon for the Passover feast beginning after sunset that evening. We may speculate that the atmosphere in Jerusalem on the afternoon of Nisan 14 was comparable to that of American cities on December 24, when offices close at noon, and the streets are full of holiday spirit and crowds.

Jesus' disciples, as Jews, were eager to be ready for this great national holiday:

MARK	MATTHEW	LUKE
And the first day of	Now the first day of the Feast of	Then came the day of
Unleavened Bread, when they killed the Passover [lamb],	Unleavened Bread	Unleavened Bread when the Passover [lamb] must be killed.
his disciples	the disciples came to Jesus,	L 22:7
said unto him, "Where wilt thou that we go and prepare that thou	saying unto him, "Where wilt thou that we prepare for thee	

MARK (cont.)	MATTHEW (cont.)	LUKE (cont.)
mayest eat	to eat	
the Passover?"	the Passover?"	
Mk 14:12	*Mt 26:17*	

Jesus sent two of his disciples, Peter and John, telling them:

Go prepare us the Passover, that we may eat. *L 22:8*

They asked:

Where wilt thou that we prepare? *L 22:9*

All three synoptic gospels have Jesus' answer:

MARK	MATTHEW	LUKE
Go ye	Go	Behold, when
		ye are entered
into the city,	into the city	into the city,
and there shall meet		there shall
you a man	to such a man,	a man meet you,
bearing		bearing
a pitcher of water.		a pitcher of water.
Follow him.		Follow him
And wheresoever		into the house where
he shall go in,		he entereth in.
say ye to	and say unto	And ye shall say unto
the goodman	him,	the goodman
of the house,		of the house,
:The Master saith,	"The Master saith,	"The Master saith
	My time is at hand;	unto thee,
Where is the guest-		Where is the guest-
chamber,		chamber,
where I shall eat	I will keep	where I shall eat
the Passover	the Passover	the Passover
	at thy house	
with my disciples?"	with my disciples."	with my disciples?"
	Mt 26:18	
And he will		And he shall

MARK (cont.)	MATTHEW (cont.)	LUKE (cont.)
shew you		shew you
a large upper room		a large upper room
furnished		furnished.
and prepared.		
There		There
make ready for us.		make ready.
Mk 14:13–15		*L 22:10–12*

Jesus' instruction to look for "a man bearing a pitcher of water" suggests an espionage movie. *Mk 14:13; L 22:10* The man is the contact, and the two disciples are to follow him to the house of one of Jesus' secret followers in the city (the safe house), and the disciples are then to give that follower, the householder, the password:

> The Master saith, "Where is the guestchamber, where I shall eat the Passover with my disciples?" *Mk 14:14 (Mt 26:18; L 22:11)*

The reason for all these precautions is that Jesus knew, or at least sensed, that the chief priests and scribes were already planning "how they might take him by craft, and put him to death." *Mk 14:1 (Mt 26:4; L 22:2)*

Mark quotes Jesus as telling his disciples at about this time:

> Ye know that two days is the Feast of the Passover, and the Son of man is betrayed to be crucified. *Mt 26:2*

The gospel accounts continue:

MARK	MATTHEW	LUKE
And his disciples	And the disciples	And they
went forth	did as Jesus had	went
and came	appointed them;	
into the city,		
and found		and found
as he had said		as he said
unto them;		unto them;
and they made ready	and made ready	and they made ready

MARK (cont.)	MATTHEW (cont.)	LUKE (cont.)
the Passover.	the Passover.	the Passover.
And in the evening he cometh with the Twelve. *Mk 14:16–17*	Now when the even was come, he sat down with the Twelve. *Mt 26:19–20*	And when the hour was come, he sat down and the Twelve apostles with him. *L 22:13–14*

Once the arrangement for the guest room had been made, Jesus and his disciples waited until evening to come into the city, presumably because it was safer for them after dusk.

This was a Thursday evening. All the Gospel accounts agree that Jesus was crucified the next day, Friday. *Mk 15:42; Mt 27:62; L 23:54; J 19:31* According to John, that Friday was the day before Passover, the day of preparation: "It was the preparation of the Passover." *J 19:14* Since, by Jewish reckoning, a day began at sunset, according to John the Passover began at sunset that Friday. John also expressly states that the next day, the Sabbath, "was an high day." *J 19:31* The other three gospels seem to imply that Passover had begun at sunset the evening before, that is, Thursday evening. *Mk 14:12; Mt 26:17; L 22:7* If that were the case, the Last Supper was technically a Passover meal, while John's account is clear that the Last Supper was simply a meal preparatory to Passover, which began at sunset on Friday, the next day.

Scholars dispute whether the Last Supper was, or was not, an actual Passover meal and then draw theological conclusions about the Last Supper from the results reached. We believe the focus should be, instead, on what Jesus actually said and did at his last meal with his disciples, his Last Supper.

The Last Supper

The supper that Thursday evening began with Jesus' solemn announcement:

> With desire I have desired to eat this Passover with you before I suffer. For I say unto you, I will not any more eat thereof, until it be fulfilled in the Kingdom of God. *L 22:15–16*

He then took a cup of wine and gave thanks, and said:

> Take this, and divide it among yourselves. For I say unto you, I will not drink of the fruit of the vine, until the Kingdom of God shall come. *L 22:17–18*

Despite the somberness of this beginning, we do know that before the meal was over that there was "strife" among the disciples present over "which of them should be accounted the greatest." *L 22:24* Jesus' rebuke was remembered:

> The kings of the Gentiles exercise lordship over them; and they that exercise authority upon them are called benefactors. But ye shall not be so; but he that is greatest among you, let him be as the younger; and he that is chief, as he that doth serve. For whether is greater, he that sitteth at meat, or he that serveth? Is not he that sitteth at meat? But I am among you as he that serveth.

> Ye are they which have continued with me in my temptations. And I appoint unto you a kingdom, as my Father hath appointed unto me, that ye may eat and drink at my table in my kingdom, and sit on thrones judging the twelve tribes of Israel. *L 22:25–30*

The precise order of events at the Last Supper is unknown, but we may speculate that Jesus at this point decided to emphasize what he had just said with an acted parable.

The custom of that hot and dusty country was that a servant should wash the guests' feet before the meal began. Jesus and the disciples had assembled by stealth at dusk at the borrowed guest room in a stranger's house. Under these circumstances, it would not be surprising if no servant had done the foot-washings. After all, there were thirteen unknown guests and the arrangements may not have been clear.

All we do know is that during the course of the supper Jesus stood up, laid aside his outer garments and girded himself with a towel. J 13:4 He then poured water into a basin and began to wash the disciples' feet and wipe them with his towel. J 13:5

When he came to Peter, the following dialogue occurred:

PETER: Lord, dost though wash my feet?

JESUS: What I do knowest not now; but thou shalt know here-after.

PETER: Thou shalt never wash my feet.

JESUS: If I wash thee not, thou hast no part with me.

PETER: Lord, not my feet only, but also my hands and my head.

JESUS: He that is washed needeth not save to wash his feet, but is clean every white; and ye are clean, but not all. J 13:6–10

John explains this saying as follows:

For he knew who should betray him; therefore said he, "Ye are not all clean." J 13:11

After he had washed the disciples' feet, he dressed and sat down again. J 13:12 He then explained his object lesson:

Know ye that I have done to you?

Ye call me "Master" and "Lord," and ye say well, for so am I.

If I then, your Lord and Master, have washed your feet, ye also ought to wash one another's feet. For I have given you an example, that ye should do as I have done to you.

Verily, verily, I say unto you, the servant is not greater than his lord; neither is he that is sent greater than he that sent him.

If ye know these things, happy are ye if ye do them. *J 13:12–17*

Jesus was seizing his last opportunity to teach his disciples. His example taught them indelibly that they "should do as I have done to you." *J 13:15* But the somber thread of betrayal by one of his own was repeatedly woven into his conversation that night. He continued:

I speak not of you all. I know whom I have chosen; but that the Scripture may be fulfilled, "He that eateth bread with me hath lifted up his heel against me."

Now I tell you before it come, that, when it is come to pass, ye may believe that I am he.

Verily, verily, I say unto you, he that receiveth whomsoever I send receiveth me; and he that receiveth me receiveth him that sent me. *J 13:18–20*

As Jesus finished speaking "he was troubled in spirit" and he could no longer suppress his overwhelming perception of his imminent betrayal and he said bluntly that one of those present would betray him. *J 13:21*

The gospel accounts of this statement vary slightly:

MARK	MATTHEW	LUKE	JOHN
Jesus said:	He said,	[Jesus said]	[Jesus said]
"Verily	"Verily	"But, behold,	"Verily, Verily,
I say	I say	the hand of	I say
unto you,	unto you,	him that	unto you,
one of you	that one of you		that one of you
which eateth			
with me shall	shall		shall

MARK (cont.)	MATTHEW (cont.)	LUKE (cont.)	JOHN (cont.)
betray me."	betray me."	betrayeth me is with me on the table.	betray me." J 13:21
And they began to be sorrowful, and	And they were exceeding sorrowful, and began every one of them		
to say unto him one by one, "Is it I?" and another said, "Is it I?"	to say unto him, "Lord, is it I?"		
And he answered and said unto them, "It is one of the Twelve, that dippeth	And he answered and said, "He that dippeth his hand		
with me in the dish.	with me in the dish, the same shall betray me.	And truly	
The Son of man indeed goeth, as it is written of him: but woe to that man by whom the Son of man is betrayed!	The Son of man goeth as it is written of him: but woe unto that man by whom the Son of man is betrayed!	the Son of man goeth as it was determined: but woe unto that man by whom he is betrayed!" L 22:21–22	

MARK (cont.)	MATTHEW (cont.)	LUKE (cont.)	JOHN (cont.)
Good were it for that man if he had never been born." Mk 14:18–21	It had been good for that man if he had not been born."		
	Then Judas, which betrayed him, answered and said, "Master, is it I?" He said unto him, "Thou has said." Mt 26:21–25		

John and Luke give us further details:

And they began to enquire among themselves, which of them it was should do this thing. L 22:23

Then the disciples looked one on another, doubting of whom he spoke. J 13:22

At this point Peter beckoned an unnamed disciple, presumably John Zebedee, to ask Jesus:

Lord, who is it? J 13:23–5

Jesus answered:

He it is, to whom I shall give a sop, when I have dipped it. J 13:26

Jesus then dipped a sop and gave it to Judas, murmuring:

That thou doest, do quickly. J 13:27

In the bustle of the supper, the men present did not hear exactly what Jesus had said to Judas:

> Now no man at this table knew for what intent he spake this unto him. For some of them thought, because Judas had the bag, that Jesus had said unto him, "Buy those things that we have need of against the feast"; or, that "he should give something to the poor." *J 13:28–29*

Judas took the sop and left immediately. *J 13:30* By this time it was night. *J 13:30*

After Judas left, the supper continued:

MARK	MATTHEW	LUKE
And *as they* did eat,	And *as they* were eating,	And
Jesus took bread,	Jesus took bread	he took bread,
and blessed,	and blessed it	and gave thanks,
and brake it,	and brake it,	and brake it,
and gave to them,	and gave it to the disciples,	and gave unto them,
and said,	and said,	saying,
"Take, eat: this is my body."	"Take, eat: this is my body."	"This is my body which is given for you; this do in remembrance of me."
Mk 14:22	*Mt 26:26*	*L 22:19*

After the supper had ended, Jesus took another cup of wine, "the cup after supper." *L 22:20; 1 Corinthians 11:25* The gospel accounts state:

MARK	MATTHEW	LUKE
And he took the cup, and when	And he took the cup,	

MARK (cont.)	MATTHEW (cont.)	LUKE (cont.)
he had given thanks,	and gave thanks,	
he gave it to them:	and gave it to them,	
and they all drank		
of it.		
And he said	saying,	
	"Drink ye all of it.	
unto them,		
"This is my blood	For this is my blood	This cup is
of the new testament,	of the new testament,	the new testament
		in my blood,
which is shed	which is shed	which is shed
for many.	for many	for you.
	for the remission	*L 22:20*
	of sins.	
Verily I say	But I say	
unto you,	unto you,	
I will drink no more	I will not drink	
	henceforth	
of the fruit	of this fruit	
of the vine,	of the vine,	
until that day	until that day	
when I drink it	when I drink it	
new	new with you	
in the Kingdom	in my Father's	
of God."	Kingdom."	
Mk 14:23–25	*Mt 26:27–29*	

In a letter to the church at Corinth, Greece, written in A.D. 54 or 55, Paul included an account of the supper which he, as a convert, had received around A.D. 33:

> That the Lord Jesus the same night in which he was betrayed took bread; and when he had given thanks, he brake it, and said,

> "Take, eat. This is my body, which is broken for you. This do in remembrance of me."

After the same manner also he took the cup, when [after] he had supped, saying:

"This cup is the new testament in my blood. This do ye, as oft as ye drink it, in remembrance of me." *1 Corinthians 11:23–25*

John sums up the Last Supper as follows:

Now before the Feast of the Passover when Jesus knew that his hour was come that he should depart out of this world unto the Father, having loved his own which were in the world, he loved them unto the end. And supper being ended, the Devil having now put into the heart of Judas Iscariot, Simon's son, to betray him; Jesus knowing that the Father had given all things into his hands, and that he was come from God, and went to God. *J 13:1–3*

The supper ended simply:

And when they had sung a hymn, they went out into the Mount of Olives. *Mk 14:26; Mt 26:30*

Jesus' Teachings on the Mount of Olives

The Mount of Olives is a ridge east of Jerusalem about 2,680 feet high and is separated from the city by a valley in which the brook Kidron flows in a general southerly direction. Jesus often withdrew to the Mount of Olives. *L 22:39* He went there after the Last Supper. *L 22:39*

The night of the Last Supper was the night of either Nisan 13/14 or Nisan 14/15. The moon must have been full, or nearly full, since Passover began with the full moon on Nisan 14. Spring comes early in that latitude, but allowance must be made for Jerusalem's elevation. We know that it was cold that night. *J 18:18* The officers and servants in the court of the high priest's palace had a warming fire going. *J 18:18*

Matthew and Mark imply that it was on the Mount of Olives that Jesus said:

Mark	Matthew
All ye shall be offended [turn away] because of me this night. For it is written, "I will smite the shepherd, and the sheep shall be scattered."	All ye shall be offended [turn away] because of me this night. For it is written, "I will smite the shepherd, and the sheep of the flock shall be scattered abroad."
But after that I am risen I will go before you into Galilee. *Mk 14:27–28*	But after I am risen again, I will go before you into Galilee. *Mt 26:31–32*

All four gospels report the next episode, but with variances:

Mark	Matthew	Luke	John
But Peter said unto him,	Peter answered said unto him,	And he said unto him,	Peter said unto him,

MARK (cont.)	MATTHEW (cont.)	LUKE (cont.)	JOHN (cont.)
"Although all shall be offended [turn away] yet will not I."	"Though all men shall be offended [turn away] because of thee, yet will I never be offended."	"Lord, I am ready to go with thee, both into prison, and to death."	"Lord, why can not I follow thee now? I will lay down my life for thy sake."
And Jesus saith unto him,	Jesus said unto him,	And he said,	Jesus answered him, "Wilt thou lay down thy life for my sake?
"Verily I say unto thee that this day, even in this night before the cock crow twice, thou shalt deny me thrice."	Verily I say unto thee that this night before the cock crow, thou shalt deny me thrice."	"I tell thee, Peter the cock shall not crow this day before that thou shalt thrice deny that thou knowest me." L 22:33–34	Verily, verily I say unto thee the cock shall not crow till thou hast denied me thrice." J 13:37–38
But he spake the more vehemently, "If I should die with thee, I will not deny thee	Peter said unto him, "Though I should die with thee, Yet will I not deny thee."		

MARK (cont.)   **MATTHEW** (cont.)   **LUKE** (cont.)   **JOHN** (cont.)

in any wise."

Likewise   Likewise
also said   also said
they all.   all the disciples.
Mk 14:29–31   *Mt 26:33–35*

Luke's account continues:

JESUS: When I sent you without purse, and scrip, and shoes, lack ye
    any thing?
DISCIPLES: Nothing.
JESUS: But now, he that hath a purse, let him take it, and likewise
    his scrip. And he that hath no sword, let him sell his garment,
    and buy one. For I say unto you, that this that is written must
    yet be accomplished in me, 'And he was reckoned among the
    transgressors' for the things concerning me have an end.
DISCIPLES: Lord, behold, here are two swords.
JESUS: It is enough. *L 22:35–38*

The next verse in Luke states:

And he came out, and went as he was wont, to the Mount of Olives;
and his disciples also followed him. *L 22:39*

This verse implies that the sections just quoted from Luke's
record what had occurred in the upper room where the Last Supper was held. John implies that the sections just quoted from his
gospel were said "after he was gone out" from the upper room. *J
13:31* The "he" is ambiguous and could refer to either Jesus or Judas. If "he" refers to Judas' leaving the upper room, Jesus' statements were made in the upper room; if it refers to Jesus' leaving
the upper room, Jesus' statements were made somewhere else.

The place where Jesus made the statements recorded by Luke and John is immaterial. What is material is that they were spoken on the night of Jesus' arrest. According to John, Jesus said that night:

Now is the Son of man glorified, and God is glorified in him. If God be glorified in him, God shall also glorify him in himself, and shall straightway glorify him.

Little children, *yet a little while I am with you*. Ye shall seek me: and as I said unto the Jews, "Whither I go ye cannot come"; so now I say unto you. A new commandment I give unto you, That ye love one another; as I have loved you, that ye also love one another. By this shall all men know that ye are my disciples, if ye have love one to another. *J 13:31–35*

Simon Peter then asked:

Lord, whither goest thou? *J 13:36*

Jesus answered:

Whither I go, thou canst not follow me *now*; but thou shalt follow me *afterwards*. *J 13:36*

Jesus said a little later that night:

Let not your heart be troubled. Ye believe in God, believe also in me. In my Father's house are many mansions [abiding places]. If it were not so, I would have told you.

I go to prepare a place for you. And if I go and prepare a place for you, I will come again, and receive you unto myself; that where I am, there ye may be also. And whither I go ye know, and the way ye know. *J 14:1–4*

Thomas then said to Jesus,

Lord, we know not whither thou goest; and how can we know the way? *J 14:5*

Jesus replied:

I am the way, the truth, and the life. No man cometh unto the Father but by me. If ye had known me, ye should have known my Father also: and from henceforth ye know him, and have seen him. *J 14:6–7*

Philip then said:

Lord, show us the Father, and it sufficeth us. *J 14:8*

Jesus replied:

Have I been so long time with you, and yet has thou not known me, Philip? He that hath seen me hath seen the Father; and how sayest thou then, "Shew us the Father"?

Believest thou not that I am *in the Father*, and the Father *in me*? The words that I speak unto you I speak not of myself: but the Father that dwelleth in me, he doeth the works. Believe me that I am *in the Father*, and the Father *in me*; or else believe me for the very works' sake.

Verily, verily I say unto you, he that believeth on me, the works that I do shall he do also; and greater works than these shall he do; because I go unto my Father."

And whatsoever ye shall ask in my name, that will I do, that the Father may be glorified in the Son. If ye shall ask anything in my name, I will do it. *J 14:9–14*

THE NEW ERA OF THE SPIRIT

Jesus then spoke of the new era in which the Spirit of Truth would be his followers' Comforter:

If ye love me, keep my commandments. And I will pray the Father, and he shall give you another Comforter, that he may abide with

you for ever, even the Spirit of Truth, when the world can not receive, because it seeth him not, neither knoweth him; but ye know
him, for he dwelleth with you, and shall be in you. *J 14:15–17*

That same night Jesus also spoke of the Comforter as follows:

But when the Comforter is come, whom I will send unto you from
the Father, even the Spirit of Truth, which proceedeth from the
Father, he shall testify of me. And ye also shall bear witness, because ye have been with me from the beginning. *J 15:26–27*

According to Jesus he had to go away before the Comforter
could come:

Nevertheless, I tell you the truth, it is expedient for you that I go
away; for if I go not away, the Comforter will not come unto you;
but if I depart, I will send him unto you.

And when he is come, he will reprove the world of sin, and of
righteousness, and of judgment:

Of sin, because they believe not on me;

Of righteousness, because I go to my Father, and ye see me no
more;

Of judgment, because the prince of this world is judged.

I have yet many things to say unto you, but ye can not bear them
now. Howbeit when he, the Spirit of Truth, is come, he will guide
you into all truth; for he shall not speak of himself; but whatsoever
he shall hear, that shall he speak; and he will show you things to
come.
He shall glorify me. For he shall receive of mine, and shall shew it
unto you. All things that the Father hath are mine. Therefore said I,
that he [the Spirit of Truth] shall take of mine, and shall shew it
unto you. *J 16:7–15*

That night Jesus also said:

> I will not leave you comfortless. I will come to you. Yet a little while, and *the world seeth me no more; but ye* [will] *see me*: because I live, ye shall live also. At that day ye shall know that I am in my Father, and ye in me, and I in you.

> He that hath my commandments, and keepeth them, he it is that loveth me, and he that loveth me shall be loved of my Father, and I will love him, and *will manifest myself* to him. *J 14:18–21*

Judas, not Iscariot, said "How is it that thou wilt manifest thyself unto us, not unto the world?" *J 14:22*

Jesus answered him:

> If a man love me, he will keep my words, and my Father will love him, and *we will come unto him and make our abode with him.* He that loveth me not keepeth not my sayings.

> And the word which ye hear is not mine, but the Father's which sent me. These things I have spoken unto you, being yet present with you. But the Comforter, which is the Holy Spirit, whom the Father will send in my name, he shall teach you all things, and bring all things to your remembrance, whatsoever I have said unto you. *J 14:23–26*

Expect the Hate of the World

Although Jesus had spoken of the Comforter that was to come, he also warned his followers that same night to expect the hate of the world:

> If the world hate you, ye know that it hated me before it hated you. If ye were of the world, the world would love his own; but because ye are not of the world, but I have chosen you out of the world, therefore the world hateth you.

> Remember the word that I said unto you, "The servant is not greater than his lord." If they have persecuted me, they will also persecute

you; and if they have kept my saying, they will keep yours also.
[They won't follow your teaching any more than they have mine.]

But all these things will they do unto you for my name's sake, because they know not him that sent me. If I had not come and spoken unto them, they had not had sin; but now they have no cloak for their sin.

He that hateth me hateth my Father also. If I had not done among them the works which none other man did, they had not had sin; but now have they both seen and hated both me and my Father. But this cometh to pass, that the word might be fulfilled that is written in their Law, "They hated me without a cause." *J 15:18–25 [Psalm 35:19; 69:4]*

Jesus, a little later, returned his prediction of impending inevitable conflict:

These things have I spoken unto you, that ye should not be offended. They shall put you out of the synagogues. Yea, the time cometh, that whosoever killeth you will think that he doeth God service.

And these things will they do unto you, because they have not known the Father, nor me. But these things have I told you, that when the time shall come, ye may remember that I told you of them. And these things I said not unto you at the beginning, because I was with you. *J 16:1–4*

Legacy of Peace

Although the conflict with the world was inevitable, Jesus also spoke that night of the legacy of peace that he was leaving to his disciples:

Peace I leave with you, my peace I give unto you, not as the world giveth, give I unto you. Let not your heart be troubled, neither let it be afraid.

Ye have heard how I said unto you, "*I go away, and come again unto you.*" If ye loved me, ye would rejoice, because I said "*I go unto the Father*" for my Father is greater than I.

And now I have told you before it came to pass, that, when it is come to pass, ye might believe. Hereafter I will not talk much with you for the Prince of this world cometh, and hath nothing in [over] me. But that the world may know that I love the Father, and as the Father gave me commandment, even so do I. *J 14:27–31*

John then states that Jesus said: "Arise, let us go hence." *J 14:31* Some scholars suggest that this sentence is not in its proper time sequence in the present text and suggest that chapters 15 and 16 should be placed ahead of this sentence.

We do know that some time that night Jesus said:

A little while, and ye shall not see me; and again a little while, and ye shall see me, because I go to the Father. *J 16:16*

John writes of the puzzlement which this cryptic saying caused the disciples:

Then said some of his disciples among themselves, "What is this that he saith unto us, 'A little while, and ye shall not see me; and again a little while, and ye shall see me'; and, 'Because I go to the Father?'" They said therefore, "What is this that he saith, 'A little while?' We can not tell what he saith."

Now Jesus knew that they were desirous to ask him, and said unto them, "Do ye enquire among yourselves of that I said, 'A little while, and ye shall not see me; and again, a little while, and ye shall see me?'" *J 16:17–19*

Jesus continued:

Verily, verily, I say unto you, that ye shall weep and lament, but the world shall rejoice; and ye shall be sorrowful, but your sorrow shall be turned into joy.

A woman when she is in travail hath sorrow, because her hour is come; but as soon as she is delivered of the child, she remembereth no more the anguish, for joy that a man is born into the world.

And ye now therefore have sorrow; *but I will see you again*, and your heart shall rejoice, and your joy no man taketh from you.

And *in that day* ye shall ask me nothing. Verily, verily I say unto you, Whatsoever ye ask the Father in my name, he will give it you. Hitherto have ye asked nothing in my name: ask, and ye shall receive, that your joy may be full. ·

These things I have spoken unto you in proverbs; but the time cometh, when I shall no more speak unto you in proverbs, but I will show you plainly of the Father.

At that day ye shall ask in my name; and I say not unto you, that I will pray the Father for you; for the Father himself loveth you, because ye have loved me, and have believed that I have come from God.

I came forth from the Father, and am come into the world; again, I leave the world, and *go to the Father. J 16:20–28*

This was clear enough for the disciples and they said to him:

Lo, now speakest thou plainly, and speakest no proverb. Now are we sure that thou knowest all things, and needest not that any man should [have to] ask thee. By this we believe that thou camest forth from God. *J 16:29–30*

Despite the subtleties of teaching in parables and proverbs, Jesus' own disciples are finally convinced that Jesus came "forth from God."
Jesus was intrigued:

Do ye *now* believe? Behold, the hour cometh, yea, is now come, that ye shall be scattered, every man to his own, and shall leave me alone; and yet I am not [will not be] alone, because the Father is with me. These things I have spoken unto you, that in me ye might have peace. In the world ye shall have tribulation; but be of good cheer; I have overcome the world. *J 16:31–33*

John then records what has come to be known as Jesus' "high priestly" prayer, and John is not explicit where Jesus prayed that prayer. The only clue is John's introduction which states: "These words spake Jesus, and lifted up his eyes to *heaven*, and said: . . ." *J 17:1*

This implies that Jesus was out of doors, and the natural inference is that he was out of doors on the Mount of Olives. Perhaps he withdrew a little from his disciples and prayed alone, but in the stillness of that moonlit night his disciples could hear his prayer:

Father, the hour is come. *Glorify* thy Son, that thy Son also may *Glorify* thee . . .

I have *glorified* thee on the earth: I have finished the work which thou gavest me to do. And now, O Father, *glorify* thou me with thine own self with the *glory* which I had with thee before the world was . . .

And all mine are thine, and thine and mine; and I am *glorified* in them. And now I am no more in the world, but these are in the world, and *I come to thee.*

Holy Father, keep through thine own name those whom thou hast given me, that they may be one, as we are. While I was with them in the world I kept them in thy name: those that thou gavest me I have kept, and none of them is lost, but the son of perdition, that the Scripture might be fulfilled.

And *now come I to thee*; and these things I speak in the world, that they might have my joy fulfilled in themselves . . .

And the *glory* which thou gavest me I have given them; that they may be one, even as we are one: I in them, and thou in me, that they may be made perfect in one; and that the world may know that thou hast sent me, and hast loved them, as thou hast loved me.

Father, I will that they also, whom thou hast given me, be with me where I am; that they may behold my *glory*, which thou hast given me: for thou lovest me before the foundation of the world.

O righteous Father, the world hath not known thee: but I have known thee, and these have known that thou hast sent me. And I have declared unto them thy name, and will declare it: that the love wherewith thou hast loved me may be in them, and I in them."
J 17:1, 4–5, 10–13, 22–26

There are many tangled skeins of thought in the prayer. Here I have focused upon the theme of glory, of Jesus' being sent from the Father and returning to him. The verses omitted: John 17:2–3, 6–9 and 14–21, focus on other themes: eternal life, the choosing of Jesus' own out of the world and his prayer for them, and their receipt of the Father's word. These themes have been treated elsewhere.

Jesus wished to return to the glory he had with the Father before the world began. *J 17:5, 24* This glory was the Father's self and the Father's love. *J 17:5, 23* This glory Jesus had given to his disciples but he still wished them to see his preexistent glory with the Father. *J 17:22, 24* That is why earlier that evening Jesus had told his disciples:

In my Father's house are many mansions [abiding places]: . . . I go to prepare a place for you. And if I go and prepare a place for you, I will come again, and receive you unto myself; that where I am, there ye may be also. [Beholding my glory which my Father hast given me] J 14:2–3

. . .that they may behold my glory, which thou hast given me *J 17:24*

Jesus was about to walk the road to that glory:

Now is the Son of man *glorified*, and God is *glorified* in him. If God be *glorified* in him, God shall also *glorify* him in himself, and shall straightway *glorify* him. *J 13:31–32*

GETHSEMANE

The night of the Last Supper, Jesus spoke repeatedly of his coming return to glory with his Father. Gethsemane was another stop on that glory road.

Both Matthew and Mark write of a place called or named Gethsemane:

MARK	MATTHEW
And they came	Then cometh Jesus with them
to a place	unto a place
which was named	called
Gethsemane,	Gethsemane,
and he saith to his disciples,	and saith unto the disciples,
"Sit ye here,	"Sit ye here,
while I shall pray."	while I go and pray yonder."
Mk 14:32	*Mt 26:36*

The precise site of the "place called Gethsemane" (literally, *oil press*) is not known, and it may have been on the west (Jerusalem) side of the brook Kidron. That would account for John's statement that Jesus "went forth with his disciples over the brook Kidron, where was a garden, into the which he entered, and his disciples." *J 18:1* They had been upon the slopes of the Mount of Olives, on the east side of the brook Kidron. They then started back (west) towards Jerusalem and then *crossed* the brook Kidron.

The phrase "where there was a garden" probably refers to a grove of olive trees. This place was known to Judas "for Jesus offtimes resorted thither with his disciples." *J 18:2*

When Jesus got to the Garden of Gethsemane that night, he told his disciples, "Pray that ye enter not into temptation," meaning probably, "Pray that ye will not be tested." *L 22:40*

He then told his disciples to sit down "while I go and pray yonder." *Mt 26:36 (Mk 14:32)* Jesus then took Peter and the Zebedee brothers, James and John, aside and "Began to be sorrowful and very heavy." *Mt 26:37 (Mk 14:33)* Jesus then said to them:

214

MARK
My soul is
exceeding sorrowful
unto death:
tarry ye here, and watch.
Mk 14:34

MATTHEW
My soul is
exceeding sorrowful,
even unto death
tarry ye here, and watch
with me.
Mt 26:38

Here the accounts vary slightly. Matthew and Mark state that Jesus went forward a little and fell on the ground. *Mk 14:35; Mt 26:39* ("fell on his face") Luke says that he kneeled down. *L 22:41*

All three gospels state that Jesus then prayed as follows:

MARK
Abba, Father
all things
are possible unto thee;
take away this cup
from me;
nevertheless not
what I will,
but what thou wilt.
Mk 14.36

MATTHEW
O, my Father,

if it is possible,
let this cup
pass from me;
nevertheless not
as I will,
but as thou wilt.
Mt 26:39

LUKE
Father,
if thou
be willing,
remove this cup
from me;
nevertheless not
my will,
but thine, be done.
L 22:42

While Jesus prayed that hour might pass from him, probably at greater length than is stated in the terse gospel summaries, his disciples, exhausted with sorrow, went to sleep, and asleep they were when Jesus returned. *L 22:45* Before they dozed off to sleep, Peter, James, and John, who were closest to him, may have heard the first part of Jesus' prayer.

When Jesus returned to his disciples, he said:

MARK
Simon, sleepest
thou? Couldest not
thou watch ye

and pray,

MATTHEW
What,
could ye not
watch with me one
hour?

Watch and pray,

LUKE
Why sleep
ye?

Rise and pray,

MARK (cont.)	MATTHEW (cont.)	LUKE (cont.)
lest ye enter	that ye enter not	lest ye enter
into temptation.	into temptation.	into temptation.
The spirit truly	The spirit indeed	*L 22:46*
is ready, but	is willing, but	
the flesh is weak.	the flesh is weak.	
Mk 14:37–38	*Mt 26:40–41*	

Jesus' anguish at his sleepy-headed disciples is understandable. Luke states that he had been praying so earnestly that "his sweat was as it were great drops of blood falling down to the ground." *L 22:44* He had just seen an angel from heaven who strengthened him in his agony, but his own disciples could not even stay awake. *L 22:43–45*

Jesus went back again to pray alone:

> O, my Father, if this cup may not pass away from me, except I drink it, thy will be done. *Mt 26:42*

Later on, the writer of the book of Hebrews summarized the early church's understanding of Jesus' agony that night when he wrote of the Christ "who in the days of his flesh, when he had offered up prayers and supplications with strong crying and tears unto him that was able to save him from death and was heard in that he feared." *Hebrews 5:7*

Jesus returned a second time and again found his disciples drowsy with sleep and speechless with embarrassment. *Mk 14:40; Mt 26:43* Jesus went again to his lonely prayer.

When Jesus returned the third time from his ordeal by prayer, he was resigned to his disciples' self-indulgence and said:

MARK	MATTHEW
Sleep on now,	Sleep on now,
and take your rest.	and take your rest.
It is enough,	Behold
the hour	the hour
is come.	is at hand,

MARK (cont.)	MATTHEW (cont.)
Behold the Son of man	and the Son of man
is betrayed	is betrayed
into the hands of sinners.	into the hands of sinners.
Rise up,	Rise, `
let us go;	let us be going;
lo, he that	behold, he is
betrayeth me	at hand
is at hand.	that doth betray me.
Mk 14:41–42	*Mt 26:45–46*

Before Jesus could finish speaking, a large, armed arresting party appeared. This arresting party was not just a casual crowd. It had been sent by the Jewish religious authorities and was guided by Judas:

MARK	MATTHEW	LUKE
And immediately,	And	And
while he yet spake,	while he yet spake,	while he yet spake,
cometh Judas,	lo, Judas	behold
one of the Twelve,	one of the Twelve, came,	a multitude,
and with him	and with him	and he that
a great multitude	a great multitude	
		was called Judas,
		one of the Twelve,
		went before them,
with swords	with swords	
and staves,	and staves,	and drew near
from the chief priests	from the chief priests	
and the scribes		
and the elders.	and elders	unto Jesus,
Mk 14:43	of the people.	to kiss him.
	Mt 26:47	*L 22:47*

The final act in Jesus' life was about to begin. He was about to be arrested by order of the religious authorities of his people, the Jews.

THE ARREST AND PROCEEDINGS AGAINST JESUS

The arrest and the proceedings against Jesus had been planned by the Jewish establishment for some time but, as late as the Wednesday before the crucifixion on Friday, had been deferred:

MARK	MATTHEW	LUKE
After two days was the Feast of the Passover, and of Unleavened Bread;		Now the Feast of
		Unleavened Bread drew nigh, which is called the Passover.
	Then assembled together	
and the chief priests and the scribes	the chief priests, and the scribes, and the elders of the people, unto the palace of the high priest who was called Caiaphas,	And the chief priests and scribes
sought how *they might take* *him* *by craft,* *and put him to death.*	*and consulted that* *they might take* *Jesus* *by subtelty* *and kill him.*	*sought how* *they might* *kill him;*
But they said, "Not on the feast day, lest there be an uproar of the people."	But they said, "Not on the feast day, lest there be an uproar among the people."	for they feared the people.
Mk 14:1–2	*Mt 26:3–5*	*L 22:1–2*

218

At this point, probably later on Wednesday, the establishment had an unexpected break. One of Jesus' twelve key followers, Judas Iscariot, defected and offered his services as an informer:

MARK	MATTHEW	LUKE
And Judas Iscariot,	Then	Then entered Satan into Judas
one of the Twelve,	one of the Twelve, called Judas Iscariot,	surnamed Iscariot; being of the number of the Twelve.
went	went	And he went his way,
unto	unto	and communed with
the chief priests,	the chief priests,	the chief priests and captains
	and said unto them, "What will ye give me, and I will	
to betray him	deliver him	how he might betray him
unto them.	unto you?"	unto them.
Mk 14:10	*Mt 26:14–15*	*L 22:3–4*

The offer was accepted, and the price, thirty pieces of silver, was either paid or promised by the chief priests. They decided to move immediately despite the coming festival if Judas could arrange a delivery in the absence of the crowd:

MARK	MATTHEW	LUKE
And when they heard it,	And they	And they
they were glad		were glad,
and promised	covenanted	and covenanted
to give him	with him for	to give him
money.	thirty pieces of silver.	money.
	And from that time	And he promised
And he sought	he sought	and sought
how he might	opportunity	opportunity

MARK (cont.)	MATTHEW (cont.)	LUKE (cont.)
conveniently betray him. Mk 14:11	to betray him. Mt 26:15–16	to betray him unto them *in the absence of the multitude.* L 22:5–6

Judas' opportunity came during the Last Supper that Thursday night. He apparently learned that Jesus and disciples planned to go, as he often did, to the Mount of Olives later that evening. L 22:39; J 18:2 John states flatly that Judas "knew the place." J 18:2

This place provided ideal conditions for an arrest: a crowd-free site at night in an open area away from buildings and people.

Judas left the Last Supper as soon as he could and slipped out into the night to notify the authorities. J 13:30 An official arresting party was formed immediately, and Judas led them to Jesus. Mk 14:43; Mt 26:47; L 22:47; J 18:3

The official arresting party was accompanied by "a great multitude with swords and staves." Mk 14:43; Mt 26:47; L 22:47 That multitude included scribes, elders, and Pharisees. Mk 14:43; Mt 26:47; J 18:3

The official arresting party were "officers from the chief priests." J 18:3, 12 (Mk 14:43; Mt 26:47) At least one of the high priests' servants was present. Mk 14:47; Mt 26:51; L 22:50 Luke goes further and states that the chief priests themselves were present, as well as the captains of the Temple. L 22:52

John calls the official arresting party simply the "officers of the Jews" and notes that they came equipped with lanterns, torches, and weapons. J 18:3, 12 John alone of the Gospels notes that the party was accompanied by Roman soldiers: "a band of men." J 18:3, 12 The word translated "band" literally means "cohort," which was a Roman army unit with a nominal strength of 600 men. John states that they were led by the captain. J 18:12 The word translated "captain" literally means "tribune," the commander of a cohort. We do not know whether this cohort, garrisoned in Jerusalem, was at full strength of 600 men or whether all of that cohort was deployed that night. Perhaps only one of its six centuries (100 men units) was on duty that night. John's wording does not necessarily mean that all 600 men of the cohort were present. The tribune's presence does, however, indicate that this was an important operation. It had been prearranged between the official arresting party and Judas that he would identify Jesus by a kiss. Judas had told them, "Whomsoever I shall kiss, that same is he; take him, and lead him away safely." *Mk 14:44; (Mt 26:48)*

Judas immediately went up to Jesus and said, "Master, master" or "Hail, master" and kissed him. *Mk 14:45; Mt 26:49; L 22:47*

Jesus replied, "Friend, wherefore art thou come" *(Mt 26:50)* or "Judas, betrayest thou the Son of Man with a kiss?" *(L 22:48)*

The arresting party immediately laid hands on Jesus and took him. *Mk 14:46; Mt 26:50*

Jesus then seized the initiative and asked, "Whom seek ye?" *J 18:4*

They answered: "Jesus of Nazareth."

Jesus then said: "I am he." *J 18:5*

They were taken aback. John writes, "As soon then as he had said unto them, 'I am he,' they went backward and fell to the ground." *J 18:6*

Jesus then asked again, "Whom seek ye?" *J 18:7*

They said again, "Jesus of Nazareth." *J 18:7*

Jesus then said: "I have told you that I am he. If therefore ye seek me, let these go their way." *J 18:8*

There was a brief flurry of resistance when one of Jesus' followers drew a sword and smote a servant of the high priest. *Mk 14:47; Mt 26:51; L 22:50; J 18:10* This ended abruptly when Jesus ordered his follower to sheath his sword. *Mt 26:52–54; J 18:11 ("Suffer ye thus far." L 22:51)*

At this time the arresting party bound Jesus. *J 18:12* Apparently it was then that Jesus said:

MARK	MATTHEW	LUKE
Are ye come out as against a thief, with swords and	Are ye come out against a thief with swords	Be ye come out, as against a thief, with swords

MARK (cont.)	MATTHEW (cont.)	LUKE (cont.)
with staves to take me?	and staves for to take me?	and staves?
I was daily with you in the Temple teaching, and ye took me not,	I sat daily with you teaching in the Temple, and ye laid no hold on me.	When I was daily with you in the Temple, ye stretched forth no hands against me;
but	But all this was done that	but this
the Scriptures	the Scriptures of the Prophets	is your hour, and the power
must be fulfilled.	might be fulfilled.	of darkness.
Mk 14:48–49	Mt 26:55–56	L 22:52–53

As soon as Jesus said this all of his disciples fled. Mk 14:50; Mt 26:56 Despite Jesus' plea to let his followers go, the arresting party apparently attempted to seize them, too, and in fact tore one man's garment off as he fled, leaving him naked. Mk 14:51–52 All disciples escaped, as Jesus had said. J 17:12, 18:9

Jesus was then led to Annas, the father-in-law of the high priest, Caiaphas. J 18:13 Annas had been high priest himself some years earlier, i.e., from about A.D. 6 to 15, and his power evidently continued through his son-in-law, Caiaphas, the high priest then in office. J 11:49; L 3:2 He evidently retained the courtesy title of high priest. Acts 4:6 John hence describes him as "the high priest" in John 18:19 even though it is clear from John 18:13 that he knew Caiaphas was then the high priest actually in office.

Annas conducted a preliminary interrogation, asking Jesus "of his disciples, and of his doctrine." J 18:19

Jesus answered him:

I spake openly to the world; I ever taught in the synagogue, and in the Temple, whither the Jews always resort; and in secret have I said nothing.

Why asketh thou me? Ask them which heard me, what I have said unto them: behold, they know what I said. *J 18:20–21*

One of the officers standing by them struck Jesus with the palm of his hand, saying:

Answerest thou the high priest so? *J 18:22*

Jesus replied:

If I have spoken evil, bear witness of the evil; but if well, why smitest thou me? *J 18:23*

Jesus was apparently bound during this interrogation. In any case, he was brought to Annas bound, and Annas sent him bound to Caiaphas. *J 18:12–13, 24*

It is misleading to think of this informal preliminary interrogation as the first trial of Jesus. The arresting party, probably acting under instructions, simply brought Jesus in so that Annas could have a first-hand look at the man who was supposed to be misleading the people. The reason for this was that Annas was probably the man in actual control of the Jewish establishment, even though, technically, his son-in-law, Caiaphas, was the high priest.

If Annas was acting in any judicial capacity, it was not to try Jesus but simply like a magistrate to conduct a brief preliminary hearing. It seems unlikely that Annas was so acting since the questioning seems as informal as the officer striking Jesus in the course of the interrogation.

The first three gospels omit the preliminary interrogation by Annas and pick up the story as Jesus was brought to Caiaphas:

Mark	Matthew	Luke
And they led	And they that had laid hold on	Then took they him, and led him,
Jesus away to	Jesus led him away to Caiaphas,	and brought him into
the high priest . . .	the high priest . . .	the high priest's house.
Mk 14:53	*Mt 26:57*	*L 22:54*

223

Caiaphas had previously advised the Jews "that it is expedient for us, that one man should die for the people, and that the whole nation perish not." *J 11:50; 18:14* By the time Jesus arrived before Caiaphas, "all the chief priests and elders and the scribes" had assembled although it was late at night, almost certainly after midnight. *Mk 14:53* (". . .the scribes and elders . . ." *Mt 26:57*)

They had no doubt expected to be summoned ever since Judas had defected on Wednesday, but neither they nor Judas knew when Judas would be able to pass the word that Jesus could be arrested in the absence of the multitude. *L 22:6 (Mk 14:11; Mt 26:16)*

Even though Jesus' arrest was anticipated, it would have taken some time to assemble the 71 member Sanhedrin in the middle of the night. Whether they were all present or only assembling, it was a hasty gathering. Judas had not slipped out of the Last Supper until after dark. *J 13:30* Even then the exact time of arrest still would not have been known. The Last Supper had probably gone on several hours after Judas left, and then Jesus and his party would still have had to make their way to the Mount of Olives. *Mk 14:26; Mt 26:30; L 22:39*

But now that they had Jesus in custody and they meant to act quickly. We have only two accounts:

MARK	MATTHEW
And the chief priests	Now the chief priests,
	and elders
and all the council	and all the council
[Sanhedrin] sought	[Sanhedrin] sought
for witnesses against Jesus,	false witnesses against Jesus,
to put him to death,	to put him to death,
and found none.	but found none;
Mk 14:55	yea, though many
	false witnesses came,
	yet found they none.
	Mt 26:59–60

The problem was not the lack of witnesses; the problem was the quality of witnesses. Mark writes:

For many bare false witness against him, but their witness *agreed not together*. And there arose certain, and bare false witness against him, saying, "We heard him say, 'I will destroy this Temple that is made with hands, and within three days I will build another made without hands.'"

But neither so did their witness *agree together*." *Mk 14:56–59*

They needed two or three witnesses who agreed since their law required that "at the mouth of two witnesses, or at the mouth of three witnesses, shall the matter be established." *Deuteronomy 19:15* Matthew writes that they did finally get two witnesses:

At the last came two false witnesses, and said, "This fellow said, 'I am able to destroy the Temple of God, and to build it in three days.'" *Mt 26:60–61*

At this point, Matthew's and Mark's accounts converge. The high priest stood up in the midst of the assembly and said to Jesus:

	MARK	MATTHEW
HIGH PRIEST:	Answerest thou nothing? What is it which these witness against thee?	Answerest thou nothing? What is it which these witness against thee?
	[Jesus did not answer.]	[Jesus did not answer.]
	Art	I adjure thee by the living God, that thou tell us whether
	thou the Christ, the Son of the Blessed?	thou be the Christ, the Son of God.
JESUS:	I am.	Thou hast said. Nevertheless I say unto you,
	And ye shall see the Son of man sitting	hereafter shall ye see the Son of man sitting

225

	MARK (cont.)	MATTHEW (cont.)
	on the right hand of power	on the right hand of power
	[of God]	[of God]
	and coming in	and coming in
	the clouds of heaven.	the clouds of heaven.
HIGH PRIEST:	[renting his clothes]	[renting his clothes]
		He hath spoken
		blasphemy.
	What need	What further need
	we any	have we
	further witnesses?	of witnesses?
		Behold,
	Ye have heard	now ye have heard
	the blasphemy.	his blasphemy.
	What think ye?	What think ye?
SANHEDRIN:	[They found him	He is
	guilty of death.]	guilty of death.
	Mk 14:60–64	*Mt 26:62–66*

Jesus was then physically abused apparently by, and certainly in the presence of, the Sanhedrin:

MARK	MATTHEW	LUKE
And some began to	Then did they	And the men that
spit on him	spit in his face,	held Jesus
and to cover his face		
and to buffet him,	and buffeted him;	mocked him;
and to say unto him,		
"Prophesy," and	and	and
the servants did strike	others smote him	smote him.
him with the palms	with the palms	And when they
		had blindfolded him,
of their hands.	of their hands.	they struck him
Mk 14:65		on the face,
		and asked him, saying,
	Saying,	"Prophesy,
	"Prophesy unto us,	

MARK (cont.)	MATTHEW (cont.)	LUKE (cont.)
	thou Christ,	
	who is he	who is it
	that smote thee?"	that smote thee?"
	Mt 26:67–68	*L 22:63–64*

This was not a trial as such, but simply an effort to procure enough evidence to justify the execution of Jesus. They were unhappy with the witnesses they had, but Jesus himself had conveniently supplied the desired evidence by answering the high priest's question. The Sanhedrin was happy to find that this evidence was sufficient to justify a death sentence.

Their exultation was shown by their physical abuse of Jesus and a continuing torrent of verbal abuse. Luke writes:

And many other things blasphemously spake they against him.
L 22:65

This interrogation and the abuse of Jesus took place in the palace of the high priest. *L 22:54 (Mk 14:53–54; Mt 26:57–58)* For legal reasons, the evidence obtained had to be repeated during the daytime in the Sanhedrin's official council chamber, the Hall of Hewn Stones.

Accordingly ,as soon as it was day the Sanhedrin reconvened in its council chamber and had Jesus led in to repeat in formal surroundings what had been developed in the night session in Caiaphas' palace. *L 22:66* According to Luke, the interrogation there went as follows:

SANHEDRIN: Art thou the Christ? Tell us.
JESUS: If I tell you, ye will not believe. And if I also ask you, ye will not answer me, nor let me go. Hereafter shall the Son of man sit on the right hand of the power of God.
SANHEDRIN: Art thou then the Son of God?
JESUS: Ye say that I am.
SANHEDRIN: What need we any further witnesses? For we ourselves have heard out of his own mouth. *L 22:67–71*

Matthew and Mark do not record this dawn hearing and simply say that there was a further consultation by the council (the Sanhedrin):

MARK	MATTHEW
And straightway	When the morning
in the morning	was come,
the chief priests	all the chief priests
held a consultation	
with the elders and scribes	and elders of the people
and the whole council, . . .	*took counsel*
Mk 15:1	against Jesus
	to put him to death, . . .
	Mt 27:1–2

The accounts continue:

MARK	MATTHEW	LUKE
And [they]	And when they	And
bound Jesus,	had bound him,	
		the whole multitude
		of them arose,
and		and
carried him away	they led him away,	led him
and delivered him	and delivered him	
to Pilate.	to Pontius Pilate.	unto Pilate.
Mk 15:1	Mt 27:2	L 23:1

John adds further details:

Then led they Jesus from Caiaphas unto the [Roman] Hall of Judgment; and it was early; and they themselves went not into the judgment hall, lest they should be defiled [by entering a Gentile building]; but that they might eat the Passover. J 18:28

The Trial Before Pilate

Pilate accommodated himself to the religious scruples of the assembled Jewish leaders and went outside to hear their charge. *J 18:29*

PILATE: What accusation bring ye against this man?
JEWS: If he were not a malefactor, we would not have delivered him up unto thee.
PILATE: Take ye him, and judge him according to your law.
JEWS: It is not lawful for us to put any man to death. *J 18:29–31*

Pilate went back into the Hall of Judgement, and had Jesus brought in. Pilate then questioned him, himself:

PILATE: Art thou the King of the Jews?
JESUS: Sayest thou this thing of thyself, or did others tell it thee of me?
PILATE: Am I a Jew? Thine own nation and the chief priests have delivered thee unto me. What hast thou done?
JESUS: My kingdom is not of this world. If my kingdom were of this world, then would my servants fight, that I should not be delivered to the Jews: but now is my kingdom not from hence. [but my kingdom is not so based]
PILATE: Art thou a king then?
JESUS: Thou sayest that I am a king. To this end was I born, and for this cause came I into the world, that I should bear witness unto the truth. Every one that is of the truth heareth my voice."
PILATE: What is truth? *J 18:33–38*

Pilate then abruptly recessed the hearing and went out of the Hall of Judgment and told the Jews:

I find in him no fault at all. But ye have a custom, that I should release unto you one at the Passover. Will ye therefore that I release unto you the "King of the Jews?" *J 18:38–39*

The Jews shouted:

Not this man, but Barabbas. *J 18:40*

The first three gospels pick up the story after Jesus was brought into the Hall of Judgment. They agree with John that Pilate's first question to Jesus was, "Art thou the King of the Jews?" and that Jesus made a noncommittal reply:

	MARK	MATTHEW	LUKE
PILATE:	Art thou the King of the Jews?	Art thou the King of the Jews?	Art thou the King of the Jews?
JESUS:	Thou sayest it.	Thou sayest. *Mt 27:11*	Thou sayest it. *L 23:3*

Apparently, Pilate asked Jesus about many other accusations made by the chief priests. *Mk 15:3–4; Mt 27:12–13* Only Luke gives any specific details of the accusations:

We found this fellow perverting the nation, and forbidding to give tribute to Caesar, saying that he himself is Christ a King. *L 23:2*

Jesus did not respond to any of the accusations except to the charge of being King of the Jews. Pilate was, however, impressed with the number of the other accusations and gave Jesus a second chance to respond, but to Pilate's amazement, "Jesus yet answered nothing." *Mk 15:5 (Mt 27:14)*

After Pilate had told the Jews, "I find no fault in this man," the Jews became more strident, saying, "He stirreth up the people, teaching throughout all Jewry, beginning from Galilee to this place." *L 23:4–5 (J 18:38)*

As soon as Pilate heard the word *Galilee*, he asked whether Jesus was a Galilean to see if he could dispose of an awkward case on the jurisdictional grounds that he did not rule Galilee. *L 23:6–7*

The Tetrarch of Galilee was Herod Antipas. It was especially convenient that Herod was in Jerusalem at the time.

Pilate immediately remanded Jesus to Herod. According to Luke "when Herod saw Jesus, he was exceeding glad, for he was desirous to see him for a long season, because he had heard many things of him; and he hoped to have seen some miracle done by him." *L 23:8*

Herod questioned Jesus at length, but Jesus "answered him nothing." *L 23:9* The chief priests and scribes were allowed to be present and stood by "vehemently" accusing him. *L 23:10*

The interrogation ended with Herod joining his soldiers to "set him at nought, and arrayed him in a gorgeous robe, and sent him again to Pilate." *L 23:11* Luke adds that Pilate's gesture ended the enmity which was existed between Pilate and Herod. *L 23:12* Pilate now had no escape from his duty of decision, and he did not shirk it. He directed the chief priests, the rulers and the people to assemble *(L 23:13)* and said to them:

> Ye have brought this man unto me, as one that perverteth the people; and behold, I having examined him before you, have found no fault in this man touching those things whereof ye accuse him. No, nor yet Herod, for I sent you to him; and, lo, nothing worthy of death is done unto him. I will therefore chastise him, and release him. *L 23:14–17*

Pilate had found Jesus not guilty under Roman law; but he had taken the time of, and caused trouble to, the Roman authorities by having been the subject of a criminal proceeding, and so he would be scrouged (flogged) before being released.

Pilate also had in custody a notorious man, a robber named Barabbas. He was one of a group of insurrectionists who had committed murder in the course of a recent insurrection. *Mk 15:7; Mt 27:16; L 23:19,25; J 18:40*

It was, of course, the time of the Passover festival; and a crowd had gathered at Judgment Hall (the Praetorium) to ask Pilate to observe his custom of releasing at the time of the festival, one prisoner of the Jews' choice. *Mk 15:6,8; Mt 27:15; L 23:17*

Pilate with heavy-handed imperial humor asked these colonials:

MARK	MATTHEW	JOHN
		But ye have a custom, that I should release you one at the Passover.
Will ye that I release unto you	Whom will ye that I release unto you? Barabbas or	Will ye therefore that I release unto you
the King of the Jews? *Mk 15:9*	Jesus which is called Christ? *Mt 27:17*	the King of the Jews? *J 18:39*

In his sardonic Roman way Pilate wanted this inferior colonial people to seethe. He knew that calling Jesus "King of the Jews" would infuriate them. This was the very charge that they had made against Jesus.

Some manuscripts indicate that Barabbas' first name was Jesus. *Mt 27:27* Matthew's version then becomes more pointed:

Whom will ye that I release unto you? [Jesus] Barabbas or Jesus which is called Christ? *Mt 27:17*

Pilate no doubt knew that referring to Jesus as the Jesus called Christ (the Messiah) would also infuriate the Jews, but Pilate was rather enjoying twitting Jesus' rabid accusers. Matthew and Mark state:

MARK	MATTHEW
For he knew that the chief priests had delivered him for envy. *Mk 15:10*	For he knew that for envy they had delivered him. *Mt 27:18*

Matthew reports that Pilate asked the crowd:

Whether of the twain [two] will ye that I release unto you? *Mt 27:21*

The chief priests and elders organized the crowd to demand release of Barabbas. *Mk 15:11; Mt 27:20* The result was a shout that Barabbas be released. *Mt 27:21* Luke has it:

And they cried out all at once, saying, "Away with this man, and release unto us Barabbas." *L 23:18*

The first three gospels continue the story:

MARK	MATTHEW	LUKE
And Pilate answered and said again unto them, "What will ye then that I should do unto him whom ye call the King of the Jews?"	Pilate said unto them "What shall I do then with Jesus which is called Christ?"	Pilate therefore, willing to release Jesus spake again to them.
And they cried out again, "Crucify him."	They all say unto him, "Let him be crucified."	But they cried, saying, "Crucify him, crucify him."
Then Pilate said unto them,	And the governor said,	And he said unto them the third time,
"Why, what evil hath he done?"	"Why, what evil hath he done?"	"Why, what evil hath he done? I have found no cause of death in him. I will therefore chastise him, and let him go."

MARK (cont.)	MATTHEW (cont.)	LUKE (cont.)
And they	But they	And they
cried out	cried out	were instant with
the more	the more,	loud voices,
exceedingly,	saying,	requiring that
"Crucify him."	"Let him be crucified."	he might be crucified.
And so Pilate,	When Pilate saw	And the voices
willing	that he could	of them and of the
to content	prevail nothing,	chief priests prevailed.
the people,	but that rather	
	a tumult was	
	made, . . .	
released	Then released	And Pilate gave
Barabbas	he Barabbas	sentence that it
unto them	unto them;	should be as they
and	and	required.
	when he	L 23:20–24
delivered Jesus,	had scourged Jesus,	
when he had scourged	he delivered	
him,	him	
to be crucified.	to be crucified.	
Mk 15:12–15	Mt 27:22–24, 26	

Only Matthew describes a gesture which Pilate made to show his deep abhorrence of Jews' persecution of Jesus:

> When Pilate saw that he could prevail nothing, but that rather a tumult was made, he took water, and washed his hands before the multitude, saying, "I am innocent of the blood of this just person; see ye to it."

> Then answered all the people, and said, "His blood be on us, and on our children." Mt 27:24–25

By Pilate's order Jesus was then scourged. Mk 15:15; Mt 27:26; J 19:1 This scourging was apparently in public view outside the Praetorium (Judgment Hall). Jesus was then taken inside its courtyard by the soldiers, and as a precaution, the whole cohort was formed up around him. *Mk 15:16; Mt 27:27*

A cohort, if at full strength, would have been 600 men. Such a number was not unlikely considering that Jerusalem was then full of Jews in for the Passover Festival, and the crowd had been shouting its demands at the Roman procurator, Pilate. *L 23:18, 21* After all, they had to march Jesus through the city to the crucifixion site.

While they waited for the whole cohort to form up, the soldiers having Jesus in custody began to abuse him:

MARK	MATTHEW	JOHN
	And they stripped him,	
And they clothed him with purple,	and put on him a scarlet robe.	And they put on him a purple robe.
and platted a crown of thorns and put it about his head,	And when they had platted a crown of thorns, they put it upon his head, and a reed in his right hand;	[And the soldiers platted a crown of thorns, and put it on his head,]*
and began to salute him,	and they bowed the knee before him, and mocked him, saying,	And said,
"Hail, King of the Jews!"	"Hail, King of the Jews!" And they spit upon him and took the reed,	"Hail, King of the Jews!"
And they smote him on the head with a reed, and did spit upon him, and bowing	and smote him on the head	And they smote him with their hands. J 19:2–3 * Conformed to Mark's order

235

MARK (cont.)	MATTHEW (cont.)	JOHN (cont.)
their knees worshipped him.		

And when	And after
they had mocked him,	they had mocked him,
they took off	they took
the purple from him,	the robe off from him,
and put	and put
his own clothes	his own raiment
on him,	on him,
and led him out	and led him away
to crucify him.	to crucify him.
Mk 15:17–20	*Mt 27:28–31*

According to John, Jesus was led outside again before he was marched off to the place of crucifixion:

Pilate therefore went forth again, and saith unto them, "Behold, I bring him forth to you, that ye may know that I find no fault in him."

Then came Jesus forth, wearing the crown of thorns, and the purple robe. And Pilate saith unto them, "Behold the man!"

When the chief priests therefore and officers saw him, they cried out, saying, "Crucify him, crucify him!"

"Pilate saith unto them, "Take ye him, and crucify him; for I find no fault in him."

The Jews answered him, "We have a law, and by our law he ought to die, because he made himself the Son of God.

When Pilate therefore heard that saying, he was more afraid; and went again into the Judgment Hall [the Praetorium] and saith unto Jesus, "Whence art thou?"

But Jesus gave him no answer. Then saith Pilate unto him, "Speakest thou not unto me? Knowest thou not that I have power to crucify thee, and have power to release thee?"

Jesus answered,"Thou couldest have no power at all against me, except it were given thee from above. Therefore he that delivered me unto thee hath the greater sin."

And from thenceforth Pilate sought to release him; but the Jews cried out, saying, "If thou let this man go, thou art not Caesar's friend; whosoever maketh himself a king speaketh against Caesar."

When Pilate therefore heard that saying, he brought Jesus forth, and sat down in the judgment seat [on an elevated dais] in a place that is called "The Pavement," but in the Hebrew, "Gabbatha."

And it was the preparation [day] of the Passover, and about the sixth hour [noon] and he saith unto the Jews, "Behold your King!"

But they cried out, "Away with him, away with him, crucify him."

Pilate saith unto them, "Shall I crucify your king?"

The chief priests answered, "We have no king but Caesar."

Then delivered he him therefore unto them to be crucified. And they took Jesus and led him away. *J 19:4–16*

When Pilate had sat on the judgment seat at the Pavement earlier that morning, his wife had sent him an urgent message, "Have thou nothing to do with that just man; for I have suffered many things this day in a dream because of him." *Mt 17:19* Dreams and portents obsessed pagans of the Roman world. So when later the Jews told Pilate that Jesus had "made himself the Son of God," it deepened Pilate's superstitious fear, he was "more afraid," and he walked back to ask Jesus "Whence art thou?" *J 19:7–9*

THE CRUCIFIXION

The crucifixion of Jesus on a Roman cross is a unique and exalted part of the Christian gospel. However, there was nothing unique about crucifixion itself. It was a common method of execution used by the Romans. For example, in A.D. 70 during the siege of Jerusalem by the Romans under the Titus, at least 500 Jews a day were crucified before the city wall. Josephus, a contemporary Jewish historian, wrote that "their multitude was so great, that room was wanting for the crosses." *Josephus, Wars of the Jews, Book V, Ch. XI, Sec. 1*

From the Roman point of view, Jesus' crucifixion was a routine execution in an occupied country. He was technically charged with being "King of the Jews." *Mk 15:26; Mt 27:37; L 23:38; J 19:19* The two others crucified with him are described in Mark and Matthew as "thieves" and in Luke as "malefactors"; but they are more accurately described as "bandits" or "insurrectionists." *Mk 15:27; Mt 27:38; L 23:32, 33, 39* They spoke to Jesus. *L 23:39–42*

Jesus had been tried by Pilate early on the morning of the crucifixion. At that time there were other men in custody awaiting execution, one of whom was Barabbas. This is the man who was released by demand of the crowd rather than Jesus. *Mk 15:15; Mt 27:26; L 23:25* It seems likely that the two men crucified with Jesus were part of the group that Mark refers to in describing Barabbas as one who "lay bound with *them* that had made insurrection with him, who had committed murder in the insurrection." *Mk 15:7* The two men crucified with Jesus fulfilled the scripture *(Isaiah 53:12)*, ". . .and he was numbered with the transgressors." *Mk 15:28*

As part of Roman legal procedure, Pilate wrote out the charge against Jesus and had it posted on the cross above his head. *Mk 15:26; Mt 27:37; J 19:19* The inscription was trilingual, being written in Hebrew and Greek as well as in Latin. *L 23:38; J 19:20*

Our sources do not agree on the exact wording of the superscription:

MARK	MATTHEW	LUKE	JOHN
	This is Jesus	This is	Jesus of Nazareth
The King	the King	the King	the King
of the Jews.	of the Jews.	of the Jews.	of the Jews.
Mk 15:26	*Mt 27:37*	*L 23:38*	*J 19:19*

The chief priests objected to Pilate's wording and told him, "Write not 'The King of the Jews'; but that he said, 'I am King of the Jews.'" *J 19:21* Pilate answered, "What I have written I have written." *J 19:22*

Jesus and the two insurrectionists were taken to the execution site followed by a large crowd which included wailing women. Luke describes the way of the cross as follows:

And there followed him a great company of people, and of women, which also bewailed and lamented him. But Jesus turning unto them said:

"Daughters of Jerusalem, weep not for me, but weep for yourselves, and for your children,

For, behold, the days are coming, in which they shall say, 'Blessed are the barren, and the wombs that never bare, and the paps which never gave suck.'

Then [as Hosea 10:8 says] shall they begin to say to the mountains, 'Fall on us'; and to the hills, 'Cover us.'

For if they do these things in a green tree, what shall be done in the dry?" *L 23:27–31*

Modern translations render Jesus' closing remark as contrasting green and dry wood, rather than as contrasting a green and a dry tree. His meaning is not known for sure, but he was apparently applying a proverbial saying to his situation. Perhaps he meant: A dry tree (dry wood) burns better than a green tree (green wood); the present situation, the green tree, is bad enough, but the future situation, the dry tree, will be devastating. Dry trees burn fiercely: that is the shape of things to come. Weep for yourselves and your children.

Each of the first three gospels mention a man named Simon of Cyrene. Cyrene was a North African town in Libya having a Jewish colony, and Simon was probably one of those Jews on pilgrimage to Jerusalem for the Passover. The gospel accounts state:

MARK	MATTHEW	LUKE
And they compel one	And as they came out they found a man	And as they led him away, they laid hold upon one
Simon, a Cyrenian, who passed by, coming out of the country, the father of Alexander and Rufus, to bear his cross.	of Cyrene, Simon by name: him they compelled to bear his cross.	Simon, a Cyrenian, coming out of the country, and on him they laid the cross that he might bear it after Jesus.
Mk 15:21	Mt 27:32	L 23:26

The site of the crucifixion was near Jerusalem but outside its walls. J 19:20; Hebrews 13:12 The site, probably routinely used for executions, was just off a heavily traveled road. Mt 27:39

This place was called in Hebrew (Aramaic) "Golgotha" — the Skull. Mk 15:22; Mt 27:33; J 19:17 Luke's gospel has "Calvary" instead. L 23:33 Modern revisions omit the word "Calvary," and replace it with the phrase "the Skull" since the word *Calvary* is a derivative of the Latin word *calvaria* that means *a bare skull*. The Latin word itself was a translation of the original gospel's Greek word *kranion* that itself was a translation of the Aramaic place name, "Golgotha" — the Skull.

The exact hour of Jesus' crucifixion is not certain. Mark states that it was at "the third hour" (9:00 A.M.), while John indicates that it was sometime after "the sixth hour" (noon). Mk 15:25; J 19:14

It is certain that the two insurrectionists were crucified with Jesus: one on his right and one on his left. *Mk 15:27; J 19:14* Apparently the executions were carried out by one centurion and three squads of four soldiers each, one for each execution. We do know that four soldiers crucified Jesus, and a centurion was present to watch him die. *J 19:23; Mk 15:39; Mt 27:54; L 23:47*

The gospel accounts of the crucifixion are terse:

MARK	MATTHEW	LUKE	JOHN
And they bring him	And when they were come	And when they were come	And he bearing his cross went
unto the place	unto a place called	to the place, which is	into a place
Golgotha, which is, being interpreted,	Golgotha, that is to say,	called Calvary,	called
"The place of a skull," and they gave him to drink wine mingled with myrrh: but	"A place of a skull," they gave him vinegar to drink mingled with gall: and when he had tasted thereof		"The place of a skull," which is called in the Hebrew Golgotha:
he received it not.	he would not drink.		
And when they had crucified him,	And they crucified him,	there they crucified him, . . .	where they crucified him, . . . Then the soldiers, when they had crucified Jesus,
they parted his garments,	and parted his garments,	And they parted his raiment,	took his garments,

MARK (cont.)	MATTHEW (cont.)	LUKE (cont.)	JOHN (cont.)
casting lots	casting lots:	and cast lots.	and made
upon them,		*L 23:33–34*	four parts,
what every man			to every soldier
should take.			a part;
And it was			and also
the third hour,			his coat:
and they			now the coat
crucified him.			was without
Mk 15:22–25			seam, woven
			from the top
			throughout.
			They said
			therefore
			among
			themselves,
			"Let us not
			rend it,
			but cast lots
			for it,
			whose it
			shall be":
	that		that the
	it		Scripture
	might be		might be
	fulfilled		fulfilled,
	which was spo-		which
	ken		saith,
	by the Prophet,		
	"They parted		"They parted
	my garments		my raiment
	among them,		among them,
	and upon		and for
	my vesture		my vesture
	did they		they did
	cast lots."		cast lots."
	[Psalm 22:18]		*[Psalm 22:18]*
	And sitting		

MARK (cont.)	MATTHEW (cont.)	LUKE (cont.)	JOHN (cont.)
	down		These things
	they watched		therefore
	him there.		the soldiers did.
	Mt 27:33–36		J 19:17–18, 23–24

All four gospels add the detail of the two thieves:

MARK	MATTHEW	LUKE	JOHN
And with him	Then there were	There they	Where they
they crucify	two thieves	crucified him,	crucified him,
two thieves;	crucified with	and the	and two other
	him,	malefactors,	with him,
the one on	one on	one on	on either side
his right hand,	the right hand,	the right hand,	one,
and the other	and another	and the other	
on his left.	on the left.	on the left.	
Mk 15:27	Mt 27:38	L 23:33	and Jesus
			in the midst."
			J 19:18

Only Luke records Jesus' statement as he hung on his cross:

Father, forgive them; for they know not what they do. L 23:34

Luke adds:

And the soldiers also mocked him, coming to him, and offering him vinegar, and saying, "If thou be the King of the Jews, save thyself." L 23:36–37

The crowd stared, gawked, railed and reviled him:

MARK	MATTHEW	LUKE
And they that	And they that	And the people stood
passed by	passed	beholding.
railed on him,	reviled him	
wagging their heads,	wagging their heads	

MARK (cont.)	MATTHEW (cont.)	LUKE (cont.)
and saying:	and saying:	
"Ah, thou that	"Thou that	
destroyest the Temple	destroyest the Temple,	
and buildest it	and buildest it	
in three days,	in three days,	
save thyself,	save thyself.	
	If thou be	
	the Son of God,	
and come down	come down	
from the cross."	from the cross."	
Likewise also	Likewise, also	
the chief priests	the chief priests	
mocking	mocking him,	
said among		
themselves		And the rulers
with the scribes:	with the scribes	also with them
	and elders, said:	derided him, saying,
"He saved others;	He saved others;	"He saved others;
himself he	himself he	let him
cannot save.	cannot save.	save himself,
Let Christ	If he be	if he be Christ,
the King	the King	the chosen
of Israel	of Israel,	of God . . ."
	let him now	
descend now	come down	
from the cross	from the cross,	
that we may see	and we will	
and believe."	believe him.	
	He trusted in God;	
	let him deliver him	
	now,	
	if he will have him:	
	for he said, 'I am	
	the Son of God.'"	
And they	The thieves also,	
that were crucified	which were crucified	
with him	with him,	
reviled him.	cast the same	

MARK (cont.)	MATTHEW (cont.)	LUKE (cont.)
	in his teeth.	
And when	Now from the	And it was about
the sixth hour [noon]	sixth hour [noon]	the sixth hour [noon],
was come		and
there was darkness	there was darkness	there was darkness
over the whole land	over all the land	over all the earth
until the ninth hour	until the ninth hour	until the ninth hour
[3 P.M.].	[3 P.M.].	[3 P.M.],
		and the sun
		was darkened,
		and the veil
		of the Temple
		was rent in the midst.
"And at	And about	
the ninth hour	the ninth hour	
Jesus cried	Jesus cried	
with a loud voice	with a loud voice,	
saying,	saying	
"Eloi, Eloi,	"Eli, Eli,	
lama sabachthani?"	lama sabachthani?"	And when Jesus
which is,	that is to say,	had cried with
being interpreted		a loud voice,
[translated]		he said,
"My God, My God,	"My God, my God,	"Father, into
why hast thou	why hast thou	thy hands,
forsaken me?"	forsaken me?"	I commend my spirit."
		And having said thus,
And some of them	Some of them	he gave up the ghost.
that stood by,	that stood there,	L 23:35, 44–46
when they head it,	when they heard that	
said,	said,	
"Behold, he calleth	"This man calleth	
Elijah."	for Elijah."	
	And straightway	
And one ran	one of them ran,	
and filled a sponge	and took a sponge and	
full	filled it	
of vinegar	with vinegar,	

MARK (cont.)	MATTHEW (cont.)	LUKE (cont.)
and put it	and put it	
on a reed,	on a reed,	
and gave him	and gave him	
to drink,	to drink.	
saying,	The rest said,	
"Let alone:	"Let be,	
let us see whether	let us see whether	
Elijah will come	Elijah will come	
and take him down."	to save him."	
And Jesus	Jesus, when he	
cried with	had cried again	
a loud voice,	with a loud voice,	

and gave up the ghost.	yielded up the ghost.	
And the veil	And behold, the veil	
of the Temple	of the Temple	
was rent in twain	was rent in twain	
from the top	from the top	
to the bottom.	to the bottom,	
Mk 15:29–38	and the earth	
	did quake,	
	and the rocks rent;	
	and the graves	
	were opened,	
	and many bodies	
	of the saints	
	which slept	
	arose and came out	
	of the graves	
	after his resurrection,	
	and went into	
	the holy city,	
	and appeared	
	unto many.	
	Mt 27:39–53	

By this time, the four crucifying soldiers had taken Jesus' clothes and divided them among themselves, casting lots for his tunic so that it would not have to be torn into four parts.

John writes:

Then the soldiers, when they had crucified Jesus, took his garments, made four parts, to every soldier a part; and also his coat: now the coat was without seam, woven from the top throughout. They said therefore among themselves, "Let us not rend it, but cast lots for it whose it shall be." J 19:23–24 (Mk 15:24; Mt 27:35)

John, alone, has the following further details as to what happened while Jesus was on the cross. Jesus saw his mother standing by the cross with two other women, Mary, his mother's sister, and Mary Magdalene, and with one of his disciples, John Zebedee. Jesus then said to his mother, "Woman, behold thy son!" and he then said to John, "Behold thy mother!" J 19:25–27

John then writes:

And from that hour that disciple took her unto his own home. J 19:27

John continues:

After this, Jesus knowing that all things were now accomplished, that the Scriptures might be fulfilled, saith, "I thirst."

Now there was set a vessel full of vinegar; and they filled a sponge with vinegar and put it upon hyssop and put it to his mouth. When Jesus therefore had received the vinegar, he said, "It is finished"; and he bowed his head and gave up the ghost. J 19:28–30

The centurion in charge of the crucifixion detail was facing Jesus and then said:

MARK

Truly this man was
the Son of God.
Mk 15:39

LUKE

Certainly this was
a righteous man.
L 23:47

The soldiers were equally impressed. Matthew states:

Now when the centurion and they that were with him watching
Jesus, saw the earthquake, and those things that were done, they
feared greatly, saying "Truly this was the Son of God." *Mt 27:54*

The crowd then melted away. Luke writes:

And all the people that came together to that sight, beholding the
things that were done, smote their breasts, and returned. *L 23:48*

That crowd included "all his acquaintance, and the women that
followed him from Galilee." They were afraid and "stood afar off,
beholding these things." *L 23:49 (Mk 15:40; Mt 27:55)*

The Jewish authorities did not want the three bodies to remain
on their crosses since the Sabbath was to begin at sunset, especially since that Sabbath was also a high day. *J 19:31* Deuteronomy
21:23 provided that when a man was executed by hanging upon a
tree that his body should not "remain all night upon the tree, but
thou shalt in any wise bury him that day." Josephus notes that the
Jews "took down those that were condemned and crucified, and
buried them before the going down of the sun." *Josephus, Wars of the
Jews, Book IV, Ch. V, Sec. 2*

Since it was already late afternoon speed was urgent, and accordingly the Jewish authorities asked Pilate to authorize breaking the men's leg to induce immediate death. John writes:

Then came the soldiers, and brake the legs of the first, and of the
other which was crucified with him. But when they came to Jesus,
and saw that he was dead already, they brake not his legs. But one of
the soldiers with a spear pierced his side, and forthwith came there
out blood and water. *J 19:32–34*

John's Gospel lists certain things that had happened as the Jewish Old Testament scriptures had foretold:

> For these things were done, that the Scripture should be fulfilled.
> J 19:36

John then gives examples:

1. A bone of him shall not be broken. J 19:36 (Exodus 12:46; Numbers 9:12; Psalms 34:20)

Jesus' legs were not broken.

2. They shall look on him whom they pierced. J 19:37 (Zechariah 12:10)

The crowd saw the soldier shove a lance into Jesus' side.

3. They parted my raiment among them, and for my vesture they did cast lots. J 19:24 (Psalms 22:18)

The soldiers divided Jesus' clothes, and cast lots for his tunic. Although John's Gospel lists the prophecies which were fulfilled, it is also at pains to state that its record of the crucifixion is objectively true and based upon testimony of the eyewitness:

> And he that saw it bare record, and his record is true; and he knoweth that he saith true, that ye might believe. J 19:35

THE BURIAL

Jesus had given up the ghost on his cross at about "the ninth hour" (3:00 P.M.). *Mk 15:34–37; Mt 27:46–49; L 23:44–46* The Jewish authorities had interceded with Pilate to have the legs of the men on the crosses broken to induce immediate death so that their bodies could be removed from the crosses before sunset. *J 19:31* The soldiers assigned this task found Jesus dead already. *J 19:31*

Shortly thereafter Joseph of Arimathea went to Pilate to ask for the body of Jesus. *Mk 15:42–43, Mt 27:57–58; L 23:50–52, J 19:38* Pilate doubted that Jesus was already dead, and called the centurion in charge of the crucifixion detail to verify the death. *Mk 15:44* Upon so confirming Jesus' death, Pilate released Jesus' body to Joseph. *Mk 15:45; Mt 27:58, J 19:38*

Joseph was "a rich man of Arimathea." *Mt 27:57* Arimathea was a Jewish provincial town. Joseph lived there but was also probably a member of the national Jewish Council (Sanhedrin) sitting in Jerusalem. That is why Mark describes him as "an honourable counsellor" and Luke describes him as "counsellor." *Mk 15:43; L 23:50* His status was such that Luke feels obliged to explain that Joseph "had not consented to the counsel and deed of them" (the other Council members). *L 23:51*

Luke also describes Joseph as "a good man, and a just." *L 23:50* Both Matthew and John describe Joseph as a disciple of Jesus. *Mt 27:57; J 19:38* John adds that Joseph was a secret disciple "for fear of the Jews." *J 19:38*

Joseph took Jesus' body down and "wrapped it in linen." *L 23:53* Matthew describes the wrapping "as a clean linen cloth." *Mt 27:59 See also Mk 15:46; Mt 27:59; J 19:38.*

Mark's account is as follows:

> And he brought fine linen and took him down and wrapped him in the linen, and laid him in a sepulchre which was hewn out of a rock, and rolled a stone unto the door of the sepulchre. *Mk 15:46*

Matthew adds the detail that it was Joseph's "own new tomb, which he had hewn out in the rock." *Mt 27:60* No one had ever yet laid in that tomb. *L 23:53; J 19:41*

According to John, Nicodemus, a Pharisee and a ruler of the Jews who had previously come to Jesus by night, accompanied Joseph when he took the body and "wound it in linen clothes with the spices, as the manner of the Jews is to bury." *J 19:40* For this purpose Nicodemus had brought "a mixture of myrrh and aloes, about an hundred pound weight." *J 19:39*

This suggests that Joseph and Nicodemus had together planned the removal and the burial, but the first three gospels do not mention Nicodemus' part and tacitly assume that Joseph performed the task alone. This seems unlikely since taking the body down from the cross and carrying it some distance would be a difficult task even for two men, and there is no hint of the gospel accounts that Joseph brought any servants with him. The cooperation of Joseph and Nicodemus also seems likely since John describes Joseph as "being a disciple of Jesus, but secretly for fear of the Jews." *J 19:38 See also Mt 27:57* Mark and Luke add the detail that Joseph "waited for the kingdom of God." *Mk 15:43; L 23:51*

Nicodemus, while not described as a secret disciple of Jesus, probably was such a disciple. The only two mentions of him in the New Testament are as follows.

First, he came to Jesus by night at the beginning of Jesus' ministry and asked him, "Rabbi, we know that thou art a teacher come from God; for no man can do these miracles that thou doest, except God be with him." *J 3:2*

Second, he raised the question before the chief priests and Pharisees when Jesus was suspected, "Doth our law judge any man, before it hear him, and know what he doeth?" *J 7:51*

These two incidents clearly show that Nicodemus was favorably disposed toward Jesus and probably was as much a secret disciple of Jesus as Joseph of Arimathea.

Once Joseph and Nicodemus laid the body in the tomb, it was closed. Matthew and Mark's accounts as to *how* differ slightly:

MARK	MATTHEW
. . . and rolled a stone	. . . and he rolled a great stone
unto the door	to the door
of the sepulchre	of the sepulchre, and departed.
Mk 15:46	*Mt 27:60*

The tomb itself was in a garden. *J 19:41* John indicates that this garden was "in the place where he was crucified." *J 19:41* While this does not agree with popular picturizations of the crucifixion, it is intrinsically likely. The special high day was about to begin at sunset. There was no time to carry the body very far. John explicitly states that "the sepulchre was nigh at hand." *J 19:42*

The burial in that garden tomb was observed by Mary Magdalene and one other woman. *Mk 15:47; Mt 27:61* Matthew refers to that woman as simply "the other Mary." *Mt 27:61* Mark describes her as "Mary, the mother of Joses." *Mk 15:47* Luke simply says:

> And the women also, which came with him from Galilee, followed after, and beheld the sepulchre, and how his body was laid. *L 23:55*

Apparently, after having observed the burial, the women left since the high day was about to begin. The tomb was apparently left unattended that Friday night but with the "great stone" blocking its door. Sometime the next day, the chief priests and the Pharisees secured leave from Pilate to post a watch at the tomb which they did and at which time they sealed the stone. *Mt 27:66*

The full account of the precautions taken by the Jewish establishment is as follows:

> Now the next day, that followed the day of the preparation, the chief priests and Pharisees came together unto Pilate, saying, "Sir, we remember that that deceiver said, while he was yet alive, 'After three days I will rise again.' Command therefore that the sepulchre be made sure until the third day, lest his disciples come by night, and steal him away, and say unto the people, 'He is risen from the dead': so the last error shall be worse than the first."

Pilate said unto them, "Ye have a watch: go your way, make it as sure as ye can."

So they went, and made the sepulchre sure, sealing the stone, and setting a watch. *Mt 27:62–66*

CHAPTER 4

JESUS' RESURRECTION AND ASCENSION

RAISING OF THE DEAD

Jesus claimed to have raised the dead. When John the Baptist sent his disciples to ask Jesus if he was the Messiah, Jesus told them:

> Go your way, and tell John what things ye have seen and heard: how the blind see, the lame walk, the lepers are cleansed, the deaf hear, *the dead are raised*, to the poor the gospel is preached. *L 7:22 (Mt 11:5)*

Luke places this incident shortly after Jesus had raised a widow's son at Nain, a village in Galilee near Nazareth. As he approached the city gate with his disciples and the following crowd, the boy's body was carried out in procession. *L 7:11–12* Luke states:

> And when the Lord saw her [the widow], he had compassion on her, and said unto her, "Weep not." And he came and touched the bier, and they that bare him stood still. And he said, "Young man, I say unto thee, Arise." And he that was dead sat up, and began to speak. And he delivered him to his mother. *L 7:13–15*

It is easy to explain this raising as a simple combination of immediate burial (on the day of "death") and lack of adequate medical techniques to determine death.

Jesus, himself, recognized the possibility of an incorrect diagnosis of death. Jairus, a synagogue ruler (president), bowed at Jesus' feet and pleaded urgently for his help:

> My little daughter lieth at the point of death; I pray thee, come and lay thy hands on her, that she may be healed; and she shall live. *Mk 5:22–23 (Mt 9:18; L 8:41)*

This was Jairus' only daughter, and she was twelve. *Mk 5:42; L 8:42* Jesus got up and followed Jairus but so did Jesus' disciples and whole multitude. *Mk 5:24; Mt 9:19; L 8:42*

Jesus was delayed by a woman in the crowd and while he spoke to her, messengers came up from Jairus' house, reporting to Jairus:

> Thy daughter is dead. Why troublest thou the Master [Teacher or Rabbi] any further? *Mk 5:35 (L 6:49)*

Jesus overheard the message and said:

MARK	LUKE
Be not afraid,	Fear not:
only believe.	believe only,
Mk 5:36	and she shall
	be made whole.
	L 8:50

Jesus took three of his disciples, Peter, James, and John, and proceeded to Jairus' house. *Mk 5:37–38* The tumult, weeping and wailing of the ancient Near East for the dead had already begun. *Mk 5:38; Mt 9:23; L 8:52* The flute players had already arrived. *Mt 9:23*

Jesus said to those present at the house:

MARK	MATTHEW	LUKE
Why make ye	Give place:	Weep not;

MARK (cont.)	MATTHEW (cont.)	LUKE (cont.)
this ado and weep?	for	
The damsel	the maid	she
is not dead,	is not dead,	is not dead,
but sleepeth.	but sleepeth.	but sleepeth.
Mk 5:39	*Mt 9:24*	*L 8:52*

All three gospels state: "And they laughed him to scorn." *Mk 5:40; Mt 9:24; L 8:53* Luke adds: "knowing that she was dead." *L 8:53* This was no faith-healer's suggestible crowd.

Like a physician, Jesus first put the crowd out. *Mk 5:40; Mt 9:25* He then took the girl's parents and the three disciples he had brought with him into the room where the girl was. His treatment was simple. He took her hand where she lay and said:

MARK	MATTHEW
Damsel,	Maid,
I say unto thee,	
arise.	arise.
Mk 5:41	*L 8:54*

She immediately got up and walked. *Mk 5:42; Mt 9:25; L 8:55* Jesus then prescribed that "something should be given to her to eat." *Mk 5:43 (L 8:55)* He was not interested in exploiting this raising. Two of the gospels state:

MARK	MATTHEW
And they	And her parents
were astonished	were astonished.
with a great astonishment.	
And he charged them	But he charged them
straitly that	that they should tell
no man should know it; . . ."	no man what was done.
Mk 5:42–43	*L 8:56*

This raising, of course, could not be hid, and "the fame hereof went abroad into all that land." *Mt 9:26* This was exactly what happened after the raising of the son of the widow of Nain:

And there came a fear on all: and they glorified God, saying, that "A great prophet is risen up among us"; and that "God hath visited his people."

And this rumor of him went forth throughout all Judea, and through-out all the region round about. And the disciples of John shewed him of all these things. *L 7:16–18*

It could hardly have been otherwise. Jairus' daughter was an only daughter, and the widow of Nain's son was an only son. *L 7:12; 8:42*

It can be argued that these were both cases of resuscitation since the girl had just "died," and the boy would have "died" the same day as his funeral under the local custom. However, the same easy explanation does not fit the case of Lazarus.

Lazarus had been dead four days. *J 11:39* When Jesus ordered the removal of the stone from the mouth of the burial cave, Lazarus' sister, Martha objected: "Lord, by this time he stinketh: for he hath been dead four days." *J 11:39*

Nor can the Lazarus' appearance be explained as a mere apparition. Later on Lazarus attended a supper where a number of persons were present:

Then Jesus six days before the Passover came to Bethany, where Lazarus was which had been dead, whom he raised from the dead. Then they made him a supper, and Martha served; but Lazarus was one of them that sat at the table with him. *J 12:1–2*

As might be expected, such a stupendous miracle aroused popular interest:

Much people of the Jews therefore knew that he was there; and they came not for Jesus' sake only, but that they might see Lazarus also, whom he had raised from the dead. *J 12:1–2*

In those days, of course, people were prepared to consider the possibility that the dead might rise. The Roman tetrarch, Herod

Antipas, was perplexed when he heard of Jesus' highly successful ministry "because it was said of some, that John was risen from the dead; and of some that Elijah had appeared; and of others that one of the old prophets was risen again." *L 9:7–8 Compare Mk 6:14–16 and Mt 14:1–2*

The Jews were familiar with the idea of personal resurrection. When Jesus sought to comfort Martha on the death of her brother Lazarus he said, "Thy brother shall rise again." *J 11:23* Martha interpreted this as a pious statement of Jewish belief and answered, "I know that he shall rise again in the resurrection at the last day." *J 11:24*

The Old Testament book of Daniel taught a resurrection:

And many of them that sleep in the dust of the earth shall awake, some to everlasting life, and some to shame and everlasting contempt. *Daniel 12:2*

Not all Jews believed as did Martha "in the resurrection at the last day." *J 11:24* One Jewish sect, the Sadducees, held that there was no resurrection. *Mk 12:18; Mt 22:23; L 20:27; Acts 23:8*

The Sadducees had a stock question for Pharisees and other believers in the resurrection that was supposed to demonstrate that the resurrection was contrary to the law of Moses. That law in Deuteronomy 25:5 provided for Levirate marriage, which is a brother should preserve the male line of a deceased brother by marrying his widow if he died without begetting a son.

The Sadducees asked Jesus that question. That question went like this:

Now there were seven brethren; and the first took a wife, and dying left no seed. And the second took her, and died, neither left he any seed; and the third likewise. And the seven had her, and left no seed. Last of all the woman died also.

In the resurrection therefore, when they shall rise, whose wife shall she be of them? For the seven had her to wife. *Mk 12:20–23 (Mt 22:25–30; L 20:29–33)*

Jesus answered the question in this way:

MARK	MATTHEW	LUKE
Do ye not therefore err, because ye know not the Scriptures, neither the power of God?	Ye do err, not knowing the Scriptures nor the power of God.	The children of this world marry and are given in marriage, but they which shall be accounted worthy to obtain that world, and
For when they shall rise from the dead, they neither marry, nor are given in marriage;	For in the resurrection they neither marry, nor are given in marriage	the resurrection from the dead, neither marry, nor are given in marriage; neither can they die any more: for they are equal
but are as the angels	but are as the angels of God	unto the angels, and are children of God, being the children
which are in heaven.	in heaven.	of the resurrection.
And as touching the dead, that they rise,	But as touching the resurrection of the dead,	Now that the dead are raised,
have ye not read in the book of Moses, how in the bush	have ye not read that which was spoken	even Moses showed at the bush,

MARK (cont.)	MATTHEW (cont.)	LUKE (cont.)
God spake unto him saying,	unto you by God, saying,	when he calleth the Lord
"I am the God of Abraham, and the God of Isaac, and the God of Jacob"? (*Exodus 3:6*)	"I am the God of Abraham, and the God of Isaac, and the God of Jacob"? (*Exodus 3:6*)	the God of Abraham, and the God of Isaac, and the God of Jacob. (*Exodus 3:6*)
He is not the God of the dead, but the God of the living. Ye therefore do greatly err. *Mk 12:24–27*	God is not the God of the dead, but of the living. *Mt 22:29–32*	For he is not a God of the dead, but of the living: for all live unto him. *L 20:34–38*

Jesus' answer strongly affirms ("ye therefore do *greatly* err") that the dead do rise ("And as touching the dead, that they rise"), that they do rise by "the power of God" and that in this spiritual state ordinary human concerns, marriage and giving in marriage, are irrelevant.

The rest of Jesus' answer is devoted to answering these Sadducees in terms of their own theology. They accepted as Scripture only the book of Moses, a general title for the first five books of the Old Testament. They did not find the doctrine of a resurrection in their Scripture. Jesus argued from their Scripture in their own rabbinical way against their position. He quoted a statement found in that Scripture, in Exodus 3:6, that, "I am the God of Abraham, and the God of Isaac, and the God of Jacob," and argued that this God is "the God of the living," that is, the God of the patriarchs who (you know) still live, and a God of power. If so, why do you doubt the power of that God to raise the dead?

Jesus' answer shattered the Sadducees' cherished question, and their Jewish adversaries appreciated that. Luke writes:

> Then certain of the scribes answering said, "Master, thou hast well said." And after that they durst not ask him any question at all. *L 20:39–40*

These "scribes" were almost certainly Pharisees, and that sect believed in the resurrection. However, Jesus' answer went beyond the stock Jewish teaching on the resurrection. Matthew writes:

> And when the multitude heard this [Jesus' answer], they were astonished at his doctrine. *Mt 22:33*

Jesus' own teaching about the resurrection was:

> And this is the will of him that sent me, that every one which seeth the Son, and believeth on him, may have everlasting life; and I will raise him up at the last day. *J 6:40*

Jesus did not, like some of his latter day followers, doubt the power of God to raise the dead. He taught it was the will of God that those who believe on Jesus will be raised by him at the last day.

Jesus also taught:

> For the hour is coming, in the which all that are in the graves shall hear his [Son of man's] voice, and shall come forth: they that have done good, unto the resurrection of life; and they that have done evil, unto the resurrection of damnation. *J 5:28–29*

He taught that those who invite the poor, the maimed, the lame and the blind to a feast shall "be recompensed at the resurrection of the just." *L 14:13–14*

Jesus' own teaching about the resurrection culminates in his famous reply to Martha's statement about her brother, "I know that he shall rise again in the resurrection at the last day":

> I am the resurrection, and the life: he that believeth in me, though he were dead, yet shall he live; and whosoever liveth and believeth in me shall never die. *J 11:25–26*

Jesus' statement has two aspects: a statement that "whosoever liveth and believeth in me shall never die," referring to eternal life; and a statement that "he that believeth in me, though he were dead, yet shall he live," referring to resurrection. The opening statement in some ancient manuscripts, is simply "I am the resurrection," omitting "and the life."

In substance, Jesus told Martha that I am the resurrection, and if a man dies he shall rise at the resurrection at the last day if he believes in me. Jesus' statement bonds his own person to the resurrection of men.

For Christians the resurrection of men is based upon Jesus' own resurrection. Paul summarizes the earliest Christian gospel as follows:

> For I delivered unto you first of all that *which I also received* [was taught], how that Christ died for our sins according to the scriptures; and that he was buried, and that he rose again the third day according to the scriptures, and that he was seen of Cephas, then of the Twelve. After that, he was seen of above five hundred brethren at once, of whom the greater part remain unto this present, but some are fallen asleep. After that, he was seen of James, then of all the apostles. And last of all he was seen of me also, as of one born out of due time." *1 Corinthians 15:3–8*

Jesus rebuked Sadducees for doubting "the power of God" to raise the dead. *Mk 12:24* Paul also referred to that power when he wrote:

> And God hath both raised up the Lord, and will also rise up us by his own power. *1 Corinthians 6:14*

Just as the Sadducees in Jewry denied the resurrection, so also some members of the earliest Christian churches asserted that "there is no resurrection of the dead." *1 Corinthians 15:12*

Even today many Christians repeat this old heresy. This old heresy makes any faith in Christ vain:

> But if there is no resurrection of the dead, then is Christ not risen. And if Christ be not risen, then is our preaching vain, and your faith is also vain. Yea, and we are found false witnesses of God, because we have testified of God that he raised up Christ, whom he raised not up, if so be that the dead rise not. For if the dead rise not, then is not Christ raised: And if Christ be not raised, your faith is vain; ye are yet in your sins." *1 Corinthians 15:13–17*

JESUS' PREDICTION OF HIS RESURRECTION

Jesus, in his lifetime, repeatedly predicted his own resurrection, but usually it was part of a statement that he would be killed. In their revulsion at his prediction of his killing, the disciples apparently glossed over the companion prediction of his resurrection.

The classic instance is the interchange between Jesus and Peter:

MARK	MATTHEW	LUKE
	From that time forth	
And he began to teach them	began Jesus to shew unto his disciples, how that he must go unto Jerusalem,	Saying,
that the Son of man must suffer many things, and be rejected of the elders and of the chief priests and scribes, and be killed, and after three days rise again. And he spake that saying openly. And Peter took him, and began to rebuke him. *Mk 8:31–32*	and suffer many things of the elders and chief priests and scribes, and be killed, and be raised again the third day. Then Peter took him, and began to rebuke him, saying, "Be it far from thee, Lord: this shall not be unto thee." *Mt 16:21–22*	"The Son of man must suffer many things, and be rejected of the elders and chief priests and scribes and be slain, and be raised the third day." *L 9:22*

265

On another occasion Jesus predicted his resurrection, and the accounts make it clear that his disciples did not understand the prediction and were afraid to ask about it:

MARK	MATTHEW	LUKE
For he taught his disciples, and	And while they abode in Galilee,	But while they wondered every one at all things which Jesus did,
said unto them,	Jesus said unto them,	he said unto his disciples, "Let these sayings sink into your ears: for
"The Son of man is delivered into the hands of men, and they shall kill him; and after that he is killed, he shall rise the third day."	"The Son of man shall be betrayed into the hands of men, and they shall kill him; and the third day he shall be raised again."	the Son of man shall be delivered into the hands of men."
But they understood not that saying,	And they were exceedingly sorry. *Mt 17:22–23*	But they understood not this saying, and it was hid from them, that they perceived it not; and they feared to ask him of that saying. *L 9:43–45*
and were afraid to ask him. *Mk 9:31–32*		

266

Luke quotes Jesus as saying only that he should "be delivered into the hands of men" omitting Jesus' statement that he should "rise the third day." The focus of the disciples' memory was on the prediction of Jesus' being killed, not upon his being resurrected the third day. All three accounts quoted above show the disciples as shattered and puzzled. That is why they did not come to the tomb *expecting* to find Jesus resurrected.

On a third occasion Jesus predicted his resurrection, and Luke states that they "understood none of these things":

MARK	MATTHEW	LUKE
	And Jesus going up to Jerusalem	
And he took again	took	Then he took unto him
the Twelve, and began	the Twelve disciples apart in the way,	the Twelve,
to tell them what things should happen unto him, saying,	and said	and said
"Behold, we go up to Jerusalem,	unto them, "Behold, we go up to Jerusalem,	unto them, "Behold, we go up to Jerusalem
and the Son of man shall be delivered unto the chief priests and unto the scribes;	and the Son of man shall be betrayed unto the chief priests and unto the scribes	and all things that are written by the prophets concerning the Son of man shall be accomplished.
and they shall condemn him to death, and shall deliver him to the Gentiles; and they shall mock him,	and they shall condemn him to death, and shall deliver him to the Gentiles to mock,	For he shall be delivered unto the Gentiles, and shall be mocked, and spitefully entreated [treated],

MARK (cont.)	MATTHEW (cont.)	LUKE (cont.)
and shall scourge him,	and to scourge,	and spitted on;
and shall spit		and they shall
upon him,		scourge him,
and shall kill him:	and to crucify him:	and put him to death:
and the third day	and the third day	and the third day
he shall rise again."	he shall rise again."	he shall rise again."
Mk 10:32–34	*Mt 20:17–19*	
		And they *understood*
		none of these things:
		and this saying
		was hid
		from them, neither
		knew they the things
		which were spoken.
		L 18:31–34

So far as Jesus' resurrection is concerned, the point is that the disciples and Jesus' other followers did not have his predictions of his resurrection in mind, and accordingly, Easter morning they did not expect any resurrection.

These clear and specific predictions by Jesus of his resurrection were made on his final journey to Jerusalem. (". . . In the way going up to Jerusalem" *Mk 10:32;* ". . . Going up to Jerusalem." *Mt 20:17*)

The statements Jesus made after he reached Jerusalem on the night he was betrayed are not so clear and specific. On that night after the Last Supper Jesus said to the disciples:

MARK	MATTHEW
All ye	All ye
shall be offended	shall be offended
because of me	because of me
this night:	this night:
for it is written,	for it is written,
"I will smite	"I will smite
the shepherd,	the shepherd,
and the sheep	and the sheep

268

MARK (cont.)

shall be
scattered."
[*Zechariah 13:7*]
But *after* that
I am risen,
I will go before you
into Galilee.
Mk 14:27–28

MATTHEW (cont.)
of the flock
shall be
scattered abroad."
[*Zechariah 13:7*]
But *after*
I am risen again,
I will go before you
into Galilee.
Mt 26:31–32

Later on that same evening, John quotes Jesus as saying: "*A little while*, and ye shall not see me; and again, *a little while*, and ye shall see me, because I go to the Father." *J 16:16*

John then writes:

Then said some of his disciples among themselves, "What is this that he saith unto us, 'A little while, and ye shall not see me; and again, a little while, and ye shall see me,' and, 'because I go to the Father'?"

They said therefore, "What is this that he saith, 'A little while'? We can not tell what he saith."

Now Jesus knew that they were desirous to ask him, and said unto them:

"Do ye enquire among yourselves of that I said, 'A little while, and ye shall not see me; and again, a little while, and ye shall see me'?

Verily, verily, I say unto you, that ye shall weep and lament, but the world shall rejoice; and ye shall be sorrowful, but your sorrow shall be turned into joy.

A woman when she is in travail hath sorrow, because her hour is come; but as soon as she is delivered of the child, she remembereth no more the anguish, for joy that a man is born into the world.

And ye now therefore have sorrow; but I will see you again, and your heart shall rejoice, and your joy no man taketh from you."
J 16:17–22

These quotations can not now be read after nineteen centuries of Christian history without reading back into them the events that began the next day: Jesus' disappearance which began with his death on the next day, a Friday, and lasted "a little while," and his reappearance in "a little while" on Sunday morning.

A disappearance for "a little while" was then vague and ambiguous. Even now with the benefit of hindsight, it is cryptic. It is no wonder that the resurrection was not in the minds of the women who went to the tomb that Sunday morning or in the minds of the disciples when they heard the report of the women.

The Disciples Did Not Expect Jesus' Resurrection

The women came to Jesus' tomb to embalm his body and were concerned about how they could move the heavy closure stone to get at it. *Mk 16:1, 3–4* They did not expect anything unusual.

Luke's account of the women at the tomb states that the two "men" said to them:

Why seek ye the living among the dead?

He is not here, but is risen. Remember how he spake unto you when he was yet in Galilee, saying, "The Son of man must be delivered into the hands of sinful men, and be crucified, and the third day rise again."

And *they remembered his words*, and returned from the sepulchre, and *told all these things* unto the Eleven, and to all the rest." *L 24:5–9*

Jesus had, of course, repeatedly predicted his resurrection. (See section Jesus' Prediction Of His Resurrection pp 265–270.) The two "men" reminded the women of these predictions, and they included these predictions in their report. However, their report was not believed by the Eleven:

And their words seemed to them as idle tales, and they believed them not. *L 24:11*

Two disciples left Jerusalem for Emmaus after the women had made their report. Their statement about the women's report is equally negative:

Yea, and certain women also of their company made us astonished, which were early at the sepulchre; and when they found not his body, they came, saying, that they had seen a vision of angels, which said that he was alive. *L 24:22–23*

Nevertheless, according to the Emmaus two, the women's report was investigated:

> And certain of them which were with us went to the sepulchre, and found it even so as the women had said: but him they saw not. *L 24:24*

No credulity here; just a terse factual report: body gone; Jesus not sighted.

Peter and John were the disciples who went to the tomb to investigate. *L 24:12; J 20:3–4* Luke states that after Peter looked into the tomb and saw grave clothes laid by themselves he "departed, wondering in himself at that which was come to pass." *L 24:12*

At this point John's gospel explains:

> For as yet they knew not *the Scripture*, and that he must rise again from the dead. *J 20:9*

While they did not know the Scripture yet, they must have been reminded of Jesus' predictions by the report of the women. However, a fair reading of the Gospel accounts shows that despite Jesus' predictions of his resurrection his disciples did not expect it and were, instead, puzzled by the facts of the empty tomb and the empty grave clothes. *L 24:12*

Mary Magdalene did not expect to see a risen Jesus, and when she did see him supposed him to be the gardener. *J 20:13–15*

Thomas, called Didymus (the Twin), adamantly refused to believe the report of the other ten disciples that they had seen the risen Jesus, and Thomas has become a proverbial example of the will to skepticism:

> Except I shall see in his hands the print of the nails, and put my finger into the print of the nails, and thrust my hand into his side, I *will not* believe. *J 20:25*

IS JESUS' RESURRECTION A POSSIBILITY?

It is an objective fact of historical scholarship that the heart of the earliest Christian preaching was that:

> This Jesus hath God raised up, whereof we all [the apostles] are witnesses. *Acts 2:32*

That question is different from the question whether Jesus' resurrection actually did occur. Before we examine the evidence, it is fair to point out that the factuality of Jesus' resurrection raised the same doubts in the ancient world that it does today.

In about A.D. 50, Paul was in Athens and engaged in religious discussions daily in the market place, the Agora. Acts states:

> Then certain philosophers of the Epicureans, and of the Stoics, encountered him. And some said, "What will this babbler say?" Other some, "He seemed to be a setter forth of strange gods," because he preached unto them Jesus, and the resurrection.
>
> And they took him, and brought him unto Areopagus, saying, "May we know what this new doctrine, whereof thou speakest, is? For thou bringest certain strange things to our ears; we would know therefore what these things mean." *Acts 17:18–20*

"Areopagus" was the common way to refer to an Athenian city court that had formerly met on Mars' hill. In this case, however, its meeting place simply provided a forum to hear Paul's doctrine.

Paul began appropriately in the classic Greek way, "Ye men of Athens," praised their religiosity, and referred to an Athenian altar inscribed "To An Unknown God." *Acts 17:22–23* He then proceeded to identify that God with the Christian God, "him declare I unto you," and stated that this God "hath appointed a day, in which he will judge the world in righteousness by *that man* whom he hath ordained; whereof he hath given assurance unto all men, in that he hath raised him from the dead." *Acts 17:23, 31*

Although Paul had not yet identified "that man" as Jesus, there was an immediate end to the discussion:

> And when they heard of the resurrection of the dead, some mocked: and others said, "We will hear thee again of this matter." *Acts 17:32*

Intellectuals really haven't changed: some of their minds were closed; others politely put the matter off.

Some years later in about A.D. 58, Paul was in Roman custody in Caesarea, a Roman administrative town on the coast of Palestine, charged with being "a pestilent fellow, and a mover of sedition among all the Jews throughout the world, and a ringleader of the sect of the Nazarenes." *Acts 24:5*

Paul's case was ultimately heard by Porcius Festus, the Roman procurator for Judea. He in turn briefed the matter for King Herod Agrippa II, stating that Paul's accusers "brought none accusation of such things as I supposed: but had certain questions against him of their own superstition, and of one Jesus, which was dead, whom *Paul affirmed to be alive.*" *Acts 25:18–19*

Agrippa himself then heard Paul's defense. Part of that defense was Paul's question:

> Why should it be thought a thing incredible with you, that God should raise the dead? *Acts 26:8*

That is really the crucial question still: Why should it be thought incredible that God should raise the dead?

The answer is that God's raising the dead is unbelievable, not that it is impossible. It is impossible only if we *assume* it is impossible. If we assume it is impossible, there is nothing to investigate.

The usual scientific method is to first investigate the evidence and then draw conclusions. We have one specific case to investigate, the alleged resurrection of Jesus. The question is: Does the evidence support the alleged resurrection of Jesus?

The Evidence as to the Resurrection

The crucifixion of Jesus Christ is a historical fact, and is not often disputed. The resurrection of Jesus Christ is also a historical fact, but is often disputed.

To resolve the dispute, we turn to the evidence. That evidence is found in the four Christian gospels and in certain other books of the Christian New Testament. While obviously these books were written by Christians, and as such, interested persons, this does not disqualify them as witnesses but only goes to the weight of their testimony.

We begin with the evidence as to the burial of Jesus Christ. According to Jewish practice based on Deuteronomy 21:23, the body of an executed man had to be buried on the day of execution and not left overnight. The matter of Jesus' burial was even more urgent. His crucifixion had occurred on a Friday. That particular Friday was not only the day of Preparation for the Sabbath the next day but for the Passover that year, since the next day was not only a Sabbath, but a high day. *J 19:14, 31*

The gospel accounts agree that Jesus died on the cross at about 3:00 P.M. *Mk 15:33–37; Mt 27:45–50; L 23:44–46* The Sabbath began at sunset. In that interval, it was necessary to get the permission of the Roman procurator, Pilate, to remove Jesus' body from the cross, then remove the body, and bury the body. *Mk 15:42–47; Mt 27:5–61; L 23:50–56; J 19:38–42*

Joseph of Arimathaea secured the necessary permission and, with the assistance of Nicodemus, removed the body. They then embalmed and buried it. The account in the Gospel of John is as follows:

> And after this Joseph of Arimathaea, being a disciple of Jesus, but secretly for fear of the Jews, besought Pilate that he might take away the body of Jesus: and Pilate gave him leave. He came therefore, and took the body of Jesus.

And there came also Nicodemus, (which at first came to Jesus by night), and brought a mixture of myrrh and aloes, about an hundred pound weight. Then took they the body of Jesus and wound it in linen clothes with the spices, as the manner of the Jews is to bury.

Now in the place where he was crucified there was a garden; and in the garden a new sepulchre, wherein was never man yet laid. There laid them Jesus therefore because of the Jews' Preparation day, for the sepulchre was nigh at hand. *J 19:38–42*

The day of Preparation was about to end, and the high Sabbath was about to begin at sunset. The burial had to be hasty, and a nearby tomb had to be used.

Certain women followers of Jesus watched his burial, apparently from a distance. In any case they did not know that Joseph and Nicodemus had used a large quantity of myrrh and aloes to embalm the body. *Mk 15:46–47; Mt 27:59–61; L 23:53–55*

Luke's Gospel has this statement:

And that day was the [day of] Preparation, and the Sabbath drew on. And the women also, which came with him from Galilee, followed after, and beheld the sepulchre, and how his body was laid. And they returned, and *prepared spices and ointments*; and rested the Sabbath Day according to the commandment.

Now upon the first day of the week, very early in the morning, they came unto the sepulchre, bringing *the spices which they had prepared*, and certain others with them. And they found the stone rolled away from the sepulchre. And they entered in, and found not the body of the Lord Jesus. *L 23:54–56; L 24:1–3*

Mark also mentions that the women "brought sweet spices, that they might come and anoint him." *Mk 16:1*

The obvious and indisputable fact is that the women came to the tomb to embalm the body of Jesus and that they expected to find his corpse, nothing else.

All the gospel accounts agree that Mary Magdalene came to the tomb; they do not agree in their lists of the other women who came:

MARK	MATTHEW	LUKE	JOHN
Mary Magdalene	Mary Magdalene	Mary Magdalene	Mary Magdalene *J 20:1–2*
Mary the mother of James	the other Mary *Mt 28:1*	Mary the mother of James	
Salome *Mk 16:1*		Joanna	
		other women that were with them *L 24:10*	

The "other Mary" mentioned by Matthew is probably the "mother of James" listed by Mark and Luke. The basis for this statement is as follows. Two women watched the burial of Jesus. Mark and Matthew describes them as follows:

MARK	MATTHEW
Mary Magdalene and Mary the mother of Joses. *Mk 15:47*	Mary Magdalene, and the other Mary *Mt 27:61*

Just previously Matthew writes that "many women" watched the crucifixion, and specifically names "Mary Magdalene, and Mary the mother of James and Joses, and the mother of Zebedee's children." *Mt 27:56* From the foregoing, I conclude that "Mary the mother of James and Joses" is "the other Mary" listed in Matthew.

In addition to the various women specifically named by the various Gospels as present at the tomb, there were probably other women present. Luke lists the women present as "Mary Magdalene, and Johanna and Mary, the mother of James, *and other women that were with them.*" L 24:10

The other Gospels do not mention the "other women" probably because their writers are focusing on the main participants, the chief of whom was Mary Magdalene. Indeed, John so focuses his account that he does not expressly mention any other women, although their presence shines through when she reports to Simon Peter and another disciple: ". . . *we* know not where they have laid him." *J 20:2*

It is not clear from the Gospel accounts who first came to the tomb on Easter morning: whether it was Mary Magdalene alone or a group of women which included Mary Magdalene. According to Luke, the women present were: Mary Magdalene, Joanna, Mary, the mother of James "and other women that were with them." L 24:10 The problem of who came first to the tomb is compounded by the state of the manuscript evidence of Mark's Gospel. The best manuscripts of Mark omit the part of Mark included in older versions as chapter 16:9–20. That section states that Jesus appeared *first* to Mary Magdalene:

> Now when Jesus was risen early the first day of the week, he appeared *first* to Mary Magdalene, out of whom he had cast seven devils. And she went and told them that had been with him, as they mourned and wept. And they, when they had heard that he was alive, and had been seen of her, believed not. *Mk 16:9–11*

John agrees that it was Mary Magdalene who first came to the tomb alone:

> The first day of the week cometh Mary Magdalene early, when it was yet dark, unto the sepulchre, and seeth the stone taken away from the sepulchre. Then she runneth, and cometh to Simon Peter, and to the other disciple, whom Jesus loved, and saith unto them, "They have taken away the Lord out of the sepulchre, and we know not where they have laid him." *J 20:1–2*

However, Matthew, Luke, and the part of Mark before Mark 16:9–11 agree that it was a group of women, not Mary Magdalene alone, who went to the tomb:

MARK	MATTHEW	LUKE
And when	In the end	Now . . .
the Sabbath	of the Sabbath . . .	they came . . .
was past,	came	
Mary Magdalene,	Mary Magdalene,	
and Mary,	and the other Mary	[and certain others
the mother of James,		with them,]
and Salome,		
had brought		[bringing
sweet spices,		the spices
that they		which they
might come		had prepared,]
and anoint him.		
And very early	[as it began	[very early
in the morning	to dawn toward	in the morning]
the first day	the first day	[upon the first day
of the week	of the week,]*	of the week,]*.
they came	to see	
unto the sepulchre	the sepulchre.	unto the sepulchre.
at the rising	Mt 28:1	L 24:1
of the sun.	*Conformed to Mark's	*Conformed to Mark's
Mk 16:1–2	order	order

John's account clearly implies that Mary Magdalene came *alone* to the tomb "when it was yet dark." J 20:1 John does not mention that she brought spices. Perhaps Mary came first, and saw that the tomb-sealing stone had been taken away. J 20:1 Perhaps she paused, puzzled, and the other women then arrived with the spices "at the rising of the sun." Mk 16:2 (Mt 28:1; L 24:1)

However, John's account implies that immediately after her discovery that the tomb-sealing stone had been taken away, she ran to Simon Peter and the other disciple, whom Jesus loved, and reported:

> They have taken away the Lord out of the sepulchre, and *we* know not where they have laid him. *J 20:2*

It seems unlikely that "we" is editorial and instead probably implies that she is reporting what the group of women observed. Furthermore, the report states that the Lord's body had been removed from the tomb, not simply that she had observed "the stone taken away." *J 20:1* Therefore, it seems likely that Mary Magdalene had arrived first alone and that there was a time gap of a few minutes between John 20:1 and 20:2 and that the "then" *(John 20:2)* of the King James Version does not mean a time gap but is only connective.

In the time gap, the other woman arrived, and the group, including Mary Magdalene, entered the tomb and found the body missing. *L 24:3 (Mk 16:6; Mt 28:6)* Mary Magdalene then ran to tell Peter and the other disciple.

The way the accounts refer to Mary Magdalene subtly suggest that she was an independent person and not quite one of the group of women. If this is true, it would be expected that she would be the one to run off and report the astonishing news. She was, however, a Galilean, since her name was really Mary of Magdala, a town on the west side of the Sea of Galilee. Although she had a unique personal history (she had been cured of "seven devils" by Jesus, *L 8:2; Mk 16:9*), Peter considered her report reliable enough to require immediate investigation. *J 20:3-4*

The rest of the group of women stayed at the tomb, "much perplexed thereabout." *L 24:4* At this point, they saw either one "man" or two "men." The accounts differ:

MARK	MATTHEW	LUKE
And entering into the sepulchre, they saw a young man	And, behold, there was a great earthquake: for the angel of the Lord descended from	And they entered in, and found not the body of the Lord Jesus. And it came to pass, as they were much

MARK (cont.)	MATTHEW (cont.)	LUKE (cont.)
	heaven, and came	perplexed thereabout,
	and rolled back	behold,
	the stone from	two men
	the door,	
sitting	and sat upon it.	stood
on the right side,		by them
	His countenance	
	was like lightning,	
clothed in	and his raiment	in
a long white garment;	white as snow:	shining garments:
and they were	and for	and as they were
affrighted.	fear of him	afraid,
	the keepers	and bowed down their
	did shake, and	faces to the earth,
	became as dead men.	
And he	And the angel	they
	answered and	
saith unto	said unto	said unto
them,	the women,	them,
"Be not affrighted:	"Fear not ye:	"Why
	for I know that	
ye seek	ye seek	seek ye
Jesus of Nazareth,	Jesus	the living
which was crucified.	which was crucified.	among the dead?
He is risen;	He is not here:	He is not here,
he is not here:	for he is risen,	but is risen.
	as he said.	
behold the place	Come, see the place	
where they laid him.	where the Lord lay.	
But go your way,	And go quickly,	
tell his disciples	and tell his disciples	
and Peter		
	that he is risen	
	from the dead;	
that he goeth	and behold, he goeth	
before you	before you	

Mark (cont.)	Matthew (cont.)	Luke (cont.)
into Galilee:	into Galilee;	
there ye shall see	there ye shall see	
him,	him:	
as he said unto you."	lo, I have told you."	
Mk 16:5–7	Mt 28:2–7	
		Remember how
		he spake unto you
		when he was
		yet in Galilee,
		saying,
		'The Son of Man
		must be delivered
		into the hands of
		sinful men,
		and be crucified,
		and the third day
		rise again.'"
		L 24:3–7

It is a familiar principle of psychology that a sudden or traumatic event will be perceived differently by different people. In legal terms eyewitness accounts often disagree. Luke's witnesses reported two men "in shining garments." Mark's witnesses reported one young man clothed in "a long white garment." Matthew's witnesses described the "man" as an angel but agree that his raiment was "white as snow." Mt 28:3

The accounts agree that this was an awesome experience generating fear. Despite minor differences, the accounts generally agree upon what was said to the women.

In weighing this evidence, it is important to stress that the record is undisputable that the women did not come to the tomb expecting anything unusual. The record is indisputable that the women expected to find a corpse since they came with spices to embalm Jesus' body. Mk 16:1; L 24:1 The record is indisputable that the concern of the women as they approached the tomb was how they would, as women, be able to roll away the heavy grave-closure stone to get at Jesus' body.

Mark writes:

> And they said among themselves, "Who shall roll us away the stone from the door of the sepulchre?" *Mk 16:3*

Mark describes the stone as "very great." *Mk 16:4* The women were surprised to find that the stone had already been rolled away:

> And when they looked, they saw that the stone was rolled away: for it was very great. *Mk 16:4 (L 24:2)*

Whatever exactly the women saw and heard when they entered the tomb, the record is indisputable that they did not find Jesus' body there. *L 24:3 (Mk 16:6; Mt 28:6)*

The record is clear that they then left the tomb:

MARK	MATTHEW	LUKE
And they went out quickly and fled from the sepulchre, for they trembled and were amazed: neither said they any thing to any man, for they were afraid. *Mk 16:8*	And they departed quickly from the sepulchre with fear and great joy,	And they returned from the sepulchre,
	and did run to bring his disciples word. *Mt 28:8*	and told all these things unto the Eleven, and to all the rest. *L 24:9*

Luke identifies the women who brought the news as follows:

283

It was Mary Magdalene, and Joanna, and Mary the mother of James, and other women that were with them, which told these things unto the apostles. *L 24:10*

Luke also states that it was *after* the women had heard the voice at the tomb that they remembered Jesus' words that he must "be crucified, and the third day rise again." *L 24:7–8*

Matthew adds the detail that on the way back to the disciples the women encountered Jesus himself:

And as they went to tell his disciples, behold, Jesus met them, saying, "All hail."

And they came and held him by the feet, and worshipped him. Then said Jesus unto them, "Be not afraid: go tell my brethren that they go into Galilee, and there shall they see me." *Mt 28:9–10*

The greeting by Jesus translated as "All hail" was an everyday greeting and meant literally *be glad*. The appearance of Jesus himself surprised the women; but his words, as they remembered them, are low key and prosaic without a hint of sensationalism. In substance they remembered Jesus as saying:

Greetings. Don't be afraid. Tell my brethren to go to Galilee and they will see me there.

Although the women did not expect to find anything unusual at the tomb, they were bereaved, and the crucifixion two days before must have devastated them. Evidence of these women in such circumstances is to be viewed with caution, although they claimed not only to have heard Jesus speak, but also to have gripped his feet. *Mt 28:9* In fact, the disciples themselves went further and dismissed the women's reports as "idle tales":

And their words seemed to them as idle tales, and they believed them not. *L 24:11*

Peter's Investigation

The disciples, as a group, considered the women's reports "idle tales," not worthy of belief. *L 24:11* Peter and one other disciple were not so sure, and ran to the tomb to investigate.

We have two accounts:

LUKE	JOHN
Then arose Peter, and ran	Peter therefore went forth
	and that other disciple,
unto the sepulchre;	and came to the sepulchre.
	So they ran both together,
	and the other disciple
	did outrun Peter,
	and came first
	to the sepulchre.
	And he stooping down,
	and looking in,
	saw the linen clothes lying;
	yet went he not in.
	Then cometh Simon Peter
	following him,
and stooping down,	and went into the sepulchre,
he beheld	and seeth
the linen clothes	the linen clothes lie,
	and the napkin,
	that was about his head
laid by	not lying with
themselves.	the linen clothes,
	but wrapped together
	in a place by itself.
	Then went in also
	that other disciple
	which came first
	to the sepulchre,
	and he saw,
	and believed.

LUKE (cont.)

JOHN (cont.)
For as yet they knew not
the Scripture,
that he must rise again
from the dead.

Then the disciples

and departed,
wondering in himself
at that which
was come to pass.
L 24:12

went away again
unto their own home.
J 20:3–10

Luke has it that Peter "departed, wondering in himself at that which was come to pass." L 24:12 John simply states that both Peter and the other disciple "went again unto their own home." J 20:10 John expressly states that "as yet they knew not the Scripture, that he must rise again from the dead." J 20:9 The same point is easily inferable from Luke's statement that Peter left "wondering in himself at that which was come to pass." L 24:12

To sum up, the report of the women was received by the disciples with skepticism. Two disciples ran to investigate and confirmed that the body was gone, but the grave clothes were still in the tomb.

THE CASE OF THE CURIOUS GRAVE CLOTHES

The accounts differ on whether Peter actually went into the tomb. *L 24:12; J 20:6* As a minimum, he stooped down and looked in. *L 24:12* Though not explicitly stated, it is clear that he found the body missing. The grave clothes remained.

The accounts agree that Peter was impressed by the peculiar position of the grave clothes. Luke's account just states that they were "laid by themselves." *L 24:12* John's account is more detailed and states that Peter not only saw the grave clothes lying but that "the napkin, that was about his head, not lying with the linen clothes, but wrapped together in place by itself." *J 20:7*

The evidence as to grave clothes is impressive. If the body was stolen, why were the grave clothes left and the head napkin neatly rolled up by itself?

It should be noted that the grave clothes were not just a burial smock but were linen strips wound about the body as part of the embalming process. Joseph of Arimathaea and Nicodemus had taken "the body of Jesus, and wound it in linen clothes with the spices, as the manner of the Jews is to bury." *J 19:40 (Mk 15:46; Mt 27:59; L 23:53)*

The Appearance to Mary Magdalene

After Peter and the other disciple went home, Mary Magdalene stayed at the tomb, standing outside. *J 20:10–11*

She had been deeply moved and was weeping. However, she stooped down and looked into the tomb. Here is what she saw as reported by John:

> And seeth two angels in white sitting, the one at the head, and the other at the feet, where the body of Jesus had lain.
>
> And they say unto her, "Woman, why weepest thou?"
>
> She saith unto them, "Because they have taken away my Lord, and *I know not where they have laid him.*"
>
> And when she had thus said, she turned herself back, and saw Jesus standing, and *knew not that it was Jesus.*
>
> Jesus saith unto her, "Woman, why weepest thou? Whom seekest thou?"
>
> She *supposing him to be the gardener*, saith unto him, "Sir, if thou have borne him hence, *tell me where thou has laid* him, and I will take him away."
>
> Jesus saith unto her, "Mary."
>
> She turned herself, and saith unto him, "Rabboni," which is to say "Master."
>
> Jesus saith unto her, "Touch me not, for I am not yet ascended to my Father; but go to my brethren, and say unto them, 'I ascend unto my Father, and your Father, and to my God, and your God.'" *J 20:12–17*

It is clear from Mary's statement that:

1. She assumed simply that Jesus' body had been moved, not that any resurrection had occurred.

2. She was not expecting to see Jesus, and when she saw him and heard his voice, supposed that it was simply the gardener.

John's report continues:

> Mary Magdalene came and told the disciples that she had seen the Lord, and that he had spoken these things unto her. *J 20:18*

That is all. John's narrative then abruptly shifts to the evening of that day and to an appearance behind closed doors to the disciples. Mark does refer tersely to the conversation between Jesus and Mary Magdalene when he writes:

> Now when Jesus was risen early the first day of the week, he appeared first to Mary Magdalene, out of whom he had cast seven devils. And she went and told them that had been with him, as they mourned and wept. And they, when they had heard that he was alive, and had been seen of her, *believed not. Mk 16:9–11*

Peter had believed Mary enough to investigate her report that the closure stone had been taken away from the tomb, but the disciples were not prepared to believe that Jesus had appeared to Mary, even though her report of her conversation with Jesus was apparently after the report to the disciples by the group of women, including Mary Magdalene, of their hearing at the tomb either one or two "men" speaking.

That conversation initially produced great fear. Mark reports:

> And they went out quickly, and fled from the sepulchre, for they trembled and were amazed; neither said they anything to any man, for they were afraid. *Mk 16:8*

The fear was soon succeeded by joy and Matthew condenses the fear-to-joy sequence into a single sentence:

> And they departed quickly from the sepulchre with fear and great joy, and did run to bring his disciples word. *Mt 28:8*

As they ran, Jesus appeared to them, saying:

> All hail. [pause] Be not afraid: go tell my brethren that they go into Galilee, and there shall they see me. *Mt 28:9–10*

Luke is more historical. He sketches the interval between the conversation with the woman and their report to the disciples in grey, sober prose:

> And they remembered his words, and returned from the sepulchre, and told all these things unto the Eleven, and to all the rest. It was Mary Magdalene, and Joanna, and Mary, the mother of James, and other women that were with them, which told these things unto the apostles. *L 24:8–10*

On that Easter morning the sequence of events was, apparently:

1. Mary Magdalene arrived first at the tomb "when it was yet dark." *J 20:1*

2. The other women arrived a few minutes later "at the rising of the sun." *Mk 16:2*

3. They found the closure stone rolled back and the tomb open. *Mk 16:4; Mt 28:2; L 24:2; J 20:1*

4. The women entered the tomb, found the body gone, and heard a voice. *Mk 16:5–8; Mt 28:5–7; L 24:3–7*

5. The women reported to the disciples but were not believed. *Mk 16:8; Mt 28:8; L 24:8–11* Their report of seeing Jesus on the way back apparently was also disbelieved. *Mt 28:9*

6. Mary Magdalene apparently outdistanced the rest of the group of women and met Peter and another disciple, presumably John, and reported to them that the tomb was open and Jesus' body was gone. *J 20:2*

7. Peter and John investigated and entered the tomb and found the body gone and the grave clothes lying in a peculiar manner. *J 20:3–8*

8. They returned to disciples' lodgings, puzzled. *J 20:10 Compare L 24:12*

9. Mary Magdalene stayed at the tomb and had a conversation with Jesus. *J 20:11–17*

10. She reported to the disciples who were mourning and weeping, but they disbelieved her. *J 20:18; Mk 16:9–11*

As of perhaps midmorning there had been only one appearance of Jesus himself, and that was the appearance to Mary Magdalene whom the disciples disbelieved, just as they had dismissed as "idle tales" the report by the group of women of a voice at the tomb. *L 24:11* The only facts that they had were that the stone had been moved, the tomb was empty and the body was gone.

By this time it had become common knowledge that the body was gone, and the Jewish establishment acted. Matthew has this report:

Now when they were going, behold, some of the watch [tomb guards] came into the city, and shewed unto the chief priests all the things that were done. And when they were assembled with the elders, and had taken counsel, they gave large money unto the soldiers, saying, "Say ye, 'His disciples came by night, and stole him away while we slept,' and if this comes to the governor's ears, we will persuade him, and secure you."

So they took the money, and did as they were taught: and this saying is commonly reported among the Jews until this day. *Mt 28:11–15*

THE REPORT OF THE EMMAUS TWO

Despite the report that Jesus' body was missing, two of the disciples left their group to walk to a village called Emmaus whose precise location is disputed but which was about seven miles from Jerusalem. As they walked they talked of the astounding events of that morning. L 24:14–15

Luke quotes them as telling a man they met on the journey:

Yea, and certain women also of our company made us astonished, which were early at the sepulchre; and when *they found not his body*, they came, saying, that they had also *seen a vision of angels*, which said that he was alive.

And certain of them which were with us [Peter and John] went to the sepulchre, and found it even so as the women had said, *but him they saw not*." L 24:22–24

The conversation between the two disciples (one named Cleopas) with the stranger began like this:

STRANGER: What manner of communications are these that ye have one to another, as ye walk, and *are sad*?
CLEOPAS: Art thou only a stranger in Jerusalem, and hast not known the things which are come to pass in these days?
STRANGER: What things?
TWO DISCIPLES: Concerning Jesus of Nazareth, which was *a prophet* mighty in deed and word before God and all the people, and how the chief priests and our rulers delivered him to be condemned to death, and crucified him. But we trusted that it had been he which should have redeemed Israel. And beside all this, *today is the third day since these things were done*." L 24:17–21

These two disciples were sad: Jesus' crucifixion on Friday was their concern; not the Sunday morning fact that his body was missing. They, like the rest of the disciples, were not impressed with the women's report of "a vision of angels." L 24:23 They must have left before Mary Magdalene had reported her vision of Jesus because the last word they had was that the disciples investigating the empty tomb had reported "but him they saw not."

The stranger exploded:

> O fools, and slow of heart to believe all that the prophets have spoken. Ought not Christ to have suffered these things, and to enter into his glory? *L 24:25*

The disciples did not recognize this stranger as Jesus for some time, but by evening they made the astounding connection. Here is what happened as they walked. The stranger expounded to them, "beginning at Moses and all the prophets" the things in the Jewish scriptures concerning the Christ, the annointed one. *L 24:27*

Luke continues:

> And they drew nigh unto the village, whither they went, and he made as though he would have gone further. But they constrained him, saying, "Abide with us: for it is toward evening, and the day is far spent."

> And he went in to tarry with them. And it came to pass, as he sat at meat with them, he took bread, and blessed it, and brake, and gave to them. And their eyes were opened, and they knew him; and he vanished out of their sight.

> And they said one to another "Did not your heart burn within us, while he talked with us by the way, and while he opened to us the Scriptures?"

> And they rose up the same hour, and returned to Jerusalem, and found the Eleven gathered together, and them that were with them, saying, "The Lord is risen indeed, and hath appeared to Simon."

> And they told what things were done in the way, and how he was known of them in breaking of bread. *L 24:28–35*

It was "towards evening" as they approached the village of Emmaus. *L 24:28–29* The stranger agreed to dine with them there.

After he took bread and blessed it, and broke it, and gave it to them, he vanished. *L 24:30–31*

They then realized who the stranger really was, saying to each other:

> Did not our heart burn within us, while he talked with us by the way, and while he opened to us the Scriptures? *L 24:32*

The obvious thing to do was to go tell the Eleven what had happened. So they left immediately for Jerusalem. It was a seven mile walk back, and their arrival in Jerusalem must have been late evening.

The Eleven, and other followers, were gathered together in a room with doors shut "for fear of the Jews." *J 20:19* But they already knew that astonishing things were happening. They blurted out to the men from Emmaus:

> The Lord is risen indeed, and hath appeared to Simon. *L 24:34*

The men then exultantly reported "what things were done in the way, and how he was known of them in breaking bread." *L 24:35* The very next thing that happened is that Jesus himself, stood in the midst of the gathering and said:

> Peace be unto you. *L 24:36*

In this atmosphere it is hard to believe that the Emmaus men were disbelieved, but this is what one account states:

> After that [the appearance to Mary Magdalene] he appeared in another form unto two of them, as they walked, and went into the country. And they went and told it unto the residue: neither believed they them. *Mk 16:12–13*

The best manuscripts of Mark do not contain Mark 16:9–20; that is why some modern versions treat these verses specially. This section obviously includes the verses we are discussing, Mark 16:12–13. The inferior manuscript evidence for these verses and the clarity and detail of Luke's account make it probable that Luke's account is correct, and the verses in Mark, as they now stand, garble the facts.

The appearance of Jesus to the two men on the way to Emmaus is impressive evidence for the resurrection of Jesus:

1. They did not know of Jesus' appearance to Peter. *L 24:34*
2. They did not know of Jesus' appearance to Mary Magdalene *L 24:22–24*
3. They were sad at Jesus' death three days before, and they accepted the report of the disciples investigating Jesus' empty tomb that they did not see Jesus. *L 24:24*
4. They regarded Jesus as "a prophet mighty in deed and word before God and all the people," but felt that his death had ended his mission. *L 24:19, 20–21* They did not recognize Jesus. *L 24:16*
5. It was daylight and they were walking in the open country. *L 24:13, 29*
6. The conversation with the stranger on the road was natural and ordinary in form:

    STRANGER: What manner of communications are these that ye have one to another, as ye walk, and are sad?
    CLEOPAS: Art thou only a stranger in Jerusalem, and hast not known the things which are come to pass there in these days?
    STRANGER: What things? *L 24:17–19*

7. They had an extended discussion with the stranger, and he expounded texts from the Scriptures of Israel. *L 24:25–27*
8. The stranger did ordinary acts of a pious Jew:

    He sat at meat with them, he took bread, and blessed it, and brake, and gave to them. *L 24:30*

The Appearance to Peter

Between the time the Emmaus men had left Jerusalem, perhaps around midmorning, and their return that night, Jesus had appeared to Peter (also known as Simon or Cephas). When they returned to the Eleven, they were greeted with the startling news:

The Lord is risen indeed, and hath appeared to Simon. *L 24:34*

Oddly enough, this crucial appearance to Peter is not otherwise included in the Gospel accounts but does appear prominently in a letter of Paul, 1 Corinthians, to the church at Corinth, Greece. This letter was written earlier than the Gospels, and from a technical historiographic point of view is a superior source. In that letter Paul wrote about what "I also received" as a convert within two or three years after Jesus' crucifixion:

. . .that he rose again the first day according to the Scriptures and that he was seen of Cephas, *then* of the Twelve: . . . *1 Corinthians 15:4–5*

We do have statements in Acts that quote Peter stating that he was a witness to the resurrection of Jesus. The first statement is in a speech Peter gave to a large crowd in Jerusalem about fifty days after Jesus' crucifixion. He said:

This Jesus hath God raised up, whereof we all are witnesses. *Acts 2:32*

The "we all" refers back to the Eleven disciples, Matthias having been inducted to replace Judas. *Acts 1:25–26; 2:14* Acts states that Peter "standing up with the Eleven" began this speech. *Acts 2:14*

Peter made another statement about Jesus' resurrection that is quoted in Acts. About fifteen years later, he was outlining Jesus' life to a Roman centurion. He referred to Jesus' crucifixion and then continued:

> Him God raised up the third day, and shewed him openly, not to all the people, but unto witnesses chosen before God, *even to us*, who did eat and drink with him after he rose from the dead. *Acts 10:40–41*

The Appearance to The Disciples

The appearance to Peter and the appearance to the Emmaus men are preludes to the appearance to eleven key disciples "and to them that were with them." *L 24:33* They were exalted by Peter's report, but they were hiding behind locked doors "for fear of the Jews." *J 20:19*

It was evening, probably late evening. According to Mark, they were eating supper. *Mk 16:14* Then it happened. As the Emmaus men made their report, Jesus appeared. *L 24:36*

Luke states that "they were terrified and affrighted, and supposed that they had seen a spirit." *L 24:37*

We have two detailed accounts of what happened:

LUKE	JOHN
And as they thus spake, Jesus himself stood in the midst of them, and saith unto them: "Peace be unto you. . . . Why are ye troubled? And why do thoughts arise in your hearts? Behold my hands and my feet, that it is I myself: handle me, and see, for a spirit hath not flesh and bones, as ye see me have."	Came Jesus and stood in the midst, and saith unto them: "Peace be unto you."
And when he had thus spoken he shewed them his hands and his feet.	And when he had so said, he shewed unto them his hands and his side.
And while they yet believed not for joy, and wondered, he said unto them,	Then were the disciples glad, when they saw the Lord.

LUKE (cont.)   **JOHN** (cont.)

"Have ye here any meat?"

And they gave him
a piece of a broiled fish,
and of an honeycomb.
And he took it,
and *did eat before them.*

And he said unto them,
"These are the words which
I spake unto you,
while I was yet with you,
that all things
must be fulfilled,
which were written
in the Law of Moses,
and in the Prophets
and in the Psalms,
concerning me."

Then opened he   Then said Jesus to them again,
their understanding
that they might understand
the Scriptures,
and said unto them,
"Thus it is written,
and thus it behoved
Christ
to suffer,
and to raise from the dead
the third day.

And that repentance
and remission of sins
should be preached
in his name among all nations,   "Peace be unto you:
beginning at Jerusalem.   as my Father hath sent me,

LUKE (cont.)

And ye are witnesses
of these things.

And, behold, I send the promise
of my Father upon you.
But tarry ye
in the City of Jerusalem,
until ye be endued
with power from on high."
L 24:36–49

JOHN (cont.)

even so send I you."

And when he had said this,
he breathed on them,
and saith unto them,

"Receive ye the Holy Spirit,
whose soever sins ye remit,
they are remitted unto them;
and whose soever sins ye retain,
they are retained."
J 20:19–23

Mark has only a terse summary of this appearance:

Afterward he appeared unto the Eleven as they sat at meat, and up-
braided them with their unbelief and hardness of heart, because they
believed not them which had seen him after he was risen. Mk 16:14

Again we have a manuscript problem, with modern versions
omitting this verse since the better manuscripts omit it. By this
time Jesus had appeared to Peter who, of course, was one of the
Eleven referred to by Mark 16:14.

Despite Jesus' appearance to Peter and the exultation it produced, there were still undercurrents of doubt and skepticism
among the Eleven. Luke, in his fuller account, records Jesus as
saying to them:

Why are ye troubled?

And why do *thoughts* arise in your hearts?

Behold my hands and feet, that it is I myself; handle me, and see:
for a spirit hath not flesh and bones, as ye see me have. L 24:38–39

Their muted doubt, despite Peter's report, makes the evidence of Jesus' appearance to them behind locked doors more impressive. There was not a united will to believe, but an unexpected occurrence.

The details support this analysis. They had been eating. *Mk 16:14* Jesus asked for food, and they offered him a piece of broiled fish. *L 24:41–42* The account continues:

And he took it, and did *eat before them*. *L 24:43*

This detail rebuts their supposition that "they had seen a spirit." *L 24:37* It also rebuts persons who question the factuality of Jesus' appearance that evening.

The facts as stated in the record show that the body of Jesus was in a transitional state away from his human body which had died on the cross and which had left its grave clothes in the tomb:

1. This body entered behind locked doors without having to open them. *J 20:19*
2. This body still had the stigmata of the crucifixion in its hands, feet and sides. *L 24:39–40; J 20:20*
3. This body had flesh and bones. *L 24:39*
4. This body could now be touched. *L 24:39; J 20:20* About twelve hours earlier Jesus had specifically charged Mary Magdalene:

   Touch me not, for I am not yet ascended to my Father: . . . *J 20:17*

5. This body could ingest food, and did ingest a piece of broiled fish. *L 24:43*

Skepticism was not invented in the twentieth century. Despite these objective facts, even Jesus' closest disciples were skeptical about his appearances after his resurrection.

John reports:

But Thomas, one of the Twelve called Didymus [the Twin], was not with them when Jesus came [appeared that night].

The other disciples therefore said unto him, "We have seen the Lord."

But he said unto them, "Except I shall see in his hands the print of the nails, and put my finger into the print of the nails, and thrust my hand into his side, I will not believe." J 20:24–25

The Appearance to the Disciples Eight Days Later

The next appearance of Jesus is recorded only in John's Gospel which tersely states:

> And after eight days again his disciples were within, and Thomas with them; then came Jesus, the doors being shut, and stood in the midst, and said, "Peace be unto you."

> Then saith he to Thomas: "Reach hither thy finger, and behold my hands; and reach further thy hand, and thrust it into my side: and be not faithless, but believing."

> And Thomas answered, and said unto him: "My Lord and My God."

> Jesus saith unto him, "Thomas, because thou hast seen me, thou hast believed; blessed are they which have not seen, and yet have believed." J 20:26–29

The touchability of Jesus' resurrection body is strong evidence that it was not a spirit, an apparition, or a ghost. The disciples themselves originally held that view but had had to abandon it in view of the touchability of Jesus' body, its stigmatic characteristics and its ability to ingest food.

The Appearance to the Eleven in Galilee

Matthew reports:

Then the eleven disciples went away into Galilee, into a mountain where Jesus had appointed them. And when they saw him they worshipped him, but *some doubted. Mt 28:16–17*

As in any group there were differences of opinions. The existence of doubt on the part of some shows that the Eleven were not simply a credulous group. It is likely that it took time for all of them to be convinced by the facts. Thomas was probably not alone.

The Appearance to Seven Disciples
In galilee at the Sea of Tiberias

The Sea of Tiberias was another name for the Sea of Galilee and is about sixty-five miles northeast of Jerusalem where the first appearances of Jesus occurred. Again the appearance is recorded only in John's Gospel.

The persons present were Peter, the Zebedee brothers, Thomas the Twin, Nathanael of Cana and two other disciples who were also probably Galileans. *J 21:2* Peter and the Zebedee brothers were commercial fishermen and partners. *L 5:3, 10*

Here is what happened. Peter said, "I go a fishing." *J 21:3*

The others said, "We also go with thee." *J 21:3*

They immediately put out in what must have been the partnership boat. It was probably late afternoon or early evening, time to go out for a night of fishing. They fished that night but caught nothing. *J 21:3*

At daybreak when they were about one hundred yards off shore, they saw a figure on the shore. *J 21:4, 8* The figure hailed them and the conversation went this way:

FIGURE: Children, have ye any meat? *J 21:5*

DISCIPLES: No. *J 21:5*

FIGURE: Cast the net on the right side of the ship, and ye shall find.
J 21:6

They cast as directed, and the net was so full of fish (fifty-three large fish) that they could not draw the net into the boat. *J 21:6, 11*

John Zebedee then said to Peter, "It is the Lord." *J 21:7*

Peter girt on his outer coat and plunged into water and headed for the shore and the Lord. *J 21:7*

The rest of the men stayed in the boat and dragged the net full of fish to the shore. *J 21:8* When they got ashore they saw a fire which was down to the coals. Fish and bread were laid on the coals. *J 21:9*

The figure said: "Bring the fish which ye have now caught." *J 21:10*

Peter stepped into the boat that was apparently beached with the net at its offshore end. *J 21:11* He then pulled the net up onto the shore and apparently gave the figure some of the fish to broil with the other fish. *J 21:11*

The figure then said: "Come and dine." *J 21:12*

No one said anything to the figure. John states:

> And none of the disciples durst ask him, "Who art thou?" Knowing that it was the Lord. *J 21:12*

John continues:

> Jesus then cometh, and *taketh bread*, and *giveth them, and fish like-wise.*

> This is now the third time Jesus shewed himself to his disciples, after that he was risen from the dead.

> So when *they had dined*, Jesus saith to Simon Peter, . . . *J 21:13–15*

The plain implication is that Jesus ate of both the bread and fish. This is evidence of the factuality of Jesus' resurrection: his resurrected body was seen to ingest food not only one evening in a closed room in Jerusalem, but one morning on an open lake shore in Galilee.

The Other Appearances

Paul's list of the appearances of Jesus states:

And that he was seen of Cephas, *then* of the Twelve.

After that, he was seen of above five hundred brethren at once; of whom the greater part remain until this present [about twenty-five years later, i.e., around A.D. 54], but some are fallen asleep [have died].

After that, he was seen of James; *then* of all the apostles.

And *last of all* he was seen of me also, as one born out of due time. *1 Corinthians 15:5–8*

Paul lists six appearances and is careful to list them in time sequence:

1. Peter (Cephas)
2. The Twelve (really the Eleven)
3. Five hundred brethren
4. James
5. All the apostles
6. Paul.

Paul's list does not precisely match the lists in the Gospels, but Paul wrote in 1 Corinthians what he had "received" when he was converted several years after the resurrection. *1 Corinthians 15:3* It is obvious that Paul did not necessarily, as a convert, *receive* accounts of all the appearances. If Jesus had indeed risen on the third day, and this was indubitably established by evidence of five key appearances, the other appearances were cumulative for purposes of instructing a convert.

This is not to say that other appearances did not occur. The early church did preserve accounts of those other appearances that are listed in the Gospels, which were probably all written after Paul's letter to the Corinthians.

Paul does not state that his list of appearances is exhaustive. He simply lists the key appearances he received as a convert and rushes on to his point:

> Now if Christ be preached that he rose from the dead, how say some among you that there is no resurrection of the dead?
> *I Corinthians 15:12*

There is no need to harmonize the accounts of the appearances as Paul listed them and as the Gospels state them. We simply have different accounts of various appearances; some are included only once and others may be duplicate accounts.

The following tabulation of appearances, in estimated time sequence, may be helpful (see Fig. 4.1 on the next four pages rotating the book so the "Paul" column is on your left).

Figure 4.1

PAUL	MARK	MATTHEW	LUKE-ACTS	JOHN
		To several women, including Mary Magdalene on the way back from the tomb (early Easter morning) Mt 28:1–10		To Mary Magdalene alone at the tomb (mid-morning Easter) J 20:11–18
	To Mary Magdalene (early Easter morning) Mk 16:9–10			
			Two disciples on the road to Emmaus (Easter day) L 24:13–35	

Figure 4.1 (cont.)

Peter		Peter (Easter before evening) L 24:34	
"The Twelve"	"The Eleven" Mk 16:14	"The Eleven" and other disciples (Easter evening) L 24:36–51	"the disciples," Thomas absent (Easter evening) J 20:19–23
			"his disciples," Thomas present (Eight days later) J 20:26–29

Figure 4.1 (cont.)

Paul	Mark	Matthew	Luke-Acts	John
		"The Eleven" on a mountain in Galilee *Mt 28:16*		Peter and six other disciples on the shore of the Sea of Galilee ("the third time Jesus showed himself to his disciples") *J 21:1–14*
			Intermittent appearances for forty days *Acts 1:3–5*	

Figure 4.1 (cont.)

		"The apostles," "They" *Acts 1:2, 6*	
"five hundred brethren at once"	James	"all the apostles"	Paul (several years later) 1 Corinthians *15:5–8*

Except for Paul's sequence, the appearances Easter day and evening and eight days later, and John's statement that the Sea of Galilee appearance was "the third time Jesus showed himself to his disciples," we have no information about the order of the appearances.

The disorderly and fragmentary state of the written evidence as to Jesus' appearances makes it obvious that it was not something contrived by the early church to prove a point.

After some hesitation, the disciples were convinced beyond a reasonable doubt that Jesus had risen from the dead and had repeatedly appeared to them in a bodily form. Luke sums up the view of the early church as to Jesus' appearances writing of "the apostles whom he had chosen to whom also he showed himself alive after his passion [death] *by many infallible proofs*, being seen of them forty days, and speaking of the things pertaining to the Kingdom of God." *Acts 1:2–3*

Accordingly, when a replacement disciple for Judas was chosen, one of his qualifications was "to be a witness with us of his resurrection." *Acts 1:22* The disciples regarded themselves as witnesses bound to tell the truth about the astonishing fact of Jesus' resurrection.

Peter and the apostles were laymen, not ecclesiastics. Peter's speeches recorded in the early chapters of Acts are often described as sermons. They do relate Jesus to the religious traditions of Israel, but the major thrust of the speeches is simply to tell the astonishing facts of Jesus' resurrection which the apostles had witnessed:

This Jesus hath God raised up, whereof *we all are witnesses* . Acts 2:32

And [ye] killed the Prince of life, whom God raised from the dead; whereof *we are witnesses*. Acts 3:15

About fifteen years after Jesus' resurrection, Peter outlined Jesus' life to a Roman centurion. Here is part of what he said:

And we are *witnesses* of all things which he did both in the land of the Jews, and in Jerusalem, whom they slew and hanged on a tree:

314

him God raised up the third day, and shewed him openly; *not to all the people*, but unto *witnesses chosen before God, even to us*, who did eat and drink with him after he rose from the dead. *Acts 10:39–41*

The apostles were chosen witnesses as to the resurrection. Jesus' resurrection was not apparent to all the people, only to selected witnesses. This does not detract from the evidence of those witnesses. For most events there are only a few witnesses since usually only a few people are in a position to see or hear what happened. It was no different with Jesus' resurrection.

The crucial question is the quality of the testimony of such witnesses as do exist. Here the quality of the testimony is very high. Peter and the apostles had not expected the resurrection, did not believe the first reports after it happened, had differences of opinion about the resurrection after several of Jesus' appearances, and on several occasions ate and drank with the resurrected Jesus: once in a locked room in Jerusalem and once on a lake shore in Galilee. This so impressed Peter that he mentions it when he summarized to the Roman officer saying the apostles "did eat and drink with him after he arose from the dead." *Acts 10:41*

In addition, we have some accounts of what Jesus said on certain of those appearances. These statements are detailed and specific. The statements on the shore of the Sea of Galilee continued after Jesus and seven disciples had dined, as follows:

Jesus: Simon, son of Jonas, lovest thou me more than these?
Simon (Peter): Yea, Lord, thou knowest that I love thee.
Jesus: Feed my lambs . . . Simon, son of Jonas, lovest thou me?
Peter: Yea, Lord, thou knowest that I love thee.
Jesus: Feed my sheep . . . Simon, son of Jonas, lovest thou me?
Peter: Lord, thou knowest all things; thou knowest that I love thee.
Jesus: Feed my sheep . . . Verily, verily, I say unto thee, when thou wast young, thou girdedst thyself, and walked whither thou wouldest; but when thou shalt be old, thou shalt stretch forth thy hands, and another shall gird thee, and carry thee whither thou wouldest not . . . Follow me.

Peter: [seeing John Zebedee] Lord, and what shall this man do?
Jesus: If I will that he tarry till I come, what is that to thee? . . .Follow
thou me. *J 21:15–22*

We have a realistic and credible interchange between Jesus and
Peter not simply some awesome ex cathedra pronouncement by
Jesus.

Just before Jesus' ascension, we have a report of another interchange. This time the interchange was with a group of the apostles:

Group: Lord, wilt thou at this time restore again the Kingdom of
Israel?
Jesus: It is not for you to know the times or the seasons, which the
Father hath put in his own power. But ye shall receive power,
after that the Holy Spirit is come upon you: and ye shall be
witnesses unto me both in Jerusalem, and in all Judea, and in
Samaria, and unto the uttermost part of the earth. *Acts 1:6–8*

This was an unanticipated world-wide missionary answer to some
Jews who simply wanted to know when the Kingdom of Israel would
be restored. The same unanticipated world-wide missionary emphasis
is found in two other of Jesus' post-resurrection statements:

MARK	LUKE
Go ye into all the world and preach the gospel to every creature.	These are my words which I spake unto you while I was yet with you, that all things must be fulfilled,
He that believeth and is baptized shall be saved; but he that believeth not shall be damned.	which were written in the Law of Moses, and in the Prophets, and in the Psalms, concerning me . . .
And these signs shall follow them that believe: in my name	Thus it is written, and thus it behoved Christ to suffer, and to rise from the dead

Mark (cont.)	Luke (cont.)
shall they cast out devils;	the third day:
they shall speak	and that repentance and
with new tongues;	remission of sins should be
they shall take up serpents;	*preached in his name*
and if they drink	*among all nations,*
any deadly thing,	*beginning at Jerusalem.*
it shall not hurt them;	
they shall lay hands on the sick,	And ye are witnesses
and they shall recover.	of these things.
Mk 16:15–18	L 24:44–48

Not only did Jesus make unanticipated missionary statements in his post-resurrection appearances but he also gave his disciples some very clear and exact instructions what to do immediately after his resurrection. We have what are apparently parallel accounts of what Jesus said on his Easter evening appearance to the disciples: *Luke 24:49 and Acts 1:4–5.*

The last part of Luke and the first part of Acts overlap. It is a common opinion of New Testament scholars that Luke and Acts are a single unit: Luke-Acts, having a single author, Luke.

In the Acts portion, Luke writes of one occasion of Jesus "being assembled together with them" (the apostles) apparently eating with them (the translations vary). *Acts 1:4–5* This may be the Easter evening appearance he describes more fully in Luke, mentioning that Jesus ate some broiled fish in their presence. Here are the two accounts:

Luke	Acts
And, behold, I	Commanded them
send the promise of	
my Father	
upon you:	that they
but tarry ye	should not depart
in the city of Jerusalem	from Jerusalem,
until	but wait for
	the promise of

LUKE (cont.)

ACTS (cont.)
the Father, which,
ye have heard of me.

For John truly
baptized with water; but
ye   ye
be endued   shall be baptized
with power from on high.   with the Holy Spirit
L 24:49   not many days hence.
                                  Acts 1:4–5

Most of the disciples were Galileans, inhabitants of a partly Gentile northern province several days journey distance from Jerusalem, who like other hinterland Jews, had come up to Jerusalem, the metropolis, for the great yearly Passover Festival.

Jesus had been crucified, and the Festival was over. The disciples were not wealthy, but common folk, and they all, like Peter and the Zebedee brothers, who were commercial fishermen, had their livings to make back in Galilee. The natural and obvious thing for the disciples to do would have been to go home to Galilee immediately and try to pick up their lives. The crucifixion had been a disaster, and they were in danger, meeting behind locked doors at night. J 20:19, 25

Despite all this, they obeyed Jesus' post-resurrection instruction,

Tarry ye in the City of Jerusalem until ye be endued with power from on high. L 24:49 (Acts 1:4)

They stayed at least eight days. They were still in Jerusalem when "after eight days again" the disciples, including Thomas, were in the same room, "the doors being shut," when Jesus appeared to Thomas. J 20:26

Ultimately, the disciples did return to Galilee, at least for awhile, since we have records of two post-resurrection appearances by Jesus there: the appearance to seven disciples on the shore of the Sea of

Galilee and the appearance to the Eleven on a mountain in Galilee. *J 21:1–14; Mt 28:16–20*

We do not know the location of the appearances to "above five hundred brethren at once," James, and "all the apostles." *1 Corinthians 15:6–7* Except for the appearance to Paul several years later as to "one born out of due time," we do know that Jesus' final appearance occurred near Jerusalem forty days after his passion. *Acts 1:3; 1 Corinthians 15:8*

Acts sums up the resurrection appearances of Jesus by stating that "he shewed himself alive after his passion by many infallible proofs, being seen of them [the apostles] forty days, and speaking of the things pertaining to the Kingdom of God." *Acts 1:3*

THE ASCENSION OF JESUS

The final appearance of Jesus to his disciples has wrongly come to be called his Ascension. This is wrong because, as will be demonstrated, this was not what Jesus himself meant when he referred to his Ascension.

This final appearance occurred at Bethany, a village about two miles east of Jerusalem on the east slopes of the Mount of Olives, forty days after Jesus' passion. *L 24:50; Acts 1:3, 12*

This appearance is described in both Luke and Acts:

LUKE	ACTS
And he led them	And when he had
out as far as Bethany,	spoken these things,
and he lifted up his hands,	
and blessed them.	
And it came to pass,	while they beheld,
while	
he blessed them,	
he was parted from them,	he was taken up;
and carried up	and a cloud received him
into heaven.	out of their sight.
	And while they looked
	steadfastly
	toward heaven, as he went up,
	behold, two men
	stood by them
	in white apparel,
	which also said,
	"Ye men of Galilee,
	why stand ye
	gazing up into heaven?
	This same Jesus, which is
	taken up from you into heaven,
	shall so come
	in like manner as ye have seen
	him go into heaven."

LUKE (cont.)

And they worshipped him,
and returned
to Jerusalem
with great joy,

and were continually in
the Temple, praising and
blessing God. Amen.
L 24:50–53

ACTS (cont.)

Then returned they
unto Jerusalem
from the mount called Olivet,
which is from Jerusalem
a Sabbath day's journey.

And when they were
come in, they
went up into an upper room,
where abode both Peter,
and James, and
John, and Andrew, Phillip
and Thomas,
Bartholomew, and Matthew,
James the son of Alphaeus,
and Simon Zelotes,
and Judas, the brother of James.

These all continued
with one accord
in prayer and supplication,
with the women,
and Mary, the mother of Jesus,
and with his brethren."
Acts 1:9–14

Mark does not consider important the detail of Jesus' final appearance to his disciples. Instead he describes the ascension in terms much like Jesus himself used:

So then after the Lord had spoken unto them, he was received up into heaven, and sat on the right hand of God. *Mk 16:19*

It will no doubt be objected that this is childish anthropomorphism: God does not have a hand like a man, so how could he have a right hand?

"The right hand of God" is, of course, a figure of speech which conveys the idea of utmost closeness and great authority. This is how Jesus himself used such words. When he was interrogated by the Jewish authorities shortly before his crucifixion, the questioning went like this:

MARK	MATTHEW	LUKE
Q.	I adjure thee by the living God, that thou tell us whether	
Art thou the Christ, the Son of the Blessed?	thou be the Christ, the Son of God.	Art thou the Christ?
A. I am.	Thou hast said: nevertheless I say unto you,	If I tell you, ye will not believe; and if I also ask you, ye will not answer me, nor let me go.
And ye shall see the Son of man *sitting on* *the right hand* *of power,* and coming in the clouds of heaven. *Mk 14:61–62*	hereafter shall ye see the Son of man *sitting on* *the right hand* *of power* and coming in the clouds of heaven. *Mt 26:63–64*	Hereafter shall the Son of man *sit on* *the right hand* *of the power of God.* *L 22:67–70*

The "right hand of God" meant, for Jesus, "the right hand of the power of God" or literally "on the right hand of the Power."

322

Jesus considered that his place near "the Power" (Almighty God) was simply a restoration to his former place of honor with God.
For Jesus said:

> I have glorified thee on earth: I have finished the work which thou gavest me to do.

> And now, O Father, glorify thou me with thine own self with the glory which I had with thee *before the world was.* J 17:4–5

In technical theological terms Jesus was saying:

1. He was pre-existent with God "before the world was."
2. He had finished the work on earth that God had given him to do.
3. He asked to be restored to his former glory in the presence of God.

Jesus came down from his pre-existence status in heaven to do God's work and will:

> For I came down from heaven, not to do mine own will, but the will of him that sent me. J 6:38

Early in his ministry Jesus told Nicodemus, a prominent Pharisee:

> Art thou a master of Israel, and knowest not these things?

> Verily, verily, I say unto thee, we speak that we *do know*, and testify that *we have seen*; and ye receive not our witness.

> If I have told you earthly things, and ye believe not, how shall ye believe, if I tell you of heavenly things?

> And no man hath *ascended up to heaven, but he that came down from heaven*, even the Son of Man *which is in heaven*. And as Moses lifted

up the serpent in the wilderness, even so must the Son of Man be *lifted up*: that whosoever believeth in him should not perish, but have eternal life." *J 8:10–15*

Some manuscripts omit the phrase translated "which is in heaven." If they are correct, it makes Jesus' statement simpler and easier to understand. Jesus then simply said in substance, "No one has ascended up to heaven, except the Son of man who came down from heaven."

A dialogue of Jesus with some hostile Jews ended this way:

Jews: Thou art not yet fifty years old, and thou hast seen Abraham?
Jesus: Verily, verily, I say unto you, before Abraham was, I AM.
J 8:57–58

By his ascension Jesus meant simply his return to heaven whence he came where he pre-existed as "I AM." *J 8:58* Jesus anticipated that even his own disciples would not be able to understand the fact of his ascension back to heaven.

This is shown by the following incident. While teaching in the synagogue at Capernaum, Jesus had asserted:

Verily, verily I say unto you, except ye eat the flesh of the Son of man, and drink his blood, ye have no life in you. *J 6:53*

Many of Jesus' disciples murmured that, "This is an hard saying: who can hear it?" *J 6:60*

When Jesus heard their murmurings he said:

Doth this offend you?
What and if ye shall see the Son of man ascend up where he was before?" *J 6:61–62*

Jesus' ascension up to heaven happened after Jesus' resurrection, although not immediately thereafter. Jesus told Mary Magdalene on the first Easter morning:

Touch me not, for *I am not yet ascended to my Father*; but go to my brethren, and say unto them, *I ascend* unto my Father, and your Father; and to my God, and your God. *J 20:17*

We know that by eight days later the resurrected Jesus specifically directed Thomas to touch his hands and side. *J 20:26–27* Contrasting Jesus' direction to Thomas with Jesus' caution to Mary Magdalene, it seems clear that Jesus' ascension, in the sense of his receipt of his former power and glory, had occurred in that eight day interval.

To Jesus his ascension was this reinstatement of his former power and glory, not his last post-resurrection appearance to his disciples outside Jerusalem at Bethany forty days after his resurrection.

Luke-Acts does not speak of this final appearance as Jesus' ascension. It simply states:

Luke	Acts
He was parted from them,	Which is taken up
and carried up	from you
into heaven.	into heaven.
L 24:51	*Acts 1:11*

Acts repeatedly uses the phrase "was taken up." *Acts 1:2, 9, 22* This is a convenient divider, marking the end of Jesus' ministry:

The former treatise [Book of Luke] have I made, O Theophilus, of all that Jesus began both to do and teach, *until* the day in which he was taken up, . . ." *Acts 1:1*

Beginning from the baptism of John, *unto* the same day that he was taken up from us, . . ." *Acts 1:22*

Acts does state:

And when he had spoken these things, while they beheld, he was taken up; and a cloud received him out of their sight. *Acts 1:9*

The conventional artistic representation showing Jesus ascending off the Mount of Olives into the sky as the disciples watch misstates the essence of what happened. This was simply the last time the disciples saw Jesus after his resurrection. They remembered the occasion vividly. Jesus did disappear from their sight into a cloud just as he had previously disappeared from the locked doors of the disciples' upstairs common room. *Acts 1:9; J 20:29*

The point is not the mechanics of his disappearance from his disciples' sight or the mechanics of his ultimate return "in like manner." *Acts 1:11* Once Jesus had ascended to his Father, his body was different. *L 24:36; J 20:19, 26*

The ascension in the sense Jesus used the term had occurred about forty days before. Jesus had already been reinstated in his pre-existent power and glory. That is why some time previously he had been able to tell the Eleven on the mountain in Galilee:

All power is given unto me in heaven and in earth. *Mt 28:18*

The earliest preaching of the earliest church was the resurrection of Jesus. Jesus' last appearance to his disciples after his resurrection is wrongly called his ascension. His true ascension was his return to the right hand of God.

Acts quotes Peter as preaching:

This Jesus hath God raised up, whereof we all are witnesses. Therefore being by the right hand of God exalted, . . . *Acts 2:32–33*

Ephesians states that "the God of our Lord Jesus Christ, the Father of glory" as "according to the working of his mighty power" raised up Jesus from the dead and "set him at his own right hand in the heavenly places far above all principality, and power, and might, and dominion, and every name that is named, not only in this world but also in that which is to come." *Ephesians 1:17, 19–21*

CHAPTER 5

JESUS' MOVEMENT AND ITS ORGANIZATION

JESUS AND THE JEWISH RELIGIOUS ORGANIZATION

People often have the impression that Jesus was a wandering teacher at odds with Israel's religious system. The truth is that he regularly attended the synagogues and taught and preached in them.

Luke reports that on one Sabbath Jesus read the lesson in the Nazareth synagogue:

> And he came to Nazareth, where he had been brought up; and, *as his custom was*, he went into the synagogue on the Sabbath day, and stood up for to read. And there was delivered unto them the book of the prophet Isaiah. *L 4:16–17*

Jesus then read to the congregation from Isaiah. *L 4:18–20* Luke introduces this episode by stating that Jesus had returned to Galilee.

> And there went out a fame of him through all the region round about. And he taught in their synagogues, being glorified of all. *L 4:14–15*

In short, Jesus was enthusiastically received in the synagogues in Galilee. Mark's Gospel also states that Jesus ministered in the synagogues in Galilee:

And he preached in their synagogues throughout all Galilee, and cast out devils. *Mk 1:39*

The King James Version of Luke at chapter 4:44 states that "he preached in the synagogues of Galilee." Upon the basis of the manuscript evidence, modern versions change this to the synagogues of *Judea*. This shows that Jesus' synagogue ministry was not confined to Galilee but also included Judea.

Jesus not only preached in the synagogues but he taught in them:

And he was *teaching in one of the synagogues* on the Sabbath. *L 13:10*

And Jesus went about all Galilee, *teaching in their synagogues*, and preaching the gospel of the Kingdom, and healing all manner of sickness and all manner of disease among the people. *Mt 4:23*

And Jesus went about all the cities and villages, *teaching in their synagogues*, and preaching the gospel of the Kingdom, and healing every sickness and every disease among the people. *Mt 9:35*

And he went out from thence, and came into his own country; and his disciples followed him. And when *the Sabbath day was come, he began to teach in the synagogue*; and many hearing him were astonished, saying, "From whence hath this man these things? And what wisdom is this which is given unto him, that even such mighty works are wrought by his hands?" *Mk 6:1–2 (Mt 13:54)*

And they went into Capernaum, and straightway *on the Sabbath day he entered into the synagogue, and taught*. And they were astonished at his doctrine: for he taught them as one that had authority, and not as the scribes." *Mk 1:21–22 (L 4:31–32)*

We have a sample of what Jesus taught in the synagogues. Jesus' teaching had raised fierce disputes over this question:

How can this man give us his flesh to eat? *J 6:52*

While teaching in the synagogue at Capernaum Jesus gave this answer:

Verily, verily, I say unto you, except ye eat the flesh of the Son of man, and drink his blood, ye have no life in you. Whoso eateth my flesh, and drinketh my blood hath eternal life; and I will raise him up at the last day. For my flesh is meat indeed; and my blood is drink indeed.

He that eateth my flesh and drinketh my blood, dwelleth in me, and I in him. As the living Father hath sent me, and I live by the Father: so he that eateth me, even he shall live by me.

This is that bread which came down from heaven, not as your fathers did eat manna, and are dead; he that eateth of this bread shall live for ever. *J 6:53–58*

John adds:

These things said he in the synagogue, as he taught in Capernaum. *J 6:59*

The first three Gospels all report that on one Sabbath Jesus healed a man with a withered hand *in a synagogue. Mk 3:1–5; Mt 12:9–14; L 6:6–11* Luke reports that Jesus healed a crippled woman *in a synagogue. L 13:10–13* Mark and Luke report that Jesus healed a man of an evil spirit *in a synagogue. Mk 1:23–27; L 4:33–36* Jesus also healed the blind and the lame *in the Temple* in Jerusalem. *Mt 21:14* Jesus associated with synagogue people:

And, behold, there came a man named Jairus, and he was *a ruler of the synagogue*; and he fell down at Jesus' feet, and besought him that he would come into his house. *L 8:41*

The synagogue ruler wanted Jesus to heal his dying daughter, and Jesus did. *L 8:49–56*

Later on, Jesus did come into direct conflict with the administrators of Israel's national religious system. They had him arrested. The details are stated in the chapter entitled "The Arrest And Proceedings Against Jesus" (pp. 218–228). Shortly after his arrest, the high priest "asked Jesus of his disciples and his doctrine." *J 18:19* Jesus answered him:

> I spake openly to the world; *I ever taught in the synagogue, and in the Temple*, whither the Jews always resort; and in secret have I said nothing. Why askest thou me? Ask them which heard me, what I have said unto them: behold, they know what I said. *J 18:20–21*

The clear implication is that in both synagogue and the Temple the attenders had listened to Jesus with care. Passages have previously been quoted that the Nazareth synagogue congregation had not simply listened with care but with wonder and astonishment. *Mk 6:2; Mt 13:54; L 4:22*

It was the same when he taught in the Temple:

> And he *taught daily in the Temple*. But the chief priests and the scribes and the chief of the people sought to destroy him, and could not find what they might do: for all the people *were very attentive to hear him. L 19:47*

> And in the day time he was teaching in the Temple; and at night he went out and abode in the mount that is called the Mount of Olives. And all the people came *early in the morning to him in the Temple, for to hear him. L 21:37–38*

This was not an occasional thing. The first three gospels all state that when Jesus was arrested at Gethsemane he said he had been in the Temple daily:

> I was daily with you in the Temple teaching . . ." *Mk 14:49; Mt 26:55; L 22:53*

Jesus had a great respect for the Temple. This is shown by his cleansing of the Temple. All of the first three gospels have accounts of this, but Mark's account is the fullest:

> And they come to Jerusalem: and Jesus went into the Temple, and began to cast out them that sold and bought in the Temple, and overthrew the tables of the moneychangers, and the seats of them that sold doves, and would not suffer that nay man should carry any vessel [take a short-cut] through the Temple. And he taught, saying unto them, "Is it not written, my house shall be called of all nations the house of prayer? But ye have made it a den of thieves."
> *Mk 11:15–17 (Mt 21:12–13; L 19:45–48)*

Earlier in his ministry, on another occasion, Jesus had cleansed the Temple, but its bazaar-like atmosphere had returned. *J 2:13–22* The first cleansing had occurred when Jesus went up to Jerusalem for the great religious Feast of the Passover. In the Temple he found oxen-sellers, sheep-sellers, dove-sellers, and money-changers doing business there. *J 2:14* It was all very convenient: animals and doves for the required sacrifices and the proper non-pagan coins to pay the Temple tax.

John states:

> And when he had made a scourge of small cords, he drove them all out of the Temple, and the sheep, and the oxen, and poured out the changers' money, and overthrew the tables, and said unto them that sold doves. "Take these things hence; make not my Father's house an house of merchandise." *J 2:15–16*

To Jesus, the Temple was not just a national shrine; it was his Father's House. It was not to be a big bazaar but the House of Prayer.

Up until the very end of his ministry, Jesus taught in the Temple just as he frequented and taught and healed in synagogues. *Mk 14:49; Mt 26:55; L 22:53* Jesus not only taught in the Temple and cleansed it, but he also paid the annual Temple tax. *Mt 17:24–25*

Up until the very end of his ministry, Jesus worked within the framework of the existing Jewish religious organization, whether in synagogues or in the Temple. After Jesus' resurrection, his disciples at first continued to attend the Temple all day, daily. *L 24:53; Acts 2:46*

JESUS AND THE PUBLICANS

One of Jesus' twelve disciples was "Matthew the publican." *Mt 10:3 (Mk 3:18; L 6:15)* He was recruited at Capernaum in Galilee when Jesus "saw a man, named Matthew, sitting at the receipt of custom." *Mt 9:9* The parallel accounts of his recruitment in Mark and Luke, for reasons unknown, name Matthew as "Levi" but agree he was "sitting at the receipt of custom." *Mk 2:14; L 5:27*

The "custom" involved was probably an internal custom duty collected at various points as a convenient way to collect taxes rather than the custom duties collected at a country's frontier in the usual modern manner. These collectors of taxes should not be confused with modern bureaucratic tax officials. They were different. They were either contractors or employees of contractors with the Roman occupation authorities who had purchased the right to collect Roman taxes and were entitled to keep any excess collected over what they had agreed to pay to the Roman authorities.

The opportunities for overreaching the conquered Jewish population were obvious. Publicans were despised for this reason and also because they were collaborators with the Roman (heathen) occupation. Once while condemning certain conduct by disciples, Jesus said to some disciples, "Let him be unto thee as a heathen man and a publican." *Mt 18:17*

Despite this implicit condemnation of publicans as being the same as heathens, Jesus had a reputation, according to his enemies, of being "a friend of publicans and sinners." *Mt 11:19; L 7:34* A more accurate statement is that Jesus regarded publicans as exemplifying garden-variety worldliness:

> For if ye love them which love you, what reward have ye? Do not even *the publicans* the same? And if ye salute your brethren only, what do ye more than others? Do not even *the publicans* so? *Mt 5:46–47*

But Jesus preferred these worldly wealthy men to proud religious righteous men. Jesus told this story to persons who "trusted in themselves that they were righteous, and despised others":

> Two men went up into the Temple to pray: the one a Pharisee, and the other a publican.
>
> The Pharisee stood and prayed thus with himself, "God, I thank thee, that I am not as other men are, extortioners, unjust, adulterers, or even as this publican. I fast twice in the week, I give tithes of all that I possess."
>
> And the publican, standing afar off, would not lift up so much as his eyes unto heaven, but smote upon his breast, saying, "God, be merciful to me a sinner."
>
> I tell you, this man went down to his house justified rather than the other: for every one that exalteth himself shall be abased; and he that humbleth himself shall be exalted. *L 18:9–14*

On another occasion Jesus was at the Temple himself, and he told the Jewish religious authorities ("the chief priests and the elders of the people" *Mt 21:23*):

> Verily I say unto you, that the publicans and the harlots go into the Kingdom of God before you. *Mt 21:31*

Despite their obvious flaws, some publicans had accepted the call of John the Baptist to repent and to be baptized, saying to John: "Master, what shall we do?" *L 3:12 (Mt 21:32)* John's reply was: "Exact no more than that which is appointed you." *L 3:13*

Despite the fact that some publicans had repented, the general belief was that they were "sinners." Luke wrote:

> Then drew near unto him [Jesus] all the publicans and sinners for to hear him. And the Pharisees and scribes murmured, saying, "This man receiveth sinners, and eateth with them." *L 15:1–2*

Now it was true that Jesus did eat with publicans. Just after he had recruited Matthew as a disciple, he, along with his disciples, went to eat at Matthew's house. *Mk 2:15* In fact, Matthew made "a great feast" for him. *L 5:29* Here is how the gospels describe the other guests:

MARK	MATTHEW	LUKE
		. . . a great company
. . . many publicans	. . . many publicans	of publicans
and sinners.	and sinners.	and of others.
Mk 2:15	*Mt 9:10*	*L 5:29*

For the scribes and Pharisees, being a publican was synonymous with being a sinner, and they asked Jesus' disciples:

MARK	MATTHEW	LUKE
How is it that	Why	Why do
he eateth	eateth	ye eat
and drinketh	your Master	and drink
with publicans	with publicans	with publicans
and sinners?	and sinners?	and sinners?
Mk 2:16	*Mt 9:11*	*L 5:30*

Jesus heard of their question, and his reply has reverberated down the centuries since:

MARK	MATTHEW	LUKE
They that	They that	They that
are whole	be whole	are whole
have no need	need not	need not
of the physician,	a physician,	a physician;
but they that	but they that	but they that
are sick,	are sick . . .	are sick.
I came not	For I am not come	I came not
to call the righteous,	to call	to call
but sinners	the righteous,	the righteous,
to repentance.	but sinners	but sinners
Mk 2:17	to repentance.	to repentance.
	Mt 9:12–13	*L 5:31–32*

335

Towards the end of Jesus' ministry as he passed through Jericho on his way to Jerusalem, Jesus was still dining with publicans. *L 19:1–10* Luke writes:

> And, behold, there was a man named Zacchaeus, which was the chief among the publicans, and he was rich. And he sought to see Jesus who he was, and could not for the press, because he was little of stature. And he ran before, and climbed up into a sycamore tree to see him: for he was to pass that way.
>
> And when Jesus came to the place, he looked up, and saw him, and said unto him, "Zacchaeus, make haste, and come down, for today I must abide at thy house."
>
> And he made haste, and came down, and received him joyfully. And when they saw it, they all murmured, saying, that "He was gone to be guest with a man that is a sinner."
>
> And Zacchaeus stood, and said unto the Lord: "Behold, Lord, the half of my goods I give to the poor; and if I have taken any thing from any man by false accusation, I restore him fourfold."
>
> And Jesus said unto him, "This day is salvation come to this house, forsomuch as he also is a son of Abraham. For the Son of man is come to seek and to save that which was lost." *L 19:2–10*

A GALILEAN MOVEMENT

Humanly speaking Jesus was not only a Jew, he was a Galilean Jew, a resident of the most northerly area of Palestine. He grew up in Nazareth, a town in Galilee. *L 2:39–52; Mt 2:23* He came "from Nazareth of Galilee" to be baptized by John the Baptist. *Mk 1:9; Mt 3:13*

Jesus returned to Galilee to preach in the synagogues "throughout all Galilee." *Mk 1:39 (Mt 4:23; L 4:44)* Later on, he made his headquarters at Capernaum in Galilee. *Mt 4:13; 9:1* When Jesus returned home to Galilee after his first Judean ministry, he was enthusiastically received by his fellow Galileans since they had been at Jerusalem for the great national Passover festival (feast) and "had seen all the things he did at Jerusalem at the feast." *J 4:45* Since he had made good in the capital city, he was no longer a prophet without honor "in his own country." *J 4:44*

Geographically speaking, Galilee was divided into two parts: Upper Galilee (northern Galilee); Lower Galilee (southern Galilee). Jesus' activities were centered in Lower Galilee.

Josephus, the first century Jewish historian, described Upper and Lower Galilee as follows:

> 2. These two Galilees, of so great largeness, and encompassed with so many nations of foreigners have been always able to make a strong resistance on all occasions of war; for the Galileans are inured to war from their infancy, and have been always very numerous; nor hath the country ever been destitute of men of courage, or wanted a numerous set of them; for their soil is universally rich and fruitful, and full of plantations of trees of all sorts, insomuch that it invites the most slothful to take pains in its cultivation, by its fruitfulness; accordingly, it is all cultivated by its inhabitants, and no part of it lies idle. Moreover, the cities lie here very thick, and the very many villages there are here, are everywhere so full of people, by the richness of their soil, that the very least of them contain about fifteen thousand inhabitants." *Wars of the Jews, Book III, Ch. III, Sec. 2*

To the occupying Romans, Galilee was the Tetrarchy of Galilee; to the strict Jews, it was "Galilee of the Gentiles" because of the large numbers of non-Jews living there. This was true even in the olden times of Isaiah. *Mt 4:15 (Isaiah 9:1; around 700* B.C.)

To the Jews, strange movements had arisen in Galilee before. When the Sanhedrin was contemplating action against the apostles soon after Pentecost, one learned Jew argued that Judas of Galilee in the days of the taxing had drawn away "much people after him: he also perished; and all, even as many as obeyed him were dispersed." *Acts 5:37* The revolt was put down, and Judas' two sons were crucified. *Josephus, Antiquities, Book XX, Ch. V, Sec. 2* The revolt was caused by a Roman tax census in A.D. 6. Jesus would then have been about twelve years old, having been born in about 6 B.C.

Josephus writes of the revolt as follows:

> Under his [Coponius'] administration it was that a certain Galilean, whose name was Judas prevailed with his countrymen to revolt; and said they were cowards if they would endure to pay a tax to the Romans, and would, after God, submit to mortal men as their lords. This man was a teacher of a peculiar sect of his own, and was not at all like the rest of those their leaders. *Wars of the Jews, Book II, Ch. VIII, Sec. 1*

Josephus describes this sect as follows:

> These men agree in all other things with the Pharisaic notions; but they have an inviolable attachment to liberty; and they say that God is to be their only Ruler and Lord. They also do not value dying any kinds of death, nor indeed do they heed the deaths of their relations and friends, nor can any such fear make them call any man Lord; . . ." *Antiquities, Book XVIII, Ch. I, Sec. 6*

This sect was the origin of the later Jewish resistance group, the Zealots. One of Jesus' twelve disciples was, according to Luke, "Simon called Zelotes." *L 6:15; Acts 1:13* In short, one of Jesus' Twelve was a Zealot.

The very fact that Jesus did come from Galilee and was supported by Galileans seemed proof to the Jews that Jesus was not the expected Christ:

But some said, 'Shall Christ come out of Galilee? *J 7:41*

When Nicodemus argued for a hearing for Jesus ("Doth our law judge any man before it hear him, and know what he doeth?"), the Pharisees replied:

Art thou also of Galilee? Search and look: for out of Galilee ariseth no prophet. *J 7:51–52*

In the last days of Jesus, anyone speaking with a Galilean accent was suspected of being one of Jesus' followers. Just after Jesus' arrest, the bystanders outside the high priest's palace challenged Peter:

MARK	MATTHEW
Surely thou art one of them: for thou art a Galilean, and thy speech agreeth thereto. *Mk 14:70*	Surely thou also art one of them: for thy speech betrayeth thee. *Mt 26:73*

Luke reports what is perhaps a distinct incident at about the same time and place. Someone at the palace said of Peter:

Of a truth this fellow also was with him: for he is a Galilean. *L 22:59*

Not only did the maids in the high priest's palace consider Peter a follower of Jesus since Peter spoke the Galilean dialect but one serving maid also referred to Jesus as "Jesus of Galilee":

Thou also wast with Jesus of Galilee. *Mt 26:69*

Shortly thereafter Jesus was tried before Pontius Pilate. After Pilate acquitted Jesus, the multitude remonstrated and said: "He stirreth up the people, teaching throughout all Jewry, beginning from Galilee to this place." *L 23:5*

Luke continues:

When Pilate heard of Galilee, he asked whether the man was a Galilean. And as soon as he knew that he belonged unto Herod's jurisdiction, he sent him to Herod, who himself also was at Jerusalem at that time.

And when Herod saw Jesus, he was exceeding glad: for he was desirous to see him of a long season, because he had heard many things of him; and he hoped to have seen some miracle done by him. Then he questioned with him in many words; but he answered him nothing.

And the chief priests and scribes stood and vehemently accused him. And Herod with his men of war set him at nought, and mocked him, and arrayed him in a gorgeous robe, and sent him again to Pilate. *L 23:6–11*

This Herod was Herod Antipas, and he was Tetrarch of Galilee from 4 B.C. to A.D. 39. *L 3:1* Pontius Pilate was governor (procurator) of Judea (the southern part of Palestine). We know that he was not adverse to slaughtering Galileans in Judea, even though Galilee was out of his jurisdiction. *L 13:1*

Luke records that "the women that followed him from Galilee" stood and watched the crucifixion of Jesus and that these women "which came with him from Galilee" followed Jesus' body to the grave. *L 23:49, 55* Matthew and Mark agree that the women from Galilee had followed Jesus to Jerusalem and were present but "afar" from the crucifixion. *Mk 15:40–41; Mt 27:55*

When some of the women came to Jesus' tomb on the first Easter, an angel told them that Jesus was risen and that they should go and tell his disciples that "he goeth before you into Galilee." *Mk 16:7; Mt 28:7* Some time before, Jesus had told his disciples that after he was risen, that "I will go before you into Galilee." *Mk 14:28; Mt 26:32*

When Peter explained Christianity to Cornelius, a Roman centurion, he stated that it "began from Galilee, after the baptism which John preached." *Acts 10:37* When Paul summarized the gospel to a synagogue congregation in Asia Minor, he stated that the witnesses of the resurrection were Galileans:

But God raised him from the dead. And he was seen many days of them which came up with him from Galilee to Jerusalem, who are his witnesses unto the people. *Acts 13:30–31*

Paul was no Galilean, but the disciples were. When the disciples saw Jesus for the last time after his resurrection, the angels said to them as they lost sight of him:

Ye men of Galilee, why stand ye gazing up into heaven? *Acts 1:11*

Not more than seven weeks later, at the time of the Jewish feast of Pentecost, the disciples received the gift of tongues, and the Jews from every nation who were in Jerusalem for the feast heard this speaking in tongues, and were amazed and said:

Behold, are not all these which speak Galileans? And how hear we every man in our own tongue, wherein we were born? *Acts 2:6–8*

JESUS' RECRUITMENT OF HIS DISCIPLES

Some time during his first Galilean ministry, Jesus began to recruit a more or less permanent group of disciples. He had already invited Andrew, Peter, Philip, and Nathanael to follow him. *J 1:38–51*

This did not mean that they immediately abandoned their occupations to spend full time with Jesus as he taught in the synagogues of Galilee and pursued his ministry of preaching and healing. He was apparently alone when he visited his hometown synagogue at Nazareth. *L 4:16–31*

As Jesus walked near the Sea of Galilee, he saw Peter and Andrew casting a net into the sea as they followed their trade as fishermen. He then called these two men, whom he already knew, to follow him and to leave their trade as fishermen and "become fishers of men." *Mk 1:16–20; Mt 4:18–19*

A little further along the shore, he saw two other fishermen, the Zebedee brothers, James and John. They were mending their nets. And again, he called these two men to leave their trade. *Mk 1:19–20; Mt 4:21–22*

It seems likely that Jesus already knew James and John, as he did Peter and Andrew, and that he had come to the shore where he knew that he would find the four men because he had decided that the time had come for them to leave their trade and stay with him. In any case, they all went together to Capernaum where Peter and Andrew then had a house, although they were originally from Bethsaida. *Mk 1:21, 29; J 1:44*

Matthew is not as precise as Mark in his setting of Jesus' recruitment of James, John, Andrew, and Peter. The two accounts are as follows:

MARK	MATTHEW
Now as he walked	And Jesus, walking
by the Sea of Galilee,	by the Sea of Galilee,
he saw	saw two brethren,
Simon and Andrew	Simon called Peter, and Andrew
his brother	his brother,

MARK (cont.)
casting a net
into the sea:
for they were fishers.

And Jesus said
unto them,
"Come ye after me, and
I will make you to become
fishers of men."

And straightway they
forsook their nets,
and followed him.
And when he had gone
a little farther thence, he saw
James,
the son of Zebedee,
and John his brother,
who also were in the ship

mending their nets.

And straightway
he called them,
and they left
their father Zebedee in the ship
with the hired servants,
and went after him.
Mk 1:16–20

MATTHEW (cont.)
casting a net
into the sea:
for they were fishers.

And he saith
unto them,
"Follow me, and
I will make you
fishers of men."

And they straightway
left their nets,
and followed him.
And going on
from thence, he saw
other two brethren, James,
the son of Zebedee,
and John his brother,
in a ship with Zebedee
their father,
mending their nets;

and
he called them.
And they immediately left
the ship and their father

and followed him.
Mt 4:18–22

The four fishermen apparently stayed with Jesus at least until the next Sabbath when they all went to the synagogue, and Jesus taught there. *Mk 1:21, 29* Jesus was in and about Capernaum. *Mk 1:21,29, 39; 2:1; L 4:31, 44; J 2:12* After a time, the fishermen may have decided to go back to fishing for a while perhaps to have money to support themselves while they learned from their teacher, Jesus.

Luke's account omits the calling of the fishermen as Mark and Matthew heard it and is our only source for another similar but apparently later call. This time Jesus was definitely not alone but a crowd of people "pressed upon him to hear the word of God" as he stood on the lakeshore. *L 5:1*

Jesus saw two boats beached on the shore while their crews were washing their nets. *L 5:2* Jesus entered one of the two boats, Peter's, and asked him to thrust out a little. *L 5:3* Peter did so, and Jesus sat down and taught from the boat. Andrew is not mentioned but was probably present since Peter and Andrew worked together. *Mk 1:16; Mt 4:18*

After the teaching was over, Jesus told Peter:

Launch out into the deep, and let down your nets for a draught. *L 5:4*

Peter was skeptical:

Master, we have toiled all the night, and have taken nothing: nevertheless at thy word I will let down the net. *L 5:5*

They (Peter and presumably Andrew) got so many fish that "their net broke." *L 5:6* They beckoned to "their partners," the Zebedee brothers, to come out with the other boat:

And they came, and filled both the ships, so that they began to sink. When Simon Peter saw it, he fell down at Jesus' knees, saying, "Depart from me, for I am a sinful man, O Lord." For he was astonished, and all that were with him, at the draught of the fishes which they had taken. *L 5:7–9*

Jesus then said to Peter:

Fear not; from henceforth thou shalt catch men. *L 5:10*

Luke concludes:

When they had brought their ships to land, *they* forsook all, and followed him. *L 5:11*

344

"They" was apparently at least Simon Peter, Andrew and the Zebedee brothers, and perhaps some of their hired hands. *Compare Mk 1:20*

We must remember not to project our own preconceptions of what the discipleship was like. We should not assume that Jesus always had the same disciples and that all disciples accompanied him everywhere. We do know that certain disciples left him permanently. *J 6:66* It is reasonable to assume that fishermen like Peter and Andrew and the Zebedee brothers only gradually reached the point where they stayed with Jesus continuously.

Thus it was that Jesus on the third call finally acquired Peter as a full time follower. First, Jesus met Peter as a disciple of John the Baptist at Bethany beyond Jordan. *J 1:40–42* Second, Jesus, as a dramatic object lesson, called Peter and his brother, Andrew, as they were casting a net. *Mk 1:16–20; Mt 4:18–22* Third, Peter is impressed with a miracle and finally decides to forsake all and follow Jesus. *L 5:5–11*

Andrew and the Zebedee brothers probably also followed the in-and-out pattern of Peter. Andrew, as a disciple of John, had met Jesus at Bethany beyond Jordan. *J 1:40* He and Peter were both the recipients of Jesus' object lesson as they cast their net together. *Mk 1:16–20; Mt 4:18–22* Andrew was probably called a third time on the day of the miraculous haul. *L 5:1–11*

The first call of the Zebedee brothers was immediately after Jesus had called Andrew and Peter. Andrew and Peter had been casting a net. *Mk 1:16; Mt 4:18* The Zebedee brothers were in their boat mending their nets. *Mk 1:19; Mt 4:21* Their second call was on the day of miraculous haul. This time they were out of their boat and were washing their nets. *L 5:2, 7, 10*

Some time later, Jesus acquired another disciple by the lakeshore: Levi (Matthew), a tax collector. *Mk 2:13–14; Mt 9:9; L 5:27–28* As he passed by, Jesus saw Levi "sitting at the receipt of custom," i.e., collecting internal tariffs in a tax booth by the roadside. *Mk 2:14; Mt 9:9; L 5:27*

Jesus said: "Follow me." *Mk 2:14; Mt 9:9; L 5:27*

Levi arose and followed him. *Mk 2:14; Mt 9:9; L 5:28* Luke adds that Levi "left all," presumably including his tax business. *L 5:28*

This time there is no hint that Jesus had ever spoken to the man before. However, Levi probably had seen him many times as Jesus passed back and forth along the lakeshore, and Levi could not have been ignorant of Jesus' fame in Galilee. *Mk 1:28; L 4:37*

Our sources do not tell us how the rest of Jesus' twelve special disciples were recruited. Some time later on during his second Galilean ministry, he actually designated this special twelve. We are simply told that he called the company of his disciples together, and "*of them* he chose twelve, whom also he named apostles." *L 6:13, 17*

While modern usage distinguishes between "Apostles" and "Disciples" Luke here uses them as alternate titles as do certain ancient manuscripts of Mark 3:14. Matthew introduces his list by simply saying, "Now the names of the twelve *apostles* are: . . ." *Mt 10:2*

Each of the synoptic gospels has a list of these twelve men. The following tabulation follows Mark's order:

	MARK	MATTHEW	LUKE
1.	Simon he surnamed Peter	Simon who is called Peter	Simon whom he also named Peter
2.	James the son of Zebedee	James the son of Zebedee	James
3.	John the brother of James	John [James' brother]	John
4.	Andrew	Andrew [Peter's brother]	Andrew [Peter's brother]
5.	Philip	Philip	Philip
6.	Bartholomew	Bartholomew	Bartholomew
7.	Matthew	Matthew the publican	Matthew

MARK (cont.)	MATTHEW (cont.)	LUKE (cont.)
8. Thomas	Thomas	Thomas
9. James the son of Alphaeus	James the son of Alphaeus	James the son of Alphaeus
10. Thaddaeus	Lebbaeus whose surname was Thaddaeus	Judas the brother of James
11. Simon the Canaanite	Simon the Canaanite	Simon called Zelotes
12. Judas Iscariot *Mk 3:16–19*	Judas Iscariot *Mt 10:2–4*	Judas Iscariot *L 6:14–16 (Acts 1:13)*

Each name and description has been quoted exactly except for punctuation, while bracketed material has been paraphrased to fit the format. The Twelve break down into groups.

The earliest disciples were Andrew, Peter, and Philip, with Andrew being the very first. *J 1:40–43* All three men were from the same Galilean town, Bethsaida, and all three men were apparently disciples of John the Baptist when they were recruited. *J 1:37–44* Peter and Andrew, and James and John of Zebedee were two pairs of fishermen brothers. Peter, at least, was a business partner of the Zebedee brothers. *L 5:10* Andrew and Philip are the only two disciples having Greek names. Peter and the Zebedee brothers constituted the inner circle of the Twelve. In the following sections, everything stated in the New Testament as to the Twelve is collected and analyzed, beginning with Peter, their leader.

Peter

Peter is the first disciple named in the list of Jesus' twelve key disciples, but each gospel describes him differently:

MARK	MATTHEW	LUKE
And Simon he surnamed Peter; . . . *Mk 3:16*	The first, Simon, who is called Peter, . . . *Mt 10:2*	Simon, (whom he also named Peter,) . . . *L 6:14*

It was Jesus himself who gave Simon a new name "Peter," not a surname in our present usage but a nickname. Jesus gave this nickname to Simon when they met for the first time:

Thou art Simon the son of Jona: thou shalt be called Cephas, . . .
J 1:42

John's Gospel inserts immediately after the quoted word "Cephas" the phrase "which is by interpretation, 'A stone.'" *J 1:42* "Interpretation" is meant in the sense of "translation," and John is simply explaining that the Aramaic word *Cephas* , which he left untranslated into Greek, means "a stone" or "a rock." *Peter* is the Greek word for "a rock." Paul, for example, uses the Aramaic word *Cephas* interchangeably with the Greek *Peter*. *Galatians 2:6–14* Sometimes Peter's first name, Simon, and his nickname, Peter, are combined as "Simon Peter." *L 5:8; J 13:6; 20:2, 21:15* Peter's true name was actually Simon Bar-Jona, meaning "Simon, Son of Jonah." *Mt 16:17* It is not certain whether his father's name was Jonah or John. *J 1:42; 21:15*

It was through his brother, Andrew, that Peter first met Jesus. *J 1:41–43* Each brother became one of Jesus' twelve key disciples. *Mk 1:16; Mt 4:18*

At the time Peter became Jesus' disciple he was a married man, and he still kept his wife at the time Paul wrote 1 Corinthians some thirty years later. *Mk 1:30; Mt 8:14; L 4:38; 1 Corinthians 9:5* At the time he became a disciple he had a house in Capernaum, Galilee, and lived there with his brother, Andrew. Peter's mother-in-law lived with them. *Mk 1:21, 29–30; Mt 8:14; L 4:38*

Peter and Andrew were originally from Bethsaida, a town in Galilee. *J 1:44* They worked together as fishermen on the Sea of Galilee. *Mk 1:16; Mt 4:18* Peter had his own boat. *L 5:3* He was in partnership with the Zebedee brothers, James and John. *L 5:10* He was not an educated man. *Acts 4:13*

Peter was, by his own testimony, "a sinful man" when he was called to be a disciple. *L 5:8* Much later when he attempted to walk on the water to Jesus and failed, Jesus called him "of little faith".

Oh thou of little faith, wherefore didst thou doubt? *Mt 14:31* .

When Jesus explained how hard it is for the rich to enter the Kingdom of God, all of the disciples were amazed, but it was Peter who said:

MARK	MATTHEW	LUKE
Lo, we have	Behold, we have	Lo, we have
left all,	forsaken all,	left all,
and	and	and
have followed thee.	followed thee;	followed thee.
Mk 10:28	what shall we	L 18:28
	have therefore?	
	Mt 19:27	

Peter was looking out for himself: "What shall *we* have therefore?"

It was Peter who asked for an arbitrary rubric on forgiveness:

Lord, how oft shall my brother sin against me, and I forgive him? Till seven times? *Mt 18:21*

Peter was respectful and for the life of him could not see why Jesus should wash any disciple's feet. The dialogue went like this:

PETER: Lord, dost thou wash my feet?

JESUS: What I do thou knowest not now; but thou shalt know hereafter.

PETER: Thou shalt never wash my feet.

JESUS: If I wash thee not, thou hast no part with me.

PETER: Lord, not my feet only, but also my hands and my head.
    J 13:6–9

Peter's loyalty later led him into error. In the Garden of
Gethsemane near Jerusalem when Jesus was arrested, Peter drew
his sword and cut off the ear of the high priest's servant. *J 18:10* It is
characteristic of Peter's persistent misunderstanding of Jesus' mission that Peter happened to have a sword that night and used it.
    Jesus had to say to Peter:

Put up thy sword into the sheath: the cup which my Father hath
given me, shall I not drink it? *J 18:11*

Shortly before Gethsemane, Jesus had said of Peter:

Simon, Simon, behold, Satan hath desired to have you, that he may
sift you as wheat. But I have prayed for thee, that thy faith fail not;
and when thou art converted, strengthen thy brethren. *L 22:31–32*

Peter did not admit his weakness and instead said, "Lord, I am
ready to go with thee, both into prison, and to death." *L 22:33* Jesus
knew better:

I tell thee, Peter, the cock shall not crow this day, before that thou
shalt thrice deny that thou knowest me. *L 22:34*

This saying stuck in the minds of the disciples. *Mk 14:30; Mt
26:34* Luke breaks off his narrative at this point. However, both
Mark and Matthew record Peter's reply, which he said "more vehemently": "If I should die with thee, I will not deny thee in any
wise." *Mk 14:31 (Mt 26:35)*

Peter was no more dedicated than the rest of the disciples for Mark and Matthew add: "Likewise also said they all." *Mk 14:31 (Mt 26:35)*

Jesus had just told them:

All ye shall be offended because of me this night: for it is written, "I will smite the shepherd, and the sheep shall be scattered." *Mk 14:27 (Mt 26:31)*

According to Mark and Matthew, Peter then replied: "Although all shall be offended, yet will not I." *Mk 14:29 (Mt 26:33)*

As Mark and Matthew have it, this brought on Jesus' prediction about three denials before the next dawn. John has the story differently. According to him, the conversation went like this:

PETER: Lord, whither goest thou?
JESUS: Whither I go, thou canst not follow me now; but thou shalt follow me afterwards.
PETER: Lord, why cannot I follow thee now? I will lay down my life for thy sake,
JESUS: Wilt thou lay down thy life for my sake? Verily, verily, I say unto thee, the cock shall not crow till thou hast denied me thrice. *J 13:36–38*

It was an old story to Jesus. Earlier in the ministry, Jesus had taught his disciples "that the Son of man must suffer many things and be rejected of the elders, and of the chief priest, and scribes, and be killed, and after three days rise again." *Mk 8:31–32 (Mt 16:21–22; L 9:22)*

Peter rebuked Jesus for this teaching, saying:

Be it far from thee, Lord; this shall not be unto thee. *Mt 16:22 (Mk 8:32)*

Jesus' rebuke to Peter was curt:

MARK	MATTHEW
Get thee behind me Satan;	Get thee behind me, Satan;
	thou art an offense unto me:
for thou savorest not	for thou savorest not
the things of God,	the things that be of God,
but the things that be of men.	but those that be of men.
Mk 8:33	Mt 16:23

Peter did, however, stay with Jesus after his arrest:

And Peter followed him afar off, even unto the palace of the high priest; and he sat with the servants, and warmed himself at the fire. *Mk 14:54 (Mt 26:58; L 22:54)*

Matthew adds that Peter went in "to see the end." *Mt 26:58* The other disciples had fled except for another unknown disciple, who was probably John. John's Gospel states:

And Simon Peter followed Jesus, and so did another disciple: that disciple was known unto the high priest, and went in with Jesus into the palace of the high priest. But Peter stood at the door without. Then went out that other disciple, which was known unto the high priest, and spake unto her that kept the door, and brought in Peter.

Then saith the damsel that kept the door unto Peter, "Art not thou *also* one of this man's disciples?" He saith, "I am not." *J 18:15–18*

It seems obvious that the damsel knew that "the other disciple" was a disciple of Jesus. It seems probable that she was friendly or at least not ill-disposed: she had, at the request of the "other disciple," admitted Peter. Yet Peter did not hesitate to lie.
John continues:

And the servants and officers stood there, who had made a fire of coals, for it was cold; and they warmed themselves, and Peter stood with them, and warmed himself . . .

And Simon Peter stood and warmed himself. They said therefore unto him, "Art not thou also one of his disciples?" He denied it, and said, "I am not."

One of the servants of the high priest, being his kinsman whose ear Peter cut off, saith, "Did not I see thee in the garden with him?"

Peter then denied again: and immediately the cock crew. *J 18:18, 25–27*

The other three gospels have the story differently, and they focus on Peter's remembrance of Jesus' prediction of Peter's thrice denial before the cock crew. John does not even mention that; he is content to say: "And immediately the cock crew." *J 18:27* The other three gospels vary slightly in their account of what happened. Mark tells the story as follows:

And as Peter was beneath in the palace, there cometh one of the maids of the high priest. And when she saw Peter warming himself, she looked upon him and said, "And thou also wast with Jesus of Nazareth."

But he denied it, saying, "I know not neither understand I what thou sayest." And he went out into the porch; and the cock crew.

And a maid saw him again, and began to say to them that stood by, "This is one of them." And he denied it again.

And a little after, they that stood by said again to Peter, "Surely thou art one of them: for thou art a Galilean, and thy speech [accent] agreeth thereto." But he began to curse and to swear, saying, "I know not this man of whom ye speak."

And the second time the cock crew. And Peter called to mind the word that Jesus said unto him, "Before the cock crew twice, thou shalt deny me thrice." And when he thought thereon, he wept. *Mk 14:66–72 (Mt 26:69–75; L 22:55–62)*

The two other synoptic accounts vary in many details, but a reading will show them as variances to be expected when three different men report the same episode. Both Mark and Matthew add after the bystander's statement:

MARK	MATTHEW
Surely thou art one of them:	Surely thou also art
for thou art a Galilean,	one of them:
and thy speech	for thy speech
agreeth thereto.	betrayeth thee.
Mk 14:70	Mt 26:73

However, Luke just generalizes:

Of a truth this fellow also was with him: for he is a Galilean. L 22:59

On the other hand, only Luke has the statement that at the time the cock crowed for the second time:

"And the Lord turned, and looked upon Peter. And Peter remembered the word of the Lord, how he had said unto him, 'Before the cock crow, thou shalt deny me thrice.'" L 22:61

It is impossible to write of Peter without mentioning the claims that have been made for him by certain Christians that have divided the church of Jesus Christ for many centuries. The question is whether Peter is the rock upon which Jesus founded his church. The answer depends on what Jesus meant when he talked with his disciples near the city of Caesarea Phillipi:

MARK	MATTHEW	LUKE
And Jesus went out,	When Jesus came	And it came to pass as he was alone praying,
and his disciples, into the towns of Caesarea Phillipi;	into the coasts of Caesarea Phillipi,	his disciples

MARK (cont.)	**MATTHEW** (cont.)	**LUKE** (cont.)
		were with him;
and by the way		
he asked his disciples,	he asked his disciples,	and he asked them,
say unto them,	saying,	saying,
"Whom do men say	"Whom do men say	"Whom say the people
that I	that I the Son of man	that I
am?"	am?"	am?"
And they answered,	And they said,	They answering said,
	"Some say that	
	thou art	
"John the Baptist,	John the Baptist;	"John the Baptist;
but some say Elijah;	some, Elijah;	but some say, Elijah;
and others,	and others, Jeremiah,	and others say that
one of	or one of	one of
the prophets."	the prophets."	the old prophets
		is risen again."
And		
he saith unto them,	He saith unto them,	He said unto them,
"But whom	"But whom	"But whom
say ye that I am?"	say ye that I am?"	say ye that I am?"
And Peter	And Simon Peter	Peter
answereth	answered	answering
and saith unto him,	and said,	said,
"Thou art the Christ."	"Thou art the Christ,	"The Christ
	the Son of	of
	the living God."	God."
	And Jesus answered	
	and said unto him,	
	"Blessed art thou,	
	Simon Bar-Jona:	
	for flesh and blood	
	hath not revealed it	
	unto thee,	
	but my Father	

MARK (cont.)	MATTHEW (cont.)	LUKE (cont.)
	which is in Heaven. And I say also unto thee, that thou art Peter, and upon this rock I will build my church; and the gates of Hell shall not prevail against it. And I will give unto thee the keys of the Kingdom of Heaven: and whatsoever thou shalt bind on earth shall be bound in Heaven; and whatsoever thou shalt loose on earth shall be loosed in Heaven."	
And he charged them that they should tell	Then charged he his disciples that they should tell	And he straitly charged them, and commanded them to tell
no man of him. *Mk 8:27–30*	no man that he was Jesus the Christ. *Mt 16:13–20*	no man that thing . . . *L 9:18–21*

The crucial text is:

Thou art Peter [Greek *Petros*], and upon this rock [Greek *petra*] I will build my church . . . *Mt 16:18*

The problem is to get back behind the Greek text of Matthew to what Jesus actually said in Aramaic. We do not have what Jesus actually said in Aramaic but instead have a Greek approximation, so pressing the gender and other linguistic subtleties of the Greek text is inappropriate. For example, Aramaic does not have a gender distinction as to the word rock: *Petros* (Greek) would be *Kêphā'* (Aramaic); and *petra* (Greek) would be *kêphā'*(Aramaic).

We do know that Jesus applied nicknames to his disciples. He whimsically called the Zebedee brothers "Boanerges," which is, "The sons of thunder." *Mk 3:17* Mark also states:

And Simon he surnamed Peter. *Mk 3:16*

"Surnamed" is a misleading translation here. We would now say Jesus nicknamed Simon "Peter," just as he nicknamed the Zebedee brothers "The sons of thunder."

The full story of Peter's naming is found in John. When Jesus and Peter first met, Jesus quipped:

Thou art Simon the son of Jona: thou shalt be called Cephas [Aramaic], . . . *J 1:42*

John then adds an explanation in Greek:

Which is by interpretation [translation], "a stone." *J 1:42*

We are now ready to consider the meaning of Matthew 16:18. Jesus probably said something like this:

Thou art "Rock," and upon rock I will build my church.

This reconstruction replaces "this rock" with "rock," but do we know that Jesus said in Aramaic "this rock" rather than "rock"? If Jesus did not say *this* rock" there is no reference back to Peter. The question then becomes, what is the rock Jesus spoke of?

The context is crucial to the answer. Jesus was engaged in a teaching dialogue with his disciples. He had asked, in effect, "Have you learned the basic premise of my teaching?"

But, whom say ye that I am? *Mt 16:15 (Mk 8:27; L 9:18)*

Only Peter answered; and his answer was unequivocal:

Thou art the Christ, the Son of the living God. *Mt 16:16 (Mk 8:29; L 9:20)*

Jesus rewarded Peter with a teacher's praise for an apt pupil, using Peter's nickname "Rock" as a play on words for his rock-like answer: "Thou art the Christ, the Son of the living God." It is this rock-like answer upon which Jesus said, "I will build my church," not upon the disciple who gave the answer.

After stating the foundation rock of his church, Jesus' next sentence deals with the keys of the Kingdom of Heaven. In order to understand that sentence, we must compare it with a similar sentence of Jesus reported by Matthew 18:18:

MATTHEW 16:19	MATTHEW 18:18
And I will give	Verily I say
unto thee	unto you,
the keys of the Kingdom	
of Heaven:	
and whatsoever	whatsoever
thou shalt bind on earth	ye shall bind on earth
shall be bound in Heaven;	shall be bound in Heaven;
and whatsoever	and whatsoever
thou shalt loose on earth	ye shall loose on earth
shall be loosed in Heaven.	shall be loosed in Heaven.

Matthew 18:18 is found in a block of sayings unmistakably directed to all disciples of Jesus, not just Peter. The power to bind and loose was conferred upon all disciples of Jesus, not on Peter alone as Matthew 16:19 implies, if it is read alone. But there can be no doubt when the two passages are read together that the "thee" of Matthew 16:19 is not to be read as excluding all disciples, except Peter.

Comparing the two passages it seems unlikely that the keys of the Kingdom was meant by Jesus to mean anything other than what is meant by bind and loose. To him it was another metaphor for the same power, not a special legal title deed to Peter. In any case, it is inescapable that Jesus did not mention Peter's successors.

Peter was not singled out when Jesus appeared after his resurrection to all the disciples assembled in a closed room:

Peace be unto you; as my Father hath sent me, even so I you.

And when he had said this, he breathed on *them*, and saith unto *them*, "Receive ye the Holy Spirit; whose soever sins ye remit, they are remitted unto them; and whose soever sins ye retain, they are retained." *J 20:21–23*

The two verses following Matthew 18:18 confirm that Jesus does not operate juridically through a formal ecclesiastical structure centered in one disciple or his successors:

Again I say unto you, that if two of you shall agree on earth as touching anything that they shall ask, it shall be done for them of my Father which is in Heaven. For where two or three are gathered together in my name, there am I in the midst of them. *Mt 18:19–20*

The Holy Spirit was given to all the disciples, not just to Peter. Jesus did not conceive of his church legalistically or in terms of organization charts. Instead, he conceived of it as an organism consisting of cells of "two or three gathered together in my name" where he personally would be present, and if even two there agreed on what to ask, Jesus' Father would grant the asked-for thing without going through any ecclesiastical channels. *Mt 18:20*

Jesus' post-resurrection appearance to Peter and six other disciples at the Sea of Galilee does not suggest otherwise. Jesus asked them to "come and dine." *J 21:12* After they had dined, Jesus had a dialogue with Peter as follows:

JESUS: Simon, son of Jonas, lovest thou me more than these?
PETER: Yea, Lord; thou knowest that I love thee.
JESUS: Feed my lambs.
JESUS: Simon, son of Jonas, lovest thou me?
PETER: Yea, Lord; thou knowest that I love thee.
JESUS: Feed my sheep.
JESUS: Simon, son of Jonas, lovest thou me?
(Peter was grieved because he said unto him the third time, 'Lovest thou me.')
PETER: Lord, thou knowest all things; thou knowest that I love thee.
JESUS: Feed my sheep. *J 21:15–17*

The repeated charge to Peter to "Feed my sheep" did not impress Peter as conferring upon him any special power or position in the church. Some thirty years later, toward the end of his ministry, he still regarded himself as simply a fellow elder or fellow presbyter. He then wrote from Rome to certain Christian congregations scattered throughout Asia Minor a letter which closes:

The elders which are among you I exhort, *who am also an elder*, and a witness of the sufferings of Christ, and also a partaker of the glory that shall be revealed: feed the flock of God which is among you, taking the oversight thereof, not by constraint, but willingly; not for filthy lucre, but of a ready mind; neither as being lords over God's heritage, but being ensamples to the flock. And when *the chief Shepherd* shall appear, ye shall receive a crown of glory that fadeth not away. *1 Peter 5:1–4*

Peter's letter recalls Jesus' own teaching: "I am the good shepherd." *J 10:11, 14* Jesus said:

> I am the good shepherd, and know my sheep, and am known of mine. As the Father knowest me, even so know I the Father; and I lay down my life for the sheep. And other sheep I have which are not of this fold; them also I must bring, and they shall hear my voice; there shall be one fold, and one shepherd. *J 10:14–16*

According to Jesus, he was the one shepherd of the one fold. Peter was not named. Peter did ask Jesus once, "Behold we have forsaken all, and followed thee; what shall we have therefore?" *Mt 19:27*

When Jesus answered he did not single out Peter. Jesus' answer treated all twelve disciples equally:

> Verily I say unto you, that ye which have followed me, in the regeneration when the Son of man shall sit in the throne of his glory, ye also shall sit upon twelve thrones, judging the twelve tribes of Israel. *Mt 19:28*

Later on at the Last Supper Jesus again told all his twelve disciples that they would "sit on thrones judging the twelve tribes of Israel." *L 22:30* Their function was not, however, limited to the twelve tribes of Israel.

The Kingdom of Heaven itself was appointed to them, all of them, not just to Peter. Jesus' whole statement was:

> Ye are *they* which have continued with me in my temptations; and I appoint unto you *a kingdom*, as my Father hath appointed unto me, that ye may eat and drink at my table in *my kingdom*, and sit on thrones judging the twelve tribes of Israel. *L 22:28–30*

This method of group judgment was indeed the way the earliest Christian church was run when the church at Rome was still a mission church and Peter was still living in Jerusalem.

When a dispute arose in Antioch, Syria, in about A.D. 49 as to whether Gentiles had to be circumcised to be saved, Paul, Barnabas, and certain others were sent to Jerusalem to consult "the apostles and elders about this question." *Acts 15:2* Acts states:

> And the apostles and elders came together for to consider of this matter. *Acts 15:6*

Peter spoke, but so did James, Jesus' brother. *Acts 15:7–21* The decision, however, was made by "the apostles and elders, with the whole church" not by Peter. *Acts 15:22* Acts states:

> Then pleased it the apostles and elders, with the whole church, to send chosen men of their own company to Antioch with Paul and Barnabas: namely, Judas surnamed Barsabas, and Silas, chief men among the brethren. *Acts 15:22*

The decision was in the form of letters which began:

> The *apostles and elders and brethren* send greeting unto the brethren which are of the Gentiles in Antioch and Syria and Cilicia:
>
> For as much as *we* have heard, that certain which went out from *us* have troubled you with words, . . .
>
> It seemed good unto *us, being assembled with one accord*, to send chosen men unto you with our beloved Barnabas and Paul, . . .
>
> *We* have sent therefore Judas and Silas, who shall also tell you the same things by mouth.
>
> For it seemed good to the Holy Spirit, and to *us*, to lay upon you no greater burden than these necessary things; . . . *Acts 15:23–28*

It was Paul's judgment that Peter (Cephas) was only one of the three key men in the mother church in Jerusalem:

> And when James, Cephas and John, *who seemed to be pillars*, perceived the grace that was given unto me, *they* gave to me and

Barnabas the right hands of fellowship, that we should go unto the heathen, and *they* unto the circumcision. *Galatians 2:9*

According to Paul, "the gospel of the uncircumcision" was committed to him, while "the gospel of the circumcision was unto Peter." *Galatians 2:7*

About A.D. 51 Paul founded a church at Corinth, Greece that included some Jewish converts. *Acts 18:1–11* After Paul left Corinth, he had occasion to write letters to that church. The occasion for one of his letters, 1 Corinthians, which was written around A.D. 55, was certain divisions in that church. One of those divisions was a party favoring Peter (Cephas). Paul wrote:

Now this I say, that every one of you saith, I am of Paul; I am of Apollos; and I of Cephas; and I of Christ. *I Corinthians 1:12*

Later in that same letter Paul wrote:

Therefore let no man glory in men. For all things are yours: whether Paul, or Apollos, or Cephas, or the world, or life, or death, or things present, or things to come; all are yours; and ye are Christ's, and Christ is God's. *1 Corinthians 3:21–23*

That is a suitable epitaph to the long historical division of Christians over Peter and his place in the church. No Christian should say "I am of Cephas." All Christians should say I am Christ's.

The Kingdom is appointed to all disciples. No disciple is the rock upon which the Kingdom is built. There is no keykeeper. The twelve disciples will sit upon thrones of judgment judging the twelve tribes of Israel. No throne is any higher than the others.

In the first days after the resurrection of Jesus, Peter was the leader of the disciples just as he had been during Jesus' ministry:

1. He suggested that the brethren select a replacement for Judas Iscariot; and "they appointed two" and from those two selected the replacement by lot. *Acts 1:15–26*

2. Peter "standing up with the Eleven" explained Pentecost to the Jews and their need to repent and be baptized in the name of Jesus Christ. *Acts 2:14, 38*
3. It was Peter "filled with the Holy Spirit" who spoke in his own defense and John's when they were taken into custody for preaching in the Temple. *Acts 4:8–12*
4. It was Peter who rebuked Ananias and Sapphira for keeping back part of the proceeds of the sale of some property. *Acts 5:1–11*

As the church at Jerusalem became more organized, Peter's position was that of one of three influential "pillars" but not the head of the organization. *Galatians 2:9* It was the Twelve who called the rest of the disciples and stated the necessity for appointing deacons, but it was "the whole multitude" who chose them and it was "the apostles" who ordained them. *Acts 6:2–6* It was "the apostles which were at Jerusalem" who sent Peter and John to Samaria. *Acts 8:14* It was "the apostles and brethren that were in Judea" that heard and passed judgment on Peter's mission contacts with Gentiles. *Acts 11:1–18*

Along with others in the early church, Peter had the gift of healing. *Acts 3:1–11; 5:15; 9:33–35; 9:36–41* Along with others in the early church, Peter was miraculously released from prison. *Acts 12:4–18* Along with others in the early church, Peter received visions and ministered to the Gentiles. *Acts 10:1–48*

Peter was, however, a key witness to the resurrection. In 1 Corinthians, Paul wrote what he had been taught as a convert:

How that Christ died for our sins according to the scriptures; and that he was buried, and that he rose again the third day according to the scriptures; and *that he was seen of Cephas, then* of the Twelve: . . . " *1 Corinthians 15:3–5*

Jesus' own last words to Peter were:

Verily, verily, I say unto thee, when thou wast young, thou girdest thyself, and walkest whither thou wouldst; but when thou shalt be old, thou shalt stretch forth thy hands, and another shall gird thee, and carry thee whither thou wouldest not. *J 21:18*

John's Gospel continues:

This spake he, signifying by what death he should glorify God. And when he had spoken this, he saith unto him, "Follow me."

Then Peter, turning about, seeth the disciple whom Jesus loved following, which also leaned on his breast at supper, and said, "Lord, which is he that betrayeth thee?"

Peter seeing him saith to Jesus, "Lord, and what shall this man do?"

Jesus saith unto him, "If I will that he tarry till I come, what is that to thee? Follow thou me." *J 21:19–22*

We know that Peter did die a martyr, but the details of his death are not found in the New Testament. The Greek word *martyros* has passed into English as *martyr*, but its Greek meaning then was simply, "a witness." Peter did witness until his death, obeying Jesus' last words to him:

Follow thou me. *J 21:22*

JAMES AND JOHN

In the list of the Twelve, Matthew and Mark list "James the son of Zebedee, and John, his brother." *Mt 10:2 (Mk 3:17)*. These Zebedee brothers were Galilean fishermen. *Mk 1:16; Mt 4:18; L 5:1–2, 10* They were in the fishing business with their father. *Mk 1:19–20; Mt 4:21–22*

Apparently, the family business was part of a partnership with Andrew and Peter. Luke states that James and John were partners with Peter. *L 5:10* Earlier in the same passage, it is stated of those in Peter's boat that "*they* beckoned unto *their* partners, which were in the other ship, that they should come and help them." *L 5:7* Presumably, "they" included Andrew, since Peter and Andrew fished together. *Mk 1:16; Mt 4:18* The Zebedee-Peter-Andrew business was large enough to have two boats. *L 5:7 (Mk 1:19–20; Mt 4:21–22)* At least the Zebedee segment of the business was prosperous enough to have some hired men. *Mk 1:20*

These fisher folk knew each other's families. James and John naturally accompanied their partners, Peter and Andrew, to Peter and Andrew's house when Peter's wife's mother lay sick of fever. *Mk 1:29–30*

James and John were recruited by Jesus as his disciples as they worked mending their nets on the shore of the Sea of Galilee. *Mk 1:19–20; Mt 4:21–22* After a miraculous draft of fishes, which was apparently some time later, they, along with Peter and Andrew, abandoned the fishing business. As Luke has it, "they forsook all, and followed him." *L 5:11*

Jesus nicknamed James and John, "The sons of thunder." *Mk 3:17* As the following incident shows, they were impetuous men. Jesus was on his way to Jerusalem for the last time and had sent an advance party into a Samaritan village to make arrangements for accommodations. The Samaritan villagers would not help a party of Jews headed for Jerusalem. James and John immediately said to Jesus, "Lord, wilt thou that we command fire to come down from heaven, and consume them, even as Elijah did?" *L 9:54*

Jesus rebuked them:

Ye know not what manner of spirit ye are of. For the Son of man is not come to destroy men's lives, but to save them. *L 9:55–56*

James and John, along with Peter, constituted a sort of inner circle within the Twelve. When Jesus went to raise Jairus' daughter, "he suffered no man to follow him, save Peter and James, and John, the brother of James." *Mk 5:37 (L 8:51)* Jesus picked the same three men to accompany him to a high mountain where he was transfigured.

Mark's account states:

And after six days Jesus taketh with him Peter, and James, and John, and leadeth them up into an high mountain apart by themselves: and he was transfigured before them. *Mk 9:2 (Mt 17:1; L 9:28)*

After the transfiguration and accompanying vision were over and they were coming down the mountain, Jesus charged this inner circle "that they should tell no man what things they had seen, till the Son of man were risen from the dead." *Mk 9:9 (Mt 17:9)*

Mark continues:

And they kept that saying *with themselves*, questioning one with another what the rising from the dead should mean. *Mk 9:10*

It was the same inner circle, plus Andrew, Peter's brother, who "asked him *privately*, 'Tell us, when shall these things be; and what shall be the sign when all these things shall be fulfilled?'" *Mk 13:3*

That was Tuesday. On Thursday night Jesus went to a place named Gethsemane. *Mk 14:32; Mt 26:36* The hour of his agony was at hand. He told his disciples: "Sit ye here, while I shall pray." *Mk 14:32 (Mt 26:36)*

Mark continues:

And he taketh with him Peter and James and John, and began to be sore amazed, and to be very heavy, and saith unto them, "My soul is exceeding sorrowful unto death; tarry ye here, and watch." *Mk 14:33–34 (Mt 26:37–38)*

Even this inner circle did not watch. Jesus found them sleeping. *Mk 14:37; Mt 26:40; L 22:45* This happened three times. *Mk 14:37–42; Mt 26:40–46*

Although both Zebedee brothers were part of Jesus' inner circle of disciples, they, at first, missed the essence of Jesus' teaching. This is shown by the following incident.

According to Mark, "the sons of Zebedee" approached Jesus and the following dialogue ensued:

JAMES AND JOHN: Master, we would that thou shouldest do for us whatsoever we shall desire.

JESUS: What would ye that I should do for you?

JAMES AND JOHN: Grant unto us that we may sit, one on thy right hand, and the other on thy left hand, in thy glory.

JESUS: Ye know not what ye ask. Can ye drink of the cup that I drink of? And be baptized with the baptism that I am baptized with?

JAMES AND JOHN: We can.

JESUS: Ye shall indeed drink of the cup that I drink of; and with the baptism that I am baptized withal shall ye be baptized. But to sit on my right hand and on my left hand is not mine to give; but it shall be given to them for whom it is prepared. *Mk 10:35–40 (Mt 20:21–23)*

Mark adds:

And when the ten heard it, they began to be much displeased with James and John. *Mk 10:41 (Mt 20:24)*

According to Matthew, it was the mother of James and John rather than James and John who made the request. *Mt 20:20* She was apparently also a follower of Jesus, and we do know that she was present at his crucifixion. *Mt 27:56* Jesus replied to her request as follows:

And he said unto her, "What wilt thou?" She saith unto him, "Grant that these my two sons may sit, the one on thy right hand and the other on the left, in thy kingdom." *Mt 20:21*

The conceit of James and John was shown not only by the request but also by their answer to Jesus:

MARK	MATTHEW
We can.	We are able.
Mk 10:39	*Mt 20:22*

James' name is not listed in the New Testament except in connection with his brother John. Both Mark and Luke record an incident mentioning only John:

MARK	LUKE
And John answered him, saying, "Master, *we* saw one casting out devils in thy name, and he followeth not us; and *we* forbad him, because he followeth not us."	And John answered and said, "Master, *we* saw one casting out devils in thy name; and *we* forbad him, because he followeth not with us."
But Jesus said, "Forbid him not: for there is no man which shall do a miracle in my name, that can lightly speak evil of me. For he that is not against us is on our part."	And Jesus said unto him, "Forbid him not: for he that is not against us is for us."
Mk 9:38–40	*L 9:49–50*

We may reasonably suppose that "we" is at least John and his brother James. On occasion Jesus did entrust key jobs to Peter and

John alone. Peter and John were sent into Jerusalem to make the arrangements for the disciples' Passover celebration. *L 22:8–13* This turned out to be the Last Supper.

At that Supper John (cryptically referred to as the disciple "whom Jesus loved") at Peter's request asked who would betray Jesus: "Lord, who is it?" *J 13:23–25*

After Jesus' arrest in the Garden of Gethsemane, Peter followed him to the high priest's palace:

> And Simon Peter followed Jesus, and so did *another disciple*: That disciple was known unto the high priest, and went in with Jesus into the palace of the high priest. But Peter stood at the door without. Then went out *that other disciple*, which was known unto the high priest, and spake unto her that kept the door, and brought in Peter. *J 18:15–16*

It is often supposed that this unnamed "other disciple" was John. If so, John was acquainted enough with the high priest, Caiaphas, to have easy admittance to his palace.

If, as is commonly supposed, John is the disciple cryptically referred to in John's Gospel as the "disciple whom Jesus loved," there are some further mentions of John in that gospel:

1. At the cross Jesus entrusted his mother to John:

    > When Jesus therefore saw his mother, and the *disciple* standing by, *whom he loved*, he saith unto his mother, "Woman, behold thy son!" Then saith he to the disciple, "Behold, thy mother!" And from that hour that disciple took her into his own home. *J 19:26–27*

2. After Mary Magdalene found the stone taken away from Jesus' sepulchre, John's Gospel states:

    > Then she runneth, and cometh to Simon Peter, and to *the other disciple, whom Jesus loved*, and saith unto them, "They have taken away the Lord out of the sepulchre, and we know not where they have laid him."

Peter therefore went forth, and *that other disciple*, and came to the sepulchre. So they ran both together, and *the other disciple* did outrun Peter, and came first to the sepulchre. And he stooping down, and looking in, saw the linen clothes lying; yet went he not in . . . [Peter went in] . . . Then went in also *that other disciple*, which came first to the sepulchre, and he saw, and believed. *J* 20:2–5, 8

3. After Jesus' resurrection, seven of his disciples were back by the Sea of Galilee. This group included Peter and "the sons of Zebedee." *J* 21:1–2 Peter said, "I go a fishing," and the others said, "We also go with thee." *J* 21:3 They got into a boat and fished all night, but caught nothing. At daybreak Jesus stood on the beach, but they did not recognize him. *J* 21:4 He told them, "Cast the net on the right side of the ship, and ye shall find." *J* 21:6
John writes:

They cast therefore, and now they were not able to draw it for the multitude of fishes. Therefore *that disciple whom Jesus loved* saith unto Peter, "It is the Lord." *J* 21:6–7

4. Later on, on that same occasion on the shore of the Sea of Galilee, Peter and Jesus were talking, and Peter turned about and "seeth the disciple whom Jesus loved following" and said to Jesus, "Lord, and what shall this man do?" *J* 21:20–21 Jesus answered:

If I will that he tarry till I come, what is that to thee? Follow thou me. *J* 21:22

John's Gospel continues:

Then went this saying abroad among the brethren, that that disciple should not die: yet Jesus saith not unto him, "He shall not die;" but, "If I will that he tarry till I come, what is that to thee?"

371

> This is the disciple which testified of these things, and wrote these things; and we know that his testimony is true. *J 21:23–24*

We do know that John, along with his brother James, witnessed Jesus' ascension into heaven and that they abode with the rest of the remaining eleven disciples in an upper room in Jerusalem. *Acts 1:11–13*

Both brothers were leaders in the Jerusalem church. James' church life was short. Acts states:

> Now about that time Herod the king [Herod Agrippa, the grandson of Herod the Great] stretched forth his hands to vex certain of the church. And he killed James the brother of John with the sword. *Acts 12:1–2*

This was around A.D. 44. An early Christian historian quotes a narrative giving further details of James' death:

> He says that the man who led him to the judgment seat, seeing him bearing his testimony to the faith, and moved by the fact, confessed himself a Christian. Both therefore, says he, were led away to die. On their way, he entreated James to be forgiven of him, and James considered a little, replied, "Peace be to thee," and kissed him; and then both were beheaded at the same time. *Eusebius, Ecclesiastical History, Book II, Ch. IX*

John long remained a pillar of the Jerusalem church. Paul wrote in Galatians that "James, Cephas and John, who seemed to be pillars" endorsed Paul's mission to the Gentiles. *Galatians 2:9* By this time, James the brother of John was dead, and the "James" Paul mentions is Jesus' brother.

Acts states:

> Now when the apostles which were at Jerusalem heard that Samaria had received the word of God, they sent unto them Peter and John, who, when they were come down, prayed for them, that they might

receive the Holy Spirit: . . . Then laid they their hands on them, and they received the Holy Spirit . . .

And they, when they had testified and preached the word of the Lord, returned to Jerusalem, and preached the gospel in many villages of the Samaritans. *Acts 8:14–15, 17, 25*

John and Peter had worked together from the very earliest days of the church. One day shortly after Pentecost, "Peter and John went up together into the Temple." *Acts 3:1* A lame beggar who sat at the Beautiful Gate of the Temple saw them and asked alms. *Acts 3:2–3* Acts continues:

And Peter, fastening his eyes upon him with John, said, "Look on us." *Acts 3:4*

The beggar was healed and in his joy held onto Peter and John. *Acts 3:6–11* A crowd gathered, and Peter preached through Jesus the resurrection from the dead. *Acts 3:12–26* As a result, both Peter and John were arrested and held until the next day. *Acts 4:3*

The next day the Jewish authorities interrogated them, and Peter responded with a brief summary of the gospel. *Acts 4:5–12* Acts then states:

Now when they saw the boldness of Peter and John, and perceived that they were unlearned and ignorant men, they marveled; and they took knowledge of them, that they had been with Jesus. *Acts 4:13*

The Jewish authorities then ordered that they must not "speak at all or teach in the name of Jesus." *Acts 4:18* Acts continues:

But Peter and John answered and said unto them, "Whether it be right in the sight of God to hearken unto you more than unto God, judge ye. For we cannot but speak the things which we have seen and heard." *Acts 4:19–20*

John not only spoke the things which he had seen and heard, he wrote what he had seen and heard. For reasons unknown, John in the last part of John's Gospel sometimes refers to himself cryptically as "the disciple whom Jesus loved." *J 13:23, 19:26–27, 20:2, J 21:7, 20*

John's Gospel refers to "the disciple whom Jesus loved" and concludes:

> This is the disciple which testified of these things, and *wrote these things*; and we know that his testimony is true. *J 21:24*

We do not know how John "wrote these things," that is, the book we call the Gospel According to John, or why this endorsement was added to what he wrote. It is disputed whether John also wrote three letters (epistles), 1 John, 2 John, and 3 John, and the Revelation of Saint John the Divine.

The Revelation states that it is "The Revelation of Jesus Christ" that he "sent and signified it by his angel unto his servant John, who bare record of the word of God, and of the testimony of Jesus Christ, and of all things that he saw." *Revelation 1:1–2*

John adds his own personal word of testimony as follows:

> I John, who also am your brother, and *companion in tribulation*, and in the kingdom and patience of Jesus Christ, was in the isle that is called Patmos, *for the word of God, and for the testimony of Jesus Christ*. I was in the Spirit on the Lord's day, and heard behind me a great voice, as of a trumpet, . . ."

> After this I looked, and, behold, a door was opened in heaven; and the first voice which I heard was as it were of a trumpet talking with me, which said, "Come up hither, and I will show thee things which must be hereafter." *Revelation 1:9–10, 4:1*

John had been exiled to the island of Patmos, which is about forty miles offshore from Asia Minor. The reason he was exiled was "for the word of God, and for the testimony of Jesus Christ." He also states he has been a "companion in tribulation." *Revelation*

1:9 This probably refers to the persecution of Christians around A.D. 93–96 in the reign of the Roman Emperor Domitian.

According to tradition, John returned from this exile to Ephesus and from there ruled the churches in Asia Minor until "the times of Trajan" who became Emperor in A.D. 98. *Eusebius, Ecclesiastical History, Book III, Ch. XXIII*

Generation after generation of Christians have turned to Revelation of John to learn the "things which must be hereafter." *Revelation 4:1* That is what is important, not when John died, or whether he was buried at Ephesus.

Andrew

Andrew was the brother of Peter and they were from Bethsaida, Galilee and worked together as fishermen. *Mk 1:16; Mt 4:18; J 1:44* Andrew was a disciple of John the Baptist when he met Jesus a day or two after John had baptised Jesus. *J 1:29–40* Andrew then told Peter:

> He first findeth his own brother, Simon, and saith unto him, "We have found the Messiah," which is, being interpreted [translated into Greek], "The Christ." *And he brought him to Jesus. J 1:41–42*

This is our first glimpse of Andrew; he drops from our sight as one of the disciples who abode in the upper room in Jerusalem after the resurrection. *Acts 1:13*

Andrew was on the fringe of the inner circle of disciples consisting of Peter and the Zebedee brothers. Mark states:

> And as he sat upon the Mount of Olives over against the temple, Peter and James and John *and Andrew* asked him *privately*, "Tell us, when shall these things be? And what shall be the sign when all these things shall be fulfilled?" *Mk 13:3–4*

Andrew is a Greek name. When some Greeks wished to see Jesus, they approached Philip, also a Greek-named man. Philip "cometh and telleth Andrew: and again Andrew and Philip tell Jesus." *J 12:22*

Andrew and Philip were apparently often together. John's Gospel reports this incident. Philip had pointed out to Jesus that 200 pennyworth of bread would not be sufficient to feed a crowd of 5,000. Andrew then said, "There is a lad here, which hath five barley loaves, and two small fishes; but what are they among so many?" *J 6:9*

Yet this practical man had first recognized Jesus' uniqueness: "We have found The Messiah." *J 1:41*

PHILIP

Both Philip and Andrew were Greek names: the only Greek names among the Twelve. Philip was from Bethsaida, Galilee, the city of Andrew and Peter. *J 1:44* Philip was recruited by Jesus himself in Galilee with the simple words: "Follow me." *J 1:43* Philip was the third disciple, and he recruited Nathanael, the fourth disciple, saying: "We have found him of whom Moses in the law, of whom the prophets did write, Jesus of Nazareth the son of Joseph." *J:45* Nathanael doubted this statement, and Philip said, "Come and see." *J 1:46*

Despite Philip's recognition of Jesus as the prophesied Messiah, Philip did not understand Jesus' unique relationship to God the Father. Towards the end of Jesus' ministry, Philip asked Jesus: "Lord, shew us the Father, and it sufficeth us." *J 14:8*

Jesus answered:

Have I been so long with you, and yet hath thou not known me, Philip? He that hath seen me hath seen the Father; and how sayest thou then, "Shew us the Father"? *J 14:9*

Philip had been bold enough to act as a spokesman for the Twelve, "Shew *us* the Father." He was also a practical man.

When a large crowd followed Jesus up a mountain, Jesus asked Philip, "Whence shall we buy bread that these may eat?" *J 6:5* Philip answered that "two hundred pennyworth of bread is not sufficient for them, that every one of them may take a little." *J 6:7*

Certain Greek converts to Judaism were in Jerusalem to worship at the Passover feast. Philip may have had a Greek background, since his name was Greek. In any case, these Greeks decided to approach Jesus through Philip, saying, "Sir, we would see Jesus." *J 12:21*

We lose sight of Philip after Jesus' resurrection, except that we know he lodged in an upper room with the other disciples where they "continued with one accord in prayer and supplication." *Acts 1:13–14*

THOMAS

Thomas is listed simply as "Thomas" in the list of the Twelve given in the first three gospels. *Mk 3:18; Mt 10:3; L 6:15* However, the Gospel of John often describes him as Thomas, called "Didymus." *J 11:16; J 20:24; J 21:2* *Didymus* means "the twin."

Thomas the Twin has gone down in history as "doubting Thomas." This unfairly focuses on his skepticism when the other disciples who had seen the resurrected Jesus told him, "We have seen the Lord." *J 20:25*

Thomas had not been present when Jesus had appeared, and he said:

Except I shall see in his hands the print of the nails, and put my finger into the print of the nails, and thrust my hand into his side, I will not believe. *J 20:25*

Eight days later, Thomas was present with the other disciples when the resurrected Jesus appeared again in their midst even though the doors of the room were shut and said, "Peace be unto you." *J 20:26*

Jesus then said to Thomas:

Reach hither thy finger, and behold my hands; and reach hither thy hand, and thrust it into my side; and be not faithless, but believing. *J 20:27*

Thomas was stunned and said:

My Lord and my God. *J 20:28*

Jesus then said:

Thomas, because thou hast seen me, thou hast believed; blessed are they that have not seen, and yet have believed. *J 20:29*

Thomas was also present when Jesus appeared a third time. This time the appearance was on the shore of the Sea of Galilee. Others present were Peter, the Zebedee brothers, Nathanael and two unnamed disciples. This suggests that Thomas was probably a Galilean like Nathanael, the Zebedee brothers, and Peter. *J 21:1–2*

After this Thomas lived in an upper room in Jerusalem along with the rest of the remaining eleven disciples and continued with them "in prayer and supplication." *Acts 1:13–14*

Thomas was a careful, cautious man; but it seems likely that the other disciples shared his uncertainty when he asked Jesus in the last days of his ministry, "Lord, we know not whither thou goest; and how can we know the way?" *J 14:5*

Thomas' question gave Jesus the chance to summarize his mission in his answer:

> I am the way, the truth, and the life; no man cometh unto the Father but by me. *J 14:6*

Despite his caution, Thomas was a brave, steadfast man. Jesus had been staying out of Judea to avoid being stoned to death by the Jews. *J 10:39–40, 11:7–8* However, a man named Lazarus had died in Bethany, a village in Judea near Jerusalem. Jesus sensed his death and said to his disciples, "Let us go into Judea again." *J 11:7*

His disciples replied, "Master, the Jews of late sought to stone thee: and goest thou thither again?" *J 11:8*

Jesus disregarded their objections and concluded "let us go unto him." *J 11:15*

Thomas was the only disciple to speak and say to the rest of the disciples, "Let us also go, that we may die with him." *J 11:16* This should be the epitaph of Thomas the Twin, not "doubting Thomas."

MATTHEW

Each of the first three Gospels record the call of Matthew. *Mk 2:13–17; Mt 9:9–13; L 5:27–32* Matthew appears in the list of the Twelve chosen by Jesus. *Mk 3:18; Mt 10:3; L 6:15* Matthew drops from sight as one of the Eleven in the upper room in Jerusalem after Jesus' resurrection. *Acts 1:13*

The ambiguity as to Matthew's name arises from the three parallel passages referring to his original recruitment by Jesus. *Mk 2:14; Mt 9:9; L 5:27* The Gospel of Matthew calls him "Matthew"; however, Mark and Luke both call him "Levi." The reason for this discrepancy is not known.

Mark goes further to state that Matthew (Levi) was "the son of Alphaeus." *Mk 2:14* Since Matthew's mother is not named in the Gospels and since a "Mary" is stated to be the mother of the disciple known as "James the son of Alphaeus," we may infer that Matthew was a half-brother of James. *Mk 3:18* For detailed explanation, see "James the son of Alphaeus," pp. 381–382.

Half the original Twelve then consisted of three sets of brothers: Peter and Andrew; James and John, the Zebedee brothers; and the two Alphaeus half-brothers, Matthew and James. It may seem strange that the nucleus of the church was half-recruited on a family basis. Yet what could be more natural? Jesus' own brothers were leaders in the early church. *Acts 1:14; 1 Corinthians 9:5, 15:5–7; Galatians 1:18–19; 2:9*

The important thing is Matthew's occupation: he is variously described as a "publican" and "sitting at the receipt of custom." *Mt 10:3; Mk 2:14; Mt 9:9; L 5:27* A publican was a tax farmer, i.e., he agreed to pay Rome a certain sum for taxes, and the rest he collected was his. The taxes Matthew collected were apparently internal customs duties.

The possibilities for abuse and extortion are obvious, and in Jewish eyes then a publican was a collaborator with the hated Roman occupation, as well as contaminated by his association with Gentiles. Nevertheless, Jesus gave him the classic invitation, "Follow me." *Mk 2:14; Mt 9:9; L 5:27*

Matthew's sins had made him wealthy: he was able to give Jesus "a great feast in his own house." *L 5:29* But Jesus was willing to go since he had come to call "sinners to repentance." *Mk 2:17; Mt 9:13; L 5:32*

JAMES THE SON OF ALPHAEUS

All four of our lists of the original Twelve uniformly describe one disciple as "James the son of Alphaeus." *Mk 3:18; Mt 10:3; L 6:15; Acts 1:13* We have no record of his father, Alphaeus. We do have a record that Jesus recruited "Levi the son of Alphaeus" as one of his first disciples. *Mk 2:14* He was one of the Twelve, and we have listed him under the name of "Matthew." *See p. 380.*

We do have numerous references to James' mother, Mary, but none of those references state any connection between Mary and Levi or Matthew. From the foregoing, we infer that James was a half-brother of Matthew, having the same father but different mothers.

We may speculate that James was recruited into the movement by his half-brother; however, except for his name being on the lists of the Twelve, there is no reference to James in the Gospels. The numerous references to his mother, Mary, do provide some further details about him.

She was in the very center of Jesus' following. She is one of the three women followers listed as having been present at Jesus' crucifixion. The other two so listed are Mary Magdalene and the mother of the Zebedee brothers. *Mk 15:40; Mt 27:56*

James's mother and Mary Magdalene were the two women who watched when Jesus was buried. *Mk 15:47; Mt 27:61* James' mother accompanied Mary Magdalene to Jesus' tomb the first Easter morning and heard the angelic announcement of Jesus' resurrection. *Mk 16:1–7; Mt 28:1–8; L 24:1–10*

Mark describes James' mother as "Mary the mother of James the less and of Joses, and Salome." *Mk 15:40* Matthew describes her as "Mary the mother of James and Joses." *Mt 27:56* Modern translations have "James the younger" for "James the less." In any case, this was the title given to James the son of Alphaeus to distinguish him from James, one of the Zebedee brothers.

The gospel references to James' mother are confusing. After his first full description of her in chapter 27:56, Matthew simply calls her "the other Mary." *Mt 27:61, 28:1* After his first full description of her in chapter 15:40, Mark refers to her as "Mary the mother of

Joses" and "Mary the mother of James, and Salome." *Mk 15:47, 16:1* It is even more confusing that the name of another son of Mary is translated as either "Joseph" or "Joses," the Greek form of Joseph, depending on the translation.

We summarize the facts as follows: James' mother, Mary, had three children, James, Joseph and Salome. Since Alphaeus himself is not mentioned in the Gospels, we may speculate that he was dead and his wife, Mary, was a widow. We do know that she was a key witness to the resurrection of Jesus. She, James and his brother, Joseph, and his sister, Salome, were one of the first Christian families.

BARTHOLOMEW

Like James the son of Alphaeus, Bartholomew is mentioned expressly only in the list of the original Twelve and as one of the remaining eleven disciples who stayed in an upper room in Jerusalem after the resurrection. *Mk 3:18; Mt 10:3; L 6:14; Acts 1:13*

Bartholomew is sometimes identified with Nathanael of Cana, who became one of Jesus' first disciples. *J 1:45–51* This, of course, does not mean that Nathaniel was necessarily chosen as one of the original Twelve, although he did remain a disciple even after Jesus' death. *J 21:1–2*

Conjecture is not proof. All we really know about Bartholomew is his name which literally menas "son of Tolmai."

SIMON

Like James the son of Alphaeus and Bartholomew, Simon is mentioned expressly only in the list of the original Twelve and as one of the remaining eleven disciples who stayed in an upper room in Jerusalem after the resurrection. *Mk 3:18; Mt 10:4; L 6:15; Acts 1:13*

Matthew and Mark refer to him as "Simon the Canaanite"; Luke, in both his Gospel and in the Book of Acts, refers to him as "Simon called Zelotes" or "Simon Zelotes." In modern English, he was either "Simon the Cananaean" or "Simon the Zealot."

The Zealots were a Jewish insurrectionary group resisting Roman rule. It is uncertain whether the description "the Cananaean" is really to be understood as such or is a confused rendering that in the original meant to convey the same idea as the other passages that are translated "the Zealot." The point is that at least one of Jesus' original Twelve was a converted revolutionary.

JUDAS

Mark and Matthew list "Thaddaeus" or "Lebbaeus" whose surname was "Thaddaeus" as the tenth disciple; Luke has "Judas the brother of James" instead, but lists him as the eleventh disciple. *Mk 3:18; Mt 10:3; L 6:16* All three Gospels place Judas Iscariot last.

"Judah" was a common Jewish name, and "Judas" is the Greek form of that name. One of Jesus' brothers was named Judas. *Mk 6:3; Mt 13:55* Judas "surnamed Barsabas" was one of the chief men among the brethren of the mother church in Jerusalem. *Acts 15:22* A Galilean who led an insurrection in A. D. 6 was named Judas. *Acts 5:37*

The King James Version describes the disciple Judas as "the brother of James" both in Luke 6:16 and Acts 1:13 but uses italics to indicate that the word *brother* is not in the Greek text. Modern versions insert *son* for "brother" so that Judas is described as the "son of James."

The church has assumed for a long time that "Thaddaeus" is the same person as this Judas. The form of the name varies in the manuscripts, and the King James Version combines the name forms as "Lebbaeus whose surname was Thaddaeus" in Matthew but has simply "Thaddaeus" in Mark. *Mt 10:3; Mk 3:18*

The only reference to Judas besides these names is found in John's Gospel where he asks an important question:

> Judas saith unto him, not Iscariot, "Lord, how is it that thou wilt manifest thyself unto us, and not unto the world?" *J 14:22*

Judas Iscariot

Judas, the son or brother of James, is not well known; but the world can never forget Judas Iscariot "who also betrayed him." *Mt 10:4; Mk 3:19; L 6:16 ("the traitor")* He was the son of Simon. *J 6:71; J 12:4, 13:26* Scholars dispute over the word *Iscariot*. The usual view is that it means "man of Kerioth." Kerioth was a Judean village. If so, Judas Iscariot was not a Galilean like most of the Twelve.

Long before his arrest, Jesus told the Twelve:

Have not I chosen you twelve, and one of you is a devil? *J 6:70*

On the evening of his arrest Jesus was troubled in spirit and said to his disciples:

Verily, verily, I say unto you, that one of you shall betray me. *J 13:21; Mt 26:21 (L 22:21)*

The disciples looked at one another, "doubting of whom he spake." *J 13:22* One disciple asked: "Lord, who is it?" *J 13:22–25*

Jesus answered:

He it is, to whom I shall give a sop, when I have dipped it. *J 13:26*

Jesus gave the sop to Judas and said:

That thou doest, do quickly. *J 13:27*

After Judas received the sop he "went immediately out: and it was night." *J 13:30* John writes:

Now no man at the table knew for what intent he spake this unto him. For some of them thought, because Judas had the bag, that Jesus had said unto him, "Buy those things that we have need of against the Feast"; or, that "He should give something to the poor." *J 13:28–29*

Just before Jesus' final entry into Jerusalem, he and his disciples had supper in Bethany. In honor of the occasion, Mary took "a pound of ointment of spikenard, very costly, and anointed the feet of Jesus, and wiped his feet with her hair." *J 12:1–3* This Mary was the sister of Lazarus and Martha. *J 11:2*

According to John it was Judas who objected:

Why was not this ointment sold for three hundred pence, and given to the poor? *J 12:5*

John continues:

This he said, not that he cared for the poor, but because he was a thief, and had the bag, and bare what was put therein. *J 12:6*

As Matthew and Mark have the story, it was the disciples generally who were indignant at this extravagance, not just Judas. *Mk 14:4–5; Mt 26:8–9* Probably Judas just voiced what they all felt. *J 11:4*

At Gethsemane just before his arrest Jesus told his disciples:

Rise up, let us go; lo, he that betrayeth me is at hand. *Mk 14:42*

Mark continues the story:

And immediately, while he yet spake, cometh Judas, one of the Twelve, and with him a great multitude of swords and staves, from the chief priests and the scribes and the elders. And he that betrayed him had given him a token, saying, "Whomsoever I shall kiss, that same is he; take him, and lead him away safely." And as soon as he was come, he goeth straightway to him, and saith, "Master, master," and kissed him. *Mk 14:43–45*

The betrayal had been planned for some time:

MARK	MATTHEW	LUKE
And	Then one of the Twelve, called	Then entered Satan into
Judas Iscariot,	Judas Iscariot,	Judas surnamed Iscariot being of the number of the Twelve.
one of the Twelve, went into	went unto	And he went his way, and communed with
the chief priests,	the chief priests	the chief priests and captains,
	and said unto them, "What will ye give me,	
to betray him unto them.	and I will deliver him to you?"	how he might betray him unto them.
And when they heard it, they were glad, and promised to give him money.	And they covenanted with him for thirty pieces of silver.	And they were glad, and covenanted to give him money.
And he sought how he might conveniently betray him.	And from that time he sought opportunity	And he promised and sought opportunity
Mk 14:10–11	to betray him. *Mt 26:14–16*	to betray him unto them in the absence of the multitude. *L 22:3–6*

According to Matthew, Judas said: "What will ye give me, and I will deliver him unto you?" *Mt 26:15* The price was "thirty pieces of silver." *Mt 26:15* The place was a garden beyond the brook Cedron. *J 18:1–2* The sign was a kiss. *Mk 14:44; Mt 26:48; L 22:47–48*

It happened like this:

MARK	MATTHEW	LUKE
JUDAS: Master, Master	JUDAS: Hail, Master	JUDAS: (drew near unto Jesus to kiss him)
(and kissed him.) *Mk 14:45*	(and kissed him.) JESUS: Friend, wherefore art thou come? *Mt 26:49–50*	JESUS: Judas, betrayest thou the Son of man with a kiss? *L 22:47–48*

After Jesus had been delivered to Pontius Pilate, the governor, Judas repented:

Then Judas, which had betrayed him, when he saw that he was condemned, repented himself, and brought again the thirty pieces of silver to the chief priests and elders, saying, "I have sinned in that I have betrayed the innocent blood."

And they said, "What is that to us? See thou to that."

And he cast down the pieces of silver in the Temple, and departed, and went and hanged himself.

And the chief priests took the silver pieces, and said, "It is not lawful for to put them into the Treasury, because it is the price of blood."

And they took counsel, and bought with them the potter's field, to bury strangers in. Wherefore that field was called, "The field of blood," unto this day. That was fulfilled that which was spoken by Jeremiah the prophet, saying, "And they took thirty pieces of silver, the price of him that was valued, whom they of the children of Israel did value, and gave them for the potter's field, as the Lord appointed me." *Mt 27:3–10*

Acts has a different version:

Now this man purchased a field with the reward of iniquity; and falling headlong, he burst asunder in the midst, and all his bowels gushed out. And it was known unto all the dwellers at Jerusalem; inasmuch as that field is called in their proper tongue, "Aceldama," that is to say, "The field of blood." *Acts 1:18–19*

Both Matthew and Acts agree that Judas' silver left him a monument: "The field of blood." *Mt 27:8; Acts 1:19* However, modern versions place the statement in Acts in parenthesis. It is obviously an explanatory insert in Peter's speech to the brethren as to the necessity of picking a successor to Judas Iscariot.

Peter's speech began as follows:

Men and brethren, this scripture must needs have been fulfilled, which the Holy Spirit by the mouth of David spake before concerning Judas, which was guide to them that took Jesus. For he was numbered with us, and had obtained part of this ministry . . . [Explanatory insert as to Judas' end] . . . For it is written in the book of Psalms, "Let his habitation be desolate, and let no man dwell therein"; and His bishoprick [office] let another take." *Acts 1:16–17, 20 (Psalms 69:25; 109:8)*

Peter does not condemn Judas and treats him with surprising mildness, saying, "he was numbered with us, and had obtained part of this ministry." *Acts 1:17* Judas had repented, and Peter knew it. *Mt 17:3-5* The apostles' prayers show that they shared this mildness:

Thou, Lord, which knowest the hearts of all men, shew whether of these two thou hast chosen, that he may take part of this ministry and apostleship, from which Judas by transgression fell, that he might go to his own place. *Acts 1:24–25*

The replacement for Judas had to be a man who like Judas "companied with us all the time that the Lord Jesus went in and out among us, beginning from the baptism of John." *Acts 1:21–22*

They had been close companions, Peter was the leader of the Twelve, and Judas had been the treasurer. *J 13:29*

Peter, no doubt, remembered that it had not been clear to the Twelve who should betray Jesus even after Judas, like the rest had asked, "Is it I?" *Mk 14:19; Mt 26:22* Luke writes:

> And they began to enquire among themselves, which of them it was that should do this thing. *L 22:23*

Peter had heard Jesus' solemn epitaph for Judas:

MARK	MATTHEW	LUKE
It is		
one of the Twelve,	He	
that dippeth	that dippeth his hand	
with me in the dish.	with me in the dish,	
	the same	
	shall betray me.	
		And truly
The Son of man	The Son of man	the Son of man
indeed goeth,	goeth	goeth,
as it is written	as it is written	as it was determined;
of him;	of him;	
but woe to	but woe unto	but woe unto
that man by whom	that man by whom	that man by whom
the Son of man	the Son of man	he
is betrayed!	is betrayed!	is betrayed!
		L 22:22
Good were it	It had been good	
for that man	for that man	
if he had	if he had	
never been born.	not been born.	
Mk 14:20–21	*Mt 26:23–24*	

Judas then asked:

> Master, is it I? *Mt 26:25*

Jesus replied:

Thou hast said. *Mt 26:25*

Jesus, that evening, gave the first communion to the Twelve, including Judas Iscariot. *Mk 14:22–25; Mt 26:26–29; L 22:19–22* He recognized that both he and Judas Iscariot were caught in a divine drama: he had chosen Judas, but Judas had betrayed him:

> If ye know these things, happy are ye if ye do them. I speak not of you all. I know whom I have chosen; but that the scripture may be fulfilled, "He that eateth bread with me hath lifted up his heel against me." *J 13:17–18 (Psalm 41:9)*

Perhaps it was too painful to Jesus to quote all of Psalm 41:9: "Yea, *mine own familiar friend, in whom I trusted*, which did eat of my bread, hath lifted up his heel against me."
We do know that Jesus felt this way:

> While I was with them in the world, I kept them in thy name: those that thou gavest me I have kept, and none of them is lost, but the son of perdition; that the Scripture might be fulfilled. *J 17:12*

The Scripture had to be fulfilled. We do not know why Judas Iscariot chose to be the one to fulfill it. Judas did repent, and Jesus himself taught:

> All manner of sin and blasphemy shall be forgiven unto men: . . . And whosoever speaketh a word against the Son of man, it shall be forgiven him. *Mt 12:31–32*

Jesus' Organization of His Movement

We tend to overlook that Jesus carefully organized his movement. Not only did he choose twelve special assistants whom he called *apostles*, literally, "ones set forth," but he also did send them forth in an organized way with specific instructions (See "The Mission Of The Twelve," pp. 399–404).

Not only did he send out the Twelve but he also later sent out either seventy or seventy-two other men with similar instructions *L 10:1* (See "The Mission Of The Seventy," pp. 405–411). The Seventy were sent out in twos as advance parties to prepare each place where Jesus was going to minister. As Luke has it, Jesus appointed and "sent them two and two before his face into every city and place, whither he himself would come." *L 10:1*

There is a persistent pattern of Jesus sending out advance parties. When Jesus was going to Jerusalem, he "sent messengers before his face; and they went, and entered into a village of the Samaritans, *to make ready for him.*" *L 9:52*

The same pattern of organization is shown on an earlier journey through Samaria. Jesus stopped and waited at Jacob's Well while his disciples went ahead into Sychar to buy meat. *J 4:5–6, 8, 30*

Jesus and his disciples maintained a common mess. On one occasion a great multitude of people had been with him for three days. *Mk 8:1–3; Mt 15:32* Jesus wanted to feed them from their stock of provisions, but his disciples doubted that they had enough, saying:

Whence should we *have* so much bread in the wilderness, as to fill so great a multitude? *Mt 15:33 (Mk 8:4)*

Jesus then asked them:

How many loaves have ye? *Mk 8:5; Mt 15:34*

They answered:

Seven, and a few small fishes. *Mt 15:34 (Mk 8:5)*

After the disciples served the seven loaves, they found that they also had on hand "a few small fishes." *Mk 8:7*

On another, similar, occasion, the disciples asked:

> Shall we go and *buy* two hundred pennyworth of bread, and give them to eat? *Mk 6:37*

To buy, the group had to have money, and this would probably have required a treasurer to hold the money. We do not know if Judas Iscariot was then treasurer. Later on, he was. John writes that Judas "had the bag, and bare what was put therein," i.e., Judas kept the money the group collected in a bag. *J 12:6, 13:29*

Apparently, they received contributions of property that were then sold and the money given to the poor. This, apparently, was when Mary used a pound of costly ointment to anoint the feet of Jesus, since Judas then asked:

> Why was not this ointment sold for three hundred pence, and given to the poor? *J 12:5*

As Mark and Matthew got the story, it was not just Judas who objected but the disciples, generally:

MARK	MATTHEW
And there were *some* that had indignation within themselves, and said,	But when his *disciples* saw it they had indignation, saying,
"Why was this waste of the ointment made?" For it might have been sold for more than three hundred pence, and have been given to the poor. And they murmured against her. *Mk 14:4–5*	"To what purpose is this waste?" For this ointment might have been sold for much, and given to the poor. *Mt 26:8–9*

There are indications that the amount in the disciples' treasury was substantial: enough to buy "two hundred penny worth of bread"; or, to consider sale of donated ointment worth "three hundred pence." *Mk 6:37, 14:5; J 12:5* The "pence" were really "denarii"; an denarius was a Roman silver coin equal in value to a vineyard laborer's wage for one day. *Mt 20:2,9,13* To get to contemporary equivalents: assume a daily wage of $50.00; multiply by 200 (two hundred pennyworth); and the result is a treasury with $10,000 on hand.

Money matters were so commonly discussed among the disciples that at the Last Supper the disciples thought Jesus had said to Judas:

> Buy those things that we have need of against the Feast; or, that he should give something to the poor. *J 13:29*

It was during the Passover festival, and the disciples thought Judas had been told to buy the food that the group would need for the festival feast. Mark and Luke report that Jesus earlier that day had sent two disciples, Peter and John, into Jerusalem to arrange for a room in which the group could have their Passover feast. *Mk 14:13; L 22:7–8*

He told them:

> Go and prepare us the Passover, that we may eat. *L 22:8*

They answered:

> Where wilt thou that we prepare? *L 22:9 (Mk 14:12; Mt 26:17)*

He replied:

> Behold, when ye are entered into the city, there shall a man meet you, bearing a pitcher of water; follow him into the house where he entereth in. *L 22:10 (Mk 14:13; Mt 26:18)*

For some time, Jesus had had to be very careful since he knew that the Sanhedrin was planning to put him to death. *J 11:47–53* John writes:

> Jesus therefore walked no more openly among the Jews; but went thence unto a country near to the wilderness, into a city called Ephraim, and there continued with his disciples. *J 11:54*

Later on, he was in and out of Jerusalem. *L 21:37* As Passover began, he waited until evening to enter Jerusalem to go to the room Peter and John had arranged for the Passover supper. *Mk 14:17 (Mt 26:20)*

When Jesus was arrested later that night, at least one of the disciples was armed with a sword and resisted, cutting off the ear of a servant of the high priest. *Mk 14:47, Mt 26:51; L 22:49–50; J 18:10* John identifies this disciple as Simon Peter and states that Jesus then told Peter, "Put up *thy* sword into the sheath: . . ." *J 18:11*

Apparently, more than one disciple had a sword because Luke states that "*they* said unto him, Lord, shall *we* smite with the sword?" *L 22:49*

Earlier that same evening, Jesus had told his disciples:

> He that *hath no sword*, let him sell his garment and buy one. *L 22:36*

The disciples had answered:

> Lord, behold, here are two swords. *L 22:38*

Jesus assumed that his disciples had money to buy swords. They were not penniless mendicants. They had individual purses as well as their common purse. Jesus told his disciples that same night:

> But now, he that *hath a purse*, let him take it, and likewise his scrip: . . . *L 22:36*

This refers back to the instructions which Jesus had given when he had several years before sent out the Twelve and the Seventy:

JESUS: When I sent you without purse, and scrip, and shoes, lacked ye anything?
DISCIPLES: Nothing.
JESUS: But *now*, he that hath a purse, let him take it, and likewise his scrip . . . L 22:35–36

While strictly speaking, it was not a matter of organization, Jesus and the Twelve were accompanied on their preaching tours by a group of healed women. Luke states:

And it came to pass afterward, that he went throughout every city and village, preaching and shewing the glad tidings of the Kingdom of God; and the Twelve were with him, and *certain women, which had been healed of evil spirits and infirmities*, Mary called Magdalene, out of whom went seven devils, and Joanna, the wife of Chuza Herod's steward, and Susanna and many others, *which ministered unto him of their substance.* L 8:1–3

To sum up, a considerable number of women who had been healed of their infirmities accompanied Jesus and his disciples and used their own property to provide for Jesus and the Twelve. They were, presumably, wealthy women. Joanna, in particular, was the wife of a key royal official and, as such, would be likely to be a woman of means.

It seems evident that Jesus and his disciples did not rely on casual hospitality or alms. These women provided the food and probably administered the common mess of Jesus' company of close disciples.

These women disciples accompanied Jesus from Galilee unto Judea to a distant view of his cross:

MARK	MATTHEW	LUKE
		And all his
There were	And	acquaintance,

MARK (cont.)	MATTHEW (cont.)	LUKE (cont.)
also women	many women were there	and the women that *followed him* from Galilee,
looking on afar off:	beholding afar off,	stood afar off, beholding these things.
		L 23:29
among whom was Mary Magdalene, and Mary the mother of James the less and of Joses, and Salome;	[among which was Mary Magdalene, and Mary the mother of James and Joses and the mother of Zebedee's children]*	
who also, when he was in Galilee, *followed him, and ministered unto him,* and many other women which came up with him unto Jerusalem.	which *followed Jesus* from Galilee, *ministering unto him.*	
Mk 15:40–41	Mt 27:55 *Conformed to Mark's order	

These dedicated women then followed Jesus' body to its grave:

And the *women* also, *which came with him from Galilee*, followed after, and beheld the sepulchre, and how his body was laid. And *they* returned, and prepared spices and ointments; . . ." L 23:55–56

The Mission of the Twelve

Jesus sent out his twelve chief disciples with these instructions:

Mark	Matthew	Luke
And commanded them that they should take nothing for their journey,	Provide	Take nothing for your journey, neither staves,
save a staff only, no scrip, no bread, no money in their purse;	neither gold, nor silver, nor brass in your purses, nor scrip for your journey;	nor scrip, neither bread, neither money;
But be shod with sandals, and not put on two coats. Mk 6:8–9	neither two coats, neither shoes, nor yet staves: for the workman is worthy of his meat. Mt 10:9–10	neither have two coats apiece. L 9:3

Jesus then instructed them in missionary technique and procedures:

Mark	Matthew	Luke
In what place soever ye enter into an house,	And into whatsoever city or town ye shall enter, enquire who in it is worthy, and	And whatsoever house ye enter into,

MARK (cont.)	MATTHEW (cont.)	LUKE (cont.)
there abide till ye	there abide till ye go thence. And when ye come into a house, salute it. And if the house be worthy, let your peace come upon it; but if it be not worthy, let your peace return to you.	there abide, and thence
depart from that place.		depart.
And whosoever shall not receive you, nor hear you, when ye depart thence, shake off the dust under your feet for a testimony against them.	And whosoever shall not receive you, nor hear your words, when ye depart out of that house or city, shake off the dust of your feet.	And whosoever will not receive you, when ye go out of that city, shake off the very dust from your feet for a testimony against them. *L 9:4–5*
Verily I say unto you, it shall be more tolerable for Sodom and Gomorrha in the day of judgment, than for that city. *Mk 6:10–11*	Verily, I say unto you, it shall be more tolerable for the land of Sodom and Gomorrha in the day of judgment, than for that city. *Mt 10:11–15*	

Modern translations omit the last sentence quoted from Mark upon the basis of the manuscript evidence, but they retain the last sentence quoted from Matthew, which is identical in meaning.

Only Matthew quotes Jesus as then limiting the mission of the Twelve to Jews:

> Go not into the way of the Gentiles, and into any city of the Samaritans [a non-Jewish group] enter ye not; but go rather to the lost sheep of the house of Israel. *Mt 10:5–6*

Both Matthew and Luke indicate that they were to preach the Kingdom and to heal:

MATTHEW	LUKE
And as ye go, preach, saying, "The Kingdom of Heaven is at hand."	And he sent them to preach the Kingdom of God, and
Heal the sick, cleanse the lepers, raise the dead, cast out devils: *freely ye have received, freely give.* Mt 10:7–8	to heal the sick. L 9:2

Matthew makes it clear that the healings were to be without charge: "freely ye have received, freely give." *Mt 10:8* All of the first three Gospels specifically say that the Twelve were given special healing power:

MARK	MATTHEW	LUKE
. . . gave them *power* over unclean spirits. Mk 6:7	. . . gave them *power* against unclean spirits, to cast them out, and to heal all manner	. . . gave them *power* and authority over all devils, and to cure

Mark (cont.)	Matthew (cont.)	Luke (cont.)
	of sickness	
	and all manner	
	of disease.	diseases.
	Mt 10:1	*L 9:1*

Mark and Luke sum up the mission of the Twelve as follows:

Mark	Luke
And they went out,	And they departed,
and	and went through the towns,
preached that men	preaching
should repent.	the gospel,
And they cast out many devils,	
and anointed with oil	
many that were sick,	
and healed them.	and healing everywhere.
Mk 6:12–13	*L 9:6*

Mark's and Luke's accounts of the charge to the Twelve are quite brief, while Matthew's is long. Part of Jesus' charge to the Twelve is found only in Matthew and to make matters more complicated, Matthew has inserted in his charge material which the other two synoptic Gospels have in other contexts:

Matthew's Charge	Synoptic Parallels		
	Mark	Matthew	Luke
Mt 10:16			L 10:3
Mt 10:17–22	Mk 13:9, 11–13		L 21:12–19
Mt 10:24			L 6:40
Mt 10:26b–33			L 12:2–9
Mt 10:34–36			L 12:51–53
Mt 10:37			L 14:26
Mt 10:38	Mk 8:34	Mt 16:24	L 9:23
Mt 10:39	Mk 8:35	Mt 16:25	L 9:24, 17:33

Omitting this material and the parts of Matthew's charge already quoted, his charge states:

> ... But when they persecute you in *this* [that] *city* flee ye into another: for verily I say unto you, ye shall not have gone over the cities of Israel, till the Son of man be come. ...

> It is enough for the disciple that he be as his master, and the servant as his lord. If they have called the master of the house "Beelzebub," how much more shall they call them of his household?

> Fear them not therefore: ...

> He that receiveth you receiveth me, and he that receiveth me receiveth him that sent me. He that receiveth a prophet in the name of a prophet shall receive a prophet's reward; and he that receiveth a righteous man in the name of a righteous man shall receive a righteous man's reward.

> And whosoever shall give to drink unto one of these little ones a cup of cold water, only in the name of a disciple, verily I say unto you, he shall in no wise lose his reward. *Mt 10:23, 25–26a, 40–42*

In some way, Mark has gotten this "reward" saying intermingled in an account of a teaching episode involving the example of a little child:

Mark	Matthew
For whosoever shall give	And whosoever shall give
you	unto one of these little ones
a cup of water	[a cup of cold water
to drink in my name,	to drink]*
because ye belong to Christ,	only in the name of a disciple,
verily I say unto you,	verily I say unto you,
he shall not lose	he shall in no wise lose
his reward.	his reward.
Mk 9:41	*Mt 10:42*
	*Conformed to Mark's order

Modern translations make it clear that the "little ones" in Matthew's quote are Jesus' disciples. Accordingly, both Matthew and Mark say the same thing: whoever shall give you a cup of water to drink *because you are my disciples* shall not lose his reward.

The point is that those who help Jesus' disciples in Jesus' name shall be *rewarded* just as he that receives a prophet's emissary in the name of a prophet shall receive a prophet's *reward* and he that receives a righteous man's emissary in the righteous man's name shall receive a righteous man's *reward*. The reason for the reward to Jesus' Twelve is "he that received you receiveth me." They are his emissaries—the "sent" ones.

The scribes who came up to Galilee from Jerusalem had said of Jesus, "He hath Beelzebub, and by the prince of the devils casteth he out devils." *Mk 3:22* The Pharisees had said, ". . . he casteth out devils through the prince of devils." *Mt 9:34*

Jesus accordingly told the Twelve, "If they have called the master of the house 'Beelzebub,' how much more shall they call *them of his household*? *Mt 10:25*

The point is that the Twelve could expect to be accused as untruly and unfairly as the scribes and Pharisees had accused Jesus. The servant is not above his lord.

But it was not to be all heartache. Already the popular opinion was that Jesus was a great prophet. They were saying, "That a great prophet is risen among us"; and, "that God hath visited his people." *L 7:16* Jesus, himself, claimed that title for himself, saying, "A prophet is not without honor, but in his own country, and among his own kin, and in his own house." *Mk 6:4 (Mt 13:57)*

The people would honor the Twelve so as to receive the reward of one who they deemed to be a prophet, namely Jesus. At least the Twelve would be rewarded by the people as the emissaries of a righteous man.

At the end to Jesus' charge to the Twelve, Matthew writes:

And it came to pass, when Jesus had made an end of commanding his twelve disciples, he departed thence to teach and to preach in their cities. *Mt 11:1*

The Mission of the Seventy

After Jesus sent out the Twelve, he sent out either seventy or seventy-two others. *L 10:1* These are referred to as the Seventy. Mark's charge to the Twelve and Luke's charge to the Seventy both state that they were to go "two and two." *Mk 6:7; L 10:1* Luke's charge to the Seventy is paralleled for the most part by Matthew's charge to the Twelve. One part of Matthew not included in his charge to the Twelve also parallel Luke's charge to the Seventy. That part of Matthew is marked with an asterisk in the following comparison:

MATTHEW	LUKE
CHARGE TO THE TWELVE	CHARGE TO THE SEVENTY
The harvest truly is plenteous,	The harvest truly is great,
but the laborers are few;	but the laborers are few;
pray ye therefore	pray ye therefore
the Lord of the harvest,	the Lord of the harvest,
that he will send forth	that he would send forth
laborers into his harvest.	laborers into his harvest.
Mt 9:37–38*	
Behold,	Go your ways: behold,
I send you forth	I send you forth
as sheep	as lambs
in the midst of wolves:	among wolves.
be ye therefore	
wise as serpents, and	
harmless as doves.	
Mt 10:16	
Provide neither gold, nor silver,	Carry neither purse,
nor brass in your purses,	nor scrip,
nor scrip for your journey,	nor shoes,
neither two coats, neither shoes,	and salute no man by the way.
nor yet staves: . . .	
Mt 10:9–10	

And when ye come into a house	And into whatsoever house
	ye enter, first say, "Peace be to this house."
salute it.	
And if the house be worthy, let your peace come upon it; but if it be not worthy, let your peace return to you. *Mt 10:12–13*	And if the son of peace be there, your peace shall rest upon it; if not, it shall turn to you again.
And into whatsoever city or town ye shall enter, enquire who in it is worthy; and there abide till ye go thence. *Mt 10:11*	And in the same house remain, eating and drinking such things as they give:
. . .for the workman is worthy of his meat. *Mt 10:10*	for the laborer is worthy of his hire. Go not from house to house.
And as ye go, preach,	And into whatsoever city ye enter, and they receive you, eat such things as are set before you, and heal the sick that are therein,
saying, "The Kingdom of Heaven is at hand." *Mt 10:7*	and say unto them, "The Kingdom of God is come nigh unto you."

	But into
And whosoever	whatsoever city ye enter,
shall not receive you,	and they receive you not,
nor hear your words,	
when ye depart out	go your ways out
of that house or city,	into the streets of the same,
	and say,
shake off the dust	"Even the very dust of your city,
of your feet.	which cleaveth on us,
Mt 10:14	we do wipe off against you:
	notwithstanding
	be ye sure of this,
	that the Kingdom of God
	is come nigh unto you."

Verily I say unto you,	But I say unto you,
it shall be more tolerable	that it shall be more tolerable in
for the land of Sodom	that day for Sodom,
and Gomorrha	
in the day of judgment,	
than for that city.	than for that city.
Mt 10:15	*L 10:2–12*

He that receiveth you	He that heareth you
receiveth me, and	heareth me;
he that receiveth me	
receiveth him that sent me.	
Mt 10:40	and he that despiseth you
	despiseth me; and
	he that despiseth me
	despiseth him that sent me.
	L 10:16

Jesus told the Seventy essentially the same things he told the Twelve but in variant phrases. The parallelism of Matthew's charge to the Twelve and Luke's charge to the Seventy does not prove that Luke mislabeled his material, since we would expect Jesus, in his human aspect, to repeat himself just as any other man does. If he had first sent out Twelve and he later sent out a larger group of Seventy, he would be likely to repeat himself.

The Seventy were told to heal the sick. *L 10:9* The Twelve were given the power to heal. *Mt 9:10; Mk 6:7; L 9:1* They did heal. *Mk 6:13 L 9:6*

The Twelve were given power over unclean spirits. *Mk 6:7; Mt 10:1; L 9:1* (*devils*) When the Seventy returned to Jesus they reported:

Lord, even the devils are subject unto us through thy name. *L 10:17*

But, the essential work of the Twelve and the Seventy was not to cure demon possession or to heal, but to act as advance parties for the Kingdom of God. The Seventy were sent to every city and place where Jesus himself was going to go. *L 10:1*

Both the Twelve and the Seventy were to preach the near approach of the Kingdom of God:

MATTHEW	LUKE
The Kingdom of Heaven is at hand. *Mt 10:7*	The Kingdom of God is come nigh unto you. *L 10:9, 11*

Jesus' teaching of the coming of the Kingdom of God is usually thought of as a gentle happy thing; but an intrinsic part of that Kingdom, so far as Jesus was concerned, was a savage judgment of God. In Luke's charge to the Seventy Jesus moved from an instruction in Luke 10:11 to declare that "the Kingdom of God is come nigh unto you" to a solemn warning to cities that did not accept the Kingdom in Luke 10:12, and this warning has its parallel in Matthew's charge to the Twelve:

MATTHEW	LUKE
Verily I say unto you, it shall be more tolerable for the land of Sodom	But I say unto you, that it shall be more tolerable in that day for Sodom,

MATTHEW (cont.)	LUKE (cont.)
and Gomorrha	
in the day of judgment,	
than for that city.	than for that city.
Mt 10:15	*L 10:12*

Luke's charge to the Seventy then continues with a solemn warning to specific cities, and these warnings are paralleled in Matthew but are not included in his charge to the Twelve:

MATTHEW	LUKE
Woe unto thee, Chorazin!	Woe unto thee, Chorazin!
Woe unto thee, Bethsaida!	Woe unto thee, Bethsaida!
For if the mighty works,	For if the mighty works
which were done in you,	
had been done	had been done
in Tyre and Sidon,	in Tyre and Sidon,
	which have been done in you,
they would have repented	they had a great while ago
long ago	repented
in sackcloth and ashes.	sitting in sackcloth and ashes.
But I say unto you,	But
it shall be more tolerable	it shall be more tolerable
for Tyre and Sidon	for Tyre and Sidon
at the day of judgment,	at the judgment,
than for you.	than for you.
And thou, Capernaum,	And thou, Capernaum,
which art exalted unto heaven,	which art exalted to heaven,
shalt be brought down to hell:	shalt be thrust down to hell.
for if the mighty works	*L 10:13–15*
which had been done in thee,	
had been done in Sodom,	
it would have remained	
until this day.	
Mt 11:21–24	

Matthew introduces the statement just quoted by saying:

Then began he to upbraid the cities wherein most of his mighty works were done, because they repented not. *Mt 11:20*

The preaching of the Kingdom of God required repentance in Chorazin, Bethsaida, and Capernaum and, in fact, in every city. Both the Twelve and the Seventy were told to perform a solemn rite of warning for those persons and towns who rejected their missions: shake off the dust from their feet as evidence against them. *Mt 10:14; Mk 6:11; L 9:5 (the Twelve); L 10:11 (the Seventy)*

Paul and Barnabas performed this rite when they were expelled from Antioch in Pisidia:

They shook off the dust of their feet against them. *Acts 13:51*

Today this spirit has gone out of Christianity. But Jesus did teach:

Give not that which is holy unto the dogs, neither cast ye your pearls before swine, lest they trample them under their feet, and turn again and rend you. *Mt 7:6*

Jesus' statements like these, his statement that it shall be more tolerable for Sodom in the day of judgment than for an unrepentant city, and his warnings such as: "Woe unto thee, Chorazin! Woe unto thee, Bethsaida!" are read out of the New Testament by people who see Jesus as only a gentle itinerant preacher of parables. *Mt 11:21, 10:15; L 10:12* But Jesus' mission was not that. Jesus' mission was:

I am come to send fire on the earth; and what will I, if it be already kindled? But I have a baptism to be baptized with; and how am I straightened till it be accomplished! Suppose ye that I am come to give peace on earth? I tell you, Nay; but rather division . . ." *L 12:49–51*

Jesus' mission was: "Fire on the earth!" not "Peace on earth." Jesus told the Twelve and the Seventy to shake off the dust of unreceptive cities as a warning of the judgment to come upon those who would neither receive nor hear them. Are Christians today to solemnly perform this rite of warning against the sickness of cities and their culture or are Christians only to be God's anonymous underground? Are Jesus' warnings, "Woe unto thee, Los Angeles! Woe unto thee, Tokyo! Woe unto thee, Moscow! Woe unto thee, London! Woe unto thee, Bombay!"?

The Harvest Jesus Saw

In the Samaritan town of Sychar Jesus told his disciples:

Say not ye, "There are yet four months, and then cometh the harvest?"

Behold, I say unto you, "Lift up your eyes and look at the fields; for they are white already to harvest."

And he that reapeth receiveth wages, and gathereth fruit unto life eternal: that both he that soweth and he that reapeth may rejoice together. And herein is that saying true, "One soweth, and another reapeth." [*Job 31:8; Micah 6:15*]

I sent you to reap that whereon ye bestowed no labor: other men labored, and ye entered into their labors. *J 4:35–38*

The obvious reference of Jesus' words was to the Samaritans: they are the grain that was white for harvest. He had just announced to a Samaritan woman at the well in that Samaritan town that he was the Messiah (the Christ), and she had left her waterpot at the well and was busily announcing to anyone who would hear her, "Come, see a man, which told me all things that ever I did: is not this the Christ?" *J 4:29*

The Samaritan townspeople came out of the town to see Jesus and prevailed upon him to stay two days. Many of them believed because of the woman's words, "and many more believed because of his own word." *J 4:39, 41* They later told the woman, "Now we believe, not because of thy saying, for we have heard him ourselves, and know that is indeed the Christ, the saviour of the world." *J 4:42*

When Jesus told his disciples to, "Lift up your eyes, and look on the fields; for they are white already to harvest" he meant the Samaritans. *J 4:35*

Later on when he commissioned his twelve disciples he instructed them:

> The harvest truly is plenteous, but the laborers are few; pray ye therefore the Lord of the harvest, that he will send forth laborers into his harvest. *Mt 9:37–38*

Here, when Jesus spoke of the harvest, he meant the multitudes who had been listening to him. Matthew states that "he was moved with compassion on them, because they fainted, and were scattered abroad, as sheep having no shepherd." *Mt 9:36*

Jesus gave the Seventy the same instructions he had given the Twelve:

> The harvest truly is great, but the laborers are few. Pray ye therefore the Lord of the harvest, that he would send forth laborers into his harvest. *L 10:2*

The harvest the Twelve and the Seventy were sent to were to Jews — "the lost sheep of the house of Israel." *Mt 10:6; 15:24* Within twenty-five years after Jesus' death and resurrection his followers were mostly Gentiles and so it has remained to the twentieth century.

Is this what Jesus intended?

The Time for Israel to Repent

There is a cryptic parable of Jesus that is recorded only in Luke:

A certain man had a fig tree planted in his vineyard; and he came and sought fruit thereon, and found none.

Then said he unto the dresser of his vineyard, "Behold, these three years I come seeking fruit on this fig tree, and find none; cut it down. Why cumbereth it the ground?"

And he answering said unto him, "Lord, let it alone this year also, till I shall dig about it, and dung it. And if it bear fruit, well; and if not, then after that thou shalt cut it down." *L 13:6–19*

Jesus had just spoken of the absolute necessity that his hearers repent, or perish. Probably what was in his mind in this parable is his hearers collectively, that is, the nation of Israel. Three years had gone by with no fruit. Some commentators flatly assert that these three years do not refer to the three years of Jesus' ministry. It is true that three is a common number in stories, but the question is: what was in the mind of Jesus when he spoke?

Is the vineyard owner, God the Father, who had planted a fig tree (Israel) in his world? Is Jesus the vinedresser who pleads for another year before God the Father's judgment shall fall on Jesus' people, Israel?

Jesus had just spoken of the need to repent. Was he here in a cryptic way telling Israel that it must repent — its fruitlessness must end?

Later in his ministry, Jesus told another parable of warning that is found only in Matthew. The chief priests and elders had just refused to say whether the baptism of John was "from Heaven, or of man" and Jesus had accordingly refused to state his own authority. *Mt 21:25–27*

Jesus then said:

But what think ye? A certain man had two sons; and he came to the first, and said, "Son, go work today in my vineyard."

He answered and said, "I will not," but afterward he repented, and went.

And he came to the second, and said likewise. And he answered and said, "I go, sir," and went not.

Whether of them twain did the will of his father?" *Mt 21:28–31*

They replied:

The first. *Mt 21:31*

Jesus replied:

Verily I say unto you, that the publicans and the harlots go into the Kingdom of God before you. For John came unto you in the way of righteousness, and ye believed him not; but the publicans and the harlots believed him: and ye, when ye had seen it, repented not afterward, that ye might believe him. *Mt 21:31–32*

The publicans and prostitutes had by their occupations said that they would not work in God's vineyard, but they had, in fact, done so because they had accepted John's call to repentance. The chief priests and elders each had, in effect, said to God, "I go, sir," but had not. They had not accepted John's call to repentance. Accordingly, the publicans and prostitutes were already in the Kingdom of God, and the chief priests and elders were not.

Matthew then has another parable of warning, but that parable is also found in Mark and Luke:

MARK	MATTHEW	LUKE
	There was	
A certain man	a certain householder,	A certain man
planted	which planted	planted

MARK (cont.)	MATTHEW (cont.)	LUKE (cont.)
a vineyard	a vineyard	a vineyard,
and set an hedge	and hedged it	
about it,	round about,	
and digged	and digged	
a place		
for the winefat [vat],	a winepress in it,	
and built a tower,	and built a tower,	
and let it out	and let it out	and let it forth
to husbandmen,	to husbandmen,	to husbandmen
and went into	and went into	and went into
a far country.	a far country.	a far country
		for a long time.
And at the season	And when the time	And at the season
	of the fruit drew near,	
he sent	he sent his servants	he sent a servant
to the husbandmen	to the husbandmen,	to the husbandmen,
a servant,		
that he	that they	that they
might receive	might receive	should give him
from the husbandmen		
of the fruits	the fruits	of the fruit
of the vineyard.	of it.	of the vineyard.
And they	And the husbandmen	But the husbandmen
caught him	took his servants,	
and beat him, and	and beat one	beat him, and
	and killed another,	
sent him away empty.		sent him away empty.
And again		And again
he sent unto them		he sent
another servant'		another servant;
and at him		
they cast stones,	and stoned another.	and they beat
and wounded him		him also,
in the head,		and entreated
		[treated]
		him shamefully,

MARK (cont.)	MATTHEW (cont.)	LUKE (cont.)
and sent him away shamefully handled.		and sent him away empty.
And again he sent another and him they killed, and many others: beating some, and killing some.	Again he sent other servants more than the first; and they did unto them likewise.	And again he sent a third; and they wounded him also, and cast him out.
Having yet therefore		Then said the lord of the vineyard, "What shall I do?
	But last of all he sent unto them	I will send
one son, his wellbeloved, he sent him also last unto them, saying, "They will reverence my son."	his son, saying, "They will reverence my son."	my beloved son; it may be they will reverence him when they see him."
But these husbandmen said among themselves:	But when the husbandmen saw the son, they said among themselves:	But when the husbandmen saw him, they reasoned among themselves, saying,
"This is the heir; come, let us kill him, and the inheritance	"This is the heir; come, let us kill him, and let us seize on his inheritance."	"This is the heir; come, let us kill him, that the inheritance

MARK (cont.)	MATTHEW (cont.)	LUKE (cont.)
shall be ours."		may be ours."
And they took him,	And they caught him,	So they
and killed him		
and cast him out	and cast him out	cast him out
of the vineyard.	of the vineyard,	of the vineyard,
	and slew him.	and killed him.
What shall	When the lord	What
therefore	therefore	therefore
the lord		shall the lord
of the vineyard	of the vineyard	of the vineyard
	cometh,	
do?	what will he do	do unto them?
	unto those	
He will come and		He shall come and
destroy the		destroy these
husbandmen,	husbandmen?	husbandmen
and will give	*Mt 21:33–40*	and shall give
the vineyard		the vineyard
unto others.		to others."
Mk 12:1–9		*L 20:9–16*

Jesus' listeners then said:

MATTHEW
He will
miserably
destroy
those wicked men,
and will let out
his vineyard
unto other husbandmen
which shall render him
the fruits
in their seasons.
Mt 21:41

Jesus continued:

MARK	MATTHEW	LUKE
And have ye not read this Scripture, "The stone which the builders rejected is become the head of the corner: this was the Lord's doing, and it is marvellous in our eyes"? Mk 12:10–11 (Psalm 118:22–23)	Did ye never read in the Scriptures, "The stone which the builders rejected, the same is become the head of the corner: this is the Lord's doing, and it is marvellous in our eyes"? (Psalm 118:22-23)	What is this then that is written, "The stone which the builders rejected the same is become the head of the corner"? (Psalm 118:22)
	Therefore say I unto you, the Kingdom of God shall be taken from you, and given to a nation bringing forth the fruits thereof. And whosoever shall fall on this stone shall be broken; but on whomsoever it shall fall, it will grind him to powder. Mt 21:42–44	Whosoever shall fall upon that stone shall be broken; but on whomsoever it shall fall, it will grind him to powder. L 20:17–18

In this parable, the owner of the vineyard is God the Father. The beloved son is Jesus. The husbandmen who had leased the vineyard on shares is meant to be the nation of Israel, collectively its religious establishment.

The Gospel accounts record the reaction of the Jewish religious establishment to Jesus' parable as follows:

MARK	MATTHEW	LUKE
	And when	And the chief priests
And they	the chief priests	and the scribes
	and Pharisees	
	had heard	
	his parables,	
	they perceived	
	that he spake	the same hour
	of them.	
sought	But when they sought	sought
to lay hold on him,	to lay hands on him,	to lay hands on him:
but feared	they feared	and they feared
the people:	the multitude,	the people:
for they	because they	for they
knew	took him	perceived
that he had spoken	for a prophet.	that he had spoken
the parable	*Mt 21:45–46*	this parable
against them,		against them.
and they left him		*L 20:19*
and went their way.		
Mk 12:12		

This parable was uttered in Jerusalem, in the Temple itself. The key members of Israel's religious establishment, the chief priests, the scribes and the elders, had just challenged Jesus' authority, and he had refused to answer unless they were willing to answer his own question respecting the significance of the baptism of John the Baptist. *Mk 11:27–33; Mt 21:23–27; L 20:1–8*

Matthew quotes Jesus as pronouncing judgment on Israel as follows:

> Therefore say I unto you, the Kingdom of God shall be taken from you, and given to a nation bringing forth the fruits thereof. *Mt 21:43*

The nation or people referred to is the Christian church. After Jesus' resurrection, Peter, writing in 1 Peter, referred back to this teaching of Jesus:

> Wherefore also it is contained in the Scripture, "Behold, I lay in Zion a chief corner stone, elect, precious; and he that believeth on him shall not be confounded." [*Isaiah 28:16*]
>
> Unto *you* therefore *which believe* he is precious, but unto them which be disobedient, "the stone which the builders disallowed, the same is made the head of the corner, [*Psalm 118:22*] and, "a stone of stumbling and a rock of offence," [*Isaiah 8:14*], even to them which stumble at the word, being disobedient; whereunto also they were appointed.
>
> But ye [who believe in Jesus] are a chosen generation, a royal priesthood, *an holy nation, a peculiar people*; that ye should show forth the praises of him who hath called you out of darkness into his marvellous light.
>
> [*You*] *Which in time past were not a people, but are now the people of God: which had not obtained mercy, but now have obtained mercy."*
> 1 Peter 2:6–10

Jesus as the Christ is still "a stone of stumbling, and a rock of offence" to Jews. The Christian church has become the nation or people of God. The Kingdom of God has been taken from Israel and given to the Christian church to bring forth the fruits of God's vineyard.

JESUS AND THE GENTILES

Ethnically, Jesus was a Jew. Paul wrote of his kinsmen, the Jews, that "of whom as concerning the flesh Christ came." *Romans 9:5*

Jesus thought of himself as a Jew, and this is shown by the way he used Gentile practices and attitudes as examples that his followers should avoid.

In the Sermon on the Mount, he said:

Therefore, take no thought, saying, "What shall we eat?" or, "What shall we drink?" or, "Wherewithal shall we be clothed?" For after all these things do the Gentiles seek . . . But seek ye first the Kingdom of God, and his righteousness; and all these things shall be added unto you. *Mt 6:31–33*

Jesus instructed his disciples against seeking places of honor and authority by telling them not to exercise lordship over others like the rulers of the Gentiles:

MARK	MATTHEW	LUKE
Ye know that	Ye know that	
they	the princes	The kings
which are accounted	*of*	*of*
to rule over		
the Gentiles	*the Gentiles*	*the Gentiles*
exercise lordship	exercise dominion	exercise lordship
over them;	over them;	over them;
and their great ones	and they that are great	and they that
exercise authority	exercise authority	exercise authority
upon them.	upon them.	upon them
		are called benefactors.
But so shall	But it shall	But ye shall
it not be	not be so	not be so: . . .
among you: . . .	among you: . . .	*L 22:25–26*
Mk 10:42–43	*Mt 20:25–26*	

It does not require much imagination to see that Jesus' reference to the rulers "of the Gentiles" exercising authority over their subjects is to the Roman authorities; and the accolade, "benefactors," rings like the title of a Roman emperor. The point, however, is that these Roman attitudes were non-Jewish attitudes, which were therefore inappropriate.

In two places in the Sermon on the Mount, Jesus was probably referring to the Gentiles, although the King James Version uses the phrases, "the heathen" and "the publicans":

But when ye pray, use not vain repetitions, as *the heathen* do: for they think that they shall be heard for their much speaking. Be not ye therefore like unto them: . . . Mt 6:7–8

And if ye salute your brethren only, what do ye more than others? Do not even *the publicans* so? Mt 5:47

Jesus was also probably referring to a Gentile when he is reported to have said with respect to the wrongdoing brother:

And if he shall neglect to hear them [the corroborating witnesses], tell it unto the church; but if he neglect to hear the church, let him be unto thee as *an heathen man* and a publican. Mt 18:17

Modern translations of these three quotations from Matthew use a variety of words for words I have emphasized in each quotation: Gentiles, pagans, and heathen. Whatever words they use for their English translations, Jesus' point was clear. He told his followers again and again: don't act like non-Jews.

It is not surprising, then, that Jesus explicitly instructed his twelve closest disciples:

Go not into the way of the Gentiles, and into any city of the Samaritans enter ye not; but go rather to the lost sheep of the house of Israel. Mt 10:5–6

Jesus did not mean "the way of the Gentiles" as a concept but simply that his twelve should not walk down any road (way) to a

Gentile town, for example, to Scythopolis, one of the ten Greek-speaking towns of the Decapolis (Ten Towns). Jesus did not live in a purely Jewish area. Galilee was predominantly Jewish, but many Gentiles lived there. Perhaps this is why it was known as "Galilee of the Gentiles." *Mt 4:15 (Isaiah 9:1)* Two of Jesus' twelve disciples had Gentile (Greek) names: Andrew and Phillip.

Jesus, at that time, thus forbade a mission to the Gentiles. The Twelve were not to go into any Samaritan town, either, and Jesus mentioning them in the same breath as the Gentiles is significant.

Although the Samaritans accepted the first five books of the Old Testament as authoritative for their religion, the Jews regarded the Samaritans as heretics and foreigners. Jesus himself referred to a Samaritan man as "this stranger," meaning "this foreigner." *L 17:18*

When the Jews wanted to insult Jesus, they said, "Say we not well thou art a Samaritan, and hast a devil?" *J 8:48* John understatingly writes that the Jews had "no dealings with the Samaritans." *J 4:9* However, the territory of the Samaritans lay between Galilee and Jerusalem and had to be crossed unless a long detour was taken by going along the east side of the Jordan River. That is why Jesus happened to be in the Samaritan town of Sychar where he talked to the Samaritan woman at Jacob's well. He had left Judea northbound for Galilee "and he must needs go through Samaria." *J 4:4*

The Samaritans, themselves, were hostile to Jesus. Once, Jesus' advance party was unable to arrange accommodations for him in a Samaritan village and had to go to another village (probably in Judea) because he was headed for Jerusalem, the shrine city of the religion that the Samaritans rejected. *L 9:51–56*

Jesus' own disciples were amazed that he would even talk to a Samaritan woman. *J 4:27* Jesus did not mince words and told her flatly that "salvation is of the Jews." *J 4:22* He immediately made his point:

> But the hour cometh, and now is, when the true worshippers shall worship the Father in spirit and in truth: for the Father seeketh such to worship him. *J 4:23*

The implication is clear that even Samaritans could now be "true worshippers." These could now be gathered "unto life eternal" by the disciples. *J 4:36* They had not sown these "true worshippers," but it was their duty now to reap. In the same way, it was the duty of the Twelve and the Seventy to harvest the multitudes of Jewish common folk. *Mt 10:6; 15:24*

Jesus, himself, ministered to Samaritans on occasion. Jesus healed ten lepers in a village near the border of Galilee and Samaria. *L 17:11–12* Luke writes that "one of them, when he saw that he was healed, turned back, and with a loud voice glorified God, and fell down on his fact at his feet, giving him thanks: and he was a Samaritan." *L 17:15–16*

Jesus was impressed, and said:

Were there not ten cleansed?

But where are the nine?

There are not found that returned to give glory to God, save this stranger. *L 17:17–18*

Jesus then said to him:

Arise, go thy way. Thy faith has made thee whole. *L 17:19*

The Samaritan was a "true worshipper," and Jesus recognized that faith was not restricted to Jews.

Jesus was aware that his co-religionists could, on occasion, fail to measure up, while a Samaritan acted out the true faith. Jesus told a story of a man, presumably a Jew, who was robbed and left half-dead on the Jerusalem-Jericho road in Jewish territory:

And by chance there came down a certain [Jewish] priest that way; and when he saw him, he passed by on the other side.

And likewise a Levite [a Jewish religious functionary], when he was at the place, came and looked on him, and passed by on the other side.

> But a certain *Samaritan* [of all people], as he journeyed, came where he was; and when he saw him, he had compassion on him, and went to him, and bound up his wounds, pouring in oil and wine, and set him on his own beast, and brought him to an inn, and took care of him. *L 10:31–34*

This was a parable, but Jesus may be reflecting what he had already seen of the faith operating in Samaritans. Part of the village of Sychar had been converted. Later on, after Jesus' resurrection, Peter, John and Philip all preached in Samaria. *Acts 8:5, 14, 25*

It can be argued that Samaritans were Jewish heretics and not really Gentiles. Jesus' attitude toward a certain Gentile woman is therefore instructive. Matthew describes her simply as "a woman of Canaan," while Mark is more explicit, listing her as "a Syrophenician by nation." *Mt 15:22; Mk 7:26*

Phoenicia was the costal strip of Syria, a Gentile land north of Israel. On a journey toward Tyre and Sidon, which were seacoast towns in Phoenicia, James "entered into a house, and would have no man know it: but he could not be hid." *Mk 7:24*

The Gentile woman in question had a young daughter who, Luke says, had "an unclean spirit," or, as Matthew has it, was "grievously vexed with a devil." *Mk 7:25; Mt 15:22* This woman heard of Jesus and wanted his help for her daughter. *Mk 7:25* After she had prostrated herself at his feet, she cried out:

> Have mercy on me, O Lord, thou son of David; my daughter is grievously vexed with a devil. *Mt 15:22 (Mk 7:25)*

Jesus did not even answer her, and the reaction of his disciples was negative:

> Send her away, for she crieth after us. *Mt 15:23*

Jesus agreed:

> I am not sent but unto the lost sheep of the house of Israel. *Mt 15:24*

The woman followed them and persisted:

Lord, help me. *Mt 15:25*

Jesus still gave a Jewish answer:

MARK	MATTHEW
Let the children [the Jews] first be filled,	
for it is not meet	It is not meet
to take the children's bread	to take the children's bread
and to cast it	and cast it
unto the dogs [Gentiles].	to the dogs [Gentiles].
Mk 7:27	*Mt 15:26*

Both Matthew and Mark have the woman's reply:

MARK	MATTHEW
Yes, Lord.	Truth, Lord,
Yet the dogs	Yet the dogs
under the table	
eat of	eat of
the children's crumbs.	the crumbs which fall
Mk 7:28	from their masters' table.
	Mt 15:27

Jesus then said:

MARK	MATTHEW
For this saying go thy way;	O woman, great is thy faith;
the devil is gone out	be it unto thee
of thy daughter.	even as thy wilt.
Mk 7:29	*Mt 15:28*

It is almost an anti-climax that the woman's daughter "was made whole from that very hour." *Mt 15:28* Mark has more details: "And when she was come to her house, she found the devil gone out, and her daughter laid upon the bed." *Mk 7:30*

Here Jesus, only after the entreaties of a desperate woman, retreated from his statement, "I am not sent but unto the lost sheep of the house of Israel [i.e., to lost Jews]." *Mt 15:24* There is, however, a slight reminiscence of his statement to the Samaritan woman that a new age was dawning, "when the true worshippers shall worship the Father in spirit and in truth," when he said to the Phoenician woman, "Let the children *first* be filled, . . ." *Mk 7:27*

The children referred to must be "the lost sheep of the house of Israel." The fact that they shall *first* be filled implies that others, to wit, the Gentiles, like this Phoenician woman, will have their turn.

And so it has happened. Relatively few lost sheep of the house of Israel ever followed Jesus. Within about twenty-five years after Jesus' death and resurrection, his church had become mostly a Gentile church, and so it has remained ever since. Accordingly, when John's Gospel looks back at Jesus' ministry, it states, "He came unto his own and *his own* [people] received him not." *J 1:11*

Even in Jesus' own days, he recognized that the Christian faith was not to be confined to Israel. This is demonstrated by the case of a centurion of the Roman occupation army who may have commanded its detachment in Capernaum. He was probably a partial convert, at least, to Judaism, because he sent Jewish elders to Jesus, who stated that he was a worthy man, "for he loveth our nation [the Jews] and he hath built us a synagogue [in Capernaum?]." *L 7:5*

There are minor differences in Luke's and Matthew's accounts of this incident. Matthew indicates that the centurion met Jesus in Capernaum and said, "Lord, my servant lieth at home sick of the palsy, grievously tormented," and Jesus had replied, "I will come and heal him." *Mt 8:6-7* Luke indicates that the message came to Jesus through the Jewish elders the centurion sent. *L 7:3*

Luke and Matthew also disagree as to whether the centurion told Jesus directly of his unworthiness, or relayed the message by friends who met Jesus on the way:

MATTHEW	LUKE
Lord,	Lord, trouble not thyself:
I am not worthy	for I am not worthy
that thou shouldest	that thou shouldest
come under my roof,	enter under my roof,
	wherefore neither thought
	I myself
	worthy to come unto thee;
but speak the word only,	but say in a word,
and my servant shall be healed.	and my servant shall be healed.
For I am a man	For I also am a man
under authority	set under authority,
having soldiers under me:	having under me soldiers,
and I say to this man, "Go,"	and I say unto one, "Go,"
and he goeth;	and he goeth;
and to another, "Come,"	and to another, "Come,"
and he cometh;	and he cometh;
and to my servant, "Do this,"	and to my servant, "Do this,"
and he doeth it.	and he doeth it.
Mt 8:8–9	*Luke 7:6–8*

Jesus was astonished and turned to his followers and said:

MATTHEW	LUKE
Verily I say unto you,	I say unto you,
I have not found	I have not found
so great faith,	so great faith,
no, *not in Israel.*	no, *not in Israel.*
	L 7:9

And I say unto you,
that many shall come
from the east and west,
and shall sit down
with Abraham,
and Isaac, and Jacob,
in the Kingdom of Heaven.

But the children of the Kingdom
shall be cast out

MATTHEW (cont.)   LUKE (cont.)
into other darkness:
there shall be weeping
and gnashing of teeth.
Mt 8:10–12

In another context, Luke has material that parallels what Matthew has about those who shall come from east and west to sit down in the Kingdom. Jesus had been asked, "Lord, are there few that be saved?" *L 13:23*

Jesus replied:

Strive to enter in at the strait gate: for many, I say unto you, will seek to enter in, and shall not be able.

When once the master of the house is risen up, and hath shut to the door, and ye begin to stand without, and to knock at the door, saying, "Lord, Lord, open unto us;" and he shall answer and say unto you, "I know you not whence ye are."

Then shall ye begin to say, "We [Jews] have eaten and drunk in thy presence, and thou hast taught in *our* streets [in Israel].

But he shall say, "I tell you, I know you not whence ye are; depart from me, all ye workers of iniquity."

There shall be weeping and gnashing of teeth, when ye shall see Abraham, and Isaac, and Jacob [your Jewish patriarchs], and all the [your Jewish] prophets, in the Kingdom of God, and *you yourselves* thrust out. And they, [the Gentiles?] shall come from the east, and from the west, and from the north, and from the south, and shall sit down in the Kingdom of God.

And, behold, there are last which shall be first, and there are first which shall be last. *L 13:24–30*

It is instructive to compare Jesus' two statements about sitting down in the Kingdom:

MATTHEW	LUKE
That many shall come from the east and west,	And they shall come from the east, and from the west, and from the north, and from the south,
and shall sit down . . . [in the Kingdom of Heaven . . .]*	and shall sit down in the Kingdom of God. L 13:29
with	
	When ye shall see
Abraham, and Isaac, and Jacob.	Abraham, and Isaac, and Jacob, and all the prophets,
But the children of the Kingdom	in the Kingdom of God and you yourselves
shall be cast out into outer darkness: there shall be weeping and gnashing of teeth. Mt 8:11–12 *Conformed to Luke's order	thrust out . . . [There shall be weeping and gnashing of teeth, when ye shall see . . .]* L 13:28 *Conformed to Matthew's order

Matthew uses the phrase "Kingdom of Heaven" for the same realm for which Luke uses the phrase "Kingdom of God." Summarizing both Matthew and Luke, Jesus told Jewish audiences that Abraham, Isaac and Jacob (Luke adds, "and all the prophets") will be in that kingdom along with certain other persons from all points of the compass, but "you yourselves [his listeners, i.e., Jews - the natural children of the Kingdom] thrust out." L 13:28 (Mt 8:12)

As a Jew, Jesus probably never ate with Gentiles, and we know that he hardly ever walked in any street outside of Israel. As he made his way to Jerusalem, teaching in the towns and villages, Jesus taught that it will be Jews who will argue against his judgment by saying:

> We have eaten and drunk in thy presence, and thou hast taught in our streets. *L 13:26*

The point of the centurion story is that a Gentile who was not even a member "in Israel" had great faith, indeed, greater than any Jesus had found in Israel:

> Verily I say unto you, I have not found so great faith, no, not in Israel. *Mt 8:10*

Jesus then told the centurion:

> Go thy way; and as thou hast believed, so be it done unto thee. *Mt 8:13*

Accordingly, when the centurion's friends returned, they found "the servant whole that had been sick," healed "in the self-same hour." *L 7:10; Mt 8:13*

To sum up, Jesus' attitude towards the Gentiles in relation to his own mission was as follows:

1. In the first instance, he was sent to the lost sheep of the house of Israel. *Mt 10:6; 15:24*
2. He recognized that the hour had arrived when true worshippers, even heretics, like Samaritans, should worship the Father in spirit and in truth. *J 4:23*
3. Later on, as he neared the end of his ministry, he went further and recognized that he was, indeed, sent not only to Jews, but also to Gentiles. In the closing days of his ministry, he said:

> I am the good shepherd, and know my sheep, and am known of mine. As the Father knoweth me, even so know I the Father:

and I lay down my life for the sheep. *And other sheep I have which are not of this fold: them also I must bring, and they shall hear my voice*; and there shall be one fold, and one shepherd. *J 10:14–16*

The final phrase "one fold, and one shepherd" is an ancient mistranslation which modern versions correct to "one flock, and one shepherd," but they leave intact the earlier phrase "other sheep I have which are not of this *fold.*" Here our focus is on the earlier phrase:

And other sheep I have which are not of this fold: them also I must bring, and they shall hear my voice; . . . *J 10:16*

The crucial point is what Jesus meant by other sheep "not of this fold." By "this fold," Jesus meant the house of Israel. The "other sheep" that he has and must bring are thus the Gentiles. And they shall hear his voice. The history of Christianity is that the Gentiles have heard his voice.

4. Finally, he recognized that his human ministry to his fellow countrymen, the Jews, would fail, as it did; and that later on, after the Gentiles from all points of the compass had joined the Jewish patriarchs and prophets in the Kingdom of God, the Jews would rail at their exclusion, which would occur by their own choice despite their neighborly acquaintance with Jesus: eating and drinking together; walking the same streets. *Mt 8:11–12; L 13:24–29*

Early in his ministry Jesus recognized he would not be accepted by his own countrymen:

Verily I say unto you, no prophet is accepted in his own country.

But I tell you of a truth, many widows were in Israel in the days of Elijah, when the heaven was shut up three years and six months, when great famine was throughout all the land. But unto none of them was Elijah sent, save unto Sarepta, a city of Sidon, unto a woman that was a widow.

And many lepers were in Israel in the time of Elisha the prophet; and none of them was cleansed, saving Naaman the Syrian. *L 4:24–27*

The point is that two Gentile individuals had received what his countrymen had been unable to accept: a Syrophoenician woman from the Gentile region of Sidon and Tyre; and Naaman, a Syrian man.

When the Pharisees plotted against Jesus, Jesus continued with his healing ministry but gave instructions that his presence was not to be made known so that Isaiah's prophecy of the redemption of the Gentiles might be fulfilled in him, Jesus. *Mt 12:14–17* He quoted the prophecy as follows:

Behold my servant, whom I have chosen; my beloved, in whom my soul is well pleased. I will put my spirit upon him, and *he shall shew judgment to the Gentiles.*

He shall not strive, nor cry; neither shall any man hear his voice in the streets. A bruised reed shall he not break, and smoking flax shall he not quench, till he send forth judgment unto victory. *And in his name shall the Gentiles trust. Mt 12:18–21 (Isaiah 42:1–4)*

So it has been for many centuries. This was foreshadowed by Jesus' own final instructions which state:

Go ye therefore, and teach *all nations*, baptizing them in the name of the Father, and of the Son, and of the Holy Spirit: teaching them to observe all things whatsoever I have commanded you; and, lo, I am with you always, even to the end of the world. *Mt 28:19*

The familiar phrase "all nations" meant "all nations not just Israel." This is obvious since Jesus was then speaking to his remaining eleven key disciples who were Jews. They should have understood his instruction to mean: teach everyone, even the Gentiles. Gentiles were to receive the Gospel, too.

Earlier in the last week of his life Jesus had made the same point:

MARK	MATTHEW
"And the Gospel	And this Gospel
must first	of the Kingdom
be published	shall be preached
	in all the world
	for a witness
among *all nations*."	unto *all nations*;
Mk 13:10	and then shall
	the end come."
	Mt 24:14

CHAPTER 6

THE BACKGROUND FOR UNDERSTANDING JESUS' TEACHINGS

SECTS AND DIVISIONS OF JUDAISM IN JESUS' DAY

Before the teachings of Jesus can be examined, they must be placed in context. An important part of that context is the sects and divisions of Judaism in Jesus' day. There are five divisions in that Judaism which need to be mentioned: Pharisees, Sadducees, Essenes, Herodians and Zealots.

PHARISEES

The Pharisees were a Jewish sect in Jesus' time. Paul, who had been a Pharisee, considered the Pharisees the strictest sect of the Jewish religion. *Acts 26:5* The Pharisees' name, like the name of Christians, began as a term of derision: they were called in Hebrew *Perushim,* literally, "the separated ones," meaning that they were apart from the priestly party and, according to Josephus, appeared "more religious than others." *Wars of the Jews, Book I, Ch. V, Sec. 2*

The Pharisees first appeared under that name about 125 years before the birth of Jesus and disappeared as a separate sect after the fall of Jerusalem to the Romans in A.D. 70, but their attitudes and doctrines lived on thereafter in Judaism.

Josephus was a Jewish historian who was born in A.D. 37. Between the ages of sixteen and nineteen, he made trial, he writes, of three sects "that were among us": the Pharisees, Sadducees and Essenes. *Life of Flavius Josephus, Sec. 2* He continues, "For I thought that by this means I might choose the best, if I were once acquainted with them all." *Op. cit., Sec. 2*

Josephus' comments on the Pharisees give us a near contemporary view of the Pharisees Jesus interacted with:

> 3.   Now, for the Pharisees, they live meanly, and despise delicacies in diet; and they follow the conduct of reason; and what that prescribes to them as good for them, they do; and they think they ought earnestly to strive to observe reason's dictates for practice. They also pay a respect to such as are in years; nor are they so bold as to contradict them in anything which they have introduced; and, when they determine that all things are done by fate, they do not take away the freedom from men of acting as they think fit; since their notion is, that it hath pleased God to make a temperament, whereby what he wills is done, but so that the will of men can act virtuously or viciously. They also believe that souls have an immortal vigour in them, and that under the earth there will be rewards or punishments, according as they have lived virtuously or viciously in this life; and the latter are to be detained in an everlasting prison, but that the former shall have power to revive and live again; on account of which doctrines, they are able greatly to persuade the body of the people, and whatsoever they do about divine worship, prayers, and sacrifices, they perform them according to their direction; insomuch that the cities gave great attestations to them on account of their entire virtuous conduct, both in the actions of their lives and their discourses also. *Josephus, Antiquities of the Jews, Book XVIII, Ch. I, Sec. 3*

In the Antiquities, Josephus also describes the Pharisees as a sect "who valued themselves highly upon the exact skill they had in the law of their fathers, and made men believe they were highly favored by God." *Book XVII, Ch. II, Sec. 4* Josephus continues that they had "a capacity of greatly opposing kings" and refused to swear allegiance to Caesar and Herod's government. *Op. cit., Sec. 4* Josephus adds that "a cunning sect they were, and soon elevated to a pitch of open fighting and doing mischief." *Op. cit., Sec. 4*

In another book of the Antiquities, Josephus describes the Pharisees as follows:

> What I would now explain is this, that the Pharisees have delivered to the people a great many observances by succession from their fathers, which are not written in the law of Moses.; and for that reason it is that the Sadducees reject them, and say that we are to esteem those observances to be obligatory which are in the written word, but are not to observe what are derived from the tradition of our forefathers; and concerning these things it is that great disputes and differences have arisen among them, while the Sadducees are unable to persuade none but the rich, and have not the populace obsequious of them, *but the Pharisees have the multitude of their side*: but about these two sects, and that of the Essens, I have treated accurately in the second book of Jewish affairs." *Book XIII, Ch. X, Sec. 6*

The second book of Jewish affairs to which Josephus refers is his *Wars Of The Jews, Book II, Chap. VIII, Sec. 14.* He writes there as to Pharisee and Sadducee "orders":

> 14. But then as to the two other orders (other than the Essenes) at first mentioned; the Pharisees are those who are esteemed most skilful in the exact explication of their laws, and introduce the first sect. These ascribe all to fate [or providence,] and to God, and yet allow, that to act what is right, or the contrary, is principally in the power of men, although fate does co-operate in every action. They say that all souls are incorruptible; but that the souls of good men are only removed into other bodies, - but that the souls of bad men are subject to eternal punishment. But the Sadducees are those that compose the second order, and take away fate entirely, and suppose that God is not concerned in our doing or not doing what is evil; and they say, that to act what is good, or what is evil, is at men's own choice, and that the one or the other belongs so to every one, that they may act as they please. They also take away the belief of the immortal duration of the soul, and the punishments and rewards of

Hades. Moreover, the Pharisees are friendly to one another, and are for the exercise of concord and regard for the public. But the behaviour of the Sadducees one towards another is in some degrees wild; and their conversation with those that are of their own party is as barbarous as if they were strangers to them. And this is what I had to say concerning the philosophic sects among the Jews. *Op. cit., Book II, Ch. VIII, Sec. 14*

SADDUCEES

In addition to contrasting Sadducees with the Pharisees, Josephus drew on his experience to describe the Sadducees as follows:

4. But the doctrine of the Sadducees is this: That souls die with the bodies; nor do they regard the observation of anything besides what the law enjoins them; for they think it an instance of virtue to dispute with those teachers of philosophy whom they frequent; but this doctrine is received but by a few, yet by those still of the greatest dignity; but they are able to do almost nothing of themselves; for when they become magistrates, as they are unwillingly and by force sometimes obliged to be, they addict themselves to the notions of the Pharisees, because the multitude would not otherwise bear them. *Josephus, Antiquities of the Jews, Book XVIII, Ch. I, Sec. 4*

Paul's contrast of the Sadducees and Pharisees is familiar:

For the Sadducees say that there is no resurrection, neither angel, nor spirit; but the Pharisees confess both. *Acts 23:8*

The first three gospels all state the Sadducees denied that there is any resurrection. *Mk 12:18; Mt 22:23; L 20:27* The Sadducees were accordingly deeply offended when Peter and John:

. . .preached through Jesus the resurrection from the dead. *Acts 4:1–2*

The Sadducees were few in number, while the Pharisees had the multitude on their side. *Josephus, Antiquities of the Jews, Book XVIII,*

Ch. I, Sec. 4, and Book XIII, Ch. X, Sec. 6 The Sadducees were wealthy and "of the greatest dignity." *Op. cit., Book XVIII, Ch. I, Sec. 4* They were the priestly party. Accordingly, in Acts we find "the priests and the captain of the Temple, and the Sadducees" jointly coming to arrest Peter and John. *Acts 4:1* Later on when the apostles were arrested, those accompanying the high priest were of "the sect of the Sadducees." *Acts 5:17*

Both the Sadducees and Pharisees had religious aspirations and were moved to partake of John the Baptist's baptism of repentance. John was not impressed:

> But when he saw many of the Pharisees and Sadducees come to his baptism, he said unto them, "O generation of vipers, who hath warned you to flee from the wrath to come?
>
> "Bring forth therefore fruits meet for repentance, and think not to say within yourselves, 'We have Abraham to our father': for I say unto you, that God is able of these stones to raise up children unto Abraham.
>
> "And now also the axe is laid unto the root of the trees; therefore every tree which bringeth not forth good fruit is hewn down and cast into the fire." *Mt 3:7–10*

ESSENES, HERODIANS, ZEALOTS

The third sect or order among the Jews that Josephus mentions is the Essenes. *Wars of the Jews, Book II, Ch. VIII, Sec. 2–13* This ascetic sect lived in monastic groups but are not mentioned in the New Testament.

The Herodians are mentioned in the New Testament. They are mentioned three times: each time they are noted to have acted with the Pharisees against Jesus. *Mk 3:6; 12:13; Mt 22:16* Mark writes:

> And the Pharisees went forth, and straightway took counsel with the Herodians, how they might destroy him. *Mk 3:6*

The other two references to Herodians, Mark 12:13 and Matthew 22:16, are parallel accounts of a single incident. It is clear from these accounts that the Herodians, on one occasion, conspired with the Pharisees to attempt to entrap Jesus:

MARK	MATTHEW
And they	And they [the Pharisees]
send	sent out
unto him	unto him
certain of the Pharisees,	their disciples
and of the Herodians	with the Herodians,
	saying, . . .
to catch him	*Mt 22:16*
in his words.	
Mk 12:13	

The preceding verse in Matthew states that the object of the conspiracy was to "entangle him in his talk." *Mt 22:15*

Jesus also bracketed the two groups together when he said:

Take heed, beware of the leaven of the Pharisees, and of the leaven of Herod [Herodians]. *Mk 8:15*

However, unlike the Pharisees, the Herodians were not a sect but rather a politically oriented group that took its name from the Herod family who collaborated with the Romans from 4 B.C. to A.D. 37. His sons each were willed and then governed parts of his kingdom: Archelaus governed Judea as Ethnarch from 4 B.C. to A.D. 6; Herod Antipas governed Galilee and Perea as Tetrarch from 4 B.C. to A.D. 39; and Phillip governed Iturea and Trachonitis as Tetrarch from 4 B.C. to A.D. 34.

Finally, there are the Zealots, a group resisting the Roman rule. The group is included in the "fourth sect of Jewish philosophy" that Josephus describes as follows:

6.   But of the fourth sect of Jewish philosophy, Judas the Galilean was the author. These men agree in all other things with the Phari-

saic notions; but they have an inviolable attachment to liberty; and they say that God is to be their only Ruler and Lord. They also do not value dying any kinds of death, nor indeed do they heed the deaths of their relations and friends, nor can any such fear make them call any man Lord; and since this immovable resolution of theirs is well known to a great many, I shall speak no further about that matter; nor am I afraid that anything I have said of them should be disbelieved, but rather fear, that what I have said is beneath the resolution they shew when they undergo pain; and it was in Gessius Florus's time that the nation began to grow mad with this distemper, who was our procurator, and who occasioned the Jews to go wild with it by the abuse of his authority, and to make them revolt from the Romans; and these are the sects of Jewish philosophy. *Josephus, Antiquities of the Jews, Book XVIII, Ch. I, Sec. 6*

The founder of the Zealots, "Judas the Galilean," rose up "in the days of the taxing (A.D. 6), and drew away much people after him: he also perished; and all, even as many as obeyed him, were dispersed." *Acts 5:37*

Galilee, Jesus' home province, had thus been a center of Zealot resistance to the Roman occupation. One of Jesus' disciples, Simon, was a Zealot. *L 6:15; Acts 1:13*

Jesus and the Pharisees

Jesus apparently had much more interaction with the Pharisees than the Sadducees. He told his disciples to beware of the leaven (doctrine) of the Pharisees and Sadducees. *Mt 16:6, 12* He went further against the Pharisees: "Beware ye of the leaven of the Pharisees *which is hypocrisy.*" *L 12:1*

Again and again, Jesus charged the Pharisees with hypocrisy, and in the strongest terms.

Woe 1: But woe unto you, scribes and Pharisees, *hypocrites*! For ye shut up the Kingdom of Heaven against men: for ye neither go in yourselves, neither suffer ye them that are entering to go in. *Mt 23:13*

Luke has a variant saying:

Woe unto you, lawyers [legalists]! For ye have taken away the key of knowledge: ye entered not in yourselves, and them that were entering in ye hindered. *L 11:52*

Woe 2: Woe unto you, scribes and Pharisees, *hypocrites*! For ye devour widow's houses, and for a pretense make long prayer: Therefore ye shall receive the greater damnation. *Mt 23:14*

Woe 3: Woe unto, scribes and Pharisees, *hypocrites*! For ye compass sea and land to make one proselyte, and when he is made, ye make him twofold more the child of hell than yourselves. *Mt 23:15*

Woe 4: Woe unto you, ye blind guides, which say, "Whosoever shall swear by the Temple, it is nothing; but whosoever shall swear by the gold of the Temple, he is a debtor!"

Ye fools and blind: for whether is greater, the gold, or the temple that sanctifieth the gold?

And, "Whosoever shall swear by the altar, it is nothing; but whosoever sweareth by the gift that is upon it, he is guilty."

Ye fools and blind: for whether is greater, the gift or the altar that sanctifieth the gift? Whoso therefore shall swear by the altar, sweareth by it, and by all things thereon. And whoso shall swear by the Temple, sweareth by it, and by him that dwelleth therein. And he that shall swear by heaven, sweareth by the throne of God, and by him that sitteth thereon. *Mt 23:16–22*

Woe 5:	MATTHEW	LUKE
	Woe unto you,	But woe unto you,
	scribes and Pharisees,	Pharisees!
	hypocrites!	
	For ye pay tithe of mint	For ye tithe mint
	and anise	and rue
	and cumin	and all manner of herbs
	and have omitted	and pass over
	the weightier matters	
	of the law,	
	judgment,	judgment
	mercy, and faith:	and the love of God:
	these ought ye to have done	these ought ye to have done,
	and not to leave	and not to leave
	the other undone.	the other undone.
		L 11:42
	Ye blind guides,	
	which strain at a gnat,	
	and swallow a camel.	
	Mt 23:23–24	

Woe 6:	MATTHEW	LUKE
	Woe unto you,	Now do ye,
	scribes and Pharisees	Pharisees
	hypocrites!	
	For ye make clean	make clean
	the outside of the cup	the outside of the cup
	and of the platter,	and the platter,

Matthew (cont.)	Luke (cont.)
but within they are	but your inward part is
full of extortion	full of ravening
and excess.	and wickedness.

Thou blind Pharisees,	Ye fools,
cleanse first	did not he that made
that which is within	that which is without
the cup and platter,	make that which
that the outside of them	is within
may be clean also.	also?
Mt 23:25–26	But rather give
	alms of such things
	as ye have;
	all things are clean unto you.
	L 11:39–41

Woe 7:

Matthew	Luke
Woe unto you,	Woe unto you,
scribes and Pharisees,	scribes and Pharisees!
hypocrites!	*hypocrites*!
For ye are like unto	For ye are as
whited sepulchres	graves
which indeed appear	which appear not,
beautiful outward,	and the men
but are within	that walk over them
full of dead men's bones,	are not aware of them.
and of all uncleanness.	L 11:44
Even so ye also	
outwardly appear	
righteous unto men,	
but within ye are	
full of *hypocrisy*	
and iniquity.	
Mt 23:27–28	

Woe 8:

Matthew	Luke
Woe unto you,	Woe unto you!
scribes and Pharisees,	

MATTHEW (cont.)	LUKE (cont.)
hypocrites!	
Because ye build	For ye build
the tombs	the sepulchres
of the prophets	of the prophets,
and garnish the sepulchres	
of the righteous,	
and say, "If we had been	
in the days of our fathers,	and your fathers
we would not have been	
partakers with them	
in the blood	killed
of the prophets."	them.
Wherefore ye be witnesses	Truly ye bear witness
unto yourselves,	that ye allow
that ye are the children	the deeds
of them	of your fathers:
which killed the prophets.	for they indeed killed them,
Fill ye up then	and ye build
the measure of your fathers.	their sepulchres.
Ye serpents,	*L 11:47–48*
ye generation of vipers,	
how can ye escape	
the damnation of hell?	
Mt 23:29–33	

Jesus' identification of Pharisees as hypocrites is indelible. The Greek word literally means "actors." Jesus said: "Beware ye of the leaven of the Pharisees, which is hypocrisy." *L 12:1*

The basic sin of the Pharisees was hypocrisy: ". . . ye outwardly appear righteous unto men, but within ye are full of hypocrisy and iniquity." *Mt 23:28*

The outside is beautiful, but the inside is full of uncleanness, extortion and excess. *Mt 23:25, 27* The religious rules are followed meticulously: mint is tithed; vows are made according to the proper formula; cup and platter are kosher; long prayers are said; proselytes are made; and shrines to prophets of olden time are built and kept decorated; but widows' estates are devoured. *Mt 23:14*

The weightier matters of justice, mercy, and faith are omitted; but the religious rules are kept. This spiritual schizophrenia had secondary and derived symptoms:

1. Heavy and impractical ritual purity requirements:

MATTHEW	LUKE
	Woe unto you also,
	ye lawyers!
For they bind	For ye lade men
heavy burdens and grievous	with burdens grievous
to be borne, and	to be borne, and
lay them on men's shoulders;	
but they themselves will not	ye yourselves touch not
move them with	the burden with
one of their fingers.	one of your fingers.
Mt 23:4	*L 11:46*

2. Piety on their sleeves and religious exhibitionism:

But all their works they do for to be seen of men: they make broad their phylacteries, and enlarge the borders of their garments, . . . *Mt 23:5*

3. Love of place and status:

MATTHEW	LUKE
	Woe unto you, Pharisees!
And love the uppermost	For ye love the uppermost
rooms of feasts, and the	
chief seats in the synagogues	seats in the synagogues,
and greetings in the markets,	and greetings in the markets.
and to be called of men,	*L 11:43*
"Rabbi, Rabbi."	
Mt 23:6–7	

4. The Pharisees were covetous and money-lovers and accordingly derided Jesus for teaching that a man can not serve both God and mammon (money). Jesus replied to their derision:

> Ye are they which justify yourselves before men; but God knoweth your hearts: for that which is highly esteemed among men is abomination in the sight of God. *L 16:15*

5. They trusted themselves that they were righteous, and despised others:

> The Pharisee stood and prayed thus with himself [silently], "God, I thank thee, that *I am not as other men are*, extortioners, unjust, adulterers, or even as this publican. I fast twice in the week, I give tithes of all that I possess." *L 18:11–12 (L 18:9)*

The Pharisees shut up the Kingdom of Heaven against lesser men and then refused to go in themselves. *Mt 23:13* Jesus did not mince words when it came to the Pharisees. He called them, "Ye fools." *L 11:40* He called them, "Ye fools and blind" twice. *Mt 23:17, 19* Twice he called them, "Ye blind guides." *Mt 23:16, 24* Once he called them collectively, "Thou blind Pharisee." *Mt 23:26*

Jesus once asked:

> Can the blind lead the blind? Shall they not both fall into the ditch? *L 6:39*

Matthew states that Jesus once told the multitude:

> Hear, and understand: not that which goeth into the mouth defileth a man; but that which cometh out of the mouth, this defileth a man. *Mt 15:10–11 (Mt 7:14)*

Jesus' disciples then asked Jesus:

> Knowest thou that the Pharisees were offended, after they heard this saying? *Mt 15:12*

Jesus then passed judgment on the Pharisees:

Every plant, which my heavenly Father hath not planted, shall be rooted up. Let them alone: *they* be *blind* leaders of the *blind*. And if the *blind* lead of the *blind*, both shall fall into the ditch. *Mt 15:13–14*

There can be no doubt that Jesus considered the Pharisees to be spiritually blind. After Jesus had healed the man born blind, Jesus said:

For judgment I am come into this world, *that they which see not might see*; and that they which see might be made blind. *J 9:39*

Some Pharisees heard Jesus and asked him:

Are we also blind? *J 9:40*

Jesus answered:

If ye were blind [like this man], ye should have no sin; but now ye say, "We see"; therefore your sin remaineth. *J 9:41*

The Pharisees were blinded by the tradition of the elders that they had constructed. Matthew and Mark have an account of an incident in Galilee in which some scribes from Jerusalem and some local Pharisees questioned Jesus. *Mk 7:1; Mt 15:1*

Mark states:

And when they saw some of his disciples eat bread with the defiled, that is to say, with unwashen, hands, they found fault. *Mk 7:2*

The question of the scribes and Pharisees was:

MARK	MATTHEW
Why walk not thy disciples according to	Why do thy disciples transgress

450

MARK (cont.)	MATTHEW (cont.)
the tradition of the elders,	*the tradition of the elders?*
but eat bread	For they wash not their hands
with unwashen hands?	when they eat bread.
Mk 7:5	Mt 15:2

According to Matthew, Jesus' reply was:

Why do ye also transgress the commandment of God by *your tradition?* Mt 15:3

Matthew and Mark have the rest of Jesus' reply in different sequences. Here I have followed Mark's sequence and conformed Matthew's to it:

MARK	MATTHEW
Well hath Isaiah	Ye hypocrites, well
prophesied of you	did Isaiah prophesy of you,
hypocrites,	
as it is written,	saying,
"This people	"This people draweth nigh
	unto me with their mouth and
honoreth me with their lips,	honoreth me with their lips,
but their heart is far from me.	but their heart is far from me.
Howbeit in vain	But in vain
do they worship me,	they do worship me,
teaching for doctrines	teaching for doctrines
the commandments of men."	the commandments of men."
	Mt 15:7–9

For laying aside
the commandment of God,
ye hold the tradition of men,
as the washing of pots and cups,
and many other such things
ye do.

Full well ye reject
the commandment of God,

MARK (cont.)	MATTHEW (cont.)
that ye may keep *your own tradition.*	
For Moses said, "Honor thy father and thy mother"; and, "Whoso curseth father or mother, let him die the death."	For God commanded, saying, "Honor thy father and mother," and, "He that curseth father or mother, let him die the death."
But *ye say,* "If a man shall say to his father or mother, 'It is Corban,' that is to say, 'a gift,' by whatsoever thou mightest be profited by me;	But *ye say,* "Whosoever shall say to his father or his mother, 'It is a gift,' by whatsoever thou mightest be profited by me, and honor not his father or his mother,
he shall be free."	he shall be free."
And ye suffer him no more to do ought for his father or his mother.	
Making the word of God of none effect *through your tradition,* . . . and many such like things do ye. *Mk 7:6–13*	Thus have ye made the commandment of God of none effect *by your tradition.* *Mt 15:4–6*

Even friendly Pharisees could not understand Jesus' attitude toward their traditions. They murmured about Jesus eating and drinking with tax collectors and sinners, and they wondered why his disciples did not fast. *Mk 2:16, 18; Mt 9:11; L 5:30* A Pharisee invited Jesus to dinner, and Jesus simply went in and sat down to eat. Luke writes:

> And when the Pharisee saw it, he marvelled that he had not first washed before dinner. *L 11:38*

SABBATH OBSERVANCE

Not only did Pharisees stress the ritual washings imposed by tradition but they revelled in a minute observance of all the rules by which "tradition" embalmed the Jewish Sabbath. Jesus was not such a traditionist, and consequently, our sources show continuous conflict between the Pharisees and Jesus over the Sabbath.

Sometimes the conflict is implied in our sources rather than actually stated. On one Sabbath, Jesus ate at the house of one of the chief Pharisees, and "they watched him." *L 14:1* A man who had the dropsy happened to be present. *L 14:2* Was this a trap?

Jesus said to "the lawyers and Pharisees": "Is it lawful to heal on the Sabbath day?" *L 14:3*

Luke records, "And they held their peace." *L 14:4* Jesus then healed the man and asked:

> Which of you shall have an ass or an ox fallen into a pit, and will not straightway pull him out on the Sabbath day? *L 14:5*

Once, Jesus, on a Sabbath, healed an adult man who had been blind from birth. When some of the Pharisees learned that Jesus had done "work" in putting the healing clay upon the man's eyes, they said, "This man is not of God because he keepeth not the Sabbath day." *J 9:16* But other Pharisees said, "How can a man that is a sinner do such miracles?" *J 9:16*

On another Sabbath, Jesus even healed a man with a withered hand in a *synagogue. Mk 3:1–5; Mt 12:9–13; L 6:6–11*

Earlier on that same Sabbath, Jesus' disciples in his presence had picked some heads of grain to eat as they walked through some grainfields. The Pharisees captiously considered this prohibited work (harvesting) on the Sabbath and wanted to know why his disciples were allowed to do this religiously unlawful act. *Mk 2:23–24; Mt 12:1–2; L 6:1–2*

The Pharisees asked Jesus for a "sign from heaven" attesting his status. *Mk 8:11; Mt 16:1; Mt 12:38 ("a sign")* But they were sure he could not be even a prophet. When Nicodemus asked them to withhold judgment until Jesus was tried, their reply was:

> Art thou also of Galilee? Search and look: for out of Galilee ariseth no prophet. *J 7:52*

When Jesus cured a man of demon possession, the Pharisees said, "He casteth out devils through the prince of devils." *Mt 9:34*

Not All Contacts Were Hostile

Not all of Jesus' contacts with the Pharisees were hostile. Once he went to the house of one of the chief Pharisees to eat bread on the Sabbath day. *L 14:1* Pharisees invited Jesus to eat. *L 7:36; 11:37*

One leading Pharisee, Nicodemus, came to Jesus by night and addressed Jesus as follows:

> Rabbi, we know that thou art a teacher come from God: for no man can do these miracles that thou doest, except God be with him. *J 3:2*

This was early in the ministry, but later on Nicodemus interceded with his fellow Pharisees for Jesus, arguing: "Doth our law judge any man, before it hears him, and know what he doeth?" *J 7:51*

Nicodemus was not the only Pharisee who helped Jesus. Luke writes:

> That same day there came certain of the Pharisees, saying unto him, "Get thee out, and depart hence: for Herod will kill thee." *L 13:31*

The Pharisees were, however, as a whole, hostile to Jesus. Their test questions were no accident. The first three Gospels all report this hostility in one parallel section:

MARK	MATTHEW	LUKE
And the Pharisees went forth, and straightway took counsel with the Herodians against him, how they might destroy him.	Then the Pharisees went out, and held a council against him, how they might destroy him.	And they were filled with madness and communed one with another what they might do to Jesus.
Mk 3:6	*Mt 12:14*	*L 6:11*

In Jesus' lifetime he told the people and his disciples:

> The scribes and the Pharisees sit in Moses' seat. All therefore whatsoever they bid you observe, that *observe and do*; but do not ye after their works: for they say and do not. *Mt 23:2–3*

Jesus recognized that the scribes and Pharisees sat in Moses' seats in the synagogues as teachers of the Law from which not "one jot or one tittle" should pass "till all be fulfilled." *Mt 5:18* Accordingly, the Law of Moses, as expounded by the scribes and Pharisees, was to be adhered to "till all be fulfilled."

After Jesus' resurrection, some of the Pharisees became believers and members of the church. *Acts 15:5* Characteristically, they took the position that Gentile converts had to be circumcised and commanded to keep the Law of Moses. *Acts 15:5* Paul himself had been a Pharisee, and was the son of a Pharisee. *Acts 23:6; Philippians 3:5*

THE PHARISEES: THE CONCLUSION

Although all contacts between Jesus and the Pharisees were not hostile, it is an inescapable fact that Jesus was bitterly opposed to them as a group and their doctrines. He repeatedly called them hypocrites. *Mt 23:13, 14, 15, 23, 25, 27, 29* He said that they were "fools and blind." *Mt 23:17, 19* He said that they were spiritually "blind" or "blind guides." *Mt 23:16, 24, 26* He called them:

> O generation of vipers, . . . *Mt 12:34*

> Ye serpents, ye generation of vipers, . . . *Mt 23:33*

"Generation of vipers" has acquired a soft metaphysical ring. It should be remembered that a viper is a deadly poisonous snake. Jesus' image was that Pharisees were a sinister brood of vipers slithering around spreading spiritual poison.

SCRIBES AND PHARISEES

Jesus often lumped "scribes and Pharisees" together. *Mt 5:20; 23:2* Jesus' repeated phrase, "scribes and Pharisees, hypocrites," has burned itself into the conscience of Christendom as a single category. *Mt 23:14, 15, 23, 25, 27, 29; L 11:44* Jesus vehemently denounced both scribes and Pharisees as hypocrites, fakes, literally actors. They collaborated to monitor Jesus' conduct and teaching in the light of their pietistic legalism. *Mk 2:16; L 5:30, 6:7, 11:53, 14:3, 15:2*

Despite this collaboration between scribes and Pharisees, there were differences between them. Pharisees were a strict sect in Judaism; scribes were the ecclesiastical lawyers of Judaism. Scribes were usually Pharisees, but each Pharisee was not a scribe, sōphēr, literally a writer or a clerk. Scribes were laymen who not only copied the Law but also expanded it into a great corpus of detailed rules, the tradition of the elders. Unlike Jesus, they were merely expositors:

MARK	MATTHEW
For he taught them	For he taught them
as one	as one
that had authority,	having authority,
and not	and not
as the scribes.	as the scribes.
Mk 1:22	*Mt 7:29*

The scribes (lawyers) considered themselves to be distinct from the Pharisees. Once after Jesus had denounced the Pharisees, Luke reports:

Then answered one of the lawyers, and said unto him, "Master, thus saying thou reproachest us *also*." *L 11:45*

The scribes were part of the religious establishment of Israel. In Galilee late in Jesus' ministry they argued with his disciples as he returned from the Mount of Transfiguration. *Mk 9:14–16* Earlier in Jesus' ministry in Galilee, Mark reports that "the scribes which came down from Jerusalem" had charged Jesus with being possessed by the devil: "He hath Beelzebub, and by the prince of the devils casteth he out devils." *Mk 3:22*

The Gospels are full of phrases like:

. . . of the elders, and of the chief priests, and scribes . . . *Mk 8:31* (*Mt 16:21; L 9:22*)

. . . unto the chief priests, and unto the scribes . . . *Mk 10:33; Mt 20:18*

. . . the chief priests, and the scribes, and the elders . . . *Mk 11:27* (*L 20:1, 19*)

. . . the scribes and chief priests . . . *Mk 11:18 (Mt 21:15)*

. . . the chief priests and the scribes and the chief of the people . . . *L 19:47*

. . . the chief priests and the scribes . . . *Mk 14:1 (Mt 26:3; L 22:2)*

. . . all the chief priests and the elders and the scribes . . . *Mk 14:53* (*Mt 26:57*)

. . . the elders and scribes and the whole council . . . *Mk 15:1* (*Mt 27:1; L 22:66*)

As part of that establishment, the scribes questioned Jesus' authority. *Mk 11:27–28; L 20:1–2* As part of that establishment, they charged him with blasphemy:

MARK	MATTHEW	LUKE
But there were certain	And, behold, certain	And
of the scribes	of the scribes	the scribes and the Pharisees
sitting there,		began

MARK (cont.)	MATTHEW (cont.)	LUKE (cont.)
and reasoning	said	to reason,
in their hearts.	within themselves,	saying,
"Why doth		"Who is
this man	"This man	this
thus speak		which speaketh
blasphemies?"	blasphemeth."	blasphemies?"
Mk 2:6–7	*Mt 9:3*	*L 5:21*

As part of that establishment, they laid down the official interpretation of the Jewish scripture. Jesus asked:

MARK	MATTHEW
Why say	Why then say
the scribes	the scribes
that Elijah	that Elijah
must first come?	must first come?
Mk 9:11	*Mt 17:10*

Jesus, of course, challenged their interpretations, asking, "How say the scribes that Christ is the Son of David?" *Mk 12:35 (L 20:41)* He went beyond challenge of their interpretations to scathing denunciation of their conduct:

MARK	LUKE
Beware of *the scribes*,	Beware of *the scribes*,
which love to go	which desire to walk
in long clothing,	in long robes,
and love	and love
salutations	greetings
in the marketplaces,	in the markets,
and the chief seats	and the highest seats
in the synagogues,	in the synagogues,
and the uppermost	and the chief
rooms at feasts;	rooms at feasts;
which devour	which devour
widows' houses,	widows' houses,
and for a pretence	and for a shew

MARK (cont.)	LUKE (cont.)
make long prayers:	make long prayers:
these shall receive	the same shall receive
greater damnation.	greater damnation.
Mk 12:38–40	*L 20:46–47*

Jesus passed solemn judgment on scribes, the ecclesiastical lawyers of his time and place, saying:

Woe unto you also, ye lawyers! For ye lade men with burdens grievous to be borne, and ye yourselves touch not the burdens with one of your fingers.

Woe unto you! For ye build the sepulchres of the prophets, and your fathers killed them.

Truly ye bear witness that ye allow the deeds of your fathers: for they indeed killed them, and ye build their sepulchres. *L 11:46–48*

For their part, the scribes, as a group, bitterly opposed Jesus:

And as he said these things unto them, *the scribes* and the Pharisees began to urge him vehemently, and to provoke him to speak of many things: laying wait for him, and seeking to catch something out of his mouth, that they might accuse him. *L 11:53–54*

The scribes were movers in the final conspiracy against Jesus. As he was teaching in the Temple, "the chief priests and *the scribes* the same hour sought to lay hands on him." *L 20:1, 19* Before Herod "the chief priests and *scribes* stood and vehemently accused him." *L 23:10*

Despite these indisputable facts, there were individual scribes who followed Jesus:

And a certain scribe came and said unto him, "Master, I will follow thee whithersoever thou goest." *Mt 8:19*

Jesus recognized such scribes:

Therefore every scribe which is instructed unto the Kingdom of Heaven is like unto a man that is a householder, which bringeth forth out of his treasure things new and old. *Mt 13:52*

Jesus did not resent their test questions, like:

Which is the first commandment of all? *Mk 12:28 (Mt 22:36)*

In turn, certain scribes accepted his answers. Mark reports the reaction of one such scribe:

Well, Master, thou hast said the truth: for there is one God, and there is none other but he; and to love him with all the heart, and with all the understandings, and with all the soul, and with all the strength, and to love his neighbor as himself, is more than all whole burnt offerings and sacrifices. *Mk 12:32–33*

Jesus approved his statement, saying:

Thou art not far from the Kingdom of God. *Mk 12:31*

But his group indictment of scribes remains:

MATTHEW	LUKE
But woe unto you, scribes and Pharisees, hypocrites!	Woe unto you, lawyers!
For ye shut up the Kingdom of Heaven against men:	For ye have taken away the key of knowledge;
for ye neither go in yourselves,	ye entered not in yourselves,
neither suffer ye them that are entering to go in.	and them that were entering in ye hindered.
Mt 23:13	*L 11:52*

HOSTILE QUESTIONS

In order to understand Jesus' teaching, it must be stressed that he was often answering hostile questions of religious adversaries. The questions were often traps, and Jesus' answers must be understood accordingly.

One of the best examples is the question put to Jesus whether or not it was lawful to give tribute to Caesar. Matthew introduces this question by writing:

> Then went the Pharisees, and took counsel how they might *entangle him in his talk.* Mt 22:15

Luke states:

> And they [the chief priests and the scribes] watched him, and sent forth spies, which should feign themselves just men, *that they might take hold of his words,* that so they might deliver him unto the power and authority of the governor. L 20:20

The gospels then continue:

Mark	Matthew	Luke
And they	And they [the Pharisees]	And they [the spies]
send unto him certain of the Pharisees,	sent out unto him their disciples	
and of the Herodians,	with the Herodians,	
to catch him in his words. And when they were come,		
they say unto him,	saying,	asked him, saying,
"Master, we know that thou art true,	"Master, we know that thou art true,	"Master, we know that thou sayest and teachest rightly,

462

MARK (cont.)	MATTHEW (cont.)	LUKE (cont.)
and carest	[neither carest	neither acceptest
for	thou for	thou
no man:	for any man:	
for thou regardest not	for thou regardest not	
the person of men,	the person of men.]*	the person of any,
but teachest	and teachest	but teachest
the way of God	the way of God	the way of God
in truth.	in truth.	truly.
	Tell us, therefore,	
	what thinkest thou?	
Is it lawful	Is it lawful	Is it lawful for us
to give	to give	to give
tribute to Caesar,	tribute unto Caesar,	tribute unto Caesar,
or not?	or not?"	or no?"
	Mt 22:16–17	L 20:21–22
	*Conformed to Mark's	
Shall we give, or	order	
shall we not give?"		
Mk 12:13–15		

The gospels continue:

MARK	MATTHEW	LUKE
But he,	But Jesus	But he
knowing	perceived	perceived
their hypocrisy,	*their wickedness*,	*their craftiness*,
said unto them,	and said,	and said unto them,
"Why *tempt* ye me?	"Why *tempt* ye me,	"Why tempt ye me?
	ye hypocrites?	
Bring me	Shew me	Shew me
a penny,	the tribute money."	a penny.
	Mt 22:18–19	
that I may see it."		Whose image and
Mk 12:15		superscription
		hath it?"
		L 20:23

Jesus was brought a Roman coin, a denarius. *Mk 12:16; Mt 22:18*
The confrontation continued:

JESUS: Whose is this image and superscription?
INTERROGATORS: Caesar's.
JESUS: Render to Caesar the things that are Caesar's, and to God the
things that are God's. *Mk 12:16–17 (Mt 22:20–21; L 20:24–25)*

Jesus was not deceived by the oozing and obvious guile of the
Pharisees and Herodian agent provocateurs. The flattery was a trap
designed to impale Jesus on the alternative of counseling resistance to the Roman occupation by withholding the tribute money
or of offending the Jewish people who loathed the "unclean" Gentile oppressors.

This hostile context must be considered in evaluating Jesus'
famous answer, "Render to Caesar the things that are Caesar's, and
to God the things that are God's." *Mk 12:17 (Mt 22:21; L 20:25)*

The same insincerity is present in the question about the adulterous woman. The "scribes and Pharisees" brought him the
woman, stating:

> Master, this woman, was taken in adultery, in the very act. Now
> Moses in the law commanded us that such should be stoned; but
> what sayest thou? *J 8:3–5*

Would Jesus counsel violation of the sacred law, or would he
spare the woman?

John comments, "This they say, *tempting him*, that they might
accuse him." *J 8:6*

The same pattern of questioning was followed with divorce:

MARK	MATTHEW
And the *Pharisees*	The *Pharisees* also
came to him,	came unto him, . . .
and asked him,	and saying unto him,
"Is it lawful for a man	"Is it lawful for a man

MARK (cont.)	**MATTHEW** (cont.)
to put away his wife?"	to put away his wife
	for every cause?"
tempting him.	[*tempting* him.]*
Mk 10:2	Mt 19:3
	*Conformed to Mark's order

Would Jesus contradict Moses who allowed bills of divorcement, or would he condemn divorce and the adultery involved?

After Jesus openly and specifically denounced the Pharisees, Luke records:

And as he said these things unto them, *the scribes and the Pharisees* began to urge him vehemently, and to provoke him to speak of many things: laying wait for him, and seeking to catch something out of his mouth, that they might accuse him. *L 11:53–54*

John records:

And many of the people believed on him, and said, "When Christ cometh, will he do more miracles than these which this man hath done?" The Pharisees heard that the people murmured such things concerning him, and the Pharisees and the chief priests sent officers to take him. *J 7:31–32*

When the officers reported to the chief priests and Pharisees that they had not seized Jesus, saying, "Never man spake like this man." *J 7:45–46*

It was not the chief priests, but the Pharisees who answered:

Are ye also deceived? Have any of the rulers or of the Pharisees believed on him? But this people who knowest not the Law are cursed. *J 7:47–49*

The Pharisees sometimes seemed to have almost collaborated with the Sadducees in baiting Jesus. We catch only brief cryptic glimpses. Matthew writes, "But when the Pharisees had heard that

he had put the Sadducees to silence, they were gathered together."
Mt 22:34

Matthew further writes, "The Pharisees also with the Sadducees came, and *tempting* desired him that he would shew them a sign from heaven." *Mt 16:1*

The word *tempting* in this context is archaic and a more accurate translation would be *testing* him. This is true of all the above quoted questions of the Pharisees: they are test questions.

Jesus warned his disciples, "Take heed and beware of the leaven of the Pharisees and of the Sadducees." *Mt 16:6 (Mk 8:15)* It was some time before his disciples realized that Jesus meant beware "of the doctrine of the Pharisees and of the Sadducees." *Mt 16:22*

The Sadducees followed the same pattern of baiting questions. We simply have fewer reports of incidents. One incident is described in all the first three gospels. The Sadducees asked the following question:

Master, Moses wrote unto us, "If a man's brother die, and leave his wife behind him, and leave no children, that his brother should take his wife, and raise up seed unto his brother.

Now there were seven brethren: and the first took a wife, and dying left no seed. And the second took her, and died, neither left he any seed: and the third likewise. And the seven had her, and left no seed: last of all the woman died also.

In the resurrection therefore, when they shall raise, whose wife shall she be of them? For the seven had her to wife. *Mk 12:19–23 (Mt 22:24–28; L 20:28–33)*

The question was obviously a contrived question designed to embarrass Jesus since the Sadducees did not believe in any resurrection and wanted to force Jesus to concede that the doctrine of the resurrection was untenable.

Sadducees, Herodians and Pharisees all asked Jesus trick or test questions designed to entrap and embarrass him. This hostile context must be considered in evaluating what Jesus meant by his answers to such questions. In analyzing Jesus' teaching, not only is this hostile context important but it is also important to understand one of Jesus' key teaching devices, his parables.

TEACHING IN PARABLES

Jesus' characteristic teaching tool was a parable. He did not invent the parable since parables are also found in the Old Testament. For example, there is Nathan's story of the rich man taking the poor man's one little lamb and ending with the indictment of David: "Thou art the man." *II Samuel 12:1–7*

A parable is a simple, vivid story used to make a point. The word *parable* is derived from a Greek word meaning "to place beside", that is, to compare. Jesus used such simple stories and comparisons as teaching devices. For example, during his second ministry in Galilee the gospels report:

Mark	MATTHEW	LUKE
And he began again to teach	The same day went Jesus out of the house,	
by the seaside: and there was gathered unto him a great multitude,	and sat by the seaside, and great multitudes were gathered together unto him,	And when much people were gathered together, and were come to him out of every city,
so that he entered into a ship, and sat in the sea; and the whole multitude was by the sea on the land.	so that he went into a ship, and sat; and the whole multitude stood on the shore.	
And he taught them many things	And he spake many things unto them	he spake
by parables, and said unto them	*in parables,* saying, . . . When he had finished	*by a parable:* . . . *L 8:4*
in his doctrine, . . . *Mk 4:1–2*	*these parables,* . . . *Mt 13:1–3; 53*	

Jesus then told a number of parables: the parable of the sower, the lamp under the bush, the tares, the growing seed, the mustard seed, the leaven, the treasure hidden in a field, the pearl of great price and the net. *Mk 4:3–32; Mt 13:3–50; L 8:5–18* These parables were told to simple folk, "the great multitude." *Mk 4:1; Mt 13:2; L 8:4* Jesus wanted these folks to understand his teaching, so he used simple comparisons and picture stories, parables, to do this.

Most parables are clear, so clear that twenty centuries later they are still clear because of their simple, vivid imagery. Here are some examples of how Jesus spoke "in parables":

And he called them unto him, and said unto them *in parables*, "How can Satan cast out Satan? And if a kingdom be divided against itself, that kingdom cannot stand." *Mk 3:23–24*

And he began to speak unto them *by parables*. "A certain man planted a vineyard, and set a hedge about it, and digged a place for the winefat [wine press], and built a tower, and let it out to husbandmen, and went into a far country." *Mk 12:1*

And Jesus answered and spake unto them again *by parables*, and said, "The Kingdom of Heaven is like unto a certain king, which made a marriage for his son, and sent forth his servants to call them that were bidden to the wedding: and they would not come." *Mt 22:1–2*

There are many other instances when Jesus taught by the use of parables. All of the first three gospels have the parable of the fig tree. *Mk 13:28–31; Mt 24:32–35; L 21:29–33* Luke is full of parables Jesus spoke that are not even mentioned in other gospels; for example, the parable of the Good Samaritan, the friend who wants to borrow bread at midnight, the rich fool, the waiting servants, the faithful steward, the fruitless fig tree, the supper guests who gave excuses, the lost coin, the prodigal son, the rich man and Lazarus, the unjust judge and the persistent widow, the Pharisee and the publican. *L 10:25–37, 11:5–13, 12:16–21, 12:35–40, 12:42–48, 13:6–9, 14:16–24, 15:8–10, 15:11–32, 16:19–31, 18:1–8, 18:9–14* These, and the other parables Jesus spoke, have passed into our language and culture because of their vivid power.

While Jesus usually used parables as teaching tools, it is also true that Jesus used parables to challenge his enemies:

MARK	LUKE
And they	And the chief priests
	and the scribes the same hour
sought to lay hold	sought to lay hands
of him,	on him;
but feared the people:	and they feared the people:
for they knew that	for they perceived that
he had spoken *the parable*	he had spoken *this parable*
against them: . . .	against them.
Mk 12:12	L 20:19

It is clear from a study of the parables that their purpose was to explain to Jesus' listeners his teaching. However, there are some statements in the Gospels that seem to imply that parables are secret lore designed to conceal, rather than to convey, Jesus' teaching.

After Jesus had told the parable of the sower, his disciples asked for an explanation why he spoke to the crowd in parables:

Why speakest thou unto them *in parables*? Mt 13:10

Jesus' answer was:

MARK	MATTHEW	LUKE
Unto you	Because it is given	Unto you
it is given	unto you	it is given
to know	to know	to know
the *mystery* of	the *mysteries* of	the *mysteries* of
the Kingdom	the Kingdom	the Kingdom
of God:	of Heaven,	of God:
but unto them	but to them	but to others
that are without,	it is not given . . .	
all these things		

Mark (cont.)	Matthew (cont.)	Luke (cont.)
are done	Therefore speak I to them	
in parables: ...	*in parables:* ...	*in parables;* ...
Mk 4:11	*Mt 13:11–13*	*L 8:10*

Nowhere else is Jesus quoted as using the words translated *mystery* or *mysteries*. It is often wrongly assumed that Jesus was using the words as referring to secret lore like that of a lodge, and this raises questions of fairness–why are people allegedly excluded from knowledge of the Kingdom?

The answer is that Jesus was not using "mysteries of the Kingdom of God" to refer to some body of secret lore but rather to refer to the subtle principles of the Kingdom, much as we might refer to the mysteries of plant growth. It is to be noted that this saying occurred immediately after he had told the parable of the sower, which essentially states that some seeds grow and others don't. The subtle principles of the Kingdom are known to the disciples because they have had much greater opportunity to learn them from Jesus' teaching, but to the bystanders, their introduction to the subtle principles of the Kingdom must be by parables, simple picture stories.

All three gospels, however, have Jesus' answer to the question why he spoke in parables, continuing beyond the mysteries of the Kingdom statement:

Mark	Matthew	Luke
"That seeing they may see, and not perceive; and hearing they may hear and not understand; lest at any time they should be converted,	Because "they seeing see not; and hearing they hear not, neither do they understand."	"That seeing they might not see and hearing they might not understand." *L 8:10* (Isaiah 6:9)

471

MARK (cont.)	MATTHEW (cont.)	LUKE (cont.)
and their sins should be forgiven them."		
Mk 4:11–12		
(Isaiah 6:9–10)	And in them is fulfilled the prophecy of Isaiah, which saith,	
	"By hearing ye shall hear, and shall not understand; and seeing ye shall see, and shall not perceive: for this people's heart is waxed gross, and their ears are dull of hearing, and their eyes they have closed; lest at any time they should see with their eyes, and hear with their ears, and should understand with their heart, and should be converted, and I should heal them."	
	Mt 13:11–15	
	(Isaiah 6:9–10)	

It is made explicit by Matthew that Jesus was here quoting Isaiah 6:9–10. In the other two gospels quote marks need to be inserted to remind us of this fact. Isaiah 6:9–11 states:

And he said, "Go, and tell this people, Hear ye indeed, but understand not; and see ye indeed, but perceive not. Make the heart of this people fat, and make their ears heavy, and shut their eyes; lest they see with their eyes, and hear with their ears, and understand with their heart, and convert, and be healed."

Then said I, "Lord, how long." *Isaiah 6:9–11*

This was judgment on the people Isaiah spoke to because they heard, and would not understand, and who saw, but would not perceive. There are similar judgments by Jeremiah and Ezekiel on their hearers:

Hear now this, O foolish people, and without understanding; which have eyes, and see not; which have ears and hear not: Fear ye not me? saith the Lord: . . . *Jeremiah 5:21–22*

The word of the Lord also came unto me, saying, "Son of man thou dwellest in the midst of a rebellious house, which have eyes to see, and see not; they have ears to hear, and hear not: for they are a rebellious house." *Ezekiel 12:1–2*

The reason Jesus quotes the words of Isaiah from the religious traditions of his people is that he did not want such judgment to fall on his listeners. He wanted them to understand, not simply hear. Therefore, he used parables so they would understand and would perceive.

He blessed his disciples because they did see and heard with understanding. After Jesus' quotation from Isaiah ends, Matthew quotes Jesus as saying:

But blessed are your eyes, for they see, and your ears, for they hear. For verily I say unto you, that many prophets and righteous men have desired to see those things which ye see, and have not seen them; and to hear those things which ye hear, and have not heard them. *Mt 13:16–17*

As it turned out, the disciples did not meet this standard. They did not even understand some of Jesus' parables. After Jesus told the parable of the sower, it was *his disciples* who asked for an explanation:

Mark	Matthew	Luke
And	And	And
when he was alone,		his disciples
they that were	the disciples	
about him	came	
with the Twelve		
asked of him	and said unto him, "Why speakest thou unto them	asked him, saying, "What might
the parable.	*in parables?"*	*this parable* be?"
Mk 4:10	*Mt 13:10*	*L 8:9*

In two of the gospel accounts it is clear that the disciples are the ones who ask for an explanation of the parable. *Mk 4:10; L 8:9* In Matthew the ostensible question is not this but, "Why speakest thou *unto them* in parables?" *Mt 13:10*

This difference is probably more apparent than real. This was probably a face-saving way for the disciples *themselves* to ask the meaning of the parable.

The disciples themselves had trouble understanding some of Jesus' parables. In the interchange with Jesus after he had told the parable of the sower, Mark records this statement:

And he said unto them, "Know ye not this parable? And how then will ye know all parables?" *Mk 4:13*

Cutting through the archaic King James language, Jesus simply said, "if you don't understand this parable, how will you understand my other parables?"

Matthew writes:

Then Jesus sent the multitude away, and went into the house; and his disciples came unto him, saying, "Declare unto us the parable of the tares of the field." *Mt 13:36*

After Jesus had taught the multitude that the things which proceed out of a man are the things which defile him, we find his disciples needing an explanation:

MARK	MATTHEW
And when he was entered into the house from the people, his disciples asked him concerning the parable.	Then answered Peter and said unto him,
	"Declare unto us this parable."
And he saith unto them, "Are ye so without understanding *also?*"	And he said, "Are ye *also yet* without understanding?"
Mk 7:17–18	*Mt 15:15–16*

The parable of the sheepfold was also puzzling to the disciples:

This parable spake Jesus unto them: but they understood not what things they were which he spake unto them. *J 10:6*

Sometimes it was the application of a parable which puzzled the disciples. Peter once asked:

Lord, speakest thou this parable unto us, or even to all? *L 12:41*

The message to be ready when the Son of man comes was clear, but it was not clear to Peter, to whom it was sent. *L 12:35–41*

At the time of Jesus' second ministry in Galilee he spoke to the crowds only in parables:

Mark	MATTHEW
	All these things
	spake Jesus
And with	unto the multitude
many such parables	in parables;
spake he	
the word	
unto them,	
as they were able	
to hear it.	
But without a parable	*and without a parable*
spake he not	*spake he not*
unto them: . . .	*unto them,* . . .
Mk 4:33–34	*Mt 13:34*

Matthew continues with an explanation for the use of parables:

That it might be fulfilled which was spoken by the prophet, saying, "I will open my mouth in parables; I will utter things which have been kept secret from the foundation of the world." *Mt 13:35 (Psalm 78:2)*

Jesus taught in parables to explain the things that had been kept secret from the foundation of the world. This teaching to the multitude was "as they were able to hear it." *Mk 4:33* This does not imply any discrimination against the multitude in favor of his disciples, since even they were puzzled by the parables, too, and had to ask Jesus what the parables meant. *Mk 4:10, 4:13, Mk 7:17–18; Mt 13:36, 15:15–16; L 8:9, 12:41; J 10:6* Jesus' ministry emphasized that nothing can remain secret or hidden. *Mk 4:22; L 8:17*

Jesus taught in parables to explain the secret things of God. In a sense, the Kingdom is a mystery but only to those who will not see and will not hear.

Jesus specifically instructed his disciples that:

What I tell you in darkness, that speak ye in light: and what ye hear in the ear, that preach ye upon the housetops. *Mt 10:27*

This applies to Jesus' private explanations of parables of the Kingdom which his disciples received. The Kingdom was to be preached and not hidden as mysterious lore for the initiated only.

Jesus' Background

Humanly speaking, Jesus was a Jew; and as such, he was familiar with the religious heritage of his people, including its Scriptures, the Old Testament. It is to be expected that his speech would reflect the language of those Scriptures, particularly in times of stress.

The first stressful time of which we have record is his temptation. In his need Jesus' recourse was to those Scriptures and he said:

Matthew	Luke
It is written,	It is written, that
"Man shall not	"Man shall not
live by bread alone,	live by bread alone,
but by every word	but by every word
that proceedeth out	
of the mouth of God."	of God."
Mt 4:6 (Deuteronomy 8:3)	*L 4:4 (Deuteronomy 8:3)*
It is written again,	It is said,
"Thou shalt not tempt	"Thou shalt not tempt
the Lord thy God."	the Lord thy God."
Mt 4:7 (Deuteronomy 6:16)	*L 4:12 (Deuteronomy 6:16)*
Get thee hence, Satan;	Get thee behind me, Satan;
for it is written,	for it is written,
"Thou shalt worship	"Thou shalt worship
the Lord thy God,	the Lord thy God,
and him only	and him only
shalt thou serve."	shalt thou serve."
Mt 4:10 (Deuteronomy 6:13)	*L 4:8 (Deuteronomy 6:13)*

The most stressful time in Jesus' life was as he hung on the cross and in his agony cried out with a loud voice:

My God, my God, why has thou forsaken me? *Mk 15:34; Mt 27:46*

Jesus' original Aramaic words are quoted in our Greek text Gospels:

Eloi, Eloi, Lama Sabachthani? *Mk 15:34 (Mt 27:46)*

Some manuscripts of Matthew have the Hebrew "Eli, Eli" for the Aramaic "Eloi, Eloi," and the King James Version follows manuscripts using the Hebrew form. The important point is that in Jesus' terrible ordeal the opening lines of Psalm 22 surged out in his cry: "My God, my God, why hast thou forsaken me?" *Psalm 22:1*

Likewise, Jesus turned to the prophet Zechariah when he tried to explain to his disciples on the night before his cross, his coming passion:

Mark	Matthew
All ye shall be offended because of me this night. For it is written, "I will smite the shepherd, and the sheep	All ye shall be offended because of me this night. For it is written, "I will smite the shepherd, and the sheep of the flock
shall be scattered." *Mk 14:27 (Zechariah 13:7)*	shall be scattered abroad." *Mt 26:31 (Zechariah 13:7)*

Jesus obviously knew Zechariah well enough to quote it from memory, just as he knew Isaiah well enough to find and expound Isaiah 61:1–2 when the scroll was handed to him to read to the congregation in the synagogue in Nazareth at the beginning of his ministry. *L 4:1–21* The depth of Jesus' knowledge is shown by where he stopped quoting. In the Nazareth synagogue the last words he read from Isaiah were: "to preach the acceptable year of the Lord"; but he did not continue with "and the day of vengeance of our God." *Isaiah 61:2* When Jesus quoted Zechariah to his disciples after repeating the words about "the sheep shall be scattered," he did not continue with "and I will turn mine hands upon the little ones." *Zechariah 13:7; Mk 14:27; Mt 26:31*

In the Sermon on the Mount the thrust of Jesus' preaching was the contrast between the Old Testament rules that he cited as the sayings by "them of old times" and his own teaching:

Ye have heard that it was said by them of old time, "Thou shalt not kill; and whosoever, shall kill shall be in danger of the judgment"; but I say unto you, . . .

Ye have heard that it was said by them of old times, "Thou shalt not commit adultery"; but I say unto you, . . .

It hath been said, "Whosoever shall put away his wife, let him give her a writing of divorcement"; but I say unto you, . . .

Again, ye have heard that it hath been said by them of old time, "Thou shalt not forswear thyself, but shall perform unto the Lord thine oaths"; but I say unto you . . .

Ye have heard that it hath been said, "An eye for an eye, and a tooth for a tooth"; but I say unto you, . . .

Ye have heard that it hath been said, "Thou shalt love thy neighbor, and hate thine enemy"; but I say unto you . . . *Mt 5:21 (Exodus 20:13), 5:27 (Exodus 20:14; Deuteronomy 5:18), 5:31 (Deuteronomy 24:1), 5:33 (Leviticus 19:12), 5:38 (Exodus 21:24; Leviticus 24:20; Deuteronomy 19:21), 5:43 (Leviticus 19:18)*

Jesus not only knew the first five books of the Old Testament, the Law, he knew the Prophets that under the nomenclature then used included all of the rest of the Old Testament except the Writings: Psalms, Song of Solomon, Proverbs and Ecclesiastes. *cf. L 24:44* He once quickly summarized the Law and the Prophets, when challenged: "Which is the first commandment of all?" *Mk 12:28* ("Which is the greatest commandment in the Law?" *Mt 22:36)*

Jesus answered:

MARK	MATTHEW
The first of all commandments is,	
"Hear, O Israel, the Lord our God is one Lord.	
And thou shalt love the Lord thy God with all thy heart, and with all thy soul, and with all thy mind, and with all thy strength."	Thou shalt love the Lord thy God with all thy heart, and with all thy soul, and with all thy mind.
This is the first commandment.	This is the first and great commandment.
And the second is like, namely this, "Thou shalt love thy neighbor as thyself."	And the second is like to it, "Thou shalt love thy neighbor as thyself."
There is none other commandment greater than these.	On these two commandments hang all the Law and the Prophets.
Mk 12:29–31	*Mt 22:37–40*

The challenging scribe applauded Jesus' answer, saying:

Well, Master, thou hast said the truth: . . . *Mk 12:32*

The first part of Jesus' answer was to quote the beginning verses of the Shema (literally *Hear*) that was the affirmation of faith repeated twice daily by a devout Jew. The whole Shema is found in Deuteronomy 6:4–9, 11:13–21, and Numbers 15:37–41, but Jesus quoted only Deuteronomy 6:4–5. He then continued with a quotation of the part of Leviticus 19:18 that states, "thou shalt love thy neighbor as thyself."

It is probable that Jesus was the first to make this two proposition summary of the Law and the Prophets. In the Sermon on the Mount his summary was even terser:

Therefore all things whatsoever ye would that men should do to you, do ye even so to them: for this is the Law and the Prophets. *Mt 7:12*

Jesus did not simply summarize and restate the Law and the Prophets. He quoted with approval those parts of his heritage that were consistent with his own message and mission. He quoted Hosea 6:6 at least twice:

They that be whole need not a physician, but they that are sick. But go ye and learn *what that meaneth*, "I will have mercy, and not sacrifice." For I have not come to call the righteous, but sinners to repentance. *Mt 9:12–13*

But if ye had known *what this meaneth*, "I will have mercy, and not sacrifice; ye would not have condemned the guiltless. *Mt 12:7*

Jesus quoted Isaiah 56:7 ("a house of prayer") and Jeremiah 7:11 ("a den of robbers") when he cleansed the Temple:

MARK	MATTHEW	LUKE
And he taught,	And	
saying unto them,	said unto them,	Saying unto them,
"Is it not written	"It is written,	"It is written,
'My house	'My house	'My house
shall be called	shall be called	is
of all nations		
the house of prayer?'	the house of prayer.'	the house of prayer.'
But ye	But ye	But ye
have made it	have made it	have made it
'a den of thieves.'"	'a den of thieves.'"	'a den of thieves.'"
Mk 11:17	*Mt 21:13*	*L 19:46*

Jesus' knowledge and reliance extended beyond the Law and the Prophets to the Psalms. When the chief priests and scribes "were sore displeased" that the children were crying in the Temple that he was the Son of David, his answer was to quote Psalm 8:2 to them:

> Yea; have ye *never read*, "Out of the mouth of babes and sucklings thou hast perfected praise"? *Mt 21:16*

Once after Jesus had told a parable, he quoted Psalm 118:22–23 as the key to its meaning:

MARK	MATTHEW	LUKE
And	Did	What is this then
have ye not read	ye never read	
this Scripture:	in the Scriptures,	that is written,
"The stone which	"The stone which	"The stone which
the builders rejected	the builders rejected,	the builders rejected,
is become	the same is become	the same is become
the head	the head	the head
of the corner.	of the corner.	of the corner."
This was	This is	*L 20:17*
the Lord's doing,	the Lord's doing,	
and it is marvellous	and it is marvellous	
in our eyes"?	in our eyes"?	
Mk 12:10–14	*Mt 21:42*	

This is not an exhaustive list of the times Jesus turned to his Jewish heritage. There are many other references and echoes of that heritage in Jesus' statements recorded in the Gospels. Some of these references and echoes are very clear; others are disputed. The problem is complicated by the fact that we do not know precisely from which version or Targum Jesus learned those scriptures.

The important point is this: To understand what Jesus said we must remember that, humanly speaking, his statements reflect his Jewish background which is as much an objective fact as the fact that he spoke Aramaic. Jesus was often engaged in colloquial controversies that arose out of that background. That background is as essential to understanding his statements as the facts that he was often answering hostile or entrapping questions and that he often used parables to make his points.

Finally, since Jesus' knowledge of the Jewish Scriptures was a natural and inevitable part of his speech, it is error to assume, as some scholars arbitrarily do, that the early church or some hypothetical anonymous "editors" simply inserted in the Gospels the Old Testament quotations which those Gospels place on his lips.

Although Jesus was not a technically trained scribe (*J 7:15*), the Gospels show that he knew the Scriptures well and that he construed those Scriptures as foreshadowing his own special mission. Two examples must suffice.

1. In the Nazareth synagogue at the beginning of his ministry he read Isaiah 61:1–2 and then told the congregation:

    This day is this Scripture fulfilled in your ears. *L 4:21*

2. Early in his ministry in Galilee he asserted:

    Search the Scriptures; for in them ye think ye have eternal life: and *they are they which testify of me. J 5:39*

We know that Jesus relied upon the Scriptures in his disputes with his people. Once he argued, rather tartly:

MARK	MATTHEW
Do ye not therefore err, because	Ye do err,
ye know not the Scriptures	not knowing the Scriptures,
neither	nor
the power of God?	the power of God.
Mk 12:29	*Mt 22:29*

His knowledge of the Scriptures allowed him to make a devastating retort to some scribes and Pharisees who had complained that his disciples transgressed "the tradition of the elders." *Mk 7:5; Mt 15:2:*

MARK	MATTHEW
Well hath Isaiah	Ye hypocrites,
prophesied of	well did Isaiah
you hypocrites,	prophesy of you,
as it is written,	saying,
"this people	"this people
honoreth me	draweth might
	unto me
	with their mouth,
	and honoreth me
with their lips,	with their lips;
but their heart	but their heart
is far from me.	is far from me.
Howbeit in vain	But in vain
do they	they do
worship me,	worship me,
teaching	teaching
for doctrines	for doctrines
the commandments	the commandments
of men."	of men."
Mk 7:6–7 (Isaiah 29:13)	*Mt 15:7–8 (Isaiah 29:13)*

Jesus cites this passage in Isaiah 29:13 in support of his answer to these scribes and Pharisees, and it was also his answer to Jewish culture generally:

MARK	MATTHEW
Full well	Why do
ye reject	ye also transgress
the commandment of God,	the commandment of God
that ye may keep	by
your own tradition.	your own tradition?
Mk 7:9	*Mt 15:3*

To a certain extent Jesus participated in that culture. He probably wore garments having fringes laced with blue as required by Numbers 15:38–39 whose purpose was "remember all the commandments of the Lord, and do them." *Mt 9:20, 14:36 (". . . the hem of his garment . . .")* He customarily attended synagogue services on the Sabbath. *L 4:16* He made yearly pilgrimages to Jerusalem for Passover. *J 2:13, 2:23, 11:55, 12:12, 13:1; L 22:15* We have record that he attended at least two other Jewish religious feasts in Jerusalem: the Feast of Tabernacles (Harvest) in the autumn before he was crucified the following spring; and the Feast of Dedication (Hanukkah) in the intervening winter. *J 7:2, 10:14, 10:22–23*

It is a mistake to stress Jesus' Jewish background and then stop there. It is a mistake because a fair reading of the Gospels shows that Jesus himself did not stop there. A fair summary of Jesus' mission is that he said he came to give a *new* commandment and to make a *new* covenant. He said:

> A *new* commandment I give unto you, that ye love one another; as I have loved you, that ye also love one another. *J 13:34*

The familiar words of the King James Version have Jesus announcing at the Last Supper "the new Testament" of his blood. *Mk 14:24; Mt 26:28; L 22:20* Modern translations consider a more accurate translation to be "the new covenant" of his blood. With the greatest of solemnity, Jesus at the Last Supper announced a new covenant, his own.

The old covenant was superseded. The old Jewish wineskins were inadequate and had to be discarded:

> And no man putteth new wine into old bottles: else the new wine doth burst the bottles, and the wine is spilled, and the bottles will be marred (will burst); but new wine must be put into new bottles. *Mk 2:22 (Mt 9:17; L 5:37)*

KINGDOM TOPICS

JESUS THE KING

Very early in Jesus' ministry some persons were recognizing him as the expected "King of Israel." A few days after Jesus' baptism, Nathanael, whom Jesus characterized as "an Israelite indeed, in whom is no guile" J 1:47, said to Jesus:

Rabbi, thou art the Son of God; thou art the King of Israel. J 1:49

Jesus' answer was noncommittal. J 1:50–51 The impression that Jesus was the expected king was reinforced by his miracles. After Jesus had fed the five thousand, John wrote:

Then those men, when they had seen the miracle that Jesus did, said, "This is of a truth that prophet that should come into the world."

When Jesus therefore perceived that they would come and take him by force, to make him a king, he departed again into a mountain himself alone. J 6:14–15

Later on, when Jesus made his triumphant entry into Jerusalem at Passover just before his arrest, many Jews in Jerusalem for that holiday "took branches of palm trees, and went forth to meet him, and cried, 'Hosanna: Blessed is the King of Israel that cometh in the name of the Lord.'" *J 12:13* Jesus' entry riding on an ass's colt was later regarded by his disciples as a fulfillment of Zechariah 9:9:

> Fear not, daughter of Zion: behold, thy King cometh, sitting on an ass's colt. *J 12:15–16*

The crowd of disciples also shouted:

> Blessed be the King that cometh in the name of the Lord; peace in heaven, and glory in the highest. *L 19:38*

Some Pharisees asked Jesus to rebuke his disciples for so shouting. *L 19:39* Jesus answered:

> I tell you that if these should hold their peace, the stones would immediately cry out. *L 19:40*

The unsophisticated popular feeling that Jesus was somehow an uncrowned king of Israel was easily perverted into a charge that Jesus himself had royal ambitions:

> And the whole multitude of them arose, and led him unto Pilate. And they began to accuse him, saying, "We found this fellow perverting the nation, and forbidding to give tribute to Caesar, saying that *he himself is Christ a King.*" *L 23:1–2*

> And from thenceforth Pilate sought to release him; but the Jews cried out, saying, "If thou let this man go, thou are not Caesar's friend. Whosoever *maketh himself a king* speaketh against Caesar." *J 19:12*

There can be no question that this charge was the heart of Pilate's investigation. All four Gospels report his key question to Jesus as:

> Art thou the King of the Jews? *Mk 15:2; Mt 27:11; L 23:3; J 18:33*

Three of the four Gospels report Jesus' reply as a noncommittal:

Thou sayest it. *Mk 15:2; L 23:3 (Mt 27:11)*

John has a fuller account:

Sayest thou this thing of thyself, or did others tell it thee of me? *J 18:34*

Pilate responded with exasperation:

Am I a Jew? Thine own nation and the chief priests have delivered thee unto me. What hast thou done? *J 18:35*

Jesus replied:

My kingdom is not of this world. If my kingdom were of this world, then would my servants fight, that I should not be delivered to the Jews; but now is my kingdom not from hence [here]. *J 18:36*

Pilate pressed Jesus:

Art thou a king then? *J 18:37*

Jesus answered, again noncommittally:

Thou sayest that I am a king. To this end was I born, and for this cause came I into the world, that I should bear witness unto the truth. Every one that is of the truth hearesth my voice. *J 18:37*

That is where Jesus left it and where we should leave it. The trilingual Roman legal notice, "The King Of The Jews," posted on his cross was just that, a legal notice. *Mk 15:26 (Mt 27:42; L 23:38; J 19:19–20)* The derision of the bystanders, Jewish and Roman, that Jesus was the King of Israel or the King of the Jews, was just that, derision. *Mk 15:31–32; Mt 27:41–42; L 23:36–37* Jesus was not a king in any ordinary sense, but he had, and has, a kingdom that was not, and is not, an ordinary realm. It was, and is, the rule of God himself, which, of course, already exists in Heaven but is subject to God's self-imposed restrictions on Earth. A large part of Jesus' teachings were devoted to explaining, by parables and otherwise, the nature of that kingdom and when it would come.

JESUS' TIMETABLE FOR THE COMING OF THE KINGDOM OF GOD

The question when the Kingdom of God is to come is a favorite question of scholars. The learned of Jesus' day asked him this very question:

> And when he was demanded of [asked by] the Pharisees, when the Kingdom of God should come, he answered them and said, "The Kingdom of God cometh not with observation; neither shall they say, 'Lo here!' or, 'Lo there!' for, behold, the Kingdom of God is *within you.*" *L 17:20–21*

The passage seems clear enough that the Kingdom is simply an inward and spiritual thing. However, the various versions of the New Testament translate "within you" differently, as "in the midst of you" or "among you." This is an old dispute that is based upon the ambiguity of Jesus' original Aramaic words as we have them and in the Greek rendering of them in the manuscripts, but it is clear that Jesus did not then answer when the Kingdom of God would come.

Before we consider Jesus' other statements we should note the popular expectations about the coming of the Kingdom. Late in his ministry Jesus felt he had to tell some of his hearers a parable "because he was nigh to Jerusalem, and because they thought that the Kingdom of God should immediately appear." *L 19:11* Jesus himself stated that the Kingdom of God had only been preached since the days of John the Baptist. *L 16:16 (Mt 11:12)*

Early in his ministry, all three synoptic gospels have a statement of Jesus about the time of the coming of the Kingdom of God:

MARK	MATTHEW	LUKE
Verily I say	Verily I say	But I tell
unto you,	unto you,	you of a truth,
that there be	there be	there be
some of them	some	some

MARK (cont.)	MATTHEW (cont.)	LUKE (cont.)
that stand here	standing here,	standing here,
which shall not	which shall not	which shall not
taste of death,	taste of death,	taste of death,
till they have	till they	till they
seen	see	see
the Kingdom	the Son of Man	the Kingdom
of God	coming in	
come *with power*.	his kingdom.	of God.
Mk 9:1	*Mt 16:28*	*L 9:27*

The heart of this saying is Jesus' flat statement that some persons then living ("standing here") would not die ("taste of death") till they saw a kingdom. Mark and Luke are clear that this kingdom is the Kingdom of God. Matthew is not so clear, but probably refers to the same kingdom. Mark and Luke differ on whether that kingdom was already present but powerless (Mark) or was just then arriving (Luke).

Mark suggests that the Kingdom of God was then present, but latent in form with the activating power to come soon. Jesus' own wonderworking acts, such as his casting out of devils, were the first spurts of that activating power:

MATTHEW	LUKE
But if I	But if I
	with the finger of God
cast out devils	cast out devils,
by the Spirit of God,	
then	no doubt
the Kingdom of God	the Kingdom of God
is come unto you.	is come upon you.
Mt 12:28	*L 11:20*

Jesus, himself, had opened his ministry by proclaiming:

The time is fulfilled, the Kingdom of God is *at hand*: repent ye, and believe the gospel. *Mk 1:15*

The Law and the Prophets were until John: since that time the King-dom of God is preached, and every man presseth into it. *L 16:16*

The sequence seems clear:

1. Jesus preaches the Kingdom of God.
2. It is near but has not yet come with power.
3. It was, however, present as a latent infiltrating event.

According to Luke, Jesus compared the nearness of the King-dom to spring, just before the trees suddenly leaf out:

Behold the fig tree, and all the trees; when they now shoot forth, ye see and know of your own selves that summer is now nigh at hand. So likewise ye, when ye see these things come to pass, know ye that the Kingdom of God is nigh at hand. *L 21:29–31*

Mark writes:

Now after that John was put in prison, Jesus came into Galilee, preaching the gospel of the Kingdom of God. *Mk 1:14*

Matthew writes that "Jesus went about all Galilee, teaching in their synagogues, and preaching the gospel of the Kingdom." *Mt 4:23 (Mt 9:35)*

Matthew records Jesus as saying:

And this gospel of the Kingdom shall be preached in all the world for a witness unto all nations; and then shall the end come. *Mt 24:14*

Luke writes of Jesus telling the people in Capernaum, Galilee:

I must preach the Kingdom of God to other cities also: for therefore am I sent. *L 4:43*

And he did. Luke writes that "he went throughout every city and village, preaching and shewing the glad tidings of the Kingdom of God: and the Twelve were with him." *L 8:1* Later on Jesus sent the Twelve "to preach the Kingdom of God." *L 9:2*

When the people followed him he "spoke unto them of the Kingdom of God." *L 9:11* When the seventy disciples were sent out, Jesus instructed them:

> And into whatsoever city ye enter, and they receive you, eat such things as are set before you, and heal the sick that are therein, and say unto them, "The Kingdom of God *is come nigh* unto you."

> But into whatsoever city ye enter, and they receive you not, go your ways out into the streets of the same, and say, "Even the very dust of your city which cleaveth on us, we do wipe off against you; notwithstanding be ye sure of this, that the Kingdom of God *is come nigh* unto you." *L 10:8–11*

Even though the disciples were to tell the Galilean villagers that the Kingdom of God had come near to them, the disciples were taught by Jesus to pray to God:

> Thy Kingdom come! *Mt 6:10; L 11:2*

Many Jews were then looking for the Kingdom. One of these was Joseph of Arimathaea, who begged the body of Jesus. He "also waited for the Kingdom of God." *Mk 15:43 (L 23:51)* One of the guests at a dinner Jesus attended at the house of one of the chief Pharisees said to Jesus, "Blessed is he that shall eat bread in the Kingdom of God." *L 14:15*

Certainly that Kingdom had come at the time Jesus died. It was no longer just "near." At his Last Supper with his disciples, he said of the Passover wine:

MARK	MATTHEW	LUKE
Verily I say unto you, I will drink no more	But I say unto you, I will not drink henceforth	For I say unto you, I will not drink

Mark (cont.)	Matthew (cont.)	Luke (cont.)
of the fruit	of this fruit	of the fruit
of the vine,	of the vine,	of the vine,
until that day	until that day	until
that I drink	when I drink it new	
it new	with you	
in the Kingdom	in my Father's	the Kingdom
of God.	Kingdom.	of God
Mk 14:25	*Mt 26:29*	shall come.
		L 22:18

After Jesus' resurrection, there are two recorded instances when Jesus ate with his disciples. Luke states that on one occasion he ate "a piece of broiled fish, and a honeycomb." *L 24:42–43* John states that on another occasion Jesus said, "Come and dine," and he gave the disciples bread and fish. *J 21:12–13* In neither case is it expressly stated that Jesus drank wine, but the implication is likely in Luke's account. *L 24:42–43*

Acts states that Jesus "shewed himself alive after his passion by many infallible proofs, being seen of them forty days, and speaking of the things pertaining to the Kingdom of God." *Acts 1:3* This clearly suggests that the Kingdom had indeed come, and it was necessary to indoctrinate its earliest subjects with the rules of the realm.

Even after Jesus' resurrection, some of his disciples still confused the Kingdom of God with the restoration of the Kingdom of Israel as a Jewish theocratic state in Palestine. After Jesus' resurrection, his disciples asked him:

Lord, wilt thou at this time restore again the Kingdom of Israel?
Acts 1:6

Such disciples must have been the despair of Jesus, since Acts states he had been "speaking of the things pertaining to the Kingdom of God" for forty days. *Acts 1:3* Paul had a truer apprehension of the Kingdom of God. Acts writes of Paul's teaching "that we must through much tribulation enter into the Kingdom of God." *Acts 14:22*

The Kingdom of God was then existing so far as Paul was concerned. He urged the church at Thessalonica, Greece, that "ye may be counted worthy of the Kingdom of God, for which ye also suffer: . . ." *2 Thessalonians 1:5* Paul exhorted that church to "walk worthy of God, who hath called you into his Kingdom and glory." *I Thessalonians 2:12*

It remained for latter-day Christians to assert that the church is the Kingdom. Paul thought otherwise:

> For the Kingdom of God is not meat and drink; but righteousness, and peace, and joy in the Holy Spirit. *Romans 14:17*

That is why Christians still pray as Jesus taught:

Thy Kingdom come! *Mt 6:10; L 11:2*

Jesus' Gospel of the Kingdom

After John the Baptist was imprisoned Jesus "came into Galilee, preaching the *gospel* of the Kingdom of God." *Mk 1:14* Jesus preached:

> The time is fulfilled, and the Kingdom of God is at hand: repent ye, and believe *the gospel* . . . *Mk 1:15*

The gospel Jesus preached was the gospel of the Kingdom of God. Matthew twice states that Jesus went around "preaching the gospel of the Kingdom." *Mt 4:23, 9:35* This was the gospel he sent the Twelve to preach. *L 9:2, 6*

Jesus had claimed that he had been anointed "to preach the gospel to the poor." *L 4:18* Both Matthew and Luke quoted Jesus having directed the disciples of John the Baptist to report to him that the gospel had been preached to the poor:

MATTHEW	LUKE
The poor have the gospel preached to them. *Mt 11:5*	To the poor the gospel is preached. *L 7:22*

Jesus twice referred to sacrifices for "the gospel's sake"":

> Whosoever shall lose his life for my sake *and the gospel's*, the same shall save it. *Mk 8:35*

> Verily I say unto you, there is no man that hath left house, or brethren, or sisters, or father, or mother, or wife, or children, or lands, for my sake, *and the gospel's*, but he shall receive an hundredfold now in this time . . . ; and in the world to come eternal life. *Mk 10:29–30*

What did Jesus mean by "the gospel's sake"? The parallel passages in Matthew and Luke to Mark 8:35 simply say "for my sake" not "for my sake and the gospel's." *Mt 16:25; L 9:24*

The parallel passages to Mark 10:29–30 have, instead of "for my sake, and the gospel's":

MATTHEW	LUKE
For my	For the Kingdom
name's sake	of God's sake
Mt 19:29	*L 18:29*

These variants help us to determine what Jesus meant by his gospel. It is the gospel of the Kingdom of God.

In Bethany a woman anointed Jesus' head and feet with a precious ointment. *Mk 14:3–9; Mt 26:6–13; J 12:1–8* His disciples, especially Judas Iscariot, were severely critical. Jesus rebuked them, and two of the Gospels quote him as ending the rebuke with this statement:

MARK	MATTHEW
Verily I say unto you,	Verily I say unto you,
wheresoever *this gospel*	wheresoever *this gospel*
shall be preached	shall be preached
throughout the whole world,	in the whole world,
this also that	there shall also this,
she	that this woman
hath done	hath done,
shall be spoken of	be told
for a memorial of her.	for a memorial of her.
Mk 14:9	*Mt 26:13*

Of the last week of Jesus' life at Jerusalem, Luke writes:

And it came to pass, that on one of those days, as he taught the people in the temple, and *preached the gospel*, the chief priests and the scribes came upon him with the elders, and spake unto him, saying, "Tell us, by what authority doest thou these things?" or "Who is he that gave thee this authority?" *L 20:1–2*

In that same week, Jesus predicted the destruction of the Temple in Jerusalem. *Mk 13:1–2, Mt 24:1–2, L 21:5–6* His disciples asked him

privately when was this to happen. *Mk 13:3; Mt 24:3; L 21:7* He told
them that one of the things that had to happen first was the world–
wide preaching of the gospel:

MARK	MATTHEW
And *the gospel*	And *this gospel of the Kingdom*
must first be published	shall be preached
among all nations.	in all the world
Mk 13:10	for a witness
	unto all nations;
	and then shall
	the end come.
	Mt 24:14

After Jesus' resurrection he instructed his disciples:

Go ye into all the world, and *preach the gospel* to every creature.
Mk 16:15

Jesus himself preached "this gospel of the Kingdom" in his lifetime. This is how he began his preaching. *Mk 1:14–15; Mt 4:23, 9:35*
This is the gospel he sent the Twelve to preach. *L 9:2, 6* The gospel
that must be preached to all nations before the end can come is the
gospel of the Kingdom of God. That was Jesus' gospel. *Mt 24:14*

THE GOSPEL OF THE KINGDOM AFTER JESUS' RESURRECTION

Everyone agrees that teaching as to the Kingdom of God was one of Jesus' great themes. What is often forgotten is that the early church not only preached and taught "Christ crucified" and "Jesus and the resurrection" but also preached and taught the Kingdom of God. *1 Corinthians 1:23; Acts 17:18*

After Jesus' resurrection, Acts quotes him as teaching, during the forty days of his appearances, "the things pertaining to the Kingdom of God." *Acts 1:3*

Paul, both at Ephesus and at Rome, spent months teaching about the Kingdom of God. At Ephesus Paul spent three months at the local synagogue "disputing and persuading the things concerning the Kingdom of God." *Acts 19:8* Shortly after Paul arrived in Rome and while he was under house arrest, many came to his lodging "to whom he expounded and testified the Kingdom of God, persuading them concerning Jesus, both out of the Law of Moses, and out of the Prophets, from morning till evening." *Acts 28:23 (See verse 16 as to house arrest)*

The preaching about Jesus was intermingled with the preaching about the Kingdom of God. In the City of Samaria, Philip preached "the things concerning the Kingdom of God, and the name of Jesus Christ." *Acts 8:12*

Paul speaks of certain persons active in the early church as "my fellow workers unto the Kingdom of God." *Colossians 4:11* Several times Paul describes of the persons who are excluded from the Kingdom of God:

> Know ye not that the unrighteous shall not *inherit* the Kingdom of God?

> Be not deceived: neither fornicators, nor idolaters, nor adulterers, nor effeminate, nor abusers of themselves with mankind, nor thieves, nor covetous, nor drunkards, nor revilers, nor extortioners, shall *inherit* the Kingdom of God. *1 Corinthians 6:9–10*

For this ye know, that no whoremonger, nor unclean person, nor covetous man, who is an idolater, hath any *inheritance* in the Kingdom of Christ and of God. *Ephesians 5:5*

Now the works of the flesh are manifest, which are these: adultery, fornication, uncleanness, lasciviousness, idolatry, witchcraft, hatred, variance, emulations, wrath, strife, seditions, heresies, envyings, murders, drunkenness, revellings, and such like: of the which I tell you before, as I have told you in time past, that they which do such things shall not *inherit* the Kingdom of God. *Galatians 5:19–21*

Paul states that the unrighteous will not inherit the Kingdom of God. James states that "the poor of this world rich in faith" will inherit that Kingdom:

Hearken, my beloved brethren, hath not God chosen the poor of this world rich in faith, and *heirs of the Kingdom* which he hath promised to them that love him? *James 2:5*

The heirs of the Kingdom are those who love God. The Kingdom of God is an inheritance, and certain persons cannot inherit. But the class of those who cannot inherit is larger than the persons named in Paul's lists.

Paul, himself, concluded:

Now this I say, brethren, that *flesh and blood* can not inherit the Kingdom of God; neither doth corruption inherit incorruption. *1 Corinthians 15:50*

This brings us to the nature of the Kingdom of God. How did Paul understand this key teaching of Jesus?

In Asia Minor, at Lystra, Iconium and Antioch, Paul taught his converts "that we must through much tribulation enter into the Kingdom of God." *Acts 14:22*

Not only is the entrance into the Kingdom attended with hardship, it also requires that the persons who have entered the Kingdom to be worthy of it. Paul twice entreated the church at Thessalonika to be worthy of the Kingdom of God. He entreated them:

> That ye walk worthy of God, who hath called you unto his Kingdom and glory. *1 Thessalonians 2:12*

> That ye may be counted worthy of the Kingdom of God, for which ye also suffer. *2 Thessalonians 1:5*

In two famous sayings, Paul summed up what he knew of the Kingdom of God's nature:

> For the Kingdom of God is not meat and drink; but righteousness, and peace, and joy in the Holy Spirit. *Romans 14:17*

> For the Kingdom of God is not in word, but in power. *1 Corinthians 4:20*

The Kingdom of God was, for Paul, righteousness, and peace, and joy in the power of the Holy Spirit. According to Paul, God has "delivered us from the power of darkness, and hath translated us into the Kingdom of his dear Son: in whom we have redemption through his blood, even the forgiveness of sins: who is the image of the invisible God, . . ." *Colossians 1:13–15*

God has seized Christians from the realm of darkness and deported them into Christ's Kingdom.

This is an everlasting kingdom. Peter writes of the believer's entrance "into the everlasting Kingdom of our Lord and Saviour Jesus Christ". *2 Peter 1:11*

This is an unconquerable Kingdom:

> Wherefore we receiving *a Kingdom which cannot be moved*, let us have grace, whereby we may serve God acceptably with reverence and godly fear: for our God is a consuming fire. *Hebrews 12:28–29*

This Kingdom is apocalyptic. Paul wrote:

> I charge thee therefore before God, and the Lord Jesus Christ, who shall judge the quick and the dead at his appearing and his Kingdom: . . . *2 Timothy 4:1*

Both the living and dead shall be judged by Jesus' Kingdom. The end of the whole matter is this:

> For as in Adam all die, even so in Christ shall all be made alive. But every man in his own order: Christ the firstfruits; afterwards they that are Christ's at his coming. *Then* cometh the end, *when he shall have delivered up the Kingdom* to God, even the Father; when he shall have put down all rule and all authority and power. For he must reign, till he hath put all enemies under his feet. The last enemy that shall be destroyed is death. *1 Corinthians 15:22–25*

THE NATURE OF THE KINGDOM: PART 1

After Jesus had answered a scribe's question, "Which is the first commandment of all?", with two quotations from the Law (*Deuteronomy 6:4–5 and Leviticus 19:18*), the scribe then said:

> Well, Master, thou hast said the truth: for there is one God; and there is none other but he. And to love him with all the heart, and with all the soul, and with all the strength, and to love his neighbor as himself, is more than all whole burnt offerings and sacrifices. *Mk 12:32–33*

Jesus approved the scribe's statement and said to him:

> Thou are not far from the Kingdom of God. *Mk 12:34*

The scribe's statement must then be regarded as a first approximation of the nature of the Kingdom. It was not a definitive statement of the nature of the Kingdom but we have Jesus' own word that it was "not far from the Kingdom of God."

THE NATURE OF THE KINGDOM: PART II

For Paul, the Kingdom of God is "righteousness, and peace, and joy in the Holy Spirit." *Romans 14:17* He also wrote:

For the Kingdom of God is not in word, but in power. *1 Corinthians 4:20*

The power of God surges into the universe through the Holy Spirit. Jesus himself used three parables to explain how the Kingdom of God surges into our world with wonder-working power from small and obscure beginnings.

In the first parable, Jesus compared the Kingdom to the growth of a tiny mustard seed:

MARK	MATTHEW	LUKE
Whereunto shall we liken		Unto what is
the Kingdom of God	The Kingdom of Heaven	the Kingdom of God like,
Or with what comparison		and whereunto shall I resemble it?
shall we compare it?		
It is like a grain	is like to a grain	It is like a grain
of mustard seed,	of mustard seed,	of mustard seed,
which, when	which	which
	a man took,	a man took,
it is sown	and sowed	and cast
in the earth,	in his field,	into his garden;
	which indeed	
is less than	is the least	
all the seeds	of all seeds,	
that be in the earth;		
but when it is sown,	but when	
it groweth up,	it is grown,	and it grew,
and becometh	it is	and waxed

Mark (cont.)	Matthew (cont.)	Luke (cont.)
greater than	the greatest	
all herbs,	among herbs,	
and shooteth out	and becometh	
great branches,	a tree,	a great tree
so that the fowls	so that the birds	and the fowls
of the air	of the air come	of the air
may lodge under	and lodge in	lodged in
the shadow of it.	the branches thereof.	the branches of it.
Mk 4:30–32	*Mt 13:31–32*	*L 13:18–19*

The second parable is found only in Matthew and Luke:

Matthew	Luke
	Whereunto shall I liken
The Kingdom of Heaven	the Kingdom of God?
is like unto leaven,	It is like leaven,
which a woman took,	which a woman took
and hid in	and hid in
three measures of meal,	three measures of meal,
till the whole was leavened.	till the whole was leavened.
Mt 13:33	*L 13:20–21*

"Three measures" of meal would be about a bushel or about fifty pounds.

The third parable is found only in Mark:

So is the Kingdom of God, as if a man should cast seed into the ground, and should sleep, and rise night and day, and the seed should spring [sprout] and grow up, *he knoweth not how.* For the earth bringeth forth fruit of herself; first the blade, then the ear, after that the full corn in the ear. But when the fruit is brought forth, immediately he putteth in the sickle, because the harvest is come. *Mk 4:26–29*

Reading the three parables together, Jesus explains that the Kingdom grows explosively from tiny beginnings in ways we know not how. The grain shoots up, the tiny mustard seed becomes a big shrub, and the pinch of starter raises fifty pounds of meal.

To a prescientific age, the growth of seeds and the fermentation of yeast were mysteries. Although we now understand these processes, Jesus used those illustrations that his hearers would deem mysteries to explain the Kingdom and its astonishing results. The Kingdom seethes into the inert meal of the world and leavens it. The true analogies of the Kingdom are biological, not the crude categories of human logic.

There is a statement by Jesus about "violence" and the Kingdom that is quoted differently by Matthew and Luke:

Matthew	Luke
And from the days of John the Baptist until now the Kingdom of Heaven suffereth violence and the violence take it by force.	Since that time the Kingdom of God is preached and every man presseth into it
For all the Prophets and the Law prophesied until John. *Mt 11:21*	The Law and the Prophets were until John *L 16:16*

Our inquiry is the nature of the Kingdom. The Greek of Matthew is obscure and various interpretations of it are possible. Luke is simpler and clearer. Scholars speculate that Matthew's version, because of prolixity, is the original form of the saying. They also speculate that both quotes are variants of a single saying found in the hypothetical document Q. Despite these contentions, it is possible, and indeed likely, that Jesus made his point in variant forms at different times and places in his ministry: once in the context of John's imprisonment *(Mt 11:2–20)*; and once in the course of a dispute with some Pharisees. *(L 16:14–18)* The real question is what was Jesus' point.

Since our record is so obscure (a "hard saying" in the traditional jargon), we need to remember that we look at these verses through a thick and cloudy three-layer lens: the basic layer of Jesus' actual Aramaic words that we do not have; the middle layer of the Greek words of the text whose meanings are obscure; and the top layer of the English distorted by the translators' varying responses to the obscure Greek text.

If we move from words to ideas, the ideas are quite simple and such that Jesus might well have stated repeatedly: the Kingdom is such a desirable thing that everyone who appreciates its worth is determined to get in, "violently," if necessary; and that Kingdom had only been preached since the days of John the Baptist.

The great desirability of the Kingdom is consistent with the two parables of Jesus that teach the great joy of finding the Kingdom, a delirious joy like finding hidden treasure:

Again, the Kingdom of Heaven is like unto treasure hid in a field, the which when a man hath found, he hideth, and *for joy thereof* goeth and selleth all that he hath, and buyeth that field. *Mt 13:44*

Again, the Kingdom of Heaven is like unto a merchant man seeking goodly pearls, who, when he had found *one* pearl of great price, went and sold all that he had, and bought it. *Mt 13:45–46*

These parables teach the supreme worth of the Kingdom—the one thing most needful to man. In each case, the man in the parable sold all that he had so that he could buy the field or the pearl.

Both parables teach the ecstatic joy of the man in finding the Kingdom. The joy of finding the Kingdom is like finding 1,000 gold coins in a field, and being able to buy that field. The joy of finding the Kingdom is like a broker finding a perfect pearl in a bag of seconds and being able to raise enough money to buy that perfect pearl.

The Kingdom is a joyful thing. As Paul wrote, the Kingdom is not only a righteousness and peace, it is "joy in the Holy Spirit." *Romans 14:17* We tend to think that Gospel and the Kingdom are separate things. However, both Matthew and Mark write that Jesus came preaching the gospel of the Kingdom. *Mk 1:14 (". . . gospel of the Kingdom of God. . .")*; *Mt 4:23, 9:35, 24:14 (". . . gospel of the Kingdom . . .")* Luke writes that Jesus "went throughout every city and village, preaching and shewing *the glad tidings* of the Kingdom of God." *L 8:1*

The Anglo-Saxon root of the word *gospel* is "gôd-spell," meaning "good tidings." Newer translations modernize "glad tidings" lamely to "good news." The Kingdom is more that good news, it is joy!

The Kingdom is also crucial. We have Jesus' own words:

And this gospel of the Kingdom shall be preached in all the world
for a witness unto all nations: and then shall end come. *Mt 24:14*

It should be noted that the Kingdom of God and the Kingdom of Heaven are one and the same. Matthew, writing a gospel for Jews, usually uses "Kingdom of Heaven" to avoid writing, contrary to Jewish scruples, the unspeakably holy name of God, while the other gospels use the "Kingdom of God" in the same contexts. Matthew does, however, also use the phrase "Kingdom of God." For example, see Matthew 6:33; 12:28; 19:24; and 21:31, 43.

Some examples show that Kingdom of God and Kingdom of Heaven are equivalent phrases:

MARK	MATTHEW	LUKE
	Repent: for	
The Kingdom	the Kingdom	
of God	of Heaven	
is at hand:	is at hand.	
repent ye, . . .	*Mt 4:17*	
Mk 1:15		
	And as ye go,	And he sent them
	preach, saying,	to preach
	"The Kingdom	the Kingdom
	of Heaven	of God, . . .
	is at hand."	*L 9:2*
	Mt 10:7	
Suffer	Suffer	Suffer
the little children	little children	little children

MARK (cont.)	MATTHEW (cont.)	LUKE (cont.)
to come unto me,		to come unto me,
and forbid them not:	and forbid them not,	and forbid them not:
	to come unto me:	
for such is	for of such is	for of such is
the Kingdom	the Kingdom	the Kingdom
of God	of Heaven.	of God.
Mk 10:14	*Mt 19:14*	*L 18:16*

One day Jesus was teaching in parables by the Sea of Galilee. *Mt 13:1–3* After telling four parables, including the parable of the tares, Jesus sent the multitude away and went into the house where he was staying, and his disciples came in to ask for an explanation of the parable of the tares, saying:

Declare unto us the parable of the tares of the field. *Mt 13:36*

Jesus explained that parable and then told three new parables: treasure hid in a field, one pearl of great price and the net.

Matthew then records the following interchange between Jesus and his disciples:

JESUS: Have ye understood all these things?
DISCIPLES: Yea, Lord.
JESUS: Therefore every scribe which is instructed unto the Kingdom of Heaven is like unto a man that is an house holder, which bringeth forth out of his treasure things new and old. *Mt 13:51–52*

Jesus said that every scholar of the Jewish Law who was indoctrinated with precepts of the Kingdom, as by these parables, added to his old store of learning, new concepts.

For such scholars, and indeed for everyone, the pressing question is how to move from knowledge about the Kingdom to entering it.

BIRTH INTO THE KINGDOM OF GOD

It was Jesus himself who taught that men must be born again to enter into the Kingdom of God. He taught:

> Verily, verily, I say unto thee, except a man *be born again,* he cannot see the Kingdom of God . . .

> Verily, verily, I say unto thee, except a man be *born of water and of the Spirit,* he can not enter into the Kingdom of God. That which is born of the flesh is flesh; and that which is born of the Spirit is spirit. Marvel not that I said unto thee, "Ye must be *born again."*

> The wind bloweth where it listeth, and thou hearest the sound thereof, but canst not tell whence it cometh, and whither it goeth: so is every one that is *born of the Spirit. J 3:3, 5–8*

The Greek word translated *again* is ambiguous and can mean "from above." That is why some modern translations give "from above" as an alternative rendering of Jesus' own words. However, we do not have Jesus' own Aramaic words, only the Greek translation of them that are the Gospels.

A fair reading of Jesus' words does, however, show that he used "born of the Spirit" as synonymous with "born again." By Spirit, he means the Holy Spirit. Simply stated, Jesus taught to be born again or to be born from above means to be born spiritually by the act of the Holy Spirit.

This spiritual birth is the indispensable condition for entrance into the Kingdom of God:

> Verily, verily, I say unto thee,
> except a man be born
> again,
> he can not see
> the Kingdom of God.
> J 3:3

> Verily, verily, I say unto thee,
> except a man be born
> of water and of the Spirit,
> he can not enter into
> the Kingdom of God
> J 3:5

The word *water* suggests baptism. It is hard to know from these few sentences of Jesus whether or not he meant to refer to baptism here. Considering this passage as a whole, Jesus may be using "water" as a symbol of the spiritual washing necessarily incident to birth by the Spirit somewhat as Paul writes in Titus:

> Not by works of righteousness which we have done, but according to his mercy he saved us, *by the washing of regeneration, and renewing of the Holy Spirit. Titus 3:5*

In short, both phrases "born *of water* and *of the Spirit*" describe a single birth process and not a birth by the Spirit *and* a separate rite of water.

The focus of Jesus' sentences here is on the necessity for spiritual birth in order to enter the Kingdom. The phrase "he can not see the Kingdom of God" means the same as "he can not enter the Kingdom of God."

Jesus said:

> That which is born of the flesh is flesh; and that which is born of the Spirit is spirit. *J 3:6*

Echoing those words, Peter later wrote:

> Seeing ye have purified your souls in obeying the truth through the Spirit unto unfeigned love of the brethren, see that ye love one another with a pure heart fervently: *being born again*, not of corruptible seed, but of incorruptible, by the word of God, which liveth and abideth for ever. *1 Peter 1:22–23*

That which is born of the corruptible seed, sperm, is flesh, while that which is born of the eternal Word of God is spirit. It is as Paul wrote:

> Now this I say, brethren, that flesh and blood can not inherit the Kingdom of God; neither doth corruption [flesh] inherit incorruptiom [spirit]. *1 Corinthians 15:50*

It is only by a spiritual birth after and beyond their physical birth that man can enter into the Kingdom of God. The process of spiritual birth into that Kingdom may be as traumatic as a physical birth. That is why some men speak again and again of their spiritual birth.

Snide remarks about "born-again" Christians ignore the fact that it was Jesus *himself* who taught that men must "be born again." *J 3:3, 7* It was Jesus *himself*, who said:

Marvel not that I said unto thee, "Ye must be born again." *J 3:7*

Adoption into the Kingdom of God

John's Gospel describes Jesus' mission as follows:

But as many received him, to them gave he power to become the sons of God, even to them that believe on his name, which were born, not of blood, nor of the will of the flesh, nor of the will of men, but of God. *J 1:12–13*

Only those that believe on Jesus' name have the power to become the sons of God. It is only a pagan anthropological sense that all men are the sons of God. Jesus taught that a man's physical birth is insufficient to make him a subject of the Kingdom of God. *J 3:3–8*

Jesus recognized that all men were not children of the Kingdom of God. He explained his parable of the tares of the field as follows:

The field is the world, and the good seed are the children of the Kingdom; but the tares are the children of the wicked one. *Mt 13:38*

The sower of the good seed "is the Son of Man"; the sower of the tares "is the devil." *Mt 13:37, 39* Both the good seed and the tares are in the world; but all men are not children of the Kingdom of God, only those sown by the Son of Man.

One test for children of God is given by Jesus in the Beatitudes:

Blessed are the peacemakers: for they shall be called the children of God. *Mt 5:9*

In Luke, Jesus is reported to have said that those worthy of the other world and the resurrection from the dead "are the children of God, being children of the resurrection." *L 20:36*

As Paul looked back to Jesus, he wrote:

For ye are all the children of God by faith in Christ Jesus. *Galatians 3:26*

514

John wrote in his first epistle:

Whosoever believeth that Jesus is the Christ is born of God: . . .
1 John 5:1

Paul used the analogy of adoption to explain the process of becoming a child of God:

For as many as are led by the Spirit of God, they are the sons of God. For ye have not received the spirit of bondage again to fear; but ye have received the *Spirit of adoption*, whereby we cry, "Abba, Father." The Spirit itself beareth witness with our spirit, that we are the [adoptive] children of God. *Romans 8:14–16*

Even so we, when we were children, were in bondage under the elements of the world; but when the fulness of the time was come, God sent forth his Son, made of a woman, made under the Law, to redeem them that were under the Law, that we might receive *the adoption of [as] sons*; and because ye are sons, God hath sent forth the Spirit of his Son into your hearts, crying, "Abba, Father." *Galatians 4:3–6*

Both passages leave untranslated the Aramaic word for father, *Abba*, and produce a sort of liturgical repetition of the cry, "Father." The point is that we become adoptive children of God through the operation of the Holy Spirit. More succinctly, God has "predestinated us unto adoption of [as] children by Jesus Christ to himself." Ephesians 1:5

All men are not children of God; only those who consent to God's adoption of them are the children of God. This consent is given by believing in Jesus' name. The children of God are those persons who have been adopted into the Kingdom of God, and as adoptive children, they will inherit the Kingdom of God:

The Spirit itself beareth witness with our spirit, that we are the [adoptive] children of God: and if [adoptive] children, then heirs, heirs of God, and joint heirs with Christ . . . *Romans 8:16–17*

ENTRANCE INTO THE KINGDOM OF GOD

Jesus did not explain entrance into the Kingdom of God solely in terms of the analogy of birth or adoption. On many occasions, and in many different ways, Jesus explained how to enter into the Kingdom of God.

One that is indelibly burned into the world's consciousness is Jesus and the little children:

MARK	MATTHEW	LUKE
Verily, I say unto you,	Verily I say unto you, except ye be	Verily I say unto you,
whosoever shall not receive the Kingdom of God as a little child, he shall not *enter* therein. *Mk 10:15*	converted and become as little children, ye shall not *enter* into the Kingdom of Heaven. *Mt 18:3*	whosoever shall not receive the Kingdom of God as a little child shall in no wise *enter* therein. *L 18:17*

The condition of entrance into the Kingdom of God is having the willing faith of a little child. The entrant must come "as" or "like" a little child. The word *conversion* has become a technical theological word but it simply means "a turning." For Jesus, conversion was not a topic of abnormal psychology but a deliberate decision to enroll in God's Kingdom.

There is no verbal entrance test for the Kingdom that is sufficient:

Not every one that saith unto me, "Lord, Lord", shall enter into the Kingdom of Heaven; but he that doeth the will of my Father which is in heaven. Many will say to me in that day, "Lord, Lord, have we not prophesied in thy name and in thy name cast out devils and in thy name done many wonderful works?" And then I will profess unto them, "I never knew you: depart from me, ye that work iniquity," *Mt 7:21–23*

Workers of iniquity, even if they use the right verbal formulas, shall not enter the Kingdom. Religiosity is not enough:

> For I say unto you, that except your righteousness shall exceed the righteousness of the scribes and Pharisees, ye shall in no case enter into the Kingdom of Heaven. *Mt 5:20*

This proud religiosity not only caused the scribes and Pharisees to fail the Kingdom entrance test themselves, it also caused them to bar the door to others:

> But woe unto you, scribes and Pharisees, hypocrites! For ye shut up the Kingdom of Heaven against me: for ye neither go in yourselves, neither suffer ye them that are entering to go in. *Mt 23:13*

This same proud religiosity also caused Jesus to tell the chief priest and elders:

> Verily I say unto you, that the publicans and the harlots go into the Kingdom of God before you. *Mt 21:31*

Rich men also have problems entering the Kingdom. It is exceedingly difficult for a rich man to enter into the Kingdom:

MARK	MATTHEW	LUKE
	Verily I say unto you, that a rich man	
How *hardly* shall they that have riches enter into the Kingdom of God! *Mk 10:23*	shall *hardly* enter into the Kingdom of Heaven. *Mt 19:23*	How *hardly* shall they that have riches enter into the Kingdom of God! *L 18:24*

Easy exegesis diffuses Jesus' blunt statement that it is *hard* for a rich man to enter the Kingdom of God. Jesus immediately followed his statement of "hardness" with a contrasting statement to emphasize this point:

MARK	MATTHEW	LUKE
	And again	
	I say unto you,	
It is *easier*	it is *easier*	For it is *easier*
for a camel	for a camel	for a camel
to go through	to go through	to go through
the eye of a needle,	the eye of a needle	a needle's eye
than	than	than
for a rich man	for a rich man	for a rich man
to enter into	to enter into	to enter into
the Kingdom of God.	the Kingdom of God.	the Kingdom of God.
Mk 10:25	*Mt 19:24*	*L 18:24*

Jesus was speaking in hyperbole: how can a great ungainly camel squeeze through a space in a woman's sewing needle? Many ingenious ways have been devised to soften the impact of this hard and clear saying, but any fair reading of of it leads to the conclusion that Jesus was saying that it is almost impossible for a rich man to enter into the Kingdom of God.

It will no doubt be argued that Jesus did not condemn rich men as such but only those that trust in riches, citing Mark 10:24 where Mark quotes Jesus as saying:

> Children, how hard it is for them that *trust* in riches to enter into the Kingdom of God. *Mk 10:24*

The manuscripts of Mark are divided, and some omit the words translated "for them that trust in riches." Modern translations follow those manuscripts, and so we are left with Jesus having said:

> Children, how hard it is . . . to enter into the Kingdom of God. *Mk 10:24*

Whatever manuscripts are chosen as correctly reporting Jesus' words in Mark 10:24, there is no doubt about his clear statement in Mark 10:23:

How hardly shall they that have riches enter into the Kingdom of. God!

Mark records that this statement "astonished" Jesus' disciples. *Mk 10:24* Matthew has it that "they were exceedingly amazed." *Mt 19.25*
All three gospels record the depth of the disciples' astonishment by quoting them as saying:

Who then can be saved? *Mk 10:26; Mt 19:25; L 18:26*

Jesus responded by saying, in effect, that it is possible for even a rich man to be saved:

MARK	MATTHEW	LUKE
With men	With men	The things
it is impossible,	this is impossible;	which are impossible
but not	but	
with God:	with God	with men
For with God		
all things	all things	are possible
are possible	are possible.	with God.
Mk 10:27	*Mt 19:26*	*L 18:27*

Jesus' original disciples were astonished at his teaching that it is exceedingly hard for a rich man to enter into the Kingdom. Present-day disciples struggle to find ways around these plain verses.

While it is hard for a rich man to enter into the Kingdom, it is urgent that everyone enter into the Kingdom.

Jesus said:

If thine eye offend thee, pluck it out; it is better for thee to *enter* into the Kingdom of God with one eye than having two eyes to be cast into hell fire. *Mk 9:47*

It must be stated flatly that Jesus did not mean that anyone should pluck out his eye, whatever his offense. He would have been astounded that anyone would construe his words that way. He was, simply, in the language of his time and place making a point. That point was the urgency and importance of everyone entering into the Kingdom. That is still his point.

THE KINGDOM IS AN INHERITANCE

Entrance into the Kingdom is not with doubts and questionings but with the free and open faith with which children accept a gift. *Mk 10:15; Mt 18:3; L 18:17* The Kingdom is, in fact, a gift, an inheritance. Jesus said:

> Come ye blessed of my Father *inherit* the Kingdom prepared for you from the foundation of the world. *Mt 25:34*

Paul also taught that the Kingdom of God was an inheritance:

> Now this I say, brethren, that flesh and blood *can not inherit* the Kingdom of God; neither doth corruption inherit incorruption.
> *1 Corinthians 15:50*

Paul lists various works of the flesh such as murders, drunkenness and hatred and then states that "they which do such things *shall not inherit* the Kingdom of God." *Galatians 5:21* Paul also gives lists of specific types of unrighteous persons who "shall not *inherit* the Kingdom of God" or have "any *inheritance* in the Kingdom of Christ and of God." *1 Corinthians 6:9–10; Ephesians 5:5* Finally, he also affirms that Christians "have obtained an *inheritance*." *Ephesians 1:11*

Peter refers to this inheritance when he writes that Christians have "an inheritance incorruptible, and undefiled, and that fadeth not away, reserved in heaven for you." *1 Peter 1:4*

Like some inheritances, there are certain conditions to be met. This is not unreasonable. The conditions must be met or the legacy is not received.

Not many people will refuse an inheritance. Some will. The Kingdom is an inheritance which ought not to be renounced lightly.

The Kingdom is like a treasure hidden in a field or pearl of great price:

> Again, the Kingdom of Heaven is like unto treasure hid in a field: the which when a man hath found, he hideth, and for joy thereof goeth and selleth all that he hath, and buyeth that field.

Again, the Kingdom of Heaven is like unto a merchant man, seeking goodly pearls: who, when he had found one pearl of great price, went and sold all that he had, and bought it. *Mt 13:44–46*

Jesus, in effect, says: "My Father gives and bequeaths to you one pearl of great price."

Many people renounce this legacy. The Kingdom is not only a legacy, it is also a gift. Jesus told his followers:

Fear not, little flock: for it is your Father's good pleasure *to give* you the Kingdom. *L 12:32*

People are not simply born or adopted into the Kingdom. These analogies are essential and true, but in our day are distorted by the emphasis on the birth trauma or the adoption process. Jesus also taught that other analogies of the Kingdom are essential and true. One of these analogies is that the entrance into the Kingdom is like receiving an inheritance, a legacy from God the Father.

Whose is the Kingdom?

Jesus spoke of how to enter the Kingdom and who would or would not enter the Kingdom, and he also sometimes described who would possess the Kingdom.

It is certain that Jesus said the Kingdom belongs to the poor; it is not certain what he meant by poor:

Matthew	Luke
Blessed are the poor in spirit:	Blessed be ye poor:
for theirs is	for yours is
the Kingdom of Heaven.	the Kingdom of God.
Mt 5:3	L 6:20

It is disputed whether or not "in spirit" is a gloss. It is certain, however, that the Hebrew word behind the word translated "poor" in both Matthew and Luke does not mean simply "have-nots" but pious poor. Poverty alone is not virtue; the humility that may come with poverty is. It is not enough to be poor without being rich in faith. The Kingdom belongs to those who are rich in faith.

James wrote his Christian brethren:

Hath not God chosen the poor of this world [who are] *rich in faith*, and [as such] heirs of the Kingdom which he hath promised to them that love him? *James 2:5*

The context of Jesus' own words in Luke suggests that Jesus meant the materially poor since his next sentence in Luke refers to those who "hunger now," and a few sentences later he pronounced "woes" upon the materially rich:

But woe unto you that are rich! For ye have received your consolation.

Woe unto you that are full! For ye shall hunger. L 6:24–25

Jesus' saying in Matthew is in the Sermon on the Mount where it stated as part of a whole series of Jesus' sayings, the Beatitudes, defining the spiritually happy. Jesus was not content there to say, simply, to the "poor in spirit" that "theirs" is the Kingdom. He went on to say:

> Blessed are they which are persecuted for righteousness' sake: for theirs is the Kingdom of Heaven. *Mt 5:10*

In each case we have the identical conclusion, "For theirs is the Kingdom of Heaven." *Mt 5:3, 10* The "poor in spirit" along with those "persecuted for righteousness' sake" are dual aspects of a single thing, persons who are qualified to possess the Kingdom.

This brings us to the most famous group of all, the little children. Again, Jesus did not mean to be literal. He did not mean the Kingdom of God was sort of a Disney-like Kingdom belonging to infants. He meant that their simple acceptance of the gift of the Kingdom defined the kind of people who would be acceptable as subjects of the Kingdom:

MARK	MATTHEW	LUKE
	Then were	
And they brought	there brought	And they brought
young children	unto him	unto him
to him,	little children,	also infants,
that he should	that he should	that he would
	put his hands	
touch them;	on them,	touch them;
	and pray;	
and his disciples	and his disciples	but when his disciples
		saw it, they
rebuked	rebuked	rebuked
those that brought		
them.	them.	them.
But when Jesus	But Jesus	But Jesus
saw it, he was much		
displeased,		

524

MARK (cont.)	MATTHEW (cont.)	LUKE (cont.)
		called them unto him,
and said unto them,	said,	and said:
"Suffer	"Suffer	"Suffer
the little children	little children,	little children
to come unto me,		to come unto me,
and forbid them not:	and forbid them not,	and forbid them not:
	to come unto me:	
for of such is	for of such is	for of such is
the Kingdom	the Kingdom	the Kingdom
of God.	of Heaven."	of God.
Verily I say		"Verily I say
unto you,		unto you,
whosoever		whosoever
shall not receive		shall not receive
the Kingdom of God		the Kingdom of God
as a little child,		as a little child
he shall not enter		shall in no wise enter
therein."		therein."
		L 18:15–17
And he took them up	And he	
in his arms,		
put his hands	laid his hands	
upon them,	on them,	
and blessed them.		
Mk 10:13–16	and departed thence.	
	Mt 19:13–15	

Jesus' words form a mosaic of the characteristics of persons who possess the Kingdom: those who do not put their trust either in riches, or themselves; those who are persecuted for righteousness' sake; those who accept the Kingdom without pride or pretension, even intellectual pride. These are the persons who are fit for the Kingdom. But even these must not look back to the world:

No man having put his hand to the plough, and looking back, is fit for the Kingdom of God. L 9:62

THE KINGDOM INCLUDES EVIL PERSONS

Just preceding the parables of the mustard seed and the leaven, Matthew has one of the longest parables of the Kingdom:

> The Kingdom of Heaven is likened unto a man which sowed good seed in his field; but while men slept, his enemy came and sowed tares among the wheat, and went his way. But when the blade was sprung up, and brought forth fruit, then appeared the tares (darnel, a wheat-like weed) also. So the servants of the householder came and said unto him, "Sir, didst not thou sow good seed in thy field? From whence then hath it tares?"
>
> He said unto them, "An enemy hath done this." The servants said unto him, "Wilt thou then that we go and gather them up?"
>
> But he said, "Nay; lest while ye gather up the tares, ye root up also the wheat with them. Let both grow together until the harvest; and in the time of harvest *I will say to the reapers*, Gather ye together first the tares, and bind them in bundles to burn them, but gather the wheat into my barn." *Mt 13:24–30*

At the request of his disciples, Jesus later gave his explanation of this parable:

> He that soweth the good seed is the Son of Man. The field is the world; the good seed are the children of the Kingdom, but the tares are children of the wicked one. The enemy that sowed them is the Devil; the harvest is the end of the world; and the reapers are the angels. As therefore the tares are gathered and burned in the fire, *so shall it be in the end of this world.* The Son of Man shall send forth his angels, and they *shall gather out of his Kingdom all things that offend, and them which do iniquity*, and shall cast them into a furnace of fire: there shall be wailing and gnashing of teeth. Then shall the righteous shine forth as the sun in the Kingdom of their Father. Who hath ears to hear, let him hear. *Mt 13:37–43*

It would be presumptuous to explain Jesus' own explanation. It clearly states, ". . . so shall it be in the end of this world." Matthew also has the parable of the net:

Again, the Kingdom of Heaven is like unto a net, that was cast into the sea, and *gathered of every kind*; which, when it was full, they drew to shore, and sat down, and *gathered the good into vessels, but cast the bad away. So shall it be at the end of the world*: the angels shall come forth, and sever the wicked from among the just; and shall cast them into the furnace of fire; there shall be wailing and gnashing of teeth. *Mt 13:47–50*

Both the parable of the sower and the net speak of what "shall be at the end of the world" and how the Son of man shall send forth his angels to rid his Kingdom of the wicked and "cast them into the furnace of fire." Both continue that "there shall be wailing and gnashing of teeth."

The Kingdom, as Jesus taught it, is not some invisible kingdom of the redeemed or elect or the true believers. That Kingdom is not simply some pure leaven yeasting the evil world in which we live. No. That Kingdom includes the evil ones, those sown by the Devil.

Jesus' explanation of the parable of the sower states:

The Son of man shall send forth his angels, and they shall gather *out of his Kingdom* all things that offend, and them which do iniquity; . . . *Mt 13:41*

In the net parable Jesus says:

The Kingdom of Heaven is like unto a net, that was cast into the sea, and *gathered of every kind*: which, when it was full, they drew to shore, and sat down, and gathered the good into vessels, *but cast the bad away* . . . *Mt 13:47–48*

THE KINGDOM IS TO BE PURGED

The Kingdom itself must be purged of unworthy subjects. Jesus explained the parable of the tares as follows:

> The Son of man shall send forth his angels, and they shall gather *out of his Kingdom* all things that offend, and *them which do iniquity*; and shall cast them into a furnace of fire: There shall be wailing and gnashing of teeth. Then shall the righteous shine forth as the sun in the Kingdom of their Father. *Mt 13:41–43*

Jesus explained the parable of the Kingdom of Heaven being like a net that "gathered of every kind" *(Mt 13:47)* from the sea but the bad were then thrown away *(Mt 13:48)*:

> So shall it be at the end of the world: the angels shall come forth, and *sever* the wicked from among the just. And shall cast them into the furnace of fire: there shall be wailing and gnashing of teeth. *Mt 13:49–50*

Both Matthew and Luke quote a saying of Jesus but in two completely different contexts:

MATTHEW	LUKE
And I say unto you, that many shall come from the east and west,	
	There shall be weeping and gnashing of teeth,
and shall sit down with Abraham, and Isaac, and Jacob,	when ye shall see Abraham, and Isaac, and Jacob, and all the prophets,
in the Kingdom of Heaven. But the *children of the Kingdom* shall be *cast out into* outer darkness:	in the Kingdom of God, and *you yourselves thrust out.*

MATTHEW (cont.)
there shall be weeping
and gnashing of teeth.
Mt 8:11–12

LUKE (cont.)

And they shall come from
the east, and from the west,
and from the north,
and from the south,
and shall sit down in
the Kingdom of God.
L 13:28–29

Matthew quotes the saying in Jesus' response to a Roman centurion, where Jesus said to him, "Verily I say unto you, I have not found so great faith, no, not in Israel." *Mt 8:10* Luke omits the saying in his version of the centurion story. *L 7:1–10* Luke does have the saying as part of Jesus' answer to the question, "Lord, are there few that be saved?" *L 13:23*

It is obvious that Jesus could have said essentially the same thing in two different contexts. If the context is not certain, Jesus' teaching may nevertheless be clear.

To understand the teaching, the two versions may be compared analytically:

MATTHEW

1. "There shall be weeping and gnashing of teeth." *Mt 8:12*

2. "But the children of the Kingdom shall be cast out into outer darkness." *Mt 8:12*

3. "That many shall come from east and west,

and shall sit down . . . in the Kingdom of Heaven." *Mt 8:11*

LUKE

1. "There shall be weeping and gnashing of teeth." *L 13:28*

2. "When you shall see . . . you yourselves thrust out [of the Kingdom of God]."

3. "And they shall come from the east, and from the west, and from the north, and from the south, and shall sit down in the Kingdom of God." *L 13:29*

The teaching is clear enough that many from all directions shall sit down in the Kingdom, but some of those who had eaten with Jesus and heard him teach in the streets, i.e., certain Jews, will be thrust out of the Kingdom into the outer darkness, weeping and gnashing their teeth.

This is not an accidental variation in Jesus' teaching. He had the same thing to say of the unready steward:

> And [his lord] shall cut him asunder, and appoint him his portion with the hypocrites; there shall be weeping and gnashing of teeth.
> *Mt 24:51*

The Mysteries of the Kingdom

We have Jesus' own word that the Kingdom of God is a "mystery" or "mysteries." He told his disciples:

MARK	MATTHEW	LUKE
	Because	
Unto you	it is given	Unto you
it is given	unto you	it is given
to know	to know	to know
the mystery	the mysteries	the mysteries
of the Kingdom	of the Kingdom	of the Kingdom
of God;	of Heaven,	of God;
but unto them	but to them	but to others
that are without,		
all these things	it is not given.	
are done	*Mt 13:11*	
in parables.		in parables.
Mk 4:11		*L 8:10*

The discussion of these verses usually focuses on the parts referring to parables and whether the mysteries of the Kingdom were to be concealed from outsiders. For the discussion of these issues, see "Teaching In Parables," pp. 468–477, especially 470–473. Here it is sufficient to state that Jesus' parables, simple stories with a point, were designed to explain the Kingdom, not to mystify his listeners.

Modern translations of these verses consider "secret" or "secrets" to be a more appropriate translation than the King James Version's "mystery" or "mysteries." This is to be doubted since "secrets" suggest esoteric lore, like those of a lodge or a secret society. Jesus did not mean that; he meant that the mysteries of the Kingdom are its paradoxical principles, its unfamiliar theorems of an unseen spiritual universe centering in and radiating from God the Father himself.

It is hard to be more specific since we only have Jesus' own phrase "the mystery or mysteries of the Kingdom of God." *Mk 4:11; L 8:10 (Mt 13:11)* In a sense, the Kingdom is an invisible empire or a worldwide underground of God. The word *kingdom* connotes a realm, although it is not an ordinary kingdom, not even a Messianic kingdom. It is the realm of God like a sort of vast spiritual magnetic field emanating from and strong in Heaven, but in Jesus' lifetime, beginning to surge into our earth world and continuing into even our future as a sort of biosphere of the Spirit of God.

Jesus taught Christians to pray:

Thy Kingdom come. Thy will be done on earth as it is in Heaven.
Mt 6:10 (L 11:2)

The will of God is, of course, done in Heaven, because there God is King, and Christians look for the day when his Kingdom comes to earth and the will of God as King of Heaven is done here.

UNJUST RULES OF THE KINGDOM

Many rules of the Kingdom, humanly speaking, seem unjust. One rule is that many are called but few are chosen. That rule is taught by the parable of the wedding feast. Many "both bad and good" were invited, but only one was punished: a man who did not come in wedding garb. *Mt 22:10–13*

The whole parable reads as follows:

The Kingdom of Heaven is like unto a certain king, which made a marriage for his son, and sent forth his servants to call them that were bidden to the wedding; and they would not come.

Again, he sent forth other servants, saying, "Tell them which are bidden, Behold, I have prepared my dinner: my oxen and my fatlings are killed, and all things are ready; come unto the marriage."

But they made light of it, and went their ways, one to his farm, another to his merchandise; and the remnant took his servants, and entreated [treated] them spitefully, and slew them.

But when the king heard thereof, he was wroth; and he sent his armies, and destroyed those murderers, and burned up their city.

Then saith he to his servants, "The wedding is ready, but they which were bidden were not worthy. Go ye therefore unto the highways, and as many as ye shall find, bid to the marriage."

So those servants went out into the highways, and gathered together all as many as they found, both bad and good; and the wedding was furnished with guests.

And when the king came in to see the guests, he saw there was a man which had not on a wedding garment. And he saith unto him, "Friend, how camest thou in hither not having a wedding garment?"

And he was speechless.

Then said the king to the servants, "Bind him hand and foot, and take him away, and cast him into outer darkness; there shall be weeping and gnashing of teeth."

For many are called, but few are chosen. *Mt 22:2–14*

Offhand it seems unfair and unjust that "many are called, but few are chosen." That is the summary; the parable's lesson is not so simple. The king's first invitation to the feast was spurned by those invited; the second invitation provided the feast with many guests off of the streets. But even one of these was not chosen. He did not come prepared, in wedding garb, while the first invitees were not chosen at all in the sense that "they would not come." *Mt 22:3* Instead, they made light of the invitation and went their respective ways, one to his farm, another to his merchandise. *Mt 22:5* They were "called" since they were invited, but they were not "chosen" since they would not come.

The conclusion of this parable that "many are called, but few are chosen" is also found at the end of another long parable of the Kingdom:

For the Kingdom of Heaven is like unto a man that is an house-holder, which went out early in the morning to hire laborers into his vineyard. And when he had agreed with the laborers for a penny [a denarius—a day's wage for a laborer] a day, he sent them into his vineyard.

And he went out about the third hour [about 9:00 A.M.], and saw others standing idle in the marketplace, and said unto them: "Go ye also into the vineyard, and whatsoever is right I will give you."

And they went their way.

Again he went out about the sixth [about 12 noon] and ninth hour [about 3:00 P.M], and did likewise. And about the eleventh hour [about 5:00 P.M.] he went out, and found others standing idle, and saith unto them, "Why stand ye here all the day idle?"

They say unto him, "Because no man hath hired us."

He saith unto them, "Go ye also into the vineyard; and whatsoever is right, that shall ye receive."

So when even [evening] was come, the lord of the vineyard saith unto his steward, "Call the laborers, and give them their hire, beginning from the last unto the first."

And when they came that were hired about the eleventh hour [about 5:00 P.M.], they received every man a penny. But when the first came, they supposed that they should have received more; and they likewise received every man a penny.

And when they had received it, they murmured against the goodman of the house, saying, "These last have wrought but one hour, and thou hast made them equal unto us, which have borne the burden and heat of the day."

But he answered one of them, and said, "Friend, I do thee no wrong: didst not thou agree with me for a penny? Take that thine is, and go thy way; I will give unto this last, even as unto thee. Is it not lawful for me to do what I will with mine own? Is thine eye evil, because I am good?"

So the last shall be first, and the first last: for many are called, but few are chosen. *Mt 20:1–16*

Modern translations omit, on the basis of the manuscript evidence, the phrases "for many are called, but few chosen." The other summation phrase "so the last shall be first, and the first last" does seem a more appropriate summation. However, that summation was applied by Jesus in two other contexts as well: Mk 10:31; Mt 19:30; and L 13:30.

In the first context, residents of first century Galilee are said to have no advantage although they heard and saw Jesus in person. The Gentiles from east and west, north and south, will come into the Kingdom ahead of them: the first shall be last. *L 13:29–30*

In Matthew and Mark, the context of the phrases about the "many that are first shall be last; and the last first" seem to refer back to the rich young ruler in contrast to those who have left house and kin for Jesus' sake. *Mk 10:17–31; Mt 19:16–30*

Since the saying about "the last shall be first, and the first last" occurs in other contexts, it may not be the key to the parable of the vineyard workers. What then is that parable telling us the Kingdom "is like"? Its point is that the Kingdom, as God's rule, can treat persons differently (pay the worker who starts at 5:00 P.M. the same as the worker who has "borne the burden and heat" of the whole day), since God's promises to each person in the Kingdom are always kept (the whole day worker got what was agreed).

There is another parable that also illustrates the injustice of the Kingdom in a human sense: that is the parable of the sower found in all three synoptic gospels:

MARK	MATTHEW	LUKE
Hearken! Behold, there went out	Behold	
a sower	a sower went forth	A sower went out
to sow.	to sow.	to sow his seed.
And it came to pass, as he sowed, some fell	And when he sowed some seeds fell	And as he sowed, some fell
by the way side,	by the way side,	by the way side; and it was trodden down,
and the fowls of the air came and devoured it up.	and the fowls came and devoured them up.	and the fowls of the air devoured it.
And some fell on stony ground,	Some fell upon stony places,	And some fell upon a rock;

MARK (cont.)	**MATTHEW** (cont.)	**LUKE** (cont.)
where it had not	where it had not	
much earth;	much earth;	
and	and	and
immediately it	forthwith they	as soon as it
sprang up,	sprung up,	was sprung up,
because it had	because they had	
no depth of earth.	no deepness of earth.	
But when the sun	And when the sun	
was up,	was up,	
it was scorched;	they were scorched;	
and because	and because	it withered away
it had no root,	they had no root	because
it withered away.	they withered away.	it lacked moisture.
And some fell	And some fell	And some fell
among thorns;	among thorns;	among thorns;
and the thorns	and the thorns	and the thorns
grew up	sprung up,	sprang up
and choked it,	and choked them.	with it, and choked it.
and it yielded no fruit.		
And other fell	But other fell	And other fell
on good ground,	into good ground	on good ground,
and did	and	and sprang up
yield fruit	brought forth fruit,	and bare fruit
that sprang up		
and increased,		
and brought forth,		
some thirty,	some an hundredfold,	
and some sixty,	some sixtyfold,	
and some an hundred.	some thirtyfold.	an hundredfold.
He that	Who	He that
hath ears to hear,	hath ears to hear,	hath ears to hear,
let him hear.	let him hear.	let him hear.
Mk 4:3–9	Mt 13:3–9	L 8:5–8

Later on, Jesus gave his disciples his explanation of the parable:

MARK	MATTHEW	LUKE
	Hear ye therefore the parable of	Now the parable is this:
The sower soweth the word.	the sower.	The seed is the word of God.
And these are they		Those
	[This is he which receiveth seed	
by the wayside, where the word is sown; but when they have heard,	by the wayside.]*	by the wayside
	When any one heareth the word of the Kingdom, and understandeth it not,	are they that hear;
Satan cometh immediately and taketh away the word that was sown in their hearts.	then cometh the wicked one, and catcheth away that which was sown in his heart.	then cometh the Devil, and taketh away the word out of their hearts, lest they should believe and be saved.
And these are they likewise which are sown on stony ground, who, when they have heard the word, immediately receive it with gladness, and have no root in themselves,	But he that receiveth the seed into stony places, the same is he that heareth the word, and anon with joy receiveth it. Yet hath he not root in himself,	They on the rock are they, which, when they hear, receive the word with joy; and these have no root, which

538

MARK (cont.)	MATTHEW (cont.)	LUKE (cont.)
and so endure	but dureth	
but for a time.	for a while:	for a while believe,
Afterward,	for	and
when affliction	when tribulation	in time of temptation
or persecution ariseth	or persecution ariseth	
for the word's sake,	because of the word,	
immediately	by and by	
they are offended.	he is offended.	fall away.
And these are they	He also that	And that
which are sown	received seed	which fell
among thorns:	among the thorns	among thorns
such as	is he that	are they which,
hear the word,	heareth the word,	when they have heard,
		go forth,
and the	and the	and are choked
cares of this world,	cares of this world,	with cares
and the deceitfulness	and the deceitfulness	
of riches,	of riches,	and riches
and the lusts		and pleasures
of other things		of this life,
entering in,		
choke the word,	choke the word,	
and it becometh	and he becometh	and bring
unfruitful.	unfruitful.	no fruit to perfection.
And these are they	But he	But that
which are sown	that received seed	
on good ground:	into good ground	on the good ground
such as hear	is he that heareth	are they,
the word,	the word,	
and receive it,	and understandeth it,	which in
		an honest
		and good heart,
	which also	having heard
		the word,
		keep it,
and bring forth fruit,	beareth fruit,	and bring forth fruit
	and bringeth forth,	with patience.
		L 8:11–15

MARK (cont.)	MATTHEW (cont.)	LUKE (cont.)
some thirtyfold,	some an hundredfold,	
some sixty,	some sixty,	
and some an hundred.	some thirty.	
Mk 4:14–20	Mt 13:18–23	
	* Conformed to	
	Mark's order	

Jesus' explanation of this parable may be summarized as follows:

1. The seed is the word of the Kingdom. Mt 13:19 (". . . word of God." L 8:11)
2. There are four categories of people who hear the word:

   A. The waysiders. Satan is symbolized as "fowls of the air" that pick up the seed, i.e., pluck the word out of their hearts.
   B. The stony grounders. The seed falls in stony ground where the soil is shallow, is quickly warmed and immediately sprouts like the instant joy of the new believers; but their shallowness does not allow the word to root down in them so that they can endure the scorching sun of persecution.
   C. The thorn patchers. The word is sown among thorns in the forms of the deceitfulness of riches, the cares of this world and the pleasures of this life, and they choke out the sprouts from the seed.
   D. The good grounders. The seed is sown in good ground, those who hear and understand the word; and the harvest is bountiful, up to a hundredfold.

This parable of the sower teaches us that the word of the Kingdom is sown but the harvest varies. Some, the good grounders, produce a bountiful Kingdom harvest. Mk 4:8, 20 ; Mt 13:8, 23 ; L 8:8,

15 Others, the thorn patchers and the stony grounders, do not produce a crop since they do not nurture the word of the Kingdom. *Mk 4:5–7, 16–19; Mt 13:5–7, 20–22; L 8:6–7, 13–14*

The waysiders do not produce a crop because Satan snatches the word that was sown in their hearts. *Mk 4:15; Mt 13:19; L 8:12* In short, Satan is allowed to act even though the word of the Kingdom has been sown. This is analogous to the parable of the tares in which Satan is permitted to sow tares (a grainfield weed that looks like wheat) among the wheat at night and nothing can be done about it until the harvest since the removal of the tares will also destroy the wheat. *Mt 13:25–30, 37–43*

It seems unjust that Satan is permitted by the Kingdom rules to uproot "the word of the Kingdom" from the hearts of those who have received, but do not understand it. *Mt 13:19* It also seems unjust that some persons are good ground while others are stony ground or beset with "the cares of this world." *Mk 4:19*

In a way, the problem of unequal backgrounds is like the problem put by the parables of the talents and the pounds. Jesus told these two parables to illustrate a rule of the Kingdom, which, humanly speaking, seems outrageously unjust: From him that has not, shall be taken even what he has.

Jesus' own words stating this conclusion of those two parables are as follows:

MATTHEW	LUKE
For unto every one	That unto every one
that hath	which hath
shall be given,	shall be given;
and he shall have abundance;	
but from him	and from him
that hath not	that hath not,
	even that he hath
shall be taken away	shall be taken away
	from him.
even that which he hath.	*L 19:26*
Mt 25:29	

The parable of the talents is built around a large silver monetary unit used in New Testament times weighing over fifty pounds and equal to about 3,600 shekels. The parable states:

> For the Kingdom of Heaven is as a man traveling into a far country, who called his own servants, and delivered unto them his goods. And unto one he gave five talents, to another two, and to another one; to every man according to his several ability, and straightway took his journey.
>
> Then he that had received the five talents went and traded with the same, and made them other five talents.
>
> And likewise he that had received two, he also gained other two.
>
> But he that had received one went and digged in the earth, and hid his lord's money.
>
> After a long time the lord of those servants cometh, and reckoneth with them [settled accounts].
>
> And so he that had received five talents came and brought other five talents, saying, "Lord, thou deliveredst unto me five talents: behold, I have gained beside them five talents more."
>
> His lord said unto him, "Well done, thou good and faithful servant; thou hast been faithful over a few things, I will make thee ruler over many things; enter thou into the joy of thy lord."
>
> He also that had received two talents came and said, "Lord, thou deliveredst unto me two talents; behold, I have gained two other talents beside them."
>
> His lord said unto him, "Well done, good and faithful servant; thou hast been faithful over a few things, I will make thee ruler over many things; enter thou into the joy of thy lord."
>
> Then he which had received the one talent came and said, "Lord, I knew thee that thou art a hard man, reaping where thou hast not

sown, and gathering where thou hast now strawed [winnowed]; and I was afraid, and went and hid thy talent in the earth: lo, there thou hast that is thine."

His lord answered and said unto him, "Thou wicked and slothful servant, thou knewest that I reap where I sowed not, and gather where I have not strawed [winnowed]. Thou oughtest therefore to have put my money to the exchangers, and then at my coming I should have received mine own with usury. Take therefore the talent from him, and give it unto him which hath ten talents."

For unto every one that hath shall be given, and he shall have abundance; but from him that hath not shall be taken away even that which he hath. And cast ye the unprofitable servant into outer darkness: there shall be weeping and gnashing of teeth. *Mt 25:14-30*

Luke has a similar parable in which he states that Jesus spoke because his hearers "thought that the Kingdom of God should immediately appear." *L 19:11* This parable is stated in terms of "pounds" (literally "minas") instead of talents. A "mina" was a lesser monetary unit, being equal to 1/60th of a talent or 60 shekels.

The parable of the pounds is as follows:

A certain nobleman went into a far country to receive for himself a kingdom, and to return. And he called his ten servants, and delivered them ten pounds, and said unto them, "Occupy [trade with the money] till I come."

But his citizens hated him, and sent a message after him, saying, "We will not have this man to reign over us."

And it came to pass, that when he was returned, having received the kingdom, then he commanded these servants to be called unto him, to whom he had given the money, that he might know how much every man had gained by trading.

Then came the first, saying, "Lord, thy pound hath gained ten pounds."

And he said unto him, "Well, thou good servant, because thou hast been faithful in a very little, have thou authority over ten cities."

And the second came, saying, "Lord, thy pound hath gained five pounds."

And he said likewise to him, "Be thou also over five cities."

And another came, saying, "Lord, behold, here is thy pound, which I have kept laid up in a napkin: for I feared thee, because thou art an austere [hard] man; thou takest that thou layedst not down, and reapest that thou didst not sow."

And he saith unto him, "Out of thine own mouth will I judge thee, thou wicked servant. Thou knewest that I was an austere man, taking up that I laid not down, and reaping that I did not sow. Wherefore, then gavest not thou my money into a bank, that at my coming I might have required mine own with usury?"

And he said unto them that stood by, "Take from him the pound, and give it to him that hath ten pounds."

And they said unto him, "Lord, he hath ten pounds."

For I say unto you, "That unto every one which hath shall be given; and from him that hath not, even that he hath shall be taken away from him. But those mine enemies, which would not that I should reign over them, bring hither, and slay them before me." *L 19:12–27*

The parable answers those who "thought that the Kingdom of God should immediately appear" in an indirect way: the servants are to have a period of time to work with the nobleman's money, while the nobleman (Christ) is being rejected by his subjects. The parable also focuses, like Matthew's parable, on the use of one's talents—God's "money."

In the case of the parable of the talents, the servants are given unequal amounts: five, two, and one talents. *Mt 25:15* This would support the inference that even in the Kingdom men are born unequal. This is apparently not a proper inference since in the parable of the pounds each of ten servants was entrusted with one pound. *L 19:13*

God will adjust for an absolute inequity of abilities, just as he does for the smallness of a poor widow's offering:

> For all they did cast in of their abundance; but she of her want did cast in all that she had, even all of her living. *Mk 12:44 (L 21:4)*

Both parables, the parable of the talents and the parable of the pounds, state a rule of the Kingdom that each should contribute according to his ability and will be rewarded for using what he has been entrusted with. No one objects to that. It only seems right and just.

But the two parables also clearly teach what, humanly speaking, seems outrageously unjust: the one-talent servant loses everything to the five-talent servant who had doubled his five to ten talents; and one of the servants entrusted with one pound loses it to another one-pound servant who had used his pound to gain ten more.

It must be noted, however, that the losses that the one-talent servant and the servant hiding his one pound in a napkin suffer are not simply harsh punishments for nonperformance but were the result of a wrong attitude on the part of each:

MATTHEW	LUKE
Then he which	And another
had received	
the one talent	
came and said	came, saying,
"Lord,	"Lord, behold, . . .
I knew thee that	For I feared thee, because
thou art a hard man,	thou art an austere man:
reaping where	thou takest up
thou hast not sown,	that thou layedst not down,
and gathering where	and reapest
thou hast	that thou didst

MATTHEW (cont.)	LUKE (cont.)
not strawed [winnowed];	now sow.
and I was afraid,	
and went	
and hid thy talent	["Here is thy pound,
	which I have kept laid up
in the earth:	in a napkin."]*
	And he
lo, there thou hast	saith unto him,
that is thine."	
His lord answered	"Out of thine own mouth
and said unto him,	will I judge thee,
"Thou wicked and slothful	thou wicked
servant	servant.
thou knewest that	Thou knewest that
	I was an austere man,
	taking up
I reap where I sowed not,	that I laid not down,
and gather	and reaping
where I have not strawed	that I did not sow.
[winnowed].	
Thou oughtest therefore	Wherefore then
to have put	gavest not thou
my money	my money
to the exchangers,	into the bank,
and then at my coming	that at my coming
I should have received	I might have required
mine own with usury.	mine own with usury?"
	And he said unto
	them that stood by,
Take therefore the talent	"Take from him
from him,	the pound,
and give it unto him	and give it to him
which hath ten talents."	that hath ten pounds."
Mt 25:24–28	L 19:20–24
	* Conformed to Matthew's order

Both the parable of the talents and the parable of the pounds make the point that from him that has not shall be taken away even that which he had. *Mt 25:29; L 19:26*

The rules of the Kingdom go further and require severe punishment of the non-user of his own talents:

MATTHEW	LUKE
And cast ye	But those mine enemies,
the unprofitable servant	which would not
into outer darkness:	that I should reign
there shall be weeping	over them,
and gnashing of teeth.	bring hither,
Mt 25:30	and slay them before me.
	L 19:27

The Kingdom rule about "he that hath," etc., is one of Jesus' recurrent teachings. It occurs again and again in different contexts. Matthew not only has the saying at the end of the parable of the talents but has it in Jesus' answer to his disciples' question, "Why speakest thou unto them in parables?" *Mt 13:10*

Jesus' answer was:

Because it is given unto you to know the mysteries of the Kingdom of Heaven, but to them it is not given. *For whosoever hath, to him shall be given, and he shall have more abundance; but whosoever hath not. From him shall be taken away even that he hath. Mt 13:11–12*

Mark and Luke record the same saying following Jesus' teaching about the lamp that should not be covered:

MARK	LUKE
For he that hath,	For whosoever hath,
to him shall be given;	to him shall be given;
and he that hath not,	and whosoever hath not,
from him shall be taken	from him shall be taken
even that which	even that which
he hath.	he seemeth to have.
Mk 4:25	*L 8:18*

It was not harsh or unjust to insist that a person having a talent or pound use it or lose it. In the biological world, a limb not used may atrophy. Should the laws of the spiritual world, the world of the Kingdom of God, be different? Are they harsh and unjust if they are similar to biological law?

The rules of the Kingdom, like "For many are called but few are chosen" *Mt 22:14* and "The last shall be first, and the first last," *Mt 19:30, 20:16; Mk 10:31; L 13:30* are not human justice but are the rules of the Kingdom as stated by Jesus. All we can say is that God's ways are not our ways. But we can not fairly sit in judgment on God's ways until we know all the problems and considerations.

In a way, these rules are no more unjust than the Father welcoming home the prodigal son. Everyone applauds that as the very epitome of a gracious and kindly God. Yet, humanly speaking, it is unfair to receive with joy a son who has wasted his inheritance in a far country while his steady serving brother gets no celebration, not even a young goat so he could "make merry" with his friends. *L 15:11–31* The answer is, of course:

Son, thou art ever with me, and all that I have is thine. *L 15:31*

ANOTHER KINGDOM RULE: FORGIVE FROM THE HEART

Not only does the Kingdom have a rule: "use it; or lose it"; it has other rules. Matthew has a parable that shows another rule of the Kingdom:

Therefore is the Kingdom of Heaven likened unto a certain king, which would take account of his servants. And when he had begun to reckon, one was brought unto him, which owed him ten thousand talents (60,000,000 denarii—a denarius was the daily wage of a harvest laborer). But forasmuch as he had not to pay, his lord commanded him to be sold, and his wife, and children, and all that he had, and payment to be made.

The servant therefore fell down, and worshipped him, saying, "Lord, have patience with me, and I will pay thee all."

Then the lord of that servant was moved with compassion, and loosed him, and forgave him the debt.

But the same servant went out, and found one of his fellow servants, which owed him a hundred pence [100 denarii]; and he laid hands on him, and took him by the throat, saying, "Pay me what thou owest."

And his fellow servant fell down at his feet, and besought him, saying, "Have patience with me, and I will pay thee all."

And he would not, but went and cast him into prison, till he should pay the debt.

So when his fellow servants saw what was done, they were very sorry, and came and told unto their lord all that was done. Then his lord, after that he had called him, said unto him, "O thou wicked servant, I forgave thee all that debt, because thou desiredst me. Shouldest not thou also have had compassion on thy fellow servant, even as I had pity on thee?"

And his lord was wroth, and delivered him to the tormentors [tor-turers], and till he should pay all that was due unto him.

So likewise shall my heavenly Father do also unto you, if ye *from your hearts* forgive not every one of his brother their trespasses. *Mt 18:23–35*

The Kingdom is so set up that the Father is unable to forgive you unless you forgive others "from your heart." Or, more broadly, under the rules of the Kingdom, as you deal so must it be dealt to you. The teaching is the same as the line in the Lord's Prayer:

Matthew	Luke
And forgive us our debts,	And forgive us our sins;
as we forgive	for we also forgive
our debtors.	everyone that is indebted to us.
Mt 6:12	*L 11:4*

In the parable, the disparity between the debt of 60,000,000 denarii owed to the king and the debt of 100 denarii owed to the fellow servant is great. It is great because Jesus meant to teach forgiveness on our part of our fellows by suggesting how much God, the King of Heaven, has forgiven us. And forgiveness must be "from your hearts." *Mt 18:35*

Precedence in the Kingdom

Only Luke has this parable of the Kingdom:

> When thou art bidden of any man to a wedding, sit not down in the highest room, lest a more honorable man than thou be bidden of him. And he that bade thee and him come and say to thee, "Give this man place;" and thou begin with same to take the lowest room.
>
> But when thou art bidden, go and sit down in the lowest room; that when he that bade thee cometh, he may say unto thee, "Friend, go up higher." Then shalt thou have worship in the presence of them that sit at meat with thee.
>
> For whosoever exalteth himself shall be abased; and he that humbleth himself shall be exalted. *L 14:8–11*

The physical setting of this parable was this: Jesus was dining in the house of one of the chief Pharisees on a Sabbath. *L 14:1* Some lawyers and Pharisees were also guests and "they watched him" as he healed a man who had dropsy. *L 14:1–3* Jesus had noticed when the other guests had scrabbled for the preferred places at the dinner:

> And he put forth a parable to those which were bidden [the other guests], when he marked how they chose out the chief rooms, saying unto them: . . . *L 14:7*

The intellectual setting of this parable was his and their common knowledge of the book of Proverbs, which stated:

> Put not forth thyself in the presence of the king, and stand not in the place of great men: for better it is that it be said unto thee, "Come up hither," than that thou shouldest be put lower in the presence of the prince whom thine eyes have seen. *Proverbs 25:6–7*

After having brought to mind this Jewish scripture on the un-seemliness of striving for place and precedence, Jesus then stated the point of his parable:

> For whosoever exalteth himself shall be abased; and he that humbleth himself shall be exalted. *L 14:11*

This point was a recurrent teaching of Jesus:

MATTHEW	MATTHEW	LUKE	LUKE
Whosoever therefore shall humble himself as this little child, the same is greatest in the Kingdom of Heaven. *Mt 18:4*	And whosoever shall exalt himself shall be abased; and he that shall humble himself shall be exalted. *Mt 23:12*	For whosoever exalteth himself shall be abased; and he that humbleth himself shall be exalted. *L 14:11*	For every one that exalteth himself shall be abased; and he that humbleth himself shall be exalted. *L 18:14*

Only Matthew 18:4 expressly refers to the Kingdom, but the background of Luke 14:11 makes it clear that Jesus was telling this parable in the context of the Kingdom. This is shown by a comment made shortly thereafter by one guest to Jesus as follows:

> Blessed is he that shall eat bread in the Kingdom of God. *L 14:15*

The story Jesus told these guests was a parable of the King-dom, not an instruction in prudent etiquette. Striving for prece-dence has no place in the Kingdom: those who do so will be abased; but those that humble themselves will be exalted in the Kingdom.

Who is Greatest in the Kingdom?

Towards the end of his Galilean ministry as Jesus and his disciples returned to Capernaum, his disciples had had a dispute among themselves as to who among them "should be the greatest." *Mk 9:33–34 (L 9:46–47)*

Once they got to Capernaum, Jesus asked them about the dispute. *Mk 9:33* He then told the Twelve:

MARK	LUKE
If any man desire	For he that is
to be first,	least among you all,
the same	the same
shall be	shall be
last of all,	
and servant of all.	great.
Mk 9:35	*L 9:48*

According to Matthew, the disciples at this time put a question to Jesus:

Who is the greatest in the Kingdom of Heaven? *Mt 18:1*

Jesus answered them with an object lesson. He took a little child, stood him in their midst and put his arms around him. *Mk 9:36 (Mt 18:2; L 9:47)* Jesus then said, among other things:

Whosoever therefore shall humble himself as this little child, the same is greatest in the Kingdom of Heaven. *Mt 18:4*

Question/Answer: The greatest person in the Kingdom of Heaven is the person who is as humble as a little child.

The Priorioty of the Kingdom

Jesus taught that "the nations of the earth" seek after food, drink and clothing and that God the Father knows that people need all of these things. *L 12:30; Mt 6:32 (". . . the Gentiles")*
Jesus continued:

MATTHEW	LUKE
But seek ye *first* the Kingdom of God, and his righteousness; and all these things shall be added unto you." *Mt 6:33*	But rather seek ye the Kingdom of God, and all these things shall be added unto you. *L 12:31*

Matthew's account expressly states the priority of seeking the Kingdom; Luke's account implies the priority of seeking the Kingdom. Both accounts agree that the needful things required by the body will be provided, provided as a by-product of seeking the Kingdom.

The question is, what has priority? Jesus' answer is that the Kingdom of God must have priority. It is the one pearl of great price:

Again, the Kingdom of Heaven is like unto a merchant man seeking goodly pearls, who, when he had found one pearl of great price, went and sold all that he had, and bought it. *Mt 13:45–46*

Eunuchs for the Kingdom

After Jesus had answered the test question by the Pharisees about divorce by saying, in part, "Whosoever shall put away his wife, except it be for fornication, and shall marry another, committeth adultery," his disciples concluded, "If the case of the man be so with his wife, it is not good to marry." *Mt 19:9–10*

Jesus rejected this conclusion since he immediately said:

All men cannot receive this saying, save they to whom it is given. For there are some eunuchs, which were so born from their mother's womb, and there are some eunuchs, which were made eunuchs of men; and there be eunuchs, which have made themselves eunuchs for the Kingdom of Heaven's sake. He that is able to receive it, let him receive it. *Mt 19:11–12*

The interpretation of this saying has caused a mountain of heartache: who should be eunuchs for the Kingdom? Most men can not accept this status—only those who have received this special gift are able to do so, like Jesus, himself.

CHAPTER 8

JESUS' TEACHINGS ON RICHES

JESUS AND RICHES

Both Matthew and Luke have this saying of Jesus:

No man can serve two masters: for either he will hate the one, and love the other; or else he will hold to the one, and despise the other. Ye can not serve God and mammon. *Mt 6:24*

Luke's version is identical except that he substitutes "No servant" for "No man." *L 16:13* This saying has burned itself into the consciousness of Christendom. Nothing else needs to be said about it, except to point out that *mammon* means money or property.

If a man can not serve both God and money, can a rich man be saved? According to Jesus it is possible, but unlikely.

A rich young ruler asked Jesus:

Good Master, what shall I do that I may inherit eternal life? *Mk 10:17 (Mt 20:1; L 18:18)*

After Jesus told him to keep the commandments of the Jewish law and he said that he had, Jesus continued:

MARK	MATTHEW	LUKE
	"If thou wilt be perfect,	
"One thing thou lackest:		"Yet lackest thou one thing:

MARK (cont.)	MATTHEW (cont.)	LUKE (cont.)
go thy way,	go and	
sell whatsoever	sell that	sell all that
thou hast, and	thou hast, and	thou hast, and
give to	give to	distribute unto
the poor;	the poor;	the poor;
and thou shalt	and thou shalt	and thou shalt
have treasure	have treasure	have treasure
in heaven;	in heaven;	in heaven,
and come,	and come	and come,
take up the cross,		
and follow me."	and follow me."	follow me."
And he was sad at	But when the	And when he
	young man heard	heard this,
that saying,	that saying,	
and went away	he went away	he was
grieved:	sorrowful:	very sorrowful:
for he had	for he had	for he was
great possessions.	great possessions.	very rich.
Mk 10:21–22	*Mt 19:21–22*	*L 18:22–24*

The rich young man was plainly told to dispose of his wealth as a condition of discipleship. When he refused, Jesus generalized on how *hard* it is for any rich man to enter the Kingdom of God:

MARK	MATTHEW	LUKE
	Verily I say	
	unto you,	
	that a rich man	
How *hardly*	shall *hardly*	How *hardly*
shall they		shall they
that have riches		that have riches
enter into	enter into	enter into
the Kingdom of God!	the Kingdom	the Kingdom
	of Heaven.	of God!
	And again	

MARK (cont.)	**MATTHEW** (cont.)	**LUKE** (cont.)
	I say unto you,	
. . . It is *easier*	it is *easier*	For it is *easier*
for a camel	for a camel	for a camel
to go through	to go through	to go through
they eye of a needle,	the eye of a needle,	a needle's eye,
than	than	than
for a rich man	for a rich man	for a rich man
to enter into	to enter into	to enter into
the Kingdom of God.	the Kingdom of God.	the Kingdom of God.
Mk 10:23, 25	*Mt 19:23–24*	*L 18:24–25*

These passages have been analyzed in detail in *Entrance Into The Kingdom*, pp. 516–520. Jesus' conclusion was that while it is exceedingly hard for a rich man to enter into the Kingdom of God, it is possible, because "with God all things are possible." *Mk 10:27; Mt 18:26 (L 18:27)*

The basic problem is one of conflicting loyalties: treasure on earth or treasure in heaven. Jesus pointed out that a man's heart will be with whichever treasure he selects:

MATTHEW	**LUKE**
Lay not up for yourselves	Sell that you have,
treasures upon earth,	and give alms;
where moth and rust	provide yourself bags
doth corrupt,	which wax not old,
and where thieves	
break through and steal.	
But lay up	
for yourselves	
treasures in heaven,	a treasure in the heavens,
where neither	
moth nor rust	
doth corrupt,	that faileth not,
and where thieves	where no thief
do not break through	approacheth,
nor steal.	
	neither moth corrupteth.

MATTHEW (cont.)	LUKE (cont.)
For where your treasure is, there will your heart be also. *Mt 6:19–21*	For where your treasure is, there will your heart be also. *L 12:33–34*

Basically, Jesus taught that men should be rich towards God, not in earthly assets. The rich young ruler had great wealth, apparently inherited. Jesus also told the story of a rich farmer who was actively engaged in the production of wealth, a successful farmer:

> The ground of a certain rich man brought forth plentifully, and he thought within himself, saying, "What shall I do, because I have no room where to bestow my fruits?"

> And he said, "This will I do: I will pull down my barns, and build greater; and there will I bestow all my fruits and my goods.

> "And I will say to my soul, 'Soul, thou hast much goods laid up for many years; take thine ease, eat, drink, and be merry.'"

> But God said unto him, "Thou fool, this night thy soul shall be required of thee; then whose shall those things be, which thou hast provided?"

> So is he that layeth up treasure for himself, and is not rich toward God. *L 12:16–21*

The point: be rich toward God. Deposit your treasure in heaven. Don't trust in earthly assets; otherwise you will end up despising God.

That is why it is so hard for a rich man to enter into the Kingdom of God. It is possible for a rich man to be saved, but not likely. We are not to magnify the needle-eye exception for a rich man or two.

THE LAZARUS LESSON

Jesus told a story about a rich man, often known as "Dives," the Vulgate's Latin adjective for *rich*, and a beggar named Lazarus:

There was a certain rich man, which was clothed in purple and fine linen, and fared sumptuously every day. And there was a certain beggar named Lazarus, which was laid at this gate, full of sores, and desiring to be fed with the crumbs which fell from the rich man's table; moreover the dogs came and licked his sores.

And it came to pass, that the beggar died, and was carried by the angels into Abraham's "bosom" [presence]; the rich man also died, and was buried.

And in hell he lifted up his eyes, being in torments, and seeth Abraham afar off, and Lazarus in his "bosom" [presence]. *L 16:19–23*

The following dialogue ensued:

RICH MAN: Father Abraham, have mercy on me, and send Lazarus, that he may dip the tip of his finger in water, and cool my tongue: for I am tormented in this flame.

ABRAHAM: Son, remember that thou in thy lifetime receivedst thy good things, and likewise Lazarus evil things; but now he is comforted, and thou art tormented. And besides all this, between us and you there is a great gulf fixed so that they which would pass from hence to you can not; neither can they pass to us, that would come from thence.

RICH MAN: I pray thee therefore, Father, that thou wouldest send me to my father's house, for I have five brethren, that he may testify unto them, lest they also come into this place of torment.

ABRAHAM: They have Moses and the Prophets; let them hear them.

561

Rich man: Nay, Father Abraham. But if one went to them from the dead, they will repent.

Abraham: If they hear not Moses and the Prophets, neither will they be persuaded, though one rose from the dead. *L 16:24–31*

That, in fact, has been the history of the Jews since the resurrection of Jesus. They will not be persuaded since they have not "Moses and the Prophets," only Moses.

Jesus had already taught that the Jews would reject him and be thrust out of the Kingdom of God:

> There shall be weeping and gnashing of teeth, when ye shall see Abraham, and Isaac, and Jacob, and all the prophets, in the Kingdom of God, and you yourselves thrust out. *L 13:28*

> And I say unto you, that many shall come from the east and west, and shall sit down with Abraham, and Isaac, and Jacob, in the Kingdom of Heaven. But the [natural-born] children of the Kingdom shall be cast out into outer darkness: there shall be weeping and gnashing of teeth. *Mt 8:11–12*

The rich man had laid up treasure for himself and was "not rich toward God." *L 12:21* Jesus had flatly stated:

> Verily I say unto you, that a rich man shall hardly enter into the Kingdom of Heaven. And again I say unto you, it is easier for a camel to go through the eye of a needle than for a rich man to enter into the Kingdom of God. *Mt 19:23–24 cf. Mk 10:23–25; L 18:24–25.*

This rich man was not one of those who could slip through the eye of a needle, and so ended in hell. In hell, he could see Lazarus afar off in the presence of Abraham, the father of all Jews.

Lazarus had lived miserably, but was now rewarded as Jesus taught:

> Blessed be ye poor: for yours is the Kingdom of God.

Blessed are ye that hunger now: for ye shall be filled. *L 6:20–21*

The point of the story is not the great gulf fixed or the scenery of Shoel; but at one level the inevitable contradiction between earthly wealth and the eternal realm of the God and at another level the fact that Israel, with all her riches of the Law and the Prophets, would reject Jesus whom its prophets foretold.

Rich and Poor:
The Covetous Ones

While the rich have more to covet than the poor, both can covet. Jesus said:

> That which cometh out of the man, that defileth the man. For from within, out of the heart of men, proceed . . . covetousness . . . All these evil things come from within, and defile the man. *Mk 7:20–23*

The normal context of covetousness is riches, or at least, things. One of his disciples asked Jesus to speak to his brother to give the disciple his share of the family inheritance. This seems just, but Jesus used this request to teach his disciples:

> Take heed, and beware of covetousness: for a man's life consisteth not in the abundance of the things which he possesseth. *L 12:15*

Jesus was against the thralldom of things. Covetousness is an evil from within and consists in being obsessed with the abundance of things possessed.

CHAPTER 9

CHURCH TOPICS

JESUS' WORDS

Although we cherish the mission of Jesus and dwell on the theological effects of his life, death and resurrection, we can not ignore what he said while he was on earth. While Jesus had a "person," as theologians say, Jesus himself attached equal importance to his words, saying:

MARK	LUKE
Whosoever therefore	For whosoever
shall be ashamed	shall be ashamed
of me	of me
and of my words	*and of my words,*
in this adulterous	
and sinful generation,	
of him also	of him
shall the Son of man	shall the Son of man
be ashamed,	be ashamed,
when he cometh	when he shall come
	in his own glory,
in the glory of his Father	and in his Father's,
with the holy angels.	and of the holy angels.
Mk 8:38	*L 9:26*

The phrase "in this adulterous and sinful generation" does not limit Jesus' words to his own time. He taught, and we should agree, that his words have eternal significance since he said:

> Heaven and earth shall pass away, but *my words* shall not pass away.
> *Mk 13:31; Mt 24:35; L 21:33*

In light of Jesus' own statement, what are we to make of theologians and preachers who ignore Jesus' words? His words are not, and cannot be, nullified by the doctrines of men, whether they are theological time classifications like dispensations or scholarly dogmas that restrict his words to his own time and place.

Jesus' position was that his words are eternally valid and will continue in force until "the last day":

> And if any man *hear my words*, and believe not, I judge him not: for I came not to judge the world, but to save the world. He that rejecteth me, and *receiveth not my words*, hath one that judgeth him; *the word that I have spoken*, the same shall judge him *in the last day*. *J 12:47–48*

Jesus' words are not restricted to his coming cross, although he did say:

> Let *these sayings* sink down into your ears: for the Son of Man shall be delivered into the hands of men. *L 9:44*

Luke continues:

> But they understood not this saying, and it was hid from them, that they perceived it not; and they feared to ask him of that saying. *L 9:45*

With a few exceptions, Jesus' sayings are now found only in the four Gospels. These sayings are not restricted to his words about or from the cross, or to the woman taken in adultery. Jesus' words are the best way, indeed the only objective way, to bridge the twenty centuries since he lived and to know him as he actually was, and is.

For many Christians, the Gospels are mainly the Christmas and Easter stories and sayings of Jesus which fill the Gospels are, in effect, superseded by the Epistles of Paul. This was not Paul's own view since he himself considered "the words of our Lord Jesus Christ" the ultimate test, calling them "wholesome words." *1 Timothy 6:3* Accordingly, at Miletus he charged the elders of the church at Ephesus "to remember *the words* of the Lord Jesus, how he said, 'It is more blessed to give than to receive.'" *Acts 20:35*

Paul, himself, clearly distinguished between his own words and the superior words of his Lord and deferred to those words. *1 Corinthians 7:10–12, 25* See Chapter 1, "The Record," pp. 24–25 for a detailed analysis.

For many Christians, the New Testament is the constitution of Jesus' church; but it is an indisputable fact of history that Jesus' church existed and throve for many years before there was a New Testament, before there were any Paulene Epistles. But Jesus' church did have Jesus' own words, both from the memory of persons still living and the numerous writings that preceded our present Gospels. Luke states:

Forasmuch as *many* have taken in hand to set forth in order a declaration of those things which are most surely believed among us . . . *L 1:1*

Acts quotes Peter as saying:

Then, remembered I *the word of the Lord*, how that he said, "John indeed baptized with water, but ye shall be baptized with the Holy Spirit." *Acts 11:16*

Jesus is reported to have told a disciple that the Holy Spirit will "bring all things to your remembrance, *whatsoever I have said unto you*." *J 14:26* For our own times this has been done by the Gospels since they were written by men of the early church "as they were moved by the Holy Spirit." *2 Peter 1:21*

The reason Jesus considered his words so important is that they were his Father's words, not his own words:

> I speak to the world those things which I *have heard* of him. *J 8:26*

> He that loveth me not keepeth not my sayings; and *the word* which ye hear is not mine but the Father's which sent me. *J 14:24*

> For I have given unto them *the words* which thou gavest me; and they have received them, and have known surely that I came out from thee, and they have believed that thou didst send me. *J 17:8*

Jesus was even more explicit:

> My doctrine is not mine, but *his* that sent me. *J 7:16*

> For I have not spoken of myself; but the Father which sent me, he gave me a commandment, *what I should say, and what I should speak*. And I know that his commandment is life everlasting; whatsoever I speak therefore, even as the Father said unto me, so I speak. *J 12:49–50*

In plain English, Jesus claimed to speak for God the Father. He went further: he claimed that the specific words he spoke were God's words. Those that love Jesus will keep the words he received from God:

> If a man love me, he will keep *my words* . . . *J 14:23*

Jesus' sayings were controversial in his lifetime and still are. After he told some Jews that "I have power to lay it [my life] down, and I have power to take it again" and "This commandment have I received of my Father," *J 10:18*, John records that:

> There was a division therefore again among the Jews *for these sayings*. And many of them said, "He hath a devil and is mad; why hear ye him?" *J 10:19–20*

Any fair reading of the Gospels shows that Jesus placed great emphasis on his own words and considered them binding on his followers then and now since he said:

Verily, verily, I say unto you, he that heareth *my word*, and believeth on him that sent me, hath everlasting life and shall not come into condemnation, but is passed from death unto life. *J 5:24*

It is the spirit that quickeneth; and flesh profiteth nothing. *The words that I speak unto you*, they are spirit, and they are life. *J 6:63*

Now ye are clean through *the word which I have spoken* unto you. *J 15:3*

If ye abide in me, *and my words* abide in you, ye shall ask what ye will, and it shall be done unto you. *J 15:7*

Jesus' words to his Jewish disciples then apply to all his disciples now:

If ye continue *in my word*, then are ye my disciples indeed; and ye shall know the truth, and the truth shall make you free. *J 8:31–32*

Some Jews told Jesus, "We be of Abraham's seed" and, "We have one Father, even God." *J 8:33, 41* Jesus' response was:

My word hath no place in you. *J 8:37*

"Why do ye not understand *my speech*? Even because ye can not hear *my word*." *J 8:43*

Jesus concluded his statement to them by saying:

Verily, verily I say unto you, if a man keep *my saying*, he shall never see death. *J 8:51*

This saying was unacceptable to those Jews and is unacceptable to many persons today. They reject Jesus' sayings like:

Verily, verily, *I say* unto you, he that believeth on me hath everlasting life. *J 6:47*

Jesus' question to everyone is:

And if *I say* the truth, why do ye not believe me? *J 8:46*

Jesus' question to Christians is:

And why call ye me, Lord, Lord, and do not the things which *I say*? *L 6:46*

JESUS' CHILDREN

Jesus sometimes fondly called his disciples "little children":

Little children, yet a little while I am with you. *J 13:33*

After Jesus pronounced "woes" upon the Galilean cities of Chorazin, Bethsaida and Capernaum because they had ignored his mighty works and had not repented, he said:

MATTHEW	LUKE
I thank thee, O Father,	I thank thee, O Father,
Lord of heaven and earth,	Lord of heaven and earth,
because thou hast hid	that thou hast hid
these things	these things
from the wise and prudent,	from the wise and prudent,
and hath revealed them	and hast revealed them
unto babes.	*unto babes.*
Even so, Father:	Even so, Father:
for so it seemed good	for so it seemed good
in thy sight.	in thy sight.
Mt 11:25–26	*L 10:21*

"Babes" is here used in contrast to "the wise and prudent" not in contrast to adults. The "babes" are those who accepted the revelation of Jesus' mighty works in simple faith, not the religiously learned.

Jesus was not speaking of children, but of his disciples, when he said:

MARK	MATTHEW	LUKE
And whosoever	But whoso	[than that he
shall offend	shall offend	should offend
one of	one of	one of
these little ones	*these little ones*	*these little ones]**
that believe in me,	*which believe in me,*	

MARK (cont.)	MATTHEW (cont.)	LUKE (cont.)
it is better	it were better	It were better
for him that	for him that	for him that
a millstone	a millstone	a millstone
were hanged	were hanged	were hanged
about his neck,	about his neck	about his neck
and he	and that he	and he
were cast	were drowned	cast
into	in the depth	into
the sea.	of the sea.	the sea . . ."
Mk 9:42	*Mt 18:6*	*L 17:2*
		* Conformed to
		Mark's order

Luke has this saying in a different context from Matthew and Mark. The wording, however, is almost identical. The only significant omission in Luke is the phrase "that believe in me." Luke may have simply summarized out that phrase, since it simply explains what Jesus meant by his phrase "these little ones." It means Jesus' followers.

The key idea is unmistakable: A terrible fate awaits any one who "offends" against Jesus' followers. The King James Version uses the word *offend* in a sense which is now archaic and fails to convey the meaning of the Greek, which is simply not to cause these little ones (followers) to stumble.

According to Matthew, Jesus continued his discourse, saying:

> Take heed that ye despise not one of *these little ones*: for I say unto you that in heaven their angels do always behold the face of my Father which is in heaven. *Mt 18:10*

Jesus was not speaking of children, but of his disciples who have their angels in heaven in the very presence of Jesus' Father.

Jesus called his disciples "little children," "babes," "little ones" and even "children."

> And *the disciples* were astonished at his words. But Jesus answereth again and saith unto them, "*Children*, how hard it is for them that trust in riches to enter into the Kingdom of God!" *Mk 10:24*

Jesus thought of his disciples as his children, because they were willing to receive in trust, like children, those things which the Father had decided to reveal. The religious learned of his day were not willing, but he told his disciples:

Fear not, *little flock*: for it is your Father's good pleasure to give you the Kingdom. *L 12:32*

Jesus not only thought of his disciples as trustful like children, but also as "the children of light":

While ye have light, believe in the light, that ye may be *the children of light*. *J 12:36*

Paul picked up Jesus' phrase "children of light" and used it twice to describe Christians. *1 Thessalonians 5:5; Ephesians 5:8* Jesus also said that "the children of this world [age] are in their generation [with their own people] wiser than the children of light." *L 16:8*

Christians are the children of light, and that light is Jesus Christ.

THE TRUE CHURCH OF JESUS CHRIST

The true church of Jesus Christ are those persons whom the Father gives him and to whom Jesus manifests the Father's name. The true church of Jesus Christ was described by him as follows:

> I have manifested thy name unto the men which thou gavest me out of the world: thine they were, and thou gavest them me; and they have kept thy word. Now they have known that all things whatsoever thou hast given me are of thee. For I have given unto them the words which thou gavest me; and they have received them, and have known surely that I came out from thee, and they have believed that thou didst send me. *J 17:6–8*

Jesus' description does not contain the word *church*, and that word occurs only two places in the Gospels. In Matthew 16:18, Jesus is quoted as saying:

> Thou art Peter, and upon this rock I will build my church; and the gates of hell shall not prevail against it.

A detailed discussion of this statement is found in the sub-chapter "Peter" in Chapter 5, pp 357–358. Here it is sufficient to note that Jesus did not there describe "my church" but only referred to it.

The same is true of the other reference in the Gospels to "church." Again Jesus is quoted and his statement was:

> And if he [a wrongdoer] shall neglect to hear them, tell it unto the church; but if he neglect to hear the church, let him be unto thee as an heathen man and a publican. *Mt 18:17*

In John, Chapter 17, Jesus did describe his church in detail. Basically, Jesus described his church as those men which God the Father had given him. A reasonable extension of this statement is that Jesus' church is a group of persons which God gave Jesus, not only in first-century Palestine, but in the centuries since.

When Jesus said that "I have manifested thy name unto the men which thou gavest me out of the world," he used "men" in the broad sense of persons. *J 17:6* When he referred to "the men which thou gavest me out of the world" he did not mean to exclude from his church, future disciples, since he continued:

> Neither pray I for these alone [those then given], but for them also which shall believe on me through their word. *J 17:20*

Present-day Christians are the historical successors through many generations of those who believed on Jesus through the word of his first-century men.

While Jesus does not use the word *church* as such in John, Chapter 17, he there, always and repeatedly, refers to these God-given men as a group since the plural is always used: "the men," "they," "them," "those," "they may be one," "themselves," "their sakes," "their word." *J 17:6–26*

In John, Chapter 17, Jesus is repeatedly quoted as saying that this is a group that God gave him:

> "... the men which thou *gavest me* out of the world ..." *J 17:6*

> "... them which thou hast *given me* ..." *J 17:9*

> "... those whom thou hast *given me* ..." *J 17:11*

> "... those that thou *gavest me* ..." *J 17:12*

The true church of Jesus Christ is that group of persons that God gave Jesus in his lifetime and that God has given Jesus since. The true church of Jesus Christ is not a casual group of individuals who have each accepted Jesus as Lord, or at least claim to follow his teachings.

Jesus did teach:

> Ye are *my friends*, if ye do whatsoever I command you. Henceforth I call you not servants, for the servant knoweth not what his lord

575

doeth; but I have called you *friends*, for all things that I have heard of my Father I have made known unto you. *J 15:14–15*

"Friends" does suggest a casualness, but the condition of Jesus' friendship is to do what he commands. This emphasis on obedience is also found in a famous freedom passage of Jesus' teaching. Jesus told some Jews who "believed on him":

If ye continue in my word, then are ye *my disciples indeed*; and ye shall know the truth, and the truth shall make you free. *J 8:31–32*

Disciples "indeed," true disciples, must continue in Jesus' word. Jesus' word was that he left a group of his people, the church, in the world, and this group has special functions on earth and will behold Christ's glory in heaven.

In the meantime this group has Christ's present presence, even when only two or three individuals of that group are meeting together:

For where two or three are gathered together in my name, there am I in the midst of them. *Mt 18:20*

This is the group which is doing the will of Jesus' Father and is the true holy family and true brethren of Jesus. Jesus taught:

MARK	MATTHEW	LUKE
For whosoever	For whosoever	My mother and
shall do	shall do	my brethren
the will of God,	the will of my Father	are those
	which is in heaven,	which hear
the same is	the same is	the word of God,
my brother,	my brother,	and do it.
and my sister,	and sister,	*L 8:21*
and mother.	and mother.	
Mk 3:35	*Mt 12:50*	

The true church of Jesus Christ is not simply a collection of individual friends, or true brethren but is the group of persons that God has given Jesus out of the world. Jesus has given this group the glory that the Father has given him. *J 17:22* This group is sanctified by the Father's truth. *J 17:17, 19*

This group was left by Jesus in the world with the word from his Father that Jesus gave them. *J 17:8, 14–15* Like Jesus, this group is not of the world. *J 17:14, 16* Jesus has sent this group into the world. *J 17:18* Unlike the world, this group knows that the Father sent Jesus:

> O righteous Father, the world hath not known thee; but I have known thee, and *these* have known that thou hast sent me. *J 17:25*

Jesus' mission was to declare to his church the Father's name:

> I have manifested *thy* name unto the men which thou gavest me out of the world . . . *J 17:6*

> While I was with them in the world, I kept them in *thy name*: . . . *J 17:12*

> And I have declared unto them *thy name*, and will declare it: that the love wherewith thou has loved me may be in them, and I in them. *J 17:26*

Jesus also gave to his church the words he had from the Father:

> For I have given unto them *the words* which thou gavest me: and they have received them, . . ." *J 17:8*

> I have given them *thy word*; . . . *J 17:14*

Jesus' church knows surely that he was sent by the Father:

> [They] have known surely that I come out from thee, and they have believed that thou didst send me. *J 17:8*

> . . . these have known that thou hast sent me. *J 17:25*

Jesus also prayed that:

They also may be one in us: that the world may believe that thou
hast sent me. J 17:21

Jesus in turn sends his church into the world:

As thou hast sent me into the world, even so have I also sent them
into the world. J 17:18

Although his church has been sent into the world, it is not of
the world, and the world, accordingly, has hated it:

The world hath hated them, because they are not of the world, even
as I am not of the world. J 17:14

They are not of the world, even as I am not of the world. J 17:16

On another occasion Jesus told his disciples:

If ye were of the world, the world would love his own; but because
ye are not of the world, but I have chosen you out of the world,
therefore the world hateth you. J 15:19

Jesus did pray for his church and not for the world (J 17:9), but
he did not pray that his church should be taken out of the world:

I pray not that thou shouldest take them out of the world, but that
thou shouldest keep them from the evil [one]. J 17:15

His church also receives the glory which the Father gave Jesus:

And the glory which thou gavest me I have given them; . . . J 17:22

Finally, his church is to behold Jesus' ultimate glory in Heaven.

Father, I will that they also, whom thou hast given me, be with me
where I am, that they may behold my glory, which thou hast given
me: . . ." J 17:24

While his church waits to behold Jesus' glory in heaven, he has given his church this duty:

> Go ye therefore, and *teach* all nations, *baptizing* them in the name of the Father, and of the Son, and of the Holy Spirit, *teaching* them to observe all things whatsoever I have commanded you; and, lo, I am with you always, even unto the end of the world. *Mt 28:19–20*

This very familiarity of this Great Commission blinds us to a large part of it. Modern translations uniformly translate "teach all nations" as "make disciples" of them. This discipleship instruction merges into "baptizing them," all races and colors. What is read out of the Great Commission is that Jesus, also required his followers to *teach* all nations "to observe *all* things whatsoever I have commanded you." These things are not restricted to his death and resurrection. The Gospels are full of things that Jesus has commanded, but Christian sermons and books routinely do not teach, or even mention those other commandments. Instead they are full of churchy and churchly things, theological lore and sociological cliches.

If the Great Commission is mentioned at all, it is as a "missions" goal to baptize as many people as possible. The coequal charge to teach *all* commandments that *Jesus taught* is shirked; but these were his last words, and his church ignores them at its peril.

The church's solemn duty in this present age, Jesus said, is to be "witnesses unto me" not only "in Jerusalem, and in all Judea, and in Samaria" but "unto the uttermost part of the earth." *Acts 1:8* Jesus summarized to his disciples the Jewish Scriptures requiring that he, as the Christ, the Anointed One, suffer and rise "from the dead the third day" and that "repentance and remission of sins should be preached in his name among all nations, beginning at Jerusalem." *L 24:47*

And so it has been, and will be. His church's duty is stern, yet simple:

> *And ye are witnesses of these things. L 24:48*

579

THE ORGANIZATION OF THE TRUE CHURCH OF JESUS CHRIST

Jesus was not an organization man. He did not declare the apostolic succession, or the primacy of bishops, or the powers of councils and popes. He left no organization charts for his church since he has no subordinates, only friends. Jesus clearly rejected the authority principle in Christian organizations and, in particular, in his church.

During Jesus' ministry either the Zebedee brothers, James and John, or their mother, petitioned Jesus:

	MARK	MATTHEW
REQUEST:	Grant unto us that we may sit, one on thy right hand, and the other on thy left hand in thy glory. *Mk 10:37*	Grant these my two sons may sit, the one on thy right hand, and the other on the left, in thy kingdom. *Mt 20:21*
JESUS:	To sit on my right hand and on my left hand is not mine to give; but it shall be given to them for whom it is prepared. *Mk 10:40*	To sit on my right hand, and on my left, is not mine to give, but it shall be given to them for whom it is prepared of my Father. *Mt 20:23*

The other ten disciples were indignant at James' and John's presumption. To soothe the situation, Jesus said:

MARK	MATTHEW
Ye know that they which are accounted to rule over the Gentiles exercise lordship	Ye know that the princes of the Gentiles exercise domination

MARK (cont.)	MATTHEW (cont.)
over them;	over them;
and their great ones	and they that are great
exercise authority	exercise authority
upon them.	upon them.
But so shall it not be	*But it shall not be so*
among you:	*among you:*
but whosoever will be	but whosoever will be
greater among you,	great among you,
shall be your minister;	let him be your minister;
and whosoever of you	and whosoever
will be	will be
the chiefest,	chief among you,
shall be	let him be
servant of all.	your servant.
Mk 10:43–44	*Mt 10:25–27*

This squabble among the Twelve apparently continued until the Last Supper. Luke reports:

> And there was also a strife among them, which of them should be accounted the greatest. And he said unto them: "The kings of the Gentiles exercise lordship over them; and they that exercise authority upon them are called 'Benefactors.' *But ye shall not be so*, but he that is greatest among you, let him be as the younger; and he that is chief, as he that doth serve." *L 22:24–26*

Jesus was born in the reign of the first Roman emperor, Augustus, and lived in a country under Roman occupation. There is an imperial ring in "Benefactors," the title that Jesus mentions. To Jesus, the exercise of lordship (authority) was a Gentile sin. The Romans were famous for their law and their rule, but Jesus rejected those principles for his church. Jesus rejected the concept of authority as the organizational principle of his church.

All three quotes are emphatic on this point:

MARK	MATTHEW	LUKE
But so shall it	But it shall	But ye shall

Mark (cont.)	Matthew (cont.)	Luke (cont.)
not be	not be so	not be so: . . .
among you: . . .	among you: . . .	L 22:26
Mk 10:43	Mt 20:26	

The great in Jesus' church are to be servants. The word translated as "minister" was not then a church organization title. Modern translations of these passages use *servant* for "minister" and *slave* for "servant" Mk 10:43–44; Mt 20:26–27. Jesus summed up:

> And whosoever of you will be the chiefest, shall be servant of all.
> Mk 10:44

No doubt Peter was the chief disciple in Jesus' lifetime, but it is equally without doubt that even before the end of Jesus' earthly ministry, Jesus had abandoned the concept of master/servant as applied to his church:

> Henceforth I call you not servants, for the servant knoweth not
> what his lord doeth; but I have called you friends; . . . J 15:15

Jesus did not organize his church on the ordinary principles of management and control. If the members of his church are not to be his servants, it would seem to follow that no member of his church is to be a servant of another member of his church. Instead, he conceived of his church as a group of his friends and brethren with whom he would deal personally and directly and not through an organizational structure:

> For where two or three are gathered together in my name, there am
> I in the midst of them. Mt 18:20

Why then are the churches of Jesus Christ so concerned with organization and who has authority in the organization? And with titles?

Jesus expressly rejected the religious titles of Judaism and, by obvious inference, titles in his own church. He is quoted by Matthew as saying:

> But be not ye called "Rabbi": for one is your master, even Christ; *and all ye are brethren*. And call no man your father upon earth: for one is your Father, which is in heaven. Neither be ye called masters: for one is your master, even Christ. But he that is the greatest among you shall be your servant. *Mt 23:8–11*

Jesus gave as his reason for the rejection of titles the fact that "all ye are brethren." *Mt 23:8* It is very difficult to say that this principle does not also apply to Jesus' own church, reverend doctors, bishops, elders, pastors, fathers and eminences to the contrary notwithstanding.

The principles Jesus laid down for his church are quite clear and simple. No titles. No exercise of lordship or dominion over the brethren. No exception was made for Peter or his successors. The power to bind and loose was given to all disciples, not just to Peter. *Mt 16:19, 18:18*

Peter is dead, and Jesus did not confer any powers on his successors. Whatever special instructions he gave to Peter are subject to Jesus' clear and simple general instruction that his church is based not upon the concept of master/servant but upon the concept of friends/brethren.

Jesus conceived of his church as his friends and brethren and not as hierarchy of master/servant relationships. Jesus announced that he would deal directly with his followers, not through an organizational structure:

> For where two or three are gathered together in my name, there am I in the midst of them. *Mt 18:20*

The proper Christian practice as to hierarchy is simply this:

> But he that is greater among you shall be your servant. And whosoever shall exalt himself shall be abased; and he that shall humble himself shall be exalted. Mt 23:11–12

It would seem that titles like *Bishop* [Overseer] and *Reverend Doctor* would be as objectionable to Jesus as "master" and "Rabbi." Despite Jesus' clear statements, churchmen continue to love and cherish titles. Despite Jesus' express directions the relationships within churches are often, and indeed characteristically, authoritarian, whether in constitutional theory or in practical fact.

This is wrong because Jesus repudiated that authoritarian principle as being inconsistent with the controlling principle that "all ye are brethren"—brothers—and hence equals, being sons of one Father, the Father in Heaven. *Mt 23:8*

The Unity of the True Church of Jesus Christ

Since Jesus was not an organization man, he was not as concerned as some of his present-day followers are with just who was or was not in the organization. To him, his church was not a sort of lodge.

John, one of Jesus' key disciples, reported to Jesus:

	MARK	LUKE
JOHN:	Master, we saw one casting out devils in thy name, and he followeth not us; and we forbad him, because he followeth not us.	Master, we saw one casting out devils in thy name; and we forbad him because he followeth not with us.
JESUS:	Forbid him not: for there is no man which shall do a miracle in my name, that can lightly speak evil of me. For he that is not against us is on our part. *Mk 9:38–40*	Forbid him not: for he that is not against us is for us. *L 9:49–50*

Jesus thus recognized that outsiders who do miracles in his name have difficulty in speaking evil of him.

Jesus did, however, insist upon personal loyalty in no uncertain terms:

MATTHEW	LUKE
He that is not with me is against me; he that gathereth not with him scattereth abroad. *Mt 12:30*	He that is not with me is against me; and he that gathereth not with me scattereth. *L 11:23*

Loyalty to Jesus is not the same as organizational unity in Jesus' church. The unity of Jesus' church is mystical, not organizational. This is what Jesus himself taught. He prayed for his followers:

> That *they all may be one*; as thou, Father, art in me, and I in thee, that they also may be *one in us*: that the world may believe that thou hast sent me. And the glory which thou gavest me I have given them, that they *may be one, even as we are one*: I in them, and thou in me, that they may be made perfect *in one*; and that the world may know that thou hast sent me, and hast loved them, as thou hast loved me. *J 17:21–23*

The unity of the church is a unity like the unity of Jesus and the Father:

> That they may be one, even as we are one. *J 17:22 (17:11)*

This unity is really a three-fold unity, Jesus in the church, and the Father in Jesus:

> I in them, and thou in me, that they may be made perfect in one. *J 17:23*

The idea is not perfection but that the church be completely and perfectly one. On another occasion Jesus mentioned this three-fold unity:

> At that day ye shall know that I am in my Father, and ye in me, and I in you. *J 14:20*

This is a mystical and not an organizational unity and fits closely with Jesus' statement:

> For where two or three are gathered together in my name, there am I in the midst of them. *Mt 18:20*

Jesus did not speak of his church in organizational terms. He preferred the simpler, more organic concept of a shepherd and his sheep.

Here is what he actually said:

> I am the good shepherd, and know my sheep, and am known of mine. As my Father knoweth me, even so know I the Father, and I lay down my life for the sheep. And other sheep I have which are not of this fold, them also I must bring, and they shall hear my voice; and there shall be one fold, and one shepherd. *J 10:14–15*

Modern versions correct the ancient mistranslation of the final clause of this quotation by substituting *flock* for *fold* so that it reads:

> . . . and there shall be one flock [fold], and one shepherd. *J 10:15*

Jesus, humanly speaking, a Jew, was then speaking to Jews, but he recognized that there were other sheep he had which were not of the flock of Israel. The common interpretation is that these other sheep were the Gentiles who, accordingly, were to hear his voice and become, with believing Jesus, part of the one flock of which Jesus is shepherd.

When Jesus did lay down his life for his sheep, he did not leave his flock without a shepherd. He sent the Holy Spirit to take care of his flock.

> Nevertheless I tell you the truth; it is expedient for you that I go away: for if I go not away, the Comforter will not come unto you; but if I depart, I will send him unto you. *J 16:7*

The unity of Jesus' church does not consist of any clear and cohesive organization but rather in the mysterious movings of the Holy Spirit, the Comforter Jesus sent to guide his church.

Husbandman—Vine—Branches

Jesus again and again stressed a three-fold relationship between God his Father; himself as God's Son; and his followers, God's family. This is taught by his parable of the True Vine where the three-fold relationship is taught by an analogy: husbandman-vine-branches. Jesus said:

I am the true vine, and my Father is the husbandman. *J 15:1*

I am the vine, ye are the branches. *J 15:5*

Every branch in me that beareth not fruit, he taketh away [cuts off]; and every branch that beareth fruit, he purgeth it [trims back], that it may bring forth more fruit. *J 15:2*

As the branch cannot bear fruit of itself, except it abide in the vine, no more can ye, except ye abide in me . . . He that abideth in me, and I in him, the same bringeth forth much fruit: for without me ye can do nothing. *J 15:4–5*

If a man abide not in me, he is cast forth as a branch, and is withered; and men gather them, and cast them into the fire, and they are burned. *J 15:6*

The foregoing sentence order has been altered to produce a systematic statement rather than a discourse. These ideas may be summarized as follows:

1. God, Jesus' Father, watches and manages the vine's branches.
2. God prunes off the unfruitful branches.
3. God trims from the fruitful branches some tips and spurs to increase the yield of fruit.
4. No branch can yield anything unless it takes nourishment from its vine, Jesus. If it does take such nourishment the branch will have a high yield.

5. If a branch does not take nourishment from its vine, it withers and has to be cut off and burned.

The remaining verses of Jesus' discourse fit together in a simple way to point the moral:

Abide in me, and I in you. *J 15:4*

If ye abide in me, and my words abide in you, ye shall ask what ye will, and it shall be done unto you. *J 15:7*

Now ye are clean through the word which I have spoken unto you. *J 15:3*

Herein is my Father glorified, that ye bear much fruit; so shall ye be my disciples. *J 15:8*

Fruit is the proof of discipleship. The unfruitful branches wither and have to be cut off and disposed of. But note that the fruitful and unfruitful branches are both cut by the Father: the fruitful to increase their yield; the unfruitful to seal their chosen death. The life principle for the branches is to abide in the Vine and thus avoid the necessary pruning of God, Jesus' Father.

GOOD TREES; BAD TREES

Every tree is known by its fruits. So are false prophets, pretenders. Both Matthew and Luke have sayings of Jesus on this:

MATTHEW	LUKE
Beware of false prophets, which come to you in sheep's clothing, but inwardly they are ravening wolves. Ye shall know them by their fruits.	For every tree is known by his own fruit. For of thorns men do not gather figs, nor of a bramble bush gather they grapes. L 6:44
Do men gather grapes of thorns, or figs of thistles? Even so every good tree bringeth forth good fruit, but a corrupt tree bringeth forth evil fruit. A good tree cannot bring forth evil fruit; neither can a corrupt tree bring forth good fruit. Every tree that bringeth not forth good fruit is hewn down, and cast into the fire. Wherefore by their fruits ye shall know them. Mt 7:15–20	For a good tree bringeth not forth corrupt fruit; neither doth a corrupt tree bring forth good fruit. L 6:43

In another place Matthew has a succinct saying of Jesus which summarizes the point of the foregoing quotations:

> Either make the tree good, and his fruit good, or else make the tree corrupt, and his fruit corrupt: for the tree is known by his fruit. *Mt 12:33*

The quotations also state the theme of judgment on the unproductive. This repeats a theme stated by John the Baptist before Jesus' own ministry:

> And now also the axe is laid unto the root of the trees; therefore every tree which bringeth not forth good fruit is hewn down and cast into the fire. *Mt 3:10 (L 3:9)*

The poor-yielding tree is cut down and burned. Jesus, himself, consigned prunings to the fire. It matters not what he spoke of withered vine branches rather than trees:

> If a man abide not in me, he is cast forth as a branch, and is withered; and men gather them, and cast them into the fire, and they are burned. *J 15:6*

So with withered branches, bad trees, wolf prophets disguised as sheep and with all unproductive persons:

> Wherefore by their fruits ye shall know them. *Mt 7:20*

YE ARE THE SALT OF THE EARTH

In the Sermon on the Mount Jesus said:

Ye are the salt of the earth; but if the salt had lost his savour, wherewith shall it be salted? It is thenceforth good for nothing, but to be
cast out, and to be trodden under foot of men. *Mt 5:13*

Luke has another "salt" saying immediately after Jesus' saying
that whosoever has not forsaken "all that he hath, he cannot be
my disciple":

Salt is good, but if the salt have lost his savour, wherewith shall it be
seasoned? It is neither fit for the land, nor yet for the dunghill; but
men cast it out. He that hath ears to hear, let him hear. *L 14:34–35*

Mark has a third series of "salt" sayings following his section
dealing with the extreme urgency of avoiding Hell and "the fire
that never shall be quenched":

For every one shall be salted with fire, and every sacrifice shall be
salted with salt.

Salt is good, but if the salt have lost his saltiness, wherewith will ye
season it?

Have salt in yourselves and have peace one with another. *Mk 9:49–50*

Mark alone has two of these sayings:

For every one shall be salted with fire, and every sacrifice shall be
salted with salt . . .

Have salt in yourselves and have peace one with another. *Mk 9:49–50*

There is no consensus exactly what these two verses mean.
Perhaps we can say that the last verse means: be "salty" as Chris-

tians are supposed to be and you will have peace with each other. Modern translations omit "and every sacrifice shall be salted with salt," as not supported by the manuscripts.

This leaves only the verse: "For every one shall be salted with fire." *Mk 9:49* The question is whether this verse belongs with the preceding section which records Jesus' statement as to Hell and "the fire that shall never be quenched" *(Mk 9:43–48)*, or with Jesus' salt saying *(Mk 9:49–50)* that follows. "Salted with fire" could fit with the preceding section, meaning figuratively "burned with fire," perhaps like salt burns a wound. On the other hand, if "salted with fire" means something like "fired or glazed with salt" then Jesus' words mean something like, "For every one of you, like pottery, shall be glazed with salt," and belongs with Jesus' salt sayings.

All three synoptic gospels have Jesus' saying which may be summarized "if salt loses its saltiness, how will such salt be salted?" The gospels' record of the form of this saying varies:

MARK	MATTHEW	LUKE
Salt is good,	Ye are the salt of the earth;	Salt is good,
but if the salt have lost his saltiness wherewith will ye season *it*? *Mk 9:50*	but if the salt have lost his savour, wherewith shall *it* be salted? It is thenceforth good for nothing,	but if the salt have lost his savour wherewith shall *it* be seasoned? It is neither fit for the land, nor fit for the dunghill; but men cast it out. *L 14:34–35*
	but to be cast out, and to be trodden under foot of man. *Mt 5:13*	

Easy exegesis makes Christians "the salt of the earth" just as they are "the light of the world." *Mt 5:13–14* It is true. Jesus did say that Christians are the salt of the earth. But he said more. He said, if this "salt" loses its saltiness, how will this "salt" regain it? Essentially, Jesus said this "salt" can not be reconstituted. it is useless and must be discarded, thrown out like garbage on a village street, to be trodden under foot by passers-by. Not a very pretty picture.

Both "salt" and "light" are regarded as affirmative images for Christians and the church. These phrases do capsulate Jesus' cheerful image for his people — his friends and brethren — but they are also parables of warning to these friends and brethren. They are the light of the world not a secret society under a blanket. They are the salt of the earth not a bland, neutral compound that is good for nothing.

YE ARE THE LIGHT OF THE WORLD

In the Sermon on the Mount Jesus said:

Ye are the light of the world. A city that is set on a hill cannot be hid. Neither do men light a candle, and put it under a bushel [container], but on a candlestick; and it giveth light unto all that are in the house. Let your light so shine before men, that they may see your good works, and glorify your Father which is in heaven. *Mt 5:14–16*

Luke has a saying which parallels part of the foregoing quotation:

MATTHEW	LUKE
Neither do men light a candle, and put it	No man when he hath lighted a candle, putteth it in a secret place,
under a bushel, but on a candlestick;	neither under a bushel, but on a candlestick
and it giveth light to all that are in the house. *Mt 5:15*	that they which come in may see the light. *L 11:33*

A man does not light a candle and put it in the cellar or under a meal tub. He puts it on a candlestick to light the house.

Both Mark and Luke have another saying of Jesus that reiterates the same idea:

MARK	LUKE
	No man when he hath lighted a candle,
Is a candle brought to be put under a bushel [container], or under a bed,	covereth it with a vessel, or putteth it under a bed,

MARK (cont.)	LUKE (cont.)
and not to be set	but setteth it
on a candlestick?	on a candlestick,
	that they which enter in
	may see the light.
For there is nothing hid	For nothing is secret,
which shall not be manifested;	that shall not be made manifest;
neither was any thing	neither any thing
kept secret,	hid,
but that it	that shall not be known
should come abroad.	and come abroad.
Mk 4:21–22	*L 8:16–17*

The hiding is over. Christians are the light of the world. They are like a hilltop village ablaze with holiday light above the darkness of the countryside. They should allow the light of their good works to glorify God their Father, not hide them under buckets or beds.

NOTHING CAN REMAIN SECRET OR HIDDEN: NEITHER HYPOCRISY, NOR THE GOSPEL

Jesus charged the Twelve that "what ye hear in the ear that preach ye upon the housetops." *Mt 10:27* Later on after the scribes and Pharisees began to lay in wait in order to catch something out of Jesus' mouth so that they might accuse him, Jesus warned his disciples about the Pharisees in words reminiscent of his charge to the Twelve. *L 12:1–3*

Our texts state:

MATTHEW	LUKE
If they have called the master of the house Beelzebub, how much more shall they call them of his household? Fear them not therefore: for there is nothing covered, that shall not be revealed; and hid, that shall not be known.	Beware ye of the leaven of the Pharisees, which is hypocrisy. For there is nothing covered, that shall not be revealed; neither hid, that shall not be known.
What I tell you in darkness, that speak ye in light; and what ye hear in the ear, that preach ye upon the housetops. *Mt 10:25–27*	Therefore whatsoever ye have spoken in darkness shall be heard in the light, and that which ye have spoken in the ear in closets shall be proclaimed upon the housetops. *L 12:1–3*

Jesus warned his disciples about the hypocrisy of the Pharisees. Their whisperings in secret against Jesus were revealed. Hypocrisy will out. But this was a lesson for his disciples, too. Just as the Pharisees' hypocrisy had been revealed, so also will the things which his disciples had learned confidentially ("in the ear") from Jesus be preached by them upon the housetops.

Jesus told a parable to show that secrecy is no part of his gospel. We have two accounts:

MARK	LUKE
	No man,
Is a candle brought	when he hath lighted a candle,
to be put under a bushel,	covereth it with a vessel,
or under a bed?	or putteth it under a bed,
And not to be set	but setteth it
on a candlestick?	on a candlestick,
	that they which enter in
	may see the light.
For there is nothing hid,	For nothing is secret,
which shall not be manifested;	that shall not be made manifest;
neither was any thing	neither any thing
kept secret,	hid,
but that it	that shall not be known
should come abroad.	and come abroad.
Mk 4:21–22	*L 8:16–17*

Everything hidden and secret will become known, especially the gospel. The gospel is like a candle to the world, and to be put on a candlestick, and not under a pot or a bed. That is why it is to be preached upon the housetops.

BE YE DOERS OF THE WORD

Both Matthew and Luke have the parable of the house built upon a rock:

MATTHEW	LUKE
Therefore whosoever	Whosoever cometh to me,
heareth	and heareth
these sayings of mine,	my sayings,
and doeth them,	and doeth them,
I will liken him	I will shew you
	to whom he is like:
unto a wise man,	he is like a man
which built	which built
his house	an house,
	and digged deep,
	and laid the foundation
upon a rock.	on a rock;
And the rain descended,	
and the floods came,	and when the flood arose,
and the winds blew,	the stream
and beat upon	beat vehemently upon
that house;	that house,
and it fell not:	and could not shake it:
for it was	for it was
founded upon a rock.	founded upon a rock.
And every one	But he
that heareth	that heareth,
these sayings of mine,	
and doeth them not,	*and doeth not*,
shall be likened	is like
unto a foolish man,	a man
	that without a foundation
which built	built
his house	an house
upon the sand:	upon the earth;
and the rain descended	against which
and the floods came,	the stream

Matthew (cont.)	Luke (cont.)
and the winds blew,	
and beat upon that house;	did beat vehemently,
and it fell;	and immediately it fell;
and great was	and the ruin of that house
the fall of it.	was great.
Mt 7:24–27	*L 6:47–49*

The parable could be called the parable of two houses in a wadi. In a semi-desert climate the rare rainstorm brings a flash flood that sweeps away everything in the usually dry streambed (wadi), everything that is not built on rock.

Jesus introduced this parable as reported in Luke with an unanswerable question which still haunts Christians:

> And why call ye me,"Lord, Lord," and do not the things which I say? *L 6:46*

This is no new problem. Jesus had followers like that in his lifetime. He said then:

> Not every one that saith unto me, "Lord, Lord," shall enter into the Kingdom of Heaven; but he that doeth the will of my Father which is in heaven. Many will say to me in that day, "Lord, Lord, have we not prophesied in thy name? And in thy name have cast out devils? And in thy name done many wonderful works?"

> And then will I profess unto them, "I never knew you; depart from me, ye that work iniquity." *Mt 7:21–23*

Jesus quoted the words, "Depart from me, ye that work iniquity," from Psalm 6:8. He also quoted Psalm 6:8 in a statement reported by Luke:

> Then shall ye begin to say, "We have eaten and drunk in thy presence, and thou hast taught in our streets."

But he shall say, "I tell you, I know you not whence ye are; depart from me, all ye workers of iniquity." *L 13:26–27*

The parable of the house built on the rock teaches that whoever hears Jesus' sayings and does them is a wise man. His brother, James, later wrote:

Be ye doers of the word, and not hearers only, deceiving your own selves. For if any be a hearer of the word, and not a doer, he is like unto a man beholding his natural face in a glass: for he beholdeth himself, and goeth his way, and straightway forgetteth what manner of man he was. But whoso looketh into the perfect law of liberty, and continueth therein, he being not a forgetful hearer, but a doer of the work, this man shall be blessed in his deed. *James 1:22–25*

HATED OF ALL MEN

It is clear that Jesus taught that his followers would be hated by all men for his name's sake. The context of this teaching varies, but the words are the same:

MARK	MATTHEW	MATTHEW	LUKE
And ye shall be hated of all men for my name's sake;	And ye shall be hated of all men for my name's sake;	And ye shall be hated of all nations for my name's sake . . .	And ye shall be hated of all men for my name's sake . . .
but he that shall endure unto the end, the same shall be saved. *Mk 13:13*	but he that endureth to the end shall be saved. *Mt 10:22*	But he that shall endure unto the end, the same shall be saved. *Mt 24:9, 13*	
			In your patience possess ye your souls. *L 21:17, 19*

The reason for this hate is simply that Christians are not "of the world." Jesus stated:

I have given them thy word; and the world hath hated them, because they are not *of this world*, even as I am not *of the world. J 17:14*

If ye were *of the world*, the world would love his own; but because ye are not *of the world*, but I have chosen you out of the world, therefore the world hateth you. *J 15:19*

The hate of the world for Christians is inevitable: they are differentiated from the world by Jesus' choice of them out of the other people. That choice by Jesus is resented, as well as the separateness from the world it requires. Christians are foreigners and outlanders of the world because they have received God's word through Jesus. The world does not know God, and hence does not know his people. Jesus said:

> But all these things will they do unto you for my name's sake, because they know not him that sent me. *J 15:21*

Jesus continued:

> If I had not done among them the works which none other man did, they had not had sin; but now have they both seen and hated *both* me and my Father. But this cometh to pass, that the word [of the Old Testament] might be fulfilled that is written in *their* law, "They hated me without a cause." *J 15:24–25*

"Their law" here is used broadly of the Jewish scriptures and includes the Psalms. Jesus quotes a saying embedded in two Psalms 35:19 and 69:4. That saying is not a Messianic saying but instead refers to the natural mechanism of hate in men who "hate me without a cause."

The source of the hate of first-century Jews for Jesus was, according to Jesus, his special works, which convicted them of sin. The hate of Jesus was not confined to first century Jews, but is also a characteristic of "the world" generally:

> The world can not hate you; but me it hateth, because I testify of it, that the works thereof are evil. *J 7:7*

To paraphrase Jesus, the world can not hate you like it hates me since I speak the test of sin. That is not to say that you will not be "hated of all men for my name's sake." *Mk 13:13: Mt 10:22 (Mt 24:9)* The source of this hatred is my and my followers' differences from the world. *J 17:14; 15:19* The world first hated me and that hatred now extends to my followers:

> If the world hate you, ye know that it hated me *before* it hated you. *J 15:18*

According to Jesus, this hate for Jesus necessarily includes hate for his Father:

He that hateth me hateth My Father also. *J 15:23*

The same persons who hate Jesus must also hate God his Father. Christians, Jesus, and his Father are and will be hated by the world. It can not be otherwise.

Happiness in Persecution

Christians should expect to be persecuted. Jesus taught that some persecution is blessed:

MATTHEW

Blessed are they
which are persecuted
for righteousness' sake:
for theirs is
the Kingdom of Heaven.
Blessed are ye,
when men shall revile you,
and persecute you,

and shall say all
manner of evil
against you falsely,
for my sake.

Rejoice,
and be exceeding glad:
for great is
your reward
in Heaven,
for so persecuted

they the prophets
which were before you.
Mt 5:10–12

LUKE

Blessed are ye,
when men shall hate you,
and when they
shall separate you
from their company,
and shall reproach you,
and cast out your name as evil,
for the Son of man's sake.

Rejoice ye in that day,
and leap for joy:
for, behold,
your reward is great
in Heaven,
for in the like manner
did their fathers
unto the prophets.
L 6:22–23

Woe unto you,
when all men
shall speak well of you!
For so did their fathers
to the false prophets.
L 6:26

The subtle delicacy of the way Jesus' teaching web together is shown by the foregoing quotations. Matthew 5:10 belongs to the

605

Beatitudes that have gone before, yet its thought mingles with the key idea of the following passage — reproach "for the Son of man's sake." This is close to persecution "for righteousness' sake."

Peter's letter has the same juxtaposition:

1. But and if ye suffer *for righteousness' sake*, happy are ye, and be not afraid of their terror, neither be troubled: . . . *1 Peter 3:14*

2. If ye be reproached *for the name of Christ*, happy are ye: . . . *1 Peter 4:14*

Matthew does not have Luke's closing sentence, and, indeed, even in Luke that sentence does not follow immediately the main teaching in Luke 6:22–23. But it is obvious symmetry: If you are to rejoice because you are persecuted like the prophets, so also ought you to be embarrassed when "all men" shall speak well of you since the false prophets also pleased all men. *L 6:26*

Difficult Christians must remember that the persecution referred to must be "for the Son of Man's sake" not for their own sake. *L 6:22*

A Christian's Duty

Jesus taught:

But which of you, having a servant plowing or feeding cattle, will say unto him, by and by, when he is come from the field, "Go and sit down to meat?"

And will not rather say unto him, "Make ready wherewith I may sup, and gird thyself, and serve me, till I have eaten and drunken; and afterward thou shalt eat and drink?"

Doth he thank that servant because he did the things that were commanded him? I trow [think] not.

So likewise ye, when ye shall have done all those things which are commanded you, say, "We are unprofitable servants: we have done that which was our duty to do." *L 17:7–10*

This parable teaches that a Christian should not expect thanks from God for doing what, in any case, was his duty. The background of the parable is this: a slave or serf not only had to do the field work but also to perform household tasks for his master. Despite the serf's weariness at the close of a day in the field he still had his household duties to perform. He could expect no thanks for doing his duty, so it is with Christians. They cannot expect thanks from God for doing what is their duty in any case. Their proper epitaph is: "We have done that which was our duty to do."

The Relation of Disciple and Lord

Jesus taught:

MATTHEW	LUKE
The disciple	The disciple
is not	is not
above his master,	above his master,
nor the servant	
above his lord.	
It is enough	but everyone
for the disciple	that is perfect [fully discipled]
that he be	shall be
as his master,	as his master.
and the servant	L 6:40
as his lord.	
Mt 10:24–25	

John's record of this teaching is as follows:

Verily, verily,	Remember the word
I say unto you,	that I said unto you,
The servant is not	"The servant is not
greater than his lord;	greater than his lord."
neither he	
that is sent	
greater than he	
that sent him.	
J 13:16	
	If they have persecuted me,
	they will also persecute you;
	if they have kept my saying,
	they will keep yours also.
	J 15:20

The disciple is not above his master, nor is the servant greater than his lord. Those sent by the Lord are not greater than the Lord that sent them.

That is true, true, but Jesus also said that those disciples who are fully instructed shall be as their master, and their sayings will be kept like his: ignored and distorted.

THE CONDITIONS OF DISCIPLESHIP: CROSS-BEARING?

A man Matthew identifies as "a scribe" came up to Jesus and said:

Master, I will follow thee whithersoever thou goest. *Mt 8:19 (L 9:57)*

Jesus replied:

The foxes have holes, and the birds of the air have nests; but the Son of man hath not where to lay his head. *Mt 8:20 (L 9:58)*

The scribe's assertion that he would follow Jesus anywhere is often ignored, and Jesus' answer is viewed abstractly as a statement that he, as the Son of man, did not have even so much as a hole or a nest for his home. When the scribe's assertion is ignored, Jesus' point is lost.

Jesus' point was the hardship of following Jesus, since even he, the Son of man, had not even a hole or a nest to call home; so what could a follower expect?

Matthew and Luke continue their accounts:

MATTHEW	LUKE
	And he said unto another "Follow me."
And another of his disciples said unto him,	But he said,
"Lord, suffer me first to go and bury my father."	"Lord, suffer me first to go and bury my father."
But Jesus said unto him, "Follow me;	Jesus said unto him,
and let the dead bury their dead."	"Let the dead bury their dead;
Mt 8:21–22	but go thou and preach the Kingdom of God."
	L 9:59–60

Only Luke's account continues, with an interchange with a third man:

> And another also said, "Lord, I will follow thee; but let me first go bid them farewell, which are at home at my house."

> And Jesus said unto him, "No man, having put his hand to the plough, and looking back, is fit for the Kingdom of God." *L 9:61–62*

It was not just "blood, sweat and tears," but no home and no turning back, even to say, "Farewell"; no, not even to bury your father. This was no gracious invitation from the kindly Man of Galilee, but a stern and austere summons to serve under the Son of man.

Jesus did not mince words on the standards to be his disciple; he told the "great multitudes with him" *(L 14:25)*:

MATTHEW	LUKE
He that loveth father or mother more than me is not worthy of me; and he that loveth son or daughter more than me is not worthy of me. *Mt 10:37*	If any man come to me, and hate not his father, and mother, and wife, and children, and brethren, and sisters, yea, and his own life also, he cannot be my disciple. *L 14:26*

Luke quotes Jesus as using the word "hate" for family and one's own life, while Matthew quotes Jesus as saying that those who love their family more are "not worthy" of Jesus. The literal truth of what Jesus meant falls between his two statements. We interpolate that "hate" was not meant literally, but to convey the terrible urgency of discipleship, and that "not worthy" conveys in a restrained way the same urgency.

The feel of Jesus' rhetoric is succinctly caught in this quotation from John's Gospel:

> He that loveth his life shall lose it; and he that hateth his life in this world shall keep it unto life eternal. If any man serve me, let him follow me; . . . *J 12:25–26*

Jesus told the rich young ruler:

MARK	MATTHEW	LUKE
One thing thou lackest:	If thou wilt be perfect,	Yet lackest thou one thing:
go thy way,	go and	
sell whatsoever thou hast,	sell that thou hast,	sell all that thou hast,
and give to the poor,	and give to the poor,	and distribute unto the poor
and thou shalt have treasure in heaven;	and thou shalt have treasure in heaven;	and thou shalt have treasure in heaven;
and come,	and come	and come,
take up the cross,		
and follow me.	and follow me.	follow me.
Mk 10:21	*Mt 19:21*	*L 18:22*

The cost of being a disciple has to be counted. Jesus said:

> For which of you, intending to build a tower, sitteth not down first, and counteth the cost, whether he have sufficient to finish it? Lest haply, after he hath laid the foundation, and is not able to finish it, all that behold it begin to mock him, saying, "This man began to build, and was not able to finish."

> Or what king, going to make war against another king, sitteth not down first, and consulteth whether he be able with ten thousand to meet him that cometh against him with twenty thousand? Or else, while the other is yet a great way off, he sendeth an ambassage, and desireth conditions of peace.

So likewise, *whosoever he be of you that forsaketh not all that he hath,
he cannot be my disciple. L 14:28–33*

Calculate the cost of discipleship. Be warned that this cost includes forsaking all you have. Jesus comes first. There can be no
other conclusion.

Jesus also taught unequivocally that cross-bearing is required
for discipleship:

MARK	MATTHEW	LUKE
Whosoever	If any man	If any man
will come	will come	will come
after me,	after me,	after me,
let him	let him	let him
deny himself	deny himself,	deny himself,
and take up	and take up	and take up
his cross,	his cross,	his cross daily,
and follow me.	and follow me.	and follow me.
Mk 8:34	*Mt 16:24*	*L 9:23*

He made other statements to the same effect:

MATTHEW	LUKE
[To the Twelve]	[To "great multitudes"]
And he that	And whosoever
taketh not his cross	doth not bear his cross,
and followeth me after me,	and come after me,
is not worthy of me.	cannot be my disciple.
Mt 10:38	*L 14:27*

We interpolate that "cannot be my disciple" means the same as
the more restrained "is not worthy of me" despite the meaning
absolute of "cannot."

Jesus told the rich young ruler not only to sell what he had and
give it to the poor, but also:

And come, take up the cross, and follow me. *Mk 10:21*

What did Jesus mean by his repeated instructions to his disciples to take up "his cross?" Jesus' own cross was yet to come; he refers to each disciple's own cross. This was a cruel metaphor in which the Roman occupation had instructed Jesus' countrymen.

In Judea the Roman occupation forces had crucified thousands of Jews. For example, Josephus, the Jewish historian, writes of one incident during Archelaus' reign as Ethnarch of Judea (4 B.C. to A.D. 6), in which Varus took custody of great numbers of rebelling Jews, "but such as were the most guilty he crucified; these were in number about two thousand." *Josephus, Wars Of The Jews, Book II, Ch. V, Sec.3.*

The Romans required the person to be crucified to carry his cross to the site of crucifixion. The sight of Jews bearing their crosses to the crucifixion sites must have been common. So common that Jesus could use those crosses as a vivid metaphor to explain what following him meant. Jesus offered his followers discipleship as grievous as Roman crosses.

Easy exegesis has deformed the metaphor "take up your cross" into "bear your afflictions stoically." Christians no doubt bear afflictions, but Jesus meant more: to follow him is to deny yourself, and bear your cross of discipleship.

Jesus laid down the conditions of that discipleship succinctly:

Whosoever will come after me, let him deny himself, and take up his cross, and follow me. *Mk 8:34 (Mt 16:24; L 9:23)*

This is to be done "daily." *L 9:23* But in this service there is rest for your soul:

Come unto me, all ye that labor and are heavy laden, and I will give you rest.

Take my *yoke* upon you, and learn of me: for I am meek and lowly in heart; and ye shall find rest unto your souls. For my *yoke* is easy, and my burden is light. *Mt 11:28–30*

Since there are so many references in the Gospels to taking up your cross and since Jesus went on to his own cross, we tend to ignore Jesus' clear teaching that you are to take up his yoke as well as your cross. Taking his yoke and bearing your cross appear to be different metaphors for the same truth.

The condition of discipleship stated in terms taking up your cross may seem harsh, but we have Jesus' own express words that its equivalent, his yoke, "is easy," and that his burden "is light." *Mt 11:30* If, as is probable, Jesus worked in Joseph's village carpenter shop as a young man it is likely that he worked making yokes since they were then a staple carpenter shop product in a rural area. *Mk 6:3; Mt 13:55* If yokes were well made they were "easy" for the oxen that could then plow well since their burden was "light." *cf. L 14:19*

Jesus' point is that his followers will not find his yoke onerous. The hair shirt saints are wrong. Not only is Jesus' yoke easy and his burden light but there are great rewards. He said, "I will give you rest," that is, "rest unto your souls." *Mt 11:28–29*

Scholars and commentaries do their best to hide Jesus' clear light under bushel baskets of conjectures. They conjecture that his yoke is the yoke of the Kingdom of God, although Jesus himself was content to call it simply "my yoke." In fact, he twice calls it "my yoke." *Mt 11:29–30*

They conjecture that Jesus was referring here to the "yoke of the Law," which other New Testament "yoke" passages do. *Acts 15:10; Galatians 5:1* The question is what Jesus meant here, and all he said is "my yoke."

Some point out that there was a Jewish wisdom writing, Sirach (Ecclesiasticus), written before Jesus' time that referred to the yoke of wisdom. *See 51:23–27* In Jewish thinking, the yoke of wisdom was the yoke of the Law. They then leap to the conclusion that Jesus was quoting this Jewish wisdom book. Jesus was, of course, familiar with cultural heritage of his people and his speech pattern no doubt reflected that heritage, but that is different from saying he was just quoting Sirach (Ecclesiasticus) 51:23–27. A comparison of that text with Matthew 11:28–30 will show that Jesus was not quoting but stating a new teaching, his own.

Jesus explained his yoke by reference to his own nature: "for I am meek and lowly in heart." *Mt 11:29* He invited "all ye that labor and are heavy laden" to take his yoke and "learn of me." *Mt 11:28–29* This is the great invitation that even scholars should accept. This is the ultimate condition of discipleship: take up Jesus' yoke and so learn of him and his nature. The reward for meeting this condition is "rest unto your souls." *Mt 11:29*

Jesus does not simply promise easy yokes, light burdens and rest unto your souls. He promises more; he promises: Joy!

Here are some neglected statements of his as to the joy of his followers:

> These things have I spoken unto you, that *my joy* might remain in you, and that *your joy* might be full. *J 15:11*
> And now come I to thee; and these things I speak in the world, that they might have *my joy* fulfilled *in themselves. J 17:13*

Stated simply, Jesus said that he wanted his own joy to be in his followers, fully and completely. Jesus, at least twice, said it was his plan that his followers' joy "be full." *J 15:11; 16:24*

The somber centrality of Jesus' cross has blinded Christians, and the world, to his gift of his joy.

Are his followers' crosses heavy? Yes.

Are his followers' yokes easy? Yes.

Are his followers' burdens light? Yes.

Are his followers given Jesus' joy? Yes.

But the greatest of these is: Joy!

HOW TO ABIDE IN JESUS' LOVE

In his farewell address to his disciples after the Last Supper, Jesus said:

> As the Father hath loved me, so have I loved you. Continue ye in my love. If ye keep my commandments, *ye shall abide in my love*; even as I have kept my Father's commandments, and abide in his love. These things have I spoken unto you, that my joy might remain in you, and that your joy might be full. *J 15:9–11*

Elsewhere in that same address Jesus said:

> If you love me, keep my commandments. *J 14:15*

> He that hath my commandments, and keepeth them, he it is that loveth me; and he that loveth me shall be loved of my Father, and *I will love him, and will manifest myself to him. J 14:21*

> If a man love me, he will keep my words; and my Father will love him, and we will come unto him, and *make our abode with him.* He that loveth me not keepeth not my sayings: . . . *J 14:23–24*

Jesus' guiding principles may be summarized as follows:

1. If ye love me, keep my commandments.
2. Then you will abide in my love.
3. Both I and my Father will then love you and abide with you.
4. When Jesus abides in you, you acquire his joy.

Jesus' abiding in the persons keeping his commandments repeats Jesus' own experience with his Father:

> If ye keep my commandments, ye shall abide in my love, even as I have kept my Father's commandments, and abide in his love. *J 15:10*

CHAPTER 10

SPIRITUAL LAWS

THE HAPPY ONES

Jesus twice described those who are spiritually happy. His word for them is, "Blessed." These sayings are known as the Beatitudes and are enshrined on millions of wall plaques. What did Jesus actually say, and what did Jesus actually mean in those sayings?

The beatitudes are reported by Matthew and Luke with different wordings. In addition, in Luke they are matched with certain woes that are the converse of Luke's beatitudes. Each woe clarifies the meaning of the matching beatitude.

Two of the beatitudes are as follows:

MATTHEW	LUKE	LUKE
Blessed are	Blessed are	Woe unto
they that mourn:	ye that weep *now*:	you that laugh *now*:
for they	for ye	for ye
shall be comforted.	shall laugh.	shall mourn and weep.
Mt 5:4	*L 6:21*	*L 6:25*
Blessed are	Blessed are	Woe unto
they which	ye that	you that
do hunger and thirst	hunger *now*:	are full:
after righteousness:		
for they shall be filled.	for ye shall be filled.	for ye shall hunger.
Mt 5:6	*L 6:21*	*L 6:25*

Those that weep and mourn now will, in the future, laugh and be comforted. Their spiritual winter will become a spiritual spring. This is a very present word of comfort, but Jesus did not teach bland hope, for he noted that those who laugh now (wickedly?) "shall mourn and weep." L 6:25

Who is it, then, who will pass into the delights of a spiritual spring? Those happy persons will be those who *now* "hunger and thirst after righteousness." Mt 5:6 They shall then be filled with righteousness. They shall then shine forth as the sun in the Kingdom of their Father. Mt 13:43

The crucial issue is: What did Jesus mean by "righteousness"? The first clue is found four verses later where he repeats the word: "Blessed are they which are persecuted for *righteousness'* sake . . ." Mt 5:10 The second clue is found elsewhere in the Sermon on the Mount where he again used the word: "But seek ye first the kingdom of God and His *righteousness*; and all these things shall be added unto you." Mt 6:33 Finally, in the same sermon he said "except your *righteousness* shall exceed the *righteousness* of the scribes and Pharisees, ye shall in no case enter into the kingdom of Heaven." Mt 5:20 I conclude that by "righteousness" Jesus meant righteous acts, justice in accordance with rules of God's kingdom.

There is a third beatitude which Matthew and Luke share and for which Luke has a matching woe:

MATTHEW	LUKE	LUKE
"Blessed are ye,	Blessed are ye	Woe unto you,
when men	when men	when all men
shall revile you,	shall hate you	shall speak
and persecute you	and when they	well of you!
	shall separate you	
	from their company,	
and shall say	and shall	
all manner	reproach you,	
of evil against you	and cast out	
falsely,	your name as evil,	
for	for	
my sake	the Son of man's sake.	

MATTHEW (cont.)	LUKE (cont.)	LUKE (cont.)
Rejoice,	Rejoice ye	
and be	in that day	
	and	
exceedingly glad;	leap for joy:	
for	for, behold,	
great is	your reward	
your reward	is great	
in heaven:	in heaven:	
for so	for in the like manner	for so
persecuted they	did their fathers	did their fathers
	unto	to
the prophets	the prophets"	the false prophets
which were	L 6:22–23	L 6:26
before you."		
Mt 5: 11–12		

Followers enduring persecution *for Jesus' sake* are to "Rejoice and be exceedingly glad" because they have his promise of their great reward in heaven.

Matthew alone has another "persecution" beatitude:

Blessed are they which are persecuted for righteousness' sake: for theirs is the Kingdom of Heaven. *Mt 5:10*

This is not persecution for Jesus' sake, but "for righteousness' sake. This "righteousness" is God's righteousness and must "exceed the righteousness of the scribes and Pharisees." *Mt 5:20, 6:33*

This persecution beatitude looks back to Matthew's first beatitude; they both end with the phrase: "for theirs is the Kingdom of Heaven." *Mt 5:3,10* Matthew's first beatitude relates to "the poor in spirit" and is the fourth instance in which there is a parallel beatitude and woe in Luke:

MATTHEW	LUKE	LUKE
"Blessed are	"Blessed be	"But woe unto you
the poor	ye poor:	that are rich!
in spirit:		

Matthew (cont.)	Luke (cont.)	Luke (cont.)
for theirs is	for yours is	For ye have received
the Kingdom	the Kingdom	your consolation."
of Heaven"	of God."	*L 6:24*
Mt 5:3	*L 6:20*	

Did Jesus mean the literally "poor", or those "poor in spirit"? The question whether Matthew's phrase "in spirit" is a gloss on Jesus' own words is discussed in the section, "Whose Is the Kingdom?", pp. 523–524. We believe the proper assumption is that Jesus did not always state his explanation of "Blessed" in identical words.

What is indisputable is that Jesus taught that humbleness is an indispensable attribute of any one who has status in the Kingdom. He taught:

> "Whosoever therefore shall humble himself as this little child, the same is the greatest in the Kingdom of Heaven." *Mt 18:4*

Matthew alone has the following three beatitudes:

> "Blessed are the merciful: for they shall obtain mercy. Blessed are the pure in heart: for they shall see God. Blessed are the peacemakers: for they shall be called the children of God. *Mt 5:7–9*

The phrase "pure in heart" evokes Psalm 24:4–5 which states, "He that hath . . . a pure heart . . . shall receive the blessing from the Lord and righteousness from the God of his salvation." Jesus turned receiving "the blessing form the Lord" into something different, "Blessed are the pure in heart: for they shall see God." They shall become acquainted with God, not simply be the recipients of his blessing. If the lens of a telescope is not clouded you can see the heavens; if the heart is pure you can see God.

The most famous beatitude is:

> Blessed are the meek: for they shall inherit the earth. *Mt 5:5*

The problem is the word *meek*. Modern pagans titter at such nonsense as the meek inheriting the earth; preachers struggle to escape the negative image of the word, *meek*, and to distinguish Christians from Uriah Heeps.

Who, then, are "the meek"? The various translations struggle to find an equivalent English adjective: non-assertive, gentle, humble and patient.

To understand what Jesus was saying we must remember his knowledge of the Psalms. See Jesus' background, p. 483. Here he used a phrase from Psalm 37:11 and added to it the words "blessed are" to make it his own teaching. Psalm 37:11 states:

> But the meek shall inherit the earth, and shall delight themselves in the abundance of peace. *Psalm 37:11*

The true meaning of "the meek" is shown by a comparison of Psalm 37:9 and 37:11:

NINTH	ELEVENTH
. . . those that wait upon the Lord they shall inherit the earth.	. . . the meek shall inherit the earth.
Psalm 37:9	*Psalm 37:11*

The "meek" are "those that wait upon the Lord." So what Jesus is saying is:

> Blessed are those that wait upon the Lord: for they shall inherit the earth.

This is the true meaning of *meek*: not meek–humble–gentle but patient acceptors of and servants of the Lord. They shall *inherit* the earth as a matter of right, the right of inheritance.

What did Jesus mean by "the earth"? Since Jesus had used a phrase from Psalm 37:11 he may have had other verses of Psalm 37 in mind, such as:

> For such as be blessed of him shall *inherit the earth*; and they that be cursed of him shall be cut off. *Psalm 37:22*

The righteous shall *inherit the land*, and dwell therein for ever. *Psalm 37:29*

Wait on the Lord, and keep his way, and he shall exalt thee to *inherit the land*; when the wicked are cut off, thou shalt see it. *Psalm 37:34*

These quotations suggest that Jesus meant that "the earth," which is to be inherited, is a material, physical thing like "the land" of Israel, which the Jews were to inherit.

The beatitudes are Jesus' own way of describing the subjects of the Kingdom of God even though only two of them expressly mention that Kingdom. *Mt 5:3,10; L 6:20* It is implied in the other beatitudes since all of the beatitudes are tied together but the same introductory phrase, "Blessed are." The beatitudes fit together into a mosaic describing the subjects of the Kingdom: the humble in spirit, those that wait upon the Lord, those that mourn, those that hunger and thirst after righteousness and are persecuted for righteousness' sake, the merciful, the pure in heart and the peacemakers. These subjects of the Kingdom will be rewarded, receiving mercy, the sight of God and the accolade, "the children of God."

These persons who see God and are his children shall own his Kingdom and shall obtain mercy and shall inherit the earth. To attain this state it is necessary to hunger and thirst after righteousness. Their present sorrow shall become eternal happiness in the Kingdom of their Father.

THE OTHER BEATITUDES

In addition to the traditional "Beatitudes", Jesus also taught other beatitudes. The Greek words of the gospels translated *Blessed* are in turn translating the common Hebrew word *ashre*, meaning "Happy!", or "How happy!" or "Oh, the happiness of."

For example, a man said to Jesus, "Blessed is he that shall eat bread in the Kingdom of God." *L 14:15* Another time a woman lifted up her voice and said to Jesus, "Blessed is the womb that bare thee, and the paps which thou hast sucked." *L 11:27* Jesus picked up the word *blessed* and applied it, saying:

Yea, rather, *blessed* are they that hear the word of God, and keep it.
L 11:28

This beatitude deserves to be added to the "Beatitudes", as do the following statements of Jesus:

1. To Thomas after Jesus had shown him his pierced hand and side:

Thomas, because thou hast seen me, thou hast believed; *blessed* are they that have not seen, and yet have believed. *J 20:29*

2. To his disciples:

MATTHEW	LUKE
But *blessed* are your eyes,	*Blessed* are the eyes which see the things that ye see!
for they see; and your ears, for they hear.	
For verily I say unto you, that many prophets and righteous men have desired to see those things which ye see,	For I tell you, that many prophets and kings have desired to see those things which ye see,

MATTHEW (cont.)	LUKE (cont.)
and have not seen them;	and have not seen them;
and to hear those things	and to hear those things
which ye hear,	which ye hear,
and have not heard them.	and have not heard them.
Mt 13:16–17	*L 10:23–24*

3. To disciples of John the Baptist when they came to inquire whether Jesus was "the Christ—the Anointed One":

And *blessed* is he, whosoever shall not be offended in me. *L 7:23*

4. To one of the chief Pharisees who had invited Jesus and other guests to dinner at his house on a Sabbath:

When thou makest a dinner or a supper, call not thy friends, nor thy brethren, neither thy kinsmen, nor thy rich neighbors; lest they also bid thee again, and a recompense be made thee. But when thou makest a feast, call the poor, the maimed, the lame, the blind.

And thou shalt be *blessed* for they can not recompense thee: for thou shalt be recompensed at the resurrection of the just. *L 14:12–14*

5. In a parable teaching the importance of readiness for his return:

MATTHEW	LUKE
Who then is	Who then is
a faithful and wise	that faithful and wise
servant,	steward,
whom his lord	whom his lord
hath made ruler	shall make ruler
over his household,	over his household,
and give them	to give them
meat	their portion of meat
in due season?	in due season?
Blessed is that servant	*Blessed* is that servant,

Matthew (cont.)	**Luke** (cont.)
whom his lord	whom his lord
when he cometh	when he cometh
shall find so doing.	shall find so doing.
Verily I say unto you,	Of a truth I say unto you,
that he shall make him	that he will make him
ruler over all his goods.	ruler over all that he hath.
Mt 24:45–47	*L 12:42–43*

These other beatitudes, like "The Beatitudes", refer both to the apocalyptic future when Jesus will return and when the pure in heart shall see God, and to this present age when it is blessed not to be offended with Jesus and when the humble in spirit are filing into the Kingdom of Heaven and when the merciful are obtaining mercy both here and now and forever.

Soul Light

Jesus discussed the illumination of the soul as follows:

MATTHEW	LUKE
The light of the body	The light of the body
is the eye.	is the eye.
If therefore	Therefore when
thine eye	thine eye
be single [clear],	is single [clear],
thy whole body	thy whole body
shall be	also is
full of light.	full of light;
But if thine eye	but when thine eye
be evil [clouded],	is evil [clouded],
thy whole body	thy body
shall be	also is
full of darkness.	full of darkness.
If therefore	Take heed therefore
the light that is in thee	that the light which is in thee
be darkness,	be not darkness.
how great	
is that darkness!	
Mt 6:22–23	
	If thy whole body
	therefore be
	full of light,
	having no part dark,
	the whole shall be
	full of light,
	as when
	the bright shining
	of a candle
	doth give thee light.
	L 11:34–36

If the eye is clear, the whole body is full of light. If the eye is clouded, the whole body is full of darkness.

Actually, Jesus was not speaking of the body but of the soul. The eye of the soul admits light of God. If the eye of the soul is evil, that light can not enter and the soul is full of darkness. How great is that darkness!

Jesus said:

MATTHEW	LUKE
But if thine eye	But when thine eye
be evil,	is evil,
thy whole body	thy body
shall be	also is
full of darkness.	full of darkness.
Mt 6:23	*L 11:34*

The evil eye referred to was not the evil eye of witchcraft and occult phenomena. In Jewish religious tradition, the phrase translated "evil eye" referred to a wicked heart, not to witchcraft:

Because that there be not a thought in thy wicked heart, saying, The seventh year, the year of release, is at hand; and *thine eye be evil* against thy poor brother, and thou givest him nought; and he cry unto the Lord against thee, and it be sin into thee. *Deuteronomy 15:9*

Eat thou not the bread of him that hath *an evil eye*, neither desire thou his dainty meats: for as he thinketh in his heart, so is he: Eat and drink, saith he to thee; but his heart is not with thee. *Proverbs 23:6–7*

And that hasteth to be rich hath *an evil eye*, and considereth not that poverty shall come upon him. *Proverbs 28:22*

Jesus used the phrase "evil eye" in the manner of that tradition. He once said:

That which cometh out of a man, that defileth the man. For from within, out of the heart of men, proceed evil thoughts, adulteries, fornications, murders, thefts, covetousness, wickedness, deceit, lasciviousness, *an evil eye*, blasphemy, pride, foolishness. All these evil things come from within and defile the man. *Mk 7:20–23*

Modern translations of this quotation render "an evil eye" as "envy." This meaning is consistent with the meaning of Jesus' question at the end of the parable about the laborers in the vineyard:

Is thine eye evil, because I am good? *Mt 20:15*

Jesus taught that if the eye is evil, the whole body, the whole soul, shall be full of darkness. The eye is like a window into the tower of the soul. The light of God shines through that window, if clear, down inside that tower, lighting its inner gloom, leaving "no part dark" and "the whole shall be full of light." *L 11:36*

The Treasure of the Heart

Jesus spoke of the treasure of a man's heart:

MATTHEW	LUKE
A good man	A good man
out of	out of
the good treasure	the good treasure
of the heart	of his heart
bringeth forth	bringeth forth
good things;	that which is good;
and an evil man	and an evil man
out of	out of
the evil treasure	the evil treasure
	of his heart
bringeth forth	bringeth forth
evil things.	that which is evil:
Mt 12:35	
For out of	for of
the abundance	the abundance
of the heart	of the heart
the mouth	his mouth
speaketh.	speaketh.
Mt 12:34	*L 6:45*

Both Matthew and Luke place this saying about the "overflow" from the heart near Jesus' saying about good and corrupt trees, but the treasure of the heart sayings seem to stand alone, particularly in Matthew, who introduces the saying with the statement:

O generation of vipers, how can ye, being evil, speak good things?
For out of the abundance of the heart the mouth speaketh. *Mt 12:34*

The focus of Jesus here seems to be on the heart of man, not on the point that good produces good and evil produces evil. The heart is primary. Things are nurtured in the heart, and proceed from it, welling out in speech and actions.

WHAT COMETH FROM THE HEART DEFILETH A MAN

Some local Pharisees, along with some scribes who had come up to Galilee from Jerusalem, asked Jesus this question:

MARK	MATTHEW
Why walk not	Why do
thy disciples	thy disciples
according to	transgress
the tradition of the elders,	the tradition of the elders?
but eat bread	For they wash not thy hands
with unwashed hands?	when they eat bread.
Mk 7:5	*Mt 15:2*

In substance, the question was why Jesus' disciples did not, before eating, do the ritual washings prescribed by Jewish religious tradition. Mark explains this tradition as follows:

For the Pharisees, and all the Jews, except they wash their hands oft, eat not, holding the tradition of the elders. *Mk 7:3*

These ritual washings were required for religious, not hygienic reasons. The hand washing was part of the religious act of thanking God for the food that was to be eaten. This ritual had gotten extended, as rituals will, from the washing of hands to "the washing of cups, and pots, brasen vessels, and of tables." *Mk 7:4*

Jesus' reply to the question of the scribes and Pharisees about eating with unwashed hands was:

MARK	MATTHEW
For laying aside	Why do ye also transgress
the commandment of God,	the commandments of God
ye hold	
the tradition of men,	by your tradition?
as washing of pots and cups;	*Mt 15:3*
and many other such like things	
ye do.	
Mk 7:8	

The point for us is found in Jesus' explanation immediately made to the listening multitude:

MARK	MATTHEW
Hearken unto me	Hear, and understand:
every one of you,	
and understand:	
there is nothing	not that which
from without a man,	
that entering into him	goeth into the mouth
can defile him;	defileth a man;
but the things	but that
which come out of him,	which cometh out of the mouth,
those are they that	
defile the man.	this defileth a man.
	Mt 15:10–11
If any man	
have ears to hear,	
let him hear.	
Mk 7:14–16	

Later on, in a house away from the multitude, the disciples, through Peter, asked Jesus about his statement:

Declare unto us this parable. *Mt 15:15 (Mk 7:17)*

Jesus answered:

MARK	MATTHEW
Are ye so	Are ye also
without understanding also?	yet without understanding?
Do ye not perceive,	Do not ye yet understand,
that whatsoever thing	that whatsoever
from without	
entereth into the man,	entereth in at the mouth
it can not defile him,	
because it	
entereth not	

MARK (cont.)	MATTHEW (cont.)
into his heart,	
but into the belly,	goeth into the belly,
and goeth out	and is cast out
into the draught,	into the draught?
purging all meat?	

That which   *But these things which*
cometh out of the man,   *proceed out of the mouth*
                              come forth from the heart;
that defileth the man.   *and they defile the man.*
For from within,   *For*
out of the heart of men,   *out of the heart*
proceed evil thoughts,   proceed evil thoughts,
adulteries, fornications,   murders, adulteries,
murders, thefts,   fornications, thefts,
covetousness, deceit,   false witness,
lasciviousness,
an evil eye,
blasphemy,   blasphemies:
pride, foolishness:
all these evil things   *these are the things*
come from within,
and defile the man.   *which defile a man;*
Mk 7:18–23   but to eat
                          with unwashen hands
                          defileth not a man.
                          Mt 15:16–20

The King James Version of Mark lists "an evil eye" as one of the evil things coming out of a man which defile him. Witchcraft is not meant here, and modern translations consider "envy" a more accurate translation than the King James' "an evil eye."

Things taken by mouth can not defile a man because they "entereth not into his heart." *Mk 7:19* However, this implies that things taken by mouth can defile if they do enter into the heart, i.e., the mind of man.

Things that come out of a man, out of his mouth, from within, out of his heart, do defile a man. *Mk 7:20–21; Mt 15:18*. The heart referred to in the poetic, not the physiologic heart:

MARK	MATTHEW
For from within,	For
out of the heart of men,	out of the heart
proceed evil thoughts, . . .	proceed evil thoughts . . .
Mk 7:21	*Mt 15:19*

The evil that men do proceeds from their hearts where evil thoughts moulder. Evil actions, like murders and deceit, spring from evil thoughts. The evil things that men do are those that "come from within." *Mk 7:23* They defile a man.

Brother Anger

In the Sermon on the Mount Jesus said:

Ye have heard that it was said by them of old time, "Thou shalt not kill; and whosoever shall kill shall be in danger of the judgment;" but *I say* unto you, that whosoever is angry with his brother without a cause shall be in danger of the judgment; and whosoever shall say to his brother, "Raca" [a term of abuse], shall be in danger of the council; but whosoever shall say, "Thou fool," shall be in danger of hell fire. [Greek—Gehenna]

Therefore if thou bring thy gift to the altar, and there rememberest that thy brother hath ought [anything] against thee, leave there thy gift before the altar, and go thy way. First be reconciled to thy brother, and then come and offer thy gift. *Mt 5:21–24*

Modern translations omit the phrase "without a cause" after "angry with his brother." The reason for their omission is that certain of the manuscripts that they consider most reliable omit the phrase.

This passage is an example how Jesus restated the old Jewish law. Jesus' law was not concerned with overt acts only, but also with improper inner attitudes. Anger at a brother will invoke judgment; not just murder. Insulting and abusing a brother is punishable in Hell. Even a gift at an altar should not be offered until peace is first made with your brother.

A RUBRIC OF FORGIVENESS

Disciples want rules, not principles. Peter asked Jesus:

Lord, how oft shall my brother sin against me, and I forgive him? Till seven times? *Mt 18:21*

Jesus answered:

I say not unto thee, until seven times, but until seventy times seven. *Mt 18:22*

Luke quotes Jesus as laying down this rule of forgiveness:

Take heed to yourselves: if thy brother trespass against thee, rebuke him; and *if he repent*, forgive him. And if he trespass against thee seven times in a day, and seven times in a day turn again to thee, saying, "I repent," thou shalt forgive him. *L 17:3–4*

The condition of forgiveness is that the wrongdoer repent. Repentance is to be verbalized: The offender is to say, "I repent." Forgiveness is often assumed to be a one-way street: forgive the wrongdoer; but Jesus saw it a two-way street: the wrongdoer repents, and then you forgive.

Jesus also laid down a forgiveness procedure:

Moreover if thy brother shall trespass against thee, go and tell him his fault between thee and him alone; if he shall hear thee, thou hast gained thy brother. But if he will not hear thee, then take with thee one or two more, that the mouth of two or three witnesses every word may be established. And if he shall neglect to hear them, tell it unto the church; but if he neglects to hear the church, let him be unto thee as an heathen man and a publican. *Mt 18:15–17*

The statements in both Matthew and Luke refer to sins or trespasses by a "brother." It does not seem likely that the rules Jesus announced were meant to be restricted to some brotherhood relationship, whether of his disciples then or to Christians now. On the other hand, these statements are often construed as an outline of church grievance procedure. This seems wrong since Jesus' statements were not directed at organizational or power disputes, but to a brother *sinning* against another brother, which would seem to mean inflicting a wrong on a person as distinguished from organizational disputes over policy or personnel. In short, differences over policy or personnel are not sin.

LET A MAN EXAMINE HIMSELF

Both Matthew and Luke quote Jesus as requiring a person to examine himself before condemning others:

MATTHEW	LUKE
And why	And why
beholdest thou	beholdest thou
the mote	the mote
that is	that is
in thy brother's eye,	in thy brother's eye,
but considereth not	but perceivest not
the beam	the beam
that is	that is
in thine own eye?	in thine own eye?
Or how wilt	Either how canst
thou say	thou say
to thy brother,	to thy brother,
	"Brother,
"Let me	let me
pull out	pull out
the mote	the mote
	that is
out of thine eye,"	in thine eye,"
	when thou thyself
and, behold,	beholdest not
a beam is	the beam that is
in thine own eye?	in thine own eye?
Thou hypocrite,	Thou hypocrite,
first cast out	cast out first
the beam	the beam
out of thine own eye;	out of thine own eye,
and then shalt thou	and then shalt thou
see clearly	see clearly
to cast out	to pull out
the mote	the mote that
out of thy brother's eye.	is in thy brother's eye.
Mt 7:3–5	*L 6:41–42*

639

The beam (plank or board) in your own eye interferes with removing the speck in your brother's eye. This teaching is not unique to Jesus, but is often, in effect, made the heart of his message resulting in a sort of moral paralysis.

It is part of Jesus' message, but it does not imply as is often assumed that Christians can not say anything or take any action until they themselves are impeccable. All Jesus says is, first allow for your own sin and limitations and then proceed.

Jesus charged his seventy disciples to proclaim that the Kingdom of God was near to certain cities and he told them not to be self-effacing about it:

> But into whatsoever city ye enter, and they receive you not, go your ways out into the streets of the same, and say, "Even the very dust of your city, which cleaveth on us, we do wipe off against you; notwithstanding be ye sure of this, that the Kingdom of God is come nigh unto you." L 10:10–11

Shaking off the dust was a solemn condemnation, done in the spirit of, Thus says the Lord.

Once Christians have allowed for the plank in their own eyes, Christians must proceed. For example, Jesus said:

> Take heed to yourselves: if thy brother trespass against thee, rebuke him; and if he repent, forgive him. L 17:3

Popular Christianity emphasizes the instruction, "forgive him," although often ignoring the condition "if he repent." But in the same sentence, Jesus clearly taught the duty to rebuke a brother if he has trespassed against you.

After allowing for any plank in his own eye so he sees clearly (every case has two sides), the Christian must proceed as the circumstances require, condemn the people of a city, or rebuke a brother.

The Spiritual Law of Reciprocity:
Judge Not, Receive Much

Everyone knows Jesus' statement that, "Blessed are the merciful: for they shall obtain mercy." Mt 5:7 This is a simple example of Jesus' doctrine that the spiritual universe is curved, reflecting back upon your own actions. In short, there is a spiritual law of reciprocity.

That law is the background for the Golden Rule:

Matthew	Luke
"Therefore all things whatsoever	"And as
ye would that men	ye would that men
should do to you,	should do to you,
do ye even so to them . . ."	do ye also to them likewise."
Mt 7:12	L 6:31

Jesus gave three cases illustrating this law of reciprocity: judging, forgiving and giving. Matthew and Luke have parallel passages as to judging:

Matthew	Luke
Judge not,	Judge not,
that ye	and ye shall
be not judged.	not be judged;
Mt 7:1	condemn not,
	and ye shall
	not be condemned.
	L 6:37

Matthew alone states the standard of judgment: "For with what judgment ye judge, ye shall be judged . . ." Mt 7:2

The second case illustrating the spiritual law of reciprocity is forgiving:

Mark	Matthew
"And when	"For
ye stand praying,	if ye

MARK (cont.)	MATTHEW (cont.)
forgive,	forgive men
if ye have	their tresspasses
ought against any;	
that your Father also	your Heavenly Father
which is in Heaven	
may forgive you	will also forgive you.
your trespasses.	
But if ye	But if ye
do not forgive,	forgive not men
	their tresspasses
neither will	neither will
your Father	your father
which is in Heaven	
forgive	forgive
your tresspasses."	your tresspasses."
Mk 11:25–26	*Mt 6:14–15*

Luke is more succinct than the other two gospels:

Forgive, and ye shall be forgiven. *L 6:37*

In both Matthew's and Luke's versions of the Lord's Prayer, the same requirement of reciprocity as to forgiveness is stated:

MATTHEW	LUKE
And forgive us	And forgive us
our debts	our sins,
as we forgive	for we also forgive
our	every one
debtors.	that is indebted to us.
Mt 6:12	*L 11:4*

The third case illustrating the spiritual law of reciprocity is giving:

Give and it shall be given unto you; . . . *L 6:38*

This echoes a saying of Jesus not found in the Gospels but only in Acts when Paul is quoted as saying:

> Remember the words of the Lord Jesus, how he said: It is more blessed to give than to receive. *Acts 20:35*

The spiritual law of reciprocity provides that the gift you give is the measure of what is returned to you:

MARK	MATTHEW	LUKE
With what measure ye mete,	With what measure ye mete,	For with the same measure that ye mete withal
it shall be measured to you. *Mk 4:24*	it shall be measured to you again. *Mt 7:2*	it shall be measured to you again. *L 6:38*

This principle is not restricted by Jesus to giving, but it does particularly apply to giving. Indeed, Luke quotes Jesus as saying just before the measure for measure statement:

> Give and it shall be given unto you: good measure, pressed down, and shaken together, and running over, shall men give into your bosom [lap]. *L 6:38*

It is not just measure for measure, but a generous deal: "Full measure, pressed down, and shaken together, and running over." The final phrase "shall men give into your bosom" is obscure, but placing it in the context of its time and place is enlightening. A man's loose-fitting robe-like garment was used to carry grain by folding the garment up against the upper body to make a pocket.

According to Jesus the spiritual universe is so constructed that a person's attitude and actions as to others deflects back at him, in what he, in turn, receives, whether it is giving, forgiving, judging or mercy. It may even be magnified.

Love Your Enemies: Love Is Not a Business Transaction

Matthew and Luke have parallel accounts of Jesus' teaching on loving your enemies:

MATTHEW	LUKE
You have heard that it hath been said, "Thou shalt love thy neighbor, and hate thine enemy."	
But I say unto you,	But I say unto you which hear,
love your enemies, bless them that curse you, do good to them that hate you,	love your enemies, do good to them which hate you, bless them that curse you,
and pray for them which despitefully use you,	and pray for them which despitefully use you. *L 6:27–28*
and persecute you;	
	But love ye your enemies and do good, and lend, hoping for nothing again; and your reward shall be great,
That ye may be the children of your Father which is in Heaven: for he maketh his sun to rise on the evil and on the good, and sendeth rain on the just and on the unjust.	and ye shall be the children of the Highest: for he is kind unto the unthankful and to the evil. *L 6:35*

MATTHEW (cont.)
For if ye love them
which love you,
what reward have ye?

LUKE (cont.)
For if ye love them
which love you,
what thank have ye?

For sinners also love
those that love them.

And if ye do good
to them which do good to you,
what thank have you?

Do not even the publicans
the same?   .

For sinners also do
even the same.

And if ye salute
your brethren only,
what do ye more than
the others?
Do not even the publicans so?

And if ye lend to them
of whom ye hope to receive,
what thank have ye?

For sinners also lend to sinners,
to receive as much again.
L 6:32–34

Be ye therefore perfect,
even as your Father
which is in Heaven
is perfect.
Mt 5:43–48

Be ye therefore merciful
as your Father

also is merciful.
L 6:36

The familiar words of Jesus—love your enemies, do good to them that hate you, pray for them that despitefully use you—lead to a reward: status as children of the Heavenly Father. The reason is that God the Father acts impartially and compassionately to all men, both the evil and the good; if you do likewise you will truly be a child of God the Father.

As Jesus saw it, love that expects a return has no moral value. It is simply a business transaction: you help me and I will reward you. We are to aspire to a higher standard like the Heavenly Father's mercy and provision for all men, whether or not they can or will reciprocate.

The traditional Jewish rule was:

Thou shalt not avenge, nor bear any grudge against the children of thy people, but thou shalt love thy neighbor as thyself: I am the Lord. *Leviticus 19:18*

Jesus summarized that rule as:

Thou shalt love thy neighbor, . . . *Mt 5:43*

Jesus' restatement of that rule was:

Love your enemies, . . . *Mt 5:44; L 6:27, 35*

The difference is that Jesus extended the rule of love from just your neighbors, the children of your people, to your enemies.

Giving: The Golden Rule

Jesus taught:

Matthew	Luke
Give to him	Give to every man
that asketh thee,	that asketh of thee;
and from him	and of him
that would borrow of thee,	that taketh away thy goods
turn not thou away.	ask them not again.
Mt 5:42	
Therefore all things whatsoever	And as
ye would	ye would
that men should do to you,	that men shall do to you,
do ye	do ye
even so to them:	also to them likewise.
for this is the Law	L 6:30–31
and the Prophets.	
Mt 7:12	

Both Matthew and Luke agree that Jesus taught that you should give to those who ask. Luke's statement of the Golden Rule immediately follows a statement about non-resistance to theft and the taking of property:

And him that taketh away thy cloak forbid not to take thy coat also. Give to every man that asketh of thee; and of him that taketh away thy goods ask them not again.

And *as ye would that men should do to you, do ye also to them likewise.*

For if ye love them which love you, what thank have ye? L 6:29–31

The Golden Rule looks back to Jesus' teaching about non-resistance as to theft and forward to Jesus' teaching that love to have moral value must be to those who do not love you.

THE WIDOW'S MITES

In the week of his Passion in Jerusalem, Jesus was sitting in the Temple near its treasury, as was his practice, and saw many depositing gifts. Some were rich men and cast in much. *Mk 12:41; L 21:1; J 8:20* Jesus then noticed a poor widow drop in two mites, tiny copper coins. *Mk 12:42; L 21:2*

Jesus called his disciples and said:

MARK	LUKE
Verily I say unto you,	Of a truth I say unto you,
that this poor widow	that this poor widow
hath cast more in,	hath cast in more
than all they which have cast	than they all:
into the treasury:	
for all they did cast in	for all these have
of their abundance;	of their abundance cast in
	unto the offerings of God;
but she of her want	but she of her penury
did cast in all that she had,	hath cast in all the living
even all her living.	that she had.
Mk 12:43–44	*L 21:3–4*

God's measure is not man's measure. The mites were the widow's food money, but she gave them. The gifts of the rich, though acceptable, did not appreciably deplete their abundant funds. Obviously, the widow's gift was proportionately enormously greater.

THE PARABLE OF THE FRAUDULENT STEWARD

The first part of the chapter 16 of Luke has a puzzling parable of Jesus that is stated as follows:

There was a certain rich man, which had a steward; and the same was accused unto him that he had wasted his goods.

And he called him, and said unto him:

"How is it that I hear this of thee? Give an account of thy stewardship: for thou mayest be no longer steward."

Then the steward said within himself:

"What shall I do? For my lord taketh away from me the stewardship. I cannot dig; to beg I am ashamed. I am resolved what to do, that, when I am put out of the stewardship, they may receive me into their houses."
So he called every one of his lord's debtors unto him, and said unto the first, "How much owest thou unto my lord?"

And he said, "An hundred measures of oil."

And he said unto him "Take thy bill, and sit down quickly, and write fifty."

Then said he to another, "And how much owest thou?"

And he said, "An hundred measures of wheat."

And he said unto him, "Take thy bill, and write fourscore."

And the lord commended the unjust steward because he had done wisely: for the children of this world are in their generation wiser than the children of light.

And I say unto you, Make to yourselves friends of the mammon of unrighteousness, that, when ye fail, they may receive you into everlasting habitations. *L 16:1–9*

In interpreting a parable, the rule is that its details are not to be pressed. A parable is a story told to make a point. What was the point Jesus wanted to make here?

First let us extract the essential facts in the story background. "A certain rich man", that is, an employer, learned that "a steward", that is, a key employee, "had wasted his goods", that is, mismanaged the employer's property. *L 16:1* The rich man called in the steward and told him he was terminated and demanded an account of his stewardship. *L 16:2* The steward panicked, thinking:

> What shall I do? For my lord taketh away from me the stewardship.
> I cannot dig; to beg I am ashamed. *L 16:3–4*

In short, he was physically unable to become a laborer, and he was too proud to become a beggar. So he decided to provide for his future by getting employment, or at least a place to live, from persons who owed the rich man money, and as Luke phrases it, "they may receive me into their houses." *L 16:4*

This was done by defrauding the rich man by soliciting his debtors to reduce the amounts owed by the debtors to him. The debtors would then pocket the difference but be obligated to take care of the steward, who would then make these debt writedowns effective by altering the accounts of the rich man to agree with the written down amounts.

The parable concludes:

> And the lord commended the unjust steward, because he had done wisely: . . . *L 16:8*

The lord commended the steward, not for his dishonesty, but for his cleverness in concocting the fraud. In contemporary English he said:

> You really know how to take care of number one.

Jesus then states the point of the parable for his disciples:

For the children of this world are in their generation wiser than the children of light. *L 16:8*

In short, the children of the world take better care of their own interests in the world of affairs than the children of light (his disciples) take care of their own interests in the spiritual world.

Jesus continues:

Make to yourselves *friends* of the mammon of unrighteousness, that, when ye fail, *they* may receive you into everlasting habitations . . . If therefore ye have not been faithful in the unrighteous mammon, who will commit to your trust the true riches? *L 16:9,11*

Verse 9 as we now have it, is, to say the least, obscure. It is clear from comparing verse 9 and verse 11 that "the mammon of unrighteousness" in verse 9 is the same as "the unrighteous mammon" in verse 11. *Mammon* is riches or worldly wealth, as in verse 13:

Ye cannot serve God and mammon. *L 16:13*

Some commentators think that in verse 9 Jesus was speaking of giving alms and thereby obtaining friends who intercede in Heaven. The difficulty is that Jesus did not say that.

If we take Jesus' words as they now stand in verse 9, it appears that he was speaking sardonically, saying,

Go ahead and make "friends" of unrighteous riches, that when ye fail [die], these "friends" will receive you into everlasting habitations [meaning that such "friends" don't control any "everlasting habitations"].

Here is why. Jesus taught that:

In my Father's house are many mansions: . . . I go to prepare a place for you. *J 14:2*

The word translated *mansions* can be translated as "dwellings" or "dwelling places." In Verse 9, Jesus spoke of "everlasting habitations." *L 16:9* Although the underlying Greek words are different, Jesus is probably referring to the same idea in both statements. In short, "everlasting habitations" is probably the same ideas as dwellings "in my Father's house."

Jesus' sardonic point in Verse 9 is that your mammon friends can't "receive you into the everlasting habitations", that is, into the dwelling places in my Father's house.

There is also, perhaps a subtle word play by Jesus on the story framework of the parable when he speaks of the mammon friends *receiving* "you into everlasting habitations" and the steward seeking to be *received* "into their houses." *L 16:4, 9*

Immediately after stating the point of the parable about mammon and everlasting habitations in Verse 9, Jesus continued with other points which allude to the parable but which are separate teachings.

The first point is that even mundane things like money are tests:

> He that is faithful in that which is least [money] is faithful also in much; and he that is unjust in the least [with money] is unjust also in much [the true riches]. *L 16:10*

In other parables Jesus stated the same principle more broadly as the way to spiritual rewards:

PARABLE OF THE TALENTS	PARABLE OF THE POUNDS
His lord said unto him,	And he said unto him,
"Well done, thou	"Well, thou
good and faithful servant.	good servant,
Thou hast	because thou hast
been faithful	been faithful
over a few things,	in a very little,
I will make thee	have thou
ruler over	authority over
many things.	ten cities."
Enter thou into	*L 19:17*
the joy of thy lord."	
Mt 25:21	

There is a sort of spiritual law of the inner consistency of a person that melds with another such law that those who are faithful in little things will be rewarded with larger things.

The second point Jesus made, alluding back to the parable, was this:

> If therefore [like the steward] ye have not been faithful in the unrighteous mammon, who will commit to your trust the true riches? *L 16:11*

If you can't even be honest in money matters, how can you handle "the true riches"?

There is a spiritual law of ordinary honesty. The condition of ordinary honesty in ordinary things is a prerequisite to being entrusted with true riches.

Jesus also asked:

> And if ye have not been faithful in that which is another man's [like the steward], who shall give you that which is your own [the true riches you aspire to]? *L 16:12*

Unfaithfulness in ordinary business matters raises questions about a person's spiritual qualifications.

These three points, faithfulness in handling matters for other persons, the consistency of a person's attitudes, and the relation of ordinary honesty to spirituality, all relate to the inescapable choice between God and mammon.

The point of the parable, however, is that the children of light should take as good care of their true riches as the children of the world take care of their worldly matters.

O Ye of Little Faith!

Both Matthew and Luke attest that Jesus referred to his disciples as, "O ye of little faith" when he explained why they should trust their heavenly Father for their daily needs:

Matthew	Luke
Wherefore, if God so	If then God so
clothe the grass of the field,	clothe the grass,
which today is,	which is today in the field,
and tomorrow is cast	and tomorrow is cast
into the oven,	into the oven,
shall he not much more	how much more will he
clothe you,	clothe you,
O ye of little faith?	O ye of little faith?
Mt 6:30	*L 12:28*

When Jesus' disciples had forgotten to take bread and he cryptically said, "Take heed and beware of the leaven of the Pharisees and of the Sadducees," they thought he was in some way referring to that forgotten bread. *Mt 16:6*

Jesus then said:

O ye of little faith, why reason ye among yourselves, because ye have brought no bread? *Mt 16:8*

He then reminded them of the miraculous feedings of the five thousand and the four thousand and said, "I spake it not to you concerning bread" but to beware of the doctrine of the Pharisees and Sadducees. *Mt 16:9–12*

With like language, Jesus rebuked his disciples for fear of a storm on the Sea of Galilee. The account is short. A great tempest arose and the waves were swamping the boat in which Jesus slept. *Mt 8:24* His disciples came and awoke him, saying, "Lord, save us: we perish." *Mt 8:25*

654

Jesus replied:

Why are ye fearful, O ye of little faith? *Mt 8:26*

Mark and Luke's accounts vary slightly and quote Jesus as saying to his disciples after he got the wind to stop:

MARK	LUKE
Why are ye so fearful?	
How is it that	
ye have no faith?	Where is your faith?
Mk 4:40	*L 8:25*

Finally Jesus said about the same thing to Peter in like circumstances. Peter attempted to walk on the water to Jesus. Matthew
writes:

But when he saw the wind boisterous, he was afraid, and beginning
to sink, he cried, saying, "Lord, save me."

And immediately Jesus stretched forth his hand, and caught him,
and said unto him, "O thou of little faith, wherefore did thou doubt?"
Mt 14:30–31

Jesus' disciples were not super-Christians. Even in the presence of Jesus himself, day by day he had to rebuke them, including
Simon Peter individually, as men of little faith.

They, on one occasion, asked Jesus to remedy their lack of faith.
According to Luke they said to Jesus, "Increase our faith." *L 17:5*
Jesus replied:

If ye had faith as a grain of mustard seed, ye might say unto this
sycamine tree, "Be thou plucked up by the root, and be thou planted
in the sea"; and it should obey you. *L 17:6*

Jesus taught "mustard-seed" faith to his disciples then, and that
is still his teaching to his disciples now. As with any teacher teach-

ing orally at various times and places, the wording of his metaphors varied, but his theme of faith did not. Scholars find it fascinating to argue the variety of Jesus' wordings, but the focus should be on the faith he taught:

MARK	MATTHEW	MATTHEW	LUKE
	If ye	If ye	If ye
Have faith	*have faith,*	*Have faith*	*had faith*
in God.	*and doubt not,*	*as a grain of*	*as a grain of*
	ye shall	*mustard seed,*	*mustard seed,*
	not only		
For verily	do this		
I say	which is done		
unto you,	to the fig tree,		
that whosoever	but also if ye	ye	ye
shall say unto	shall say unto	shall say unto	might say unto
this	this	this	this
mountain	mountain,	mountain,	sycamine tree,
"Be thou	"Be thou	"Remove	"Be thou
removed,	removed,	hence	plucked up
			by the root,
and be thou	and be thou		and be thou
cast into	cast into	to	planted in
the sea";	the sea";	yonder place";	the sea";
and shall not		and it	and it
doubt in		shall remove	should obey
his heart,			
but shall			
believe			
that			
those things	it		
which he saith			
shall come	shall be done.		
to pass;	*Mt 21:21*		
he shall have		and nothing	
whatsoever		shall be	
		impossible	
he saith.		unto you.	you.
Mk 11:22–23		*Mt 17:20*	*L 17:6*

Jesus predicted these results from "mustard-seed" faith:

MARK	MATTHEW
Therefore	
I say unto you,	And all things,
what things soever	whatsoever
ye desire,	ye ask
when ye pray	*in prayer*,
believe that	believing,
ye receive them,	
and	
ye shall have them.	ye shall receive
Mk 11:24	*Mt 21:22*

JESUS ON ANXIETY

Matthew and Luke quote Jesus on anxiety as follows:

MATTHEW	LUKE
Therefore I say unto you,	Therefore I say unto you,
take no thought	take no thought
for your life,	for your life,
what ye shall eat,	what ye shall eat;
or what ye shall drink;	
nor yet for your body,	neither for the body,
what ye shall put on.	what ye shall put on.
It is not the life more	The life is more
than meat, and	than meat, and
the body more than raiment?	the body is more than raiment.
Behold the fowls of the air:	Consider the ravens:
for they sow not,	for they neither sow
neither do they reap,	nor reap,
	which neither have
nor gather into barns;	storehouse nor barn;
yet your heavenly Father	and God
feedeth them.	feedeth them.
Are ye not much	How much more are ye
better than they?	better than the fowls?
Which of you	And which of you
by taking thought	with taking thought
can add	can add to
one cubit unto his stature?	his stature one cubit?

[A cubit is the length of a forearm]

MATTHEW	LUKE
And why take ye thought	If ye then are not able
for raiment?	to do that thing
	which is least,

Matthew (cont.)	Luke (cont.)
	why take ye thought
	for the rest?
Consider the lilies	Consider the lilies,
of the field,	
how they grow:	how they grow:
they toil not,	they toil not,
neither do they spin;	they spin not;
and yet I say unto you,	and yet I say unto you,
that even Solomon	that Solomon
in all his glory	in all his glory
was not arrayed	was not arrayed
like one of these.	like one of these.
Wherefore, if	If then
God so clothe	God so clothe
the grass of the field,	the grass,
which today is,	which is today in the field,
and tomorrow is	and tomorrow is
cast into the oven,	cast into the oven,
shall he not	how
much more clothe you,	much more will he clothe you,
O ye of little faith?	*O ye of little faith?*
Therefore take no	And
thought, saying,	seek not ye
"What shall we eat?"	what ye shall eat,
or, "What shall we drink?"	or what ye shall drink,
or, "Wherewithal shall we	
be clothed?"	
	neither be ye of doubtful mind.
For after all these things	For all these things
do the Gentiles seek:	do the nations of the world seek
	after,
for your heavenly Father	and your Father
knoweth that ye have need	knoweth that ye have need
of all these things.	of these things.

MATTHEW (cont.)

But seek ye first
the Kingdom of God
and his righteousness;
and all these things
shall be added unto you.
Take therefore no thought
for the morrow:
for the morrow
shall take thought
for the things of itself.
Sufficient unto the day
is the evil thereof.
Mt 6:25–34

LUKE (cont.)

But rather seek ye
the Kingdom of God,

and all these things
shall be added unto you.
L 12:22–31

We are all part of God's world: if he feeds the birds and clothes the flowers, why will he not feed and clothe us too?

It is not that we do not need to be fed and clothed. Our Father in heaven knows we do. Men who do not first seek God's Kingdom spend their time and lives, worried and anxious, seeking these things. These things are, of course, necessary, but they will be added, Jesus assures us, to those who seek first God's Kingdom.

The quotations from both Matthew and Luke about the anxiety for things each begin with the word, "Therefore." *Mt 6:25; L 12:22* The gospel accounts preceding the word, "Therefore" differ, but both accounts deal with riches.

In Matthew, Jesus had just said:

Ye cannot serve God and mammon. Therefore . . . *Mt 6:24*

In Luke, Jesus had just told a parable about "a certain rich man" who was always building bigger barns for his ever bigger crops and the parable concludes:

So is he that layeth up treasure for himself, and is not rich toward God. Therefore . . . *L 12:21*

Some modern translations of Matthew render *mammon* as simply money. Mt 6:24 The parable in Luke expressly refers to laying up "treasure" for one's self. L 12:21 In another place, Jesus once spoke of "the cares of this world, and the deceitfulness of riches." Mk 4:19

When Jesus spoke out against anxiety for things, even essential things such as food and drink, he wanted to give peace from anxiety by prescribing reliance upon God's provision. He used, as examples of God's provision, the facts that wildflowers grow without neuroses to stunning beauty and that the birds are fed without their having to plant crops.

His point was that anxiety rejected God's plan, His provision. Furthermore, it is all so futile. Your anxiety will not add an hour to your life, nor an inch to your height. Jesus taught: Do not be obsessed with your daily needs; they will be provided by your heavenly Father as you seek His Kingdom and His righteousness. Day by day, out of his abundance, the Father will provide your needs.

Jesus was once the dinner guest of a woman named Martha. Her sister, Mary, sat and listened to Jesus teach, leaving it to Martha to get the dinner ready.

With acerbity, Martha asked Jesus:

Lord, dost thou not care that my sister hath left me to serve alone? Bid her therefore that she help me. L 10:40

Jesus answered:

Martha, Martha, thou art *careful and troubled* about many things, but one thing is needful; and Mary hath chosen that good part, which shall not be taken away from her. L 10:41–42

Careful is archaic for "full of care." Translations vary as to how to render "careful and troubled": worried, anxious, upset, troubled, bothered. The cares of a hostess should yield to a chance to hear Jesus teach; just as the cares for food and clothing should yield to the quest for the Kingdom of God.

One of Jesus' most famous sayings teaches that God has concern for each person, since not even one sparrow is "forgotten before God":

MATTHEW	LUKE
Are not two sparrows	Are not five sparrows
sold for a farthing?	sold for two farthings,
and one of them	and not one of them
shall not fall on	is forgotten
the ground	
without your Father.	before God?
But the very hairs	But even the very hairs
on your head	on your head
are all numbered.	are all numbered.
Fear ye not therefore,	Fear not therefore,
ye are to more value	ye are of more value
than many sparrows.	than many sparrows.
Mt 10:29–31	*L 12:6–7*

Jesus' teaching is clear that "the very hairs on your head are all numbered"; but his followers now, as his disciples then, do not remember his words, or the numbers on their hairs.

Jesus taught that a sparrow "shall not fall on the ground without your Father", why were a boat-load of his disciples on the Sea of Galilee afraid when a sudden squall was swamping their boat?

Here is what happened:

	MARK	MATTHEW	LUKE
Disciple:	Master, carest thou not that we perish?	Lord, save us; we perish.	Master, master, we perish.
Jesus:	Peace, be still. . . Why are ye so fearful? How is it that ye have *no faith?* *Mk 4:38–40*	Why are ye fearful, O ye of *little faith?* *Mt 8:25–26*	Where is *your faith?* *L 8:24–25*

These disciples had had the benefit of day-to-day association with Jesus, yet in the crunch there was only fear verging on panic. That fear was inconsistent with the faith in the hair-numbering Father that Jesus taught:

Why are ye so fearful? How is it that ye have no faith? *Mk 4:40*

Faith is not only inconsistent with fear, it is the antithesis of doubt. Peter was a key disciple, yet in the crunch he doubted Jesus' power. The scene is again a boat on the Sea of Galilee. Again the wind came up, but Jesus was not present, and appeared like an apparition, walking on the sea. The interchange went like this:

JESUS: Be of good cheer; it is I; be not afraid.
PETER: Lord, if it be thou, bid me come unto thee on the water.
JESUS: Come.
[Peter got out of the boat and walked on the water toward Jesus, "but when he saw the wind boisterous, he was afraid; and beginning to sink" cried out.]
PETER: Lord, save me.
[Jesus reached for Peter and caught him.]
JESUS: O thou of little faith, wherefore didst thou doubt? *Mt 14:27–31*

Despite the benefit of years of close association, Peter doubted Jesus' command, "Come." *Mt 14:29* So far as Jesus was concerned, Peter doubted. Contrary to current psychology Jesus then belittled Peter, calling him, "O thou of little faith."

It was not just Peter Jesus belittled. He had belittled the disciples, saying, "O ye of little faith," when they feared drowning in their swamping boat. *Mt 8:26* He belittled the disciples on another occasion when they squabbled among themselves over what Jesus had meant when he had said to beware "of the leaven of the Pharisees and of the Sadducees", supposing he was referring to the fact that they had forgotten to bring more than one loaf of bread:

MARK	MATTHEW
	O ye of little faith,
Why reason ye,	why reason ye
because ye	among yourselves, because ye
have no bread?	have brought no bread?
Perceive ye not yet,	Do ye not yet
neither understand?	understand.
Have ye your heart yet	
hardened?	
Having eyes, see ye not?	
And having ears, hear ye not?	
And do ye not remember?	neither remember
When I brake the five loaves	the five loaves
among five thousand,	of the five thousand,
how many baskets	and how many baskets
full of fragments	
took ye up?	ye took up?
[They said, "Twelve"]	
And when the seven	Neither the seven loaves
among four thousand,	of the four thousand,
how many baskets	and how many baskets
full of fragments	
took ye up?	ye took up?
[They said, "Seven"]	
How is it that ye	How is it that ye
do not understand?	do not understand
Mk 8:17–21	that I spake it not
	to you concerning bread,
	[but] that ye should
	beware of the leaven of
	the Pharisees and of the
	Sadducees?
	Mt 16:8–11

On four occasions Jesus called his disciples men "of little faith." *Mt 6:30; L 12:28; Mt 8:26, 14:31, 16:8* Today men of little faith doubt Jesus' report of the concern of the hair-numbering Father for his human children. Men "of little faith" fear the sudden squall, doubt the power of God over the wind and the waves, forget the lessons of God's bounty, and as individuals and nations demand to know how and when they shall eat, drink, and be clothed.

This is blasphemy.

The gospel is:

But seek ye first the Kingdom of God, and his righteousness; and all these things shall be added unto you. *Mt 6:33*

The epistle is:

Be careful for nothing; but in every thing by prayer and supplication with thanksgiving let your requests be known unto God.

And the peace of God, which passeth all understanding, shall keep your hearts and minds through Christ Jesus. *Philippians 4:6–7*

CHAPTER 11

SOCIAL TOPICS

JESUS AND THE FAMILY

The church of Jesus Christ is strongly identified with the family as the key social institution. Jesus, himself, recognized that his teachings would split families. And they still do.

Jesus said:

MATTHEW	LUKE
Think not that I am come to send peace on earth.	Suppose ye that I am come to give peace on earth?
I came not to send peace, but a sword.	I tell you, "Nay"; but rather division:
For I come to set	for from henceforth there shall be five in one house divided, three against two, and two against three. The father shall be divided against the son,
a man at variance against his father, and	and the son against the father; the mother against the daughter, and
the daughter against her mother, and	the daughter against the mother; the mother-in-law against

Matthew (cont.)	Luke (cont.)
	her daughter-in-law, and
the daughter-in-law against	the daughter-in-law against
her mother-in-law.	her mother-in-law.
And a man's foes shall be they	L 12:51–53
of his own household."	
Mt 10:34–36 (Micah 7:6)	

The split in households will go as far as betrayal. Luke quotes Jesus as saying:

> And ye shall be betrayed both by *parents*, and *brethren*, and *kinsfolks* and friends; and some of you shall they cause to be put to death.
> L 21:16

The other synoptic gospels quote Jesus as saying:

Mark	Matthew
Now the brother	And the brother shall deliver up
shall betray the brother	the brother
to death,	to death,
and the father the son;	and the father the child;
and children shall rise up	and the children shall rise up
against their parents,	against their parents,
and shall cause them	and cause them
to be put to death.	to be put to death.
Mk 13:12	Mt 10:21

Both Mark and Luke have these betrayal sayings in Jesus discourse concerning the end times. Matthew has this saying in Jesus' charge to the Twelve, in which he also states that he came "not to send peace, but a sword" and that "a man's foes shall be they of his own household." Mt 10:34,36

That charge continued (with Luke's parallel) as follows:

Matthew	Luke
He that	If any man come to me,
loveth father	and hate not his father,

MATTHEW (cont.)	LUKE (cont.)
or mother	and mother,
more than me	and wife,
is not worthy of me;	
and he that loveth	
son or daughter	and children,
	and brethren, and sisters,
more than me	yea, and his own life also,
is not worthy	he cannot be
of me.	my disciple.
And he that	And whosoever
taketh not his cross,	doth not bear his cross,
and followeth after me,	and come after me,
is not worthy of me.	cannot be my disciple.
Mt 10:37–38	*L 14:26–27*

Neither Matthew nor Luke have these sayings in an apocalyptic context. It was meant by Jesus to be the stuff of ordinary Christian life.

Matthew's version is gentler than Luke's: his report is cast in terms of "worthiness", not in terms of rhetorical exaggeration of "hate." Both end on the same note, however: each disciple must take his own cross and follow Jesus.

This can not wait for family matters, not even to bury your father:

MATTHEW	LUKE
	And he said unto another,
	"Follow me."
And another of his disciples	
said unto him,	But he said,
"Lord, suffer me	"Lord, suffer me
first to go and	first to go and
bury my father."	bury my father."
But Jesus said unto him:	But Jesus said unto him,
"Follow me; and	

MATTHEW (cont.)	LUKE (cont.)
let the dead	"Let the dead
bury their dead."	bury their dead:
Mt 8:21–22	but go thou and preach
	the Kingdom of God."
	L 9:59–60

The urgency of following Jesus did not even allow time to say farewell to those at home:

And another also said, "Lord, I will follow thee; but let me first go bid them farewell, which are at home at my house."

And Jesus said unto him, "No man, having put his hand to the plough, and looking back, is fit for the Kingdom of God." L 9:61–62

Jesus' emphasis was not on the ties of family and kin but on the primacy of spiritual life. Another incident reported in all three synoptic gospels also makes this point:

MARK	MATTHEW	LUKE
There came then	While he yet talked to the people, behold,	Then came to him
his brethren and his mother, and,	his mother and his brethren	his mother and his brethren, and could not come at him for the press.
standing without, sent unto him, calling him.	stood without, desiring to speak with him.	
And the multitude sat about him, and they said unto him,	Then	And it was
	one said unto him,	told him by certain which said,
"Behold, thy mother and thy brethren without	"Behold, thy mother and thy brethren stand without,	"Thy mother and thy brethren stand without

670

MARK (cont.)	MATTHEW (cont.)	LUKE (cont.)
	desiring	desiring
seek for thee."	to speak with thee."	to see thee."
And he answered them saying,	But he answered and said unto him that told him,	And he answered and said unto them,
"Who is my mother,	"Who is my mother, and who	
or my brethren?"	are my brethren?"	
And he looked round about on them which sat about him, and said,	And he stretched forth his hand towards his disciples, and said,	
"Behold my mother and my brethren!	"Behold my mother and my brethren!	"My mother and my brethren are these which hear the word of God,
For whosoever shall do the will of God,	For whosoever shall do the will of my Father which is in heaven,	and do it." *L 8:19-21*
the same is my brother, and my sister, and mother." *Mk 3:31–35*	the same is my brother, and sister, and mother." *Mt 12:46–50*	

Jesus made his point with rhetorical exaggeration. He did not mean that he had severed his ties to his family; he did mean that doing the will of God is supremely important.

Another incident reported by Luke illustrates this point:

And it came to pass, as he spake these things, a certain woman of the company lifted up her voice, and said unto him, "Blessed is the womb that bare thee, and the paps which thou hast sucked."

But he said, "Yea rather, blessed are they that hear the word of God, and keep it." *L 11:27–28*

Jesus' point was not belittlement of his biological debt to his mother. His point again was: do the will of God.

Jesus did recognize his debt to his mother. Probably millions of sermons have made this point, citing in support of it Jesus' words from his cross when he remembered his mother and said:

When Jesus therefore saw his mother, and the disciple standing by, whom he loved, he saith unto his mother, "Woman, behold thy son!"

Then saith he to the disciple, "Behold thy mother!"

And from that hour that disciple took her unto his own home. *J 19:26–27*

Jesus' family ties were close. His mother was at his cross. *J 19:25* He provided for her, but he also taught that no one can be his disciple unless he or she understands that the truly blessed are those who hear the word of God and keep it.

Jesus and Women

It is well known and generally believed that Jesus was favorable to women, and that he, in fact, opened a new era for them. Jesus' statements and actions support this proposition.

We begin with the story of the woman taken in adultery. The scribes and Pharisees brought Jesus a woman taken in adultery, "in the very act." *J 8:4* The accusers then asked him an entrapping question:

> Now Moses in the Law commanded us, that such should be stoned; but what sayest thou? *J 8:5*

Jesus' classic reply was:

> He that is without sin among you, let him first cast a stone at her. *J 8:7*

Jesus then stooped down and wrote on the ground; and the accusers, beginning with the eldest, melted away, leaving Jesus still stooped and the woman still standing. Jesus stood up, and seeing no one but the woman, said:

> Woman, where are those thine accusers? Hath no man condemned thee? *J 8:10*

She answered:

> No man, Lord. *J 8:11*

Jesus replied:

> Neither do I condemn thee; go, and sin no more. *J 8:11*

Adultery was a capital offense under the Mosaic Law. *Leviticus 20:10; Deuteronomy 22:22* It was more than an offense; it was a grave sin. *Leviticus 18:20* Jesus recognized the woman's adultery as *sin* since he told her, "go, and sin no more."

The story about this woman is not really about women, or their place; it is a parable about condemning the sin of other persons, male or female.

So far as adultery was concerned, Jesus did recognize the same standard for both men and women. He told his disciples:

> Whosoever shall put away his wife, and marry another, committeth adultery against her. And if a woman shall put away her husband, and be married to another, she committeth adultery. *Mk 10:11–12*

Jesus did have an exalted and nonlegalistic attitude toward adultery:

> But I say unto you, that whosoever looketh on a woman to lust after her hath committed adultery with her already in his heart. *Mt 5:28*

But again Jesus' lesson was not so much on adultery, male or female, as on the heart sources of sin.

Jesus was even handed in his treatment of men and women. He resuscitated the only daughter of a male ruler. *Mk 5:22–24, 35–43; Mt 9:18–19, 23–26; L 8:41–42, 49–56* He resuscitated the only son of a widow. *L 7:11–17*

He healed a man with a withered hand on a Sabbath in a synagogue. *Mk 3:1–6; Mt 12:9–14; L 6:6–11* He healed a woman bent double eighteen years on a Sabbath in a synagogue. *L 13:10–16* He considered and said she was "a daughter of Abraham", just as he considered and said that Zacchaeus the tax collector was "a son of Abraham." *L 13:16, 19:9*

In the case of the woman, Jesus ended his argument with the synagogue president by asking him:

> And ought not this woman, being a daughter of Abraham, whom Satan hath bound, lo, these eighteen years, be loosed from this bond on the Sabbath day? *L 13:16*

Even though she was a woman, she was part of the family of Abraham and, as such, entitled to equal consideration as a family member.

Jesus recognized that women may have faith. A case in point is the woman who "had an issue of blood twelve years", had doctored to no avail, but in her simple way said, "If I may touch but his clothes, I shall be whole." *Mk 5:25–28 (Mt 9:20–21; L 8:43–44)* Jesus felt the touch and looked around. *Mk 5:30–32* The woman, "fearing and trembling", fell down before him and told her story, and how the touch had healed her. *Mk 5:33* Jesus then said:

Daughter, thy faith hath made thee whole; go in peace, and be whole of thy plague. *Mk 5:34 (Mt 9:22; L 8:48)*

An immoral woman brought an alabaster box of ointment to Jesus as he dined in a Pharisee's house. *L 7:37* She "stood at his feet behind him weeping, and began to wash his feet, and did wipe them with the hairs of her head, and kissed his feet and anointed them with the ointment." *L 7:38* Simon, the Pharisee host, fumed inwardly, "This man, if he were a prophet, would have known who and what manner of woman this is that toucheth him: for she is a sinner." *L 7:39*

Jesus did know what kind of woman she was, and that her sins were many. *L 7:47* After he had told a parable, he turned to the woman and said to Simon:

Seest thou this woman: I entered into thine house, thou gavest me no water for my feet; and she hath washed my feet with tears, and wiped them with the hairs of her head.

Thou gavest me no kiss, but this woman since the time I came in hath not ceased to kiss my feet. My head with oil thou didst not anoint, but this woman hath anointed my feet with ointment.

Wherefore I say unto thee, *her sins, which are many*, are forgiven: *for she loved much*; but to whom little is forgiven, the same loveth little. *L 7:44–47*

675

To the woman Jesus said:

Thy sins are forgiven . . . Thy faith hath saved thee; go in peace.
L 7:48, 50

Jesus was considerate of the weakness of this woman who, despite her many sins, "loved much"; but the point of the story is not Jesus' attitude toward a shunned woman. The point of the story is a paradigm of faith for everyone, male or female:

Your faith saves you. Your sins are forgiven. Therefore, go in peace.

Jesus said almost the same thing to a blind beggar man whom he healed that he had said to the shunned woman:

MARK	LUKE
Go thy way;	Receive thy sight;
thy faith	thy faith
hath made	hath saved
thee whole.	thee.
Mk 10:52	*L 18:42*

Jesus told a Samaritan man whom he had healed of leprosy:

Arise, go thy way; thy faith hath made thee whole. *L 17:19*

Just as he had told the shunned woman, "Thy sins are forgiven," he told a paralytic man who was lowered down from the rooftop in front of him:

MARK	MATTHEW	LUKE
Son,	Son,	Man,
	be of good cheer;	
thy sins	thy sins	thy sins
be forgiven	be forgiven	are forgiven
thee.	thee.	thee.
Mk 2:5	*Mt 9:2*	*L 5:20*

Jesus recognized that a woman's faith can be great. He told a Syrophoenician, a Gentile, woman whose daughter he had healed:

> O woman, great is thy faith; be it unto thee even as thou wilt.
> Mt 15:28

The story of Jesus' treatment of a Samaritan woman with deference and consideration is well known. Jesus was resting about noon at a well near Sychar, Samaria, while his disciples went into town to buy food. J 4:5–6 A local woman came to draw water. J 4:7 They had a conversation. J 4:7–26

The fact that they had a conversation at all astonished Jesus' disciples. J 4:27 She was, of course, a Samaritan, and as a woman herself remarked to Jesus, "How is it that you, being a Jew, askest drink of me, which am a woman of Samaria?" J 4:9 The hostility of Jews and Samaritans was notorious, and they had no dealings. J 4:9

More important for our purposes, she was a woman; and Jesus, as a Jewish religious teacher, would not usually even speak with a strange woman in a public place, especially this woman who, Jesus had somehow learned, had had five husbands. J 4:18

Despite her dubious marital status under the mores of that time and place (J 4:16–18), Jesus talked with her and gave her answers which have echoed down the centuries, like:

> God is a Spirit, and they that worship him must worship him in spirit and in truth. J 4:24

She, in turn, sensed that Jesus was even more than she had first thought, a prophet (J 4:19):

> Come, see a man which told me all things that ever I did. Is not this the Christ? J 4:29 (J 4:39)

It was not just a Samaritan woman who sensed Jesus' uniqueness. Once while dining in Bethany at the house of Simon the leper *(Mk 14:3; Mt 26:6)*, a woman lavished a gift upon Jesus:

MARK	MATTHEW
A woman [came] having	A woman [came] having
an alabaster box	an alabaster box
of ointment of spikenard	of very precious
very precious;	ointment,
and she brake the box,	
and poured it on his head.	and poured it on his head.
Mk 14:3	*Mt 26:7*

The ointment was expensive, being worth "more than three hundred pence." *Mk 14:5 (Mt 26:9)*

John's Gospel records a similar incident. Jesus was having supper in Bethany at the house of Mary and Martha:

> Then took Mary a pound of ointment of spikenard, very costly, and anointed the feet of Jesus, and wiped his feet with her hair: and the house was filled with the odor of the ointment. *J 12:3 (J 11:2)*

This is the Mary who, on another occasion, left Martha "to serve alone' while she "sat at Jesus' feet and heard his word." *L 10:39–40*

Jesus' theology did not distinguish between men and women. He taught:

MATTHEW	LUKE
Then shall two be	[Two men shall be
in the field;	in the field;
the one shall be taken	the one shall be taken,
and the other left.	and the other left.]*
Two women	Two women
shall be grinding	shall be grinding
at the mill;	together;
the one shall be taken,	the one shall be taken,
and the other left.	and the other left.
Mt 24:40–41	*L 17:35–36*
	* Conformed to
	Matthew's order

Jesus' even-handed theology was reflected in his ministry. When he fed the five thousand, he fed, according to Matthew, "five thousand men, *besides* women and children." *Mt 14:21* It was the same when he fed the four thousand, when, according to Matthew, it was "four thousand men, *beside* women and children." *Mt 15:38*

Women were not just passive feeders at Jesus' miracles; they were close to heart of his ministry, giving financial support and accompanying Jesus and his disciples about:

> And it came to pass afterward, that he went throughout every city and village, preaching and showing the glad tidings of the Kingdom of God; and the Twelve were with him, *and certain women, which had been healed of evil spirits and infirmities*, Mary called Magdalene, out of whom went seven devils, and Joanna, the wife of Chuza Herod's steward, and Susanna, *and many others, which ministered unto him of their substance. L 8:1–3*

In an age addicted to sensationalism, the focus in discussing Jesus' relation with women is on Mary Magdalene, out of whom he exorcised devils. *Mk 16:9; L 8:2* A fairer statement is that Jesus healed many women. This is not significant in considering his relationship to women since Jesus also healed many men.

What is more significant for Jesus' relation to women is that many women "ministered unto him of their substance." *L 8:3* Cutting through the archaic King James language, this means that they supported him financially.

We catch another glimpse of this support when Matthew and Mark describe the women present at the crucifixion and incidentally mention that some of these women had "ministered unto him." *Mk 15:41 (Mt 27:55)* We are not told what this ministry was, but it seems likely it was providing the food for Jesus and his disciples. See "Jesus' Organization Of His Movement", pp 396–398, for details.

Jesus chose all men for his Twelve and Seventy, but there were large numbers of women in his movement. The movement remembered the names of some of them, and the Gospel writers, all men, listed them. For example, at Jesus' cross the Gospels name at least three women, in addition to his mother. *Mk 15:40; Mt 27:56; J 19:25* At Jesus' tomb at least one additional woman is named. *Mk 16:1; Mt 28:1; L 24:10; J 20:1*

On Jesus' way to his cross, he was followed by "a *great company* of people, and *of women*, which also bewailed and lamented him." *L 23:27* Jesus even turned and addressed the women:

> Daughters of Jerusalem, weep not for me, but weep for yourselves, and for your children. *L 23:28*

Mark's account of the crucifixion mentions three women by name and then states that "many other women" were present who had also followed Jesus all the way from Galilee to Jerusalem. *Mk 15:41 (Mt 27:55; L 23:49)* The two disciples who were returning to Emmaus after the crucifixion refer to "certain women also *of our company.*" *L 24:22*

Two women, Mary Magdalene and Mary, the mother of Joses, had the courage and determination to watch Jesus' burial. *Mk 15:47; Mt 27:61* A short time later, some unnamed women followers from Galilee "Beheld the sepulchre, and how his body was laid." *L 23:55* They then went to prepare spices and ointments to apply to Jesus' body but stopped work at sunset when the Sabbath began. *L 23:56* Mark names three women, including Mary Magdalene, who, a day later after the Sabbath was over, bought sweet spices to anoint the body. *Mk 16:1*

Everyone knows the stories of the women who came to Jesus' tomb early on Easter morning to anoint his body. *Mk 16:1–11; Mt 28:1–10; L 24:1–11; J 20:1–18* Mary Magdalene, alone or with one or more other women, came to the tomb that morning. "See The Evidence As To The Resurrection", pp. 276–284, for a detailed analysis.

John reports that Mary Magdalene stood outside the tomb weeping and had a conversation with Jesus, whom she first supposed to be a gardener:

JESUS: Woman, why weepest thou? Whom seekest thou?
MARY: Sir, if thou have borne him hence, tell me where thou hast laid him, and I will take him away.

JESUS: Mary.

MARY: Rabboni.

JESUS: Touch me not: for I am not yet ascended to my Father; but
go to my brethren and say unto them, I ascend unto my Father,
and your Father, and to my God, and your God. *J 20:15–17*

Aside from Mary Magdalene's presence at the cross and her
actions on Easter morning, the Gospels have virtually nothing to
say about her. What they do say is either quoted or referred to in
this section. Both Mark and Luke incidentally note that Jesus had
exorcised her of seven devils:

MARK	LUKE
Mary Magdalene,	Mary called Magdalene,
out of whom	out of whom
he had cast	went
seven devils.	seven devils.
Mk 16:9	*L 8:2*

This is not particularly significant since she is only one of three
women named by Luke whom Jesus had "healed of evil spirits and
infirmities." *L 8:2* And it was not just the three named women who
were so healed, there were "many others." *L 8:3*

The situation is the same with the women at Jesus' crucifixion.
Mary Magdalene is listed by name along with several other women,
either named or described. *Mk 15:40 ("one other"); Mt 27:56 ("two others"); J 19:25 ("three others")* Again, there were many other women followers, neither named nor described, looking on. *Mk 15:40; Mt 27:55;
L 23:49*

These women, including Mary Magdalene, had followed Jesus
from Galilee to Jerusalem. *Mk 15:41; Mt 27:55; L 23:49* Mary Magdalene
was apparently a Galilean since *Mary Magdalene* probably means
Mary of "Magdala", a town in Galilee on the west shore of the Sea
of Galilee and a few miles southwest of Capernaum.

There is no basis except conjecture to identify Mary Magdalene
with the unnamed woman who anointed Jesus' feet in the house of
Simon the Pharisee and whose sins were "many." *L 7:36–50 (Mk 14:3–*

9; Mt 26:6–13) The scanty references to Mary Magdalene in the four New Testament Gospels do not support the myths and legends which surround her. There are some references to her in writings outside the New Testament, such as the Gospels of Thomas and Mary, which the Christian church has rejected but scholars have exhumed. These writings, however, are inferior as technical historical sources to the four New Testament Gospels.

We turn now to Jesus' mother, Mary. While her religious role has helped to form the attitude of millions toward women, we are left with only a few enigmatic hints in the New Testament Gospels as to how Jesus himself viewed his mother.

At the marriage feast at Cana in Galilee early in his ministry, Mary is reported to have complained to him, "They have no wine." *J 2:3*

Jesus replied:

Woman, what have I do with thee? Mine hour is not yet come. *J 2:4*

When his hour did come, his mother was there:

Now there stood by the cross of Jesus his mother; and his mother's sister, Mary the wife of Cleophas; and Mary Magdalene. When Jesus therefore saw his mother, and the disciple, whom he loved, standing by, he saith unto his mother, "Woman, behold thy son!"

Then saith he to the disciple, "Behold thy mother!" *J 19:25–27*

Despite Jesus' concern for his mother, he made it clear that, for him, biological ties were secondary to the ties of faith. Earlier in his ministry a woman bystander had cried out at him:

Blessed is the womb that bare thee, and the paps which thou hast sucked. *L 11:27*

Jesus replied:

Yea rather, blessed are they that hear the word of God, and keep it. *L 11:28*

JESUS ON DIVORCE

Both Matthew and Mark record an incident in which some Pharisees attempted to harass Jesus by asking him a test question about divorce:

MARK	MATTHEW
And the Pharisees came to him,	The Pharisees also came unto him, tempting him,
and asked him, "Is it lawful for a man to put away his wife?" tempting him.	and saying unto him, "Is it lawful for a man to put away his wife for every cause?"
Mk 10:2	*Mt 19:3*

This dialogue then followed:

	MARK	MATTHEW
Jesus:	What did Moses command you?	
Pharisees:	Moses suffered to write a bill of divorcement, and to put her away.	
Jesus:	For the hardness of your heart he wrote you this precept.	
		Have ye not read, that he which made them at the beginning
	But from the beginning of the creation God	at the beginning

Mark (cont.)
"made them
male and female."
[*Genesis 1:27*]

"For this cause
shall a man
leave his father and mother,
and cleave
to his wife;
and they twain
shall be one flesh."
[*Genesis 2:24*]
So then they
are no more twain,
but one flesh.
What therefore
God hath
joined together,
let not man
put asunder.
Mk 10:3–9

Matthew (cont.)
"made them
male and female"
[*Genesis 1:27*]
and said,
"For this cause
shall a man
leave father and mother,
and shall cleave
to his wife,
and they twain
shall be one flesh"?
[*Genesis 2:24*]
Wherefore they
are no more twain,
but one flesh.
What therefore
God hath
joined together,
let not man
put asunder.

Pharisees:

Why did Moses then
command to give a
writing of divorcement,
and to put her away?

Jesus:

Moses because of the hardness
of your hearts
suffered you to
put away your wives;
but from the beginning
it was not so.

And I say unto you,
whosoever shall put away
his wife, except it be
for fornication,
and shall marry another,

MARK (cont.)   MATTHEW (cont.)
                               committeth adultery:
                               and whoso marrieth her
                               which is put away
                               doth commit adultery.
                               Mt 19:4–9

This dialogue must be placed in its Jewish context. Jesus was, in the eyes of the Pharisees, an unordained and itinerant teacher or rabbi. They often asked him test questions, and this was one. There were then differences of opinions between rabbis over divorce. For example, the School of Shammai held that a man might not divorce his wife except for unchastity; the School of Hillel allowed divorce for trivial causes.

Matthew has the Pharisees asking, "Is it lawful for a man to put away his wife *for every cause*", i.e., for trivial cause. In effect, the question to Jesus, as reported in Matthew was: "Do you agree with the School of Hillel on divorce?"

The question to Jesus, as reported in Mark, was simply, "Is it lawful [in any circumstances] for a man to put away his wife?"

Jesus' answer, as reported in Mark, was to turn, not to the opinions of the rabbis, but the Law of Moses itself. He asked "What did Moses command you?" *Mk 10:3*

The Pharisees replied by summarizing that Law, as "Moses suffered to write a bill of divorcement and to put her away."*Mk 10:4*

This is a summary of Deuteronomy 24:1–2 that states:

> When a man hath taken a wife, and married her, and it comes to pass that she find no favor in his eyes, because he hath found some uncleanness in her: then let him write her a bill of divorcement, and give it in her hand, and send her out of his house. And when she is departed out of his house, she may go and be another man's wife.

In substance Moses recognized divorce as a right of the husband if he found "some uncleanness" in his wife, and provided a procedure, "a bill of divorcement", to establish that his wife was free to remarry.

The question put to Jesus was, "Is it *lawful* [under the Law of Moses] for a man to put away his wife?" *Mk 10:2; Mt 19:3*

Matthew and Mark disagree as to whether Jesus in his answer referred to the Law of Moses in the first instance. Mark quotes Jesus as asking, "What did Moses command you?", while Matthew has the Pharisees, not Jesus, as asking, "Why did Moses then command to give a writing of divorcement, and to put her away?" *Mk 10:3; Mt 19:7*

Jesus did not repudiate the Mosaic rule about giving a bill of divorcement, but he did state that God, through Moses, had announced that rule as an accommodation to human weakness: "the hardness of your heart", and that God's original intention was that there should be no divorce, "let not man put asunder."

Jesus' dialogue with the Pharisees about divorce did not end, according to Matthew, with Jesus' statement, "but from the beginning it was not so." *Mt 19:8* Matthew's continuation of the dialogue is paralleled by Mark's report of Jesus' answer to follow-up questions put by his disciples after they returned to their house and by another saying of Jesus found in Matthew's report of the Sermon on the Mount. *Mk 10:10 (Disciples ask again)*

Finally Luke records a similar statement of Jesus in a completely different context, immediately after he said that:

> And it is easier for heaven and earth to pass, than one tittle of the Law to fail. *L 16:17*

Jesus' final statement in the dialogue with the Pharisees, as reported by Matthew, and its parallels as found elsewhere in the gospels are as follows:

MARK [Questions by disciples]	MATTHEW [Sermon on the Mount]	MATTHEW [Dialogue with Pharisees]	LUKE [The Law cannot fail]
Whosoever	Whosoever	Whosoever	Whosoever

MARK (cont.)	MATTHEW (cont.)	MATTHEW (cont.)	LUKE (cont.)
shall put away his wife, and	shall put away his wife, saving for the cause of fornication,	shall put away his wife, except it be for fornication, and shall	putteth away his wife, and
marry another, committeth adultery against her. And if a woman shall put away her husband, and be married to another,	causeth her to commit adultery; and whosoever shall marry her that is divorced	marry another, committeth adultery; and whoso marrieth her which is put away	marrieth another, committeth adultery; and whosoever marrieth her that is put away from her husband
she committeth adultery. *Mk 10:11–12*	committeth adultery. *Mt 5:32*	doth commit adultery. *Mt 19:9*	committeth adultery. *L 16:18*

Jesus' sayings just quoted were his midrash on the Law of Moses. Luke has this saying in a dialogue with the Pharisees immediately following Jesus' statement that the Law can not fail and Matthew 5 has this saying as part of a massive comparison by Jesus between the Law of Moses ("It has been said") and Jesus' restatement of that law ("But I say unto you") on many subjects: killing, Matthew 5:21–22; adultery, Matthew 5:27–30; divorce, Matthew 5:31–32; oaths, Matthew 5:33–37; an eye for an eye, Matthew 5:38–42; and hate your enemies, Matthew 5:43–48.

The other two sayings, Mark 10:11–12 and Matthew 19:9, are either a direct or indirect continuation of Jesus' dialogue with the Pharisees that began, "Is it *lawful* for a man to put away his wife?" *Mk 10:2; Mt 19:3*

Jesus' comparison in the Sermon on the Mount between the Law of Moses and his restatement of that law did not announce a new code of rules, but rather, as Paul later wrote:

> But now ye are delivered from the Law, that being dead wherein we were held; that we should serve in newness of spirit, and not in the oldness of the letter. *Romans 7:6*

This has not stopped Christians from turning the newness of spirit into a new written code. They point to the "Matthew exception", the fact that both Matthew quotations "allow" divorce if fornication is involved:

. . . saving for the cause of fornication. *Mt 5:32*	. . . except it be for fornication. *Mt 19:9*

They point out that divorce is not prohibited, only remarriage after divorce:

MARK	MATTHEW	LUKE
. . . *and* marry another, committeth adultery. *Mk 10:11*	. . . *and* shall marry another, committeth adultery. *Mt 19:9*	. . . *and* marrieth another, committeth adultery. *L 16:18*

Paul tersely summarized Jesus' sayings about divorce, but this terse summary wrongly comes through as a command of Jesus:

> And unto the married I command, yet not I, but the Lord, "Let not the wife depart from her husband, but and if she depart, let her remain unmarried, or be reconciled to her husband; and let not the husband put away his wife." *1 Corinthians 7:10–11*

Paul's terse summary must yield to Jesus' own words. The question is what Jesus himself said. Jesus' own words were of counsel, not of command.

The hard questions in analyzing what Jesus taught on divorce is to place the specific sayings we do have in the broad context of his total teaching.

We know that much that Jesus taught was not written down, hence we can not assume that we do have, in the New Testament, everything Jesus taught on divorce. *J 21:25* We must reject the temptation to extrapolate the few sentences we do have and assume that we can confidently state Jesus' views on divorce, especially as applied to a different age and culture. We must remember that the few sentences of his we do have are terse and elliptical and are probably summaries rather than full reports of what he did say.

We know that what statements we do have were made in pre-cross contexts of rabbinical controversy. In three of the four instances he was responding to the questions or derision of Jewish legalists, the Pharisees. *Mk 10:2–12; Mt 19:3–9; L 16:14–18* In the fourth instance, the Sermon on the Mount, he was explaining how his teaching differed from the Law of Moses. *Mt 5:31–32*

In the instances of which we have record Jesus was, in effect, always being asked a rabbinical question, "Why did Moses provide for a writing of divorcement?" *Mt 5:31, 19:7* Understandably he responded with rabbinical type answers and analysis.

We know that Jesus did not come simply to restate the Mosaic Law. He also affirmed and extended the teaching of the Prophets. For example, we have record of two instances in which he quoted and extended Hosea against the Law.

The first instance was Jesus' answer to the Pharisees' question to the disciples, "Why eateth your Master with publicans and sinners?" *Mt 9:11*

Jesus' answer was:

They that be whole need not a physician, but they that are sick. But go ye and learn what that meaneth, "I will have mercy, and not sacrifice", for I am not come to call the righteous, but sinners to repentance. *Mt 9:12–13 (Hosea 6:6)*

The second instance was Jesus' answer to the Pharisees' question to him, "Behold, thy disciples do that which is not lawful to do on the Sabbath day." *Mt 12:2*

Jesus' answer was:

Have ye not read what David did, when he was an hungered, and they that were with him? How he entered into the House of God, and did eat the shewbread, which was not *lawful* for him to eat, neither for them that were with him, but only for the priests. Or have ye not read *in the Law*, how on the Sabbath days the priests in the Temple profane the Sabbath, and are blameless?

But I say unto you, that this place is one greater than the Temple. But if ye had known what this meaneth, "I will have mercy, and not sacrifice", ye would not have condemned the guiltless. For the Son of man is Lord even of the Sabbath day. *Mt 12:3–8 (Hosea 6:6)*

By this analysis the Son of man is Lord of even divorce and his requirement is "mercy, not sacrifice" of human life and hope and happiness to legalistic principle.

If Jesus did not condemn the woman "taken in adultery, in the very act", even less would he condemn those involved in divorce. *J 8:4* For them likewise, we may confidently assume he would say, "Neither do I condemn thee: go, and sin no more." *J 8:11*

Jesus did make some specific statements on divorce, but these statements must be placed in the contexts in which they were stated. Once that is done, these specific statements must then be integrated with all his teachings.

Jesus did teach that life-long marriage is God's ideal; but he also taught that people live in a world in which Satan is alive and well and active. *Mk 4:14–15; Mt 13:19; L 8:11–12; Mt 13:37–43* See "The Covert Operations of the Devil", pp. 817–823.

690

Jesus taught that weightier matters even under the Law were justice, mercy and faith; and that these basic principles were more important than specific rules. *Mt 23:23*

If, as Christians affirm, the Law is superseded and we should serve "in the newness of spirit, and not in the oldness of the letter", the weightier teachings of Jesus on divorce are justice, mercy and faith, not a divorce code of specific rules. *Romans 7:6; Mt 9:12–13; Mt 12:3–8*

JESUS AND THE SABBATH

The word *Sabbath* is derived from a Hebrew word literally mean-ing *rest*, and observance of the day of rest, the Sabbath, was one of the Ten Commandments of the Law:

EXODUS	DEUTERONOMY
Remember the Sabbath day, to keep it holy.	Keep the Sabbath day to sanctify it, as the Lord thy God hath commanded thee.
Six days shall thou labor, and do all thy work, but the seventh day is the Sabbath of the Lord thy God. In it thou shalt not do any work, thou, nor thy son, nor thy daughter, thy manservant, nor thy maidservant,	Six days thou shalt labor, and do all thy work, but the seventh day is the Sabbath of the Lord thy God. In it thou shalt not do any work, thou, nor thy son, nor thy daughter, nor thy manservant, nor thy maidservant, nor thine ox, nor thine ass,
nor thy cattle, nor thy stranger that is within thy gates:	nor any of thy cattle, nor thy stranger that is within thy gates; that thy manservant and thy maidservant may rest as well as thou.
for in six days the Lord made heaven and earth, the sea, and all that in them is, and rested the seventh day;	
	And remember that thou wast a servant in the land of Egypt, and that the Lord thy God brought thee out hence,

EXODUS (cont.)

wherefore the Lord blessed
the Sabbath day,
and hallowed it.
Exodus 20:8–10

DEUTERONOMY (cont.)
through a mighty hand
and by a stretched out arm;
therefore the Lord thy God
commanded thee to keep
the Sabbath day.
Deuteronomy 5:12–15

The great religious principle of rest laid down by the commandment had, by Jesus' time, been transformed by legalistic interpretation into an elaborate code of specific rules.

As Jesus and his disciples walked through some grainfields on
a Sabbath, his disciples plucked a few heads of grain to eat; and
they were accused of breaking the Sabbath by doing work, that is,
harvesting.

The incident is reported in all of the first three gospels:

MARK	MATTHEW	LUKE
And it came to pass, that he went	At that time Jesus went on the Sabbath day	And it came to pass on the second Sabbath after the first, he went
through the corn fields on the Sabbath day; and his disciples	through the corn;	through the corn fields;
	and his disciples were an hungered,	and his disciples
began, as they went,	and began	
to pluck the ears of corn.	to pluck the ears of corn, and to eat.	plucked the ears of corn, and did eat, rubbing them in their hands.
And the Pharisees said unto him,	But when the Pharisees saw it, they said unto him,	And certain of the Pharisees said unto them,

MARK (cont.)	MATTHEW (cont.)	LUKE (cont.)
"Behold, why do they on the Sabbath day that which is not lawful?"	"Behold, thy disciples do that which is not lawful to do upon the Sabbath day."	"Why do ye that which is not lawful to do on the Sabbath days?"
And he said unto them, "Have ye never read	But he said unto them, "Have ye not read	And Jesus answering them said, "Have ye not read so much as this,
what David did, when he had need, and was an hungered, he and they that were with him? How he went into the House of God in the days of Abiathar the high priest, and did eat	what David did, when he was an hungered, and they that were with him? How he entered into the House of God and did eat	what David did, when himself was an hungered, and they which were with him? How he went into the House of God and did take and eat
the shewbread,	the shewbread,	the shewbread, and gave also to them that were with him,
which is not lawful to eat	which was not lawful for him to eat, neither for them which were with him,	which is not lawful to eat
but for the priests, and gave also to them which were with him?"	but only for the priests?	but for the priests alone?"
	Or have ye not read	

MARK (cont.)	MATTHEW (cont.)	LUKE (cont.)
	in the Law, how that on the Sabbath days the priests in the Temple profane the Sabbath, and are blameless?	
And he said unto them, "The Sabbath was made for man, and not man for the Sabbath.	But I say unto you, that in this place is one greater than the Temple; but if ye had known what this meaneth, 'I will have mercy, and not sacrifice,' ye would not have condemned the guiltless.	And he said unto them,
Therefore the Son of man is Lord also of the Sabbath." Mk 2:23–28	For the Son of man is Lord even on the Sabbath day." Mt 12:1–8 (Hosea 6:6)	"That the Son of man is Lord also of the Sabbath." L 6:1–5

Plucking grain heads on a neighbor's field was expressly permitted by the Law so long as it was done casually by hand. *Deuteronomy 23:25* The problem was the "work" done on the Sabbath to pick the heads (harvesting) and extract the kernels of grain (threshing).

Jesus defended his disciples by citing an incident from the history of the Jews in which David, who was not a priest, unlawfully ate consecrated bread in the House of God, and allowed his followers to do likewise. *1 Samuel 21:1–6* Jesus' point was that David allowed his followers to eat forbidden bread in the House of God which was like Jesus allowing his disciples to pluck grain, an act forbidden on the Sabbath.

In both cases the human need of hunger was met despite the violations of religious law involved. This implies that human need overrides legal niceties and this principle, indeed, was specifically stated by Jesus when he said, "The Sabbath was made for man, not man for the Sabbath." *Mk 2:27*

It is unlikely that he went further and said that "man is Lord of the Sabbath." What he did say was that "the Son of man" is Lord of the Sabbath. *Mk 2:28; Mt 12:8; L 6:5* The question is: does the phrase translated "the Son of man" here mean "man" or "Jesus"? "The Son of man" is a title Jesus often claimed, and here he was arguing that he had done no wrong in permitting his disciples to pluck grain heads for lunch that Sabbath day. He was answering the Pharisees who were, he said, condemning the guiltless. *Mt 12:7* It is likely that he went a step further and said that he himself (the Son of man) was Lord of the Sabbath.

Matthew quotes Jesus as using not only the analogy of David and his use of the consecrated bread, but also the "work" of the priests offering burnt offerings on the Sabbath:

> Or have ye not read the Law, how that on the Sabbath days the priests in the Temple profane the Sabbath, and are blameless? *Mt 12:5*

The priests violated the Sabbath commandment with their burnt offerings on the Sabbath which were required by the Law. *Numbers 28:9–10* However, such actions did not violate the basic principle of the Sabbath, rest, any more than did plucking on the Sabbath a few heads of grain to eat.

Jesus applied the same sort of analysis to healing the sick on the Sabbath. The Gospels report a number of instances in which he himself healed on the Sabbath, some times as a teaching illustration to Pharisees.

In one instance Jesus went on a Sabbath day to dine at the house of a chief Pharisee. *L 14:1–6* Although Jesus' relations with the Pharisees were still friendly enough that he was being invited to their houses to dine and he was accepting *(L 7:36; 11:37)*, it seems likely that this particular invitation was a test situation with a man with the dropsy conveniently present, and not, as it appears on the surface of the text, a gratuitous challenge by Jesus to his host and the other guests.

The basis for this inference is first of all the text:

> And it came to pass, as he went into the house of one of the chief Pharisees to eat bread on the Sabbath day, that *they watched him*, and behold, there was a *certain man before him which had the dropsy*.
>
> And Jesus *answering* spake unto the lawyers and Pharisees, saying, "Is it lawful to heal on the Sabbath day?" L 14:1–3

We probably do not have a full account since the account we do have omits any question and yet has Jesus "answering." L 14:3 The words translated *they watched him* also suggests "they were ready for him", ready for him with an obviously ill man present at a Sabbath feast, ready with a question whose text we do not have.

The second basis for the foregoing inferences is that just three chapters before, Luke at the end of his account of another of Jesus' dinners at a Pharisee's house, wrote:

> And as he [Jesus] said these things unto them, the scribes and the Pharisees began to urge him vehemently, and *to provoke* him to speak of many things: *laying in wait for him*, and seeking to catch something out of his mouth, that they might accuse him. L 11:53–54

Here Jesus answered the question of the Pharisees with a question:

> Is it lawful to heal on the Sabbath day? L 14:3

Jesus' question was devastating and ended the test situation:

> And they held their peace. And he took him, and healed him, and let him go; and answered them, saying, "Which of you shall have

an ass or an ox fallen into a pit, and will not straightway pull him out on the Sabbath day?"

And they could not answer him again to these things. *L 14:4–6*

On another occasion, the Pharisees were waiting, with their question ready, for Jesus when he entered a synagogue on a Sabbath to teach. A man with a withered right hand was present. Was this man a set-up?

We have three accounts:

MARK	MATTHEW	LUKE
And he entered again into the synagogue; and there was a man there which had a withered hand.	He went into their synagogue, and, behold, there was a man which had his hand withered.	He entered into the synagogue and taught, and there was a man whose right hand was withered.
And *they watched him,* whether he would heal him on the Sabbath day, *that they might accuse him.*	And they asked him, saying, "Is it lawful to heal on the Sabbath days?" *that they might accuse him.*	And the *scribes and Pharisees watched him,* whether he would heal upon the Sabbath day, *that they might find an accusation against him.* But he knew their thoughts, and said to the man which had the withered hand, "Rise up, and stand forth in the midst."
And he saith unto the man which had the withered hand, "Stand forth."		

MARK (cont.)	MATTHEW (cont.)	LUKE (cont.)
		And he rose and stood forth
And he saith unto them,	And he said unto them,	Then said Jesus unto them, "I will ask you one thing:
"Is it lawful to do good on the Sabbath days, or to do evil; to save life, or to kill?"	"What man shall there be among you, that shall have one sheep, and if it fall into a pit on the Sabbath day, will he not lay hold	Is it lawful [to do good on the Sabbath days]* or to do evil to save life, or to destroy it?"
But they held their peace. And when he had looked round about on them with anger, being grieved for the hardness of their hearts, he saith unto the man, "Stretch forth thine hand."	on it and lift it out? How much then is a man better than a sheep? Wherefore it is lawful to do well on the Sabbath days.' Then saith he to the man, "Stretch forth thine hand."	And looking round about upon them all, he said unto the man, "Stretch forth thy hand."
And he stretched it out, and his hand was restored whole as the other. *Mk 3:1–5*	And he stretched it forth; and it was restored whole, like as the other. *Mt 12:10–13*	And he did so, and his hand was restored whole as the other. *L 6:7–10* * Conformed to Mark's order

On another occasion Jesus was teaching in a synagogue on a Sabbath. A woman who had been ill eighteen years was present and her illness had bowed her together and she could not straighten up. *L 13:11* Jesus saw the woman and without any request being made healed her by laying his hands on her.

Unlike the case of the man with the withered hand, there is no hint that this was a contrived situation. Jesus simply responded to her plight. However, the ruler of the synagogue did not approve. He was indignant because Jesus had healed on the Sabbath day, and said unto the people:

> There are six days in which men ought to work; in them therefore come and be healed, and not on the Sabbath day. *L 13:14*

Jesus answered him:

> Thou hypocrite, doth not each one of you on the Sabbath loose his ox or his ass from the stall, and lead him away to watering? And ought not this woman, being a daughter of Abraham, whom Satan hath bound, lo, these eighteen years, be loosed from this bond on the Sabbath day? *L 13:15–16*

You water stock on the Sabbath, why is it not right to heal on the Sabbath one of God's chosen people who had been ill eighteen years? Why should she wait another day?

John lists two other incidents when Jesus healed on the Sabbath. In neither of these two cases was anything contrived by others: Jesus simply healed the two men involved and it happened to be on a Sabbath. Both incidents occurred in Jerusalem.

In the first incident, Jesus was in Jerusalem for a religious festival and saw a man who had been lame thirty-eight years clustered with others who were blind, halt, and withered, waiting to be healed by stepping in a pool near the Sheep Gate reputed to be a healing shrine. *J 5:1–5*

After a brief conversation with the lame man, Jesus said to him:

> Rise, take up thy bed, and walk. *J 5:8*

John's account continues:

> And immediately the man was made whole, and took up his bed, and walked; and on the same day was the Sabbath.
>
> The Jews therefore said unto him that was cured, "It is the Sabbath day; it is not lawful for thee to carry thy bed."
>
> He answered them, "He that made me whole, the same said unto me, 'Take up thy bed, and walk.'"
>
> Then asked them they him, "What man is that which said unto thee, 'Take up thy bed, and walk?'" *J 5:9–12*

Jesus had slipped away, and the man did not know who Jesus was. He later met Jesus and then identified him to the Jews. *J 5:13–15* John's account then states:

> And therefore did the Jews persecute Jesus, and sought to slay him, because he had done these things on the Sabbath day. *J 5:16*

Jesus' answer to these Jews was:

> My Father worketh hitherto, and I work. *J 5:17*

The charge was that Jesus had broken the Sabbath by healing the man that day. Jesus' defense was that the healing on the Sabbath was proper since the Father himself was still active and had worked with Jesus in doing that work.

Jesus' defense infuriated the Jews:

> Therefore the Jews sought the more to kill him, because he had not only broken the Sabbath, but said also that God was his Father, making himself equal with God. *J 5:18*

The other healing also incidentally involved a Sabbath. On a Sabbath, Jesus healed a blind man blind from birth by anointing his eyes with clay. He then told the man to wash the clay off in the Pool of Siloam. *J 9:6–7* The account continues:

> And it was the Sabbath day when Jesus made the clay, and opened his eyes. Then again the Pharisees also asked him how he had received his sight. He said unto them, "He put clay upon mine eyes, and I washed, and do see."

> Therefore said *some* of the Pharisees, "This man is not of God, because he keepeth not the Sabbath day." *J 9:14–16*

On another occasion in Jerusalem while defending his doctrine in the Temple, Jesus said:

> I have done one work, and ye all marvel. Moses therefore gave unto you circumcision; (not because it is of Moses, but of the fathers;) and ye on the Sabbath day circumcise a man. If a man on the Sabbath day receive circumcision, that the law of Moses should not be broken, are ye angry at me, because I have made a man every whit whole on the Sabbath day?

> Judge not according to the appearance, but judge righteous judgment. *J 7:21–24*

Jesus said, "I have done one work," which apparently referred to his having healed on a Sabbath the man who had been lame thirty-eight years. *J 5:2–17* In substance, Jesus said, "Judge not this healing by its appearance of 'work' but by its essence, the religious act of restoring a man to health." *J 7:24*

Jesus had pointed out that the rite of circumcision required by the patriarchs was done on the Sabbath in certain cases. That rite had to be performed when the baby boy was eight days old. *Genesis 17:12* It was obvious that this eighth day could fall on a Sabbath.

Jesus' point was that if the ritual cutting of one organ of a baby boy did not break the Sabbath, why should the healing of the whole body of the man be judged unrighteously a violation of the Sabbath?

Jesus respected the essence of the Sabbath Commandment, rest, but he rejected legalistic interpretations of the Sabbath Commandment that construed it was forbidding the right to meet simple human needs: to eat and to be healed. His famous summary was:

The Sabbath was made for man, and not man for the Sabbath. *Mk 2:27*

But Jesus respected the Sabbath. It was his custom to go to the synagogue on the Sabbath. *L 4:16* He taught in the synagogue on the Sabbath. *Mk 6:2; L 4:31* The Sabbath was part of his life so he could naturally say of the great tribulation to come:

But pray ye that your flight be not in winter, neither on the Sabbath day. *Mt 24:20*

Jesus did more than respect the Sabbath as a Jew; he claimed to transcend the Sabbath. He claimed as Son of man to be Lord of the Sabbath. *Mk 2:28; Mt 12:8; L 6:5*

JESUS AND THE STATE

Jesus' native land was, throughout his lifetime, under Roman rule. During his ministry Judea was ruled by a Roman procurator, Pontius Pilate; and Jesus' own province, Galilee, was ruled by a Roman tetrarch, Herod Antipas, a collaborator of Edomite and Samaritan ancestry. *L 3:1*

Herod Antipas imprisoned John the Baptist and ultimately beheaded him. *Mk 6:17, 27; Mt 14:3, 10; L 3:19–20, 9:9* Some Pharisees warned Jesus that Herod Antipas planned a like fate for him, saying: "Get thee out, and depart hence: for Herod will kill thee." *L 13:31*

Jesus' reply showed his contempt. He said: "Go ye, and tell that fox, . . ." *L 13:32*

Yet there were Jews who supported the Herod family. They were called Herodians. Mark tells us that the Pharisees on one occasion "took counsel with the Herodians against him, how they might destroy him [Jesus]." *Mk 3:6*

Two of our three accounts of Jesus' "rendering unto Caesar" sayings positively identify the Herodians as participating in the question to Jesus. *Mk 12:13; Mt 22:16* The three accounts are as follows:

MARK	MATTHEW	LUKE
And they	Then	And they
send	went	watched him, and set
unto him certain	the Pharisees,	forth spies,
of the Pharisees,		which should
and of the Herodians,	and took counsel	feign themselves
		just men,
	how they might	that they might
to catch him	entangle him	take hold
in his words	in his talk.	of his words,
		that so they might
		deliver him unto
		the power and
		authority

MARK (cont.)	MATTHEW (cont.)	LUKE (cont.)
	And they sent	of the governor.
And when they	out unto him	
were come,	their disciples	
	with the Herodians,	
	saying,	And
they		they asked him,
say unto him,		saying,
"Master, we know	"Master, we know	"Master, we know
	that thou	that thou sayest
that thou	art true,	and teachest rightly,
art true,	[neither	neither
and		
carest for	carest thou	acceptest thou
no man:	any man:	the person of any,
for thou regardest	for thou regardest	
not the person	not the person	
of men,	of men]*	
but teachest	and teachest	but teachest
the way of God	the way of God	the way of God
in truth.	in truth.	truly.
	Tell us therefore,	
	what thinkest thou?	
Is it lawful	Is it lawful	Is it lawful for us
to give tribute	to give tribute	to give tribute
to Caesar, or not?	unto Caesar, or not?"	unto Caesar, or no?"
Shall we give, or		
shall we not give?"		
But he, knowing	But Jesus perceived	But he perceived
their hypocrisy,	their wickedness,	their craftiness,
said unto them,	and said,	and said unto them,
"Why tempt ye me?	"Why tempt ye me,	"Why tempt ye me?
	ye hypocrites?	
Bring me a penny,	Show me the tribute	Show me a penny.
that I may see it."	money."	
And they	And they	
brought	brought unto	
it.	him a penny.	

MARK (cont.)	MATTHEW (cont.)	LUKE (cont.)
	And he saith unto them,	
And he saith unto them,		
"Whose is this image and superscription?"	"Whose is this image and superscription?"	Whose image and superscription hath it?"
And they said unto him, "Caesar's."	They say unto him, "Caesar's."	They answered and said, "Caesar's."
And Jesus answering said unto them, "Render to Caesar the things that are Caesar's, and to God the things that are God's."	Then saith he unto them, "Render therefore unto Caesar the things which are Caesar's, and unto God the things that are God's."	And he said unto them, "Render therefore unto Caesar the things which be Caesar's, and unto God the things which be God's."
	When they had heard these words,	And they could not take hold of his words before the people,
And they marvelled at him. *Mk 12:13–17*	they marvelled, and left him, and went their way. *Mt 22:15–22* * Conformed to Mark's order	and they marvelled at his answer, and held their peace. *L 20:20–26*

The "penny" referred to as "the tribute money" was actually a small Roman silver coin, a denarius, which bore the Roman emperor's image and a superscription naming him.

The emperor's image could be considered an image prohibited by Jewish law. *Exodus 20:4* Pontius Pilate encountered massive resistance when he ordered imperial ensigns bearing the image of the emperor brought into Jerusalem.

Josephus states:

So he introduced Caesar's effigies, which were upon the ensigns,
and brought them into the city; whereas our law forbids us the
very making of images; on which account the former procurators
were wont to make their entry into the city with such ensigns as
had not those ornaments. Pilate was the first who brought those
images into Jerusalem, and to set them up there; which was done
without the knowledge of the people, because it was done in the
night–time; but as soon as they knew it, they came in multitudes
to Caesarea, and interceded with Pilate many days, that he would
remove the images; . . . *Josephus, Antiquities of the Jews, Book XVIII,
Ch. III, Sec. 1*

When Jesus was questioned about paying the tribute, he was
not only in Jerusalem, but in the Temple area; yet his questioners
had in their possession a coin that not only attested the hated Roman rule but also bore what the punctiliously scrupulous would
consider a graven image.

The question was not the coin itself, but whether the tribute,
an annual tax on every adult male, was to be paid. The tax was not
high but it was a symbol of the Roman rule.

All three accounts agree that Jesus said, in substance, "Render
to Caesar the things that are Caesar's, and to God the things that
are God's." Jesus did not give any list as to which things are Caesar's,
which things are God's. The implication is, however, that paying
the tribute tax was Caesar's thing, and that his listeners' possession of Roman coins showed that they accepted the benefits of the
Roman rule and that they ought not to quibble over paying its tax.

All three accounts agree that his questioners "marvelled" at
his deft answer to the trick question that attempted to either
impale Jesus as a traitor to the Jewish cause or a rebel against
Rome. As it later turned out, one of the charges against Jesus
before the Roman procurator, Pontius Pilate, was: "We found this
fellow perverting the nation, and forbidding to give tribute to
Caesar, . . ." L 23:2

What does this incident teach about Jesus' teaching as to the state? It teaches that he did recognize that the state does have a sphere—some things are Caesar's, but he also taught that some things are God's. Lest there be any mistake Jesus was speaking of taxes. The Romans had been ruling Judea many years, and modern versions render "tribute" as "taxes."

Jesus' basic attitude toward the state is stated in his explanation to Pontius Pilate why his followers had not resisted his arrest:

> My kingdom is not of this world. If my kingdom were of this world, then would my servants fight, that I should not be delivered to the Jews; but now is my kingdom not from hence. *J 18:36*

Jesus did not advocate civil disobedience. Jesus impliedly taught that the Roman tribute tax should be paid. Jesus expressly taught that its forced labor be done gladly and beyond what was required.

A Roman soldier could requisition the services of a civilian to carry his pack to the next village. Presumably referring to this Jesus said:

> And whosoever shall compel thee to go a mile with him, go with him twain. *Mt 5:41*

Luke's account of the incident in which Jesus stated the principle that some things are Caesar's does not positively identify Herodians and Pharisees as being involved but simply says that "the chief priests and the scribes" sent spies who were to "feign themselves just men, that they might take hold of his words, that so they might deliver him into the power and authority of the *governor*." *L 20:20*

That governor was the Roman procurator, Pontius Pilate. This was an occupied country, and repression was bloody. Some time before, Jesus had been told about some Galileans "whose blood Pilate had mingled with their sacrifices." *L 13:1* Some of Jesus' fellow Galileans apparently had been slaughtered by Pilate's order while they were in the Temple engaged in sacrifices required by their national religion.

Despite all this, Jesus did not use this incident to preach civil disobedience to the Roman rule. Instead, Jesus ignored the nationalist issue, and simply made a religious point: the slaughter of those Galileans did not show that they were worse sinners; all must repent, or they will perish like the Galileans.

Even though Jesus' basic position was that his kingdom was not of this world, Jesus directed Peter to pay the Temple tax for them both. The Temple tax was annual half–shekel poll tax levied by the Jewish authorities on every free Jewish male over the age of twenty years for the support of the national shrine, the Temple in Jerusalem. The tax went back to Exodus 30:11–16.

The collectors of this religious tax asked Peter if his master paid "the half–shekel", and Peter said, "Yes." Mt 17:24–25

Apparently Peter was concerned about the question, and when he returned to the house where Jesus was, Jesus anticipated his question:

What thinkest thou, Simon? Of whom do the kings of the earth take custom or tribute? Of their own children, or of strangers? Mt 17:25

Peter replied:

Of strangers. Mt 17:26

Jesus then said:

Then are the children free.

Notwithstanding, lest we offend them, go thou to the sea, and cast an hook, and take up the fish that first cometh up; and when thou hast opened his mouth, thou shalt find a piece of money: that take, *and give unto them for me and thee.* Mt 17:26–27

The point of Jesus' statement is found in the words emphasized. A king would not tax his children; since we are children of
the king we are not obliged to pay, but we do so to avoid offense to
the collectors. Tax protestors please take notice!

The details of how the payment of this tax for the established
religion was to be made are incidental. On its face, Jesus' language
comes through to us as a sort of fish miracle, but Jesus probably
spoke figuratively, meaning something like this: Use the first–fruits
(the first fish caught) to pay the tax; when you have removed the
hook from its mouth you will have a saleable fish, "a piece of
money" (a stater, a coin equal to a shekel); take the sale proceeds
and pay the tax.

Jesus clearly taught that "My kingdom is not of this world."
J 18:36 His followers as children of that kingdom are free of the
obligation to pay taxes, but to avoid giving offense should do so.
Christians are to pay taxes, things of Caesar, even though as citizens of heaven they are exempt.

Jesus was familiar with personnel who staff governments. He
describes one city judge as a man who "feared not God, neither
regarded man." L 18:2 This judge was repeatedly beset by a widow
who demanded, "Avenge me of mine adversary." L 18:3

The text continues:

> And he would not for a while, but afterward he said within himself,
> "Though I fear not God, nor regard man, yet because this widow
> troubleth me, I will avenge her, lest by her continual coming she
> weary me." L 18: 4–5

Jesus had no confidence that litigation before such judges would
produce just results. Accordingly, he taught:

MATTHEW	LUKE
Agree with	When thou goest with
thine adversary	thine adversary
quickly,	
	to the magistrate,

MATTHEW (cont.)	LUKE (cont.)
whiles thou art	as thou art
in the way	in the way,
	give diligence that thou mayest
	be delivered
with him;	from him;
lest at any time	lest
the adversary	
deliver thee	he hale thee
to the judge,	to the judge,
and the judge	and the judge
deliver thee	deliver thee
to the officer,	to the officer,
and thou be cast	and the officer cast thee
into prison.	into prison.
Verily I say	I tell
unto thee,	thee,
thou shalt	thou shalt
by no means	not
come out thence,	depart thence,
till thou hast paid	till thou hast paid
the utmost farthing.	the very last mite.
Mt 5:25–26	*L 12:58–59*

Jesus counseled settling rather than going to trial, perhaps because he had no confidence in judges or litigation.

There are other sayings of Jesus which go further:

MATTHEW	LUKE
And if any man	And him
will sue thee	
at the law,	
and take away	that taketh away
thy coat,	thy cloak
let him have	forbid not to take
thy cloak also.	thy coat also.
Mt 5:40	*L 6:29*

711

The first thing to note is that the principle announced is not restricted to lawsuits. Only Matthew refers to lawsuits. The principle announced is Jesus' rejection of the old law of "An eye for an eye, and a tooth for a tooth", and Jesus' statement as to taking away a garment is one of several illustrating that rejection. *Mt 5:38*

When Jesus said, "And if any man will sue thee at the law, and take away thy coat, let him have thy cloak also," he was probably using hyperbole to make his point just as when he said, "And if thy right eye offend thee, pluck it out, and cast it from thee." *Mt 5:29, 40*

Jesus' statement as quoted in Matthew in fact, only involves litigation incidentally since it says if a man sues you, "and take away thy coat", i.e. wins the case, then "let him have thy cloak also." The focus of Jesus' statement is not on the lawsuit but on the process of restoration after the lawsuit is lost.

This is consistent with Jesus' statements about settling rather than trying cases. He simply takes courts and judges as a given and focuses on the personal relations before a case is tried or after it is lost, saying:

Yea, and why even of yourselves judge ye not what is right? *L 12:57*

Consistent with this, Jesus once refused to intercede so that the Jewish law of inheritance would be carried out. He did not reject the concept of a law of inheritance, but he was more interested in why some one wanted a social wrong righted and to be sure his reasons were proper.

The story is in Luke:

And one of the company said unto him, "Master, speak to my brother, that he divide the inheritance with me." *L 12:13*

Jesus answered the man:

Man, who made me a judge or a divider over you? *L 12:14*

Jesus then explained to the company:

Take heed, and beware of covetousness: for a man's life consisteth not in the abundance of the things which he possesseth. *L 12:15*

Jesus did not dispute the principle of authority as applied to governments; he did modify that principle as applied to relations between his followers. The principle of authority governs human society in which Christians must live, but not the Christian kingdom itself. Jesus, as a Jew speaking to Jews, described human society in terms of "Gentiles" when he said:

The kings of the Gentiles exercise lordship over them; and they that exercise authority upon them are called "Benefactors." But ye shall not be so; but he that is greatest among you, let him be as the younger; and he that is chief, as he that doth serve. *L 22:25–26*

Both Matthew and Mark have a similar saying where again the occasion was a dispute between Jesus' disciples as to rank:

MARK	MATTHEW
Ye know that	Ye know that
they which are accounted	the princes
to rule	
over the Gentiles	of the Gentiles
exercise lordship	exercise dominion
over them; and	over them, and
their great ones	they that are great
exercise authority	exercise authority
upon them.	upon them.
But so shall it	But it shall not
not be among you,	be so among you,
but whosoever	but whosoever
will be great	will be great
among you,	among you,
shall be	let him be
your minister;	your minister;
and whosoever	and whosoever

MARK (cont.)	**MATTHEW** (cont.)
of you	
will be the chiefest,	will be chief
	among you,
shall be	let him be
servant of all.	your servant.
Mk 10:42–44	*Mt 20:25–27*

Jesus accepted governments as they existed because his kingdom was not and is not of this world. *J 18:36* Accordingly, Jesus recognized that certain things, like taxes, are Caesar's and are to be rendered to the Caesars and kings of this world. But he mainly taught that there are other things, the things of God, and they must be rendered to God.

JESUS AND NONVIOLENCE

Many persons see Jesus as an apostle of nonviolence. That picture is inconsistent with the historical sources for Jesus' life. The gentle Jesus of Galilee never existed. He is a myth sired by a selective reading of the Gospels. The historical Jesus did exist, and he is a different person from the gentle Jesus of Galilee.

It is true that Jesus did teach:

MATTHEW	LUKE
But I say unto you,	
that ye resist not evil;	
but whosoever	And unto him that
shall smite thee	smiteth thee
on thy right cheek,	on the one cheek,
turn to him	offer
the other also.	also the other; . . .
Mt 5:39	*L 6:29*

Modern translations of Matthew make it clear that "resist not evil" does not refer to evil in the abstract but to resisting evil persons.

What did Jesus mean by these "cheek" statements?

First, these statements are not action precepts themselves so much as teaching illustrations of a general principle. That principle is stated in both Matthew and Luke in association with the "other cheek" sayings:

MATTHEW	LUKE
But I say unto you:	But I say unto you
	which hear:
Love your enemies,	Love your enemies,
bless them	[bless them
that curse you,	that curse you,]*
do good to them	do good to them
that hate you,	which hate you,

MATTHEW (cont.)	LUKE (cont.)
and pray for	and pray for
them which	them which
despitefully use you,	despitefully use you.
and persecute you.	*L 6:27–28*
Mt 5:44	* Conformed to Matthew's order

Second, we must remember and allow for the rhetorical exaggeration that was natural in Jesus' speech. He spoke of "the beam" (the log or plank) in your own eye, and "the mote" (a small particle) in your brother's eye. *Mt 7:3-5; L 6:41–42* No one has logs or planks in his eyes, except rhetorically; but Jesus made his point by hyperbole.

Third, this teaching is in a one-for-one context of intrapersonal relations (him v. you). The question is whether this teaching was meant by Jesus to be generalized beyond that private context to public matters involving the state, directly or indirectly.

Finally, the "other cheek" statements were not all of Jesus' teachings on the use of violence and force. We have his own example. On either one or two occasions, Jesus used force, or the threat of force, to cleanse the Temple at Jerusalem.

John's Gospel places the cleansing early in Jesus' ministry; the other three gospels place it in the last days of that ministry. All four accounts are set out in tabular form below.

MARK	MATTHEW	LUKE	JOHN
Jesus went	Jesus went	He went	Jesus . . . found
into the Temple,	into the Temple of God,	into the Temple	in the Temple
and began	and	and began	
			those that sold oxen and sheep and doves, and the changers of money sitting.

Mark (cont.)	Matthew (cont.)	Luke (cont.)	John (cont.)
			And when he had made a scourge of small cords,
to cast out them that sold and bought in the Temple,	*cast out* all them that sold and bought in the Temple,	*to cast out* them that sold therein and them that bought; . . . *L 19:45*	he *drove* them all out of the Temple,
			and the sheep, and the oxen; and *poured out* the changers' money,
and *overthrew* the tables of the moneychangers, and the seats of them that sold doves; . . . *Mk 11:15*	and *overthrew* the tables of the moneychangers, and the seats of them that sold doves, . . . *Mt 21:12*		and *overthrew* the tables; . . . *J 2:13–15*

The verbs, "cast out," "drove," "poured out," and "overthrew" unmistakably connote violent action and force. Their natural and obvious meaning should not be neutralized by bland exegesis. We should not impose our own preconceptions about Jesus upon what the Gospels say he did.

Legally, there is very little difference between the use of force and the threat of the use of force. Both are forbidden. Nonviolence is a contemporary issue. It may be helpful to put what the Gospels say Jesus did in cleansing the Temple into contemporary legal English, in the form of a complaint of the disturbance of the peace:

On _____, Jesus of Nazareth did willfully and unlawfully disturb the peace and quiet of the City of Jerusalem, in that, in a public place in said city, to-wit: in the Court of the Gentiles in the Temple:

1. he did overturn certain tables used by money-changers, which were the property of A, B, C, and D, without their consent and against their wishes;
2. he did overturn certain seats used by sellers of doves, which seats were the property of E, F, and G, without their consent and against their wishes;
3. he did threaten numerous persons with a whip;
4. he did intimidate numerous persons and thereby cause them to leave said public place;

contrary to the form of the statute in such case made and provided, and against the peace and dignity of the people of the City of Jerusalem.

On the question of violence, we not only have Jesus' own example, we have the examples of the men closely associated with him, who knew his views better than we can know them.

At the time of Jesus' arrest, one of his followers, whom John identifies as Peter, was carrying a sword, drew it, "and smote the servant of the high priest, cutting off his ear." *Mk 14:47; Mt 26:51; L 22:50; J 18:10*

Luke does not expressly state that a sword was used, but the inference is clear since the preceding sentence in Luke states:

When they which were about him saw what would follow, they said unto him, "Lord, shall we smite with the sword?" *L 22:49*

This implies that Jesus' followers were armed with swords, not just the one who cut off the ear of the high priest's servant.

718

After the ear-cutting incident, Matthew and John report that Jesus said:

MATTHEW	JOHN
Put up again thy sword	Put up thy sword
into his place:	into the sheath;
for all they	
that take the sword	
shall perish	
with the sword.	
Thinkest thou that	
I can not now pray	
to my Father, and	
he shall presently	
give me more than	
twelve legions of angels?	
But how then shall	the cup
the scriptures	which my Father
be fulfilled,	hath given me,
that thus it must be?	shall I not drink it?
Mt 26:52–54	J 18:11

The basic thrust of Jesus' statement is not "they that take the sword shall perish with the sword," but submission to his Father's plan, which, in this particular instance, required Jesus' death, "that thus it must be?"

This is why Jesus at that particular time and place did not want his followers to use swords or to fight. That is why Jesus told Pilate the next morning:

> My Kingdom is not of this world. If my Kingdom were of this world, then would my servants fight, that I should not be delivered to the Jews; but now is my Kingdom not from hence. J 18:36

Jesus was explaining why his followers had not fought his arrest; he was not teaching pacifism.

The statement that "they that take the sword shall perish with the sword" was essentially an aside, and Jesus' general attitude towards the use of the sword is more accurately stated in a dialogue he had with his disciples earlier on the day of his arrest:

JESUS: When I sent you without purse, and scrip, and shoes, lack ye any thing?
DISCIPLES: Nothing.
JESUS: But *now*, he that hath a purse, let him take it, and likewise his scrip; *and he that hath no sword, let him sell his garment, and buy one.* For I say unto you, that this that is written *[Isaiah 53:12]* must yet be accomplished in me, "And he was reckoned among the transgressors" for the things concerning me have an end [are happening].
DISCIPLES: Lord, behold, *here are two swords.*
JESUS: It is enough. *L 22:35–38*

Jesus is contrasting his old instructions not to carry a purse (and impliedly, a sword) with his new instructions for the "now": take a purse and buy a sword. The "now" is the imminent end of his earthly ministry on the cross and the beginning of the era of the Holy Spirit in which we still live.

Jesus' feeling that swords would be necessary for his disciples in that era was so strong that he said that a disciple should sell his shirt to get money to buy a sword:

And he that hath no sword, let him sell his garment, and buy one. *L 22:36*

This is consistent with what Jesus had always told his disciples:

MATTHEW	LUKE
Think not that I am come to send peace on earth; I came not to send peace, but a sword. *Mt 10:34*	Suppose ye that I am come to give peace on earth? I tell you, Nay, but rather division. *L 12:51*

Jesus and the Capitalistic Ethic

The parables of the talents and pounds are parables of the Kingdom (*Mt 25:14; L 19:11*) and have been treated as such under the heading "Unjust Rules Of The Kingdom," pp. 533–548.

Here we consider Jesus' assumptions in these parables as to wealth and its use: the "talent" of Matthew's parable has, of course, passed into English and become a synonym for natural ability. However, "talents" and "pounds" (minas) were ancient measures of weight that had become, by Jesus' time, monetary units based on their weights in precious metals. Jesus used these monetary units in these parallel parables: In Matthew's parable, talents were used to state the amount of goods entrusted; in Luke's parable, money stated in pounds was entrusted.

That is not significant; nor is it significant that in Matthew's parable the servants received unequal amounts of goods while in Luke's parable each servant received the same amount of money; or that in Matthew all the man's goods were entrusted, while in Luke relatively small sums of money were entrusted.

There is much learned nonsense written about the relationship of the two parables. Here we assume, we think correctly, that Jesus told essentially the same parable twice with inconsequential variations. One of these inconsequential variations is that a talent was a much larger monetary unit than a pound, perhaps of a magnitude of about sixty times as much. Another inconsequential variation is that in Matthew only three servants are mentioned, while in Luke ten servants are mentioned, but the stewardship of only three is discussed.

Here is an abstract of the "business" aspects of the two parables:

MATTHEW	LUKE
Then he that had received the five talents went and traded	Lord, thy pound

MATTHEW (cont.)	LUKE (cont.)
with the same,	
and made them	hath gained
other five talents;	ten pounds.
and likewise he that	*L 19:16*
had received	
two,	Lord, thy pound
he also gained	hath gained
other two.	five pounds.
	L 19:18
But he that	Lord, behold
had received	here is
one	thy pound,
went	which
and digged in the earth,	I have kept
and hid	laid up in a napkin.
his lord's money.	*L 19:20*
Mt 25:16–18	

The third servant in each parable did nothing, except safekeeping of the entrusted goods or funds. Jesus severely condemned this:

MATTHEW	LUKE
	"Out of thine own mouth
	will I judge thee,
Thou wicked and	thou wicked
slothful servant,	servant.
thou knewest that	Thou knowest that
	I was an austere man,
I reap where I sowed not,	taking up that I laid not down,
and gather where	and reaping that
I have not strawed [winnowed].	I did not sow.
Thou oughtest therefore	Wherefore then
to have put	gavest not thou
my money	my money
to the exchangers,	into the bank,
and then	that
at my coming	at my coming

MATTHEW (cont.)	LUKE (cont.)
I should have received	I might have required
mine own with usury.	mine own with usury?"
	And he said unto them
	that stood by,
Take therefore	"Take from him
the talent from him,	the pound,
and give it	and give it
unto him	to him
which hath ten talents.	that hath ten pounds."
Mt 25:26–28	*L 19:22–24*

Modern translations replace *usury* with *interest* and that is more accurate since Jesus' point was not an exorbitant rate of interest but making a return on the entrusted money by putting it on deposit with someone who would pay for its use. It did not bother him that the money was to be used for trading to make trading profits. *Mt 25:16; L 19:15*

The first servant in Matthew made a 100 percent profit: he doubled the five talents entrusted. *Mt 25:16* The first servant in Luke did much better: he made a 1,000 percent profit, increasing his one pound to ten pounds. *L 19:16*

Jesus approved these profits:

MATTHEW	LUKE
Well done,	Well,
thou good and faithful servant:	thou good servant:
thou hast been faithful	because thou hast been faithful
over a few things,	in a very little,
I will make thee	have thou
ruler over many things.	authority over ten cities.
Enter thou into	*L 19:17*
the joy of thy lord.	
Mt 25:21	

The second servant in each parable made a large profit: 100 percent profit in Matthew, he had doubled the two talents entrusted;

500 percent profit in Luke, he had made five pounds on the one pound entrusted. *Mt 25:22; L 19:18*

Jesus praised these results:

MATTHEW	LUKE
Well done,	
good and faithful servant: .	
thou hast been faithful	
over a few things,	
I will make thee	Be thou
ruler over many things.	also over five cities.
Enter thou into	*L 19:19*
the joy of thy lord.	
Mt 25:23	

It is obvious that Jesus did not criticize the capitalistic ethic implicit in the two parables. It was not only right for the servants to invest the entrusted funds, it was their duty to do so, and, beyond that, there was high praise for those who invested profitably.

In these parables Jesus clearly assumed, unlike many of his modern "followers", that profits from business transactions, even very high profits, were proper. In the hypothetical examples put by the parables, he even considered business profits to be the appropriate analogy to explain the reward system of the Kingdom.

Jesus' approval of profits and investments, and, indeed, approval of a high rate of return on investment, is just as much a part of his teaching as his beatitude stating, "Blessed be ye poor: for yours is the Kingdom of God," *(L 6:20; Mt 5:3)* and his teaching of priorities, "But seek ye first the Kingdom of God and his righteousness; and all these things shall be added unto you." *Mt 6:33 (L 12:31)*

CHAPTER 12

JESUS AND GOD

THE PERSON OF JESUS
SOMETHING FOR THE THEOLOGIANS

We look at Jesus across twenty centuries and through the billions of words written about him. It is refreshing and instructive to look at what the men who lived and worked with him wrote when they described what theologians later called his "person."

Peter's Pentecost sermon to the Jerusalem Jews described Jesus as follows:

> Ye men of Israel, hear these words; Jesus of Nazareth, *a man approved of God* among you by miracles and wonders and signs, which God did by him in the midst of you, as ye yourselves also know: . . . whom God hath raised up, having loosed the pains of death, because it was not possible that he should be holden of it. *Acts 2:22, 24*

Peter continued:

> *This [same] Jesus* hath God raised up, whereof we all are witnesses. Therefore being by the right hand of God exalted, and having received of the Father the promise of the Holy Ghost, he hath shed forth this, which ye now see and hear. *Acts 2:32–33*

Peter concluded:

> Therefore let all the house of Israel know assuredly, that God hath
> made *that same Jesus*, whom ye crucified, *both Lord and Christ*.
> *Acts 2:36*

When Peter came to describe "this Jesus" to a Gentile, a Roman centurion named Cornelius, he told him "how God anointed
Jesus of Nazareth with the Holy Ghost and with power: who went
about doing good, and healing all that were oppressed of the devil;
for God was with him." *Acts 10:38*

After Peter explained how God raised Jesus from the dead, Peter continued:

> And he commanded us to preach unto the people, and to testify that
> *it is he which was ordained of God* to be the Judge of quick and dead.
> To him gave all the prophets witness, that through his name whoso-
> ever believeth in him shall receive remission of sins. *Acts 10:42–43*

Paul told a mixed audience of Jews and Gentile adherents to
Judaism in Asia Minor that Jesus had been crucified but that "God
raised him from the dead, and he was seen many days of them
which came up with him from Galilee to Jerusalem, who are his
witnesses unto the people." *Acts 13:30, 31* Paul then said:

> Be it known unto you therefore, men and brethren, that through
> *this man* is preached unto you the forgiveness of sins; and by him all
> that believe are justified from all things, from which ye could not be
> justified by the Law of Moses. *Acts 13:38–39*

In Athens Paul preached to some Greeks there and closed his
address in this manner:

> Because he [God] hath appointed a day, in which he will judge the
> world in righteousness by *that man [Jesus] whom he hath ordained*;
> whereof he hath given assurance unto all men, in that he hath raised
> him [Jesus] from the dead. *Acts 17:31*

Both Peter and Paul speak of Jesus being a man "ordained of God." *(Peter: Acts 10:42; Paul: Acts 17:31)* Jesus, himself, spoke of his divine appointment as follows:

> But I have greater witness than that of John [the Baptist]: for the works which the Father hath given me to finish, the same works that I do, bear witness of me, *that the Father hath sent me*. And the Father himself, *which hath sent me*, hath borne witness of me. Ye have neither heard his voice at any time, nor seen his shape. And ye have not his word abiding in you: *for whom he hath sent*, him ye believe not.

> Search the scriptures: for in them ye think ye have eternal life, and *they are they which testify of me*. And ye will not come to me, that ye might have life. I receive not honor from men. But I know you, that ye have not the love of God in you.

> *I am come in my Father's name*, and ye receive me not; if another shall come in his own name, he ye will receive. How can ye believe, which receive honor one of another, and seek not the honor that cometh from God only?

> Do not think that I will accuse you to the Father; there is one that accuseth you, even Moses, in whom ye trust. For had ye believed Moses, ye would have believed me; *for he wrote of me*. But if ye believe not his writings, how shall ye believe my words? *J 5:36–47*

This is, of course, not all Jesus said of his divine appointment but is a succinct summary of Jesus' mission in his own words. He considered himself sent by the Father in accordance with the Jewish scriptures which speak of his coming. He claimed to have "come in my Father's name." *J 5:43*

The Jews understood him as saying that "God was his Father", which they thought was a claim that he was "equal with God." *J 5:18* But Jesus had only said:

> My Father worketh hitherto, and I work. *J 5:17*

Jesus' answer to their charge shows the exact nature of his divine appointment:

Verily, verily, I say unto you, *The Son can do nothing of himself*, but what he seeth the Father do: for what things soever he doeth, these also doeth the Son likewise.

For the *Father loveth the Son, and sheweth him all things that himself doeth*; and he will shew him greater works than these, that ye may marvel.

For as the Father raiseth up the dead, and quickeneth them, even so the Son quickeneth whom he will.

For the Father judgeth no man, but hath committed all judgment unto the Son: that all men should honor the Son, even as they honor the Father. He that honoreth not the Son honoreth not the Father which hath sent him.

Verily, verily, I say unto you, he that heareth my word, and believeth on him that sent me, hath everlasting life, and shall not come into condemnation; but is passed from death unto life.

Verily, verily, I say unto you, the hour is coming, and *now is, when the dead shall hear the voice of the Son of God*; and they that hear shall live. *J 5:19–25*

Jesus not only claimed to have come in his Father's name, he claimed to be the Son of God. We turn now to an examination of the gospel record of that claim.

There is But One God and Jesus is His Only Son

All three synoptic gospels report that at the time Jesus was baptized by John the Baptist a heavenly voice announced to Jesus that he was the beloved Son of God:

MARK	MATTHEW	LUKE
And there came	And lo	And
a voice	a voice	a voice came
from heaven,	from heaven,	from heaven
saying,	saying,	which said,
"Thou art	"This is	"Thou art
my beloved Son,	*my beloved Son,*	*my beloved Son'*
in whom	in whom	in thee
I am well pleased."	I am well pleased."	I am well pleased."
Mk 9:7	*Mt 3:17*	*L 3:22*

Some time after Jesus was well established in his ministry, he took three of his closest disciples, Peter and the Zebedee brothers, to a high mountain alone. There they heard a voice from a cloud announce that Jesus was God's beloved son:

MARK	MATTHEW	LUKE
And	And behold	And there came
a voice	a voice	a voice
came out	out	out
of the cloud	of the cloud,	of the cloud,
saying,	which said,	saying,
"This is	"This is	"This is
my beloved Son:	my beloved Son,	my beloved Son:
	in whom	
	I am well pleased;	
hear him."	hear ye him."	hear him."
Mk 9:7	*Mt 17:5*	*L 9:35*

It is not certain from the gospel accounts whether John the Baptist heard the heavenly voice at the time of Jesus' baptism calling Jesus, "my beloved Son"; but it is certain that on the mountain

Peter and the Zebedee brothers heard the voice stating that Jesus was "my beloved Son." Mt 17:6

Shortly before the mountain incident, Jesus had conducted a dialogue with his disciples as they walked to villages near the town of Caesarea Philippi:

	MARK	MATTHEW	LUKE
Jesus:	Whom do men say that I am?	Whom do men say that I the Son of man am?	Whom say the people that I am?
Disciples:	John the Baptist; but some say Elijah; and others, one of the prophets.	Some say that thou art John the Baptist; some, Elijah; and others, Jeremiah, or one of the prophets.	John the Baptist; but some say, Elijah; and others say that one of the old prophets is risen again.
Jesus:	But whom say ye that I am?	But whom say ye that I am?	But whom say ye that I am?
Peter:	Thou art the Christ. Mk 8:27–29	Thou art the Christ, the Son of the living God. Mt 16:13–16	The Christ of God. L 9:18–20

The Greek word of the synoptic gospels *Christos,* of course, is translated *Christ* and means, literally, *anointed.* Peter spoke Aramaic, not Greek, and the Aramaic word which he spoke was *Messiah,* meaning, literally, *the Anointed One.* This is why the King James Ver-

sion has Peter saying Jesus is "the Christ", while some modern translations say "the Messiah."

"The Messiah" was a term the Jews had used in their religious
tradition describing the prophesied king and deliverer of Israel.
Jesus claimed that title for himself. The quotation from Matthew
16 continues at verse 20:

> Then charged he his disciples that they should tell no man that he
> was Jesus the Christ. *Mt 16:20 (Mt 16:17)*

Jesus also claimed this title for himself when he spoke to a
Samaritan woman at Jacob's Well near the city of Sychar:

Woman: I know that Messiah cometh, which is called Christ: when
he is come, he will tell us all things.
Jesus: I that speak unto thee am he. *J 4:25–26*

After Jesus' arrest he was interrogated by the High Priest on
this point. We have two accounts:

	MARK	MATTHEW
Q.		I adjure thee
		by the living God,
		that thou tell us
	Art thou	whether thou be
	the Christ,	the Christ,
	the Son	the Son
	of the Blessed?	of God.
A.	I am;	Thou hast said,
		Nevertheless
		I say unto you,
	and ye shall see	hereafter shall ye see
	the Son of man	the Son of man
	sitting	sitting
	on the right hand	on the right hand
	of Power,	of Power,

MARK (cont.)	MATTHEW (cont.)
and coming	and coming
in the clouds of heaven.	in the clouds of heaven.
Mk 14:61–62	*Mt 26:63–64*

According to both accounts the High Priest then rent his clothes because he considered Jesus' answer gross blasphemy, and then he said:

MARK	MATTHEW
	He hath spoken
	blasphemy;
What need	what further need
we any further	have we
witnesses?	of witnesses?
	Behold, now
Ye have heard	ye have heard
the blasphemy: . . .	his blasphemy.
Mk 14:63–64	*Mt 26:65*

Mark's account has the High Priest asking if Jesus was "the Christ, the Son of the Blessed", while Matthew has the question as asking if Jesus was "the Christ, the Son of God." *Mk 14:61; Mt 26:63* There is really no difference between Matthew and Mark since Matthew's phrase "the Son of the Blessed" with Jewish scrupulousness evades saying the unspeakable holy name of God by using instead the phrase "the Blessed." Peter's confession was that Jesus was "the Christ, the Son of the living God." *Mt 16:16*

It is evident that both the High Priest's question and Peter's confession assume that "the Christ" and "the Son of God" are equivalent expressions relating to one particular person. Both expressions have intricate historical and linguistic problems. What I am saying is that Peter and the High Priest here did not make any distinction between the two phrases.

The interrogation of Jesus by the High Priest had occurred at night. Early the next morning Jesus was interrogated by the assembly of the elders:

Q. Art though the Christ? Tell us.
A. If I tell you, ye will not believe; and if I also ask you, ye will not
    answer me, nor let me go. Hereafter shall the Son of man sit on
    the right hand of the power of God.
Q. Art thou then the Son of God?
A. Ye say that I am. *L 22:67–70*

Standing alone, Jesus' answer is equivocal. However, his listeners who were in the best position to judge had no doubt that
Jesus had claimed the title "the Son of God", since Luke continues:

And they said, "What need we any further witness? For we ourselves have heard of his own mouth." *L 22:71*

In addition, on a previous occasion while not in custody, Jesus
had expressly claimed the title "the Son of God." Jesus had restored the sight of a blind man, and as a result of the man's recognition of Jesus' power in his healing, the man had been put out of
the synagogue. Jesus heard about this and sought out the man.
    Their conversation went like this:

JESUS: Dost thou believe in the Son of God?
MAN: Who is he, Lord [sir], that I might believe upon him?
JESUS: Thou hast both seen him, and it is he that talketh with thee.
MAN: Lord, I believe. *J 9:35–38*

Later on, some Jews threatened to stone Jesus and they then
argued back and forth:

JEWS: For a good work we stone thee not, but for blasphemy; and
    because thou, being a man, makest thyself God. *J 10:33*
JESUS: Say ye of him, whom the Father hath sanctified, and sent
    into the world, "Thou blasphemist" because *I said*, "I am the
    Son of God?" *J 10:36*

After Jesus was crucified and while he hung on his cross, the chief priests, scribes, and elders mocked him, saying in part:

> He trusted in God; let him deliver him now, if he will have him: for he said, "I am the Son of God." Mt 27:43

They had no doubt as to what Jesus claimed, nor should we. The question whether Jesus was in fact "the Son of God" is a different question.

There can be no doubt that the writers of the Gospels believed this claim to be true. That is why they wrote the Gospels. John is explicit on this point.

> But these are written that ye might believe that *Jesus is* the Christ, *the Son of God*; and that believing ye might have life through his name. J 20:31

Mark begins his gospel with this statement:

> The beginning of the gospel of Jesus Christ, the Son of God; . . . Mk 1:1

One of the earliest Christian confessions of faith was:

> I believe that Jesus Christ is the Son of God. Acts 8:37

So has the church of Jesus Christ ever since believed.

The question whether this claim is true demands that one weigh all that Jesus did and said. What Jesus did and said is found in the four Gospels. This outline is an analysis of what Jesus did and said as stated in the four Gospels. The gospel writers may be interested witnesses, but they are the only witnesses we have. To say that these witnesses are interested does not justify discarding their testimony. Otherwise we will never know the truth. And as Jesus said:

> And ye shall know the truth, and the truth shall make you free. J 8:32

What Being the Only Son of God Means

Elaborate theological treatises and notes can, and no doubt have been, written as to what Jesus being the only Son of God means. Our inquiry is simpler. What did this phrase mean to three of the most influential early Christians, and more important, what did it mean to Jesus himself?

Here is what three of the most influential of the earliest Christians understood the statement that Jesus is the only Son of God to mean. Our first witness is John. He wrote:

> No man hath seen God at any time; the only begotten Son, which is in the bosom of the Father, he hath declared him. *J 1:18*

Modern translations omit the word *begotten* as redundant. Thus John wrote, in substance, that Jesus, as God's only Son, has declared him.

John also described Jesus, the Son of God, as the Word:

> And the Word was made flesh, and dwelt among us, and we beheld his glory, the glory as of the only begotten of the Father, full of grace and truth. *J 1:14*

Later on in his gospel John has a fuller statement of Jesus' status as the only Son of God:

> He that cometh from above is *above all*; he that is on the earth is earthly, and speaketh of the earth: he that cometh from heaven is *above all*.

> And what he hath seen and heard, that he testifieth; and no man receiveth *his testimony*. He that hath received *his testimony* hath set to his seal [accepts] that God is true.

> For *he whom God hath sent* speaketh the words of God: for God giveth not the Spirit by measure unto him. The Father loveth the Son, and hath given all things into his hand.

He that believeth on the Son hath everlasting life; and he that believeth not the Son shall not see life, but the wrath of God abideth on him. *J 3:31–36*

John's statement may be summarized as follows: Jesus, as the Son whom God has sent and loves, is superior to all others; and God has given him control of all things and authorized him to speak the words of God through the Spirit without measure or restriction.

Our second witness is Peter, and like John, he also relied upon the Spirit in explaining to an inquiring Roman centurion Jesus' unique status. Peter told him:

How *God anointed Jesus of Nazareth with the Holy Spirit and with power*; who went about doing good, and healing all that were oppressed of the Devil; for God was with him. . . And he commanded us to preach unto the people, and to testify that it is he which was ordained of God to be the Judge of quick and dead. *Acts 10:38, 42*

Our third witness is Paul. Both he and Peter attest that Jesus was designated Son of God by the Holy Spirit. Paul wrote:

Concerning his Son Jesus Christ our Lord, which was made of the seed of David, according to the flesh, and *declared to be the Son of God with power, according to the spirit of holiness*, by the resurrection from the dead. *Romans 1:3–4*

Jesus' designation as the Son of God was attested or declared by his resurrection from the dead. Jesus, as the Son of God, in turn, declared the Father to men. As Jesus himself said:

And I have declared unto them thy name, and will declare it: . . . *J 17:26*

Jesus made many other statements that explain in his own words his status as the Son of God.

Jesus recognized that:

My Father is greater than I. *J 14:28*

736

Consistent with this Jesus taught:

> For I came down from heaven, not to do mine own will, but the will of him that sent me. J 6:38

Jesus not only claimed to be doing the will of the Father, but also to speak on the authority of the Father, not on his own authority:

> For the Father loveth the Son, and sheweth him all things that himself doeth: . . . J 5:20

> I speak that which I have seen with my Father: . . . J 8:38

> For I have not spoken of myself; but the Father which sent me, he gave me a commandment, what I should say, and what I should speak. And I know that his commandment is life everlasting; whatsoever I speak therefore, even as the Father said unto me, so I speak. J 12:49–50

> The words that I speak unto you I speak not of myself; but the Father that dwelleth in me, he doeth the works. J 14:10

Jesus recognized his utter dependence upon the Father:

> Verily, verily, I say unto you, the Son *can do nothing of himself*, but what he seeth the Father do: for what things soever he doeth, these also doeth the Son likewise. J 5:19

> I *can of mine own self do nothing*: as I hear, I judge; and my judgment is just because I seek not mine own will, but the will of the Father which hath sent me. J 5:30

> I *do nothing of myself*; but as my Father hath taught me, I speak these things. J 8:28

Although Jesus was utterly dependent upon the Father, Jesus taught that they share all things and all persons:

All things that the Father hath are mine: . . . *J 16:15*

And all mine are thine, and thine are mine; . . . *J 17:10*

The Father sent Jesus on his mission but remained with him:

For I am *not alone*, but I and the Father that sent me. *J 8:16*

And he that sent me is with me; the Father hath *not left me alone*: for I do always those things that please him. *J 8:29*

I *am not alone*, because the Father is with me. *J 16:32*

Jesus taught that he was not alone but that the Father was with him. He taught that the Father was not simply God the Father of all men, but that God was his Father in a particular and unique way. We turn to the way Jesus stated it.

God is My Father

It is axiomatic that the core of Jesus' theology was his belief that God was his Father.

At the end of his ministry he prayed in the Garden of Gethsemane:

O my Father, if it be possible, let this cup pass from me: nevertheless not as I will, but as thou wilt. *Mt 26:39*

His last words from the cross were:

Father, into thy hands I commend my spirit. *L 23:46*

His earliest recorded words are those of a boy of twelve in the Temple responding to his mother's anguished questions why he had not left Jerusalem with his family:

How is it that ye sought me? Wist [know] ye not that I must be about my Father's business? *L 2:49*

In between those first and last words, Jesus habitually referred to God as "my Father."

Matthew	Luke	John
"my Father which is in heaven." *Mt 7:21*	"my Father" *L 10:22* *L 22:29* *L 24:49*	"my Father" *J 5:17*
"my Father which is in heaven." *Mt 10:32, 33*		"my Father's name" *J 5:43*
"my Father" *Mt 11:27* *Mt 12:50*		"my Father" *J 6:32, 65* *J 8:19, 28, 38, 49, 54* *J 10:17, 18*

MATTHEW (cont.)	LUKE (cont.)	JOHN (cont.)
"my heavenly Father" Mt 15:13		"my Father's name" J 10:25
"my Father which is in Heaven." Mt 16:17 Mt 18:10, 19		"my Father's hand" J 10:29
"my heavenly Father" Mt 18:35		"my Father" J 10:29, 30, 32, 37 J 12:26 J 14:7, 12, 20, 21, 23, 28 J 15:1, 8
"my Father" Mt 20:23 Mt 24:36 Mt 25:34		"my Father's commandments" J 15:10
"my Father's kingdom" Mt 26:29		"my Father" J 15:15, 23, 24 J 18:11 J 20:17, 21
"my Father" Mt 26:39, 42, 53		

The foregoing form of tabulation is used to save space and is not meant to imply that statements in one Gospel were made at the same time as statements in another Gospel placed in a parallel column.

It cannot be disputed that Jesus considered God to be his Father in a special and intimate way. Jesus also phrased his relationship to God the Father in another way:

I and my Father are one. *J 10:30*

Jesus saw no inconsistency in these two statements. Should we?

We turn now to an examination of what Jesus meant by saying that he and his Father were one.

I AND MY FATHER ARE ONE

Jesus taught:

I and my Father are one. *J 10:30*

This provoked a violent confrontation with some Jews, and Jesus ended his argument with them by saying:

If I do not the works of my Father, believe me not. But if I do, though you believe not me, believe the works: that ye may know, and believe, *that the Father is in me, and I in him. J 10:37–38*

Jesus' unity with God consists of God being *in him* and Jesus being *in God*. This unity is of the same general sort as the unity between Jesus and his followers. Thus Jesus' unity with the Father did not deny Jesus' humanity.

Late in his ministry Jesus prayed:

Holy Father, keep through thine own name those whom thou has given me, that they may be one, *as we are one. J 17:11*

Later on in the same prayer, Jesus prayed:

That they all may be one; as thou, Father, art *in me*, and I *in thee*, that they also may be *one in us*: . . . that they may be one, *even as we are one*: I *in them*, and thou *in me*, that they may be made perfect in one . . . *J 17:21–23*

The relationship of Jesus and the Father may be graphed as follows:

Father   Jesus

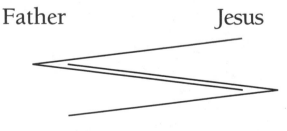

Shortly before Jesus had taught his disciples:

Yet a little while, and the world seeth me no more, but ye see me; because I live, ye shall live also. At that day ye shall know that I am *in my Father*, and ye in me, and I in you. *J 14:19–20*

Jesus had just instructed Thomas:

I am the way, the truth, and the life; no man cometh unto the Father but by me. If ye had known me, ye should have known my Father also; *and from henceforth ye know him, and have seen him.* *J 14:6–7*

This did not satisfy Philip so he said to Jesus:

Lord, shew us the Father, and it sufficeth us. *J 14:8*

Jesus replied tartly:

Have I been so long time with you, and yet hast thou not known me, Philip? He that hath seen me hath seen the Father. And how sayest thou then, "Shew us the Father?"

Believest thou not that I am *in the Father*, and the Father *in me*?

The words that I speak unto you I speak not of myself; but the Father that dwelleth in me, he doeth the works.

Believe me that I am *in the Father*, and the Father *in me*; . . . *J 14:9–11*

Earlier Jesus had said:

He that believeth on me, believeth not on me, but on him that sent me. And he that seeth me seeth him that sent me. *J 12:44–45*

On another occasion the Pharisees had sneeringly asked, "Where is *thy* Father?" *J 8:19*

Jesus answered:

> Ye neither know me, nor my Father. If ye had known me, ye should
> have known my Father also. *J 8:19*

Jesus thus claimed identity with his Father, God. This identity
allowed Jesus to properly say that he who had seen Jesus had seen
the Father. But this identity had a separateness of two beings since,
more precisely stated, Jesus taught that the Father was in him and
he was in the Father. The Father indwelt Jesus, and as a consequence Jesus did the Father's works and in so doing did not speak
for himself but for the Father. In both a practical and theological
sense Jesus and the Father were one.

Just as the Father indwelt Jesus so also has Jesus promised his
followers that he and his Father will indwell Jesus' followers:

> If a man love me, he will keep my words; and my Father will love
> him, and *we* will come unto him, and make *our* abode with him.

> He that loveth me not keepeth not my sayings; and the word which
> ye hear is not mine, but the Father's which sent me. *J 14:23–24*

Jesus Preexisted with God before the World was

Jesus did not simply teach, like a mystic, that he and God the Father were one. He claimed more. He claimed to have preexisted with God before the world began.

At the close of his ministry Jesus prayed:

And now, O Father, glorify thou me with thine own self with the glory which *I had with thee before the world was.* J 17:5

Father, I will that they also, whom thou hast given me, be with me where I am, that they may behold my glory, which thou hast given me: for *thou lovedst me before the foundation of the world.* J 17:24

Early in his ministry, in terms no Jew could misunderstand, Jesus said:

Verily, verily, I say unto you, before Abraham was, *I AM. J 8:58*

Jesus was paraphrasing one of the key sayings of the books of the Jewish Law:

And God said unto Moses, "I AM THAT I AM": and he said, "Thus shalt thou say, unto the children of Israel, I AM hath sent me unto you." *Exodus 3:14*

Jesus' claim to have preexisted before Abraham, and indeed, before the creation of the world, was the teaching John chose to introduce his gospel:

In the beginning was the Word, and the Word was *with God,* and the Word was God. The same was *in the beginning with God. J 1:1–2*

According to John, Jesus was the Word. *J 1:14, 16–18* Our English word *Word* translates John's Greek word *Logos* used to explain to a pagan world with a pagan term Jesus' unique status. It is

745

clear that this word refers to Jesus, but it was not Jesus' own word that was simply:

> Before Abraham was, I AM. *J 8:58*

Consistent with this statement, Jesus declared:

> I came forth from the Father, and am come into the world; again, I leave the world, and go to the Father. *J 16:28*

The teaching that Jesus preexisted with the Father before the creation of the world is different from, but is consistent with, the teaching that Jesus made the world. John taught that. In the prologue to his gospel John wrote:

> All things were made by him; and without him was not anything made that was made. *J 1:3*

> He was in the world, and the world was made by him, and the world knew him not. *J 1:10*

The writer of Hebrews makes the same point, writing, that God:

> Hath in these last days spoken unto us by his Son, whom he hath appointed heir of all things, *by whom also he made the worlds.* *Hebrews 1:2*

Finally, Paul in his Epistle to the Colossians ties together both Jesus' preexistence and his role in creation of the world, by writing:

> For by him were all things created, that are in heaven, and that are in earth, visible and invisible, whether they be thrones, or dominions, or principalities, or powers: *all things were created by him,* and for him; and *he is before all things*, and by him all things consist. *Colossians 1:16*

We do not often think of Jesus as creator of the universe. Paul, Hebrews and John are very clear upon this point. Jesus himself claimed to have been present at creation, present with the Father before the foundation of the world, present with the Father before the world was.

CHAPTER 13

JESUS' MISSION AND AUTHORITY

SEALED–SANCTIFIED–SENT

In addition to preexistence with God before the world was, Jesus claimed to have been "sent" from God in a special and unique way: "for him hath God the Father sealed." J 6:27 God has placed his unique seal on Jesus to show his authority just as an official receives a sealed commission from a governor.

In another place Jesus asked the Jews:

> Say ye of him, whom the Father hath sanctified, and sent into the world, "Thou blasphemest," because I said, "I am the Son of God?"
> J 10:36

"To sanctify" is literally "to make holy", and the idea is that Jesus was dedicated and consecrated to his special holy task.

Jesus was "sealed" and "sanctified" by the Father but Jesus preferred the simple formula that he was "sent" by the Father. In each of the following quotations from Jesus, emphasis has been added to the word "sent":

> My meat is to do the will of him that *sent* me, and to finish his work.
> J 4:34

He that honoreth not the Son honoreth not the Father which hath *sent* him. *J 5:23*

For I come down from heaven, not to do mine own will, but the will of him that *sent* me. And this is the Father's will which hath *sent* me, that of all which he hath given me I should lose nothing, but should raise it up again at the last day. *J 6:38–40*

No man can come to me, except the Father which hath *sent* me draw him: . . . *J 6:44*

As the living Father hath *sent* me, and I live by the Father; so he that eateth me, even he shall live by me. *J 6:57*

Ye both know me, and ye know whence I am; and I am not come of myself, but he that *sent* me is true, whom ye know not. But I know him: for I am from him, and he hath *sent* me. *J 7:28–29*

And he that *sent* me is with me; the Father hath not left me alone: for I do always those things that please him. *J 8:29*

If God were your Father, ye would love me: for I proceeded forth and came from God; neither came I of myself, but he *sent* me. *J 8:42*

For I have not spoken of myself; but the Father which *sent* me, he gave me a commandment, what I should say, and what I should speak. *J 12:49*

He that loveth me not keepeth not my sayings; and the word which ye hear is not mine, but the Father's which *sent* me. *J 14:24*

And this is life eternal, that they might know thee the only true God, and Jesus Christ, whom thou has *sent*. *J 17:3*

As thou hast *sent* me into the world, even so have I also sent them into the world. *J 17:18*

That they all may be one: as thou, Father, art in me, and I in thee, that they also may be one in us; that the world may believe that thou hast *sent* me. *J 17:21*

. . . that the world may know that thou hast *sent* me . . . *J 17:23*

Peace be unto you: as my Father hath *sent* me, even so send I you. *J 20:21*

Jesus' characteristic assertions that he was "sent" from God are not confined to his sayings recorded in John's Gospel. Both Mark and Luke record this saying:

Whosoever shall receive me, receiveth not me, but him that *sent* me. *Mk 9:37*

Whosoever shall receive me receiveth him that *sent* me. *L 9:48*

Luke also has the converse saying:

. . . he that despiseth me despiseth him that *sent* me. *L 10:16*

Matthew and John both have the saying "he that receiveth me receiveth him that *sent* me." *Mt 10:40; J 13:20*

The Father sealed, sanctified, and sent Jesus. Jesus' claims on these points are summarized by two further quotations from him:

I am *come in my Father's name*, and ye receive me not; if another shall come in his own name, him ye will receive. *J 5:43*

I *came forth from the Father*, and am come into the world; again, I leave the world, and go to the Father. *J 16:28*

JESUS' AUTHORITY

When certain Pharisees challenged Jesus permitting his disciples to pluck heads of grain on a Sabbath, Jesus, after explaining that the Sabbath was made for man and not man for the Sabbath, concluded:

> But I say unto you, that in this place is one greater than the Temple. But if ye had known what this meaneth, "I will have mercy, and not sacrifice," ye would not have condemned the guiltless. For the Son of man is Lord even of the Sabbath day. *Mt 12:6–8*

Jesus was, of course, quoting, the Old Testament to these legalists:

> For I desired mercy, and not sacrifice, and the knowledge of God more than burnt offerings. *Hosea 6:6*

God did not care for the vexatious "sacrifices" of legalistic Sabbath observance. Jesus' disciples were guiltless since he was their Lord and as Son of man was Lord of the Sabbath, as well as greater things. Jesus veiled his claim of general authority by saying:

> But I say unto you, that in this place is *one* greater than the Temple. *Mt 12:6*

Both Matthew and Luke report that Jesus also cryptically referred to his own general authority as "greater than Jonah" who was a prophet of Israel, and as "greater than Solomon," who was one of the greatest kings of Israel:

> Behold, a greater than Jonah is here. *Mt 12:41; L 11:32*

> Behold, a greater than Solomon is here. *Mt 12:42; L 11:31*

Jesus was specifically asked:

Art thou greater than our father Abraham, which is dead? And the prophets are dead. Whom makest thou thyself? *J 8:53*

Jesus did not answer directly and the interrogation continued, with the Jews asking:

Thou art not yet fifty years old, and thou hast seen Abraham? *J 8:57*

Jesus answered:

Verily, verily, I say unto you, before Abraham was, I AM. *J 8:58*

This was a claim in that Jewish culture, not simply that he had seen Abraham who had lived many centuries before, but a claim that he was God himself. *Exodus 3:14* A short time later Jesus was pressed by some Jews to state his mission:

How long dost thou make us to doubt? If thou be the Christ, tell us plainly. *J 10:24*

Jesus' answer ended with this statement:

I and my Father are one. *J 10:30*

That was Jesus' ultimate claim as to his authority.

Jesus' Verification of His Calling: The Sign of Jonah

The religious intelligentsia of Jesus' day wanted proof of his credentials. This was the normal Jewish procedure. Paul wrote that "the Jews require a sign." *1 Corinthians 1:22* Accordingly, on one occasion certain scribes and Pharisees made a request, "Master, we would see a sign from thee." *Mt 12:38*

We have two accounts of Jesus' reply:

MATTHEW	LUKE
And evil and adulterous generation seeketh after a sign; and there shall be no sign given to it, but the sign of the prophet Jonah. For as Jonah was three days and three nights in the whale's belly so shall the Son of man be three days and three nights in the heart of the earth.	This is an evil generation: they seek a sign; and there shall be no sign given to it, but the sign of Jonah the prophet. For as Jonah was a sign unto the Ninevites, so shall also the Son of man be to this generation. *L 11:29–30*
The men of Nineveh shall rise in judgment with this generation and shall condemn it: because they repented at the preaching of Jonah and, behold, a greater than Jonah is here.	The men of Nineveh shall rise up in the judgment with this generation, and shall condemn it: for they repented at the preaching of Jonah; and, behold, a greater than Jonah is here. *L 11:32*
The queen of the south shall rise up	The queen of the south shall rise up

MATTHEW (cont.)	LUKE (cont.)
in the judgment	in the judgment
	with the men
with this generation,	of this generation,
and shall condemn it:	and shall condemn them:
for she came	for she came
from the uttermost	from the utmost
parts of the earth	parts of the earth
to hear the wisdom of Solomon:	to hear the wisdom of Solomon;
and, behold,	and, behold,
a greater than Solomon	a greater than Solomon
is here.	is here.
Mt 12:39–42	L 11:31

On another occasion it was the Pharisees and the Sadducees who wanted a sign:

MARK	MATTHEW
And the Pharisees	The Pharisees
	also with the Sadducees
came forth,	came,
and began to question	and tempting [testing him]
with him,	desired him
seeking of him	that he would shew them
a sign from heaven,	a sign from heaven.
tempting him.	
And he sighed deeply	He answered
in his spirit	
and saith,	and said unto them,
	"When it is evening,
	ye say,
	'It will be fair weather:
	for the sky is red.'
	And in the morning,
	'It will be foul weather today:
	for the sky is red
	and lowering.'"

MARK (cont.)	MATTHEW (cont.)
	"O ye hypocrites,
	ye can discern
	the face of the sky;
	but can ye not discern
	the signs of the times?
"Why doth this	A wicked and adulterous
generation	generation
seek after a sign?	seeketh after a sign;
Verily I say unto you,	and
there shall be no sign	there shall be no sign
given unto this generation."	given unto it,
Mk 8:11–12	but the sign
	of the prophet Jonah."
	Mt 16:1–4

It was not just the scribes, Pharisees and Sadducees who demanded that Jesus authenticate his calling with a sign but also the people generally:

And others, tempting [testing] him, sought of him a *sign* from heaven. L 11:16

Then answered the Jews and said unto him, "What *sign* shewest thou unto us, seeing that thou doest these things?" J 2:18

They said therefore unto him, "What *sign* shewest thou then, that we may see and believe thee? What dost thou work?" J 6:30

Jesus once complained to "the people":

When ye see a cloud rise out of the west, straightway ye say, "There cometh a shower"; and so it is.

And when ye see the south wind blow, ye say, "There will be heat"; and it cometh to pass.

Ye hypocrites, ye can discern the face of the sky and of the earth;
but how is it that ye do not discern this time? *L 12:54–56*

Whether it was "the people" or the Pharisees and Sadducees
Jesus was exasperated at their failure to discern the spiritual state
of the times:

MATTHEW	LUKE
O ye hypocrites,	Ye hypocrites,
ye can discern	ye can discern
the face of the sky;	the face of the sky
	and of the earth;
but can	but how is it that
ye not discern	ye do not discern
the signs of the times?	this time?
Mt 16:3	*L 12:56*

Instead they wanted a miraculous sign "from heaven." *Mk 8:11;
Mt 16:1; L 11:16* Jesus was emphatic that no such sign would be given.
Mark reports that Jesus "sighed deeply in his spirit" and said:

Why doth this generation seek after a sign? Verily I say unto you,
there shall be no sign given to this generation. *Mk 8:12*

Some scholars eagerly contend that this statement contradicts
the three instances when Jesus is quoted as having said that no
sign would be given to his generation except "the sign of the prophet
Jonah." *Mt 12:39, 16:4 (L 11:29)* Like anyone's informal oral statements
over time, Jesus' informal oral statements varied, but there was no
inconsistency here. No miraculous sign like they sought would be
given. That is true, but it is also true that they were receiving a sign
that they did not recognize as such, the sign of Jonah. That sign
was Jesus' preaching that their generation needed to repent.

The sign of Jonah was that he had preached repentance to the
men of Nineveh. *Jonah 4; Mt 12:41; L 11:32* Jesus had preached repentance to his generation. *Mk 1:15, 2:17; Mt 4:17; L 5:32, 13:3, 5* They had
not repented. The men of Nineveh had repented. Accordingly at

the time of the final judgment, the men of Nineveh will condemn Jesus' generation for not repenting, just as the queen of the south will then condemn that generation for not recognizing Jesus as "a greater than Solomon." *Mt 12:41–42; L 11:31–32*

Luke reports that Jesus said:

> For as Jonah was a sign unto the Ninevites, so shall also the Son of man be to this generation. *L 11:30*

Jesus had preached repentance to that generation, and they had not repented. Jesus therefore indicted that generation as "an evil generation." *L 11:29; Mt 12:39 ("an evil and adulterous generation"); Mt 16:4 ("a wicked and adulterous generation")*

Is our generation also a wicked and adulterous generation? Does our generation seek a miraculous sign? Will any sign be given to our generation except Jesus' preaching that repentance is required?

Jesus' Proof That He Spoke for God

Jesus' proof for his claims was simple and pragmatic:

My doctrine is not mine, but his that sent me. *If any man will do his will*, he shall know of the doctrine, whether it be of God, or whether I speak of myself. *J 7:16–17*

The test of the truth of Jesus' doctrine, or as we would now say his teaching, is to do God's will, and the doer will learn if Jesus spoke for God or only for himself. That test is easily available to moderns. To get your answer, you must first take the test: do the will of God.

Jesus insisted that the attitude and outlook of the questioner was crucial to the questioner getting the answer about Jesus' teaching. He told Pilate:

Every one that is *of the truth* heareth my voice. *J 18:37*

In the course of a hostile confrontation with some Jews, Jesus said:

Why do you not understand my speech? Even because ye cannot hear [accept] my word. Ye are of your father the devil, and the lusts [desires] of your father ye will do. He was a murderer from the beginning, and abode not in the truth, because there is no truth in him . . .

And because I tell you the truth, ye believe me not. Which of you convinceth [convicts] me of sin? And if I say the truth, why do ye not believe me?

He that is of God heareth God's words: ye therefore hear them not, because *you are not of God*. J 8:43–47

Jesus told another group of Jews:

> But ye believe not, because *ye are not of my sheep*, as I said unto you. *My sheep hear my voice*, and I know them, and they follow me. J 10:26–27

In summary Jesus' position was: I know my sheep, and they know me; since they know me, they hear my voice.

This authentication may be unsatisfactory to skeptics, but that is different from saying that such authentication is objectively invalid. The question is really the ultimate nature of the spiritual universe. Skeptics can not prove Jesus wrong; all they can say is that his claims are unacceptable to them.

That said, Jesus did recognize that people want objective proof and he forthrightly offered such proof. His proof was "*the works which the Father hath given me* to finish, the same works that I do, *bear witness of me*, that the Father hath sent me." J 5:36 Jesus' whole statement was:

> If I bear witness of myself, my witness is not true [not admissible as evidence under Jewish legal procedures].

> There is another that beareth witness of me; and I know that the witness which he witnesseth of me is true.

> Ye sent unto John [the Baptist], and he bare witness unto the truth. But I receive not testimony from man [specifically John the Baptist]; but these things I say, that ye might be saved. He [John the Baptist] was a burning and shining light; and ye were willing for a season to rejoice in his light.

> But I have greater witness than that of John [the Baptist]: for *the works which the Father hath given me to finish, the same works that I do, bear witness of me, that the Father hath sent me.*

> And the Father himself, which hath sent me, hath borne witness of me. J 5:31–37

Jesus' key evidence (witness) for his calling were "the works which the Father has given me to finish, the same works that I do." *J 5:36*

The phrase "the works that I do" is ambiguous. It can be read as "the works that I have done" that make sense as a statement to his Jewish contemporaries. "Works" then referred to the miracles and healings he had *already* done. For example, John 2:11 (water into wine); John 4:46–54 (healing the nobleman's son); and John 5:1–17 (healing a man who had an infirmity for thirty-eight years).

Miracles and healings were the evidence Jesus cited when John the Baptist sent two of his disciples to ask, "Art thou he that should come, or do we look for another?" *Mt 11:2–3 (L 7:20)*

Jesus' answer was:

MATTHEW	LUKE
Go and show John again	Go your way and tell John
those things which	what things
ye do hear and see;	ye have seen and heard:
the blind	now that the blind
receive their sight, and	see,
the lame walk;	the lame walk;
the lepers are cleansed, and	the lepers are cleansed,
the deaf hear;	the deaf hear,
the dead are raised up, and	the dead are raised;
the poor have	to the poor
the gospel	the gospel
preached to them.	is preached.
And blessed is he	And blessed is he,
whosoever shall not	whosoever shall not
be offended in me.	be offended in me.
Mt 11:4–6	*L 7:22–23*

Some Jews asked Jesus:

If thou be the Christ; tell us plainly. *J 10:24*

Jesus replied:

> I told you, and you believed not: *the works that I do in my Father's name*, they bear witness to me. *J 10:25*

Consistent with "works" meaning healing and miracles, Jesus said that his believers will also do the same works:

> Verily, verily, I say unto you, he that believeth on me, the works that I do shall he do *also*; and greater works than these shall he do; because I go unto my Father. *J 14:12*

The phrase "the works that I do" can also be read as including the works that I have yet to do. This would include his death on the cross and his resurrection both of which were yet to come. These were "the works which the Father hath given me to finish" *J 5:36*
When his cross loomed near Jesus said:

> If I had not done among them *the works which none other man did*, they had not had sin; but now have they both seen and hated both me and my Father. *J 15:24*

Jesus returned again and again to his works as his witness:

> If I do not the *works of my Father*, believe me not. But if I do, though ye believe not me, believe *the works*: that ye may know and believe, that the Father is in me, and I in him. *J 10:37–39*

> Believest thou not that I am in the Father, and the Father in me? The words that I speak unto you I speak not of myself; but the Father that dwelleth in me, he doeth *the works*. Believe me that I am in the Father, and the Father in me; or else believe me for the *very works' sake. J 14:10–11*

Some of Jesus' Jewish contemporaries did not accept his "works" proof of his calling by God. Some Pharisees charged:

> Thou bearest record of thyself; thy record is not true. *J 8:13*

In reply Jesus summed up the evidence of his calling as follows:

> Though I bear record of myself, yet my record is true: for I know whence I came, and whether I go; but ye can not tell whence I come, and whither I go.

> Ye judge after the flesh; I judge no man. And yet if I judge, my judgment is true: *for I am not alone, but I and the Father that sent me.*

> It is also written in your law [*Deuteronomy 19:15*], that the testimony of two men is true. I am one that bear witness of myself, and *the Father that sent me* beareth witness of me. *J 8:14–18*

The Pharisees were actually making two different charges:

1. Thou bearest record of thyself. *J 8:13*
2. Thy record is not true. *J 8:13*

The first charge was that Jesus' own testimony was inadmissible in evidence under Jewish legal procedure. This rule had an exception when the challenged testimony was corroborated by another witness. Jesus in effect asserted that he was corroborated by the Father. This also met the two witness requirement of Deuteronomy 19:15. Jesus' statement was:

> I am one that bear witness of myself, and the Father that sent me beareth witness of me. *J 8:18*

As might be expected the Pharisees were not persuaded, and they simply counterattacked with a sneering question, "Where is thy Father?" *J 8–19*

The Pharisees' second charge was much more important than noncompliance with the Jewish rules of evidence. That charge was:

> Thy record is not true. *J 8:13*

Jesus' answer to this charge was:

1. I know whence I came, and whither I go, but ye can not tell
    whence I come, and whither I go. *J 8:14*
2. "I am not alone;" the Father sent me. *J 8:16,18*

Jesus relied upon his own testimony. He affirmatively stated
that "I receive not testimony from man." *J 5:34* He testified before
Pilate:

> Thou sayest that I am a king. To this end was I born, and for this
> cause come I into the world, that *I should bear witness unto the truth.*
> *J 18:37*

Any fair investigation will consider with care the testimony of
the person under investigation. Initial investigative assumptions
can not exclude rationally the possibility that the testimony is true.
That is not to say that a person's testimony in his own behalf is not
to be viewed with caution.

The Pharisees of Jesus' time went further than caution about
Jesus' testimony. They simply rejected it outright:

> Thou bearest record of thyself; thy record is not true. *J 8:13*

That was wrong then, and is wrong now. Jesus, like anyone, is
entitled to be heard on his own behalf.

The ultimate question is Jesus' credibility. No one can escape
making a judgment about his credibility, either expressly or im-
plicitly. A fair and honest judgment is important. The consequences
of an error of judgment are enormous.

JESUS' OWN VIEW OF HIS MISSION

Jesus' own view of his mission was multifaceted, not simplistic. His own view does not fit into simple verbal tags or logical formulas. It is like a diamond with many facets.

In one parable he shifted abruptly from the imagery of being like a sheepfold door to being a good shepherd of the sheep in the fold:

I am *the door* of the sheep[fold] . . .

I am *the good shepherd*: *the good shepherd* giveth his life for the sheep . . .

I am *the good shepherd*, and know my sheep, and am known of mine. As the Father knoweth me, even so know I the Father; and I lay down my life for the sheep. *J 10:7, 11, 14–15*

At that time and place a shepherd himself would act as door to protect the entrance to the fold. Jesus' statement that he is "the good shepherd" has burned itself into the consciousness of our age, as has his statement that he is "the light of the world":

I am *the light of the world*. He that followeth me shall not walk in darkness, but shall have the light of life. *J 8:12*

As long as I am in the world, I am *the light of the world*. *J 9:5*

I am come *a light into the world*, that whosoever believeth on me should not abide in darkness. And if any man hear my words, and believe not, I judge him not: for I come not to judge the world, but to save the world. *J 12:46–47*

Jesus used other metaphors to describe his multifaceted mission. Once he described his mission in horticultural terms, as he being a vine, and his disciples being branches of that vine:

I am *the true vine*, and my Father is the husbandman . . .

I am *the vine*, ye are the branches. He that abideth in me, and I in him, the same bringeth forth much fruit: for without me ye can do nothing. *J 15:1, 5*

Jesus also described himself as being "the bread of life." Some Jews asked Jesus for a sign authenticating his mission, saying, "Our fathers did eat manna in the desert; as it is written [*Exodus 16:4, Psalms 78:24*], 'He gave them bread from heaven to eat.'" *J 6:31* Jesus replied:

Verily, verily, I say unto you, Moses gave you not that bread from heaven; but my Father giveth you *the true bread from heaven*. For *the bread of God* is he which cometh down from heaven, and giveth life unto the world . . .

I am *the bread of life*. He that cometh to me shall never hunger; and he that believeth on me shall never thirst . . .

Verily, verily, I say unto you, he that believeth on me hath everlasting life. I am *that bread of life*.

Your fathers did eat manna in the wilderness, and are dead. This is *the bread which cometh down from heaven*, that a man may eat thereof, and not die.

I am *the living bread which came down from heaven*. If any man eat of *this bread*, he shall live forever; and *the bread* that I will give is my flesh, which I will give for the life of the world . . .

This is *that bread which came down from the heaven*: not as your fathers did eat manna, and are dead; he that eateth of *this bread* shall live for ever. *J 6:32–33, 35, 47–51, 58*

The theme of life "for ever" for men is intertwined in Jesus' teaching with his description of his mission. He taught:

I am the resurrection, and the life; he that believeth in me, though he were dead, yet shall he live; and whosoever liveth and believeth in me shall never die. *J 11:25–26*

The manuscripts of John's Gospel differ on whether Jesus said, "I am the resurrection and the life," or only, "I am the resurrection."

If he said, "I am the resurrection and the life," it overlaps his statement that "I am the way, the truth and the life." J 14:6 The common term between the two statements is "I am the life."

Jesus' words that "I am the way, the truth, the life and the resurrection" summarize his mission in his own way. These words together have a special essence of meaning beyond the total sum of the dictionary definitions of each separate phrase.

Jesus is the path or the way to the Father for others, yet the Father was in him, and he was in the Father. His way is the true way to life for ever. He is not the resurrection as such but the means by which the resurrection can come to man. In his way is the life for men to live on their way to life for ever.

A more literal precis of Jesus' statements would be:

1. As the good shepherd he gives his life for his sheep.
2. As the living bread he is given for the life of the world.
3. This bread gives life for ever.
4. This bread also lights the darkness of the world.
5. This bread is also the door of salvation to those who enter in.
6. There is no other way to the Father for he is the resurrection, the truth and the life.
7. Those that believe in him shall live as branches of the true vine tended by his Father.

Jesus' words as to his mission shine like facets of a diamond with a poetic glow and subtlety, because they are metaphors. Once, however, Jesus tersely summarized his mission in plain language as follows:

He that believeth on me, believeth not on me, but on him that sent me.

And he that seeth me seeth him that sent me.

I am come a light into the world, that whosoever believeth on me should not abide in darkness.

And if any man hear my words, and believe not, I judge him not: for I came not to judge the world but to save the world. He that rejecteth me, and receiveth not my words, hath one that judgeth him; the word that I have spoken, the same shall judge him in the last day. For I have not spoken of myself; but the Father which sent me, he gave me a commandment, what I should say, and what I should speak.

And I know that his commandment is life everlasting; whatsoever I speak therefore, even as the Father said unto me, so speak I. *J 12:44–50*

Jesus' statement tersely summarizes his mission. Paraphrased to break the torpor of familiar verses, Jesus taught:

1. He that believes on Jesus believes not on Jesus but on God who sent him. *J 12:44*
2. He that sees Jesus sees God. *J 12:45*
3. Jesus came as a light to the world to save men from darkness. *J 12:46–47*
4. Jesus' words were commanded by God. *J 12:49–50*
5. Jesus' words so commanded by God are the basis of judgment of men at the last day. *J 12:48–50*
6. Jesus was certain that God's commandment for men is life everlasting. *J 12:50*

Jesus did say, "I am" the good shepherd, the light of the world, the bread of life, the true vine, the resurrection, the way, the truth and the life. These are the benign and acceptable blood–free facets of Jesus' mission, but his mission also had a stern and terrible facet. Jesus taught "that the Son of man must suffer many things, and be rejected of the elders, and of the chief priests, and scribes, and be killed, and after three days rise again." *Mk 8:31 (Mt 16:21; L 9:22)*

Jesus taught that his death would be "a ransom for many":

MARK	MATTHEW
For even the Son of man	Even as the Son of man

MARK (cont.)	MATTHEW (cont.)
came not	came not
to be ministered unto,	to be ministered unto,
but to minister,	but to minister,
and to give his life	and to give his life
a ransom *for* many.	a ransom *for* many.
Mk 10:45	*Mt 20:28*

No one doubts that Jesus did, in fact, give his life. The dispute is over how Jesus' statement that he was to give "his life a ransom for many" fits into the theology of atonement. Scholars quibble over whether the Greek word translated *for* (emphasized above) should be given its literal meaning of "in place of", and whether the Greek word translated *ransom* implies a payment to someone.

The plain fact is that Jesus anticipated his own death. On the evening before his death, he gave his disciples a cup of wine to drink, saying:

MARK	MATTHEW	LUKE
This is my blood	For this is my blood	This cup is
of the new testament,	of the new testament,	the new testament
		in my blood,
which is shed	which is shed	which is shed
for many.	for many	for you.
Mk 14:24	for the remission	*L 22:20*
	of sins.	
	Mt 26:29	

So far as Jesus was concerned, the ransom was his blood: Blood money "for many for the remission of sins." This mission of Jesus, his ransom-death, is unacceptable to many because they feel either they have no sin; or, in any case, Jesus' blood can not remit such sins. Jesus disagreed.

THE LIGHT OF THE WORLD

Jesus claimed to be the light of the world. He said:

I am *the light of the world*. He that followeth me shall not walk in darkness, but shall have the light of life. *J 8:12*

I am come *a light into the world*, that whosoever believeth on me should not abide in darkness. *J 12:46*

As long as I am in the world, I am *the light of the world*. *J 9:5*

The familiar form of Jesus' claim is that he is "*the* light of the world", but his alternate statement that he "came *a* light into the world is easier to understand. *J 8:12, 12:46* Both statements lead to the same result: those that follow him will not walk or abide "in darkness."

Jesus comes as light and illuminates the darkness of the world; those who follow him no longer stumble in its darkness. They live in the light he gives, or in the King James Version quaint phrase "have light of life." *J 8:12*

John editorializes the same point:

[Jesus] was the true light which lighteth every man . . . *J 1:9*

. . . [his] life was the light of men. *J 1:4*

Jesus considered himself as light illuminating the way for men to walk. Near the end of his ministry Jesus told some Jews:

Yet a little while is *the light* with you. Walk while ye have *the light*, lest darkness come upon you: for he that walketh in darkness knoweth not whither he goeth. While ye have light, believe in *the light*, that ye may be the children of light. *J 12:35–36*

These Jews had asserted:

We have heard out of the Law that Christ abideth for ever: . . . *J 12:34*

Jesus had answered that:

Yet a little while is the light with you. *J 12:35*

This referred to his impending death, just as had his earlier assertion:

As long as I am in the world, I am the light of the world. *J 9:5*

This does not mean that the light that Jesus brought was extinguished by his death. Jesus survived his death, but the darkness of the world remains. In his place are his followers. They are now, according to Jesus, the light of the world:

Ye are the light of the world. A city that is set on a hill can not be hid. *Mt 5:14*

Jesus asserted:

I am come a light into the world, that whosoever believeth on me should not abide in darkness. *J 12:46*

The usual emphasis is on the phrase "whosoever believeth on me." It is equally worthy of emphasis that those who believe no longer live in darkness.

The prologue to John's Gospel looks back at Jesus' ministry and states, "He was in the world, . . . and the world knew him not." *J 1:10*

Jesus anticipated this lack of recognition on the part of worldly men and said:

And this is the condemnation, that *light* is come into the world, and men loved darkness rather than light, because their deeds were evil. For every one that doeth evil hateth *the light*, neither cometh to *the light*, lest his deeds should be reproved. But he that doeth truth cometh to *the light*, that his deeds may be made manifest, that they are wrought in God. *J 3:19–21*

The prologue to John's Gospel summarized Jesus' mission as the light of the world as follows:

> In him was life; and the life was the light of men. And the light shineth in darkness; and the darkness comprehended [quenches] it not . . . That was the true Light, which lighteth every man that cometh into the world. *J 1:4–5, 9*

THE BREAD OF GOD

A couple of days after the feeding of the five thousand with the loaves and fishes, Jesus was teaching in the synagogue at Capernaum, Galilee. *J 6:22–24, 59* A crowd of people had been searching for him, and when they found him there was this interchange:

CROWD: Rabbi, when camest thou hither?

JESUS: Verily, verily, I say unto you, ye seek me, not because ye saw the miracles, but because ye did eat of the loaves, and were filled. Labor not for the meat which perisheth, but for that meat which endureth unto everlasting life, which the Son of man shall give unto you: for him hath God the Father sealed.

CROWD: What shall we do, that we might work the works of God?

JESUS: This is the work of God, that ye believe on him whom he hath sent.

CROWD: What sign shewest thou then, that we may see, and believe thee? What dost thou work? Our fathers did eat manna in the desert; as it is written [in Exodus 16:4 and Psalm 78:24], "He gave them bread from heaven to eat."

JESUS: Verily, verily, I say unto you, Moses gave you not that bread from heaven; but my Father giveth you the true bread from heaven. For the bread of God is he which cometh down from heaven, and giveth life unto the world.

CROWD: Lord [Sir], evermore give us this bread.

JESUS: I am the bread of life: he that cometh to me shall never hunger; and he that believeth on me shall never thirst. *J 6:25–35*

Jesus then briefly digressed to other matters; but the crowd's mind was still on his words about bread. John states:

The Jews then murmured at him, because he said, "I am the bread which came down from heaven."

And they said, "Is not this Jesus, the son of Joseph, whose father and mother we know? How is it then that he saith, 'I came down from heaven?'" *J 6:41–42*

773

Jesus answered:

Murmur not among yourselves. *J 6:43*

Jesus then discussed other matters briefly before he continued:

Verily, verily, I say unto you, he that believeth on me hath everlasting life. I am that bread of life.

Your fathers did eat manna in the wilderness, and are dead. This is the bread which came down from heaven, that a man eat thereof, and not die.

I am the living bread which came down from heaven: if any man eat of this bread, he shall live forever; and the bread that I will give is my flesh, which I will give for the life of the world. *J 6:47–51*

This puzzled the Jewish crowd. John states:

The Jews therefore strove among themselves, "How can this man give us his flesh to eat?" *J 6:52*

Jesus overheard and answered them:

Verily, verily, I say unto you, except ye eat the flesh of the Son of man, and drink his blood, ye have no life in you. Whoso eateth my flesh, and drinketh my blood, hath eternal life; and I will raise him up at the last day.

For my flesh is meat indeed, and my blood is drink indeed. He that eateth my flesh, and drinketh my blood, dwelleth in me, and I in him.

As the living Father hath sent me, and I live by the Father: so he that eateth me, even he shall live by me. This is that bread which came down from heaven: not as your fathers did eat manna, and are dead: he that eateth of this bread shall live forever. *J 6:53–58*

Jesus' teaching that his flesh must be eaten and his blood drunk is a difficult doctrine. Many even of his disciples who heard him say it, murmured:

This is a hard saying; who can hear it? *J 6:60*

Jesus sensed their murmuring and asked:

Doth this offend you? *J 6:62*

It did. John records:

From that time many of his disciples went back, and walked no more with him. *J 6:66*

Modern "disciples" are still offended. They want no part of slaughterhouse religion and see eating flesh and drinking blood as uncouth subjects belonging in anthropology treatises, not in the teaching of Jesus. In a way, the doctrine of eating Jesus's flesh and blood was harder for his Jewish disciples than for moderns. Their ancient law stated:

And whatsoever man there be of the house of Israel, or of the strangers that sojourn among you, who eateth any manner of blood, I will even set my face against the soul that eateth blood, and will cut him off from among his people. *Leviticus 17:10*

There are many other passages to like effect. Even the new Christian church at its first council in Jerusalem in about A.D. 49 still advised Gentile converts:

For it seemed good to the Holy Spirit, and to us, to lay upon you no greater burden than *these necessary things*: that ye abstain from meats offered to idols, and from *blood*, and from things strangled, and from fornication. . . . *Acts 15:28–29*

But Jesus did say:

Verily, verily, I say unto you, except ye eat the flesh of the Son of
man, and drink his blood, ye have no life in you. Whoso eateth my
flesh, and drinketh my blood, hath eternal life; and I will raise him
up at the last day. For my flesh is meat indeed, and my blood is
drink indeed. He that eateth my flesh, and drinketh my blood,
dwelleth in me, and I in him. *J 6:53–56*

Jesus said, in substance, that his flesh was true meat and his
blood was true drink.

What did Jesus mean by this?

In that discourse that day Jesus formulated what he meant in
three different but equivalent ways. He said:

Verily, verily,		
I say unto you,	whoso eateth	
he that	my follow	If any man
believeth on me	and drinketh	eat of this bread
	my blood	he shall
hath everlasting life.	hath eternal life; . . .	live forever: . . .
J 6:47	*J 6:54*	*J 6:51 (58)*

I leave to wordsmiths the differences between "everlasting life",
"eternal life", and "live forever." Jesus was speaking Aramaic and
was not involved with subtleties of Greek words or any metaphysical differences in English between *eternal* and *everlasting*. Here,
Jesus was talking to ordinary people and his words translated "everlasting life", "eternal life", and "live forever" all meant the same
thing. Since they do mean the same thing, it follows that, for Jesus,
"believeth on me" is the same as "eateth my flesh and drinketh my
blood." Therefore he meant eating his flesh and drinking his blood
to be understood symbolically. This symbolic meaning is reinforced
by Jesus' use of a third equivalent "eat of this bread." *J 6:51 (58)*

Jesus did say that "the bread that I will give is my flesh", but he
also said that "I am the living bread which came down from heaven."

J 6:51 Bread equals flesh, but bread also equals a symbol or metaphor of the gift from heaven. Here is how Jesus phrased it:

> I am the living bread which came down from heaven: If any man
> eat of this bread, he shall live forever; the bread that I will give is my
> flesh, which I will give for the life of the world. *J 6:51*

Jesus was speaking informally that day and his discourse is sprinkled with variants of his full phrase "the living bread which came down from heaven." *J 6:51* For example, he used as alternative phrases, "that bread from heaven", "the true bread from heaven", "the bread of life", "the bread of God", "that bread of life", and "the bread which cameth down from heaven. *J 6:32, 33, 35, 48, 50* These phrases state two concepts:

1. This bread was from heaven or of God.
2. This was living bread which would give life, eternal life.

Let us not be literal–minded like the Jews, who asked:

> How can this man give us his flesh to eat? *J 6:52*

Jesus spoke figuratively. He taught that he was mystical bread and water that ends spiritual hunger and thirst forever:

> I am the bread of life: he that cometh to me shall never hunger; and
> he that believeth on me shall never thirst. *J 6:35*

The true meaning of the living bread is found in the words Jesus used at his Last Supper when he used the bread that he broke as the symbol of his body. In the same manner he used the wine offered as the symbol of his blood. We have four accounts of what Jesus said that night:

MARK	MATTHEW	LUKE	PAUL
And as they	And as they	And	The Lord Jesus
did eat,	were eating,		the same night
Jesus	Jesus	he	in which he

MARK (cont.)	MATTHEW (cont.)	LUKE (cont.)	PAUL (cont.)
			was betrayed
took bread,	took bread,	took bread,	took bread; and when
and	and	and	he had
blessed it,	blessed it,	gave thanks,	given thanks,
and brake it,	and brake it,	and brake it,	he brake it,
and gave	and gave it	and gave	
to them,	to the disciples,	unto them,	
and said,	and said,	saying,	and said,
"Take, eat:	"Take, eat;		"Take, eat;
this is	this is	"This is	this is
my body."	my body."	my body	my body,
		which is given	which is broken
		for you:	for you:
		this do	this do
		in remembrance	in remembrance
		of me."	of me."
		L 22:19	After the same manner
And	And	And	also
he took	he took	he took	he took
the cup,	the cup,	the cup,	the cup,
and when he			when he
had given	and gave	and gave	had supped,
thanks,	thanks,	thanks,	
he gave it	and gave it		
to them;	to them,		
and they all			
drank of it.			
And he said	saying,	and said,	
unto them,			
	"Drink ye	"Take this,	
	all of it;	and divide it	
		among	
		yourselves: . . ."	
		L 22:17	
			Likewise also

MARK (cont.)	**MATTHEW** (cont.)	**LUKE** (cont.)	**PAUL** (cont.)
		the cup after supper,	
"This is my blood of the new testament,	for this is my blood of the new testament,	saying, "This cup is the new testament in my blood,	saying, "This cup is the new testament in my blood:
which is shed for many.	which is shed for many for the remission of sins.	which is shed for you." *L 22:20*	
Verily I say unto you, I will drink no more of the fruit of the vine, until that day that I drink it new in the Kingdom of God." *Mk 14:22–25*	But I say unto you, I will not drink henceforth of this fruit of the vine, until that day when I drink it new with you in my Father's Kingdom." *Mt 26:26–29*	"For I say unto you, I will not drink of the fruit of the vine, until the Kingdom of God shall come." *L 22:18*	this do ye, as oft as ye drink it, in remembrance of me." *I Corinthians 11:23–25*

For easy comparison, the order of Luke's account has been conformed to the order of the other three accounts. In all the accounts, except Luke's, the bread came before the wine. This difference in order is apparent rather than real, since Luke has included, what the other accounts omit, the wine before supper. In short, Luke has two occasions when wine was drunk that night: before and after supper; the other accounts refer only to the wine after the supper, after the bread. There are further complexities that certain statements, which Luke attributes to the time before the supper, the others attribute to the time after the supper and that the fact the manuscripts of Luke vary, which variance is in turn reflected in differences in various versions of Luke.

What is important is what Jesus actually said. According to the manuscripts used for the King James Version, here is what Luke wrote that Jesus actually said:

> And he took the cup, and gave thanks, and said, "Take this, and divide it among yourselves: for I say unto you, I will not drink of the fruit of the vine, until the Kingdom of God shall come."

> And he took bread, and gave thanks, and brake it, and gave unto them, saying, "This is my body which is given for you: this do in remembrance of me."

> Likewise also the cup *after supper*, saying, "This cup is the new testament in my blood, which is shed for you." *L 22:17–20*

The four accounts obviously vary slightly. But there can be no doubt that Jesus told his disciples that the broken bread was his body ("This is my body") and that the wine was his blood, although the accounts are evenly split as to exactly how Jesus phrased it:

MARK AND MATTHEW	LUKE AND PAUL
This is my blood	This cup is
of the new testament.	the new testament
Mk 14:24; Mt 26:28	in my blood.
	L 22:20;
	I Corinthians 11:25

The word *testament* suggests a will of one who is about to die and Jesus was about to die. Many modern translations substitute for the word *testament* the word *covenant* that suggests an agreement. The Greek word used is ambiguous and can mean either a will or an agreement; but Jesus was speaking Aramaic, not Greek; and, in any case, was stating divine principles in human analogies.

A will is a unilateral act of the testator; and here, by analogy, Jesus was the testator. On the other hand, by analogy, a covenant or an agreement requires more than one party. Here, only Jesus was acting. In modern legal terms, bypassing centuries of theology and legalistic glosses, the truest analogy is "an offer." Jesus, on behalf of his Father, made an offer through his blood to every person.

The wine was symbolic of his blood, while the bread was symbolic of his flesh. The bread is superior to the manna of Moses:

> Your fathers did eat manna in the wilderness, and are dead. This is the bread which cometh down from heaven, that a man may eat thereof, and not die.

> I am the living bread which came down from heaven: if any man eat of this bread he shall live forever; and the bread I will give is my flesh, which I will give for the life of the world. *J 6:49–51*

It seems clear enough that Jesus spoke of himself as spiritual, not physical, bread. It is true that Jesus said at his Last Supper when he broke bread:

> This is my body. *Mk 14:22; Mt 26:26; L 22:19; I Corinthians 11:24*

This sentence has been a theological battleground for centuries. How is the communion wafer Jesus' flesh and the communion wine Jesus' blood? At his Last Supper, Jesus did not cut his flesh or tap his blood; instead he used that bread and wine as symbols of spiritual truth.

Jesus did say, "This is my body," but he also said, "I am the door;" and no one supposes that he was an actual physical door, whether an ordinary door or a Middle East shepherd lying across a sheepfold entrance. *J 10:9*

Jesus did say, "This is my body," but he also said, "I am the vine;" and no one supposes that he was a grape stalk. *J 15:5* His being "the vine" is simply a symbol or metaphor of spiritual truth.

Jesus did say, "This is my body," but he also said:

> I am the bread of life: he that *cometh to me* shall never hunger; and he that *believeth on me* shall never thirst. *J 6:35*

Believe ye this?

Everlasting Water

As Jesus was passing through Samaria he stopped to rest in Sychar at Jacob's Well. He said to a Samaritan woman who came to draw water, "Give me to drink." *J 4:7*

The woman asked, "How is that thou, being a Jew, asketh drink of me, which am a woman of Samaria?" *J 4:9* The Jews then had no dealings with the Samaritans, who observed only part of the Jewish religion.

Jesus answered:

If though knewest the gift of God, and who it is that saith to thee, "Give me to drink;" thou wouldest have asked of him, and he would have given thee living water . . .

Whosoever drinketh of this water shall thirst again, but whosoever drinketh of the water that I shall give him shall never thirst; but the water that I shall give him shall be in him a well of water springing up into everlasting life. *J 4:10, 13–14*

As Jesus was teaching in the synagogue in Capernaum, he stated:

I am the bread of life: he that cometh to me shall never hunger; and he that believeth on me shall never thirst. *J 6:35*

Later on at the Feast of Tabernacles, on the last, the great day of the feast, Jesus stood up and cried out:

If any man thirst, let him come unto me and drink. He that believeth on me, as the Scripture hath said, "Out of his belly [inner being] shall flow rivers of living water." *J 7:37–38*

The precise scripture Jesus referred to is uncertain. John's explanation of this saying was:

But this spake he of the Spirit, which they that believe on him should receive: for the Holy Spirit was not yet given, because that Jesus was not yet glorified. *J 7:39*

The last quotations from John's Gospel contain obscurities, but taking all of the quotations together, the main thrust of Jesus' teaching on spiritual thirst is clear:

1. If any man thirst, let him come to Jesus and drink.
2. He that believeth on Jesus shall never thirst.
3. This belief will be an inner spring of spiritual water giving him everlasting life.

CHAPTER 14

THE HOLY SPIRIT / GOD / THE DEVIL

THE HOLY SPIRIT

The King James Version of the Bible uses the phrase *Holy Ghost* for the third person of the Trinity of God. In quotations from the King James Version, I have changed that phrase to *Holy Spirit*. The reason for that change is that the general opinion is that *Holy Spirit* is a more accurate modern English translation than the Elizabethan *Holy Ghost*.

According to John's Gospel the Holy Spirit was "not yet given" in Jesus' lifetime, because he "was not yet glorified." *J 7:39* Shortly before his crucifixion, Jesus told his disciples:

The hour is come, that the Son of man should be glorified. *J 12:23*

After his crucifixion and resurrection, Jesus said to his disciples:

Receive ye the Holy Spirit. *J 20:22*

The same Holy Spirit had descended upon Jesus at the time of his baptism:

MARK	MATTHEW	LUKE
And	And	
	Jesus, when he was baptized,	Jesus also being baptized and praying,
straightway coming up out of the water, he saw	went straightway out of the water; and, lo,	
the heavens opened, and the Spirit	the heavens were opened unto him, and he saw the Spirit of God descending	the heaven was opened, and the Holy Spirit descended in a bodily shape
like a dove descending upon him. And there came a voice from heaven, saying,	like a dove and lighting upon him. And lo a voice from heaven, saying,	like a dove upon him, and a voice came from heaven, which said,
"Thou art my beloved Son, in whom I am well pleased."	"This is my beloved Son, in whom I am well pleased."	"Thou art my beloved Son; in thee I am well pleased."
Mk 1:10–11	*Mt 3:16–17*	*L 3:21–22*

After this announcement, the Holy Spirit led Jesus into the wilderness, a lonely place. Here is what the Gospel texts say:

MARK	MATTHEW	LUKE
And immediately	Then was Jesus	And Jesus being full of the Holy Spirit

MARK (cont.)	MATTHEW (cont.)	LUKE (cont.)
		returned from Jordan, and was
the Spirit	*led up* of	*led*
driveth him	the Spirit	by the Spirit
into the wilderness.	into the wilderness	into the wilderness,
Mk 1:12		being forty days
	to be tempted	tempted
	of the devil.	of the devil.
	Mt 4:1	*L 4:1*

After his temptation in the wilderness, Jesus returned to Galilee:

> And Jesus returned *in the power of the Spirit* into Galilee; and there went out a fame of him through all the region round about. *L 4:14*

Later on he taught his disciples:

> If ye then, being evil, know how to give good gifts unto your children; how much more shall your heavenly Father *give the Holy Spirit to them that ask him? L 11:13*

Jesus himself recognized that the Holy Spirit was active in the world prior to his birth. Jesus said:

> For David himself said by the Holy Spirit . . . *Mk 12:36*

According to Luke, John the Baptist was filled with the Holy Spirit, even from his mother's womb. *L 1:15* His father, Zacharias, "was filled with the Holy Spirit," and prophesied that his son should "go before the face of the Lord to prepare his ways. *L 1:67, 76*

John's mother, Elisabeth, "was filled with the Holy Spirit" when she announced to Mary, the mother of Jesus, "Blessed art thou among women, and blessed is the fruit of thy womb." *L 1:41–42*

787

The fruit of Mary's womb was planted by the Holy Spirit. *Mt 1:18*
Luke states that the angel Gabriel told Mary:

> The Holy Spirit shall come upon thee, and the power of the Highest
> shall overshadow thee: therefore also that holy thing which is born
> of thee shall be called the Son of God. *L 1:35*

After that, an angel of the Lord delivered this message to Joseph:

> Joseph, thou son of David, fear not to take unto thee Mary thy wife:
> for that which is conceived in her is of the Holy Spirit. And she shall
> bring forth a son, and thou shalt call his name Jesus: . . . *Mt 1:20–21*

After Jesus' birth, the Holy Spirit came upon a man named
Simeon. Luke writes:

> And, behold, there was a man in Jerusalem, whose name was Simeon;
> and the same man was just and devout, waiting for the consolation
> of Israel; and the Holy Spirit was upon him.

> And it was revealed unto him by the Holy Spirit, that he should not
> see death, before he had seen the Lord's Christ. And he came by the
> Spirit into the Temple; and when the parents brought in the child
> Jesus, to do for him after the custom of the law, then took he him
> up in his arms, and blessed God, and said, "Lord, now lettest thou
> thy servant depart in peace, according to thy word: for mine eyes
> have seen thy salvation, which thou hast prepared before the face of
> all people, a light to lighten the Gentiles, and the glory of thy people
> Israel." *L 2:25–32*

Despite the neat compartments of theologians, Jesus regarded
the Holy Spirit as active in certain ways even while he was still on
earth. Jesus asserted:

MATTHEW	LUKE
But if I cast out devils	But if I
by the Spirit of God,	with the finger of God
then	cast out devils, no doubt

MATTHEW (cont.)
the Kingdom of God is come
unto you.
Mt 12:28

LUKE (cont.)
the Kingdom of God is come
upon you.
L 11:20

Jesus' exorcism of devils showed the nearness of the Kingdom of God. The Holy Spirit was to control entrance to that Kingdom. Jesus taught:

Except a man be born of water and *of the Spirit*, he cannot enter into the Kingdom of God. That which is born of the flesh is flesh; and that which is born of the Spirit is spirit . . .

The wind bloweth where it listeth, and thou hearest the sound thereof, but canst not tell whence it cometh, and whither it goeth: so is every one that is born of *the Spirit. J 3:5–6*

Although the Holy Spirit was the active agent in the birth of Jesus as a man and Jesus was full of the Holy Spirit during his earthly ministry, a new era of the Holy Spirit's function began shortly after Jesus' resurrection.

In his last days Jesus had taught his disciples:

It is expedient for you that I go away: for if I go not away, the Comforter will not come unto you; but if I depart, I will send him unto you. *J 16:7*

That Comforter is the Holy Spirit. Jesus said:

These things have I spoken unto you, being yet present with you. But *the Comforter, which is the Holy Spirit*, whom the Father will send in my name, he shall teach you all things, and bring all things to your remembrance, whatsoever I have said unto you. *J 14:25–26*

But when the Comforter is come, whom I will send unto you from the Father, even the Spirit of Truth, which proceedeth from the Father, he shall testify of me. *J 15:26*

789

And I will pray the Father, and he shall give you *another* Comforter [other than Jesus], that he may abide with you forever; even the Spirit of Truth, whom the world can not receive, because it seeth him not, neither knoweth him, but ye know him: *for he dwelleth with you, and shall be in you. J 14:16–17*

Paul's understanding of and gloss on Jesus' words as to the Holy Spirit being *in* the believer are helpful:

But ye are not in the flesh, but in the Spirit, *if* so be that the Spirit of God *dwell in you.* Now if any man have not the Spirit of Christ, he is none of his. *Romans 8:9*

Jesus' doctrine of the manifestation of the Holy Spirit to his followers may be shortly summarized:

1. The Spirit could not come to his followers until Jesus left the earth.
2. The Holy Spirit–the Comforter–Spirit of Truth was to be sent by the Father at Jesus' request and in Jesus' name. The terms are used interchangeably.
3. That Spirit was to abide in and with Jesus' disciples forever.

Jesus told his disciples after his resurrection:

Receive ye the Holy Spirit: whose soever sins ye remit, they are remitted unto them; and whose soever sins ye retain, they are retained. *J 20:22–23*

Wait for the promise of the Father [as to sending the Holy Spirit], which ye have heard of me. For John truly baptized with water; but ye shall be baptized with the Holy Spirit not many days hence. *Acts 1:4–5*

John the Baptist foretold the baptism of the Holy Spirit:

MATTHEW	LUKE
He shall baptize	He shall baptize

MATTHEW (cont.)	LUKE (cont.)
you	you
with the Holy Spirit	with the Holy Spirit
and with fire,	and with fire,
whose fan is	whose fan is
in his hand;	in his hand;
and he will	and he will
thoroughly purge	thoroughly purge
his floor,	his floor,
and gather	and will gather
his wheat	the wheat
into the garner;	into his garner;
	but the chaff
he will burn up	he will burn
the chaff	
with unquenchable fire.	with fire unquenchable.
Mt 3:11–12	L 3:16–17

The "fan" is a wooden winnowing fork which was used to scoop up grain in order to throw it into the air to separate the kernels from the chaff. The "floor" is the threshing floor where the kernels fall to be swept up into the "garner", the granary.

John the Baptist's concept of the baptism of the Holy Spirit was that it would come with fire and with judgment, winnowing the grain and burning the chaff.

When the Holy Spirit did descend on Jesus' disciples about fifty days after his resurrection, it was with "cloven tongues like as of fire":

And suddenly there came a sound from heaven as of a rushing mighty wind, and it filled all the house where they were sitting. And there appeared unto them cloven tongues like as of fire, and it sat upon each of them. And they were all filled with the Holy Spirit, and began to speak with other tongues, as the Spirit gave them utterance. Acts 2:2–4

This coming of the Holy Spirit occurred on an existing Jewish holiday, the Feast of Weeks. That feast was known to Greek–

speaking Jews as "Pentecost" from the Greek word for *fiftieth*, referring to the date of the feast, fifty days after Passover.

This coming of the Holy Spirit was to give, and did give, the disciples "power":

> But ye shall receive *power*, after that the Holy Spirit is come upon you; and ye shall be witnesses unto me both in Jerusalem, and in all Judea, and in Samaria, and unto the uttermost part of the Earth. *Acts 1:8*

After the disciples had received the Holy Spirit they began to teach:

> Repent, and be baptized every one of you in the name of Jesus Christ for the remission of sins, and ye shall receive the gift of the Holy Spirit. *Acts 2:38*

The new converts were to receive the gift of the Holy Spirit and to partake of its power just as the disciples had. The receipt of the Holy Spirit was the distinctive mark of the first Christians.

Paul asked certain converts at Ephesus, a city which is now in Turkey:

> Have ye received the Holy Spirit since ye believed? *Acts 19:2*

They answered:

> We have not so much as heard whether there be any Holy Spirit. *Acts 19:2*

There was then a brief discussion of John's baptism and its being superseded by Christ Jesus, and they were then "baptized in the name of the Lord Jesus." *Acts 19:5*

Acts continues:

> And when Paul had laid his hands upon them, the Holy Spirit came on them; and they spake with tongues and prophesied. *Acts 19:6*

Peter had a similar experience a few years earlier. Acts states that the Holy Spirit moved Peter to accompany three men sent by Cornelius, a Roman centurion, and, of course, a Gentile, to bring Peter to him at Caesarea. *Acts 10:19–20* Peter explained the Christian faith to Cornelius, explaining:

> How God annointed Jesus of Nazareth with the Holy Spirit and with power, who went about doing good, and healing all that were oppressed of the devil: for God was with him. *Acts 10:38*

After recording some further statements by Peter to Cornelius, the account in Acts continues:

> While Peter yet spoke these words, the Holy Spirit fell on all of them which heard the word. And they of the circumcision which believed [Jewish Christians] were astonished, as many as came with Peter, because that on the Gentiles also was poured out the gift of the Holy Spirit. For they heard them speak in tongues, and magnify God. *Acts 10:44–46*

Peter drew the obvious conclusion:

> Can any man forbid water, that these should not be baptized, which have received the Holy Spirit as well as we? *Acts 10:47*

In each of these two cases, the Holy Spirit is said to have come upon the persons involved. *Acts 10:44 ("fell on"); 19:6 ("came on")* In his last days before his death Jesus had predicted this receipt of the Holy Spirit, the Comforter, and the Spirit of Truth. To put into Jesus' own words what had happened to these converts, the Spirit then dwelt with them and was in them. *J 14:17*

In each of these two cases, as was the case of the disciples themselves at Pentecost, this coming of the Holy Spirit was accompanied by speaking with tongues. *Acts 2:4, 10:46, 19:6* Speaking with tongues is an ecstatic phenomenon which is a subject of great dispute.

This ecstatic phenomenon is often thought of as the essence of the operation of the Holy Spirit. And it is true that Jesus said that the Holy Spirit is to "dwelleth with you" and to be "in you." *J 14:17*

Essentially, however, the operations of the Spirit are secret and covert, known only to believers. The world can not see this invisible force, or know his power: the world "seeth him not, neither knoweth him." *J 14:17* So far as the world is concerned the Spirit's function is to "reprove the world of sin, and of righteousness, and of judgment." *J 16:8* Specifically the Spirit is to reprove the world:

Of sin, because they believe not on me.

Of righteousness, because I go to my Father, and ye see me no more.

Of judgment, because the prince of this world is judged. *J 16:9–11*

The fact that the Holy Spirit is to "reprove the world of sin, and of righteousness, and of judgment" also creates the condition whereby persons who heed the reproof of the Spirit may be born into the Kingdom of God.

Paul wrote:

Wherefore I give you to understand, that no man speaking by the Son of God calleth Jesus accursed; and that no man can say that Jesus is the Lord, but by the Holy Spirit. *1 Corinthians 12:3*

Jesus summarized the essential function of the Holy Spirit as follows:

Howbeit when he, the Spirit of Truth, is come, *he will guide you into all truth*: for he shall not speak of himself; but whatsoever he shall hear, that shall he speak, and he will shew you things to come.

He shall glorify me: for he shall receive of mine, and shall shew it unto you. All things that the Father hath are mine; therefore said I, that *he shall take of mine, and shall show it unto you.* J 16:13–15

Basically the Holy Spirit is to glorify Jesus and to guide to all truth. Jesus also called the Holy Spirit, "the Spirit of Truth." J 15:26 Jesus said that this "Spirit of Truth" would "testify" of him. J 15:26

In speaking of the Holy Spirit Jesus used the word translated *testify* as synonymous with the word translated *teach*. He said that the Holy Spirit "shall testify of me" and "shall teach you all things, and bring to your remembrance, whatsoever I have said unto you." J 15:26; 14:26

The Holy Spirit did bring to the remembrance of his first disciples "whatsoever I have said unto you" with the result that the Gospels were written. The writer of John's Gospel from which I have quoted as to the Holy Spirit states:

This is the disciple which testifieth of these things, and wrote these things: and we know that his testimony is true. And there are also many other things which Jesus did, . . . J 21:24–25

In the early days of the church, and still today, the Spirit instructs believers what to do and say in certain situations:

MARK	MATTHEW	LUKE	LUKE
			But before all these they shall lay their hands
But take heed to yourselves:	But beware of men:	And when	on you, and
for they shall deliver you up to councils, and	for they will deliver you up to the councils, and they will scourge you	they bring you into	persecute you, delivering you up
in the	in their	the	to the

795

MARK (cont.)	MATTHEW (cont.)	LUKE (cont.)	LUKE (cont.)
synagogues	synagogues;	synagogues,	synagogues
ye shall			and into
be beaten;	and ye shall be	and	prisons,
and ye shall be			being
brought before	brought before	unto	brought before
rulers and	governors and	magistrates, and	kings and
kings	kings	powers,	rulers
for my	for my		for my
sake,	sake,		name's sake.
			And it shall turn
			to you
for a testimony	for a testimony		for a testimony.
against them.	against them		
And the gospel	and the		
must first			
be published			
among all			
nations.	Gentiles.		
But when they	But when they		
shall lead you,			
and deliver	deliver		
you up,	you up,		Settle it
take	take	take ye	therefore
no thought	no thought	no thought	in your hearts,
beforehand	how or	how or	not to meditate
what	what	what thing	before what
ye shall speak,	ye shall speak:	ye shall answer,	ye shall answer:
		or what	
neither do		ye shall say:	
ye meditate;	for it shall	for the	for I
but whatsoever	be given you	Holy Spirit	will
		shall teach ye	give you
shall be	in that	in the	
given you	same hour	same hour	a mouth
in that hour,	what ye	what ye ought	and wisdom,
that speak ye:	shall speak.	to say.	
		L 12:11–12	

796

MARK (cont.)	MATTHEW (cont.)	LUKE (cont.)	LUKE (cont.)
for it is not	For it is not		
ye that speak,	ye that speak,		
but	but		
the Holy Spirit.	the Spirit		
Mk 13:9–11	of your Father		
	which speaketh		
	in you.		
	Mt 10:17–20		
			which all
			your adversaries
			shall not be able
			to gainsay
			nor resist.
			L 21:12–15

The great power and majesty which Jesus attributed to the Holy Spirit is shown by this saying of Jesus:

MARK	MATTHEW	LUKE
Verily I say	Wherefore I say	
unto you,	unto you,	
all sins	all manner of sin	
	and blasphemy	
shall be forgiven	shall be forgiven	
unto the sons of men,	unto men;	
and blasphemies	but the blasphemy	
wherewith soever	against the Holy Spirit,	
they shall blaspheme;	shall not be forgiven	
	unto men.	
	And whosoever	And whosoever
	speaketh a word	shall speak a word
	against	against
	the Son of man,	the Son of man,
	it shall be	it shall be
	forgiven him;	forgiven him;
but he that shall	but whosoever	but unto him that
blaspheme against	speaketh against	blasphemeth against
the Holy Spirit	the Holy Spirit,	the Holy Spirit
hath never	it shall not	it shall not

MARK (cont.)	**MATTHEW** (cont.)	**LUKE** (cont.)
forgiveness,	be forgiven him,	be forgiven.
but is in	neither	L 12:10
danger of	in this world,	
eternal	neither	
damnation.	in the world	
Mk 3:28–29	to come.	
	Mt 12:31–32	

The Greek word from which our phrase *to blaspheme* is ultimately derived, means "to speak ill." *To blaspheme* has come to mean intentionally to revile God or his holy things. The King James Version lists "blasphemy" as one of the evil things that Jesus said comes forth from the heart and defiles a man. Mk 7:22; Mt 15:19 Modern translations often translate this word instead as "slander."

To blaspheme the Holy Spirit is to slander this person of God. Humanly speaking, Jesus was a Jew, and when he spoke of blasphemy of the Holy Spirit there was probably in his mind the following words of the third book of the Law:

> And he that blasphemeth the name of the Lord, he shall surely be put to death, and all the congregation shall certainly stone him: . . .
> *Leviticus 24:16*

Despite the neat compartments of theologians, Jesus regarded the Pharisees as *then* committing the unforgivable sin by *then* denying the presence of the Holy Spirit in assisting Jesus to cast out devils. Mt 12:28–32 To blaspheme the Holy Spirit is to deny his power and authority.

Jesus' teaching was simple: there is no forgiveness for one who speaks against the Holy Spirit, either in this world or in the world to come. This is an eternal sin.

The importance that Jesus placed upon the Holy Spirit is shown in his final instructions to his church:

> Go ye therefore, and teach all nations, baptizing them in *the name* of the Father, and of the Son, and *of the Holy Spirit*. Mt 28:19

Jesus taught that when he left, that the Holy Spirit would come. *J 14:16–17, 26; J 15:26; J 16:5–14* The Holy Spirit did come and is still active in myriad ways. When the Holy Spirit is absent, the true church does not exist, although formidable ecclesiastical organizations may thrive. The Spirit moves where it wills, and its moving is the history of the true church. The rest is simply ecclesiastical history.

The Manifestation of Jesus Christ

After Jesus was crucified, dead and buried, he made numerous appearances to his disciples over a period of forty days "speaking of things pertaining to the Kingdom of God." *Acts 1:3* In the presence of his disciples, he was taken up into the sky from the Mount of Olives near Jerusalem and "a cloud received him out of their sight." *Acts 1:9*

At the Last Supper, just prior to his crucifixion, Jesus said to his disciples:

> He that hath my commandments, and keepeth them, he it is that loveth me; and he that loveth me shall be loved of my Father, and I will love him, and *will manifest myself to him. J 14:21*

The other Judas, not Judas Iscariot, immediately picked up this point and asked:

> Lord, how is it that thou wilt manifest thyself unto us, and not unto the world? *J 14:22*

Jesus answered:

> If a man love me, he will keep my words; and my Father will love him, and we will come unto him, and make our abode with him. *J 14:23*

Jesus taught that he will manifest himself to his followers in such a way that the world does not see him. This manifestation will be by Jesus and his Father making their home with Jesus' followers.

Here is what Jesus meant by "make our abode with him":

> I will not leave you comfortless: I will come to you. Yet a little while, and the world seeth me no more, but ye see me; because I live, ye shall live also. At that day ye shall know that I am in my Father, and ye in me, and I in you. *J 14:18–20*

This continuing manifestation of Jesus Christ is by his mystical presence in the believer, "ye in me, and I in you." *J 14:20*

This mystical presence seems to be different than the dwelling of the Holy Spirit in the believer, even though Jesus discussed both things in his farewell address to his disciples that night.

That night Jesus spoke of the Holy Spirit as follows:

> And I pray the Father, that he shall give you *another* Comforter, that he may abide with you for ever; even the Spirit of Truth, whom the world can not receive, because it seeth him not, neither knoweth him; but ye know him: for he *dwelleth with you*, and shall be in you. *J 14:16–17*

Jesus taught a dual indwelling in the believer; his own dwelling in the believer; and the dwelling of the Spirit of Truth in the believer. Both are invisible to the world which naturally rejects their reality. *J 14:17, 23*

Just after Jesus had said that night that the Holy Spirit would dwell in his disciples and be in them, he continued:

> I will not leave you comfortless: I will come to you. Yet a little while, and the world seeth me no more; but ye see me; because I live, ye shall live also. At that day ye shall know that I am in my Father, and ye in me, and *I in you*. *J 14:18–20*

The close, yet separate identity of these two indwellings, of Jesus and the Holy Spirit, is shown by Jesus' statements that the Holy Spirit "dwelleth with you, and shall be in you" (*J 14:17*) and "ye shall know that I am in my Father, ye in me, and I in you" (*J 14:20*) ,and "we will come unto him, and make our abode with him" (*J 14:23*).

The indwelling of Jesus in his followers was to begin "in a little while, and the world seeth me no more, but ye see me." *J 14:19* This refers to the period after Jesus' immediately impending death and resurrection. *J 16:16–28* At about the same time as Jesus began to indwell his followers, the Holy Spirit came to dwell in Jesus' followers. In traditional language he "descended" at Pentecost. *Acts 2*

Both indwellings are invisible to the world. *J 14:17, 21–23* The world can not receive the Holy Spirit "because it seeth him not." *J 14:17* Jesus himself will manifest himself to his followers and not to the world. He will do this by he and his Father making their abode with them. *J 14:21–23* His answer to Judas' question still stands:

> If a man love me, he will keep my words; and my Father will love him, and we will come unto him, and make our abode with him. *J 14:23*

The Nature of the God Jesus Knew

Despite the volumes theologians have written about the attributes of God, it is surprising how little Jesus had to say about those attributes. The question that arises: who is right, Jesus or the theologians?

Jesus did teach that "God is good."

All three synoptic gospels record the story of the rich young ruler who unctuously asked Jesus:

Good Master, what shall I do that I may inherit eternal life?
Mk 10:17 (Mt 19:16; L 18:18)

Jesus' reaction was almost curt:

MARK	MATTHEW	LUKE
Why callest thou me good?	Why callest thou me good?	Why callest thou me good?
There is none good but one, that is, God.	There is none good but one, that is, God.	None is good, save one, that is, God.
Mk 10:18	*Mt 19:17*	*L 18:19*

We do not need to analyze here why Jesus in this interchange rejected the title "Good Master or Teacher." Here we are focusing upon Jesus' statements about God, and he simply stated that "God is good."

Jesus did say that "God is true", twice;

Ye both know me, and ye know whence I am; and I am not come of myself, *but he that sent me is true*, whom ye know not. *J 7:28*

I have many things to say and to judge of you, *but he that sent me is true*; and I speak to the world those things which I have heard from him. *J 8:26*

Jesus did affirm that:

God is a Spirit. J 4:24

The King James Version italicizes the verb *is* because it is not in the original Greek leaving us with: "God, a Spirit." Modern versions drop the article *a* and translate the verse either, "God is Spirit" or "God is spirit."

The crucial problem is the meaning of *spirit, pneuma* in the Greek, which literally means "wind." In John 3:8, *pnuema* is given both its meanings: its literal meaning of wind; and its acquired meaning of God's ever-present but inscrutable nature:

The wind [pneuma] bloweth where it listeth, and thou hearest the sound thereof, but canst not tell whence it cometh, and whither it goeth: so is everyone that is born of the Spirit [pneuma]. J 3:8

Just previously and as part of this same statement Jesus used "spirit" as the opposite of "flesh":

Except a man be born of water and of the Spirit, he cannot enter into the Kingdom of God. That which is born of the flesh is flesh; that which is born of the Spirit is spirit. J 3:5–6

Later on in his Gospel John quotes Jesus as saying:

It is the Spirit that quickeneth; the flesh profiteth nothing. The words that I speak unto you, they are spirit, and they are life. J 6:63

When Jesus said, "God is spirit," he did not mean as it may sound to our modern ears, "God is phantasm;" he meant that "God is not flesh."

This is a significant difference because it takes us out of the realm of speculative knowledge to a specific factual premise. From this specific fact Jesus drew a pragmatic conclusion: God is not to be worshipped in fleshly shrines but in spirit and in truth.

This is shown by the episode in which Jesus' statement occurred. Jesus was in Samaria talking to a Samaritan woman, i.e. a foreigner. The Samaritans had, in Samaria, their national shrine on Mt. Gerizim.

Here is what was said:

WOMAN: Our fathers worshipped in this mountain; and ye say, that in Jerusalem is the place where men ought to worship. *J 4:20*
JESUS: Woman, believe me, the hour cometh, when ye shall neither in this mountain, nor yet in Jerusalem, worship the Father . . . But the hour cometh, and now is, when the true worshippers shall worship the Father in spirit and in truth: for the Father seeketh such to worship him. God is a Spirit, and they that worship him must worship him in spirit and in truth. *J 4:21, 23–24*

Modern translations render "God is a Spirit" as "God is spirit." Since God is spirit, no man has ever seen or heard him. Jesus bluntly told the Jews:

And the Father himself, which hath sent me, hath borne witness of me. Ye have neither heard his voice at any time, nor seen his shape. *J 5:37*

On another occasion Jesus again affirmed the unseen nature of God.

Not that any man hath seen the Father, save he which is of God, he hath seen the Father. *J 6:46*

The context shows "he which is of God" is Jesus himself. The newer translations make this clear by saying he who is "from God" rather than he who is "of God."

Jesus in the Sermon on the Mount said:

Blessed are the pure in heart: for they shall see God. *Mt 5:8*

It is in the future that the Christians will see God. The last book of the Bible, The Revelation of John, says, "and they shall see his face." *Revelation 22:4* If it is objected that God has no face, John assures us that when he shall appear, "we shall see him as he is." *1 John 3:2*

It will no doubt be objected that Jesus said things inconsistent with his teaching that no man has seen God. Towards the end of John's Gospel he is quoted as saying:

And he that seeth me seeth him that sent me. *J 12:45*

Philip later asked the specific question:

Lord, shew us the Father, and it sufficeth us. *J 14:8*

Jesus answered:

Have I been so long time with you, and yet hath thou not known me, Philip? He that hath seen me hath seen the Father; and how sayest thou then, "Shew us the Father?" Believest thou not that I am in the Father, and the Father in me? The words that I speak unto you I speak not of myself; but the Father that dwelleth in me, he doeth the works. Believe me that I am in the Father, and the Father in me; or else believe me for the very works' sake. *J 14:9–11*

Jesus' answer to Philip's request to see the Father is essentially this: he that hath seen me hath seen the Father because I am in the Father and the Father is in me. In other words, Philip wanted to see God as such, and Jesus says in a sense you have seen the Father when you see me because I am specially related to the Father.

The same explanation fits John 12:45 for there the context shows the same idea. The passage starts:

He that believeth on me, believeth not on me, but on him that sent me. And he that seeth me seeth him that sent me . . . For I have not spoken of myself; but the Father which sent me, he gave me a commandment, what I should say, and what I should speak. *J 12:44–45, 49*

Essentially Jesus said he that seeth me seeth him that sent me because I carry God's message. In the introduction to John's Gospel, John summarizes Jesus' teaching as to the seeability of God.

No man hath seen God at any time; the only begotten Son, which is in the bosom of the Father, he hath declared him. *J 1:18*

In short, the Son of God, Jesus, who has the closest relation to God, has declared and taught God even though God is still not seeable as such.

Jesus did not list attributes of God the Father in the manner of systematic theologians. He taught simply that God is unknowable to any man except those to whom Jesus reveals him:

All things are delivered unto me of my Father, and no man knoweth the Son, but the Father; *neither knoweth any man the Father,* save the Son, *and he to whomsoever the Son will reveal him.* Mt 11:27	All things are delivered to me of my Father, and no man knoweth who the Son is but the Father; and *who the Father is,* but the Son, *and he to whom the Son will reveal him.* L 10:22

Jesus at first declared the Father in parables and figures of speech. It was not until the very end of his ministry that Jesus told even his disciples the plain facts as to his Father:

These things I have spoken unto you in proverbs; but the time cometh, when I shall no more speak unto you in proverbs, but I shall shew you plainly of the Father. *J 16:25*

Modern translations discard the word *proverbs* and use other words to convey Jesus' point that the time for plain talk had come and the time for parables and figures of speech was past.

Jesus did not leave us with a long list of the attributes of God; he merely mentions in passing that "God is good", "God is true", and "God is spirit." What he really taught was simply that "God is my Father."

But that is not all Jesus taught. The overlay of centuries of theological speculation and bad exegesis has buried Jesus' simple, straightforward concept of God the Father: his perfect impartiality and kindness.

Buried in one of his most famous sayings about loving your enemies are these statements of the fundamental nature of God:

MATTHEW	LUKE
But I say unto you,	But
love your enemies,	love ye your enemies,
bless them that curse you,	
do good to them	and do good, and lend,
that hate you,	hoping for nothing again;
and pray for them	and your reward
which despitefully use you,	shall be great,
and persecute you,	
that ye may be the	and ye shall be
children of your Father	the children of the Highest:
which is in heaven:	
for he maketh his sun	*for he is kind*
to rise on the evil	*unto the unthankful*
and on the good,	*and to the evil.*
and sendeth rain	
on the just	
and on the unjust.	
For if ye love them	
which love you,	
what reward have ye?	
Do not even	
the publicans the same?	

MATTHEW (cont.)	LUKE (cont.)
And if ye salute your brethren only, what do ye more than others? Do not even the publicans so?	
Be ye therefore perfect, *even as your Father* which is in heaven *is perfect.* Mt 5:44–48	Be ye therefore merciful *as your Father* also *is merciful.* L 6:35–36

The sun and the rain are not withheld from the wicked because God is kind to the unthankful and the evil, even though he himself is good. Since he is good and perfect, God is merciful to all men, good and bad. Jesus instructed us that we should strive for the perfection of God his Father by being merciful to all men, good and bad.

Jesus was not concerned, as we in our modern wisdom are, with the nature of God, with adjectives like eternal, omnipotent and omniscient. His understanding was different. For us, as it was for Philip, Jesus' answer is:

He that hath seen me hath seen the Father; and how sayest thou then, "Shew us the Father"? Believest thou not that I am *in the Father*, and the Father *in me*?" J 14:9–10

THE TRINITY

Jesus did not speak of the Trinity; nor does the Bible elsewhere use the term. That term is a shorthand verbal symbol to state the relationship of God, Jesus and the Holy Spirit.

Jesus stated flatly:

I and my Father are one. *J 10:30*

Or, phrasing it another way, he said:

The Father is in me, and I in him. *J 10:38*

He also stated that a special dynamic unity exists between himself, his Father, and his followers:

At that day ye shall know that I am *in* my Father and ye *in* me, and I *in* you. *J 14:20*

The unity of Jesus–followers–Father is as follows:

A. Jesus' followers are in him;
B. He is in them;
C. Jesus is also in his Father.

Since Jesus is in both his Father and in his followers, it is evident that they in turn are in his Father.

After Jesus' death and resurrection, the Holy Spirit (or Spirit of Truth) came. Jesus said that Spirit "dwelleth with you, and shall be *in* you. *J 14:17*

Jesus taught that "I am in the Father and the Father in me." *J 14:10–11* He also taught that the Holy Spirit shall be "in you." *J 14:17* Since the Holy Spirit is said to be one "person" of God we return to Jesus' original statement about his followers. He asked his Father:

That they all may be one; as thou, Father, art *in me*, and I *in thee*, that they also may be one *in us:* . . . that they may be one, even as

810

we are one: I *in them*, and thou *in me*, that they may be made perfect in one; . . . J 17:21–23

This statement does not speak simply of Jesus' followers having a unity, a oneness, analogous to his oneness with his Father. It goes further and speaks of the dynamic unity of Jesus–followers–Father based on the following propositions:

1. Jesus and his Father are one in each other.
2. Jesus is in his followers.

Although Jesus is one with his Father, Jesus recognized that in certain ways he and his Father were distinct:

If a man love me, he will keep my words; and my Father will love him, and *we* will come unto him, and make *our* abode with ;him. He that loveth me not keepeth not my sayings; and the word which ye hear is not *mine*, but the Father's which sent me. J 14:23–24

The third person of the Trinity, the Holy Spirit, was, according to Jesus, to be sent by his Father in Jesus' name:

But the Comforter, which is the Holy Spirit, whom the Father will send in my name, he shall teach you all things, and bring all things to your remembrance, whatsoever I have said unto you. J 14:26

After his resurrection Jesus told his eleven remaining disciples:

Go ye therefore, and teach all nations, baptizing them in the name of the Father, and of the Son, and of the Holy Spirit: . . . Mt 28:19

Jesus often spoke of his Father and his relation to him. He often spoke of the Holy Spirit's action and the Spirit's special function in the age that was to begin with his death and resurrection. He never spoke in a philosophic or logical way as to the inter–relationships of the Holy Spirit, his Father, and himself. He simply recognizes that all three exist: Father, Son, and Holy Spirit. Mt 28:19 Jesus' followers should follow his example.

JESUS AND THE DEVIL

Jesus recognized the power and reality of the devil. Moderns scoff at such a concept. The question is: Are they right?

First, we have a question of nomenclature. *Satan* simply transliterates the Hebrew word *Sâtân*, "adversary." Devil, an English word, is derived from a Greek word meaning "slanderer."

Jesus used, apparently interchangeably, the following names for the devil: Satan, the evil or wicked one, the enemy, the prince of this world, and Beelzebub. For example, Jesus told a parable of the sower about the ways of the devil, and each of the three synoptic gospels in reporting that parable used a different name for this person: Satan, *Mk 4:15*; the wicked one, *Mt 13:19*; the devil, *L 8:12*. In another place in the Gospels of Matthew and Luke, Jesus is quoted as shifting back and forth between the names Beelzebub and Satan, without making any distinction between them. *Mt 12:26–27; L 11:18–19*

Early in his ministry and shortly after his baptism, Jesus himself struggled with the devil. Mark has only the barest note of this struggle:

> And he was there in the wilderness forty days, tempted of Satan; . . .
> *Mk 1:13*

Matthew and Luke describe Jesus' temptation by the devil in detail. Their accounts have been analyzed in the section entitled "Jesus' Temptation", pp. 83–89. The temptation of Jesus was his first great battle on earth in the war between the devil and God that had been going on for a very long time.

According to Matthew, Jesus' temptation ended when "the devil leaveth him, and, behold, angels came and ministered unto him." *Mt 4:11* Luke states that "when the devil had ended all the temptation, he departed from him *for a season*." *L 4:13*

Jesus was, however, to live out his life in the territory of the devil. The devil had shown Jesus "all the kingdoms of the world." *Mt 4:8; L 4:5* Jesus did not dispute the devil's claim to control all these kingdoms and that he could give them "to whomsoever" he would. *L 4:6 (Mt 4:9)*

Later on, Jesus said:

My kingdom is not of this world: . . . *J 18:36*

The world and the kingdoms of it have been delivered to the devil. However, the power of the devil over the world was already beginning to fall in Jesus' own lifetime.

When seventy or seventy-two of Jesus' disciples were sent out as an advance party to the cities and places where he was about to go, to proclaim that "The Kingdom of God is come nigh unto you," they reported back that "even the devils are subject unto us through thy name." *L 10:1, 9, 11, 17*

Jesus then said:

I beheld Satan as lightning fall from heaven. Behold, I give unto you power to tread on serpents and scorpions, and *over all the power of the enemy*; and nothing shall by any means hurt you. *L 10:18–19*

The inference is that Jesus saw the impending defeat of Satan as these disciples moved forward proclaiming the nearness of the Kingdom of God. The Kingdom of God was near; consequently, Satan was about to fall. These disciples had been given power over the enemy who, as the statement shows, was Satan. Jesus healed a man who was "possessed with a devil, blind and dumb." *Mt 12:22 (L 11:14)* Some Pharisees charged that Jesus cast out the devils by "Beelzebub the prince of the devils." *Mt 12:24 (L 11:15)* Jesus denied the charge and said:

MATTHEW	LUKE
But if I	But if I
	with the finger of God
cast out devils	cast out devils,
by the Son of God,	no doubt
then the Kingdom of God	the Kingdom of God
is come upon you.	is come upon you.
Mt 12:28	*L 11:20*

The power of Jesus to do exorcisms was evidence, like the power of the seventy or so disciples to subdue devils, that Kingdom of God was surging in around them. *L 10:17* The nearness of the Kingdom of God presaged the coming fall of Satan. *L 10:18*

All these synoptic gospels repeat in some detail the rest of Jesus' answer when he was charged with casting out devils by Beelzebub prince of the devils:

MARK	MATTHEW	LUKE
How can Satan cast out Satan?		
And if a kingdom be divided against itself, that kingdom can not stand.	Every kingdom divided against itself is brought to desolation;	Every kingdom divided against itself is brought to desolation;
And if a house be divided against itself, that house can not stand.	and every city or house divided against itself shall not stand.	and a house divided against a house falleth.
And if Satan rise up against himself, and be divided, he can not stand, but hath an end.	And if Satan cast out Satan, he is divided against himself; how shall then his kingdom stand?	If Satan also be divided against himself, how shall his kingdom stand?
Mk 3:23–26	*Mt 12:25–26*	*L 11:17–18*

This does not tell us much about Satan. Jesus was only pointing out that he was not doing Satan's work by exorcising devils from the man. Satan would not want that!

Jesus then pointed out that he cast out devils not by Satan but by the Son of God. *Mt 12:28; L 11:20 ("the finger of God")* His ability to do so meant that Satan has been overpowered. Here is what Jesus said:

MARK	MATTHEW	LUKE
	Or else how	
No man can enter	can one enter	
into a strong man's	into a strong man's	When a strong man
		armed keepeth
house,	house, and	his palace,
and spoil his goods,	spoil his goods,	his goods are in peace.
except he will first	except he first	
bind the strong man;	bind the strong man?	
		But when
		a stronger than
		he shall come
		upon him,
		and overcome him,
		he taketh from him
		all his armour
		wherein he trusted,
and then he will	And then he will	and divideth
spoil his house.	spoil his house.	his spoils.
Mk 3:27	*Mt 12:29*	*L 11:21–22*

As the time of Jesus' crucifixion approached, he predicted the defeat of the devil:

Now is the judgment of this world; now shall *the prince of this world* be cast out. *J 12:31*

A little later, Jesus told his disciples:

Hereafter I will not talk much with you: for *the prince of this world* cometh, and hath nothing in me. But that the world may know that I love the Father, and as the Father gave me commandment, even so I do. *J 14:30–31*

The ultimate doom of the devil is sure. When Jesus spoke of the Last Judgment and the fate awaiting those who did not do the simple acts of charity, he said, speaking through the king in the parable:

> Depart from me, ye cursed, into everlasting fire, *prepared for the devil and his angels.* Mt 25:41

THE COVERT OPERATIONS OF THE DEVIL

At the end of the world, the devil and his angels will burn in the everlasting fire prepared for them. *Mt 25:41* In the meantime, the devil conducts covert operations in the world by his angels and certain persons acting as his agents. These covert or secret operations may resemble the dirty tricks of intelligence agencies.

Jesus told a parable which illustrated how the devil operates:

The Kingdom of Heaven is likened unto a man which sowed good seed in his field. *But while men slept, his enemy came and sowed tares among the wheat*, and went his way.

But when the blade was sprung up, and brought forth fruit, then appeared the tares also.

So the servants of the householder came and said unto him, "Sir, didst not thou sow good seed in thy field? From whence then hath it tares?"

He said unto them, "An enemy hath done this."

The servants said unto him, "Wilt thou then that we go and gather them up?"

But he said, "Nay; lest while ye gather up the tares, ye root up also the wheat with them. Let both grow together until the harvest; and in the time of harvest I will say to the reapers, Gather ye together first the tares, and bind them in bundles to burn them: but gather the wheat into my barn." *Mt 13:24–30*

Jesus' explanation of the parable was:

He that soweth the good seed is the Son of man.

The field is the world.

The good seed are the children of the Kingdom; but the tares are the children of the wicked one.

The enemy that sowed them is the devil.

The harvest is the end of the world, and the reapers are the angels.

As therefore the tares are gathered and burned in the fire, so shall it be in the end of this world.

The Son of man shall send forth his angels, and they shall gather out of his Kingdom all things that offend, and them which do iniquity, and shall cast them into a furnace of fire, there shall be wailing and gnashing of teeth. Then shall the righteous shine forth as the sun in the Kingdom of their Father. Who hath ears to hear, let him hear. *Mt 13:37–43*

According to Jesus, the devil secretly sowed tares in the wheat field at night after Jesus had seeded the field with wheat. The wheat and tares grow together until the harvest when the tares will be reaped, bundled and cast into a furnace of fire to burn. The tares are the children of the devil.

Jesus also told another sower parable that is recorded in all three synoptic gospels. Part of that parable states:

Behold, there went out a sower to sow. And it came to pass, as he sowed, some fell by the wayside, and the fowls of the air came and devoured it up. *Mk 4:3–4 (Mt 13:3–4; L 8:5)*

Jesus' explanation of that part of the parable was:

MARK	MATTHEW	LUKE
The sower soweth the word. And these are they by the wayside, where the word is sown;	When any one heareth the word of the Kingdom,	The seed is the word of God.

MARK (cont.)	MATTHEW (cont.)	LUKE (cont.)
	and understandeth it not,	
but when they		Those by the wayside are they that hear;
have heard,	then cometh	that cometh
Satan	*the wicked one,*	*the devil,*
cometh immediately,		
and taketh away	and catcheth away	and taketh away
the word that	that which	the word out
was sown	was sown	
in their hearts.	in his heart.	of their hearts,
Mk 4:14–15		lest they should believe and be saved.
		L 8:11–12
	This is he which receiveth seed by the wayside.	
	Mt 13:19	

This parable teaches that one reason that people can not stay with the word of God is the active intervention of Satan.

It is difficult to know when the devil is conducting secret operations. Apparently he conducts disinformation programs. Jesus himself was accused of being Beelzebub and a like fate awaits Christians:

> It is enough for the disciple that he be as his master, and the servant as his lord. If they have called the master of the house Beelzebub, how much more shall they call them of his household? *Mt 10:25*

According to Jesus, the devil does not act only through his angels but also through certain men. For example, Jesus told certain Jews who rejected his word that:

> *Ye do the deeds of your father* . . . *Ye are of your father the devil, and the lusts of your father ye will do.* He was a murderer from the beginning, and abode not in the truth, because there is no truth in him.

When he speaketh a lie, he speaketh his own: for he is a liar, and the father of it. *J 8:41, 44*

According to Jesus, there were men, certain Jews, who then did the deeds and lusts of the devil.

Even Jesus' closest disciples were used for the devil's secret operations. Peter rebuked Jesus when he began to teach his disciples that he, the Son of man, "must suffer many things, and be rejected of the elders, and of the chief priests, and scribes, and be killed, and after three days rise again." *Mk 8:31–32 (Mt 16:21–22)*

Matthew quotes Peter as saying:

Be it far from thee, Lord; this shall not be unto thee. *Mt 16:22*

Jesus then turned, and said to Peter:

MARK	**MATTHEW**
Get thee behind me, Satan:	Get thee behind me, Satan; thou art an offense unto me:
for thou savourest not the things that be of God, but the things that be of men. *Mk 8:33*	for thou savourest not the things that be of God, but those that be of men. *Mt 16:23*

The Greek word translated *an offense* means "a stumbling block." *Savourest* is an archaic word replaced in modern translations by a variety of phrases. In substance, Jesus said to Peter that he was not imparting the things of God, but of men.

Jesus' words were harsh. He called his chief disciple, Peter, "Satan" because he was acting as a Satanic stumbling block to Jesus' somber mission. In short, Satan was acting through Peter.

Both Luke and John flatly state that Satan acted through one disciple in the betrayal of Jesus to the authorities:

Then entered Satan into Judas surnamed Iscariot, being of the number of the Twelve. *L 22:3*

And when he dipped the sop, he gave it to Judas Iscariot, the son of Simon. And after the sop, Satan entered into him. *J 13:26–27*

In some cases people are not agents but rather victims of Satan. Luke writes of a woman who "had a spirit of infirmity eighteen years, and was bowed together, and could in no wise lift up herself. *L 13:11* Jesus healed her on a Sabbath and the ruler of the synagogue objected. Part of Jesus' answer was:

And ought not this woman, being a daughter of Abraham, *whom Satan hath bound*, lo, these eighteen years, be loosed from this bond on the Sabbath day? *L 13:16*

Jesus said of Peter:

Simon, Simon, behold, Satan hath desired to have you, that he may sift you as wheat, but I have prayed for thee, that thy faith fail not: . . . *L 22:31–32*

Shortly before his death Jesus prayed for his followers:

I pray not that thou shouldest take them out of the world, but that thou shouldest keep them from the evil. *J 17:15*

Modern translations correctly add to King James phrase "the evil" the word "one." Jesus' reference was not to abstract evil, but to "the evil one."

The same translation problem occurs in the Lord's Prayer:

MATTHEW	LUKE
And lead us not into temptation, but deliver us from evil: . . . *Mt 6:13*	And lead us not into temptation; but deliver us from evil. *L 11:4*

821

Some modern translations use "the evil one" for "evil" unless they follow manuscripts that omit the entire phrase translated "deliver us from evil."

The point is that Jesus recognized that "the evil one" or the devil will attack Jesus' followers, and his prayer was not that they be taken out of the world, but that they should be delivered from the temptations of the evil one.

Jesus taught his disciples:

MATTHEW	LUKE
Woe unto the world because of offenses!	It is impossible
For it must needs be that offenses come;	but that offenses will come,
but woe to that man by whom the offense cometh!	but woe unto him through whom they come!
Mt 18:7	L 17:1

The Greek word translated as *offenses* literally means "stumbling blocks." Jesus must then have said something like this, "The world is full of stumbling blocks, but woe unto the man who sets them up."

Jesus did not here say that the stumbling blocks are set up by the devil. However, the same Greek word translated as "stumbling blocks" also appears in Jesus' rebuke to Peter:

Get thee behind me, Satan: thou are an offense [stumbling block] unto me: . . . Mt 16:23

What he did say is:

Woe to that man by whom the offense cometh! Mt 18:7 (L 17:1)

Christians are not to collaborate with the devil in his activities. There is nothing in Jesus' teaching that states or implies that the secret operations of the devil do not continue until this day. Jesus' prayer for Christians was that the Father should keep them from the evil one, the devil. This is necessary since he will remain active until the end of the world, sowing tares in the darkness intermingled with the good seed sown by the Son of man.

Casting Out Demons

Movies and novels have rescued the rite of exorcism from the dogmas of an agnostic age. Demon possession now seems believable even in modern times and in urban settings and is no longer relegated to primitive cultures, the remote reaches of prehistory and the ages of myths.

The King James Version refers to demons as "devils", and modern versions correct that; but in the sense the word "devils" is more appropriate, since it suggests that this phenomena is Satanic and part of the covert operations of the devil.

In the Greco–Roman world of Jesus' time, even in Israel, demons were regarded as real. The people of Galilee did not deny the existence of demons; what amazed them was Jesus' power to exorcise them. In the synagogue in Capernaum, Jesus exorcised a man. We have two accounts of the reaction of the congregation:

MARK	LUKE
And they were all amazed,	And they were all amazed,
insomuch that they questioned	and spake
among themselves, saying,	among themselves, saying,
"What thing is this?	"What a word is this!
What new doctrine is this?	
For with authority	For with authority
	and power
commandeth he even	he commandeth
the unclean spirits,	the unclean spirits,
and they do obey him."	and they come out."
And immediately his fame	And the fame of him
spread abroad throughout	went out into
all the region	every place
round about Galilee.	of the country round about.
Mk 1:27–28	*L 4:36–37*

One of the charges of the Pharisees against Jesus was:

He casteth out devils through the prince of devils. *Mt 9:34*

On another occasion, reported in all three synoptic gospels, the Pharisees made the same charge:

MARK	MATTHEW	LUKE
He hath Beelzebub, and by the prince of the devils casteth him out devils. *Mk 3:22*	This fellow doth not cast out devils, but by Beelzebub the prince of the devils. *Mt 12:24*	He casteth out devils through Beelzebub the chief of the devils. *L 11:15*

In other cases, it was simply the crowd that made the charge:

Thou hast a devil; who goeth about to kill thee? *J 7:20*

Say we not well that thou art a Samaritan, and hast a devil? *J 8:48*

Now we know that thou hast a devil. *J 8.52*

Sometimes there was a division of opinion in the crowd:

And many of them said, "He hath a devil, and is mad. Why hear ye him?" *Others* said, "These are not the words of him that hath a devil. Can a devil open the eyes of the blind?" *J 10:20–21*

The Jews of Israel in Jesus' day did not question that demons (devils) existed. The only question for them, as these questions show, was whether Jesus himself was demon–possessed. Jesus' reply to this charge was:

MATTHEW	LUKE
And if I by Beelzebub cast out devils, by whom do your children cast them out?	And if I by Beelzebub cast out devils, by whom do your sons cast them out?

MATTHEW (cont.)	LUKE (cont.)
Therefore they shall	Therefore shall they
be your judges.	be your judges.
But if I	But if I
cast out devils	with the finger of God
by the Spirit of God,	cast out devils,
then	no doubt
the Kingdom of God	the Kingdom of God
is come unto you.	is come upon you.
Mt 12:27–28	*L 11:19–20*

On another occasion, Jesus answered the charge of demon-possession even more succinctly:

I have not a devil; but I honor my Father, and ye do dishonor me.
J 8:49

Jesus, however, had power over demons that he, in turn, delegated to his disciples:

MARK	MATTHEW	LUKE
And he	And when he	Then he
called	had called	called
unto him	unto him	
the Twelve,	his twelve disciples,	his twelve disciples together,
and began		
to send them		
forth		
by two and two;		
and gave them	he gave them	and gave them
power	power	power and authority
over	against	over
unclean spirits; . . .	unclean spirits,	all devils, . . .
Mk 6:7	to cast them out, . . .	*L 9:1*
	Mt 10:1	

Not only did the Twelve have power and authority over demons, they were specifically charged to cast them out:

Heal the sick, cleanse the lepers, raise the dead, *cast out devils*; freely ye have received, freely give. *Mt 10:8*

Not only were they charged to cast out demons, they, in fact, did so:

And they cast out many devils, and anointed with oil many that were sick, and healed them. *Mk 6:13*

Luke describes the return of the Seventy from a mission:

And the Seventy returned again with joy, saying, "Lord, even the devils are subject unto us *through thy name*." *L 10:17*

Jesus' name was so potent against demons that even non-followers could use it effectively. His disciples complained to him about it:

MARK	LUKE
Master, we saw	Master, we saw
one casting out	one casting out
devils	devils
in thy name,	*in thy name*;
and he followeth	
not us;	
and we forbad him,	and we forbad him,
because	because
he followeth not us.	he followeth not with us.
Mk 9:38	*L 9:49*

After his resurrection, Jesus told the remaining eleven of his twelve disciples:

And these signs shall follow them that believe: *In my name* shall they cast out devils; . . . *Mk 16:17*

Jesus' name and identity were crucial in the exorcism he did personally. Mark states:

> And unclean spirits, when they saw him, fell down before him, and cried, saying, "Thou art the Son of God." And he straitly charged them that they should not make him known. *Mk 3:11–12*

Luke reports that Jesus healed many persons of divers diseases by the laying on of his hands, and then continues:

> And the devils also came out of many, crying out, and saying, "Thou art Christ the Son of God."

> And he rebuking them suffered them not to speak: for they knew that he was Christ. *L 4:41*

Mark's account is much briefer:

> And he healed many that were sick of divers diseases, and cast out many devils; and suffered not the devils to speak, because they knew him. *Mk 1:34*

Matthew's account of the same incident is also brief:

> When the even was come, they brought unto him many that were possessed with devils; and he cast out the spirits with *his word*, and healed all that were sick. *Mt 8:16*

The word of exorcism that Jesus used is not recorded. We do have reports of exorcisms by Jesus when the exorcism formula used is stated.

As Jesus was teaching in the synagogue in Capernaum on a Sabbath, a demon-possessed man in the congregation shouted:

MARK	LUKE
Let us alone;	Let us alone;
what have we to do	what have we to do
with thee,	with thee,

MARK (cont.)	LUKE (cont.)
thou Jesus of Nazareth?	thou Jesus of Nazareth?
Art thou come	Art thou come
to destroy us?	to destroy us?
I know thee	I know thee
who thou art,	who thou art,
the Holy One of God.	the Holy One of God.
Mk 1:24	*L 4:34*

Jesus then exorcised the demon with this formula:

MARK	LUKE
Hold thy peace,	Hold thy peace,
and come out of him.	and come out of him.
Mk 1:25	*L 4:35*

The two Gospels describe the resulting exorcism as follows:

MARK	LUKE
And when	And when
the unclean spirit	the devil
had torn him,	had thrown him
and cried	
with a loud voice,	
	in the midst,
he came out of him.	he came out of him,
Mk 1:26	and hurt him not.
	L 4:35

Mark's account of a demon-possessed man living near some tombs in the country of the Gadarenes reports that Jesus used a formula similar to the one he used in the synagogue:

Come out of the man, thou unclean spirit. *Mk 5:9*

In this case Matthew reports Jesus as saying simply:

Go. *Mt 8:32*

Mark reports, and Luke agrees, that Jesus then said:

What is thy name? *Mk 5:9; L 8:30*

Then, there is the ambiguous case of a boy whom the Gospels describe in different ways. Mark and Luke describe him as having a spirit: "a dumb spirit", *Mk 9:17*; "a spirit taketh him", *L 9:39*. Mark reports that Jesus cured the boy with the following formula.

Thou dumb and deaf spirit, I charge thee, come out of him, and enter no more into him. *Mk 9:25*

Matthew simply states:

And Jesus rebuked the devil, and he departed out of him; and the child was cured from that very hour. *Mt 17:18*

However, Matthew begins his report of the incident by quoting the boy's father as saying:

Lord, have mercy on my son: for he is *lunatic*, and sore vexed, for ofttimes he falleth into the fire, and oft into the water. *Mt 17:15*

These and other details in the Gospel accounts are consistent with the diagnosis of epilepsy and modern translations insert this modern term for "lunatic." Accordingly, I have included the incident with the boy in the chapter on Healings under the title "The Epileptic Boy," pp. 939–943.

Sometimes Jesus' actual words of exorcism are not reported in the Gospel accounts. Sometimes the Gospels summarize that Jesus cast out or rebuked the unclean spirit, or devil. For example:

As they went out, behold they brought to him a dumb man possessed with a devil. And when the devil was cast out, the dumb spake; and the multitudes marvelled, saying, "It was never so seen in Israel." *Mt 9:32–33*

Another example is reported by both Matthew and Luke:

MATTHEW	LUKE
Then was brought	And he was
unto him one	
possessed with	casting out
a devil,	a devil,
blind,	and it
and dumb:	was dumb.
and he	And it came
healed him,	to pass,
insomuch that	when the devil
the blind	was gone out,
and dumb	the dumb
both spake	spake;
and saw,	
and all the people	and the people
were amazed, . . .	wondered.
Mt 12:22–23	L 11:14

Jesus' actual physical presence was not required for his exorcisms. While Jesus was in the region around Tyre and Sidon, a Gentile woman sought his help for her young daughter who was demon-possessed. Mk 7:28; Mt 15:22 Mark describes her as having "an unclean spirit", while Matthew states she was "grievously vexed with a devil." Mk 7:29; Mt 15:22 After an interchange between Jesus and the woman over helping her daughter, the daughter, who was home, was found healed. Mk 7:30; Mt 15:28

Here is what Jesus said to the woman:

MARK	MATTHEW
For this saying	O woman,
go thy way;	great is thy faith;
the devil is	be it unto thee
gone out	even
of thy daughter.	as thou wilt.
Mk 7:29	Mt 15:28

Each of the first three gospels has an account of Jesus exorcising an outcast man who lived among the tombs in the countryside beside the Sea of Galilee, but not in Galilee. *Mk 5:1–20; Mt 8:28–34; L 8:26–39* The spelling of the name of the area varies in manuscripts and this is reflected in the gospels. *Mk 5:1; Mt 8:28; L 8:26* Mark calls it "the country of the Gadarenes." *Mk 5:1*

The gospels describe the "man" in different ways:

MARK	MATTHEW	LUKE
. . . a man with an unclean spirit. *Mk 5:2*	. . . two possessed with devils. *Mt 8:28*	. . . a certain man which had devils a long time. *L 8:27*

Matthew's account in some way has become garbled because, as we now have it, he writes that there were "two possessed with devils", not one. *Mt 8:28* Here I assume that Mark's and Luke's manuscripts are right in stating that only one demon-possessed man was involved.

The man's reaction to Jesus was similar to the man in the synagogue. He also shouted:

MARK	MATTHEW	LUKE
What have I to do with thee, Jesus, thou Son of the most high God? I adjure thee by God, that thou torment me not. *Mk 5:7*	What have we to do with thee, Jesus, thou Son of God? Art thou come hither to torment us before the time? *Mt 8:29*	What have I to do with thee, Jesus, thou Son of God most high? I beseech thee, torment me not. *L 8:28*

The accounts continue:

MARK	MATTHEW	LUKE
Come out of the man,	"Go."	For he had
	Mt 8:32	commanded
thou unclean spirit.		the unclean spirit
		to come out
		of the man . . .
What is thy name?		"What is thy name?"
My name		
is Legion:		"Legion":
for we are m any.		because many devils
		were entered
		into him.
And he		And they
besought him much		besought him
that he would not		that he would not
send them away		command them
out of the country.		to go out
		into the deep.
Now there	And there	And there
was nigh	was a good way	was there
unto the mountains	off from them	
a great herd	an herd	an herd
of swine	of many swine	of many swine
feeding.	feeding.	feeding
		on the mountain,
And all the devils	So the devils	and they
besought him,	besought him,	besought him
saying,	saying,	that
	"If thou	he would
	cast us out,	
"Send us	suffer us	suffer them
into the swine,	to go away into	
that we may	the herd	
enter into them."	of swine."	to enter into them.
Mk 5:8–12	*Mt 8:30–31*	*L 8:29–32*

The Aramaic behind the Greek gospel words translated *enter into* may instead mean "attack." The devils thus either entered into or attacked the herd of swine and the herd then stampeded down a steep slope into the Sea of Galilee and were drowned:

MARK	MATTHEW	LUKE
And forthwith	And when	And
Jesus gave them	they were	he suffered
leave. And	come out,	them.
		Then went
the unclean spirits	they	the devils
went out,	went	out of the man,
and entered into	into	and entered into
the swine;	the herd of swine;	the swine;
and	and behold,	and
the herd	the whole herd	the herd
	of swine	
ran violently	ran violently	ran violently
down	down	down
a steep place	a steep place	a steep place
into the sea,	into the sea,	into the lake,
(they were		
about two thousand)		
and were choked	and perished	and were choked.
in the sea.	in the waters.	*L 8:32–33*
Mk 5:13	*Mt 8:32*	

It is hard for moderns to understand how demons could enter a herd of swine. However, it is really no harder than to understand how the man could be demon-possessed. Neither case fits the parameters of what we consider possible in the present state of scientific knowledge. The question, of course, is whether our present ideas of possibilities actually exhaust the categories of the possible. The history of science makes it likely that the present hypotheses of phobias, complexes and split personalities will be replaced with other and more accurate hypotheses.

What is certain is that in this case Jesus swiftly and successfully exorcised a notorious man, and all men of the Decapolis (Ten Towns) area "did marvel" at the exorcism. *Mk 5:20*

The swineherds who had lost their swine (about 2,000 head) hastened to town to tell of their loss. *Mk 5:13–14; Mt 8:33; L 8:34* The resulting crowd returned to see the man sitting at the feet of Jesus, "clothed, and in his right mind." *Mk 5:15; L 8:35*

This frightened the crowd, and they wanted Jesus to leave immediately:

MARK	MATTHEW	LUKE
		Then
And they began	. . . they	the whole multitude
		of the country
		of the Gadarenes
		round about
to pray him	besought him	besought him
	that he would	
to depart out	depart out	to depart
of their coasts.	of their coasts.	from them,
Mk 5:17	*Mt 8:34*	for they
		were taken
		with great fear; . . .
		L 8:37

The gospel descriptions of the man are vivid:

MARK	MATTHEW	LUKE
. . . who had	. . . two possessed	. . . a certain man,
	with devils	which had devils
his dwelling	coming	long time,
among the tomb;	out of the tombs,	and ware
and no man	exceeding	no clothes,
could bind him,	fierce,	neither
no, not with chains:	so that	abode
because that	no man	in any house,
he had been	might pass	but
often bound	by that way.	in the tombs.
with fetters	*Mt 8:28*	*L 8:27*

MARK (cont.)	MATTHEW (cont.)	LUKE (cont.)
and chains,		
and the chains		For oftentimes
had been plucked		it had
asunder by him,		caught him;
and the fetters		and he was
broken in pieces;		kept bound
		with chains
		and in fetters;
neither could		and he brake
any man		
tame him.		the bands,
And always,		and was driven
night and day,		of the devil
he was		into
in the mountains,		the wilderness.
and		L 8:29
in the tombs,		
crying, and		
cutting himself		
with stones.		
Mk 5:3–5		

The details are classic: a demented, fierce, shouting, uncontrollable man, without clothes, living as an outcast among the tombs, and shunned by all. Despite his condition, or perhaps rather because of it, he intuitively felt Jesus' special status and he ran up to Jesus and fell down before him, and with a loud voice, cried:

What have I to do with thee, Jesus, thou Son of the most high God?
Mk 5:7 (Mt 8:29; L 8:28)

Jesus simply proceeded with the exorcism. When the exorcism was complete, Jesus did not exploit it in any way. As Jesus was entering the boat to leave the scene, the man, now "clothed, and in his right mind", begged to go with Jesus. Mk 5:15,18; L 8:35, 38

Jesus refused. *Mk 5:19; L 8:38* Instead, he told the man:

MARK	LUKE
Go home	Return
to thy friends,	to thine own house,
and tell them	and shew
how great things	how great things
the Lord	God
hath done	hath done
for thee,	unto thee.
and hath had compassion	*L 8:39*
on thee.	
Mk 5:19	

The man did not conform to Jesus' instruction, but went his way publishing in the Decapolis "how great things Jesus had done for him." *Mk 5:20 (L 8:39)*

The Gospels tend to lump healings and exorcisms together and do not particularly stress the exorcisms. *Mk 1:32–34; Mt 8:16; L 4:40–41* For example, Matthew writes:

And Jesus went about all Galilee, teaching in their synagogues, and preaching the gospel of the Kingdom, and healing all manner of sickness and all manner of disease among the people.

And his fame went throughout all Syria, and they brought unto him all sick people that were taken with divers diseases and torments, and *those that were possessed with devils*, and those which were lunatic, and those that had the palsy; and he healed them. *Mt 4:23–24*

Many women followers of Jesus had "been healed of evil spirits and infirmities. *L 8:2–3* One was Mary, called Magdalene. *L 8:2* Two others are also specifically named: Joanna, the wife of Chuza, Herod's steward, and Susanna. *L 8:3*

Jesus himself placed exorcisms on the same plane as healings. He told certain Pharisees who had warned him that Herod would kill him:

> Go ye, and tell that fox, Behold, I cast out devils, and I do cures today and tomorrow, and the third day I shall be perfected. *L 13:32*

Jesus stated that ordinary exorcisms were not enough and that relapse was inevitable and would compound the original condition:

MATTHEW	LUKE
When	When
the unclean spirit	the unclean spirit
is gone out	is gone out
of a man,	of a man,
he [the spirit]	he [the spirit]
walketh	walketh
through dry places,	through dry places,
seeking rest,	seeking rest;
and findeth none.	and finding none,
Then he saith,	he saith,
"I will return	"I will return
into my house	unto my house
from whence	whence
I came out;"	I came out."
and when	And when
he is come,	he cometh,
he findeth it	he findeth it
empty, swept,	swept
and garnished.	and garnished.
Then goeth he,	Then goeth he,
and taketh	and taketh
with him	to him
seven other spirits	seven other spirits
more wicked	more wicked
than himself,	than himself,
and they enter in	and they enter in,

MATTHEW (cont.)
and dwell there;
and the last state
of that man
is worse than
the first.
Mt 12:43–45

LUKE (cont.)
and dwell there;
and the last state
of that man
is worse than
the first.
L 11:24–26

Here Jesus is describing exorcisms generally. The question is whether the exorcisms that Jesus did were different from exorcisms generally. The clear implication from Jesus' statements is that his exorcisms were different, since he accomplished them by the Spirit of God and these feats were signs that "the Kingdom of God is come unto you." *Mt 12:28; L 11:20*

Since Jesus exorcised demons by the Spirit of God, it can be reasonably inferred that the Spirit of God then occupied the emptiness of those exorcised. Paul wrote "the Spirit of God dwelleth in you." *1 Corinthians 3:16*

Jesus had been charged with casting out demons by the devil, by Beelzebub. *Mk 3:22; Mt 9:34, 12:24; L 11:15* He had denied the charge. *Mk 3:23; Mt 12:26–28; L 11:18–20*

He explained:

MARK	MATTHEW	LUKE
How can		
Satan		
cast out Satan?		
And if		
a kingdom	Every kingdom	Every kingdom
be divided	divided	divided
against itself,	against itself	against itself
that kingdom	is brought	is brought
can not stand.	to desolation,	to desolation,
And if	and every city	and
a house	or house	a house
be divided	divided	divided
against itself,	against itself	against a house
that house		

MARK (cont.)	MATTHEW (cont.)	LUKE (cont.)
can not stand.	shall not stand.	falleth.
And if	And if	If
Satan	Satan	Satan
rise up	cast out	
against himself,	Satan,	
and be divided,	he is divided	also be divided
	against himself;	against himself,
he can not stand,	how shall then	how shall
but hath an end.	his kingdom stand?	his kingdom stand?
	Mt 12:25–26	*L 11:17–18*
No man	Or else how	When
can enter into	can one enter into	a strong man
a strong man's house,	a strong man's house,	armed
		keepeth his palace,
and spoil his goods,	and spoil his goods,	his goods
		are in peace.
except	except	But when
he will	he	a stronger
		than he
first bind	first bind	shall come
the strong man;	the strong man?	upon him,
and then	And then	he taketh
he will spoil	he will spoil	from him
his house.	his house.	all his armor
Mk 3:23–27	*Mt 12:29*	wherein
		he trusted,
		and divideth
		his spoils.
		L 11:21–22

Jesus' point is this: Satan was not foolish enough to help destroy part of his own kingdom, the demons. By casting out demons Jesus had been able to disrupt Satan's kingdom by spoiling his demons. This was obviously done against the will of Satan, like binding a strong man to spoil his house.

Exorcism of demons can be a sensational ministry. Exorcisms are, as Jesus said, "signs" that "shall follow them that believe." Mk 16:17 The correct place of such a ministry was more fully explained by Jesus when he instructed the Seventy on this point:

SEVENTY: Lord, even the devils [demons] are subject unto us through thy name.

JESUS: I beheld Satan as lightning fall from heaven. Behold, I give you power to tread on serpents and scorpions, *and over all the power of the enemy*; and nothing shall by any means hurt you. Notwithstanding, in this rejoice not, *that the spirits [demons] are subject unto you*; but rather rejoice because your names are written in heaven. L 10:17–20

The conclusion of the whole matter is this: The ability of the Seventy to exorcise demons was evidence that Satan had lost a battle. Jesus had seen Satan's defeat as it had happened, like seeing the gun flashes of a distant battle. Notwithstanding, disciples are not to rejoice for such victories "over all the power of the enemy", but rather because their names "are written in heaven." In short, rejoice that they are saved.

CHAPTER 15

SIN / SALVATION

JESUS' OWN VIEW OF SALVATION

Jesus stated that he came to save the world. What did he mean by that?

His exact words were:

> I am come a light into the world, that whosoever believeth on me should not abide in darkness. And if any man hear my words, and believe not, I judge him not: for I come not to judge the world, but to save the world. J 12:46-47

Jesus came as a light to men, to lead them out of the darkness. This is their salvation. In this sense he is the light of men:

> I am the light of the world; he that followeth me shall not walk in darkness, but shall have the light of life. J 8:12

Jesus' own teaching of salvation was an affirmative thing: for him salvation was like stepping out of darkness into light. He specifically said he came "not to judge, but to save the world." J 12:47

Looking back at Jesus' ministry some years later, John, one of the greatest of the early Christian writers, recognized this when he wrote:

> For God sent not his Son into the world to condemn the world, but that a world through him might be saved. He that believeth on him

is not condemned: but he that believeth not is condemned already, because he hath not believed in the name of the only begotten Son of God. *J 3:17–18*

When Jesus was not received in a Samaritan village, two of his key disciples, James and John, thought fire from heaven on the villagers was indicated. Jesus refused, saying, according some manuscripts:

The Son of man is not come to destroy men's lives, but to save them. *L 9:56*

Jesus taught that it was important that people "should believe and be saved." *L 8:12* The reason is this:

MARK	MATTHEW	LUKE
For what	For what	For what
shall it profit a man,	is a man profited,	is a man advantaged,
if he shall gain	if he shall gain	if he gain
the whole world, and	the whole world, and	the whole world, and
lose his own soul?	lose his own soul?	lose himself,
Or what shall	Or what shall	or be cast away?
a man give	a man give	
in exchange for	in exchange	
his soul?	for his soul?	
Whosoever therefore		For whosoever
shall be shamed of		shall be ashamed of
me and of my words		*me and of my words*,
in this adulterous		
and sinful generation,		
of him also shall	For	of him shall
the Son of man	the Son of man	the Son of man
be ashamed		be ashamed,
when he cometh	shall come	when he shall come
in the glory	in the glory	in his own glory,

MARK (cont.)	MATTHEW (cont.)	LUKE (cont.)
of his Father	of his Father	and in his Father's,
with the holy angels.	with his angels,	and of the holy angels.
Mk 8:36–38	and then	*L 9:25–26*
	he shall reward	
	every man	
	according to	
	his works.	
	Mt 16:26–27	

The ultimate test of salvation is loyalty to Jesus and his words. In other statements, Jesus is even more explicit:

MATTHEW	LUKE
Whosoever therefore	Whosoever
shall confess me	shall confess me
before men,	before men,
him will I	him shall the Son of man
confess also	also confess
before my Father	before the angels
which is in heaven.	of God.
But whosoever	But he that
shall deny me	denieth me
before men,	before men,
him will I also deny	shall be denied
before my Father	before the angels
which is in heaven.	of God.
Mt 10:32–33	*L 12:8–9*

Confession is made by the mouth, by words. Words are important. Jesus said so:

> But I say unto you, that every idle word that men shall speak, they shall give account thereof in the day of judgment. For by thy words thou shalt be justified, and by thy words thou shalt be condemned.
> *Mt 12:36–37*

The first three gospels quote Jesus as saying:

MARK	MATTHEW	LUKE	MATTHEW	LUKE
For	For	For	He that	Whosoever
whosoever	whosoever	whosoever	findeth	shall
will save	will save	will save		seek to save
his life	his life	his life	his life	his life
shall lose it;	shall lose it,	shall lose it;	shall lose it,	shall lose it,
but	and	but	and	and
whosoever	whosoever	whosoever	he	whosoever
shall lose	will lose	will lose	that loseth	shall lose
his life	his life	his life	his life	his life
for my sake	for my sake	for my sake,	for my sake	
and				
the gospel's				
the same		the same		shall
shall save it.	shall find it.	shall save it.	shall find it.	preserve it.
Mk 8:35	*Mt 16:25*	*L 9:24*	*Mt 10:39*	*L 17:33*

How then did Jesus wish people to be saved?

The gospels record several cases in which Jesus recognized that certain specific individuals were saved. The first case is Zacchaeus, a collaborationist tax collector. When Zacchaeus repented and restored what he had wrongly exacted, Jesus said:

> This day is salvation come to this house, forsomuch as he also is a son of Abraham. For the Son of man is come to seek and to save that which was lost. *L 19:9–10*

Some manuscripts of Matthew have the same saying in a different context:

> For the Son of man is come to save that which was lost. *Mt 18:11*

There is also the episode of the sinful woman. Simon, a Pharisee, invited Jesus to his house to dine. *L 7:36* A sinful woman of the city came up behind Jesus and stood weeping and washed his feet with her tears and wiped them with her hair and kissed his feet and anointed them with ointment that she had brought in an alabaster jar. *L 7:37–38* Simon was appalled that Jesus would allow her to touch him. *L 7:39*

Jesus said to Simon:

Seest thou this woman? I entered into thine house; thou gavest me no water for my feet, but she hath washed my feet with tears, and wiped them with the hairs of her head.

Thou gavest me no kiss, but this woman since the time I came in hath not ceased to kiss my feet. My head with oil thou didst not anoint, but this woman hath anointed my feet with ointment.

Wherefore I say unto thee, her sins, which are many, are forgiven, for she loved much; but to whom little is forgiven, the same loveth little. *L 7:44–47*

And he said to her:

Thy sins are forgiven. *L 7:48*

Those at the dinner murmured:

Who is this that forgiveth sins also? *L 7:49*

Jesus then said to the woman:

Thy faith hath saved thee; go in peace. *L 7:50*

The woman's faith that she could repent and her faith in Jesus was sufficient although she said not a word.

The same phrase "thy faith hath saved thee" was also used by Jesus with respect to the healing of a blind man. On the way to Jericho, Jesus passed a blind man sitting by the wayside, begging. The blind man asked about the crowd passing by. He was told that Jesus of Nazareth was passing by. *L 18:37*

He cried out:

Jesus, thou son of David, have mercy on me. *L 18:38*

He was told to be quiet, but he cried out again:

Thou son of David, have mercy on me. *L 18:39*

Jesus stopped and directed that the blind man be brought to him, and when he came near, Jesus asked:

What wilt thou that I shall do unto thee? *L 18:41*

The man said:

Lord, that I may receive my sight. *L 18:42*

Jesus replied:

Receive thy sight: thy faith hath saved thee. *L 18:42*

Does "save" here simply mean "heal"? The sinful woman was not healed yet she also was saved. Apparently all the blind man or the sinful woman had to do was to trust in Jesus.

Almost immediately following the episode of the sinful woman, Luke has the parable of the sower that Jesus told thusly:

A sower went out to sow his seed, and as he sowed, some fell by the way side; and it was trodden down, and the fowls of the air devoured it. And some fell upon a rock; and as soon as it was sprung up, it withered away, because it lacked moisture. And some fell among thorns, and the thorns sprang up with it, and choked it. And other fell on good ground, and sprang up, and bare fruit an hundredfold. *L 8:5–8*

Jesus' explanation of the parable was this:

The seed is the word of God. Those by the way side are they that hear; then cometh the devil, and taketh away the word out of their hearts, *lest they should believe and be saved.* They on the rock are they, which, when they hear, receive the word with joy; and these have no root, which for a while believe, and in time of temptation fall away. And that which fell among thorns are they, which, when they have heard, go forth, and are choked with cares and riches and pleasures of this life, and bring no fruit to perfection. *But that on the good ground are they, which in an honest and good heart, having heard the word, keep it, and bring forth fruit with patience. L 8:12–15*

Jesus was, humanly speaking, a Jew. As such he did not scruple to speak on occasion with Jewish pride. He told a Samaritan woman:

Ye worship ye know not what. We know what we worship: for salvation is of the Jews. But the hour cometh, and *now is,* when the true worshippers shall worship the Father in spirit and in truth: for the Father seeketh such to worship him. *J 4:22–23*

Someone asked Jesus:

Lord, are there few that be saved? *L 13:23*

He answered:

Strive to enter in at the strait [narrow] gate: for many, I say unto you, will seek to enter in, and shall not be able. When once the master of the house is risen up, and hath shut to the door, and ye begin to stand without, and to knock at the door, saying, "Lord, Lord, open unto us;" and he shall answer and say unto you, "I know you not whence you are:"

Then shall ye begin to say, "We have eaten and drunk in thy presence, and thou has taught in our streets."

But he shall say, "I tell you, I know you not whence ye are; depart from me, all ye workers of iniquity."

There shall be weeping and gnashing of teeth, when ye shall see
Abraham, and Isaac, and Jacob, and all the prophets, in the Kingdom of God, and you yourselves thrust out. And they shall come
from the east, and from the west, and from the north, and from the
south, and shall sit down in the Kingdom of God. And, behold,
there are last which shall be first, and there are first which shall be
last. *L 13:24–30*

Jesus' answer clearly identifies salvation with being in the Kingdom of God with Abraham, Isaac, Jacob, the prophets, and all who
have entered through the narrow gate. His disciples thought the
same way. When Jesus taught them that it is hard for a rich man to
enter the Kingdom, they said, "Who then can be saved?" *Mk 10:26;
Mt 19:25; L 18:26*
Matthew has a saying involving the narrow gate:

Enter ye in at the strait [narrow] gate: for wide is the gate, and broad
is the way, that leadeth to destruction, and many there be which go
in thereat. Because strait is the gate, and narrow is the way, which
leadeth unto life, and few there be that find it. *Mt 7:13–14*

There is no specific mention here of the Kingdom of God, but
the narrow gate is the same gate as in Luke. The word *save* is not
used, but the narrow gate leads "unto life" while the other way
leads to destruction.
Jesus also said:

I am the door: by me if any man enter in, he shall be saved, and
shall go in and out, and find pasture. *J 10:9*

The imagery here is of a sheepfold, and "the door" spoken of is
the gate to the fold. The truth of the narrow gate to the fold was
also expressed by Jesus in another way. He said, according to some
manuscripts of Mark:

Go ye into all the world, and preach the gospel to every creature.
He that believeth and is baptized shall be saved; but he that believeth
not shall be damned. *Mk 16:15–16*

Jesus referred to John's testimony about Jesus and then concluded:

But I receive not testimony from man, but these things I say, that ye *might be saved. J 5:34*

The narrow gate of salvation is confession of Jesus before men. That narrow gate is the way of life. Salvation is passing through that gate over from death to life.

Jesus said:

Verily, verily, I say unto you, he that heareth my word, and believeth on him that sent me, hath everlasting life and shall not come into condemnation, but is passed from death unto life. J 5:24

RECEIVING JESUS AND HIS FATHER

Much is said about receiving Jesus. Jesus gave an example of how to do it. He took a little child and used the child as an object lesson, saying:

MARK	MATTHEW	LUKE
Whosoever	And whoso	Whosoever
shall receive	shall receive	shall receive
one of such children	one such little child	this child
in my name,	*in my name,*	*in my name,*
receiveth me;	receiveth me.	receiveth me;
and whosoever	*Mt 18:5*	and whosoever
shall receive me,		shall receive me,
receiveth not me,		receiveth
but him		him
that sent me.		that sent me.
Mk 9:37		*L 9:48*

It is not sufficient to receive children. All three gospels state that the reception of children must be in Jesus' name. If the Jesus' name condition is met, the receiver of children also receives Jesus himself.

Mark and Luke go further to state that "whosoever shall receive me, receiveth not me, but him that sent me." *Mk 9:37 (L 9:48)* A similar assertion of Jesus is quoted in the other two gospels, Matthew and John, but in different contexts:

He that receiveth you receiveth me, and he that receiveth me receiveth him that sent me. *Mt 10:40*

Verily, verily, I say unto you, he that receiveth whomsoever I send, receiveth me; and he that receiveth me, receiveth him that sent me. *J 13:20*

Finally, Luke has the same saying in a negative form:

He that heareth you heareth me, and he that despiseth you despiseth me; and he that despiseth me despiseth him that sent me. *L 10:16*

It is easy to summarize Jesus' statements:

Act: Receiving a little child in Jesus' name, or receiving one of Jesus' followers.
Result 1: Receiving Jesus.
Result 2: Receiving him that sent Jesus.

The way to God the Father is by receiving a little child in Jesus' name, or receiving one of Jesus' followers. As Jesus said another time:

He that believeth on me, believeth not on me, but on him that sent me.

And he that seeth me seeth him that sent me. *J 12:44–45*

What could be clearer?

God Is the Father of All Believers

God is the Father of all believers, not just Jesus' Father. Jesus expressly recognized this in the words of the model prayer he gave to his disciples:

MATTHEW
Our Father
which art in heaven, . . .
Mt 6:9

LUKE
"Our Father
which art in heaven, . . .
L 11:2

When Jesus appeared to Mary Magdalene after his resurrection, he said:

Touch me not, for I am not yet ascended to *my* Father; but go to *my* brethren, and say unto them, "I ascend unto *my* Father, and *your* Father, and to *my* God, and *your* God." *J 20:17*

Some of Jesus' most famous sayings recognize that God was not simply his Father but the Father of all believers:

Are not two sparrows sold for a farthing? And one of them shall not fall on the ground without *your* Father. *Mt 10:29*

Be not ye therefore like unto them [the heathen]: for *your* Father knoweth what things ye have need of, before ye ask him. *Mt 6:8* (*Mt 6:32, L 12:30*)

Even so it is not the will of *your* Father which is in heaven, that one of these little ones should perish. *Mt 18:14*

For if ye forgive men their trespasses, *your* heavenly Father will also forgive you; but if ye forgive not men their trespasses, neither will *your* Father forgive your trespasses. *Mt 6:14–15* (*Mk 11:25–26*)

Be ye therefore merciful, as *your* Father also is merciful. *L 6:36*

This is not an exhaustive list of the quotations in which Jesus refers to "your Father", but is sufficient to show that Jesus taught that he and his followers had the same Father.

GOD IS NOT THE FATHER OF ALL MEN

In a sense, God is the Father of all men. This is not what Jesus taught. He taught that God is only the Father of some men. Jesus told some fellow Jews:

If God were your Father, ye would love me: for I proceeded forth and came from God. Neither came I of myself, but he sent me. *J 8:42*

Later on in the same interchange Jesus told these Jews:

Ye are of your father the devil, and the lusts of your father ye will do. *J 8:44*

This is very clear. According to Jesus, these particular Jews had the devil for their father, and God was accordingly not their father.

Jesus told a parable as the good seed and the Kingdom of Heaven. *Mt 13:24–30* Jesus' explanation of that parable may also explain why he told these Jews that they were children of the devil:

He that soweth the good seed is the Son of man.

The field is the world.

The good seed are the children of the Kingdom; but the tares are the children of the Wicked One.

The enemy that soweth them is the devil. *Mt 13:37–39*

The contrast in Jesus' thought is between the children of the Kingdom and the children of the devil. Children of the Kingdom are the followers of Jesus' new law. Jesus said:

Ye have heard that it hath been said, "Thou shalt love thy neighbor, and hate thine enemy." [*Leviticus 19:18*]

But I say unto you, "Love your enemies, bless them that curse you, do good to them that hate you, and pray for them which despitefully use you, and persecute you; *that ye may be the children of your Father which is in heaven*:" for he maketh his sun to rise on the evil and on the good, and sendeth rain on the just and on the unjust. Mt 5:43–45

The followers of Jesus' new law are the children of his Father. That is why he called peacemakers children of God:

Blessed are the peacemakers: for they shall be called the children of God. *Mt 5:9*

Jesus did not teach that all men are the children of God. He taught that the children of Jesus' Kingdom are the true children of their Father which is in heaven.

Jesus and the Way To God

Jesus did not believe that there are a thousand paths to God. Jesus taught that:

No man cometh unto the Father but by me. *J 14:6*

The Father is, of course, God the Father. Jesus' enormous claim was not made in a formal, direct statement, but almost incidently in a dialogue with his disciples That went like this.

Jesus, foreseeing his own death, told his disciples that he would only be with them a little while longer and that:

Whither I go, ye cannot come. *J 13:33*

Peter then asked:

Whither goest thou? *J 13:36*

Jesus answered:

Whither I go, thou canst not follow me now, but thou shalt follow me afterwards. *J 13:36*

Peter replied:

Lord, why cannot I follow thee now? *J 13:37*

Jesus then explained that he was going to prepare a place for his disciples "in my Father's house" and concluded with the statement:

And whither I go ye know, and *the way* ye know. *J 14:4*

This was not clear to Thomas who asked:

Lord, we know not whither thou goest; and how can we know *the way*? *J 14:5*

Jesus replied:

> I am *the way*, the truth, and the life; no man cometh unto the Father
> but by me. *J 14:6*

Humanly speaking Jesus' claim on exclusiveness may seem ar-
rogant; but it is the very heart of his teaching. To reject Jesus' teaching is to reject Jesus himself. Jesus continued his dialogue with his
disciples:

> If ye had known me, ye should have known my Father also; and
> from henceforth ye know him, and have seen him. *J 14:7*

This time it was Philip who missed the point, so he said:

> Lord, shew us the Father, and it sufficeth us. *J 14:8*

Jesus replied:

> Have I been so long time with you, and yet hath thou not known
> me, Philip? He that hath seen me hath seen the Father; and how
> sayest thou then, "Shew us the Father?" *J 14:9*

What could be clearer: if the disciples had seen Jesus, they had
seen God the Father. Why quibble about the way to God?

Jesus immediately explained that he was not simply saying that
"I am the Father":

> Believest thou not that I am *in the Father*, and the Father *in me*? The
> words that I speak unto you I speak not of myself; but the Father
> that *dwelleth in me*, he doeth the works. Believe me that I am *in the
> Father*, and the Father *in me*; or else believe me for the very works'
> sake. *J 14:10–11*

To summarize, Jesus taught that he is the only way to the Father since he is in the Father, and the Father is in him, indwelling
him.

Jesus not only described himself as the only way to the Father but also as "the door" whereby men may enter in and be saved. The imagery is of a Near Eastern sheepfold, a corral of rock, and the door is the corral gate.

Jesus began this parable as follows:

Verily, verily, I say unto you, I am the door of the sheep [fold]. All that ever come before me are thieves and robbers; but the sheep did not hear them.

I am the door: by me if any man enter in, he shall be saved, and shall go in and out, and find pasture. *J 10:7–9*

There is but one way and one door to the Father, Jesus Christ. So taught Jesus. So has the Christian church taught from its earliest days:

This is "the stone which was set at naught of you builders, which is become the head of the corner [the cornerstone]." [*Psalm 118:22*]

Neither is there salvation in any other: for there is none other name under heaven given among men, whereby we must be saved. *Acts 4:11–12*

ARE THERE ANY SINNERS?

Are there any sinners?

Jesus thought so. Many of his modern "disciples" think not.

Jesus did not blush to call men to repentance. Jesus began his ministry by preaching:

MARK	MATTHEW
The time is fulfilled,	*Repent*
and the Kingdom of God	for the Kingdom of Heaven
is at hand:	is at hand.
repent ye,	
and believe the gospel.	*Mt 4:17*
Mk 1:15	

Modern scholars like to write about the Kingdom, and everyone is in favor of the Gospel, which we are told simply means, "Good news"; but Jesus did preach repentance as well as the good news of his Father and his Father's Kingdom.

Jesus, like John, came preaching that men must repent. *Mt 3:2, 8; L 3:3, 8 (John)* He was not simply the Gentle Man from Galilee. The smooth beatific image is wrong. The facts are otherwise.

Jesus came preaching with fiery denunciation. Matthew states:

Then began he to *upbraid* the cities wherein most of his mighty works were done, because they *repented not. Mt 11:20*

Jesus scathingly denounced his own generation as "this wicked generation." *Mt 12:45* This was not a stray saying, but a repeated theme of his preaching:

. . . a wicked and adulterous generation: . . . *Mt 16:4*

. . . an evil and adulterous generation . . . *Mt 12:39*

. . . an evil generation. *L 11:29*

Jesus had called his own generation to repentance, but there had been no repentance:

Matthew	Luke
The men of Nineveh	The men of Nineveh
shall rise in judgment	shall rise up in the judgment
with *this generation*,	with *this generation*,
and shall condemn it,	and shall condemn it,
because *they repented*	for *they repented*
at the preaching of Jonah;	at the preaching of Jonah;
and behold,	and, behold,
a greater than Jonah	a greater than Jonah
is here.	is here.
Mt 12:41	*L 11:32*

Jesus was not the first to preach repentance from sin; others from Jonah to John the Baptist had so preached. But Jesus taught that one "greater than Jonah" was then present, namely, himself.

There is probably no story so embedded in the concept of Jesus, both Christian and non-Christian, as the story of the woman taken in adultery. This is so, even though as modern translations note, the story is not found in the best manuscripts.

Everyone knows that Jesus said:

He that is without sin among you, let him first cast a stone at her.
J 8:7

It is easy and popular to condemn the self-righteousness of woman's accusers. What is often overlooked is that Jesus did recognize that the woman *had sinned* by her adultery:

Neither do I condemn thee; go, and *sin no more*. *J 8:11*

Jesus did not condemn the woman, but also did not deny her sin, or by obvious extension, the existence of sin generally. In fact, he recognized that sin exists and all persons are sinners:

> He that is without sin among you, let him first cast a stone at her. *J 8:7*

Sin was a reality for Jesus. He told the lame man whom he healed:

> Behold, thou art made whole; *sin no more*, lest a worse thing come unto thee. *J 5:14*

Jesus forgave the sins of the man sick of the palsy:

> Son, be of good cheer; *thy sins* be forgiven thee. *Mt 9:2 (Mk 2:5; L 5:20)*

While a sick man may have sinned and this contributed to his sickness, sickness itself was not, theologically speaking, necessarily a judgment for sin. In the case of the man born blind, Jesus was emphatic:

> Neither hath this man sinned, nor his parents . . . *J 9:3*

Jesus did, however, recognize that all are sinners and must repent. Pontius Pilate had put some Galileans to death. Jesus told those who reported this massacre:

> Suppose ye that these Galileans were sinners above all the Galileans, because they suffered such things?
>
> I tell you, "Nay;" but *except ye repent, ye shall all likewise perish.*
>
> Or those eighteen, upon whom the tower in Siloam fell, and slew them, think ye that they were sinners above all men that dwelt in Jerusalem?

I tell you, "Nay;" but, *except ye repent*, ye shall all likewise perish.
L 13:2–5

To summarize, Jesus taught:

1. The death of the massacred Galileans and the death of
   Jerusalemers killed by the fall of a tower at Siloam did not
   show above average sin on their part.
2. All men are sinners, not just these massacred Galileans and
   slain Jerusalemers.
3. All must repent, or perish.

Jesus taught that all must repent, or perish; but he did not
wallow in the sinfulness of man. To him sin was a sickness he had
to heal.

The first three gospels all report Jesus as saying:

MARK	MATTHEW	LUKE
They that are whole have no need of the physician, but they that are sick.	They that be whole need not a physician, but they that are sick.	They that are whole need not a physician, but they that are sick.
	But go ye and learn what that meaneth, "I will have mercy, and not sacrifice." [*Hosea 6:6*]:	
I came *not* to call the righteous, but sinners to repentance. Mk 2:17	for I am *not* come to call the righteous, but sinners to repentance. Mt 9:12–13	I came *not* to call the righteous, but sinners to repentance. L 5:31–32

The best manuscripts of Matthew and Mark omit "to repentance." Jesus' statement then becomes that "I came not to call the righteous, but sinners. *Mk 2:16; Mt 9:11; L 5:30*

The plain implication of Jesus' statement is that before he came there were some righteous. This causes problems for symmetrical theologians: Jesus came to save sinners; therefore, all were then sinners.

Jesus did call all men to repent. Jesus did tell the adulterous woman and the lame man to "sin no more." *J 8:11; J 5:14* But Jesus did say:

> I say unto you, that likewise joy shall be in heaven over one sinner that repenteth, more than over ninety and nine just persons, which *need no* repentance. *L 15:7*

Modern translations correctly translate "just persons" as "righteous persons." But, staying with the King James text, what about the "ninety and nine just persons, *which need no repentance*?" Was Jesus wrong? Was he misquoted? Are the manuscripts in error?

Matthew's parallel parable does not have the phrase *which need no repentance*. He simply writes of "the ninety and nine which went not astray." *Mt 18:13* But what had they to repent?

The best answer to Luke's account is that Jesus was not dealing with the universalness of sin but with a different topic. He was explaining to murmuring Pharisees and scribes why he was associating with blatant and obvious sinners. *L 15:2–3* His point was the joy over the finding of the one lost sheep, not his incidental remark about "just men", with whom the murmuring Pharisees and scribes could identify.

Jesus did not deny that there were "just men"—righteous men. *Mk 2:17; Mt 9:12; L 5:31* Jesus did affirm that righteousness is a perilous state and that publicans rather than Pharisees may qualify.

Jesus made this point by a parable that began:

> And he spoke this parable unto certain which trusted in themselves that they were righteous, and despised others. *L 18:9*

Jesus continued:

Two men went up into the Temple to pray; and the one a Pharisee, and the other a publican. The Pharisee stood and prayed thus with himself, "God, I thank thee, that I am not as other men are, extortioners, unjust, adulterers, or even as this publican. I fast twice in the week, I give tithes of all that I possess."

And the publican, standing afar off, would not lift up so much as his eyes unto heaven, but smote upon his breast, saying, "God be merciful to me a sinner."

I tell you, this man went down to his house justified rather than the other: for every one that exalteth himself shall be abased, and he that humbleth himself shall be exalted. *L 18:10–14*

Jesus said:

If I had not come and spoken unto them, they had not had sin, but now they have no cloak for their sin. *J 15:22*

This, standing by itself, seems to imply that sin began after Jesus came. This is not true since Jesus recognized that sin was part of the then existing world order:

Verily, verily, I say unto you, whosoever committeth sin is the servant of sin. *J 8:34*

Jesus assumed sin was universal:

He that is without sin among you, let him first cast a stone at her. *J 8:7*

Jesus' meaning is clearer if Jesus' two successive sentences are compared side by side:

If I had not come and spoken unto them,	If I had not done among them

the works which
none other man did,

they had not had sin;
but *now* they have
no cloak for their sin.
J 15:22

they had not had sin;
but *now* had they
both seen [my works] and
hated both me and my Father.
J 15:24

Jesus is saying, not that sin began with his coming, but that guilt for sin began with his coming:

. . . *now* they have no *cloak* for their sin. J 15:22

To Jesus this statement is equivalent to his second statement:

. . . *now* have they . . . seen [my works]. J 15:24

To Jesus ignorance was a defense to sin. He told some Pharisees:

If ye were blind, ye should have *no sin*, but now ye say, "We see;" therefore your sin remaineth. J 9:41

Since ignorance was a defense, guilt for sin began when knowledge came in the person of Jesus Christ. Jesus taught that the Comforter, the Holy Spirit, would reprove the world of sin "because they believe not on me." J 16:9 Jesus did not, like latter-day theologians, thunder about Adam and original sin. He did recognize that all men are the servants of sin. He did teach that after his coming men have no cloak for their sin.

According to Jesus, men were sinners when he came, but until he came men were not guilty of their sins. Jesus did not dwell on this guilt for sin. Instead, he stressed emancipation from sin.

Jesus' Emancipation Proclamation

Jesus taught that his true disciples were those who "continue in my word" and they should "know the truth" and that "the truth" should make them "free." *J 8:31–32*

Listening Jews objected:

We be Abraham's seed, and were never in bondage to any man. How sayest thou, "Ye shall be made free?" *J 8:33*

Jesus answered:

Verily, verily, I say unto you, *whosoever committeth sin* is the servant of sin.

And the servant abideth not in the house for ever: but the son abideth ever.

If the Son therefore shall make you *free*, ye shall be free indeed. *J 8:34–36*

Jesus was not simply saying that sin is addictive, he went further and said that to be free means to be free from sin. Jesus as the Son will free you from addiction to sin.

After Jesus briefly summarized his mission and status, he flatly stated "if ye believe not that I am he, ye shall die in your sins." *J 8:23* Jesus' whole statement was:

Ye are from beneath; I am from above.

Ye are of this world; I am not of this world.

I said therefore unto you, that ye shall die in your sins: for *if ye believe not that I am he, ye shall die in your sins. J 8:23–24*

Not only did Jesus proclaim emancipation from addiction to sin for those who believe "that I am he", he also proclaimed his and his Father's joy over the sinner who repents. Luke collects in Chapter 15 of his Gospel, three of Jesus' parables so teaching: the parables of the lost sheep, the lost coin and prodigal son.

The lost sheep parable concludes:

> I say unto you, that likewise *joy* shall be in heaven over one sinner that repenteth, more than over ninety and nine just persons, which need no repentance. *L 15:7*

The parable of the lost coin concerned a woman who had lost one of her ten silver coins and her diligent search for it. When she found it, she called her friends and neighbors together, saying:

> Rejoice with me, for I have found the piece which I had lost. *L 15:9*

Jesus then stated the point of the parable:

> Likewise, I say unto you, there is *joy* in the presence of the angels of God over one sinner that repenteth. *L 15:10*

Finally the parable of the prodigal son ends on the note of joy and gladness:

> It was meet that we should make merry, and be *glad*: for this thy brother was dead, and is *alive* again, and was lost, and is found. *L 15:32*

This joy and gladness and rejoicing in heaven ought not to obscure the indisputable fact that Jesus taught that sinners must repent.

While Jesus said that 99 out of a 100 may be righteous and "need no repentance", he also said that "he that is without sin among you, let him first cast a stone at her" and "whosoever committeth sin is the servant of sin" and that "if ye believe not that I am he, ye shall die in your sins." *L 15:7; J 8:7, 34, 24*

Jesus did preach that all men must repent. Jesus began his ministry by preaching:

MARK	MATTHEW
The time is fulfilled,	*Repent*:
and the Kingdom of God	for the Kingdom of Heaven
is at hand:	is at hand.
repent ye,	*Mt 4:17*
and believe in the gospel.	
Mk 1:15	

The risen Jesus told his disciples:

Thus it is written, and thus it behoved Christ to suffer, and to rise from the dead the third day; and that *repentance and remission of sins* should be preached in his name among all nations, beginning at Jerusalem. *L 24:46–47*

The earliest preaching of the earliest church concluded with Peter's answer to the question, "What should we do?":

Repent, and be baptized every one of you in the name of Jesus Christ *for the remission of sins*, and ye shall receive the gift of the Holy Spirit. For the promise is unto you, and to your children, and to all that are afar off, even as many as the Lord our God shall call. *Acts 2:38–39*

The Forgiveness of Sins

Each of the first three gospels has the story of the paralytic man who was healed by Jesus at Capernaum after the man was let down from the roof of the house to get through the crowd to Jesus. *Mk 2:1–12; Mt 9:2–8; L 5:17–26* Jesus said to him:

MARK	MATTHEW	LUKE
Son,	Son, be of good cheer,	Man,
thy sins	thy sins	thy sins
be forgiven thee.	be forgiven thee.	are forgiven thee.
Mk 2:5	*Mt 9:2*	*L 5:20*

This obviously meant that Jesus felt that he had power to forgive sins. His presumption offended the religious of that day:

MARK	MATTHEW	LUKE
But there were	And, behold,	And
certain of	certain of	
the scribes	the scribes	the scribes and
		the Pharisees
sitting there,	said	began to reason,
and reasoning	within themselves,	saying,
in their hearts.		"Who is
"Why doth this man	this man	this which
speak		speaketh
blasphemies?	blasphemeth.	blasphemies?
Who can forgive sins	*Mt 9:3*	Who can forgive sins,
but God only?"		but God alone?"
Mk 2:6–7		*L 5:21*

Jesus perceived their thoughts and asked:

MARK	MATTHEW	LUKE
Why reason ye	Wherefore think ye	What reason ye
these things	evil	
in your hearts?	in your hearts?	in your hearts?
Whether is it easier	For whether is easier,	Whether is easier

MARK (cont.)	MATTHEW (cont.)	LUKE (cont.)
to say	to say,	to say,
to the sick of		
the palsy,		
"Thy sins	"Thy sins	"Thy sins
be forgiven thee,"	be forgiven thee,"	be forgiven thee,"
or to say,	or to say,	or to say,
"Arise,	"Arise,	"Rise up
and take up thy bed,		
and walk?"	and walk?"	and walk?"
But that ye	But that ye	But that ye
may know that	may know that	may know that
the Son of man	the Son of man	the Son of man
hath power	hath power	hath power
on earth	on earth	upon earth
to forgive sins,	to forgive sins,	to forgive sins,
I say upon thee,		I say unto thee,
"Arise,	"Arise,	"Arise,
and take up thy bed,	take up thy bed,	and take up thy couch,
and go thy way	and go	and go
into thine house."	unto thine house."	into thine house."
Mk 2:8–11	*Mt 9:4–6*	*L 5:22–24*

In another incident Jesus again claimed the power to forgive sins. It involved a loose woman who was probably a prostitute. *L 7:37* A Pharisee had invited Jesus to his home for dinner and Jesus went. Luke's account continues:

> And, behold, a woman in the city which was a sinner, when she knew that Jesus sat at meat in the Pharisee's house, brought an alabaster box of ointment, and stood at his feet behind him weeping, and began to wash his feet with tears, and did wipe them with the hairs of her head, and kissed his feet, and anointed them with the ointment. *L 7:37–38*

According to Luke, the Pharisee thought:

> This man, if he were a prophet, would have known who and what manner of woman this is that toucheth him: for she is a sinner. *L 7:39*

Jesus then said to the Pharisee:

Simon, I have somewhat to say unto thee. *L 7:40*

Simon replied:

Master, say on. *L 7:40*

Jesus then told this story:

There was a certain creditor which had two debtors: the one owed five hundred pence, and the other fifty. And, when they had nothing to pay, he frankly forgave them both. Tell me therefore, which of them will love him most? *L 7:41–42*

Simon answered:

I suppose that he, to whom he forgave most. *L 7:43*

Jesus replied:

Thou hast rightly judged. *L 7:43*

Jesus then turned to the woman and said to Simon:

Seest thou this woman? I entered into thine house, thou gavest me no water for my feet; but she hath washed my feet with tears, and wiped them with the hairs of her head. Thou gavest me no kiss, but this woman since the time I came in hath not ceased to kiss my feet. My head with oil thou didst not anoint, but this woman hath anointed my feet with ointment.

Wherefore I say unto thee, *her sins, which are many, are forgiven*, for she loved much, but to whom little is forgiven, the same loveth little. *L 7:44–47*

Jesus then said to the woman:

Thy sins are forgiven. *L 7:48*

Luke concludes:

> And they that sat at meat with him began to say within themselves, "Who is this that forgiveth sins also?" And he said to the woman, "Thy faith hath saved thee; go in peace." *L 7:49–50*

In case of both the paralytic man and the loose woman, Jesus forgave their sins. The sins were not dwelt on and their forgiveness was immediate. Unlike some, Jesus did not question the reality of her sins (He stated that they were "many") or state that the woman had simply violated the bigoted norms of her particular society.

To Jesus, forgiveness of sins was equal to healing. This suggests that beyond our time–space horizons they are aspects of the same thing. The woman was forgiven because "she loved much" while the paralytic man was forgiven because of the faith of his four bearers:

MARK	MATTHEW	LUKE
When Jesus saw	Jesus seeing	And when he saw
their faith,	*their faith*	*their faith,*
he said unto	said unto	he said unto
the sick of palsy,	the sick of palsy,	him,
"Son,	"Son,	"Man,
	be of good cheer;	
thy sins	thy sins	thy sins
be forgiven thee."	be forgiven thee."	are forgiven thee."
Mk 2:5	*Mt 9:2*	*L 5:20*

"Their faith" does not meet the usual theology; if so, this means that the theology is too narrowly stated. In the case of the loose woman, she was the only one who had acted on faith:

> Thy faith has saved thee; go in peace. *L 7:50*

That is almost exactly what Jesus said to the woman who had had an issue of blood twelve years:

MARK	LUKE
Daughter	Daughter, be of good comfort:
thy faith	thy faith
has made thee whole;	hath made thee whole;
go in peace,	go in peace.
and be whole of thy plague.	*L 8:48*
Mk 5:34	

The woman had acted on faith. She had touched Jesus' garment, thinking, "If I may but touch his garment, I shall be whole." *Mt 9:21 (Mk 5:28; L 8:47)* There is no hint that this woman was particularly sinful. Yet Jesus' instruction both to her and to the loose woman were essentially the same. Their faith had saved them from their sickness or sin, both apparently aspects of the same matter in the eyes of Jesus in a way we do not fully understand.

In a sense, both women had met Jesus' own formula for salvation that he had stated to onlookers in the Treasury of the Temple after he said as to the woman taken in adultery, "He that is without sin among you, let him first cast a stone at her." *J 8:7*

Jesus' own formula for salvation was:

I said therefore unto you, that ye shall die in your sins: for if ye believe not that I am he, ye shall die in your sins. *J 8:24*

FORGIVENESS OF SINS—THE FINAL INSTRUCTIONS

On the evening of the first Easter, Jesus appeared to his disciples in a locked room and said, among other things:

Receive ye the Holy Spirit: Whose soever sins ye remit, they are remitted unto them; and whose soever sins ye retain, they are retained. *J 20:22*

Jesus was aware of the Jewish belief that God alone can forgive sins. *Mk 2:7; L 5:21* Jesus answered this belief with his assertion that he as the Son of man had power on earth to forgive sins. *Mk 2:10; L 5:23*

Did he then confer this power on his disciples that evening? No, not directly: only as agents of the Holy Spirit. Just before Jesus had conferred the Holy Spirit upon his disciples ("Receive ye the Holy Spirit") Jesus had said:

> Peace be unto you: as my Father hath sent me, even so send I you. *J 20:21*

Just as the Father had sent Jesus, so likewise Jesus sends his disciples as bearers of the Holy Spirit. It is the Holy Spirit that remits sins, not disciples then or now who are the bearers of the Holy Spirit.

CHAPTER 16

PRAYER

THE SPIRIT OF PRAYER

Jesus told this story:

Two men went up into the Temple to pray, the one a Pharisee, and
the other a publican.

The Pharisee stood and prayed thus with himself, "God, I thank
thee, that I am not as other men are, extortioners, unjust, adulterers, or even as this publican. I fast twice in a week, I give tithes of all
that I possess."

And the publican, standing afar off, would not lift up so much as
his eyes unto heaven, but smote upon his breast, saying, "God be
merciful to me a sinner."

I tell you, this man went down to his house justified rather than the
other: for every one that exalteth himself shall be abased; and he
that humbleth himself shall be exalted. *L 18:10–14*

The main thrust of the story is against spiritual pride, but it
also teaches that God rejects the prayer of a proud man, even the
prayer of a proud religious man.

Jesus was quite explicit that prayer should not be a self-exalting performance:

> And when thou prayest, thou shalt not be as the hypocrites are: for they love to pray standing in the synagogues and in the corners of the streets, that they *may be seen of men*. Verily I say unto you, they have their reward. But thou, when you prayest, enter into thy closet, and when thou hast shut thy door, pray to thy Father which is in secret; and thy Father which seeth in secret shall reward thee openly.
> *Mt 6:5–6*

If a person prays in private, he has no audience: he is not "seen of men." If he has no audience, he will not be tempted to be an actor, for that is the original meaning of the Greek word, hypocrite. In effect Jesus said, when you pray, don't pray as if it were a performance.

Is Prayer Necessary?

Jesus did not hold with those who say prayer is useless since God the Omniscient already knows what we want or need. Instead, Jesus used the truth that God does know as an argument against wordy prayers.

Matthew quotes Jesus as saying:

> But when ye pray, use not vain repetitions, as the heathen do: for they think that they shall be heard for their much speaking. Be not ye therefore like unto them: for your Father knoweth what things ye have need of, *before* ye ask him. *Mt 6:7*

Both Matthew and Luke have a saying of Jesus about not being anxious for what we shall eat or drink, or how we shall be clothed. This saying concludes:

(For after all these things do the Gentiles seek:) for your heavenly Father *knoweth* that ye have need of all these things. *Mt 6:32*	For all these things do the nations of the world seek after; and your Father *knoweth* that ye have need of these things. *L 12:30*

God the Father knows what his children need before they pray. However, Jesus, himself, prayed to his Father, making requests:

> Prayer that he be glorified. *J 17:5*
> Prayer for his followers. *J 17:6–19*
> Prayer for all believers. *J 17:20–23*
> Prayer to remove this cup. *Mk 14:36; Mt 26:39; L 22:42*
> Prayer to forgive them for they know not what they do. *L 23:34*

Jesus made requests of his Father by prayer. He taught his disciples to make requests of his Father by their prayers. *Mt 6:9–13; L 11:2–4* It follows that Jesus considered prayer to be necessary.

How to Pray

Jesus taught his disciples how to pray. We have two versions of a model prayer he gave his disciples. This outline of a model prayer has come to be known as the Lord's Prayer.

Matthew's version of this prayer is embedded in the Sermon on the Mount and is preceded by some general principles about prayer which we will discuss elsewhere. Luke's version of this prayer came about this way:

> And it came to pass, that, as he was praying in a certain place, when he ceased, one of his disciples said unto him, "Lord, teach us to pray, as John also taught his disciples." *L 11:1*

It is illuminating to compare the two versions of Jesus' prayer outline:

MATTHEW	LUKE
After this manner therefore pray ye:	When ye pray, say:
"Our Father Which art in Heaven, hallowed be thy Name. Thy Kingdom come. Thy will be done in earth, as it is in heaven.	"Our Father which art in Heaven, hallowed be thy Name. Thy Kingdom come. Thy will be done, as in heaven, so in earth.
Give us this day our daily bread. And forgive us our debts, as we forgive our debtors.	Give us day by day our daily bread. And forgive us our sins, for we also forgive everyone that is indebted to us.
And lead us not into temptation, but deliver us	And lead us not into temptation, but deliver us

MATTHEW (cont.)	LUKE (cont.)
from evil.	from evil."
	L 11:2–4

For thine is the Kingdom,
and the power, and the glory,
for ever. Amen.
Mt 6:9–13

The Lord's Prayer consists of four parts. The first part is the address:

Our Father which art in Heaven. *Mt 6:9; L 11:2*

The second part of the prayer outline consists of three petitions:

1. Hallowed be thy Name.
2. Thy Kingdom come.
3. Thy Will be done. *Mt 6:9–10; L 11:2*

Each of these three petitions are modified, as the Greek text shows, by the words:

MATTHEW	LUKE
In earth,	As in heaven,
as it is in heaven.	so in earth.
Mt 6:10	*L 11:2*

All of these three petitions relate to God himself: first, his Name; second, his Kingdom; and third, his Will.

The third part of the prayer outline also consists of three petitions:

1. Give us this day our daily bread.
2. Forgive us our debts.
3. Lead us not into temptation, but deliver us from evil.
   Mt 6:11–13 (L 11:3–4)

These three petitions are requests for personal needs: bread, forgiveness and deliverance from evil. Unlike the first three petitions these last three petitions vary in Matthew's and Luke's versions. These variations will be analyzed when each petition is hereafter considered separately.

The fourth part of the prayer outline is the conclusion that is found only in Matthew's version:

> For thine is the Kingdom, and the power, and the glory, for ever. Amen. *Mt 6:13*

OUR FATHER WHICH ART IN HEAVEN

In the King James Version of the Bible, the opening phrase of the Lord's Prayer in both Matthew and Luke is:

Our Father which art in Heaven. *Mt 6:9; L 11:2*

The best manuscripts of Luke, however, have in Greek simply "Father", not "Our Father which art in Heaven." For this reason many modern translations of Luke begin the Lord's Prayer with one word, "Father." The result of this choice is that their Matthews and Lukes have different versions of this part of the Lord's Prayer.

It is customarily assumed that Luke's version is what Jesus actually said since it is shorter than Matthew's version. That is an assumption since Matthew's manuscripts and some of Luke's manuscripts have the longer statement.

We do know that Jesus himself did actually use the shorter form in his own prayers: One example is found in the first three gospels, Jesus' prayer in the Garden of Gethsemane:

MARK	MATTHEW	LUKE
Abba, Father	O my Father,	Father,
all things are	if it be	if thou be
possible unto thee;	possible,	willing,
take away	let this	remove this
this cup from me: . . .	cup pass from me: . . .	cup from me: . . .
Mk 14:36	*Mt 26:39*	*L 22:42*

Abba is the Aramaic word for "Father" and is left untranslated in Mark. "Abba" in Mark is followed by the Greek word for father which is translated. "Abba" is thought to be a very personal word for "Father." Jesus spoke Aramaic, and the Aramaic word *Abba* is the very word he used for God when he was in extreme distress in the Garden of Gethsemane. *Mk 14:36*

Luke has other examples of Jesus' use of "Father" in his prayers during his last hours:

Father, forgive them, for they know not what they do. *L 23:34*

Father, into thy hands I commend my spirit. *L 23:46*

John also has numerous examples of Jesus' own use of "Father" in addressing God in prayer:

Father, save me from this hour. *J 12:27*

Father, glorify thy name. *J 12:28*

Father, the hour is come; glorify thy Son, . . .

And now, O Father, glorify thou me . . .

Father, I will that they also, whom thou hast given me, be with me where I am; . . . *J 17:1, 5, 24*

Even Matthew has an example of Jesus using the word "Father" alone in prayer:

I thank thee, O Father, Lord of Heaven and earth, . . . even so, Father: for so it seemed good in thy sight. *Mt 11:25–26*

The opening phrase in Jesus' model prayer, "Our Father which art in Heaven", expressly recognizes that God the Father is in Heaven. This does not mean that the Father is not also Lord of earth. In fact, Jesus once did pray:

MATTHEW	LUKE
I thank thee, O Father,	I thank thee, O Father,
Lord of Heaven *and* Earth,	Lord of Heaven *and* Earth,
because thou hast hid	that thou hast hid
these things	these things
from the wise and prudent,	from the wise and prudent,

Matthew (cont.)
and hast revealed them
unto babes.
Mt 11:25

Luke (cont.)
and hast revealed them
unto babes: . . .
L 10:21

The meaning of both "Father" and "Our Father which are in Heaven" is the same: Our prayers are to be addressed not to God, the neutral, unknown and omnipotent, but rather to Our Father, the head of the adoptive family of God. Paul writes of this family of God thus:

> For as many as are led by the Spirit of God, they are the *sons of God*. For ye have not received the spirit of bondage again to fear; but ye have received the Spirit of *adoption*, whereby we cry, "Abba, Father." *Romans 8:14–15*

> But when the fulness of the time was come, God sent forth his Son, made of a woman, made under the Law, to redeem them that were under the Law, that we might receive the *adoption of sons*. And because ye are sons, God hath sent forth the Spirit of his Son into your hearts, crying, "Abba, Father." *Galatians 4:4–6*

After the Lord's Prayer ceased being thought of as a prayer outline or model prayer, it became a ritual prayer, called the "Pater Noster," Latin for "Our Father."

Jesus' instruction to pray to "Our Father" was consistent with his immediately preceding instruction to "pray to *thy Father* which is in secret; and *thy Father* which seeth in secret shall reward thee openly" and "be not ye therefore like unto them, for *your Father* knoweth what things ye have need of." *Mt 6:6–8*

Jesus prayed to his "Abba", and has instructed us to begin our prayers to our "Abba" who is in Heaven.

HALLOWED BE THY NAME

Hallowed comes from an Anglo–Saxon root word meaning "holy." Hence, a simple English dictionary approach makes the first petition of the model prayer something like this, "Holy be thy name."

The Greek word translated *hallowed* is "hagio" (holy) and is the antithesis of "koinos" (common). Jesus' own word was in Aramaic, not Greek. He spoke from a Jewish background to Jews.

Jesus knew the Jewish Law. *Mt 12:5* The fourth book of that Law, Leviticus, states:

> Neither shall ye profane *my holy name*; but I will be *hallowed* among the children of Israel. I am the Lord which hallow you, that brought you out of the land of Egypt, to be your God. I am the Lord. *Leviticus 22:32–33*

Jesus also knew the Jewish prophets. *Mt 11:13; L 16:16* The prophet Ezekiel wrote:

> And I scattered them among the heathen, and they were dispersed through the countries; according to their way and according to their doings I judged them. And when they entered into the heathen, whither they went, they *profaned my holy name*, when they said to them, "These are the people of the Lord, and are gone forth out of his land."

> But I had *pity for mine holy name*, which the house of Israel had *profaned* among the heathen, whither they went. Therefore say unto the house of Israel, "Thus saith the Lord God; I do not this for your sakes, O house of Israel, but *for mine holy name's sake*, which ye have *profaned* among the heathen, whither ye went. And I will *sanctify my great name which was profaned among the heathen* which ye have *profaned* in the midst of them; and the heathen shall know that I am the Lord, saith the Lord God, when I shall be *sanctified* in you before their eyes." *Ezekiel 36:19–24*

Ezekiel also wrote for Lord God:

> So will I make *my holy name* known in the midst of my people
> Israel, and I will not let them pollute *my holy name* any more; and
> the heathen shall know that I am the Lord, the Holy One in Israel.
> *Ezekiel 39:7*

According to the Jewish Law and Prophets, God has a holy
name, and it is not to be profaned or polluted.

Jesus taught positively and exultantly that we are to pray to the
Father:

> Hallowed be thy name. *Mt 6:9; L 11:2*

The surest key to Jesus' meaning across the gap of languages
and centuries is another statement of his that probably expresses
the same idea. Shortly before his crucifixion Jesus said:

> Now is my soul troubled, and what shall I say? Father, save me
> from this hour, but for this cause came I unto this hour. *Father,
> glorify thy name. J 12:27–28*

"Glorify thy name" or "Holy be thy name" may shine with
meaning when "Hallowed be thy name" has become a smooth rote
phrase full of somber sound but signifying nothing.

God's holy name is an indispensable part of his holy nature.
Jesus therefore instructed his disciples, in praying, to recognize
God's holy name. That name is entitled to honor and respect.

Jesus, himself, addressed the Father on occasions as, "O Father, Lord of Heaven and Earth." *Mt 11:25; L 10:21* There is a certain
and proper austerity in Jesus' instruction that we are to say, in praying to the Father, "Hallowed be thy name." *Mt 6:9; L 11:2*

THY KINGDOM COME

The second petition of the Lord's Prayer is, "Thy Kingdom come", which in the Greek is modified by the words "in earth, as it is in heaven." The Kingdom referred to is the Kingdom of God, or as Matthew usually calls it, the Kingdom of Heaven. *Mt 6:10; L 11:2*

The nature of this Kingdom is a tremendous subject and is one of the main strands of Jesus' teaching. Accordingly, the nature of the Kingdom is treated in detail elsewhere (see Chapter 7: "Kingdom Topics," pp. 487–555). Here it is perhaps sufficient to quote Paul's comment that "the Kingdom of God is not meat and drink; but righteousness, and peace, and joy in the Holy Spirit." *Romans 14:17*

Early in his ministry, Jesus preached:

MARK	MATTHEW
The time is fulfilled, and	
	Repent: for
the Kingdom of God	the Kingdom of Heaven
is *at hand*;	is *at hand*.
repent ye, and believe	*Mt 4:17*
the gospel.	
Mk 1:15	

At his Last Supper, Jesus said to his disciples:

And I appoint unto you a *kingdom*, as my Father hath appointed unto me; that ye may eat and drink at my table in *my kingdom*, and sit on thrones judging the twelve tribes of Israel. *L 22:29–30*

Towards the end of the Last Supper Jesus said:

MARK	MATTHEW
Verily I say unto you,	But I say unto you,
I will drink no more	I will not drink henceforth
of the fruit of the vine,	of this fruit of the vine,
until that day that	until that day when
I drink it new	I drink it new with you
in the Kingdom of God.	*in my Father's Kingdom.*
Mk 14:25	*Mt 26:29*

During his trial before Pilate, Jesus testified:

My kingdom is not of this world. If my kingdom were of this world, then would my servants fight, that I should not be delivered to the Jews; but now is my kingdom not from hence. *J 18:36*

Jesus' kingdom is not earthly. It was appointed to him by his Father, and he, in turn, has appointed it to his followers. He has returned to his kingdom. In the meantime his followers are to pray that this kingdom will come, for and upon them, as it has already come in heaven.

Jesus' instruction to pray both that "Thy Kingdom come" and "Thy will be done" implies that there is a difference between the two. God is not only acting on earth generally and impersonally, by his will; but also through his own peculiar realm, the Kingdom of God.

Actually the injunction to pray for the coming of this peculiar realm is perhaps more fundamental than the prayer "Thy will be done" since the best manuscripts of Luke's version of the model prayer omit the petition "Thy will be done." It appears in the King James Version but is omitted by many of the modern translations.

The subtleties of scholars are fine for scholars. Here we only need to state that both versions of the model prayer have this petition:

Thy Kingdom come. *Mt 6:10; L 11:2*

Thy Will Be Done

The petition "Thy will be done" varies slightly in Matthew and Luke:

Matthew	Luke
Thy will be done	Thy will be done,
in earth,	as in heaven,
as it is in heaven.	so in earth.
Mt 6:10	*L 11:2*

Many modern versions omit this entire petition in Luke. Their omission is based on their analysis of the manuscript evidence.

If the Kingdom of God is the realm of his rule, the petition "Thy will be done" is essentially identical in meaning with the petition "Thy Kingdom come." The petition "Thy will be done" simply focuses on individual submission to that Kingdom.

The slight differences in the wording of the petition "Thy will be done" found in the King James Version of Matthew and Luke do not vary in meaning. The meaning is clear: we are to pray that God's will be done on earth as it already is in heaven.

Christians are not only to pray that God's will be done here and now on this earth, but they are also required so to act.

Jesus said that no man may enter into the Kingdom of Heaven "but he that doeth the will of my Father which is in heaven." *Mt 7:21* All such persons thereby become relatives of Jesus Christ:

Mark	Matthew	Luke
For whosoever shall	For whosoever shall	
do the will	do the will	
of God,	of my Father	
	which is *in heaven*,	My mother and
the same is	the same is	my brethren are
my brother,	my brother,	these which hear
and my sister,	and sister,	the word of God,
and mother.	and mother.	and do it.
Mk 3:35	*Mt 12:50*	*L 8:21*

Jesus' own example is the ultimate commentary on the petition that God's will be done. All three synoptic gospels record Jesus' own prayer in the Garden of Gethsemane:

MARK	MATTHEW	LUKE
Abba, Father,	O my Father,	Father,
all things are	if it be	if thou be willing,
possible	possible,	
unto thee;		
take away	let	remove
this cup	this cup	this cup
from me:	pass from me:	from me:
nevertheless not	nevertheless not	nevertheless not
what I will,	as I will,	my will,
but what thou wilt.	but as thou wilt.	but thine, be done.
Mk 14:36	*Mt 26:39*	*L 22:42*

The model prayer petition "thy will be done on earth" is Jesus' own prayer "not as I will, but as thou wilt." This prayer is not just a sterile submission but confers power, as Jesus himself, testified:

> I can of mine own self do nothing. As I hear, I judge; and my judgment is just, *because I seek not mine own will, but the will of the Father* which hath sent me. *J 5:30*

Christians, like Jesus himself, are to seek the will of the Father, and to pray that His will be done, on earth, not just in heaven.

Give Us This Day Our Daily Bread

Matthew and Luke differ in their versions of the petition for bread:

Matthew	Luke
Give us this day	Give us day by day
our daily bread.	our daily bread.
Mt 6:11	*L 11:3*

These differences relate to the adjective *daily* that translates a Greek word whose meaning is uncertain. Accordingly, scholars and versions differ on their translation of this petition. Perhaps what Jesus actually said, which was in Aramaic, and not in Greek, was something like this, "Give us each day our bread for the next day."

At least this much of the petition is clear: "Give us . . . our . . . bread." Jesus taught us to pray for the material necessities of life: food, drink, and clothing.

But both Matthew and Luke quote Jesus as saying that Christians were not to be anxious about such things; they are just to pray for them:

Matthew	Luke
Therefore take no thought, saying,	And seek not ye
"What shall we eat?"	what ye shall eat,
or, "What shall we drink?"	or what ye shall drink;
or, "Wherewithal	neither be ye
shall we be clothed?"	of doubtful mind.
Mt 6:31	*L 12:29*

Christians are not to be anxious for such things because God will answer prayers for such things:

Matthew	Luke
Or what man is there of you,	

Matthew (cont.)	Luke (cont.)
whom if his son	If a son shall
ask bread,	ask bread
	of any of you
	that is a father,
will he give him a stone?	will he give him a stone?
Or if he ask a fish,	Or if he ask a fish,
will he give him	will he for a fish give him
a serpent?	a serpent?
If ye then,	. . . If ye then,
being evil,	being evil,
know how to give	know how to give
good gifts	good gifts
unto your children,	unto your children,
how much more	how much more
shall your Father	shall your heavenly Father
which is in heaven	
give good things	give the Holy Spirit
to them that ask him?	to them that ask him?
Mt 7:9–11	*L 11:11, 13*

The Father will not give stones to those who pray to him for their daily bread. The Father will supply "good things", not stones and serpents. Even if the asking is shameless and inconvenient, bread will be supplied.

This is taught by a parable that immediately follows Luke's version of the Lord's Prayer. In this parable a friend goes to another friend's house at midnight and knocks at his door, saying, "Friend, lend me three loaves, for a friend of mine in his journey is come to me, and I have nothing to set before him." *L 11:5–6*

Jesus explained this parable thus:

Though he will not rise and give him, because he is his friend, yet because of his importunity he will rise and give him as many as he needeth. *L 11:8*

The Father, of course, does not restrict himself to loaves of bread. The promise is to supply "good things." *Mt 7:11* "Good things" include physical needs: food, drink and clothing. *Mt 6:31; L 12:29*

If even a reluctant neighbor roused at midnight will loan some bread to a friend in need, how much more will God himself give us our daily bread, if we ask! Accordingly, Christians are to pray: "Give us this day our daily bread." *Mt 6:11*

Forgive Us Our Debts

One key word differs in Matthew's and Luke's versions of the forgiveness petition:

MATTHEW	LUKE
And forgive us our *debts*,	And forgive us our *sins*;
as we forgive	for we also forgive
our	every one
debtors.	that is indebted to us.
Mt 6:12	L 11:4

Matthew has "our debts"; Luke has "our sins." Both gospels refer to debtors in the second part of the petition.

It is obvious that Jesus is not speaking of debts and debtors in a literal commercial sense, but of moral "debts"—wrongs—sins. As the Aramaic word of Jesus finally comes to us through the English translation of the Greek text Luke has "forgive us our *sins*" rather than Matthew's "forgive us our *debts*", but their meaning is identical.

The second part of the petition is also identical in meaning in both Matthew and Luke although the words vary. The meaning of the petition as recorded in both Matthew and Luke may be summarized this way: Forgive us our sins, since we have forgiven those who have sinned against us.

In his model prayer Jesus did not stop with the words "forgive us our sins" but went on to state, as a kind of postscript, the condition of that petition being granted.

The condition for the granting of teach petition for forgiveness is that we also forgive those who have sinned against or wronged us. This is made explicit by Jesus' own commentary on this prayer petition. The commentary immediately follows the Lord's Prayer in Matthew and states:

> For if ye forgive men their trespasses, your Heavenly Father will also forgive you; but if ye forgive not men their trespasses, neither will your Father forgive your trespasses. Mt 6:14–15

The word *trespass* is used in the sense of a personal wrong or offense. The word *trespasses*, however, has an archaic legalistic tinge. Accordingly, it would be better to substitute "wrongs" or "improper actions" for "trespasses."

The condition of forgiveness is mutuality: if you forgive men their wrongs to you; God will forgive your wrongs to him. Jesus expressly related the principle of forgiveness to prayer:

> And when *ye stand praying*, forgive, if ye have ought against any: that your Father also which is in heaven may forgive you your trespasses. But if ye do not forgive, neither will your Father which is in heaven forgive your trespasses. *Mk 11:25–26*

And Lead Us Not into Temptation but Deliver Us from Evil

In the King James Version both Matthew and Luke have the same wording for the final petition:

> And lead us not into temptation, but deliver us from evil. *Mt 6:13; L 11:4*

In Luke's version this petition ends the model prayer. Some manuscripts have "evil one" for "evil", and some modern versions follow suit. Upon the basis of the manuscript evidence some modern versions of Luke also eliminate the whole clause "but deliver us from evil."

This leaves us with, "And lead us not into temptation", which seems to imply that God is leading us into temptation. The problem here is the archaic language of the King James Version. The archaic meaning of tempt is "to test." The true meaning of the petition is, "Do not put me to the test."

Although the Greek word in the manuscripts for *evil* is ambiguous, Jesus meant the evil one, that is, the devil. Accordingly, the petition means: "Do not put me to the test; but deliver me from the evil one who tests me."

Jesus himself prayed:

> I pray not that thou shouldest take them out of the world, but that thou shouldest keep them from *the evil. J 17:15*

It is obvious that John's verse should be completed to read "the evil one." "Them" is of course the disciples—"the men which thou gavest me out of the world." *J 17:6*

Jesus taught his disciples to pray to God to deliver them from the evil one; and he himself prayed to God that he should keep the disciples from the evil one.

In the Garden of Gethsemane while Jesus prayed, the disciples slept. When Jesus found them asleep, he rebuked Peter, "Simon, sleepest thou? Couldest not thou watch one hour?" *Mk 14:27 (Mt 26:40)* Or, as Luke has it, he asked "them", "Why sleep ye?" *L 22:46*

Jesus then said:

MARK	MATTHEW	LUKE
Watch ye and pray,	Watch and pray,	Rise and pray,
lest ye enter into	that ye enter not into	lest ye enter into
temptation.	temptation;	temptation.
The spirit	the spirit	*L 22:46*
truly is ready,	indeed is willing,	
but the flesh is weak.	but the flesh is weak.	
Mk 14:38	*Mt 26:41*	

These disciples were to pray that they would not enter into temptation. The test of these disciples overcame the weakness of their flesh. These disciples were not tested by God but by the devil just as Jesus himself was tempted in the beginning of his ministry. *Mk 1:12–13; Mt 4:1–11; L 4:1–13*

We are not led into temptation by God but by the devil. That is how our tests come. The seventh point of Jesus' prayer outline is: if we are tested by the devil, pray that we be delivered from him.

THINE IS THE KINGDOM

The doxology that ends the Lord's Prayer is indelibly impressed in the hearts and minds of Christians:

For thine is the Kingdom, and the power, and the glory, for ever. Amen. *Mt 6:13*

Luke's version of the Lord's Prayer does not have this, or any other doxology. *L 11:2–4* Modern versions of Matthew omit this doxology upon the basis of the manuscript evidence, that is, the manuscripts that contain the doxology are late and vary its wording. This assumes, tacitly, that Jesus never spoke these words because they are omitted in the best manuscripts.

The fact that the doxology parallels phrases in *1 Chronicles 29:11* does not establish that the doxology is a later liturgical addition to Jesus' own words. First Chronicles quotes David as blessing the Lord before all the congregation of Israel, saying:

Blessed, be thou, Lord God of Israel our father, for ever and ever.

Thine, O Lord, is the greatness, and *the power, and the glory*, and the victory, and the majesty: for all that is in the heaven and in the earth is thine. *Thine is the kingdom*, O Lord, and thou art exalted as head above all. *1 Chronicles 29:10–11*

Jesus was, of course, familiar with the Jewish scriptures, the Law and the Prophets. *Mt 11:13; L 16:16* First Chronicles was one of the books of the Prophets. Jesus, himself, could have chosen certain phrases familiar to him from First Chronicles to express ideas he wanted to include in his model prayer.

Jesus often spoke of "the Kingdom"; it was one of his main topics. It would have been natural for him to use the phrase *thine is the Kingdom* from First Chronicles as a succinct prayer summary of its nature.

No one doubts that the words earlier in the prayer "Thy Kingdom Come", are Jesus' own words. It would have been fitting and likely that he would have ended his prayers with a doxology referring to that Kingdom.

It is also obvious from the Gospels that Jesus used in other contexts the remaining phrases of the doxology.

Jesus spoke of the "power of God." He told certain Sadducees that they knew "not the scriptures, neither the power of God." *Mk 12:24 (Mt 22:29)*

The word *glory* was often used by Jesus in relation to his Father. Jesus told Mary and Martha that their brother's sickness was "not unto death, but for the glory of God, that the Son of man might be glorified thereby." *J 11:4* Jesus spoke to his disciples of the Son of man coming "in the glory of his Father with the holy Angels." *Mk 8:38 (Mt 16:27; L 9:26)*

The phrase *for ever* was often used by Jesus:

He that eateth of this bread shall live for ever. *J 6:58(J 6:51)*

He shall give you another Comforter, that he abide with you for ever. *J 14:16*

The final word of Jesus' prayer is "Amen". That is Jesus' own Hebrew word transliterated into English. Jesus often used this word, which meant "truly." Accordingly, that word is usually translated in the King James Version of the Gospels as *verily*. For example, Jesus is quoted as saying:

Verily I say unto you, that there be some of them that stand here, which shall not taste of death, till they have seen the Kingdom of God come with power. *Mk 9:1 (Mt 16:28)*

The closing doxology of the Lord's Prayer parallels the first three petitions of that prayer:

PETITIONS	DOXOLOGY
Thy Kingdom come. *Mt 6:10*	Thine is the Kingdom. *Mt 6:13*
Thy will be done. *Mt 6:10*	Thine is the power. *Mt 6:13*
Hallowed be thy name. *Mt 6:9*	Thine is the glory. *Mt 6:13*

The doxology recognizes that the Father's Kingdom, power and glory will endure for ever. Verily.

PRAYER AS THANKSGIVING

Jesus did not incorporate in his outline of a model prayer any thanksgiving. *Mt 6:9–13; L 11:2–4* Jesus himself endorsed the Jewish practice of a prayer of thanksgiving before eating. That practice was to make a short prayer, such as:

> Blessed art thou, O Lord our God, king of the world, who has brought forth bread from the earth.

This is what Jesus did before he fed the Five Thousand:

MARK	MATTHEW	LUKE	JOHN
And when	And	Then	And
he had taken	took	he took	Jesus took
the five loaves	the five loaves	the five loaves	the loaves;
and the	and the	and the	
two fishes,	two fishes,	two fishes,	and when
he looked up	and looking up	and looking up	he had
to heaven,	to heaven,	to heaven,	
and blessed,	*he blessed,*	*he blessed them,*	*given thanks,*
and brake	and brake,	and brake,	
the loaves,			
and gave	and gave	and gave	he distributed
them	the loaves		
to his	to his	to the	to the
disciples . . .	disciples . . .	disciples . . .	disciples . . .
Mk 6:41	*Mt 14:19*	*L 9:16*	*J 6:11 (6:23)*

Luke, in the King James Version, states that Jesus blessed the food ("them"). This is not expressly stated in the other Gospels but is clearly implied: Jesus gave the blessing, i.e., gave thanks to God for the food, the loaves and fishes.

Jesus also prayed a prayer of thanksgiving before he fed the Four Thousand:

MARK	MATTHEW
And he took	And he took

MARK (cont.)	MATTHEW (cont.)
the seven loaves,	the seven loaves
	and the fishes,
and gave thanks,	*and gave thanks,*
and brake,	and brake them,
and gave	and gave
to his disciples, . . .	to his disciples, . . .
And they had	*Mt 15:36*
a few small fishes;	
and he blessed,	
and commanded	
to set them	
also before them."	
Mk 8:6–7	

It is obvious that "blessed" and "giving thanks" are used synonymously to refer to the prayer of thanksgiving at mealtime. At the Last Supper Jesus said prayers of thanksgiving both for the bread and the cup:

MARK	MATTHEW	LUKE
		And
		he took the cup,
		and gave thanks,
		and said, . . .
And as	And as	And
they did eat,	they were eating,	
Jesus took bread,	Jesus took bread,	he took bread,
and blessed,	*and blessed it,*	*and gave thanks,*
and brake it,	and brake it,	and brake it,
and gave	and gave it	and gave
to them,	to the disciples,	unto them,
and said,	and said,	saying,
"Take, eat:	"Take, eat;	
this is	this is	"This is
my body."	my body."	my body . . ."

Mark (cont.)	Matthew (cont.)	Luke (cont.)
And he took the cup,	And he took the cup,	Likewise also the cup after supper, . . . L 22:17, 19–20
and when he had *given thanks*, he gave it to them: . . . Mk 14:22–23	*and gave thanks*, and gave it to them, . . . Mt 26:26–27	

In Luke's account of Jesus' post–resurrection appearance to the two disciples on the road to the village of Emmaus, it is stated:

And it came to pass, as he sat at meat with them, he took bread, and *blessed it*, and brake, and gave to them. L 24:30

This is another instance when Jesus himself followed the Jewish practice of praying a prayer of thanksgiving at mealtime. We do not have its text. We do have the text of one fervent prayer of thanksgiving by Jesus himself:

Matthew	Luke
I thank thee, O Father, Lord of heaven and earth, because thou hast hid these things from the wise and prudent, and hath revealed them unto babes. Even so, Father: for so it seemed good in thy sight. Mt 11:25	I thank thee, O Father, Lord of heaven and earth, that thou hast hid these things from the wise and prudent, and hast revealed them unto babes. Even so, Father: for so it seemed good in thy sight. L 10:21

The context of this prayer of thanksgiving varies in Matthew and Luke. In Luke it follows the return of the Seventy with joy from their successful mission proclaiming the nearness of the Kingdom of God. Luke states that "Jesus rejoiced in spirit" and so prayed. *L 10:21* In Matthew the prayer is "at that time" when Jesus pronounced "Woes" upon the unrepentant cities of Chorazin, Bethsaida, and Capernaum. *Mt 11:20–25*

Jesus, himself, also prayed the fundamental prayer of thanksgiving that God hears prayers. When Lazarus was about to come forth from his grave, Jesus prayed:

> Father, I thank thee that thou hast heard me. And I knew that thou hearest me always; but because of the people which stand by I said it, that they may believe that thou hast sent me. *J 11:41–42*

Jesus "lifted up his eyes" as he prayed this prayer of thanksgiving. *J 11:41* Before he fed the Five Thousand as he prayed the prayer of thanksgiving, he "was looking up to heaven." *Mt 14:19; 1 9:16 (Mk 6:41)* This was the usual Jewish practice.

Jesus did not incorporate any thanksgiving in his model prayer. *Mt 6:9–13; L 11:2–4* This does not mean that he rejected prayers of thanksgiving. We have his own persuasive example that such prayers are appropriate, and especially the prayer of thanksgiving that:

> Father, I thank thee that thou has heard me. *J 11:41*

God Will Answer Prayer

Jesus taught that God will answer prayer:

Matthew	Luke
Ask,	Ask,
and it shall be given you;	and it shall be given you;
seek,	seek
and ye shall find;	and ye shall find;
knock,	knock,
and it shall be opened	and it shall be opened
unto you.	unto you.
For every one	For every one
that asketh	that asketh
receiveth,	receiveth,
and he that seeketh	and he that seeketh
findeth;	findeth;
and to him	and to him
that knocketh	that knocketh
it shall be opened.	it shall be opened.
Or what man is there of you,	
whom if his son	If a son
ask bread,	shall ask bread
	of any of you
	that is a father,
will give him a stone?	will he give him a stone?
Or if he ask a fish,	Or if he ask a fish,
	will he for a fish
will give him a serpent?	give him a serpent?
	Or if he shall ask an egg,
	will he offer him a scorpion?
If ye then, being evil,	If ye then, being evil,
know how to give	know how to give
good gifts	good gifts
unto your children,	unto your children,

Matthew (cont.)
how much more
shall your Father
which is in heaven
give good things
to them that ask him?
Mt 7:7–11

Luke (cont.)
how much more
shall your heavenly Father

give the Holy Spirit
to them that ask him?
L 11:9–13

Jesus taught that God will answer prayer, if the request is made, even though it may be inconvenient to do so. If the reluctant neighbor at midnight will loan needed bread to a neighbor, how much more will God himself respond to a request?

Jesus told a parable about a persistent widow to illustrate that God will, indeed, answer prayer:

There was in a city a judge, which feared not God, neither regarded man. And there was a widow in that city; and she came unto him, saying, "Avenge me of mine adversary."

And he would not for a while; but afterward he said within himself, "Though I fear not God, nor regard man, yet because this widow troubleth me, I will avenge her, lest by her continual coming she weary me." L 18:2–5

Jesus gave this explanation of the parable:

Hear what the unjust judge saith. And shall not God avenge his own elect, which cry day and night unto him, thou he bear long with them? I tell you that he will avenge them speedily. Nevertheless when the Son of man cometh, shall he find faith on the earth? L 18:6–8

It is often said that the parable about the neighbor borrowing bread at midnight and the parable about the reprobate judge teach persistence in prayer. An examination of the neighbor parable shows that there was no persistence by the borrowing neighbor, only one annoyingly urgent request.

The parable of the reprobate judge is different. The widow did persist and did prevail and the parable is introduced by the statement that Jesus "spoke a parable unto them to this end, that men ought always to pray, and not to faint." A statement that "men ought always to pray, and not to faint" does not necessarily teach persistence, but rather confidence (no fainting) that prayer will be answered. *L 18:1*

Accordingly, if even a difficult and vengeance-seeking widow ("avenge me"—not "give me my due") secured relief from a reprobate judge who acted for perverse reasons, how much more will God who is just avenge his own elect?

The widow was a nuisance and the judge was a disgrace, but the widow got relief, just as our God will respond if we ask—seek—knock.

Neither the vengeance-seeking widow nor the reprobate judge are meant, by Jesus, to be models. The persistence of the widow was as much a part of the backdrop of the parable as the perverseness of the judge, but her persistence was not Jesus' point any more than the judge's perverseness was a sketch of God.

Jesus' point was that men ought to pray with confidence that God, who is infinitely more responsive and just than a reluctant neighbor and a reprobate judge, will answer:

How *much more* shall your Father which is in heaven give good things to them that ask him? *Mt 7:11*

In another instance, Jesus taught that whatever you ask in prayer, believing, you shall receive:

MARK	MATTHEW
Have faith in God.	
For verily	Verily
I say unto you,	I say unto you,
	if ye have faith,
	and doubt not,
	ye shall not only do
	this which is done

Mark (cont.)	**Matthew** (cont.)
	to the fig tree,
that whosoever shall say	but also if ye shall say
unto this mountain,	unto this mountain,
"Be thou removed,	"Be thou removed,
and be thou cast	and be thou cast
into the sea,"	into the sea,"
and shall not doubt	
in his heart,	
but shall believe that	
those things which he saith	
shall come to pass,	it shall be done.
he shall have	
whatsoever he saith.	
	And all things,
Therefore I say unto you,	
what things soever ye desire,	whatsoever ye shall ask
when ye pray,	*in prayer,*
believe	*believing,*
that ye receive them,	
and ye shall have them.	ye shall receive.
Mk 11:22–24	*Mt 21:21–22*

John records similar teachings about the product of prayer but adjusted to prayer after Jesus' resurrection:

And in that day [after the first Easter] ye shall ask me nothing. Verily, verily, I say unto you, whatsoever ye shall ask the Father *in my name*, he will give it you. Hitherto have ye asked nothing in my name; ask, and ye shall receive, that your joy may be full . . . At that day [after the first Easter] ye shall ask *in my name*, and I say not unto you, that I will pray the Father for you: . . . *J 16:23–24, 26*

And whatsoever ye shall ask *in my name*, that will I do, that the Father may be glorified in the Son. If ye shall any thing *in my name*, I will do it. *J 14:13–14*

Ye have not chosen me, but I have chosen you, and ordained you, that ye should go and bring forth fruit, and that your fruit should remain: that whatsoever ye shall ask of the Father *in my name*, he may give it you. *J 15:16*

In our era, Christians are to ask by prayer in Jesus' name direct to the Father and whatsoever they ask the Father in Jesus' name, the Father will give them that. This is the basic rule. Elsewhere Jesus states some conditions of effective prayer:

1. *If* two of you shall agree on earth as touching any thing that they shall ask, it shall be done for them of my Father which is in heaven. *Mt 18:19*
2. *If* ye abide in me, and my words abide in you, ye shall ask what ye will, and it shall be done unto you. *J 15:7*

IS PUBLIC PRAYER CHRISTIAN?

The question whether public prayer is Christian ought to be determined by what Jesus, the founder of the Christian faith, taught about prayer. We must distinguish between Jesus' culture and his teachings.

Humanly speaking, Jesus was a Jew and attended the religious services of his people, both at the Temple and in the synagogues. *J 18:20; L 21:37, L 4:16, Mk 1:29, L 4:38; Mk 3:1; Mt 12:9; L 6:6* At such services public prayers were no doubt offered in accordance with Jewish practice.

Jesus himself mentioned those "who love to pray standing *in the synagogues*". *Mt 6:5* When Jesus cleansed the Temple late in his ministry, he quoted Isaiah 56:7 as follows:

MARK	MATTHEW	LUKE
Is it not written,	It is written,	It is written,
"My house	"My house	"My house
shall be	shall be	is
called	called	
of all nations		
the house of	*the house of*	*the house of*
prayer?"	*prayer*; . . . "	*prayer*: . . ."
Mk 11:17	*Mt 21:13*	*L19:46*

Jesus was then dealing with a Jewish problem in a Jewish context: money changers and sellers of sacrifices in the great Jewish shrine. He was not dealing with prayer as such. The question is whether public prayer was to survive in the Christian age.

The beginning point is Jesus' express instruction:

And when thou prayest, thou shalt not be as the hypocrites are: for they love to pray standing *in the synagogues and in the corners of the streets*, that they may be seen of men. Verily I say unto you, they have their reward.

But thou, when thou prayest, enter into thy closet, and when thou has shut thy door, pray to thy Father which is in secret; and thy Father which seeth in secret shall reward thee openly. *Mt 6:5–6*

What could be clearer?

Prayer is a solitary door-shut act. This was expressly endorsed, but was public prayer condemned?

Jesus did condemn certain kinds of public prayer; those kinds of prayer made that the persons praying "may be seen of men." *Mt 6:5*

Jesus did endorse certain kinds of group prayer:

Again I say unto you, that if two of you shall agree on earth as touching anything that *they shall ask* [in prayer?], it shall be done of them of my Father which is in heaven. For where *two or three are gathered together in my name*, there am I in the midst of them. *Mt 18:19–20*

Jesus' own prayer practice was in accord with his basic rule that prayer is to be solitary and private. If we start with the end of his ministry we find him praying in the Garden of Gethsemane withdrawn from his disciples "about a stone's cast." *L 22:41* Mark and Matthew have fuller accounts:

MARK	MATTHEW
And they came to a place which was named Gethsemane, and he saith to the disciples, "Sit here, while I pray."	Then cometh Jesus with them unto a place called Gethsemane, and saith unto the disciples, "Sit ye here, while I go and pray yonder."
And he taketh with him Peter and James and John, and began to be sore amazed, and to be very heavy;	And he took with him Peter and the two sons of Zebedee, and began to be sorrowful and very heavy.

MARK (cont.)	MATTHEW (cont.)
and saith unto them,	Then saith he unto them,
"My soul is exceeding	"My soul is exceeding
sorrowful unto death:	sorrowful, even unto death:
tarry ye here,	tarry ye here,
and watch."	and watch with me."
And he went forward a little,	And he went a little farther,
and fell on the ground	and fell on his face,
and prayed . . .	and prayed, . . .

[He then returned to find the three disciples sleeping and rebuked Peter.]

And again he went away,	He went away again
	the second time,
and prayed, . . .	and prayed, . . .

[Jesus then found them asleep again.]

And he cometh	And he left them,
	and went away again,
	and prayed
the third time, . . .	the third time,
Mk 14:32–35, 39, 41	saying the same words.
	Mt 26:36–39, 42, 44

Jesus apparently did the same thing on the Mount of Transfiguration, although the accounts are not so clear. Matthew and Mark do not expressly mention prayer. *Mk 9:2–8; Mt 17:1–8* Luke's account does state:

And it came to pass, about an eight days after these sayings, he took Peter and John and James, and went up into a mountain to pray. And as *he prayed*, the fashion of his countenance was altered, . . . But Peter and they that were with him were heavy with sleep; . . . *L 9:28–29, 32*

Luke records several other prayer incidents:

> And it came to pass, as he was *alone praying*, his disciples were with him; . . . L 9:18

> And it came to pass, that, as he was *praying* in a certain place, when he ceased, one of his disciples said unto him, . . . L 11:1

The same pattern is apparent in these two incidents as was the case on the Mountain of Transfiguration and in the Garden of Gethsemane: Jesus would be in the company of his disciples and then would withdraw a short way to pray, alone.

He also, on occasion, withdrew completely from the presence of his disciples to pray, alone:

> And it came to pass in those days, that he went out into a mountain to pray, and continued all night in prayer to God. L 6:12

After feeding the Five Thousand, Mark and Matthew record:

MARK	MATTHEW
And when he	And when he
had sent them away,	had sent the multitudes away,
he departed	he went up
into a mountain	into a mountain apart
to pray.	to pray;
And when even was come,	and when evening was come,
the ship was in the	
midst of the sea,	
and he *alone* on the land.	he was there *alone*.
Mk 6:46–47	Mt 14:23

This had been Jesus' practice from the beginning of his ministry:

> And in the morning, rising up a great while before day, he went out, and departed into a *solitary place*, and there prayed. And Simon and

913

they that were with him followed after him. And when they found him, they said unto him, "All men seek for thee." *Mk 1:35–37*

Jesus did sometimes pray in the presence of others. For example, Jesus apparently prayed in the presence of others when he was asked to bless some little children: "Then were there brought unto him little children, that he should put his hands on them, and pray: . . . *Mt 19:13* It is not actually stated that Jesus did pray on this occasion, but it is likely that he did so when "he laid his hands on them." *Mt 19:15*

The most famous example of Jesus praying in the presence of others is the great high priestly or intercessory prayer, prayed just before he went out to the Garden of Gethsemane. He then prayed in the presence of his disciples for them. *John 17:1; 18:1* At his Last Supper, Jesus, in the presence of his eleven disciples, blessed the bread and gave thanks for the cup. *Mk 14:22–23; Mt 26:26–27; L 22:19–20*

At his crucifixion Jesus prayed in the presence of the soldiers and bystanders, but there he had no choice if he was to pray at all. *Mk 15:34; Mt 27:46; L 23:34, 46*

Prayer in the presence of others is one thing; prayer at a formal religious service is another. We have no record of any prayer of Jesus at a formal religious service. We do know that, on occasion, he read the lesson from the scripture at a synagogue service. *L 4:16–20* We do know that he taught in the synagogues and in the Temple. *J 18:20*

We do not have any record of Jesus himself going up to the Temple to pray as did the Pharisee and the publican in a parable Jesus told. *L 18:10* Perhaps he did, but was it to pray publicly or to pray alone in some quiet corner?

We do know that after Jesus' ascension his disciples continued to attend prayers at the Temple. And they "were continually in the Temple praising and blessing God." *L 24:53*

Acts states: "Now Peter and John went up together into the Temple at the hour of prayer, being the ninth hour." *Acts 3:1*

After Jesus' resurrection, his disciples often prayed together in a group:

1. These all continued with one accord *in prayer* and supplication, with the women, and Mary the mother of Jesus, and with his brethren. *Acts 1:14*
2. And *they prayed*, and said, "Thou, Lord, which knowest the hearts of all men, shew whether of these two thou hast chosen, that he may take part of this ministry and apostleship, from which Judas by transgression fell, . . . *Acts 1:24–25*
3. And they continued steadfastly in the apostles' doctrine and fellowship, and in breaking of bread, and *in prayers*. *Acts 2:42*

In the church at Corinth, Greece in about A.D. 59 both men and women were praying publicly:

Every man *praying* or prophesying, having his head covered, dishonoreth his head. But every woman that *prayeth* or prophesieth with her head uncovered dishonoreth her head: . . . *1 Corinthians 11:4–5*

It was not long before Christians were praying "in tongues", apparently in public worship. Paul commented on this practice in his First Corinthians letter as follows:

For if I *pray* in an unknown tongue, my spirit prayeth, but my understanding is unfruitful. What is it then? I will *pray* with the spirit, and I will *pray* with the understanding also; I will sing with the spirit, and I will sing with the understanding with the spirit, and I will sing with the understanding also. Else when thou shalt bless with the spirit, how shall he that occupieth the room of the unlearned say "Amen" at thy giving of thanks, seeing he understandeth not what thou sayest? For thou verily givest thanks well, but the other is not edified. *1 Corinthians 14:14–17*

From the very first, Christians have had public prayers and prayed together in groups. The question is: Is this what Jesus taught?

The answer is that Jesus taught both private, solitary prayer and prayer in groups gathered in his name. Jesus, by his example, endorsed solitary prayer in gardens, on mountains and other solitary places.

Church prayers, however, have a family resemblance to synagogue prayers. We do know that church prayers by actors standing in pulpit and pew to be seen of men have their rewards, but Jesus did teach:

> But thou, when thou prayest, enter into thy closet, and when thou hast shut thy door, pray to thy Father which is in secret; and thy Father which seeth in secret shall reward thee openly. *Mt 6:6*

PRAYER MECHANICS

Jesus did not bother with instructions, like a prayer book, as to when to kneel. On occasion Jesus knelt to pray:

And he was withdrawn from them about a stone's cast, and kneeled down, and prayed. *L 22:41*

Jesus seems to have assumed, in accordance with the custom of his people and era, that praying, generally, would be done standing:

1. The Pharisees "stood and prayed" and "the publican, standing afar off" prayed. *L 18:11, 13*
2. Hypocrites "pray standing in the synagogues and in the corners of streets." *Mt 6:5*
3. "And when ye pray standing, forgive, . . ." *Mk 11:25*

"Standing" was not a commandment, but was simply an incidental part of the background as Jesus sketched one condition of prayer, forgiveness of others. Jesus was concerned, not with the Pharisee and the publican standing, but with the words and attitudes of their prayers.

Did Jesus condemn liturgical repetition in prayer? The King James Version of Matthew does quote Jesus saying:

When ye pray, use not vain repetitions. *Mt 6:7*

The meaning of the Greek verb translated use *vain repetitions* is obscure, but modern translations consider the word *repetitions* an inaccurate translation and do not use it. The general thrust of Jesus' point is clear, even in the King James Version, if his whole sentence is considered. For him, "vain repetitions" was equivalent to "much speaking":

But when ye pray, use not *vain repetitions*, as the heathen do: for they think that they shall be heard for their *much speaking*. *Mt 6:7*

Jesus did condemn "much speaking" in any prayer, saying, in effect, "Your Father already has the details." Here is exactly what Jesus said:

> But when ye pray, use not *vain repetitions*, as the heathen do: for they think that they shall be heard for their *much speaking*. Be not ye therefore like unto them: for your Father knoweth what things ye have need of, before ye ask him. *Mt 6:7–8*

On one occasion Jesus combined his denunciations of long prayers and praying for show. Jesus said:

MARK	MATTHEW	LUKE
	Woe unto you,	
Beware of	scribes and	Beware of
the scribes, . . .	Pharisees,	the scribes, . . .
	hypocrites!	
which devour	for ye devour	which devour
widows' houses, and	widows' houses, and	widows' houses, and
for a pretence	*for a pretence*	*for a shew [show]*
make long prayers;	*make long prayers*;	*make long prayers*;
these	therefore ye	the same
shall receive	shall receive	shall receive
greater damnation.	the greater damnation.	greater damnation.
Mk 12:38–40	*Mt 23:14*	*L 20:46–47*

Long prayers are not condemned as such. What are condemned are long prayers for show. Prayer is not to be a performance before men, but a private petition to the Father. Public prayers are risky. They are open invitations to pride and prominence. Secret prayers are safer.

Jesus condemned prayers which are a babble of many words. Jesus did not want his followers to pray, like pagans, with long, wordy prayers, nor to enjoy praying in the public eye like Jewish hypocrites. Jesus approved short, private, humble and sincere prayers like, "God, be merciful to me a sinner. *L 18:13*

CHAPTER 17

FASTING / BAPTISM /
PIOUS ACTS / CHARITY

FASTING

Jesus, himself, of course fasted: in the wilderness he fasted forty days and forty nights. *Mt 4:2* The question is what he wanted his followers to do.

Jesus' closest followers, his disciples, did not fast. *Mk 2:18; Mt 9:14; L 5:33* This was unusual; John's disciples and the Pharisees fasted. *Mk 2:18; Mt 9:14; L 5:33* Jews fasted as a religious exercise. The Day of Atonement was observed by a mandatory twenty-four hour fast. *Leviticus 12:29 (See Acts where the Day of Atonement is referred to simply as "the Fast." Acts 27:9)*

The question was put to Jesus: "Why do the disciples of John and of the Pharisees fast, but thy disciples fast not?" *Mk 2:18 (Mt 9:14; L 5:33)* Jesus' answer was:

MARK	MATTHEW	LUKE
Can	Can	Can ye make
the children	the children	the children
of the bride-chamber	of the bride-chamber	of the bride-chamber
fast while	mourn, as long	fast, while
the bridegroom	as the bridegroom	the bridegroom
is with them?	is with them?	is with them?

MARK (cont.)	MATTHEW (cont.)	LUKE (cont.)
As long as they have the bridegroom with them, they cannot fast.		
But the days will come, when the bridegroom shall be taken away from them, and then shall they fast in those days.	But the days will come, when the bridegroom shall be taken from them, and then shall they fast.	But the days will come, when the bridegroom shall be taken away from them, and then shall they fast in those days.
Mk 2:19–20	*Mt 9:15*	*L 5:34–35*

The answer is a prediction that in the future his disciples would fast. This answer is followed by a series of parables apparently meant to explain Jesus' attitude toward fasting:

MARK	MATTHEW	LUKE
No man also seweth a piece of new cloth on an old garment: else the new piece	No man putteth a piece of new cloth unto an old garment, for that which is put in	No man putteth a piece of a new garment upon an old; if otherwise they both the new
that filled it up taketh away from the old, and the rent is made worse.	to fill it up taketh from the garment, and the rent is made worse.	maketh a rent, and the piece that was taken out of the new agreeth not with the old.
And no man putteth new wine	Neither do men put new wine	And no man putteth new wine

MARK (cont.)	**MATTHEW** (cont.)	**LUKE** (cont.)
into old bottles:	into old bottles:	into old bottles:
else the new wine	else	else the new wine
doth burst the bottles,	the bottles break,	will burst the bottles,
and the wine is	and the wine	
spilled,	runneth out,	and be spilled,
and the bottles	and the bottles	and the bottles
will be marred;	perish;	shall perish.
but new wine	but they put new wine	But new wine
must be put		must be put
in new bottles.	into new bottles,	into new bottles,
Mk 2:21–22	and both	and both
	are preserved.	are preserved.
	Mt 9:16–17	

LUKE (cont.)

No man also having
drunk old wine
straightway desireth
new
for he saith,
"The old is better."
L 5:36–39

The old wine bottles of Jesus' day were old wineskins. Fasting
was like an old, dry wineskin. Jesus' new wine will burst those old
wineskins, even if men prefer the old, the familiar wine.

Fasting was important to the religious Jew. Anna the prophetess "served God with fastings and prayers night and day." *L 2:37*
Jesus quotes a Pharisee's own description of himself:

God, I thank thee, that I am not as other men are, extortioners,
unjust, adulterers, or even as this publican. *I fast twice in the week*,
I give tithes of all that I possess. *L 18:11–12*

The publican simply said:

God be merciful to me a sinner. *L 18:13*

And Jesus held:

> I tell you, this man went down to his house justified rather than the
> other: for every one that exalteth himself shall be abased; and he
> that humbleth himself shall be exalted. *L 18:13–14*

Jesus condemned the spiritual pride of a man who relied upon
his twice weekly fast. To Jesus, the fasting did not matter; what he
wanted was sincerity:

> Moreover when *ye fast*, be not, as the hypocrites, of a sad counte-
> nance: for they disfigure their faces, that they may appear unto men
> *to fast*. Verily I say unto you, they have their reward. But thou, when
> *thou fastest*, anoint thine head, and wash thy face, that thou appear
> not to men *to fast*, but unto thy Father which is in secret; and thy
> Father, which seeth in secret, shall reward thee openly. *Mt 6:16–18*

Jesus' emphasis on secrecy and sincerity in fasting is like his
teaching on prayer:

> And when thou prayest, thou shalt not be as the hypocrites are: for
> they love to pray standing in the synagogues and in the corners of
> the streets, that they may be seen of men. *Mt 6:5*

It might also be thought that Jesus regarded fasting as having a
special therapeutic value in helping a healer to heal. In the King
James Version of the Bible, Jesus is quoted as giving the following
explanation to his disciples why they had not been able to heal an
epileptic boy:

MARK	MATTHEW
This kind can	Howbeit this kind
come forth	goeth not out
by nothing,	
but prayer *and fasting*.	but by prayer *and fasting*.
Mk 9:29	*Mt 17:21*

The manuscripts for these verses vary. Modern versions of the Bible omit the words "and fasting" from Mark and the entire verse from Matthew, because they consider the manuscripts which omit these words the most reliable.

The first Christians fasted. Of the church at Antioch, Syria, it is written:

> As they ministered to the Lord, *and fasted*, the Holy Spirit said, "Separate me Barnabas and Saul for the work whereunto I have called them." And when they had *fasted and prayed*, and laid their hands on them, they sent them away. *Acts 13:2–3*

As Barnabas and Saul (Paul) had been sent on their preaching tour with prayer and fasting, so also did Barnabas and Paul ordain elders:

> And when they had ordained them elders in every church, and had *prayed with fasting*, they commended them to the Lord, on whom they believed. *Acts 14:23*

Paul wrote to the new Christians at Corinth respecting marriage and marital rights:

> Defraud ye not one the other, except it be with consent for a time, that ye may give yourselves to *fasting and prayer*; and come together again, that Satan tempt you not for your incontinency. *1 Corinthians 7:5*

In the early church, prayer and fasting went together. In the early church, fasting was part of solemn occasions, such as ordaining elders. In the early church there were soon appointed days of fasting.

An early Christian manual of instruction, The Didache, states that Chrisians fast on Wednesdays and Fridays, not like "the hypocrites" (Pharisees?) who fast on Mondays and Thursdays. *VIII, 1*

Jesus' prediction was that his disciples would fast on those days "when the bridegroom shall be taken away from them." *Mk 2:19; Mt 9:15; L 5:35* This prediction came true. The old religious forms persisted, it became Wednesdays and Fridays, rather than Mondays and Thursdays.

It is, however, certain that Jesus did not require his disciples to fast. What he did teach is that fasting must be private and without show, and that his new wine of truth and love would burst the stiff, old, dry skin bottles of religious form. New wine requires fresh wineskins.

JESUS' TEACHING ON BAPTISM

After Jesus rose from the dead, he told his disciples:

For John truly baptized with water; but ye shall be baptized with
the Holy Spirit not many days hence. *Acts 1:5*

After Jesus rose from the dead, he also instructed his disciples:

He that believeth *and is baptized* shall be saved; but he that believeth
not shall be damned. *Mk 16:16*

Go ye therefore, and teach all nations, *baptizing them* in the name of
the Father, and of the Son, and of the Holy Spirit: . . . *Mt 28:19*

In his lifetime, Jesus spoke of baptism several times. Either
James and John the sons of Zebedee, themselves, or their mother,
in their presence, asked for special status for them in Jesus' king
dom.

The dialogue went this way:

	MARK	MATTHEW
JESUS:	Ye know not what ye ask.	Ye know not what ye ask.
	Can ye drink	Are ye able to drink
	of the cup	of the cup
	that I drink of,	that I shall drink of,
	and be baptized	and to be baptized
	with the baptism	with the baptism
	that I am	that I am
	baptized with?	baptized with?
JAMES AND JOHN:	We can.	We are able.
JESUS:	Ye shall indeed	Ye shall
	drink of the cup	drink indeed of my cup,
	that I drink of,	
	and with the baptism	and be baptized

MARK (cont.)	MATTHEW (cont.)
	with the baptism
that I am baptized withal	that I am baptized with;
shall ye be baptized;	
but to sit on my right hand	but to sit on my right hand
and on my left hand	and on my left,
is not mine to give,	is not mine to give,
but it shall be given to	but it shall be given to
them for whom	them for whom
it is prepared.	it is prepared
Mk 10:38–40	of my Father.
	Mt 20:22–23

Christians can not read these statements without thinking of Jesus' question to Peter in the Garden of Gethsemane:

The cup which my Father hath given me, shall I not drink it?
J 18:11

The disciples did drink of the cup of suffering that Jesus drank. It is harder to know just what Jesus meant when he spoke of "the baptism that I am baptized with."

On the basis of the manuscript evidence, modern versions of Matthew omit the reference to baptism and quote Jesus as speaking only of the cup he was to drink.

Mark does assert that Jesus did, in fact, warn James and John that "with the baptism that I am baptized withal shall ye be baptized." *Mk 10:39* This statement, as we have it, is ambiguous: is it the literal baptism Jesus had already undergone; or is it the figurative baptism of his future suffering?

Jesus as a Jew knew the Old Testament and he may have been using "baptism" not in any technical theological sense, but only in the sense of an "ordeal" as in Isaiah 43:2 that states:

When thou passest through the waters, I will be with thee; and through the rivers they shall not overflow thee: when thou walkest through the fire, thou shalt not be burned; neither shall the flame kindle upon thee.

The only other recorded instance in which Jesus used words like "the baptism that I am baptized withal" is found in Luke and states:

> I am come to send fire on the earth; and what will I, if it already be kindled? But I have a baptism to be baptized with; and how am I straitened till it be accomplished! *L 12:49–50*

It is clear from this statement that the baptism Jesus refers to is future: it is a baptism he is "to be baptized with." It is also clear that this future baptism was a baptism in the figurative sense of an ordeal, his passion that was to come. His literal baptism had already occurred, when, at the beginning of his ministry, he had been baptized by John the Baptist. *Mk 1:9; Mt 3:16; L 3:21*

John the Baptist, as a prophet, foresaw that Jesus would:

MARK	MATTHEW	LUKE
. . . baptize you with the Holy Spirit *Mk 1:8*	. . . baptize you with the Holy Spirit, and with fire. *Mt 3:11*	. . . baptize you with the Holy Spirit and with fire. *L 3:16*

It is not clear from these quotes whether John meant: baptism with the Holy Spirit *and* with fire; or that the baptism with the Holy Spirit would be fiery.

Acts describes the appearance of the Holy Spirit as follows:

> And there appeared unto them cloven tongues *like as of fire*, and it sat upon each of them. And they were all filled with the Holy Spirit, . . . *Acts 2:3–4*

Jesus' teaching about baptism in his lifetime was short and simple:

> Verily, verily, I say unto thee, except a man be born *of water* and of the Spirit, he, cannot enter into the Kingdom of God. *J 3:5*

Water is assumed to mean the water of baptism, and we do know that Jesus' disciples in his lifetime and his presence baptized with water. *J 3:22, 4:1–2*

The early Christian preaching was:

> Repent, and be baptized every one of you in the name of Jesus Christ for the remission of sins, and ye shall receive the gift of the Holy Spirit. *Acts 2:38*

Baptism immediately followed. *Acts 2:41* The baptism required was a water baptism "in the name of Jesus Christ for the remission of sins." Once this condition was met, the persons so baptized would "receive the gift of the Holy Spirit."

This is how, immediately after Jesus' resurrection, Peter, speaking for himself and the Eleven, understood Jesus' own teaching that:

> Except a man be born of water and of the Spirit, he can not enter into the Kingdom of God. *J 3:5*

Jesus himself had been baptized in water with John's baptism because "it becometh us to fulfill all righteousness." *Mt 3:15* Jesus thereby endorsed John's baptism of repentance. But, as Paul later explained to Jesus' disciples in Ephesus, John only "baptized with the baptism of repentance" and it was necessary to be "baptized in the name of the Lord Jesus." *Acts 19:4–5*

After these men were so baptized, they received the gift of the Holy Spirit just as Peter had stated in his earliest preaching quoted above:

> Repent, and be baptized every one of you *in the name of Jesus Christ* for the remission of sins, and ye shall receive the gift of the Holy Spirit. *Acts 2:38*

In making this statement Peter followed Jesus' own words as to baptism by his church:

> And that repentance and remission of sins should be preached *in his name* among all nations, beginning at Jerusalem. *L 24:47*

> Go ye therefore, and teach all nations, baptizing them *in the name* of the Father, and of the Son, and of the Holy Spirit: . . . *Mt 28:19*

PIOUS ACTS

Jesus taught secrecy in religious practice. He gave three examples in the Sermon on the Mount: alms, prayer and fasting:

1. But when thou doest alms, let not thy left hand know what thy right hand doeth: that thine alms may be *in secret*; . . . *Mt 6:3–4*
2. And when thou prayest, thou shalt not be as the hypocrites are: for they love to pray standing in the synagogues and in the corners of the streets, that they may be seen of men. . . . But thou, when thou prayest, enter into thy closet, and when thou hast shut thy door, pray to thy Father which is *in secret*; . . . *Mt 6:5–6*
3. But thou, when thou fastest, anoint thine head, and wash thy face: that thou appear not unto men to fast, but unto thy Father which is *in secret*; . . . *Mt 6:17–18*

In each case the secret acts of religion are to be rewarded by Father:

1. Alms—"and thy Father which seeth in secret himself shall reward thee openly." *Mt 6:4*
2. Prayer—"and thy Father which seeth in secret shall reward thee openly." *Mt 6:6*
3. Fasting—"and thy Father, which seeth in secret, shall reward thee openly." *Mt 6:18*

The manuscripts of Matthew 6:4 and 6:6 are split as to whether Jesus said this reward was to be "openly" given. Modern translations consider the word "openly" a gloss on the original wording of all three quotations. Accordingly Jesus' point was not that the Father who seeth in secret will reward openly, but that he will reward.

The first verse in Matthew, Chapter 6 in the King James Version refers to doing "your alms." Modern translations regard this as a too narrow translation of Jesus' original word which probably referred to pious acts generally. If so, Matthew 6:1 is then a general introduction to specific instructions on each of the three pious acts, alms, prayer and fasting:

> Take heed that ye do not your alms [pious acts] before men, to be seen of them: otherwise ye have no reward of your Father which is in heaven. *Mt 6:1*

The condition of Father's reward for a pious act is that the act not be done so men can see and applaud it. Having stated that principle, Jesus immediately proceeded to draw this conclusion:

> Therefore when thou doest thine alms, do not sound a trumpet before thee, as the hypocrites do in the synagogues and in the streets, that they may have glory of men. Verily, I say unto you, they have their reward. *Mt 6:2*

Those who seek the glory of men in their charitable gifts have their reward, the glory of men. Their receipt of the glory of men forecloses any reward by the Father.

Jesus was severely critical of pious pomp and circumstance. He said of the scribes and Pharisees:

> But all their *works* they do for to be seen of men: they make broad their phylacteries [leather boxes containing verses of scripture worn on the forehead and left arm], and enlarge the borders of their garments, and love the uppermost rooms at feasts, and the chief seats in the synagogues, and greetings in the markets, and to be called of men, Rabbi [my great one], Rabbi [my great one]. *Mt 23:5–7*

Pious pomp and circumstance will bring judgment upon its actors:

> Woe unto you, Pharisees! For you love the uttermost seats in the synagogues, and greetings in the markets. *L 11:43*

The theme of judgment on professional piety is even stronger in the following warnings of Jesus:

Mark	Luke
Beware of the scribes,	Beware of the scribes,
which love to go in	which desire to walk in
long clothing,	long robes
and love salutations	and love greetings
in the marketplaces,	in the markets,
and the chief seats	and the highest seats
in the synagogues,	in the synagogues,
and the uppermost rooms	and the chief rooms
at feasts;	at feasts;
which devour widows' houses,	which devour widows' houses,
and for a pretense	and for a shew
make long prayers:	make long prayers:
these shall receive	the same shall receive
greater damnation.	greater damnation.
Mk 12:38–40	*L 20:46–47*

Jesus' point was that personal display voids religious acts. Since Jesus' time religion has changed little. We still have our Reverend Doctors and your Eminences.

Jesus scathingly condemned religion "for show." He taught: do not act to get the reward of men; act in secret to get the reward of God. Sound no trumpet for your gifts, not even a press release or a credit line. Even your best friend must not know. Go into your room to pray and shut the door so that you will not be seen by others. If you fast, don't publish it by looking dismal. If you act for God, he is the only one who needs to know.

Charity?

In the Sermon on the Mount, Jesus said:

> But when thou doest alms, let not thy left hand know what thy right hand doeth, that thine alms may be in secret; and thy Father which seeth in secret himself shall reward thee openly. *Mt 6:3–4*

Not only are alms to be secretly done, they must come from one's inner being. After rebuking the Pharisees for cleaning the outside of cup and platter while their inward being was full of wickedness, Jesus said:

> But rather give alms of such things as ye have; and, behold, all things are clean unto you. *L 11:41*

The King James Version, as it stands, is obscure because it seems to say the obvious: give what you have. What is implied rather than expressed is this: in giving, give of yourself, and all things will be clean for you.

Jesus taught that the reason to give is the spiritual benefit to the giver. The story of the rich young ruler who wished to inherit eternal life is familiar. *Mk 10:17–22; Mt 19:16–22; L 18:18–23* After the ruler said that he had observed all the Commandments from his youth, Jesus said to him in a kindly way:

MARK	MATTHEW	LUKE
One thing thou lackest:	If thou wilt be perfect,	Yet lackest thou one thing:
go thy way, sell whatsoever thou hast, and give to the poor, and thou shalt have treasure in heaven;	go and sell that thou hast, and give to the poor, and thou shalt have treasure in heaven;	sell all that thou hast, and distribute unto the poor and thou shalt have treasure in heaven;

MARK (cont.)	**MATTHEW** (cont.)	**LUKE** (cont.)
and come,	and come	and come,
take up		
the cross,		
and follow me.	and follow me.	follow me.
Mk 10:21	*Mt 19:21*	*L 18:22*

One of Jesus' points made to the rich young ruler was that he, as a giver, would receive spiritual benefit from his gifts, that is, treasure in heaven. Jesus' emphasis was not on the need of the poor but the spiritual benefit to the giver.

On another occasion Jesus told his "little flock":

> Sell that ye have, and give alms; provide yourself [money] bags which wax not old, a treasure in the heavens that faileth not, where no thief approacheth, neither moth corrupteth. *L 12:33*

Again Jesus makes the point that giving "provides yourself" with treasure in heaven. He did not consider this spiritual benefit to the giver as selfish, but only as an instance of how the spiritual universe operates.

Jesus gave instructions on charity, how to give alms, and his emphasis was not on the need of the recipient but on the effect of the spiritual state of the giver.

CHAPTER 18

THE HEALINGS

JESUS AND HEALING

Jesus has an indelible image as a healer of the sick. There are two common theories about Jesus as a healer: on one hand, he is viewed merely as a superpowerful healer, the best of a human series; on the other hand, his healings are denied as nonfacts explainable by psychology, psychiatry and the medical ignorance of his age. An examination of the record demonstrates that neither theory is true.

The first three gospels write of the close of a day in his early public ministry at Capernaum, Galilee:

MARK	MATTHEW	LUKE
And at even, when	When the even	Now when
the sun did set,	was come,	the sun was setting,
they brought unto him	they brought unto him	
all that	many that	all they that
were diseased,		had any sick
		with diverse diseases
and them that were	were	
possessed by devils.	possessed with devils,	brought them
		unto him;
And all the city		
was gathered		

MARK (cont.)
at the door.

And he healed many
that were sick
of diverse diseases,
and cast out
many devils;

and suffered not
the devils to speak,
because they knew
him.
Mk 1:32–35

MATTHEW (cont.)

and he cast out
the spirits
with his word
and healed all
that were sick:

LUKE (cont.)
and he laid his hands
on every one of them,

and healed them.

And
devils also came out
of many, crying out,
and saying,
"Thou art Christ
the Son of God."

And he rebuking them
suffered them not
to speak:
for they knew that
he was Christ.
L 4:40–41

that it might be
fulfilled which was
spoken by Isaiah
the Prophet, saying,
"Himself took our
infirmities, and
bare our sicknesses."
Mt 8:16–17 (Isaiah 53:4)

That, the skeptics say, is exactly what we mean. The healings are the mark of a prescientific age. Sickness shades imperceptibly into devil possession and "devils", not diseases, are cast out. Luke's account does say:

> And devils also came out of many, crying out, and saying, "Thou art Christ the Son of God."

936

And he, rebuking them, suffered them not to speak: for they knew that he was Christ. *L 4:41*

See, the skeptics say, we have "Theology", not any medically credible reports of healings. It is true that the Gospel writers were interested in the theological aspects of the healings. In the parallel passage in Matthew, he quotes the prophet Isaiah, writing that the healings were done, "that it might be fulfilled which was spoken in by Isaiah the prophet, saying, 'Himself took our infirmities, and bare our sicknesses.'" *Mt 8:17 (Isaiah 53:4)*

However, it is also noteworthy that both Matthew and Luke report certain mechanisms of healing:

MATTHEW	LUKE
He cast out the spirits *with his word*, and healed all that were sick. Mt 8:16	He *laid his hands on every one of them*, and healed them. L 4:40

Jesus' healings were not restricted to exorcisms of devils. Matthew elsewhere reports:

And Jesus went about all Galilee, teaching in their synagogues, and preaching the gospel of the Kingdom, and *healing all manner of sickness and all manner of disease* among the people. And his fame went throughout all Syria; and they brought unto him all sick people that were taken with *diverse diseases and torments*, and those which were possessed with devils, and those which were lunatic, and those that had the palsy; and he healed them. *Mt 4:23–24*

It was not just demoniacs, epileptics and paralytics, but "diverse diseases and torments." On this occasion, Mark mentions that he healed "as many as had plagues." *Mk 3:10; L 6:17 ("healed of their diseases")* Matthew, in another passage, writes of Jesus "healing every sickness and every disease among the people." *Mt 9:35*

Later on in Jesus' ministry, on a mountain near the Sea of Galilee, Matthew reports:

> And great multitudes came unto him, having with them those that were lame, blind, dumb, maimed, and many others, and cast them down at Jesus' feet; and he healed them: insomuch that the multitude wondered, when they saw the dumb to speak, the maimed to be whole, the lame to walk, and the blind to see; and they glorified the God of Israel." *Mt 15:29–31*

It is to be noted that they glorified "the God of Israel", not Jesus, personally. This reflected Jesus' own position that the healings were not so much his, as a sign that his mission was approved of God. When John the Baptist sent two of his disciples to inquire of Jesus whether Jesus was the Messiah, Jesus' answer was:

MATTHEW	LUKE
Go and show John again	Go your way and tell John
those things	what things
which ye do hear and see:	ye have seen and heard:
the blind receive their sight,	how that the blind see,
and the lame walk;	the lame walk,
the lepers are cleansed,	the lepers are cleansed,
and the deaf hear;	the deaf hear,
the dead are raised up,	the dead are raised;
and the poor	to the poor
have the gospel	the gospel
preached to them.	is preached.
And blessed is he,	And blessed is he,
whosoever shall not	whosoever shall not
be offended in me.	be offended in me.
Mt 11:4–6	*L 7:22–23*

And that very hour, according to Luke, Jesus "cured many of their infirmities and plagues, and of evil spirits; and unto many that were blind he gave sight." *L 7:21* The statement that "blind he gave sight" should not be read rationalistically as "gave spiritual sight", since the instances in which Jesus cured physical blindness are numerous and well attested.

THE BLIND RECEIVE THEIR SIGHT

Jesus claimed to give sight to the blind. This was not a spiritual claim only, but also in certain instances a physical gift of vision. The Gospels record about five cases in which Jesus gave physical sight to individuals:

1. Two blind men. *Mt 9:27–31*
2. Man both blind and dumb. *Mt 12:22–24*
3. Bartimaeus and possibly another blind beggar. *Mk 10:46–52; Mt 20:29–34; L 18:35–43*
4. Blind man at Bethsaida. *Mk 8:22–26*
5. Man born blind. *J 9:1–38*

We examine first the case of the two blind men of Matthew 9:27–31. Here is Matthew's account:

And when Jesus departed thence, two blind men followed him, crying, and saying, "Thou Son of David, have mercy on us."

And when he was come into the house, the blind men came to him; and Jesus saith unto them, "Believe ye that I am able to do this?"

They said unto him, "Yea, Lord."

Then touched he their eyes, saying, "According to your faith, be it unto you."

And their eyes were opened, and Jesus straightly charged them, saying, "See that no man know it."

But they, when they were departed, spread abroad his fame in all that country. *Mt 9:27–31*

There is no hint that these two men were not physically blind. In another incident reported only by Matthew, Jesus healed a man who was probably blind by reason of what is now called in psychiatric terms, conversion hysteria:

> Then was brought unto him one possessed with a devil, blind, and dumb; and he healed him, inasmuch that the blind and dumb both spake and saw.
>
> And all the people were amazed, and said, "Is not this the Son of David?"
>
> But when the Pharisees heard it, they said, "This fellow doth not cast out devils, but by Beelzebub the prince of the devils." *Mt 12:22–24*

This was impressive psychotherapy, but was not a miracle in twentieth-century terms, because we now understand, if crudely, the mechanisms of such healing.

This is not the case with Bartimaeus, the son of Timaeus. Late in Jesus' ministry Jesus passed through Jericho on his way to Jerusalem for the last time. As Matthew got the story there was also another blind beggar involved, but Mark and Luke mention only one man. Otherwise the three accounts are closely parallel:

MARK	MATTHEW	LUKE
		And it came to pass, that as
And they came to Jericho,		he was come nigh unto Jericho,
and as he went out of Jericho with his disciples	And as they departed from Jericho,	
and a great number of people,	a great multitude	
	followed him. And, behold,	
blind Bartimaeus, the son of Timaeus,	two blind men	a certain blind man
sat by	sitting by	sat by
the highway side	the way side,	the way side

MARK (cont.)	**MATTHEW** (cont.)	**LUKE** (cont.)
begging.		begging;
And when he heard	when they heard	and hearing
that it was	that	the multitude
		pass by, he asked
		what it meant.
		And they told him that
Jesus of Nazareth,	Jesus	Jesus of Nazareth
	passed by,	passeth by.
he began to cry out	cried out,	And he cried,
and say,	saying,	saying,
	"Have mercy on us,	
"Jesus,	O Lord,	"Jesus,
thou Son of David,	thou Son of David."	thou Son of David,
have mercy		have mercy
on me."		on me."
		And they which
And many	And the multitude	went before
charged him	rebuked them,	rebuked him,
that he should	because they should	that he should
hold his peace;	hold their peace;	hold his peace;
but he cried	but they cried	but he cried
the more a great deal,	the more, saying,	so much the more.
	"Have mercy on us,	
"Thou son of David,	O Lord,	"Thou son of David,
have mercy on me."	thou son of David."	have mercy on me."
And Jesus stood still,	And Jesus stood still,	And Jesus stood,
and commanded him		and commanded him
to be called.		to be brought
And they call		unto him;
the blind man,		
saying unto him,		
"Be of good comfort,		
rise; he calleth thee."		
And he, casting away		and when he
his garment, rose,		
and came to Jesus.		came near,

MARK (cont.)	MATTHEW (cont.)	LUKE (cont.)
And Jesus answered and said unto him, "What wilt thou that I should do unto thee?"	and called them, and said, "What will ye that I shall do unto you?"	he asked him, saying, "What wilt thou that I shall do unto thee?"
The blind man said unto him, "Lord, that I might receive my sight."	They say unto him, "Lord, that our eyes may be opened."	And he said, "Lord, that I may receive my sight."
And Jesus said unto him, "Go thy way; thy faith hath made thee whole."	So Jesus	And Jesus said unto him, "Receive thy sight; thy faith hath saved thee."
	had compassion on them, and touched their eyes;	
And immediately he received his sight, and followed Jesus in the way. *Mk 10:46–52*	and immediately their eyes received sight, and they followed him. *Mt 20:29–34*	And immediately he received his sight, and followed him, glorifying God; and all the people, when they saw it, gave praise unto God. *L 18:35–43*

It is noteworthy that all of these cases of gift of sight refer to Jesus' title as the expected Messiah of the Jews: "Son of David." *Mt 9:27, 12:23, 20:30–31; Mk 10:47–48; L 18:38–39*

In the case of the blind man who was also dumb and was possessed with a devil, it was the crowd that asked:

Is not this the Son of David? *Mt 12:23*

Matthew reports two cases of two blind men. *Mt 9:27–31, 20:29–34* In each case it was the blind men themselves who mirror the popular hope when they cry:

Thou Son of David, have mercy on us. *Mt 9:27*

Have mercy on us, O Lord, thou Son of David. *Mt 20:30*

In the case of Bartimaeus, it was he, like the two blind men of Matthew's two cases, who cries:

Jesus, thou Son of David, have mercy upon me. *Mk 10:47; L 18:38*

The invocation of the Messianic title does not seem to have been an operative element in the gifts of sight. In the case of the devil-possessed blind man, it was simply the crowd's amazed reaction to the miracle. *Mt 12:23*

While the invocation of the Messianic title does not seem to have been an operative element in these gifts of sight, it is easy to say that some of these gifts of sight are what we today would call faith healings. However, in other cases, the evidence does not support any such easy label.

We turn to the easy cases first. The first case is the case of Bartimaeus named only in Mark's Gospel, called simply "a certain blind man" by Luke and expanded to "two blind men" by Matthew. *Mk 10:46; L 18:35; Mt 20:30* Here is what happened:

	MARK	MATTHEW	LUKE
JESUS:	What wilt thou that I should do unto thee?	What will ye that I should do unto you?	What wilt thou that I should do unto thee?
BLIND:	Lord, that I may receive my sight.	Lord, that our eyes may be opened. *Mt 20:32–33*	Lord, that I may receive my sight.
JESUS:	Go thy way;		Receive

Mark (cont.)	Matt. (cont.)	Luke (cont.)
		thy sight;
thy faith		thy faith
hath made		hath saved
thee whole.		thee.
Mk 10:51–52		*L 18:41–42*

Another easy case is the case of the two blind men reported in Matthew 9:27–31. The two blind men had followed Jesus crying out, "Thou son of David, have mercy on us." *Mt 9:27* Once the blind men were in the house with Jesus, their interchange went like this:

Jesus: Believe ye that I am able to do this?
Men: Yea, Lord.
Jesus [as he touched their eyes]: According to your faith, be it unto you. *Mt 9:28–29*

In both cases of the two blind men reported by Matthew (*Mt 9:27–31 and Mt 20:29–34*), Jesus, as an incident of the healing, touched their eyes. *Mt 9:29; Mt 20:34*

When Jesus healed a man "possessed with a devil, blind and dumb," we read nothing of the man's faith. *Mt 12:22–24* There was, of course, the faith of those who brought the man to Jesus. This was also the only faith involved in the healing at Bethsaida recorded in Mark 8:22–26: the blind man's friends asked Jesus to touch the man.

The man, of course, also submitted to Jesus' treatment; however, submission to treatment did not make this healing a faith healing any more than submission to ordinary medical treatment makes such treatment faith healing. We turn to the record as to how Jesus treated the man:

And he took the blind man by the hand, and led him out of the town; and when he had spit on his eyes, and put his hands upon him, he asked him if he saw ought.

And he looked up, and said, "I see men as trees, walking."

After that he put his hands again upon his eyes, and made him look up, and he was restored, and saw every man clearly.

And he sent him away to his house, saying, "Neither go into the town, nor tell it to any in the town." *Mk 8:23–26*

Jesus acted professionally. First, he led the blind man out of the village so that he could administer the healing modalities in some privacy. The account implies, but does not state, that the man's friends were left in the town. Second, Jesus' procedures, including his questions, were clinical:

1. He administered the saliva and touched the eyes.
2. He then asked what he could see: "asked him if he saw ought." *Mk 8:23*
3. He then repeated part of the therapy: "he put his hands again upon his eyes, and made him look up." *Mk 8:25*
4. Jesus did not seek to exploit the healing in any way, and in fact specifically instructed the man not to "go into the town, nor tell it to any in the town." *Mk 8:26*

While Jesus' treatment of this man may seem primitive and repugnant, it was not a case of a faith healing. The modality of healing was the application of saliva. He used the same modality in healing the man born blind. John's account of the healing states:

When he [Jesus] had thus spoken, he spat on the ground, and made clay of the spittle; and he anointed the eyes of the blind man with the clay, and said unto him, "Go, wash in the pool of Siloam." *J 9:6–7*

The account continues:

He went his way therefore, and washed, and came seeing. *J 9:7*

There are two differences in Jesus' treatment of this man compared with his treatment of the blind man at Bethsaida recorded in

Mark 8:22–26. He mixed the saliva with earth to make a paste. *J 9:6* He had the man wash off the paste in a fresh water pool. *J 9:7*

Saliva contains, in addition to water, certain salts and enzyme ptyalin. In those times saliva was considered to have therapeutic qualities. If we are squeamish about this modality, is it any more objectionable than the physical contact required for mouth-to-mouth resuscitation?

In the case of the blind man healed at Bethsaida, the King James Version states that "he was restored, and saw every man clearly", leaving room, so far as the English is concerned, to argue that his previous sight was restored. *Mk 8:25* No such argument is possible in the case of the man born blind. He had never had vision. John's account repeatedly states that the man had been born blind. *J 9:1–2, 19–20, 32*

The circumstances of his healing are so clear and impressive that there is no escape from concluding that Jesus did a stupendous miracle, unless, of course, the easy way is taken by simply rejecting the record as preserved by John. We turn now to an examination of that record.

This healing occurred in Jerusalem on a Sabbath in the early fall shortly after an eight-day religious festival known as the Feast of Tabernacles. *J 7:2, 14, 37; J 9:2* As Jesus walked along he saw the blind man by the wayside and his entourage of disciples asked:

> Master, who did sin, this man, or his parents, that he was born blind? *J 9:2*

Jesus answered:

> Neither hath this man sinned, nor his parents, but that the works of God should be made manifest in him. I must work the works for him that sent me, while it is day; the night cometh, when no man can work. As long as I am in the world, I am the light of the world. *J 9:3–5*

Without any request from the man, or any one else, Jesus then anointed the man's eyes with a paste made of clay and spit and instructed him to wash it off in the Pool of Siloam. Jesus's account then states:

He went his way therefore, and washed, and came seeing. *J 9:7*

Some of the neighbors doubted that the man healed was the local begging blind man:

The neighbors therefore, and they which before had seen him that he was blind, said, "Is not this he that sat and begged?"

Some said, "This is he;" others said, "He is like him," but he said, "I am he."

Therefore said they unto him, "How were thine eyes opened?" *J 9:8–10*

That, of course, is exactly our question. And we do have the man's answer. He said:

A man that is called Jesus made clay, and anointed mine eyes, and said unto me, "Go to the Pool of Siloam, and wash;" and I went and washed, and I received sight. *J 9:11*

The man was brought to the Pharisees who asked how he had received his sight. *J 9:13–15* He answered:

He put clay upon mine eyes, and I washed, and do see. *J 9:15*

Some of the Pharisees then said of Jesus:

This man is not of God, because he keepeth not the Sabbath day. *J 9:16*

Other Pharisees said:

How can a man that is a sinner do such miracles? *J 9:16*

John continues:

> And there was a division among them. They say unto the blind man again, "What sayest thou of him, that he hath opened thine eyes?" He said, "He is a prophet."

> But the Jews did not believe concerning him, that he had been blind, and received his sight, until they called the parents of him that had received his sight. *J 9:16–18*

The investigators asked his parents:

Q: Is this your son, who *ye say* was born blind? How doth he now see?
A: We know that this is our son, and that he was born blind. But by what means he now seeth, we know not; or who hath opened his eyes, we know not. He is of age; ask him. He shall speak for himself. *J 9:20–21*

The questions were pointed, and the answers of the parents were cautious, restricting themselves to known facts. They had good reason to be cautious. They knew that the wrong answers would lead to their excommunication from their synagogue.
John writes:

> These words spake his parents, because they feared the Jews: for the Jews had agreed already, that if any man did confess that he was Christ, he should be put out of the synagogue. Therefore said his parents, "He is of age; ask him." *J 9:22–23*

The investigators had no choice but to return to the man himself. At this point the investigators shifted to minimizing Jesus' part in giving the man his sight. They preemptorily instructed the man, "Give God the praise; we know that this man is a sinner." *J 9:24*

The following interchange then occurred:

MAN: Whether he be a sinner or not, I know not: one thing I know, that whereas I was blind, now I see.

PHARISEES: What did he to thee? How opened he thine eyes?

MAN: I have told you already, and ye did not hear; wherefore would ye hear it again? Will ye also be his disciples?

PHARISEES: Thou art his disciple; but we are Moses' disciples. We know that God spoke unto Moses; as for this fellow, we know not from whence he is.

MAN: Why herein is a marvellous thing, that ye know not from whence he is, and yet he hath opened mine eyes. Now we know that God heareth not sinners; but if any man be a worshipper of God, and doeth his will, him he heareth. Since the world began, was it not heard that nay man opened the eyes of one that was born blind. If this man were not of God, he could do nothing.

PHARISEES: Thou wast altogether born in sins, and dost thou teach us? J 9:25–34

The account concludes: "And they cast him out." J 9:34 This probably means that they cast him out of the synagogue, which was the likely site to have conducted the investigation.

It would be hard to find a more satisfactory evidence that Jesus was able to cure blindness:

1. The man had been born blind. This was doubted by the Pharisees, but was verified by interrogating his parents who testified, "We know that this is our son, and that he was born blind." J 9:20

2. The man did not seek any healing, and the healing was incidental to a chance religious question by Jesus' disciples, "Master, who did sin, this man, or his parents, that he was born blind?" J 9:2

3. The man's blindness was a notorious neighborhood fact: he was the local blind beggar. J 9:8–9 The Pharisees had ev-

ery incentive to disprove the miracle, and they acted shrewdly and ingeniously to do so. *J 9:15–34*

4. The man repeatedly testified under hostile questioning in substance as follows:

He put clay upon mine eyes, and I washed, and do see. *J 9:15 (J 9:11, 25, 30)*

5. The man was previously unacquainted with Jesus, and referred to him as simply, "A man that is called Jesus." *J 9:11*

After the Pharisees had investigated the incident, Jesus sought the man out and the following conversation ensued:

Jesus: Dost thou believe on the Son of God? *J 9:35*
Man: Who is he, Lord, [Sir] that I might believe on him? *J 9:36*
Jesus: Thou hast both seen him, and it is he that talketh with thee. *J 9:37*

It was only then, apparently several days later, that the man believed on Jesus. *J 9:38*

This incident is a gift of sight to a man who was blind from birth. The only way the incident can be dismissed is to dismiss the record as unreliable. The detail of the account is, however, likely and persuasive to any fair–minded examination. A fair–minded examination is not possible if it assumed a priori that no such miracle is possible, that Jesus could not give sight to the blind.

The Deaf Hear

There is a report of Jesus' healing a deaf person which is difficult to explain except as authentic:

And they bring unto him one that was deaf, and had an impediment in his speech; and they beseech him to put his hand upon him.

And he took him aside from the multitude, and put his fingers into his ears, and he spit, and touched his tongue; and looking up to heaven, he sighed, and saith unto him, "Ephphatha," that is, "Be opened."

And straightway his ears were opened, and the string of his tongue was loosed, and he spake plain.

And he charged them that they should tell no man, but the more he charged them, so much the more a great deal they published it; and were beyond measure astonished, saying, "He hath done all things well; he maketh both the deaf to hear, and the dumb to speak."
Mk 7:32–37

The report reminds one of the account of the restoration of sight to the blind man at Bethsaida. In both cases the following are true:

1. The man is brought by others who ask the healing. *Mk 8:22; Mk 7:32*
2. The man is completely passive. *Mk 8:22; Mk 7:32*
3. The man is taken aside by Jesus and the healing modality is administered. *Mk 8:23; Mk 7:33*
4. One of the healing modalities was saliva. *Mk 8:23; Mk 7:33*
5. One of the healing modalities was touching the affected organ. *Mk 8:25; Mk 7:33*
6. Jesus instructed that the healing was not to be publicized. *Mk 8:26; Mk 7:36*

There are two other instances when Jesus healed persons who were "dumb" but those are explainable in modern terms as instances of conversion hysteria: Matthew 9:32–34, "a dumb man possessed with a devil"; Matthew 12:22–24, "one possessed with a devil, blind and dumb." *(L 11:14)*

The Lame Walk

Jesus listed as part of the evidence of his mission which he sent to John the Baptist that "the lame walk." *Mt 11:5; L 7:22* We have detailed accounts of three episodes of healing to support this statement.

Jesus was in Jerusalem for a religious festival. While there, he visited a popular Jewish healing shrine probably called the "Sheep Pool." The shrine consisted of five porticoes built over or around an intermittent spring. In these porticoes lay "a great multitude of impotent folk, of blind, halt, withered, waiting for the moving of the water" in the spring. *J 5:3* There was a legend that "an angel went down at a certain season into the pool, and troubled the water: whosoever then first after the troubling of water stepped in was made whole of whatsoever disease he had." *J 5:4*

Jesus saw a man who had an infirmity thirty-eight years waiting for the spring to gush and asked him, "Wilt thou be made whole?" *J 5:6*

The man replied, "Sir, I have no man, when the water is troubled, to put me in the pool; but while I am coming, another steppeth down before me." *J 5:7*

Jesus said to the man, "Rise, take up thy bed, and walk." *J 5:8*

Jesus disregarded the requirements of the shrine and its legend and healed the man immediately even though it was the Sabbath. *J 5:9* In due course the Jewish legalists learned of the healing and confronted Jesus, complaining that "he had done these things on the Sabbath day." *J 5:16*

Jesus answered:

My Father worketh hitherto, and I work. *J 5:17*

This made matters worse since the complainers then said that he had thereby implied that God was his Father. *J 5:18*

Jesus replied:

Verily, verily, I say unto you, the Son can do nothing of himself, but what he seeth the Father do: for what things soever he doeth, these also doeth the Son likewise. *J 5:19*

To paraphrase freely, Jesus could not do the healing by himself, but since he sees the Father healing, Jesus in this case did likewise.

Perhaps the best remembered incident in which Jesus healed a lame person is the case of the paralytic man who was let down on his pallet in front of Jesus after his four bearers removed the roof tiles of the house where Jesus was teaching. *Mk 2:3–4; L 5:18–19* We have three accounts and they all agree that Jesus, seeing their faith, said to the man:

Mark	Matthew	Luke
Son,	Son, be of good cheer;	Man,
thy sins be forgiven thee. *Mk 2:5*	thy sins be forgiven thee. *Mt 9:2*	thy sins be forgiven thee. *L 5:20*

This statement immediately disturbed the "Pharisees and doctors of the law sitting by, which were come out of every town of Galilee, and Judea, and Jerusalem." *L 5:17* The word that came to their minds was blasphemy. *L 5:21*

Jesus wanted to get back to the man and said to them:

What reason ye in your hearts? Whether is easier, to say, "Thy sins be forgiven thee," or to say, "Rise up and walk?" But that ye may know that the Son of man hath power upon earth to forgive sins [turning to the man], I say unto thee, "Arise, and take up thy couch, and go into thine house." *L 5:22–24*

As with the man infirm thirty-eight years, Jesus was interested in healing the person, while the Jewish legalists were raising theological questions. Jesus deflected their theological questions by saying in substance, it was as easy for the Son of man to forgive sin as to heal and that his healing would be proof of his power as Son of man to forgive sins. He did not say the sin and sickness were identical. He did, however, summarily heal the man.

The demonstration of his power was awesome:

MARK	MATTHEW	LUKE
They	They	And they
were all amazed	marvelled,	were all amazed, and they
and glorified God, saying,	and glorified God,	glorified God, and were filled with fear, saying,
"We never saw it on this fashion."	which had given such power unto men.	"We have seen strange things today."
Mk 2:12	Mt 9:8	L 5:26

In the third episode of healing the lame, Jesus was again confronted with captious, irrelevant religious arguments. The president of the synagogue, where the healing had occurred, was appalled that it had occurred on the Sabbath day.

Jesus rejected this argument as hypocritical·

Thou hypocrite [play actor], doth not each one of you on the Sabbath loose his ox or his ass from the stall, and lead him away to watering? And, ought not this woman, being a daughter of Abraham, whom Satan hath bound, lo, these eighteen years, be loosed from this bond on the Sabbath day? L 13:15–16

Luke concludes his account of the episode by saying:

And when he had said these things, all his adversaries were ashamed; and all the people rejoiced for all the glorious things that were done by him. L 13:17

The people did not doubt the cure of this synagogue parishioner. After all they had probably seen her infirmity every Sabbath for eighteen years. We do not have an exact diagnosis of the woman's condition, only that she had "had a spirit of infirmity eighteen years, and was bowed together, and could in no wise lift up herself." *L 13:11* We do not have a precise statement of the nature of her cure except that "immediately she was made straight." *L 13:13*

Here Jesus did not have to demonstrate his power to meet theological objections. As the teacher in the synagogue for that Sabbath, he simply could not bear to see a woman, probably a devout woman since she is described as "a daughter of Abraham," suffer any longer.

This same sort of compassion is evident in the case of the man infirm thirty-eight years. John writes:

> When Jesus saw him lie, and *knew that he had been now a long time in that case*, he saith unto him, "Wilt thou be made whole?" *J 5:6*

Neither the man infirm thirty-eight years, nor the woman infirm eighteen years, asked Jesus' help. In the case of the man sick of the palsy, Jesus did not act until confronted with the man by his being lowered down in front of him.

These healings, "the lame walk", were simply signs that Jesus was indeed "he that should come." *Mt 11:3; L 7:19*

The Lepers are Cleansed

There were two occasions when Jesus healed lepers, and we have detailed accounts thereof.

Early in his ministry he healed one leper. We have three accounts of that healing. They agree that the man first knelt down before Jesus, although their exact phrasing varies:

MARK	MATTHEW	LUKE
. . . beseeching him, and kneeling down to him. *Mk 1:40*	. . . worshipped him . . . *Mt 8:2*	. . . fell on his face, and besought him. *L 5:12*

The accounts agree on what the leper said:

MARK	MATTHEW	LUKE
If thou wilt, thou canst make me clean. *Mk 1:40*	Lord, if thou wilt, thou canst make me clean. *Mt 8:2*	Lord, if thou wilt, thou canst make me clean. *L 5:12*

The accounts agree on what Jesus then did and said:

MARK	MATTHEW	LUKE
Jesus put forth his hand, and touched him, and saith unto him, "I will; be thou clean." *Mk 1:41*	Jesus put forth his hand, and touched him saying, "I will; be thou clean." *Mt 8:2*	And he put forth his hand, and touched him, saying, "I will; be thou clean." *L 5:13*

The accounts agree that the healing was immediate:

MARK	MATTHEW	LUKE
And as soon as he had spoken,	And	And

MARK (cont.)	MATTHEW (cont.)	LUKE (cont.)
immediately	immediately	immediately
the leprosy	his leprosy	the leprosy
departed from him,		departed from him.
and he was cleansed.	was cleansed.	L 5:13
Mk 1:42	Mt 8:3	

The accounts agree that Jesus then directed the leper to go to the priest and told him to make the offering ordained by Moses:

MARK	MATTHEW	LUKE
	But go thy way,	But go, and
Shew thyself	shew thyself	shew thyself
to the priest	to the priest,	to the priest,
and offer for	and offer	and offer for
thy cleansing		thy cleansing,
those things which	the gift that	according as
Moses commanded,	Moses commanded,	Moses commanded,
for a testimony	for a testimony	for a testimony
unto them.	unto them.	unto them.
Mk 1:44	Mt 8:4	L 5:14

The priest was to certify the healing to the people in accordance with the Mosaic rules for the cleansing of lepers. Under those rules the priest first examined the leper to see if he was healed:

> Then shall the priest command to take for him that is to be cleansed two birds alive and clean, and cedar wood, and scarlet, and hyssop. The priest shall command that one of the birds be killed in an earthen vessel over running water. As for the living bird, he shall take it, and the cedar wood, and the scarlet, and the hyssop, and shall dip them and the living bird in the blood of the bird that was killed over the running water; and he shall sprinkle upon him that is to be cleansed from the leprosy seven times, and shall pronounce him clean, and shall let the living bird loose into the open field. *Leviticus 14:4–7*

The leper is then to wash and shave and wait seven days and then wash and shave again. *Leviticus 14:8–9* The rules further required the leper to make the offering Jesus referred to:

> And on the eighth day he shall take two he lambs without blemish, and one ewe lamb of the first year without blemish, and three tenth deals of fine flour for a meat offering, mingled with oil, and one log of oil. *Leviticus 14:10*

This was then followed by the priest presenting the leper "before the Lord, at the door of the tabernacle of the congregation." *Leviticus 14:11* An elaborate procedure of sacrifice was then followed including anointing the leper with blood of one of the sacrificial animals and with the oil offering. *Leviticus 14:12–18* The rules conclude:

> And the priest shall offer the burnt offering and meat offering upon the altar; and the priest shall make an atonement for him, and he shall be clean. *Leviticus 14:20*

On another occasion Jesus instructed ten lepers:

> Go shew yourselves unto the priests. *L 17:14*

This meant they were to comply with the Levitical ritual of purification ordained by Moses. *Leviticus 14* It is to be noted, however, that this procedure did not heal them. Luke flatly states that they were healed *before* they got to the priests:

> And it came to pass, that, *as they went*, they were cleansed. *L 17:14*

This is consistent with what had happened in the case of the one leper. He was immediately healed in the presence of Jesus even before Jesus directed him to show himself to the priest. *Mk 1:42–44; Mt 8:3–4; L 5:13–14*

In the case of both the one leper and the ten lepers there were words and acts of faith on their part. These will be treated in detail elsewhere. Here it is sufficient to note these two instances when lepers were cleansed by Jesus.

Such cleansings were part of the proof of Jesus' mission which he sent to John the Baptist. Jesus directed John's messengers to report to John that "the lepers are cleansed." *Mt 11:5; L 7:22*

Healing a Woman

All three synoptic gospels tell the story of a woman whose type is still thriving twenty centuries later. Mark's description of her is timeless. He describes her as "a certain woman, which had an issue of blood twelve years, and had suffered many things of many physicians, and had spent all that she had, and was nothing bettered, but rather grew worse." *Mk 5:25–26 (Mt 9:20; L 8:43)*

The mechanism of healing was simple, and did not involve any act on Jesus' part. The woman simply approached him from behind as the multitude "thronged him" and touched the fringe of his garment. *Mk 5:24, 27; Mt 9:21; L 8:42, 44*

The condition of the healing was belief on her part that she could and would be healed since she murmured, subaudibly, "If I may touch but his clothes, I shall be whole." *Mk 5:28 (Mt 9:21)*

Luke states, clinically, the result: "Immediately her issue of blood stanched." *L 8:44 (Mk 5:29; Mt 9:22)* She felt healed. *Mk 5:29*

The contact with Jesus was so slight that Peter and the disciples present ridiculed Jesus' question, "Who touched me?" *L 8:45 (Mk 5:30)*

They said, "Master, the multitude throng thee and press thee, and sayest thou, 'Who touched me?'" *L 8:45 (Mk 5:31)*

Jesus replied, "Somebody hath touched me; for I perceive that virtue [power] is gone out of me." *L 8:46*

He turned to see who had touched him. *Mk 5:32* Mark's account then continues:

> But the woman, fearing and trembling, knowing what was done in her, came and fell down before him, and told him all the truth. *Mk 5:33 (L 8:47)*

She made this confession publicly, before all the people. *L 8:47* Jesus then said to her:

MARK	MATTHEW	LUKE
Daughter,	Daughter,	Daughter,
	be of	be of

MARK (cont.)	MATTHEW (cont.)	LUKE (cont.)
	good comfort,	good comfort,
thy faith hath	thy faith had	thy faith had
made thee whole;	made thee whole.	made thee whole;
go in peace,	*Mt 9:22*	go in peace.
and be whole of		*L 8:48*
thy plague.		
Mk 5:34		

By use of psychiatric terms like "conversion hysteria", modern understanding of the interaction of mind and body has made the story of the instant healing believable.

The point, however, is not that Jesus operated by healing principles then unknown. The point is that the woman's faith, her believing the healing could and would happen, was sufficient to tap Jesus' unique spiritual power.

Luke quotes Jesus as saying, "I perceive that *virtue* is gone out of me." *L 8:46* Modern translations substitute "power" for "virtue." Jesus' spiritual power healed the woman on contact, without any volition on his part and apparently without having been previously acquainted with the woman and her condition. She had simply heard about Jesus and decided to touch him. *Mk 5:27*

Jesus did not exploit the healings in any way. He simply explained briefly to the woman how she had been healed, saying, "Thy faith hath made thee whole." *Mk 5:34; Mt 9:22; L 8:48*

This is in accord with Jesus' basic teaching of the wonder-working power of faith:

> Have faith in God. For verily I say unto you, that whosoever shall say unto this mountain, "Be thou removed, and be thou cast into the sea,' and shall not doubt in his heart, but shall believe that those things which he saith shall come to pass, he shall have whatsoever he saith. *Mk 11:22–23*

THE EPILEPTIC BOY

The next day after his Transfiguration, Jesus healed an epileptic boy. *L 9:37* We have three accounts of the healing. The subject was a boy. A crowd had gathered, apparently because the disciples who had not gone up the mountain had been unable to heal the boy and there was some sort of a dispute about it going on with some Jewish religious intellectuals ("scribes").

As Jesus came up, he asked the scribes:

What question ye with them? *Mk 9:16*

The boy's father stepped out of the crowd and knelt before Jesus. *Mt 17:14* He said:

MARK	MATTHEW	LUKE
Master,	Lord,	Master,
I have brought	have mercy on	I beseech thee,
unto thee		look upon
my son,	my son,	my son,
		for he is
		mine only child.
which hath	for he is lunatic,	And, lo,
a dumb spirit;	and sore vexed:	a spirit
	for ofttimes	taketh him,
and wheresoever	he falleth into the fire,	and he suddenly
he taketh him,	and oft into the water.	crieth out;
he teareth him,		and it teareth him
and he foameth		that he foameth again,
and gnasheth		and bruising him
with his teeth,		hardly departeth
		from him.
and pineth away;		
and I spake to	And I brought him to	And I besought
thy disciples that they	thy disciples,	thy disciples
should cast him out,		to cast him out,
and they could not.	and they could not	and they could not.
Mk 9:17–18	cure him.	*L 9:38–40*
	Mt 17:15–16	

Jesus replied:

MARK	MATTHEW	LUKE
O faithless generation, how long shall I be with you? How long shall I suffer you? Bring him unto me. *Mk 9:19*	O faithless and perverse generation, how long shall I be with you? How long shall I suffer you? Bring him hither to me. *Mt 17:17*	O faithless and perverse generation, how long shall I be with you, and suffer you? Bring thy son hither. *L 9:41*

The accounts continue:

MARK	MATTHEW	LUKE
And they brought him unto him, and when he saw him, straightway the spirit tare him; and he fell on the ground, and wallowed foaming. *Mk 9:20*		And as he was yet a coming, the devil threw him down, and tare him. *L 9:42*
When Jesus saw that the people came running together,		
he rebuked the foul spirit, saying unto him, "Thou dumb and deaf spirit, I charge thee, come out of him,	And Jesus rebuked the devil,	And Jesus rebuked the unclean spirit,

MARK (cont.)	MATTHEW (cont.)	LUKE (cont.)
and enter no more into him."		
And the spirit cried, and rent him sore, and came out of him;	and he departed out of him;	
and he was as one dead, insomuch that many said,	and the child was cured	and healed the child, and delivered him again
"He is dead."	from that very hour.	to his father.
But Jesus took him by the hand, and lifted him up; and he arose.	*Mt 17:18*	*L 9:42*
Mk 9:25–27		

Matthew and Luke omit the following details that Mark reports. According to Mark as soon as they brought the boy Jesus questioned his father as follows:

How long is it ago since this came unto him? *Mk 9:21*

The father replied:

Of a child. And ofttimes it hath cast him into the fire, and into the waters, to destroy him; but if thou canst do any thing, have compassion on us, and help us. *Mk 9:21–22*

Jesus then said:

If thou canst believe, all things are possible to him that believeth. *Mk 9:23*

The father cried out, and said with tears:

Lord, I believe; help thou mine unbelief. *Mk 9:24*

The father had impliedly challenged Jesus' power. The father had said to Jesus, in effect, "*If you can*, heal him."

Jesus' answer to the doubting father hands his doubts back with a ring of irony: "*If thou canst believe*, all things are possible to him that believeth." *Mk 9:23*

The father was cut to the quick. Tears came. The classic affirmation of faith was made: "Lord, I believe; help thou mine unbelief." *Mk 9:24*

What did the father believe? That Jesus was able to heal his son. This was sufficient. The son was not required to believe; nor could he as the epileptic seizure racked him.

Later the disciples asked Jesus privately in a house why they had been unable to help the boy:

	MARK	MATTHEW
DISCIPLES:	Why could not we cast him out?	Why could not we cast him out?
JESUS:		Because of *your unbelief*: for verily I say unto you, if ye have faith as a grain of mustard seed, ye shall say unto this mountain, "Remove hence to yonder place," and it shall remove; and nothing shall be impossible unto you.
	This kind can come forth by nothing, but by prayer and fasting. *Mk 9:28–29*	Howbeit this kind goeth not out but by prayer and fasting. *Mt 17:19–21*

The reason why the disciples had been unable to heal the boy was unbelief, i.e., too little faith. This explains Jesus' earlier exasperated reference to this "faithless generation." *Mk 9:19* It was not just the doubting father. It was his own disciples. According to Matthew and Luke, Jesus not only called them a "faithless generation", he called them a "faithless *and* perverse generation." *Mt 17:17; L 9:41* Are Jesus' disciples still a "faithless and perverse generation"?

HEALING WAS NOT A PERSONAL PREROGATIVE OF JESUS ONLY

Since the healings were evidence that the Kingdom of God had arrived, Jesus' disciples also had power to heal. Healing was not a personal prerogative of Jesus only. He gave his twelve disciples authority:

MARK	MATTHEW	LUKE
And	And when	Then
he called	he had called	he called
unto him	unto him	
the Twelve,	his twelve disciples,	his twelve disciples together
and began		
to send them forth		
by two and two,		
and gave them	he gave them	and gave them
power	power	power and authority
over	against	over
unclean spirits.	unclean spirits,	all devils, and
Mk 6:7	to cast them out	to cure diseases.
		And he sent them
		to preach
		the Kingdom of God,
	and to heal	and to heal
	all manner of sickness	the sick.
	and all man of disease.	*L 9:1–2*
	Mt 10:1	

Mark and Luke report:

MARK	LUKE
And they went out	And they departed, and went through the towns,
and preached that	preaching
men should repent;	the gospel,
and they cast out	
many devils,	

Mark (cont.)
and anointed with oil
many that were sick,
and healed them.
Mk 6:12–13

Luke (cont.)

and healing everywhere.
L 9:6

Later on Jesus appointed another seventy disciples and sent them out in twos as advance parties "into every city and place, whether he himself would come." *L 10:1* He gave them lengthy and detailed instructions, which included the following:

> And into whatsoever city ye enter, and they receive you, eat such things as are set before you, and heal the sick that are therein, and say unto them, "The Kingdom of God is come nigh unto you." *L 10:8–9*

The Seventy reported back:

> And the Seventy returned again with joy, saying, "Lord, even the devils are subject unto us through thy name." *L 10:17*

Jesus replied:

> I beheld Satan as lightning fall from heaven.

> Behold, I give unto you power to tread on serpents and scorpions, and over all the power of the enemy; and nothing shall by any means hurt you. Notwithstanding in this *rejoice not, that the spirits are subject unto you; but rather rejoice, because your names are written in heaven.* *L 10:18–20*

The focus was not on the power of the Seventy over devils and spirits, but on their names being "written in heaven." Jesus had instructed the Seventy to say to the sick, "The Kingdom of God is come nigh unto you." *L 10:9* Just as with Jesus' own healings the emphasis is not on the inherently sensational acts of healing but on the advent of the Kingdom of God.

Jesus Did Not Exploit His Healings

Jesus did not use his healings to publicize himself or his mission. He did not want his healings publicized. When he healed the man infirm thirty-eight years, even the man, himself, did not know that it was Jesus who had healed him: "And he that was healed wist [knew] not who it was: for Jesus had conveyed himself away, a multitude being in that place." *J 5:13*

On at least four occasions Jesus gave explicit instructions that the healing involved was not to be told:

	MARK	MATTHEW	LUKE
1. LEPER	See thou say nothing to any man; but go thy way, shew thyself to the priest. *Mk 1:44*	See thou tell no man; but go thy way, shew thyself to the priest. *Mt 8:4*	Tell no man; but go, and shew thyself to the priest. *L 5:14*
2. TWO BLIND MEN		See that no man know it. *Mt 9:30*	
3. DEAF MUTE WITH SPEECH IMPEDIMENT	And he charged them that they should tell no man. *Mk 7:36*		
4. BLIND MAN NEAR BETHSAIDA	Neither go into the town, nor tell it to any in the town. *Mk 8:26*		

Human nature being what it is, these instructions of Jesus were disregarded. The two blind men "spread abroad his fame in all that country." *Mt 9:31* The leper was told to "say nothing to any man." *Mk 1:44* Instead, as Mark reports:

> But he went out, and began to publish it much, and to blaze abroad the matter, insomuch that Jesus could no more openly enter into the city, but was without in desert places; and they came to him from every quarter. *Mk 1:45 (L 5:15)*

Luke closes his report of this commotion with Jesus' own reaction to it:

> But so much the more went there a fame abroad of him; and great multitudes came together to hear, and to be healed by him of their infirmities. And *he withdrew* himself into the wilderness, and prayed. *L 5:15–16*

Jesus did not exploit his healings; instead he withdrew from the bustling countryside to the wilderness to pray alone. The people "wondered every one at all the things which Jesus did" and "they were all amazed at the mighty power of God." *L 9:43*

Matthew states that "the multitude wondered when they saw the dumb to speak, the maimed to be whole, the lame to walk, and the blind to see; and *they glorified the God of Israel.*" *Mt 15:31*

When Jesus healed the man sick of the palsy, Matthew states that:

> But when the multitudes saw it, they marvelled, and *glorified God*, which had given such power unto men. *Mt 9:8 (Mk 2:12; L 5:26)*

The multitudes did not glorify Jesus, but "the God of Israel." When the blind man was healed near Jericho, the man followed Jesus "glorifying God, and all the people, when they saw it, gave praise unto God." *L 18:43* The woman infirm eighteen years, bowed and unable to stand straight, when healed, did not praise Jesus, but instead "glorified God." *L 13:13*

One of the group of ten lepers healed returned to Jesus to give thanks and fell down at his feet, but "with a loud voice glorified God", not Jesus. *L 17:15–16* Jesus singled out for approval this leper who "returned to give glory to God." *L 17:18*

Jesus did not exploit his healings. The people understood this. Both the people and Jesus gave the glory for his healings to the God of Israel, not to Jesus personally.

Jesus Did Not Usually Initiate His Healings

Not only did Jesus give explicit instructions that his healings were not to be told, he usually did not initiate the healing. Of the fourteen incidents of healing reported in some detail in the Gospels, in only four incidents did Jesus initiate the incident:

	MARK	MATTHEW	LUKE	JOHN
1. MAN INFIRM THIRTY- EIGHT YEARS				When Jesus saw him lie, and knew that he had been now a long time in that case, he saith unto him, "Wilt thou be made whole?" *J 5:6*
2. MAN WITH WITHERED HAND	And he saith unto the man which had the withered hand, "Stand forth." *Mk 3:3*	Then saith he to the man, "Stretch forth thine hand." *Mt 12:13*	But he knew their thoughts, and said to the man which had the withered hand, "Rise up and stand forth in the midst." *L 6:8*	

	MARK (cont.)	MATT. (cont.)	LUKE (cont.)	JOHN (cont.)
3. MAN BORN BLIND (cont.)			.	Jesus was asked a theological question involving healing. Jesus then acted to heal the man in order to demonstrate that Jesus was in the world as "the light of the world." *J 9:2–7*
4. WOMAN INFIRM EIGHTEEN YEARS			And when Jesus saw her, he called her to him, and said unto her, "Woman thou art loosed from thine infirmity." *L 13:12*	

In two of the four incidents in which Jesus initiated the healing, the place was a synagogue and the time a Sabbath. (man with withered hand, *Mk 3:1–2; Mt 12:9–10; L 6:6–7*; woman with infirm eighteen years, *L 13:10*) In the case of the man with the withered hand, it is expressly stated that the healing arose out of Jesus' continuing controversy with the scribes and Pharisees over the Sabbath day:

MARK	MATTHEW	LUKE
And they	And they	And the scribes and Pharisees
watched him,	asked him, saying,	watched him,
whether he	"Is it lawful	whether he
would heal him	to heal	would heal
on the Sabbath day,	on the Sabbath days?"	on the Sabbath day,
that they might	that they might	that they might find
accuse	accuse	an accusation
him.	him.	against him.
Mk 3:2	*Mt 12:10*	*L 6:7*

In the case of the woman infirm eighteen years, the background of the Sabbath day controversy is also evident. *L 13:14–16*

In the case of the man born blind, the healing occurred on a Sabbath, and the Pharisees argued that Jesus was "not of God, because he keepeth not the Sabbath day." *J 9:14, 16* Apparently the Sabbath day controversy was in the background of this healing, too, since Jesus acted after a chance question of his disciples gave him an opportunity to show he was in the world as "the light of the world" *(J 9:5)* by offering proof thereof in the form of a work of God, to wit: the granting of sight to the man. In short, despite the argument of the Pharisees based on Sabbath breaking, Jesus was indeed a man "of God" as this mighty work showed.

In the case of the man infirm thirty-eight years, Jesus' purpose was simple: compassion.

In the other ten of the fourteen incidents of healing, Jesus was asked, often repeatedly, to do the healing:

1. Leper. He knelt before Jesus and beseeched him to "make me clean." *Mk 1:40, Mt 8:2; Luke 5:12*

2. Man sick of palsy (a paralytic). Four men brought the man on a pallet, uncovered part of the roof tiles of the house where Jesus was, and let him down into Jesus' presence. *Mk 2:3–4; Mt 9:1–2; L 5:18–19*

3. Centurion's servant sick of palsy (paralyzed). Either the Roman centurion himself or Jewish synagogue elders acting for him asked Jesus to heal the servant. *Mt 8:5–6; L 7:3–5*

4. Woman with issue of blood. The woman touched the border of Jesus' garment for the purpose of being healed. *Mk 5:27–28; Mt 9:20–21; L 8:44, 47*

5. Two blind men. They followed Jesus as he walked along, crying, "Thou son of David, have mercy on us", and followed him into the house. *Mt 9:27–28*

6. Deaf man with a speech impediment. Some person brought the man to Jesus and they beseeched him "to put his hand upon him." *Mk 7:32*

7. Blind man near Bethsaida. Someone brought the man to Jesus and "besought him to touch him." *Mk 8:22*

8. Epileptic boy. His father begged Jesus to have mercy upon his son by healing him. *Mt 17:15 (Mk 9:17; L 9:38)*

9. Ten lepers. The lepers standing in a village street saw Jesus before he saw them and cried out, "Jesus, Master, have mercy on us." *L 17:12–14*

10. One or two blind men near Jericho. He or they were sitting by the wayside and when he or they heard Jesus was passing by, he or they cried out, "Jesus, thou son of David, have mercy on me" *(Mk 10:47; L 18:38)* or "Have mercy on us, O Lord, thou son of David." *(Mt 20:30)*

In ten of the fourteen episodes of healing recorded in some detail in the Gospels, Jesus did not initiate the healing. In the remaining four episodes, there were special circumstances that impelled Jesus to exercise his healing powers. In three of those four episodes, Jesus' controversy with the Jewish legalists over the observance of the Sabbath day was involved. From the viewpoint of those legalists even a great healing on a Sabbath was a prohibited act of work.

Jesus' Modalities of Healing

Jesus' usual modality of healing was either touching *or* use of a verbal formula. Jesus' first healing, the healing of Peter's wife's mother, is a case in point:

MARK	MATTHEW	LUKE
And forthwith, when they were come out of the synagogue, they entered into the house of Simon and Andrew, with James and John.	And when Jesus was come into Peter's house,	And he arose out of the synagogue, and entered into Simon's house.
But Simon's wife's mother lay sick of a fever, and anon they tell him of her.	he saw his wife's mother laid, and sick of a fever.	And Simon's wife's mother was taken with a great fever, and they besought him for her.
And he came and *took her by the hand, and lifted her up;* and immediately the fever left her,	And he *touched her hand,* and the fever left her; and	And he *stood over her and rebuked the fever,* and it left her; and immediately
and she ministered unto them.	she arose, and ministered unto them.	she arose and ministered unto them.
Mk 1:29–31	*Mt 8:14–15*	*L 4:38–39*

The healing modalities for the other diseases were as follows:

1. A leper:

MARK	MATTHEW	LUKE
Jesus "put forth his hand	"Jesus put forth his hand,	"And he put forth his hand

977

MARK (cont.)	MATTHEW (cont.)	LUKE (cont.)
and touched him,"	and touched him,	and touched him,
and said,	saying,	saying,
"I will;	'I will'	'I will;
be thou clean."	be thou clean.'"	be thou clean.'"
Mk 1:41	*Mt 8:3*	*L 5:13*

2. A man sick of the palsy:

MARK	MATTHEW	LUKE
"Son,	"Son,	"Man,
	be of	
	good cheer,	
thy sins	thy sins	thy sins
be forgiven	be forgiven	are forgiven
thee."	thee."	thee."
"I say unto thee,		"I say unto
Arise, and	"Arise,	thee,
take up	take up	Arise, and
thy bed, and	thy bed, and	take up
go thy way	go	thy couch, and
into	into	go into
thine house."	thine house."	thine house."
Mk 2:5–11	*Mt 9:2, 6*	*L 5:20, 24*

3. A man infirm thirty-eight years:

"Rise, take up thy bed and walk." *J 5:8*

4. A man with a withered hand:

MARK	MATTHEW	LUKE
"Stretch	"Stretch	"Stretch
forth	forth	forth
thine hand."	thine hand."	thy hand."
Mk 3:5	*Mt 12:13*	*L 6:10*

5. A centurion's servant who was sick of the palsy:

The servant was not present and Jesus talked either to the centurion (Mark) or the Jewish elders or friends acting for the centurion (Luke). Jesus neither did or said anything to effect the healing. He simply told the centurion it had been done. *Mt 8:13 (L:7:10)*

6. A woman with issue of blood for twelve years:

The woman came behind Jesus and touched his garment. *Mk 5:27; Mt 9:20; L 8:44* The healing was instantaneous and before the healing Jesus did not say anything to her or touch her. *Mk 5:25–34; Mt 9:20–22; L 8:43–48*

7. Two blind men:

"Then touched he their eyes, saying, 'According to your faith, be it unto you.'" *Mt 9:29*

8. A deaf mute man with a speech impediment:

"And he took him aside from the multitude, and put his fingers into his ears, and he spit, and touched his tongue; and looking up to heaven, he sighed, and saith unto him, 'Ephphatha,' that is, 'Be opened.'" *Mk 7:33–34*

9. A blind man at Bethsaida:

"And he took the blind man by the hand, and led him out of the town; and when he had spit on his eyes, and put his hands upon him, he asked him if he saw ought. And he looked up and said, 'I see men as trees, walking.' After that he put his hands again upon his eyes, and made him look up; and he was restored, and saw every man clearly." *Mk 8:23–25*

10. An epileptic boy:

MARK	MATTHEW	LUKE
	"And Jesus	"And Jesus
"Thou dumb and	rebuked	rebuked
deaf spirit,	the devil, and	the unclean spirit
I charge thee,	he departed	and
come out of him,	out of him;	
and enter no more	and the child	healed
into him."	was cured	the child
Mk 9:25	from that	
	very hour."	
	Mt 17:18	
"But Jesus		
took him		and delivered
by the hand,		him again
and lifted		to his father."
him up;		L 9:42
and he arose."		
Mk 9:27		

11. A man born blind:

"When he had thus spoken, he spat on the ground, and made clay of the spittle; and he anointed the eyes of the blind man with the clay, and said unto him, 'Go wash in the pool of Siloam' (which is by interpretation 'Sent'). He went his way therefore, and washed, and came seeing." J 9:6–7

12. A woman infirm eighteen years, bowed and unable to stand straight:

"And when Jesus saw her, he called her to him, and said unto her, 'Woman thou art loosed from thine infirmity.' And he laid his hands on her, and immediately she was made straight, and glorified God. L 13:12–13

13. Ten lepers:

"And when he saw them, he said unto them, 'Go shew yourselves unto the priests.' And it came to pass, that, as they went, they were cleansed." *L 17:14*

14. One or two blind men near Jericho:

MARK	MATTHEW	LUKE
"And Jesus stood still, and commanded him to be called."	"And Jesus stood still, and	"And Jesus stood, and commanded him to be brought unto him; and when he was come near,
"And Jesus answered and said unto him, 'What wilt thou that I should do unto thee?'	called them and said, 'What will ye that I shall do unto you?'	he asked him, saying, 'What wilt thou that I shall do unto thee?'
"The blind man said unto him, 'Lord, that I might receive my sight.'	"they say unto him, 'Lord, that our eyes may be opened.'	"And he said, 'Lord, that I may receive my sight.'
"And Jesus said unto him, Go thy way; thy faith hath made thee whole.'" *Mk 10:49, 51–52*	"So Jesus had compassion on them, and touched their eyes; . . ." *Mt 20:32–34*	"And Jesus said unto him, 'Receive thy sight; thy faith hath saved thee.'" *L18:40–42*

The modality of healing was not the critical factor. Jesus touched the one leper; he sent the ten lepers to the priests. (*One leper:* Mk 1:41; Mt 8:3; L 5:13) (*Ten lepers:* L 17:14) In each case the healing followed.

The woman with the issue of blood for twelve years touched Jesus' garment and was healed, but the active agent in the healing was not the touching itself but rather her faith in touching since she was saying to herself, "If I may touch but his clothes, I shall be whole." *Mk 5:28 (Mt 9:21)*

In the case of the blind he healed, Jesus always seemed to have touched their eyes:

1. The two blind men. *Mt 9:29*
2. Blind man at Bethsaida. *Mk 8:23–35*
3. Man born blind. *J 9:6*
4. Two blind men near Jericho. *Mt 20:34*

The only apparent exception is in Mark and Luke's account of the blind man near Jericho. They do not record a touching. *Mk 10:46–52; L 18:35–43* Matthew does. *Mt 20:34* However, Matthew states that there were two blind men near Jericho, and Mark and Luke in what appear to be parallel accounts describe one. *Mt 20:30; Mk 10:46; L 18:35*

The touching does not appear to have been the crucial factor in the healing, any more than the spittle used in the case of the man born blind and the blind man at Bethsaida. *J 9:6; Mk 8:23* The agent, spittle, was not used in the case of the two sets of two blind men described in Matthew 9:27–31 and 20:30–34, respectively.

The basic reason is what he said to the first set of two blind men, "According to your faith, be it unto you." *Mt 9:29*

As Jesus responded to the faith of the healed, he touched others besides the blind. He "laid his hands on" the woman infirm eighteen years. *L 13:13* He touched the tongue of the deaf mute and put his fingers into his ears. *Mk 7:33*

This leaves two categories of healed persons. To the man sick of palsy, the man infirm thirty-eight years, and the man with a withered hand, he simply said, in effect, act upon your healing: "Take up thy bed", or "Stretch forth thine hand." (*Man sick of palsy:* Mk 2:11; Mt 9:6; L 5:24) (*Man infirm thirty-eight years:* J 5:8) (*Man with a withered hand:* Mk 3:5; Mt 12:13; L 6:10)

The second category are those healed by indirection and without personal contact. The epileptic boy was healed at his father"s request; the centurion's servant was healed by a request either of the centurion himself, or Jewish elders acting for the centurion. (*Boy:* Mk 9:17–18; Mt 17:15–16; L 9:38–40) (*Servant:* Mt 8:5–6; L 7:3–5)

Minute analysis of Jesus' modalities of healing helps to strip away the background details from Jesus' power to heal and to erase easy explanations of that power. We must, however, in the last analysis, defer to Jesus' own explanation of how he healed.

Sometimes, but not often, we are left with the bare record that he laid hands on the sick and healed them:

> Now when the sun was setting, all they that had any sick with divers diseases brought them unto him; and he laid his hands on every one of them, and healed them. L 4:40

> And he could there [in his hometown synagogue] do no mighty work, save that he laid his hands upon a few sick folk, and healed them. And he marvelled because of their unbelief. Mk 6:5–6

The laying on his hands was not necessarily a healing modality for Jesus. It may have been simply a blessing which was given quite apart from the healing since he did lay hands on children simply to bless them. Mk 10:16; Mt 19:15

The laying on of hands and other modalities of healing are simply incidental details. Jesus' own view was that faith was the indispensable condition for the exercise of his healing power. See "Jesus' Own Explanation Of His Healings", pp.990–992.

Were Jesus' Modalities of Healing Sufficient of Themselves to Heal?

The modalities of healing used by Jesus were not sufficient by themselves to heal. The healings required acts or words of faith on the part of the healed or their surrogates:

1. A leper:

His words and acts of faith were:

MARK	MATTHEW	LUKE
	"Lord,	"Lord,
"If thou wilt,	if thou wilt,	if thou wilt,
thou canst	thou canst	thou canst
make me clean."	make me clean."	make me clean."
"beseeching him,		"fell on his
and kneeling	"worshipped him"	face, and
down to him."	[knelt]	besought him."
Mk 1:40	*Mt 8:2*	*L 5:12*

2. A man sick with the palsy:

We have no record that he said anything but his acts of faith were:

MARK	MATTHEW	LUKE
"And immediately	"And	"And immediately
he arose,	he arose,	he rose up
		before them,
took up the bed,		and took up
		whereon he lay,
and went forth	and departed	and departed
before them all."	to his house."	to his own house,
Mk 2:12	*Mt 9:7*	glorifying God."
		L 5:25

3. A man infirm thirty-eight years:

The man did not express any words of faith, but simply explained to Jesus that he had no one to help him get into the healing pool. *J 5:7* The man did act in faith on Jesus' instruction to, "Rise, and take up thy bed, and walk" in that he "took up his bed, and walked." *J 5:8–9*

4. A man with a withered hand:

The man said nothing, but he did act in faith:

MARK	MATTHEW	LUKE
		"And he arose and stood forth." *L 6:8*
"And he stretched it [his hand] out, and his hand was restored whole as the other." *Mk 3:5*	"And he stretched it [his hand] forth; and it was restored whole, like as the other." *Mt 12:13*	"And he did so [stretched forth his hand] and his hand was restored whole as the other." *L 6:10*

5. A centurion's servant who was sick of the palsy:

The servant was not present and in his absence the centurion besought Jesus to heal his servant and uttered the words of faith. *Mt 8:5–9* According to Luke the centurion did the beseeching and relayed his words of faith through intermediaries. *L 7:3–8* The words were:

MATTHEW	LUKE
"Lord	"Lord, trouble not thyself: for

MATTHEW (cont.)	LUKE (cont.)
I am not	I am not
worthy that	worthy that
thou shouldest	thou shouldest
come under	enter under
my roof;	my roof.
	Wherefore neither
	thought I myself
	worthy to come
but	unto thee; but
speak the word	say in a word,
only,	
and my servant	and my servant
shall be	shall be
healed."	healed."
Mt 8:8	*L 7:6–7*

6. A woman with issue of blood twelve years.

This woman acted in faith by touching Jesus' garment, and before the healing said to herself (or just thought) that this touching would produce her healing:

MARK	MATTHEW	LUKE
"If I may	"'If I may	"She declared
		unto him
		before
		all the people
		for what cause
		she had
touch but	but touch	touched him,
his clothes,	his garment,	and how she
I shall	I shall	was healed
be whole."	be whole."	immediately.
	Mt 9:21	*L 8:47*

"When she had
heard of Jesus,

MARK (cont.)	MATTHEW (cont.)	LUKE (cont.)
came in the press behind,	"came behind him,	"came behind him,
and touched	and touched the hem of	and touched the border of
his garment."	his garment."	his garment."
Mk 5:27	*Mt 9:20*	*L 8:44*

7. Two blind men:

These two men followed Jesus into a house, crying, "thou son of David, have mercy upon us." Jesus then asked them, "Believe ye that I am able to do this?" Their answer was, "Yea, Lord." *Mt 9:27–28*

8. A deaf mute man with a speech inpediment:

Others "they" brought the man to Jesus and besought him "to put his hand upon him." *Mk 7:32* The man himself simply submitted to Jesus' touching. *Mk 7:33*

9. A blind man at Bethsaida:

The words and acts of faith were those of the man's friends, "they bring a blind man unto him, and besought him to touch him." *Mk 8:22* The man himself was passive, simply allowing Jesus to lead him out of town and submitting to his therapy. *Mk 8:23–25*

10. An epileptic boy:

The words and acts of faith were not those of the boy, but his father:

MARK	MATTHEW	LUKE
"Master,	"Lord,	"Master,
I have brought unto thee	have mercy on	I beseech thee, look upon

MARK (cont.)	MATTHEW (cont.)	LUKE (cont.)
my son, which	my son for	my son: for
has a	he is	he is
	lunatic,	mine only child.
dumb spirit.	and sore vexed."	And lo,
	Mt 17:15	a spirit
(with tears)		taketh him,
"Lord, I believe		and he suddenly
help thou		crieth out."
mine unbelief."		*L 9:38–39*
Mk 9:17, 24		
"And they brought	Boy's father	
him unto him."	knelt before	
Mk 9:20	Jesus.	
	Mt 17:14	

11. A man born blind:

We have no record of any words spoken by the man before he was healed. His acts of faith were submitting to Jesus' therapy: "He went his way therefore, and washed, and came seeing." *J 9:7*

12. A woman infirm eighteen years, bowed and unable to stand straight:

We have no record of any words spoken by her, and her acts of faith were simply submitting to Jesus' therapy. *L 13:11–13*

13. Ten lepers:

They said, "Jesus, Master, have mercy on us." *L 17:13* Their acts of faith were that they came to meet Jesus, asked his help and then submitted to his directions and went to the priests. *L 17:12–14*

14. One or two blind men near Jericho:

Their words and acts of faith were:

MARK	MATTHEW	LUKE
"Jesus, thou son of David, have mercy upon me."	"Have mercy on us, O Lord, thou son of David."	"Jesus, thou son of David, have mercy upon me."
"Thou son of David, have mercy on me."	"Have mercy on us, O Lord, thou son of David."	"Thou son of David, have mercy on me."
"Lord, that I might receive my sight." *Mk 10:47, 48, 51*	"Lord, that our eyes may be opened." *Mt 20:30, 31, 33*	Lord, that I may receive my sight." *L 18:38, 39, 41*
"And he casting away his garment, rose and came to Jesus," *Mk 10:50*	[They submitted to Jesus; touching.] *Mt 20:34*	[The man allowed others to bring him near Jesus.] *L 18:40*

In each of the fourteen cases analyzed the person or their surrogates either acted or spoke in faith and usually did both.

Jesus' Own Explanation of His Healing

Faith without works is dead, so people Jesus healed usually either had to act or say something. Jesus, several times, gave us his own explanation of his healings.

In the case of the woman with the issue of blood twelve years, Jesus said:

MARK	MATTHEW	LUKE
Daughter,	Daughter,	Daughter,
	be of good	be of good
	comfort;	comfort:
thy faith hath	thy faith hath	thy faith hath
made thee whole;	made thee whole.	made thee whole;
go in peace,	*Mt 9:22*	go in peace.
and be whole of		*L 8:48*
thy plague.		
Mk 5:34		

Jesus flatly said, "Thy faith hath made thee whole." He said nothing of the woman touching his garment, although the fact that she did touch it was a manifestation of her healing faith. Jesus did not, however, question the real existence of her "plague"—which is archaic King James language for her hemorrhages.

Nor did Jesus question the real existence of the leprosy afflicting the ten lepers. He, of course, did not have available or use sulfones and antibiotics now used for treatment. He did, however, instruct the lepers to go to the priests, presumably to follow the cleansing procedure prescribed in Leviticus 14. But the healing occurred "as they went" to the priests. *L 17:14*

Only one leper turned back to thank Jesus. That man was a Samaritan, a sort of half-Jew who Jesus described as "this stranger" meaning "this outlander." *L 17:18* Jesus said to him, "Arise, go thy way; *thy faith* hath made thee whole." *L 17:19*

However, as with the woman with the issue of blood, the healed manifested their healing faith by acting: in one case, touching Jesus' garment; and in the other case, going to the priests after asking Jesus for mercy. *(Woman: Mk 5:27; Mt 9:20; L 8:44) (Lepers: L 17:13–14)*

Jesus did not doubt that Bartimaeus, the son of Timaeus, was afflicted with a real condition, blindness. *Mk 10:46–52; L 18:35–43* The dialogue of Jesus and Bartimaeus went this way:

	MARK	LUKE
JESUS:	What wilt thou that I should do unto thee?	What wilt thou that I should do unto thee?
BARTIMAEUS:	Lord, that I might receive my sight.	Lord, that I may receive my sight.
JESUS:	Go thy way; thy faith hath made thee whole. *Mk 10:51–52*	Receive thy sight; thy faith hath saved thee. *L 18:41–42*

Jesus made the same statement that he had made to the woman and the returned lepers, "Thy faith hath made thee whole." Again, the faith had been manifested in tangible acts on the part of the healed: in this case, he asked mercy, he came when Jesus called and he specifically asked to be healed. *Mk 10:47–48, 50–51; L 18:38–39, 40–41*

When the time for specific healing request arrived, Bartimaeus addressed Jesus, not as "thou son of David", but simply as "Lord", a term of respect like "Sir", "Master", or "Rabbi." *Mk 10:48, 51; L 18:37, 41* The woman healed said nothing as to Jesus' status; in fact she did not say anything until questioned. *Mk 5:33; L 8:47* The ten lepers had not assigned any particular title to Jesus, they only addressed him with respect:

Jesus, Master, have mercy on us. *L 17:13*

The faith the lepers, the woman and Bartimaeus had, was not in Jesus' messianic role but simply that he could in fact heal them if he would. And he did. Not through any act of therapy but simply by the exercise of his own inherent power.

That power was invoked in accordance with the spiritual laws of the universe which he elsewhere stated generally as follows:

MARK	MATTHEW
Have faith in God.	
For verily	Verily
I say unto you,	I say unto you,
	if ye have faith,
	and doubt not,
	ye shall not only do
	this which is done
	to the fig tree,
that whosoever shall say	but also if ye shall say
unto this mountain,	unto this mountain,
"Be thou removed,	"Be thou removed,
and be thou cast	and be thou cast
into the sea,"	into the sea,"
and shall not doubt	
in his heart,	
but shall believe that	
those things which he saith	
shall come to pass,	
he shall have	it shall be done.
whatsoever he saith.	
Therefore I say unto you,	And all things,
what things soever ye desire,	whatsoever ye shall ask
when ye pray,	in prayer,
believe	believing,
that ye receive them,	
and ye shall have them.	ye shall receive.
Mk 11:22–24	

To sum up, Jesus' healings were simply specific applications of the foregoing general spiritual law governing man and the universe.

Sickness Is Not Sin;
Sin May Cause Sickness

It should be noted that sin was not a part of Jesus' explanation of his healings. In the case of the man born blind, the references to sin focus on Jesus being "a sinner" in the eyes of the objecting Jews. They told the healed man, "Give God the praise; we know that this man is a sinner." *J 9:24* Some of the Pharisees said, "This man is not of God, because he keepeth not the Sabbath day." *J 9:16*

It is true, of course, that even Jesus' disciples assumed that sin had been the cause of the blind man's blindness. They asked Jesus, "Master, who did sin, this man, or his parents, that he was born blind?" *J 9:2*

Jesus answered, "Neither hath this man sinned, nor his parents: . . ." Jesus' own theology did not equate sin and disease. That was the old error of these "disciples of Moses" who said to the blind man, "'Thou wast altogether born in sins,' . . . ." *J 9:28, 34*

Jesus denied the blind man's sin, but said to the man sick of the palsy, "Son, thy sins be forgiven thee." *Mk 2:5* So far as Jesus was concerned, the healing formula could either "Thy sins be forgiven thee." or "Arise, take up thy bed, and walk."

Jesus said to the objecting scribes: "Whether is it easier to say to the sick of the palsy, 'Thy sins be forgiven thee;' or to say, 'Arise, and take up thy bed, and walk?'" *Mk 2:9*

To end their blasphemy objections Jesus then said to the man, "I say unto thee, arise, and take up thy bed, and go thy way unto thine house." *Mk 2:11* This was the healing formula, not Jesus' introductory remark, "Son, thy sins be forgiven thee." *Mk 2:5* Before Jesus got further with the matter, he was accused of speaking blasphemies, and proceeded to utter the healing formula after saying to the objectors that the healing would be done "that ye may know that the Son of man hath power on earth to forgive sins." *Mk 2:10* (*Mt 9:6; L 5:24*)

The introductory statement of sin appears to have been irrelevant to the healing. For Jesus disease was not sin. The fact that disease was not sin is different from the fact that Satan may act through disease. Jesus recognized that disease may be, in current intelligence terminology, a covert operation of Satan. Jesus said of the woman who had been infirm eighteen years and was bowed together that "this woman, being a daughter of Abraham, *whom Satan hath bound,* lo, these eighteen years." *L 13:16*

It is to be noted that the woman's condition was perhaps psychiatric or psychological since Luke describes her not as being simply infirm but having had "a *spirit* of infirmity." *L 13:11* However, in the case of the epileptic boy Luke describes his malady as "a spirit taketh him." *L 9:39 (Mk 9:17 "a dumb spirit"; Mt 17:15 "lunatic")*

There is no easy explanation for Jesus' statement to the man infirm thirty-eight years whom Jesus healed at the Pool of Bethesda. When Jesus met him later in the Temple Jesus said to him, "Behold, thou art made whole; sin no more, lest a worse thing come unto thee." *J 5:14*

This statement clearly implies that this man's infirmity was causally related to his sin. For example, a man might acquire a venereal disease by the sin of adultery. The disease itself would not be sin, and such a disease might be acquired without sin by the intercourse between married people.

It is interesting that Jesus used almost identical language to the woman taken in adultery as he did to the man infirm thirty-eight years. He said to her, "Neither do I condemn thee; go, and sin no more." *J 8:11*

Jesus did not deny the reality of the woman's sin by saying she had merely been sexually active. He did, however, tell her to stop her adultery: "Sin no more."

The problem with the man infirm thirty-eight years is that we do not know his sin. We do know his infirmity resulted from it. *J 5:14* It is, however, clear from Jesus' flat statement to his disciples about the man born blind, "Neither hath *this* man sinned, nor *his* parents," *(J 9:3),* that disease does not *necessarily* result from sin. The man infirm thirty-eight years is the converse case that is obvious that disease *may* result from sin either of the afflicted one or others.

JESUS' HEALINGS DID NOT TURN ON THE HEALED PERSON'S KNOWLEDGE OF JESUS' SPECIAL STATUS

Jesus himself explained three of his healings by the statement that, "Thy faith hath made thee whole." *(Woman with issue of blood: Mk 5:34, Mt 9:22, L 8:46) (Ten lepers: L 17:19) (Bartimaeus: Mk 10:52; L 18:42)*

In these cases the healings did not turn on Jesus being called upon as the Messiah. The woman said nothing. *Mk 5:25–29; Mt 9:20–22; L 8:43–44* The ten lepers said, "Jesus, Master, have mercy upon us." *L 17:13* "Master" is a term of respect, not a Messianic title.

The two blind men cried out, "Thou son of David, have mercy on us." *Mt 9:27* But when Jesus got down to the healing, the dialogue went this way:

JESUS: Believe ye that I am able to do this?
TWO BLIND MEN: Yea, Lord. *Mt 9:28*

"Lord" here is not a Messianic title, only a term of respect. Whatever conclusion is drawn from the words of the two blind men and the ten lepers, it is clear that a sick person to be healed did not have to call upon Jesus by his Messianic title.

The proof is impressive. The man infirm thirty-eight years did not know Jesus by name: ". . . he that was healed wist not who it was, for Jesus had conveyed himself away, a multitude being in that place." *J 5:13*

Wist is archaic English for "knew", and Jesus was only a man in a crowd to the infirm man. On their initial contact he addressed Jesus with simply a term of respect, "*Sir*, I have no man, when the water is troubled, to put me into the pool: . . ." *J 5:7*

The clinching proof is that the man born blind knew Jesus before his healing only as "a man that is called Jesus." *J 9:11* He referred to Jesus only as a man of God: "If this man were not of God, he could do nothing." *J 9:33*

Finally when Jesus sought out the blind man after he had been cast out following his healing, the dialogue went like this:

Jesus: Dost thou believe on the Son of God?
Man: Who is he, Lord, that I might believe on him? *J 9:35–36*

The conclusion is obvious and certain. The healings by Jesus did not depend upon the person to be healed calling on, or even knowing Jesus' special status. That does not mean that Jesus' special status did not confer on him special powers. However, since his disciples could also heal and since Jesus' own explanation of his healings was simply that the faith of the person to be healed made that person whole, the inevitable conclusion is that Jesus' healings did not depend on recognition of his special status or use of the right verbal formula. Jesus' healings were, and healings today are, specific applications of a general spiritual law: "Have faith in God.' *Mk 11:22*

Jesus' Doctrine of Healing Summarized

On three occasions Jesus expressly explained a healing of his by saying, "Your faith has made you whole." (*Woman with issue of blood: Mk 5:34, Mt 9:22, L 8:48; One of the ten lepers: L 17:19; Bartimaeus: Mk 10:51–52, L 18:41–42*)

Faith alone, however, was not sufficient. It was only an indispensable condition for the exercise of Jesus' power. Jesus claimed the power to heal. The father of the epileptic boy said to Jesus "but *if* thou canst do anything, have compassion on us, and help us." *Mk 9:22*

Jesus' reply was devastating:

If thou canst believe, all things are possible to him that believeth. *Mk 9:23*

The father was shamed to tears, and cried out:

Lord, I believe; help thou mine unbelief. *Mk 9:24*

Belief in Jesus' power to heal by someone, usually the person to be healed, was a condition of his healings. This condition was expressly stated in the case of the two blind men. When they followed Jesus into the house their interchange went this way:

Jesus: Believe ye that I am able to do this?
The blind men: Yea, Lord.
Jesus (as he touched their eyes): According to your faith, be it unto you. *Mt 9:28–29*

It was not, however, necessary that the healed person have faith in Jesus' power to heal; it was sufficient if some other person had that faith. In the case of the epileptic boy it was his father's faith. The boy himself was in the throes of an epileptic seizure: he had fallen to the ground "and wallowed foaming." *Mk 9:20*

997

Jesus' disciples had also power to heal. *Mt 10:1; Mk 6:12–13; L 9:1–2, 6* In the case of the epileptic boy, they were unable to exercise that power. Jesus explained why:

> Then came the disciples to Jesus apart, and said, "Why could not we cast him out?"

> And Jesus said unto them, "Because of your unbelief: for verily I say unto you, if ye have faith as a grain of mustard seed, ye shall say unto this mountain, 'Remove hence to yonder place;' and it shall remove, and nothing shall be impossible unto you. Howbeit this kind goeth not out but by prayer and fasting." *Mt 17:19–21*

The disciples' lack of faith prevented their healing the epileptic boy. In the case of the centurion's servant, the faith of the centurion caused the healing. Jesus was so impressed by that faith that he told the crowd:

MATTHEW	LUKE
Verily I say unto you,	I say unto you,
I have not found	I have not found
so great faith,	so great faith,
no, not in Israel.	no, not in Israel.
Mt 8:10	*L 7:9*

The faith of the centurion was as follows:

MATTHEW	LUKE
Lord,	Lord, trouble not thyself:
I am not worthy that	for I am not worthy that
thou shouldest come	thou shouldest enter
under my roof;	under my roof.
	Wherefore neither thought
	I myself worthy to come
	unto thee,
but speak the word only,	but say in a word
and my servant shall	and my servant shall
be healed.	be healed.
Mt 8:8	*L 7:6–7*

Jesus explained to the centurion how his servant would be healed by saying, "Go thy way, and as *thou hast* believed, so be it done unto thee." *Mt 8:13* This faith was a soldier's faith; the centurion was a professional soldier:

MATTHEW	LUKE
For I am a man	For I also am a man
under authority,	set under authority,
having soldiers under me,	having under me soldiers,
and I say to this man,	and I say unto one,
"Go," and he goeth;	"Go," and he goeth;
and to another,	and to another,
"Come," and he cometh;	"Come," and he cometh;
and to my servant,	and to my servant,
"Do this,"	"Do this,"
and he doeth it.	and he doeth it.
Mt 8:9	*L 7:8*

The centurion's faith was that if Jesus gave the order, the servant would be healed. He had faith that the servant's sickness was subject to Jesus' power. The same was true of the father of the epileptic boy although his faith was, at first, half-doubting. *Mk 9:22*

In two other cases the faith of others appears to have been the key factor. In the case of the deaf mute with a speech impediment, Mark's account states:

And *they* bring unto him one that was deaf, and had an impediment in his speech; and *they* beseech him to put his hand upon him. *Mk 7:32*

In the case of the blind man near Bethsaida, Mark's account states:

And *they* bring a blind man unto him, and besought him to touch him. *Mk 8:22*

Sometimes there does not appear to have been any works or acts of faith on the part of either the healed person, or any one else. In the case of the man infirm thirty-eight years, the man had a conversation with Jesus; and the man did not answer directly that he wished to be made whole, but instead he explained his difficulty in complying with the requirements of the legend about the shrine. *J 5:6–7* Jesus then told him, "Rise, take up thy bed, and walk." *J 5:8*

The account continues:

> And immediately the man was made whole, and took up his bed, and walked. *J 5:9*

The inference is that the man was healed by Jesus' power before he attempted to act on faith. The same inference may be drawn from the account of the woman infirm eighteen years:

> And when Jesus saw her, he called her to him, and said unto her, "Woman, thou art loosed from thine infirmity."
>
> And he laid his hands on her, and immediately she was made straight, and glorified God. *L 13:12–13*

The account is spare, and it is possible the woman had moved by faith close enough to him so he could touch her, but this is not stated. In the case of the man infirm thirty-eight years, he may have acted on faith to take up his bed simultaneously with Jesus' instruction to "rise, take up thy bed, and walk." *J 5:8* The account, however, implies he was healed before he acted at all. *J 5:9*

It does not appear that Jesus was required to do anything if the sick person had faith. In the case of the woman with the issue of blood, he was not sure who had touched his garment:

MARK	LUKE
And Jesus, immediately knowing in himself	And Jesus said, "Who touched me?"
	. . . "Somebody hath touched me:

Mark (cont.)

that *virtue* had gone
out of him,
turned him about in the press,
and said,
"Who touched my clothes?"
Mk 5:30

Luke (cont.)
for I perceive
that *virtue* is gone
out of me."
L 8:45–46

Modern translations use "power" instead of "virtue" to translate the Greek. The clear implication of the accounts is that the woman's touching Jesus' garment drained Jesus of force or vitality. The same was true of a crowd's touching. L 6:19

This agrees with Luke's statement in another context that Jesus' healing power was the power of God channeling itself through Jesus.

> And it came to pass on a certain day, as he was teaching, . . . and the power of the Lord was present to heal them. L 5:17

The modality that Jesus used to heal does not seem critical. One leper he touched; the ten lepers he sent to the priests. (One leper, Mk 1:41; Mt 8:3; L 5:13; Ten lepers, L 17:14) He seems always to have touched the eyes of the blind. (Two blind men, Mt 9:29; blind man near Bethsaida, Mk 8:23; man born blind, J 9:6; two blind men near Jericho, Mt 20:34; but not noted in the parallel accounts. Mk 10:52; L 18:42)

The parallel accounts as to the one or two blind men healed near Jericho diverge. Matthew states that Jesus "touched their eyes: and immediately their eyes received sight." Mt 20:34

The other two accounts do not mention any touching but simply state:

Mark
And Jesus said unto him,
"Go thy way;
thy faith hath made thee whole."

Luke
And Jesus said unto him,
"Receive thy sight;
thy faith hath saved thee."

MARK (cont.)
And immediately he
received his sight, . . .
Mk 10:52

LUKE (cont.)
And immediately he
received his sight, . . .
L 18:42–43

In the case of another two blind men reported only in Matthew, Jesus' touching of their eyes was combined with Jesus' statement that their faith was the healing agent:

Then touched he their eyes, saying, "According to your faith, be it unto you."

And their eyes were opened; . . . *Mt 9:29–30*

Sometimes Jesus used spittle and applied it to the eyes in his healing: used to make a clay ointment in the case of the man born blind, *(J 9:6)*; used directly on eyes in the case of the blind man near Bethsaida. *Mk 8:23*

Sometimes no modality at all was used, except Jesus' words. There are three such cases.

In the case of the man sick of the palsy, Jesus' words were:

I say unto thee, Arise, and take up thy bed, and go thy way into thine house. *Mk 2:11 (Mt 9:6; L 5:24)*

In the case of the man infirm thirty-eight years, Jesus' words were:

Rise, take up thy bed, and walk. *J 5:8*

In the case of the man with the withered hand, Jesus' words were:

Stretch forth thine hand. *Mk 3:5; Mt 12:13; L 6:10*

In each of the three cases just cited, the healed person was healed simply by acting upon Jesus' command to act as if he were healed.

In the case of the man born blind there was a combination of acting upon Jesus' command and various healing modalities:

> When he had thus spoken, he spat on the ground, and made clay of the spittle, and he anointed the eyes of the blind man with the clay, and said unto him, "Go, wash in the Pool of Siloam," . . . He went his way therefore, and washed, and came seeing. *J 9:6–7*

Finally in the case of the woman with the issue of blood, Jesus did nothing. The modality was the woman touching Jesus without his knowledge. *Mk 5:11; Mt 9:22; L 8:45* The woman was not responding to any command of Jesus, but simply acted on her faith. *Mk 5:27–28; Mt 9:20–21; L 8:44 ("A"crowd so acted." L 6:19)*

Sometimes there were both words and acts of faith on the part of the healed and acts on the part of Jesus. In the cases of the one leper and the ten lepers, the words of faith were:

ONE LEPER	TEN LEPERS
Lord, if thou wilt,	Jesus, Master, have
thou canst make me clean.	mercy on us.
Mt 8:2; L 5:12 (Mk 1:40)	*L 17:13*

The lepers acted on their faith: the one leper knelt to Jesus; the ten lepers went to the priests as Jesus directed. *Mk 1:40; Mt 8:2; L 5:12; L 17:14* Jesus also acted: he touched one leper *(Mk 1:41; Mt 8:3; L 8:13)*; he directed the ten lepers to the priests. *(L 17:14)*

In the case of the blind men reported by Matthew and in the case of one or two blind men near Jericho, they all uttered words of faith as a prelude to their healing. *Mt 9:28 (the Matthew two); Mk 10:51; Mt 20:33; L 18:41 (the Jericho case)*

We may attempt to categorize Jesus' healings in semi-scientific categories. Jesus, however, explained his healings as simply the result of faith, "Your faith has made you whole." *Mk 5:34 Mt 9:22; L 8:48; L 17:19; Mk 10:51–52; L 18:41–42* It was the same mustard seed faith which moves mountains. *Mt 17:20; L 17:6; Mk 11:22–23; Mt 21:21*

For Jesus himself his healings were mandated by God himself, works which he could not refuse to perform. The man born blind

was simply an opportunity to manifest God by healing him. *J 9:3*
Jesus had no choice:

> I must work the works of him that sent me." *J 9:4*

The healings, including the casting out of devils, were signs
that the Kingdom of God had arrived:

MATTHEW	LUKE
But if I	But if I
cast out devils	with the finger of God
by the Spirit of God,	cast out devils,
then	no doubt
the Kingdom of God	the Kingdom of God
is come unto you.	is come upon you.
Mt 12:28	*L 11:20*

It is also true that the coming of the Kingdom of God coin-
cided with the coming of the Messiah in the person of Jesus. According to Jesus, his healings ("the blind receive their sight, and
the lame walk, the lepers are cleansed, and the deaf hear" *Mt 11:5*)
were evidence that he was, indeed, "he that should come." *Mt 11:3;*
L 7:19

CHAPTER 19

MISCELLANEOUS
MIRACLES

THE MIRACLES OF THE LOAVES AND FISHES

All four gospels report Jesus' feeding of five thousand people. In fact it is the only miracle recorded in all four Gospels. It was the spring of the year since the Passover festival was at hand. *J 6:4* John the Baptist had just been beheaded and buried and his disciples "went and told Jesus." *Mt 14.12*

Matthew continues, "When Jesus heard of it, he departed thence by ship into a desert place apart; and when the people had heard thereof, they followed him on foot out of the cities." *Mt 14:13*

The Twelve accompanied him in the boat. *Mk 6:32* The Twelve had just returned from their preaching and healing mission. *Mk 6:30; L 9:10* They were reporting to Jesus "all things, both what they had done, and what they had taught." *Mk 6:30*

However, Jesus' own healings had attracted an immense crowd. *J 6:2* There were so many people going and coming that Jesus and his disciples "had no leisure so much as to eat." *Mk 6:31* So Jesus said to the Twelve, "Come ye yourselves apart into a desert place, and rest a while." *Mk 6:31*

To get away, Jesus and the Twelve slipped away by boat across the lake (the Sea of Galilee) to a secluded place. *Mk 6:32; Mt 14:13; L 9:12; J 6:1*

This maneuver was unsuccessful. *Mk 6:33; Mt 14:13; L 9:11; J 6:2* Mark writes:

> And the people saw them departing; and many knew him, and ran afoot thither out of all cities, and outwent them, and came together unto him.

> And Jesus, when he came out, saw much people, and was moved with compassion toward them, because they were as sheep not having a shepherd; and he began to teach them many things. *Mk 6:33–34*

The things taught included the Kingdom of God, and he also healed their sick. *L 9:11; Mt 14:14*

Later in the day the Twelve intervened and told Jesus:

MARK	MATTHEW	LUKE
This is	This is	[. . . for we are here
a desert place,	a desert place,	in a desert place.]*
and now the time	and the time	
is far passed.	is now past.	
Send	Send	Send
them away,	the multitude away,	the multitude away,
that they may go	that they may go	that they may go
into	into	into the towns
the country		and country
round about,		round about,
and into		
the villages,	the villages,	
		and lodge,
and buy themselves	and buy themselves	and get
bread:	victuals.	victuals . . .
for they have nothing	*Mt 14:15*	*L 9:12*
to eat.		* Conformed to
Mk 6:35–36		Mark's order

John does not report this conversation, nor the following dialogue between Jesus and the Twelve:

JESUS: They need not depart. *Mt 14:16*
   Give ye them to eat. *Mk 6:37; Mt 14:16; L 9:13*
THE TWELVE: Shall we go and buy two hundred penny–worth of bread, and give them to eat? *Mk 6:37 (L 9:13)*
JESUS: How many loaves have ye? Go and see. *Mk 6:38*
THE TWELVE: [After checking] Five, and two fishes. *Mk 6:38 (Mt 14:17; L 9:13)*
JESUS: Bring them hither to me. *Mt 14:18*

As John got the story, only three of the Twelve did any talking and the dialogue went like this:

JESUS: [To Philip] Whence shall we buy bread, that these may eat? *J 6:5*
PHILIP: Two hundred pennyworth of bread is not sufficient for them, that every one of them may take a little. *J 6:7*
ANDREW: There is a lad here, which hath five barley loaves, and two small fishes. But what are they among so many? *J 6:8–9*

All four gospels agree that Jesus then had the multitude sit down:

MARK	MATTHEW	LUKE	JOHN
And he commanded them to make all sit down by companies upon the green grass.	And he commanded the multitude to sit down on the grass. *Mt 14:19*	"Make them sit down by fifties in a company."	"Make the men sit down." . . .
And they		And they did so,	So the men

MARK (cont.)	MATTHEW (cont.)	LUKE (cont.)	JOHN (cont.)
		and made them	
sat down		all sit down.	sat down,
		L 9:14–15	
in ranks,			in number
by hundreds,			about five
and by fifties.			thousand.
Mk 6:39–40			*J 6:10*

The accounts continue:

MARK	MATTHEW	LUKE	JOHN
And when he	And	Then he	And Jesus
had taken	took	took	took
the five loaves	the five loaves	the five loaves	the loaves;
and	and	and	
the two fishes,	the two fishes,	the two fishes,	
he looked up	and looking up	and looking up	
to heaven,	to heaven,	to heaven,	and when
and	he	he	he had
blessed,	blessed	blessed them,	given thanks
and brake	and brake,	and brake,	
the loaves,			
and gave	and gave	and gave	he distributed
them	the loaves		
to his disciples	to his disciples,	to the disciples	to the disciples,
	and the		and the
	disciples		disciples
to set	to	to set before	to them that
before them;	the multitude.	the multitude.	were set down;
			and likewise
and			of the fishes
the two fishes			as much as
divided he			they would.
among them all.			When they
And they all	And they did	And they	
did eat,	all eat,	did eat,	
and were	and were	and were	

MARK (cont.)	MATTHEW (cont.)	LUKE (cont.)	JOHN (cont.)
filled.	filled.	all filled.	were filled, he said unto his disciples, "Gather up the fragments that remain, that nothing be lost."
And they took up	[And they took up	[And there was taken up	Therefore they gathered them together, and filled
twelve baskets full of the fragments, and of the fishes.	twelve baskets]* full of the fragments that remained	twelve baskets]* of fragments that remained to them . . . *L 9:16–17*	twelve baskets with the fragments of the five barley loaves, which remained over and above unto them
And they that did eat of the loaves were about five thousand men. *Mk 6:41–44*	And they that had eaten were about five thousand men, beside women and children. *Mt 14:19–21*		that had eaten. *J 6:11–13* * Conformed to Mark's order

The question is: did this proliferation of five barley loaves and two fish actually occur? Before that question can be considered, the reader must first decide whether or not such a thing is possible. Unless the reader is prepared to concede, as a hypothesis, that such a thing is possible there is no need to consider the evidence as to whether such proliferation did, in fact, occur.

That depends on what the witnesses say and whether they are credible. We cannot be certain whether four gospel accounts were written by eyewitnesses or whether they are simply based on the statements of eyewitnesses. If the latter is the case, the problem is much like whether you believe an Associated Press dispatch based upon what its reporters at the scene of an event learn by talking to bystanders. An Associated Press dispatch is evaluated by weighing what AP says the bystanders said.

The gospel accounts do contain convincing detail as to what Jesus and the Twelve said:

1. The miracle was not planned but arose out of the circumstances. It was getting late in this lonely place and the disciples realized that the crowd would need to eat and should be sent to the nearby villages to buy food before it got dark. *Mk 6:35–36; Mt 14:15; L 9:12* They interrupted Jesus to point this out.

2. Jesus had been absorbed in his teaching and healing and his first reaction was to feed them from the supplies his group carried, "They need not depart; give ye them to eat." *Mt 14:16 (Mk 6:37; L 9:13)* According to John, Jesus' next reaction was to buy food for them. *J 6:5–6*

3. Money was apparently not the problem although a large amount was required: two hundred pennyworth (two hundred denarii—200 Roman silver coins) *Mk 6:37; J 6:7*

4. The problem was the supply. One boy (probably a vendor following the crowd) still had five loaves and two fish. *J 6:9* Presumably these were then purchased from the boy although the accounts do not so state.

5. John's account does state that Andrew did not think that this quantity was worth bothering with: "But what are they among so many?" *J 6:9*

6. Jesus took over and had the crowd seated in groups of fifty. *Mk 6:39–40; L 9:14–15* This was probably for the purpose of counting off and suggests everyday practicality not preparation for some illusion. There were apparently about 100

groups since all four accounts agree that the crowd fed was about five thousand men. *Mk 6:44; Mt 14:21; L 9:14; J 6:10* Matthew understood that the women and children were in addition. *Mt 14:21*

7. Jesus then looked up to heaven, no doubt praying to his Father, although our accounts do not so state. *Mk 6:41; Mt 14:19; L 9:16*

8. They do state that he gave thanks for and blessed the food. *Mk 6:41; Mt 14:19; L 9:16; J 6:11* This was in accordance with Jewish practice.

9. It is clear that he then broke up the loaves and the fish and gave the fragments to his disciples to distribute. *Mk 6:41; Mt 14:19; L 9:16; J 6:11* The disciples, probably using their own provision baskets, systematically distributed the fragments to the seated groups.

10. All accounts agree that the crowd did eat and were filled. *Mk 6:42; Mt 14:20; L 9:17; J 6:12* The reasonable inference from the accounts is that their hunger was satisfied and not that they each received some tiny symbolic flake or bit:

MARK	MATTHEW	LUKE	JOHN
			[Food was distributed]
And they did all eat, and were filled.	And they did all eat, and were filled.	And they did eat, and were all filled.	As much as they would. When they were filled, . . .
Mk 6:42	*Mt 14:20*	*L 9:17*	*J 6:11–12*

11. The capstone of the miracle was the quantity of food that was left over:

MARK	MATTHEW	LUKE	JOHN
And they	And they	And there was	Therefore they

MARK (cont.)	MATT. (cont.)	LUKE (cont.)	JOHN (cont.)
took up	took up	taken up	gathered
	of the	of	them
	fragments	fragments	together,
	that	that	
	remained	remained	
		to them	and filled
twelve	twelve	twelve	twelve
baskets	baskets	baskets.	baskets
full of the	full.	*L 9:17*	with the
fragments,	*Mt 14:20*		fragments
			of
			the five
			barley
			loaves,
			which
and of			remained
the fishes.			over and
Mk 6:43			above
			unto them
			that
			had eaten.
			J 6:13

The *twelve* baskets were probably the individual provision baskets of each of the Twelve, and thus a correct detail rather than some mystical number. It was all so matter of fact. Jesus told the Twelve:

Gather up the fragments that remain, that nothing be lost. *J 6:12*

The Twelve then used the only baskets they had—their individual provision baskets. Jesus wanted the fragments saved for future use.

As John understood it, no fish were left and all the fragments were from the loaves; Mark understood that they had fragments of fish left over, too. *J 6:13; Mk 6:43*

If Jesus had the power he claimed and the Christians assume, there would be no problem in his invoking from his Father by means still unknown to science the proliferation of those five barley loaves and two fishes. Except for the highly compressed time involved it would not be a greater miracle than the proliferation that goes on in every productive barley field from planting to harvest. A great deal more is harvested than is planted or else farmers go broke. The fact that the food here was in refined form, barley loaves, rather than barley grains does not alter the fundamental point that if by ordinary biological means proliferation occurs in every field if conditions are right; so also if conditions were then right, e.g., Jesus' special relation to God, and other conditions we do not now understand, the five loaves could serve as the "seed" for an immense proliferation of the fragments.

The crowd itself was convinced that a miracle had occurred. John writes:

> Then those men, when they had seen the miracle that Jesus did, said, "This is of a truth that prophet that should come into the world."

> When Jesus therefore perceived that they would come and take him by force, to make him a king, he departed again into a mountain himself alone. J 6:14–15

Jesus did not wish to exploit the miracle in any way. He apparently regarded the miracle as a routine provision for the physical needs of his listeners, and not as a demonstration or proof of special powers on his part. Matthew and Mark write:

MARK	MATTHEW
And straightway he constrained his disciples to get into the ship, and to go to the other side before unto Bethsaida,	And straightway Jesus constrained his disciples to get into a ship, and to go before him unto the other side,

MARK (cont.)	**MATTHEW** (cont.)
while he sent	while he sent
away the people.	the multitudes away.
And when he had sent	And when he had sent
them away,	the multitudes away,
he departed into	he went up into
a mountain to pray.	a mountain apart to pray;
And when even	and when the evening
was come,	was come,
the ship was	
in the midst of the sea,	
and he alone on the land.	he was there alone.
Mk 6:45–47	*Mt 14:22–23*

It is obvious from the two accounts that Bethsaida was on the "other side" of the lake, i.e. part way around the lake. Luke describes the site of the miracle as "a desert place belonging to the city called Bethsaida." *L 9:10* Modern translations of Luke shorten this English phrase to "a town or city called Bethsaida." Reading Matthew, Mark and Luke together it seems likely that Luke meant "a desert place near to the city called Bethsaida."

The problem is complicated by the fact that there may have been more than one town named Bethsaida. *J 12:21* However, at this time there was a Roman town, Bethsaida Julius, on the northeast shore of the lake across the upper end of the lake about three miles from Capernaum. Capernaum was the destination of the disciples when Jesus sent them away after the miracle. *J 6:17*

We do know that the site was a deserted, rather than a desert, place since there was much green grass there. *Mk 6:39; J 6:10* The King James Version states that the site was "a mountain." *J 6:3* Considering the topography around the lake, it would be more accurate to say the site was on a hill.

Jesus had no need to do this particular miracle to attract support. He was already a popular figure. He was the man the disciples of John the Baptist turned to after John was executed.

Mt 14:12 His healings alone had already generated large crowds. *J 6:2 (Mk 6:31; Mt 14:14; L 9:11)*

Later on, the same sort of miracle was repeated in similar circumstances. This time only Matthew and Mark have accounts of the incident. Again, the setting is some deserted place near the Sea of Galilee probably on its east side. Again, there was a large crowd without anything to eat. This time, however, they had not just surged around the lakeshore one day to follow his boat, but they had been with him for three days.

Jesus called his disciples and told them privately:

MARK	MATTHEW
I have compassion	I have compassion
on the multitude,	on the multitude,
because	because
they have now been	they continue
with me three days,	with me now three days,
and have nothing to eat.	and have nothing to eat.
And if I send them away	And I will not send them away
fasting	fasting,
to their own houses,	
they will faint	lest they faint
by the way:	in the way.
for divers of them came	*Mt 15:32*
from far.	
Mk 8:2–3	

The dialogue with the disciples continued as follows:

	MARK	MATTHEW
DISCIPLES:	From whence can	Whence should we
	a man satisfy these	have so much
	men with bread here	bread
	in the wilderness?	in the wilderness,
		as to fill so great a
		multitude?

	MARK (cont.)	MATTHEW (cont.)
JESUS:	How many loaves have ye?	How many loaves have ye?
DISCIPLES:	Seven. *Mk 8:4–5*	Seven, and a few little fishes. *Mt 15:33–34*

The two accounts continue:

And he commanded the people to sit down on the ground; and he took the seven loaves,	And he commanded the multitude to sit down on the ground. And he took the seven loaves and the fishes,
and gave thanks, and brake, and gave to his disciples to set before them; and they did set them before the people.	and gave thanks, and brake them, and gave to his disciples, and the disciples to the multitude.
And they had a few small fishes, and he blessed, and commanded to set them also before them.	
So they did eat, and were filled; and they took up of the broken meat that was left seven baskets.	And they did all eat, and were filled; and they took up of the broken meat that was left seven baskets full.
And they that had eaten were about four thousand,	And they that did eat were four thousand men, besides women

Mark (cont.)	**Matthew** (cont.)
	and children.
and he sent them away.	And he sent away
Mk 8:6–9	the multitude . . .
	Mt 15:35–39

Again there was the same basic pattern as with the feeding of the five thousand:

1. The miracle was not planned but arose out of the circumstances. The crowd had been with Jesus for three days, and he wanted them fed since he realized that many had come too far to go home without eating. *Mk 8:2–3; Mt 15:32*
2. The disciples, as such, were prosaic-minded and raised practical difficulties: how can we feed so many from our own supply of food? "Whence should *we have* so much bread . . .?" *Mt 15:33*
3. Jesus first attempted to meet the problem in the ordinary way, asking, "How many loaves *have ye?*" *Mk 8:5; Mt 15:34* What he really asked is, "How many loaves do we have in the supplies for our common mess?"
4. Again he had the people sit down, gave thanks for the food, broke it, distributed it to the disciples and they distributed it to the people. *Mk 8:6–7; Mt 15:35–36*
5. Again it was both bread and fish which were distributed. And again all the crowd ate and "were filled", yet there were large quantities of scraps left over which were saved. *Mk 8:8; Mt 15:37* One difference is that only seven rather than twelve supply baskets full were left over, despite the fact that the crowd was smaller: about 4,000 men rather than 5,000 men. *Mk 6:43, 8:8; Mt 14:20, 15:37*
6. Again the episode ended prosaically without Jesus in any way attempting to exploit the tremendous miracle which had occurred: he simply sent the people away. They had been fed. That was enough. Not spiritual food, but carbohydrates and protein for their journeys home.

Jesus himself later referred to the two miraculous feedings pro-saically, on another occasion when his disciples had forgotten to bring bread along for Jesus' entourage:

MARK	MATTHEW
Now the disciples	And when his disciples were come to the other side [of the Sea of Galilee], they
had forgotten to take bread, neither had they in the ship with them more than one loaf. And he charged them, saying,	had forgotten to take bread.
	Then Jesus said unto them,
"Take heed, beware of the leaven of the Pharisees, and of the leaven of Herod." *Mk 8:14–15*	"Take heed and beware of the leaven of the Pharisees and of the Sadducees." *Mt 16:5–6*

Leaven (the fermenting yeast in bread) was a symbol of evil in Israel. *Exodus 12:15,19; Leviticus 2:11, 6:17, 10:12* Jesus' literal-minded disciples thought that Jesus was warning them not to eat bread ("leaven") provided by the Pharisees and Sadducees because the disciples had forgotten to bring their own bread. Actually Jesus was warning his disciples against insidiously evil doctrines of the Pharisees and Sadducees with whom he had been debating just before he had crossed the lake.

The accounts continue:

MARK	MATTHEW
And they reasoned among themselves, saying, "It is because we have no bread." And when Jesus knew it he saith unto them,	And they reasoned among themselves, saying, "It is because we have taken no bread." Which when Jesus perceived, he said unto them, "O ye of little faith,
"Why reason ye, because	why reason ye among yourselves,

MARK (cont.)
ye have no bread?"

"Perceive ye not yet,
neither understand?
Have ye your heart
yet hardened?
Having eyes, see ye not?
And having ears, hear ye not?
And do ye not remember?
When I brake the five loaves
among five thousand,
how many baskets
full of fragments
took ye up?"
They say unto him,
"Twelve."
"And when the seven
among four thousand,
how many baskets
full of fragments
took ye up?"
And they said,
"Seven."
And he said to them,
"How is it that ye
do not understand?"
Mk 8:16–21

MATTHEW (cont.)
because
ye have brought no bread?
Do ye not yet
understand,

neither remember
the five loaves
of the five thousand,
and how many baskets

ye took up?

Neither the seven loaves
of the four thousand,
and how many baskets

ye took up?

How is it that ye
do not understand
that I spake it not to you
concerning bread, that ye
should beware of the leaven
of the Pharisees
and of the Sadducees?"
Mt 16:7–11

Matthew adds:

Then understood they how that he bade them not beware of the leaven of bread, but of the doctrine of the Pharisees and of the Sadducees. *Mt 16:12*

The disciples regarded the two miraculous feedings as factual events. They remembered the number of baskets of left-overs in each case. But they did not regard this power of Jesus as a routine reliable matter: they were still carrying bread about with them, and they still worried about what to do if they forgot to lay in the necessary supply of bread.

Indeed Mark tells us that the very night after the first miracle of the loaves that "they considered not the miracle of the loaves: for their heart was hardened." *Mk 6:52* Jesus' disciples still harden their hearts and close their eyes and minds to the practical reality of his power. The miracles of the loaves are impossible to explain on any other basis than that power; otherwise they can only be accepted or rejected. Rejection, of course, has to be based on the prior assumption of impossibility.

The Miracle of Water into Wine

The same matter of fact practical approach that Jesus used in his miracles of the loaves and fishes was evident in his first miracle, the transformation of water into wine.

This first miracle occurred in Galilee at a town named Cana. J 2:1 The occasion was a marriage feast. Jesus and his disciples were invited guests, as well as Jesus' mother. J 2:2

She said to him:

They have no wine [left]. J 2:3

Jesus replied:

Woman, what have I to do with thee? Mine hour is not yet come. J 2:4

This translation follows the Greek, but the Greek can also mean, "Why should we be concerned?"

His mother did not answer Jesus, but instead told the servants:

Whatsoever he saith unto you, do it. J 2:5

Jesus said:

Fill the waterpots with water. J 2:7

The servants filled the pots to the brim and Jesus said:

Draw out now, and bear unto the governor of the feast. J 2:8

The governor of the feast tasted the sample and complimented the bridegroom:

Every man at the beginning doth set forth good wine; and when men have well drunk, then that which is worse; but thou hast kept the good wine until now. J 2:10

This miracle is not so taxing to the imagination. Five loaves and two fishes do not feed 5,000 men; instead six stone waterpots of water were transformed into wine. Conceptually this is not so difficult. Most of any wine is water. But the wine-making process was telescoped into milliseconds and the unique properties of the grapes had to be supplied or simulated. Jesus used what was at hand: not five loaves and two fishes but six empty pots used for ritual washing and water.

The result was an artificial wine which impressed the governor of the feast. Nothing has been planned; like the miracles of the loaves and fishes, the miracle arose out of an unforeseen practical problem: the wine was running out; just like darkness was about to fall when the 5,000 were fed.

Nothing is made of the miracle although each stone pot held anywhere from twenty to thirty gallons and were filled to the brim. That was a lot of wine and it must have been a large wedding involving the whole community, but the guests would not necessarily have known of the miracle, only the busy servants trying to keep the cups full. So there was no impact, except on his disciples. John writes:

> This beginning of miracles did Jesus in Cana of Galilee; and *his disciples* believed on him. *J 2:11*

JESUS AND WALKING ON WATER

On the evening after the first miracle of the loaves Jesus directed his disciples to proceed by boat across the Sea of Galilee to Bethsaida and then on to Capernaum. *Mk 6:45; Mt 14:22; J 6:16–17* As they crossed, a strong wind came up "contrary unto them" and the "sea arose" and they had to row. *Mk 6:48; Mt 14:24; J 6:18–19*

After they had rowed twenty-five or thirty stadia (a stadium was a measure of about 606 feet) they saw Jesus walking upon the water. *J 6:19* By this time it was after 3:00 a.m.; and they were far offshore. *Mk 6:47–48; Mt 14:24–25* Their immediate reaction was that this was an apparition. *Mk 6:49; Mt 14:26*

The gospel accounts speak for themselves:

MARK	MATTHEW	JOHN
But when	And when	
they saw	the disciples saw	. . . they see
him walking upon	him walking on	Jesus walking on
the sea, they	the sea, they	the sea,
		and drawing nigh
	were troubled,	unto the ship,
supposed it had	saying, "It	
been a spirit,	is a spirit;"	
and cried out:	and they cried out	and they were
	for fear.	afraid.
for they all saw		
him, and were		
troubled.		
And immediately	But straightway	But
he talked	Jesus spake	he saith
with them,	unto them,	unto them,
and said unto them,	saying,	
"Be of good cheer:	"Be of good cheer:	
it is I;	it is I;	"It is I;
be not afraid."	be not afraid."	be not afraid."

MARK (cont.)	MATTHEW (cont.)	JOHN (cont.)
And he went up unto them	. . . And when they [Jesus and Peter] were come	Then they willingly received him
into the ship, and	into the ship,	into the ship, and
the wind ceased; and they were sore amazed in themselves beyond measure, and wondered. *Mk 6:49–51*	the wind ceased. *Mt 14:26–27, 32*	
		immediately the ship was at the land whither they went. *J 6:19–21*

Matthew alone reports that Peter left the boat and attempted to walk on the water to Jesus:

And Peter answered him and said, "Lord, if it be thou, bid me come unto thee on the water."

And he said, "come."

And when Peter was come down out of the ship, he walked on the water, to go to Jesus. But when he saw the wind boisterous, he was afraid; and beginning to sink, he cried, saying, "Lord, save me."

And immediately Jesus stretched forth his hand, and caught him, and said unto him, "O thou of little faith, wherefore didst thou doubt?" *Mt 14:28–31*

The fact that Peter was able to walk part way on the water shows that Jesus' ability was not unique but was in some way related to faith. In the eras before ground effect vehicles that can skim on the water surface, walking on water seemed an absolute technical impossibility.

In one sense, a miracle is simply an event that is impossible under the current state of knowledge and technology. Graphically, this may be stated thus:

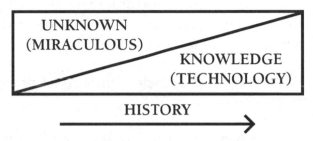

As history moves along, knowledge increases and the miraculous shrinks, assuming that the total of things to be known is constant. The point is not that Jesus' walking on water may be technologically explainable as like a special ground effect phenomenon in a high wind. The point is that Jesus at that time and age was able to so fit into the rules his Father had made for the universe that he could do it. Peter could not.

It is, however, consistent with Peter's character as it appears in the New Testament that he would make the attempt. It should be emphasized that neither he, nor the other disciples, were naively credulous. Peter is quoted as saying, "Lord, *if* it be thou, bid me come unto thee on the water." Mt 14:28

Both Matthew and Mark state that the disciples' first reaction to the sight of Jesus was that they were seeing a spirit or apparition or ghost. Mk 6:49; Mt 14:26 This was reasonable since Mark states:

> . . . and about the fourth watch of the night he cometh unto them, walking upon the sea, and *would have passed by them*. Mk 6:48

This is just when a mass hallucination might be expected. The disciples had been through a tiring crowd-filled day, they had embarked under orders about dusk but without their leader, after a while a contrary wind had come up sharply and the water had become rough and they had had to row hard to keep the boat headed into the waves. Despite this they had been able to row about three or four miles, but by 3:00 a.m. were no doubt exhausted and were still far off shore.

It was, however, no hallucination. Jesus did, in fact, come aboard. Perhaps coincidentally the wind dropped: it was getting to be morning. But the disciples were dumbfounded that Jesus was actually in the boat: "they were sore amazed in themselves beyond measure, and wondered." *Mk 6:51* Mark adds:

> For they considered not the miracle of the loaves: for their heart was hardened. *Mk 6:52*

Matthew states that the reaction of these stunned men as follows:

> Then they that were in the ship came and worshipped him, saying, "Of a truth thou art the Son of God." *Mt 14:33*

They landed at Gennesart and moored. *Mk 6:53; Mt 14:34* It had been quite a night, but no attempt was made to exploit the miracle. The crowd soon gathered again and Jesus simply continued his healing ministry that he had left off the day before. *Mk 6:54–56; Mt 14:35–36*

John's account of the miracle is very brief and matter of fact. He does, however, mention the puzzlement of the crowd left at the site of the miracle of the loaves and fishes. The next day they realized that they had seen the disciples depart the prior evening in a boat without Jesus, and there had been no other boat, yet Jesus had also disappeared. *J 6:22*

Other boats then put in from Tiberias, a Roman town across the Sea of Galilee on its southwest shore. *J 6:23* The crowd then took passage in these boats for Capernaum where they found Jesus teaching in the synagogue. *J 6:25, 59*

Their question to Jesus was:

> Rabbi, when camest thou hither? *J 6:25*

Jesus' answer was:

Verily, verily, I say unto you, ye seek me, not because ye saw the miracles, but because ye did eat of the loaves, and were filled.

Labor not for the meat which perisheth, but for that meat which endureth unto everlasting life, which the Son of man shall give unto you: for him hath God the Father sealed. *J 6:26–27*

The crowd picked up the idea of "work" from Jesus' admonition to labor for "that meat which endureth unto everlasting life" and asked:

What shall we do, that we might work the works of God? *J 6:28*

Jesus then made his point:

This is the work of God, that ye believe on him whom he hath sent. *J 6:29*

Jesus, in effect, told the crowd that they followed him to Capernaum because they had eaten their fill of the bread, and not because the proliferation of the bread was any miraculous sign to them. Jesus was correct. The crowd did not regard the miraculous proliferation of the loaves and fishes as appropriate proof God had sent Jesus since they then immediately asked for a sign just like the sign Moses had given:

What sign showest thou then, that we may see, and believe thee? What dost thou work? Our fathers did eat manna in the desert; as it is written [in the Old Testament, Nehemiah 9:15], "He gave them bread from heaven to eat." *J 6:30–31*

Jesus pointed out that the Mosaic manna was not the true bread from heaven:

Verily, verily, I say unto you, Moses gave you not that bread from heaven; but my Father giveth you the true bread from heaven. For the bread of God is he which cometh down from heaven, and giveth life unto the world. *J 6:32–33*

The listeners were touched and said:

Lord, evermore give us this bread. *J 6:34*

Jesus replied:

I am the bread of life [the true bread from heaven]. He that cometh to me shall never hunger, and he that believeth on me shall never thirst.

But I said unto you, that ye also have seen me, *and believe not*. [But so be it.]

All that the Father giveth me shall come to me; and he that cometh to me, I will in no wise cast out. *J 6:35–37*

Two Nature Miracles

All three synoptic gospels have an account of Jesus stilling a storm on the Sea of Galilee. *Mk 4:35–41; Mt 8:23–27; L 8:22–25* About evening he and his disciples had shoved off in a boat, along with other boats, to go to the other side. *Mk 4:35–36; Mt 8:18, 23; L 8:22* A big squall came up, and the waves were swamping the boat. *Mk 4:37; Mt 8:24; L 8:23*

Jesus was asleep in the stern *(Mk 4:38)*, and the disciples awakened him, saying:

MARK	MATTHEW	LUKE
Master,	Lord,	Master, master,
carest thou not	save us:	
that we perish?	we perish.	we perish.
Mk 4:38	*Mt 8:25*	*L 8:24*

The accounts continue:

MARK	MATTHEW	LUKE
And he arose,	Then he arose,	Then he arose,
and rebuked	and rebuked	and rebuked
the wind,	the winds	the wind
and said unto	and	and
the	the	the raging of the
sea,	sea;	water;
"Peace, be still."		
And the wind		and they
ceased,		ceased,
and there was	and there was	and there was
a great calm.	a great calm.	a calm.
Mk 4:39	*Mt 8:26*	*L 8:24*

Jesus' comment to his disciples was:

MARK	MATTHEW	LUKE
Why are ye	Why are ye	

MARK (cont.)	MATTHEW (cont.)	LUKE (cont.)
so fearful?	fearful,	
How is it that		Where
ye have no faith?	O ye of little faith?	is your faith?
Mk 4:40	*Mt 8:26*	*L 8:25*

The accounts close with these statements:

MARK	MATTHEW	LUKE
And they	But the men	And they
feared exceedingly,	marvelled,	being afraid
		wondered,
and said	saying,	saying
one to another,		one to another,
"What manner	"What manner	"What manner
of man	of man	of man
is this,	is this,	is this! For
that even	that even	he commandeth even
the wind	the winds	the winds
and the sea	and the sea	and water,
obey him?"	obey him!"	and they obey him."
Mk 4:41	*Mt 8:27*	*L 8:25*

Skeptics say that it was coincidence: the wind dropped just as Jesus rebuked it; the atmospheric physics were such that the wind would have dropped anyway. Christians rely on the accounts that Jesus commanded the calm and point out that Jesus had access to power which could, if desired, override the ordinary laws of atmospheric physics. If by faith mountains can be moved, as Christians affirm, why cannot a squall be stilled? Where is your faith?

The incident of the withered fig tree is often considered to be a nature miracle. We have two accounts: *Mk 11:12–14, 20–24; Mt 21:18–22* During Jesus' last days in Jerusalem, he was staying each night in Bethany, a nearby village, and coming into the city each morning. *Mk 11:11,19; Mt 21:17* One morning Jesus was hungry and saw by the roadside a fig tree in leaf. *Mk 11:13; Mt 21:18–19* He

examined the tree but found that it had no figs. *Mk 11:13; Mt 21:19*
Our two accounts differ as to what Jesus then said:

MARK	MATTHEW
No man *eat* fruit	Let no fruit *grow*
of thee	on thee
hereafter for ever.	henceforward for ever.
Mk 11:14	*Mt 21:19*

This is usually considered to be a cursing of the fig tree. That is apparently how Peter understood it because Mark quotes him as saying on the next morning as they again passed the tree:

Master, behold, the fig tree which thou cursedst is withered away.
Mk 11:21

According to Mark, it was at the same time, the next morning, that the disciples saw that the tree had "dried up from the roots."
Mk 11:20

As Matthew got the story, the tree had withered immediately after Jesus' statement the morning before:

And presently the fig tree withered away. And when the disciples saw it, they marvelled, saying, "How soon is the fig tree withered away!" *Mt 21:19–20*

The miracle, if any, was that the tree dried up after Jesus' statement. Mark's clear account that the disciples did not notice any withering until the next day, suggests the possibility of a coincidence, not a miracle. Trees can die abruptly, and the question is whether twenty-four hours were enough. Since the tree had "dried up from the roots", it may have already been essentially dried out on the first morning and the leaves then abruptly withered in the next twenty-four hours. *Mk 11:20–21*

The problem is whether Peter, a rough, impulsive man, correctly understood Jesus' words to have been a curse. Matthew understood his words as a curse *(Mt 21:19)* but Mark's account is ambiguous:

No man *eat* fruit of thee hereafter for ever. *Mk 11:14*

Since our accounts vary, it seems obvious that we do not have Jesus' exact words. Suppose he in fact said:

This tree will never bear anymore.

No one would suppose that an orchardist was cursing one of his trees if he notices with a keen eye that the tree is terminal, the roots being dead, and says:

This tree will never bear anymore.

When Peter made his comment about the fig tree, Jesus simply used it as a peg to state his teaching about faith in God:

MARK	MATTHEW
Have faith in God.	
For verily	Verily
I say unto you,	I say unto you,
	if ye have faith,
	and doubt not,
	ye shall not only do
	this which is done
	to the fig tree,
that whosoever shall say	but also if ye shall say
unto this mountain,	unto this mountain,
"Be thou removed,	"Be thou removed,
and be thou cast	and be thou cast
into the sea,"	into the sea,"
and shall not doubt	
in his heart,	
but shall believe that	
these things which he saith	

MARK (cont.)	**MATTHEW** (cont.)
shall come to pass,	it shall be done.
he shall have	*Mt 21:21*
whatsoever he saith.	
Mk 11:22–23	

It seems likely that Jesus did not in fact curse the fig tree but that his disciples, including Peter, misunderstood what he did say (as they often did). Since there was no curse, there was no miracle. Jesus used, as he often did, a chance remark to make a point. That point is, "Have faith in God", just as he said after stilling the squall on the Sea of Galilee:

How is it that ye have no faith? *Mk 4:40*

CHAPTER 20

LAW / PREDESTINATION / JUDGMENT

JESUS AND HIS LAW

To understand Jesus' teaching as to the religious law of the Jews, the Mosaic Law, the context of his teaching is important. Anyone familiar with the gospels will know how often the question was put to Jesus by his fellow Jews: "Is it *lawful* to . . . ?"

This is the way they thought, in terms of the Mosaic Law. For example:

1. The Pharisees asked him:

   Is it lawful for a man to put away his wife? *Mk 10:2*

   Is it lawful for a man to put away his wife for every cause? *Mt 19:3*

2. Pharisees and Herodians asked:

   Is it lawful to give tribute to Caesar, or not? *Mk 12:14*

   Is it lawful to give tribute to Caesar, or not? *Mt 22:17*

Is it lawful for us to give tribute unto Caesar, or no? *L 20:22*

3. In a synagogue "they" asked him:

Is it lawful to heal on the Sabbath days? *Mt 12:10*

Jesus himself used the Mosaic Law as a teaching device. An ecclesiastical lawyer asked him a test question:

Master, what shall I do to inherit eternal life? *L 10:25*

Jesus answered:

What is *written in the Law*? How readest thou? *L 10:26*

The lawyer answered by quoting two sections of the Law: Deuteronomy 6:5 and Leviticus 19:18
Jesus replied:

Thou hast answered right: this do, and thou shalt live. *L 10:26–28*

It is easy to find other examples how Jesus used the Law as a teaching device:

And he taught, saying unto them, "Is it *not written*, [*Isaiah 56:7*] "My house shall be called of all nations the house of prayer?" *Mk 11:17*

Jesus answered them, "Is it *not written in your Law* [*Psalm 82:6*], "I said, ye are gods?" *J 10:34*

John quotes some priests and Pharisees as saying of one crowd:

This people . . . knoweth not *the Law*. *J 7:49*

Jesus felt that those who did attempt to keep the Law dispensed with its crucial precepts:

MATTHEW	LUKE
Woe unto you,	But woe unto you,
scribes and Pharisees,	Pharisees!
hypocrites!	
For ye pay tithe of mint	For ye tithe mint and rue
and anise and cumin,	and all manner of herbs,
and have omitted	and pass over judgment
the weightier matters	and
of the Law,	
judgment, mercy and faith;	the love of God;
these ought ye to have done	these ought ye to have done,
and not to leave	and not to leave
the other undone.	the other undone.
Ye blind guides,	L 11:42
which strain at a gnat,	
and swallow a camel.	
Mt 23:23–24	

The scribes and Pharisees used the Law as a weapon against Jesus. They felt that he profaned the Law with his teaching, and they tried again and again to set up test cases against him.

For example, they brought him a woman taken in adultery and said:

Master [Teacher], this woman was taken in adultery, in the very act. Now Moses in the Law commanded us, that such should be stoned; but what sayest thou? This they said, tempting [testing] him, that they might have to accuse him. J 8:4–6

Jesus answered:

He that is without sin among you, let him first cast a stone at her. J 8:7

Sometimes the questions were not hostile, and we get a fair glimpse of Jesus teaching:

> And one of the scribes [a man learned in the religious law] came, and having heard them reasoning together [Jesus and the Sadducees], and perceiving that he had answered them well, asked him, "Which is the first commandment of all?" *Mk 12:28*

Jesus answered:

> The first of all the commandments is: "Hear, O Israel, the Lord our God is one Lord; and thou shalt love the Lord thy God with all thy heart, and with all thy soul, and with all thy mind, and with all thy strength." This is the first commandment.
>
> And the second is like, namely this: "Thou shalt love thy neighbor as thyself." There is none other commandment greater than these. *Mk 12:29–31*

Jesus' first commandment is a quotation of Deuteronomy 6:4–5. This is the Shema, a prayer said every morning and evening by devout Jews. *Shema* means "Hear", the first word of the prayer. Jesus' second commandment is a quotation of Leviticus 19:18.

More typically, Jesus was asked test questions that were hostile. Matthew reports one incident as follows:

> But when the Pharisees had heard that he had put the Sadducees to silence, they were gathered together. Then one of them, which was a lawyer [of the religious law], asked him a question, tempting [baiting] him, and saying, "Master, which is the great commandment in the Law?" *Mt 22:34–36*

Jesus answered:

> Thou shalt love the Lord thy God with all thy heart, and with all thy soul, and with all thy mind. This is the first and great commandment. [*Deuteronomy 6:5*]

1038

And the second is like unto it: Thou shalt love thy neighbor as thyself.

On these two commandments hang all the Law and the Prophets. [*Leviticus 19:18*] *Mt 22:37–40*

In the Sermon on the Mount, Matthew quotes a similar saying:

Therefore all things whatsoever ye would that men should do to you, do ye even so to them: for this is the Law and the Prophets. *Mt 7:12*

As Paul later wrote:

For all the Law is fulfilled in one word, even in this: Thou shalt love thy neighbor as thyself. *Galatians 5:14*

Jesus, however, felt that he had a new commandment to give, going beyond the old Jewish Law:

A new commandment I give unto you, that ye love one another; as I have loved you, that ye also love one another. By this shall all men know that ye are my disciples, if ye have love one to another. *J 13:34–35*

This is my commandment, that ye love one another, as I have loved you. Greater love hath no man than this, that a man lay down his life for his friends. Ye are my friends, if ye do whatsoever I command you . . . These things I command you, that ye love one another. *J 15:12–14, 17*

Looking back at Jesus' ministry, John later wrote:

And this is his [God's] commandment, that we should believe on the name of his Son Jesus Christ, and love one another, as he gave us commandment. *1 John 3:23*

Since Jesus in fact announced a new commandment, that ye love one another, he chose to explain this new commandment by contrast with the old commandments of the Jews. This he did in the Sermon on the Mount:

Ye have heard it was said by *them of old time*, "Thou shalt not kill, and whosoever shall kill shall be in danger of judgment" [*Exodus 20:13*]

But I say unto you, that whosoever is angry with his brother without a cause shall be in danger of the judgment; and whosoever shall say to his brother, "Raca," shall be in danger of the council; but whosoever shall say, "Thou fool," shall be in danger of hell fire. *Mt 5:21–22*

Jesus then contrasted his new commandments on adultery and divorce with the provisions of the old Law:

Ye have heard that *it was said by them of old time*, "Thou shalt not commit adultery." [*Exodus 20:14*]

But I say unto you, that whosoever looketh on a woman to lust after her hath committed adultery with her already in his heart. *Mt 5:27–28*

It hath been said, "Whosoever shall put away his wife, let him give her a writing of divorcement." [*Deuteronomy 24:1*]

But I say unto you, that whosoever shall put away his wife, saving for the cause of fornication, causeth her to commit adultery; and whosoever shall marry her that is divorced committeth adultery. *Mt 5:31–32*

Jesus' teaching as to divorce that "what therefore God hath joined together, let not man put asunder" was questioned by the Pharisees upon the ground that Moses speaking for God had provided for a "bill of divorcement." *Mk 10:4, Mt 19:7*
Jesus' answer was:

Moses because of the hardness of your hearts suffered you to put away your wives, but from the beginning it was not so.

And I say unto you, whosoever shall put away his wife, except it be for fornication, and shall marry another, committeth adultery; and whoso marrieth her which is put away doth commit adultery. *Mt 19:8–9*

The Sermon on the Mount continues with other examples of the contrast of the old law (". . .it hath been said . . .") and Jesus' new law (". . . but I say unto you . . ."):

Again, ye have heard that *it hath been said* by them of old time, "Thou shalt not forswear thyself, but shalt perform unto the Lord thine oaths."

But I say unto you, swear not at all, neither by heaven for it is God's throne, nor by the earth for it is his footstool, neither by Jerusalem for it is a city of the great King. Neither shalt thou swear by thy head, because thou canst not make one hair white or black. But let your communication be, "Yea, yea;" "Nay, nay:" for whatsoever is more than these cometh of evil. *Mt 5:33–37*

Ye have heard that *it hath been said,* "An eye for an eye, and a tooth for a tooth."

But I say unto you, that ye resist not evil; but whosoever shall smite thee on thy right cheek, turn to him the other also. And if any man will sue thee at the law, and take away thy coat, let him have thy cloak also. And whosoever shall compel thee to go a mile, go with him twain [two]. Give to him that asketh thee, and from him that would borrow of thee turn not thou away. *Mt 5:38–42*

Ye have heard that *it hath been said,* "Thou shalt love thy neighbor, and hate thine enemy."

But I say unto you, love your enemies, bless them that curse you, do good to them that hate you, and pray for them which despitefully use you, and persecute you; that ye may be the children of your Father which is in heaven: for he maketh his sun to rise on the evil and on the good, and sendeth rain on the just and on the unjust.

For if ye love them which love you, what reward have ye? Do not even the publicans the same? And if ye salute your brethren only, what do ye more than others? Do not even the publicans so? Be ye therefore perfect, even as your Father which is in heaven is perfect. *Mt 5:43–48*

The teachings which have just been quoted are introduced by these words of Jesus:

Think not that I am come to destroy the Law, or the Prophets. I am not come to destroy, but to fulfil. For verily I say unto you, till heaven and earth pass, one jot or one tittle shall in no wise pass from the Law, till all be fulfilled.

Whosoever therefore shall break one of these least commandments, and shall teach men so, he shall be called the least of the Kingdom of Heaven; but whosoever shall do and teach them, the same shall be called great in the Kingdom of Heaven. For I say unto you, that except your righteousness shall exceed the righteousness of the scribes and Pharisees, ye shall in no case enter into the Kingdom of Heaven. *Mt 5:17–20*

To understand this quotation, Jesus' religious time scale must be considered. He taught that John the Baptist was the dividing line between the age of the Law and the Prophets and the new Kingdom age.

MATTHEW	LUKE
And from	The Law and the Prophets
the days of John the Baptist	were until John;
until now	since that time
the Kingdom of Heaven	the Kingdom of God
suffereth violence,	is preached,
and the violent take it by force.	and every man presseth into it.
For all the Prophets and the Law	*L 16:16*
prophesied until John.	
Mt 11:12–13	

The quotations continue:

MATTHEW	LUKE
For verily I say unto you,	And it is easier for
till heaven and earth pass,	heaven and earth to pass,
one jot or one tittle	than one tittle
shall in no wise	
pass from the Law,	of the Law
till all be fulfilled.	to fail.
Mt 5:18	*L 16:17*

Reading the quotations from both Matthew and Luke together they have this sense: the Law is the utmost importance, it is easier for the universe to pass away than even a dot in the Law to fail, but when all is fulfilled this will happen.

Jesus did not then explain what he meant by "till all be fulfilled." *Mt 5:18* His own personal mission was involved:

I am not come to destroy, but to fulfil. Mt 5:17

This personal mission, Jesus' way to the cross and beyond, even his closest disciples, did not yet understand. *J 13:36–38; 14:1–31; 16:16–33* All was fulfilled when Jesus died and rose again: the Law was superseded and the Kingdom age began.

The Law was to be superseded when "all be fulfilled." *Mt 5:18* In the meantime, Jesus stressed the importance of the weightier matters of the Law: justice, mercy, and good faith. *Mt 23:23* But for that meantime and the new Kingdom age, he restated the Law and condensed it into the single all–pervading principle of love, a new commandment, "that ye love one another." *J 13:34*

In the new age, the Christian age, the Jewish Law is a historical curiosity; the law of the Christians is the "But I say unto you" principle of love. The new age has a new commandment:

A new commandment I give unto you, that ye love one another; as I have loved you, that ye also love one another. By this shall all men

know that ye are my disciples, if ye have love one to another.
J 13:34–35

The Law was a primitive curse, a crude first approximation.
Paul wrote:

Christ hath redeemed us from the curse of the Law, being made a
curse for us . . . *Galatians 3:13*

The Christian epitaph on the Jewish Law is this:

For the Law was given by Moses, but grace and truth came by Jesus
Christ. *J 1:17*

JOY IN HEAVEN FOR STRAYS VS. PREDESTINATION

So far as we know from the Gospels, Jesus did not use the root words from which the term "predestination" has descended to us. Jesus' own teaching does not fit into this concept of human reasoning and logic. Paul's words as translated in the King James Version do not use words *predestinate* and *predestinated*. *Romans 8:29–30; Ephesians 1:5, 11*

Discussions about predestination are often based upon what Paul wrote, but a decent respect for Jesus, Paul's Lord, requires examination of what Jesus himself said relating to predestination. John quotes Jesus as saying:

All that the Father giveth me shall come to me . . . And this is the Father's will which hath sent me, that of all which he hath given me, I should lose nothing . . . And this is the will of him that sent me, that every one which seeth the Son, and believeth on him, may have everlasting life . . . *J 6:37–40*

Jesus did not say *only* those "the Father giveth me shall come to me," but rather that "*all* that the Father giveth me shall come to me." *J 6:37* In fact, as Jesus said, it is the will of the Father "that every one which seeth the Son, and believeth on him, may have everlasting life." *J 6:40* Later on in the same chapter, John quotes Jesus as referring back to John 6:37 and 39, when he says:

But there are some of you that believe not . . . Therefore said I unto you, that no man can come unto me, except it were given unto him of my Father. *J 6:64–65*

John's next verse states:

From that time *many of his disciples* went back, and walked no more with him. *J 6:66*

These disciples apparently left over Jesus' hard saying that "whoso eateth my flesh, and drinketh my blood, hath eternal life;

and I will raise him up at the last day." *J 6:54* Humanly speaking, the disciples who left were free to go, and they did. Men are still free to reject Jesus and they do, but it is not the will of the Father that they do this.

Jesus was asked, "Lord, are there few that be saved?" *L 13:23* Jesus answered:

Strive to enter in at the strait [narrow] gate: for many, I say unto you, will seek to enter in, and shall not be able. *L 13:24*

Able is here meant in the sense of succeed, and they will not succeed because they have waited until the gate is shut:

When once the master of the house is risen up, and hath shut to the door, and ye begin to stand without, and to knock at the door, saying, "Lord, Lord, open unto us."

And he shall answer and say unto you, "I know you not whence ye are."

Then shall ye begin to say, "We have eaten and drunk in thy presence, and thou hast taught in our streets."

But he shall say, "I tell you, I know you not whence ye are; depart from me, all ye workers of iniquity." *L 13:25–27*

To Jesus the gate to the Father is narrow, but it is open to all who will meet the Father's conditions of entrance. There is no preordained list of persons authorized to enter the gate. The gate, however, is to be open for only a limited time.

Jesus' own teaching on "predestination" is tersely summarized in these words of his:

No man can come to me, *except the Father which hath sent me draw him* . . .

It is written in the prophets, "And they shall be all taught of God."

Every man therefore that hath heard, and hath learned of the Father,
cometh unto me. J 6:44–45

Jesus' own doctrine as to "predestination" consists of two propositions:

1. No one can come to Jesus unless the Father draws him, *but*
2. Everyone who heeds the Father's teaching can come to Jesus.

The Father is supreme, but every man is free to make his own choice. This is a logical contradiction from a human point of view, but it is an unjustified assumption that human rules of logic apply to this relation of God and Man. If we are discussing coins, two plus two equals four, but this logical rule fails if we are discussing rabbits and two of those rabbits are male and the other two are females in heat.

Jesus was not concerned with the logical subtleties later centuries enjoy. So far as he was concerned, it is not the will of God "your Father" that any one should perish. In fact, it is possible to repent and return to the Father; and when this happens, there is joy in Heaven.

Jesus' first proposition, that no one can come to Jesus unless drawn by the Father, is modified by Jesus' second proposition, that everyone who heeds the Father's teaching can come to Jesus. Whosoever wills, may come to Jesus.

That is why Jesus taught that the Father does not want anyone to be lost, and, in fact, actively seeks them. Jesus made this point in two twin parables: the parable of the lost sheep and the parable of the lost coin.

The parable of the lost sheep is stated in two slightly different forms in Matthew and Luke:

Matthew	Luke
How think ye?	What man of you,
If a man have a hundred sheep,	having an hundred sheep,
and one of them be gone astray,	if he lose one of them,

MATTHEW (cont.)
doth he not leave
the ninety and nine
and goeth into the mountains,
and seeketh that
which is gone astray?

And if so be that he find it,
verily I say unto you,

he rejoiceth more of that sheep,
than of the ninety and nine
which went not astray.

Even so it is not
the will of your Father
which is in heaven,
that one of the little ones
should perish.
Mt 18:12–14

LUKE (cont.)
doth not leave
the ninety and nine
in the wilderness,
and go after that
which is lost,
until he find it?

And when he hath found it,
he layeth it
on his shoulders,
rejoicing.

And when he cometh home,
he calleth together
his friends and neighbors,
saying unto them,
"Rejoice with me:
for I have found my sheep
which was lost."

I say unto you, that likewise
joy shall be in heaven
over one sinner that repenteth,
more than over
ninety and nine just persons,
which need no repentance.
L 15:4–7

The parable of the lost coin is this:

Either [or] what woman having ten pieces of silver, if she lose one piece, doth not light a candle, and sweep the house, and seek diligently till she find it?

And when she hath found it, she calleth her friends and her neighbors together, saying, "Rejoice with me: for I have found the piece which I had lost."

Likewise, I say unto you, there is *joy in the presence of the angels of God* over one sinner that repenteth. *L 15:8–10*

The parable of the lost sheep and the lost coin each teach that God actively seeks those estranged from him—like a man doggedly looking for a stray sheep, or a woman diligently searching for a lost coin.

Jesus did not teach that certain persons are predestined to spiritual death at some time prior to the beginning of the world. Jesus did not teach any iron law of predestination.

Jesus did teach that it is not the will of God, "your Father", that anyone should perish. Jesus did teach that there is joy in Heaven over the return of each stray.

The lost sheep and the lost coin parables are the first two of three parables that Jesus gave as his answer to the murmurs of the Pharisees and scribes that, "This man receiveth sinners and eateth with them." *L 15:2*

The third parable is the parable of the prodigal son. This parable states:

A certain man had two sons. The younger of them said to his father, "Father, give me the portion of goods that falleth to me."

And he divided unto them his living. And not many days after, the younger son gathered all together, and took his journey into a far country, and there wasted his substance with riotous living. And when he had spent all, there arose a mighty famine in that land; and he began to be in want. And he went and joined himself to a citizen of that country, and he sent him into his fields to feed swine. And he would fain have filled his belly with the husks that the swine did eat, and no man gave unto him.

And when he came to himself, he said, "How many hired servants of my father's have bread enough and to spare, and I perish with hunger! I will arise and go to my father, and will say unto him, 'Father, I have sinned against heaven and before thee, and am no more worthy to be called thy son. Make me as one of thy hired servants.'"

And he arose, and came to his father. But when he was yet a great way off, his father saw him, and had compassion, and ran, and fell on his neck, and kissed him. And the son said unto him, "Father, I have sinned against heaven, and in thy sight, and am no more worthy to be called thy son."

But the father said to his servants, "Bring forth the best robe, and put it on him, and put a ring on his hand, and shoes on his feet. And bring hither the fatted calf, and kill it; and let us eat, and be merry. For this my son was dead, and is alive again; he was lost, and is found."

And they began to be merry.

Now his elder son was in the field, and as he came and drew nigh to the house, he heard music and dancing. And he called one of the servants, and asked what these things meant. And he said unto him, "Thy brother is come, and thy father hath killed the fatted calf, because he hath received him safe and sound."

And he was angry, and would not go in; therefore came his father out, and entreated him.

And he answering said to his father, "Lo, these many years do I serve thee, neither transgressed I at any time thy commandment; and yet thou never gavest me a kid, that I might make merry with my friends. But as soon as this thy son was come, which hath devoured thy living with harlots, thou hast killed for him the fatted calf."

And he said unto him, "Son, thou art ever with me, and all that I have is thine. It was meet that we should make merry, and be glad: for this thy brother was dead, and is alive again; and was lost, and is found." L 15:12–32

The point of this parable is the joy of the Father at the return of the prodigal son—the return of a lost son. Not just the finding of a lost sheep, or a lost coin, but the return of a lost son. There is Joy! Joy!

Jesus' Father in the heights of heaven is always looking into the hazy distance to see if one of his children is returning from a far country. For such the narrow gate of heaven is always open, and the servants of the Father will prepare a mighty feast of welcome.

THE DAY OF JUDGMENT

Jesus repeatedly taught that there will be a Day of Judgment
for all men:

MARK	MATTHEW
And whosoever shall not receive you, nor hear you, when ye depart thence,	And whosoever shall not receive you, nor hear your words, when ye depart out of that house or city,
shake off the dust under your feet for a testimony against them.	shake off the dust of your feet.
Verily I say unto you, it shall be more tolerable for Sodom and Gomorrha *in the Day of Judgment*, than for that city.	Verily I say unto you, it shall be more tolerable for the land of Sodom and Gomorrha *in the Day of Judgment*, than for that city.
Mk 6:11	*Mt 10:14–15*

The raw power of Jesus' teaching on the Day of Judgment is
shown by these words of his:

MATTHEW	LUKE
Woe unto thee, Chorazin!	Woe unto thee, Chorazin!
Woe unto thee, Bethsaida!	Woe unto thee, Bethsaida!
For if the mighty works, which were done in you, had been done in Tyre and Sidon, *they would have repented long ago* in sackcloth and ashes.	For if the mighty works [which have been done in you]* had been done in Tyre and Sidon, *they had a great while ago repented*, sitting in sackcloth and ashes.

MATTHEW (cont.)	**LUKE** (cont.)
But I say unto you,	But
it shall be more tolerable	it shall be more tolerable
for Tyre and Sidon	for Tyre and Sidon
at the *Day of Judgment*,	at *the Judgment*,
than for you.	than for you.
And thou, Capernaum,	And thou, Capernaum,
which art exalted	which art exalted
unto heaven,	to heaven,
shall be brought down	shall be thrust down
to hell:	*to hell.*
for if the mighty works,	
which have been done in thee,	
had been done in Sodom,	
it would have remained	
until this day.	
But I say unto you,	[But I say unto you,
that it shall be	that it shall be
more tolerable	more tolerable
for the land of Sodom	
in the Day of Judgment,	*in that Day*
	for Sodom
than for thee.	than for that city.]*
Mt 11:21–24	*L 10:12–15*
	* Conformed to
	Matthew's order

Jesus contrasted the towns of his native Galilee, Chorazin, Bethsaida and Capernaum, with the pagan Phoenician seaport towns of Tyre and Sidon. In summary, Jesus preached that the failure of these Galilean towns to repent would bring down terrible retribution upon them in the Day of Judgment, worse retribution than had been visited on Sodom. Capernaum, his headquarters town, was to be thrust down to hell. *Mt 4:13, 9:1*

It can not be disputed that Jesus looked forward to a Day of Judgment. He charged his twelve disciples that whatever house or city did not receive them would suffer grievously in the Day of

Judgment. *Mk 6:11; Mt 10:14–15* He charged his seventy disciples to like effect. *L 10:10–15* Cities that did not heed his mighty works and repent were to be punished severely at the Day of Judgment. *Mt 11:20–24*

It is hard to make a stronger statement about the reality of "the Day of Judgment" than Jesus' statement that:

> But I say unto you, that every idle word that man shall speak, they shall give account thereof *in the Day of Judgment*. *Mt 12:36*

Jesus described the Day of Judgment this way:

> When the Son of man shall come in his glory, and all the holy angels with him, then shall he sit upon the throne of his glory. And before him shall be gathered all nations, and he shall separate them one from another, as a shepherd divideth his sheep from the goats. And he shall set the sheep on his right hand, but the goats on the left. *Mt 25:31–33*

To those on his right hand the Son of man shall say:

> Come, ye blessed of my Father, inherit the Kingdom prepared for you from the foundation of the world. *Mt 25:34*

Sentence will then be pronounced on those on the left hand:

> Depart from me, ye cursed, into everlasting fire, prepared for the devil and his angels. *Mt 25:41*

Jesus concluded his statement this way:

> And these shall go away into everlasting punishment, but the righteous into life eternal. *Mt 25:46*

The solemn finality of the Day of Judgment was summed up by Jesus in a single sentence:

> For the Son of man shall come in the glory of his Father with his angels, and then he shall reward every man according to his works.
> *Mt 16:27*

Jesus, himself, gave us one other detail about that Day of Judgment. He will not be sitting in judgment alone on that day; his followers will also be sitting, judging the twelve tribes of Israel. Jesus told Peter:

> Verily I say unto you, that ye which have followed me, in the regeneration when the Son of man shall sit in the throne on his glory, ye *also* shall sit upon twelve thrones, judging the twelve tribes of Israel. *Mt 19:28*

Many discussions of Jesus' statements about the Day of Judgment become lost in thickets of disputes over what exactly Jesus meant by "all nations", "the sheep", and "the goats", and when the Day is to occur. *Mt 25:31–46* Such disputes miss Jesus' main point that on the awesome Day of Judgment he will "reward *every man* according to his works." *Mt 16:27*

It is popular to talk of the gentle Jesus, but this same Jesus bluntly warned that there will be a Day of Judgment when cities, nations and men must give an account of themselves. What would he say of "disciples" who reject such a world view as naive and tiresome?

Technicolor and stereophonic sound can not convey the unspeakable majesty of that Day when Jesus "shall come in his glory, and all the holy angels with him, then shall he sit upon the throne of his glory." *Mt 25:31*

Jesus Will Judge on That Day

Not only did Jesus teach that was an awesome Day of Judgment coming, he taught that he, as the Son of Man, had been delegated by the Father to sit as judge on that day. *Mt 25:31–34, 41, 46; 16:27*

Jesus said:

For the Father judgeth no man, but hath *committed all judgment* unto the Son.

. . . For as the Father hath life in himself, so hath he given to the Son to have life in himself, and hath given him *authority to execute judgment* also, and because he is Son of man. *J 5:22, 26–27*

Jesus expressly recognized that his authority to execute judgment was not inherent but had been delegated to him by the Father:

I can of mine own self do nothing. As I hear, I judge; and my judgment is just, because I seek not mine own will, but the will of the Father which hath sent me. *J 5:30*

These acts of judgment by Jesus are in the future, on the Day of Judgment. During his ministry Jesus did not judge. Quite the contrary, he said:

And if any man hear my words, believe not, I judge him not: for I came not to judge the world, but to save the world. *J 12:47*

He told the woman caught in the act of adultery:

Neither do I condemn thee; go and sin no more. *J 8:11*

Jesus came to save the world by announcing standards of judgment so that all persons and the world may see the error of their ways.

The following interchange reported in John's Gospel is illuminating. Jesus had opened the eyes of a man born blind. The Pharisees were appalled, and after interrogating the man had cast him out. Jesus heard about this and came to see the man.

Here is what was said:

JESUS: Dost thou believe on the Son of God?
MAN: Who is he, Lord, that I might believe on him?
JESUS: Thou has both seen him and it is he that talketh with thee.
MAN: Lord, I believe.
JESUS: For judgment I am come into this world, that they which
　　see not might see, and that they which see might be made blind.
PHARISEES: Are we blind also?
JESUS: If ye are blind, ye should have no sin, but now ye say, "We
　　see;" therefore your sin remaineth. *J 9:35–41*

Jesus did not judge anyone. He did proclaim standards of judgment which he brought from the Father. He told some Pharisees:

Ye judge after the flesh; I judge no man. And yet if I judge, my
judgment is true: for I am not alone, but I and the Father that sent
me. *J 8:15–16*

On the Day of Judgment Jesus will exercise his delegated authority as Son of man to judge all nations and each person and reward them according to their works.

CHAPTER 21

HELL / HEAVEN / ETERNAL LIFE

JESUS TAUGHT HELL FIRE

Jesus taught that there will be a Day of Judgment and that he had been commissioned by the Father to execute judgment on that day. Jesus went further: he preached hell fire.

In the Sermon on the Mount he preached:

> Ye have heard that it was said by them of old time, "Thou shalt not kill, and whoever shall kill shall be in danger of the judgment." But I say unto you, that whosoever is angry with his brother without a cause shall be in danger of the judgment, and whosoever shall say to his brother, "Raca," shall be in danger of the Council; but whosoever shall say, "Thou fool," shall be in *danger of hell fire. Mt 5:21–22*

There are questions whether this statement of Jesus, as we now have it, has become garbled. These questions do not affect the point here: that Jesus preached hell fire, or literally the "Gehenna of fire."

Later on in the same Sermon, he said, and he repeated on other occasions, similar statements about hell fire.

MATTHEW (Sermon)	MATTHEW	MARK
And if thy right eye	And if thine eye	And if thine eye

MATTHEW (cont.)	MATTHEW (cont.)	MARK (cont.)
offend thee,	offend thee,	offend thee,
pluck it out,	pluck it out,	pluck it out;
and cast it	and cast it	
from thee:	from thee;	
for it is	it is	it is
profitable	better	better
for thee that	for thee	for thee
one	to enter into	to enter into
of thy members	life	the Kingdom of God
should perish,	with one eye,	with one eye,
and not that	rather than	than
thy whole body	having two eyes	having two eyes
should be	to be	to be
cast into	cast into	cast into
hell	*hell fire.*	*hell fire,*
	Mt 18:9	where
		their worm
		dieth not,
		and the fire
		is not quenched.
		Mk 9:47–48
And if	Wherefore if	And if
thy right hand	thy hand	thy hand
	or thy foot	
offend thee,	offend thee,	offend thee,
cut it off,	cut them off	cut it off;
and cast it	and cast them	
from thee:	from thee	
for it is	for it is	it is
profitable	better	better
for thee that	for thee	for thee
one	to enter	to enter
of thy members	into life	into life
should perish,	halt or maimed	maimed,
and not that	rather than	than
thy whole body	having two hands	having two hands
	or two feet	

MATTHEW (cont.)
should be
cast into
hell.
Mt 5:29–30

MATTHEW (cont.)
to be
cast into
everlasting fire.
Mt. 18:8

MARK (cont.)
to
go into
hell,
into the fire
that never
shall be quenched,
where their worm
dieth not,
and the fire
is not quenched.
And if
thy foot
offend thee,
cut it off;
it is better
for thee
to enter
halt
into life,
than having
two feet
to be
cast into
hell,
into the fire
that never
shall be
quenched,
where
their worm
dieth not,
and the fire
is not quenched.
Mk 9:43–46

In these passages, Jesus appears to use "hell" and "hell fire" interchangeably. "Hell fire" for Jesus included the idea of everlasting and unquenchable fire.

In the strongest possible language, Jesus exhorted men to avoid "hell" and "hell fire." He did not, however, by his strong language, mean that to avoid hell a person was to literally pluck out an eye or cut off a limb. That is the rhetorical exaggeration of his Aramaic speech and culture. What is not rhetoric and what is important is that Jesus taught the absolute reality of hell. This is not some later medieval error. This was Jesus' own teaching.

Unlike some of his modern disciples, Jesus did not blush to consign men to hell. His rhetorical question to the scribes and Pharisees was:

> Ye serpents, ye generation of vipers, how can ye escape the damnation of hell? *Mt 23:33*

Jesus sentenced others to "everlasting fire" and "everlasting punishment", to the "furnace of fire", to "hell fire." *Mt 25:40–41, 45–46; Mt 13:40–42, 49–50; Mk 9:47; Mt 5:22, 18:9*

Liberals close their ears to the fact that Jesus taught damnation, as well as meekness and mercy. When he sent the Twelve on a preaching tour, he charged them:

MATTHEW	LUKE
	And I say
	unto you
	my friends,
And fear not	be not afraid
them which	of them that
kill the body,	kill the body,
but are	and after that
not able	have no more
to kill	that they
the soul;	can do.
but rather	But I will
	forewarn you
	whom
	ye shall fear:
fear him	fear him,

MATTHEW (cont.)
which

is able
to destroy
both soul and body
in hell.
Mt 10:28

LUKE (cont.)
which after
he hath killed,
hath power
to cast

into hell;
yea, I say unto you,
fear him.
L 12:4–5

Fear him who has power "to cast into hell" and "to destroy both soul and body in hell"! This is not some ignorant preacher ranting, but the considered and solemn teaching of Jesus himself.

Everyone applauds Jesus' statement about works of help and mercy to the unfortunate:

Verily I say unto you, inasmuch as ye have done it unto one of the least of these my brethren, ye have done it unto me. *Mt 25:40*

But Jesus' next sentence is then read out of his Gospel:

Then shall he say also unto them on the left hand, "Depart from me, ye cursed, into *everlasting fire*, prepared for the devil and his angels." *Mt 25:41*

Not only is this sentence read out of the Gospel of Matthew, but all the other statements of Jesus about hell and hell fire quoted in this section are also read out of Jesus' Gospel.

Matthew's Gospel continues its quote of Jesus:

Verily I say unto you, inasmuch as ye did it not to one of the least of these, ye did it not to me. And these shall go away into *everlasting punishment*, but the righteous into life eternal. *Mt 25:45–46*

Jesus taught that there was an everlasting fire of everlasting punishment at a place called "Hell." Sometimes he does not use that noun, but instead uses the phrase "hell fire." There can be no doubt that Jesus, himself, not only taught judgment, but also the resulting punishment at the place called "Hell."

JESUS ON HELL

Hell is an English word. The Gospels were written in Greek. Jesus spoke Aramaic. We do not have Jesus' exact Aramaic words except by inference from the Greek words of the Gospels. The Gospels use two different Greek words for *hell*: Hades and Gehenna.

When reference is made here to the words Jesus used, it is convenient to say he used *Hades* or *Gehenna*, as the case may be, without repeating each time that Jesus actually used the Aramaic equivalents of these two words.

Four times in the Gospels, Jesus is quoted as having used the word *Hades*. That word is the equivalent of the Hebrew word *Shoel*, meaning the underground world of the dead.

Jesus used this word when he told the story of Lazarus, the beggar, and the rich man. He said:

And it came to pass that the beggar died, and was carried by the angels into Abraham's bosom. The rich man also died, and was buried.

And in *hell* he lift up his eyes, being in torments, and seeth Abraham afar off, and Lazarus in his bosom.

And he cried and said, "Father Abraham, have mercy on me, and send Lazarus, that he may dip the tip of his finger in water, and cool my tongue: for I am tormented in this flame."

But Abraham said, "Son, remember that thou in thy lifetime receivedst thy good things, and likewise Lazarus evil things; but now he is comforted, and thou art tormented. And beside all this, between us and you there is a great gulf fixed, so that they which would pass from hence to you cannot; neither can they pass to us, that would come from thence." *L 16:22–26*

Some modern English translations simply use the Greek word *Hades* for the English word *hell* used in the King James Version. *L 16:23*

Jesus is quoted as using that same word, *Hades*, three other times in the Gospels. Two of the three quotations are found in the two parallel passages from Matthew and Luke when Jesus laid woes upon certain Galilean towns:

MATTHEW	LUKE
And thou, Capernaum, which art exalted unto heaven, shall be brought down to *hell*. *Mt 11:23*	And thou, Capernaum, which art exalted to heaven, shalt be thrust down to *hell*. *L 10:15*

Here Jesus was apparently using *Hades* as a figurative word to state the depth of the town's coming plunge to judgment rather than as to the place of the dead as such.

Finally, Matthew quotes Jesus as saying:

And I say also unto thee, that thou art Peter, and upon this rock I will build my church, and the *gates of hell* shall not prevail against it. *Mt 16:18*

The literal Greek "gates of Hades" here is simply a figurative way of saying "death." The fact that death shall not prevail against Christ's church is expressed by Paul in 1 Corinthians as follows:

Then cometh the end, when he shall have delivered up the Kingdom of God, even the Father, when he shall have put down all rule and all authority and power. For he must reign, till he put all enemies under his feet. The last enemy that shall be destroyed is death. *1 Corinthians 15:24–26*

According to the Book of The Revelation, the risen Christ stated:

Behold, I am alive for evermore, Amen, and have the keys of hell and of death. *Revelation 1:18*

"Hell" here is "Hades", and some modern translations simply use the Greek word *Hades*. The "keys" of Hades and death is an image like the "gates" of Hades. The subject is simply death.

The four places in the Gospels where Jesus "used" the Greek word *Hades* have been quoted. The passages in the Gospels where Jesus "used" the Greek word *Gehenna* are much more numerous. Three of the passages where he used the Greek word *Gehenna* are as follows:

MARK	MATTHEW	MATTHEW
And if thy hand offend thee, cut it off.	Wherefore if thy hand	And if thy right hand offend thee, cut it off, and cast it from thee.
It is better for thee to enter into life maimed		For it is profitable for thee
		that one of thy members should perish and not that
than having two hands to go into *hell*, into the fire that never shall be quenched, [where their worm dieth not, and the fire is not quenched].		thy whole body should be cast into *hell*. *Mt 5:30*
And if thy foot offend thee, cut it off.	or thy foot offend thee, cut them off, and cast them from thee.	
It is better for thee	It is better for thee	

MARK (cont.)	MATTHEW (cont.)	LUKE (cont.)
to enter halt into life	to enter into life	
	halt or maimed,	
than having	rather than having	
	two hands	
two feet	or two feet	
to be cast into	to be cast into	
hell,	*everlasting fire.*	
into the fire that		
never shall		
be quenched,		
[where their worm		
dieth not,		
and the fire		
is not quenched].		
And if thine eye	And if thine eye	And if thy right eye
offend thee,	offend thee,	offend thee,
pluck it out.	pluck it out,	pluck it out,
	and cast it from thee.	and cast it from thee.
It is	It is	For it is
better for thee	better for thee	profitable for thee
to enter into	to enter into	that
the Kingdom of God	life	
with one eye,	with one eye,	one of thy members
		should perish,
	rather	and not that
than having two eyes	than having two eyes	thy whole body
to be	to be	should be
cast into *hell fire,*	cast into *hell fire.*	cast into *hell.*
[where their worm	*Mt 18:8–9*	*Mt 5:29*
dieth not, and the		
fire is not quenched].		
Mk 9:43–48		

The best manuscripts of Mark omit verses 44 and 46 but have the same phrase in verse 48. These three verses are bracketed in the above quotation and read as follows:

Where their worm dieth not, and the fire is not quenched. *Mk 9:44, 46, 48*

This is a quotation of the last verse of the last chapter of Isaiah:

And they shall go forth, and look upon the carcasses of the men that have transgressed against me: for their worm shall not die, neither shall their fire be quenched; and they shall be an abhorring unto all flesh. *Isaiah 66:24*

The idea expressed by Isaiah is the perpetuity of punishment: the worms do not cease to feed on the bodies; and their burning never stops.

Jesus' words as to self-mutilation were not meant by him to be taken literally. Jesus meant, by means of rhetorical exaggeration common to his Aramaic culture, to stress the extreme and awesome importance of avoiding Hell.

The word Jesus used for Hell in those three quotations, *Gehenna*, comes through to us in King James English as "hell" and as part of the phrase "hell fire." *(Hell, Mk 9:43,45; Mt 5:29–30; hell fire, Mk 9:47; Mt 18:9)*

Gehenna is the Greek form of the Hebrew word *Ge–Hinnon*. This word was derived from a place name, the Valley of "Hinnon", a ravine south and southwest of Jerusalem used as a rubbish dump, a loathsome place of burning and decomposition. By Jesus' time, the word *Gehenna* had become the name of the place of punishment after death, Hell.

Jesus used the word *Gehenna* when he said:

MATTHEW	LUKE
	And I say unto you,
	my friends,
And fear not them	be not afraid of them
which kill the body,	that kill the body,
but are not able	and after that have
to kill the soul;	no more that they can do.

MATTHEW (cont.)	LUKE (cont.)
but rather	But I will forewarn you
	whom ye shall fear:
fear him	Fear him
which is able	which after he
to destroy	hath killed hath power
both body and soul	to cast
in *hell*.	into *hell*.
Mt 10:28	*L 12:4–5*

Finally Jesus used the word *Gehenna* when he passed judgment on the Pharisees, when he said:

> Woe unto you, scribes and Pharisees, hypocrites! For ye compass sea and land to make one proselyte, and when he is made, ye make him twofold more the child of *hell* than yourselves.
>
> . . . Ye serpents, ye generation of vipers, how can ye escape the damnation of *hell*? *Mt 23:15, 23:33*

Hell is an English word derived from Old English root words meaning "to conceal" and evoking the shadowy world of the dead; but Jesus considered Hell (Gehenna) to be a place of unquenchable fire.

Jesus is quoted by Mark and Matthew as using Hell and unquenchable fire as equivalents:

MARK 9:43	MARK 9:45	MATTHEW 18:8
. . . to go into hell,	to be cast into hell,	to be cast into
into the fire that	into the fire that	everlasting fire.
never shall	never shall	
be quenched.	be quenched.	

The ideas of fire and Hell are combined in Jesus' phrase translated by the King James Version as "hell fire." *Mk 9:47; Mt 18:9; Mt 5:22*

Mark 9:47	**Matthew 5:22**	**Matthew 18:9**
. . . to be cast into hell fire.	. . . shall be in danger of hell fire.	. . . to be cast into hell fire.

Literally the Greek is "Gehenna of fire" so Jesus must have said a "Hell of fire" rather than "hell fire." Other times he simply used as translated, the word *Hell* or the phrases translated as "everlasting or eternal or unquenchable fire." Whatever the exact linguistics, it is clear, that not only did Jesus consider Hell to exist, but also it was a place of unquenchable fire.

Jesus also described Hell as a "furnace of fire." *Mt 13:42, 50* This occurs in two parables, the parable of the tares (weeds) and the parable of the net:

Matthew 13:40–42 (Tares)	**Matthew 13:49–50 (Net)**
So shall it be in the end of this world.	So shall it be at the end of the world.
The Son of man shall send forth his angels, and they shall gather out of his Kingdom all things that offend, and them which do iniquity.	The angels shall come forth, and sever the wicked from among the just.
And shall cast them into *a furnace of fire.*	And shall cast them into *the furnace of fire.*
There shall be wailing and gnashing of teeth. *Mt 13:40–42*	There shall be wailing and gnashing of teeth. *Mt 13:49–50*

Jesus referred to a "furnace of fire." The image is of a furnace to smelt ore, or a kiln to fire pottery. The word *Gehenna* is not used, but Jesus is describing Hell.

Jesus' image of Hell as a "furnace of fire" overlaps his image of Hell as "everlasting fire." Jesus taught:

> Verily I say unto you, inasmuch as ye have done it unto one of the least of these my brethren, ye have done it unto me. Then shall he say also to them on the left hand, "Depart from me, ye cursed, into *everlasting fire*, prepared for the devil and his angels."

> . . . Verily I say unto you, inasmuch as ye did it not to one of the least of these, ye did it not to me. And these shall go away into *everlasting punishment*, but the righteous into life eternal. *Mt 25:40–41, 45–46*

Jesus did not distinguish between "everlasting fire" and "everlasting punishment"; nor should we.

Let us be candid. The geography or thermal characteristics of Hell are not the point. The point of the objection to Hell is the judgment on sinners associated with it.

Jesus taught that there will be a Day of Judgment and that he had been commissioned by God the Father to be the judge on that Day and that Hell exists, a place of everlasting fire and everlasting punishment. Ought his followers to teach otherwise?

JESUS ON HEAVEN

Jesus was crucified with two criminals. As they hung on their crosses, one criminal said to Jesus:

Lord, remember me when thou comest into thy kingdom. *L 23:42*

Jesus replied:

Verily I say unto thee, today thou shalt be with me in Paradise.
L 23:43

Jesus thus expected to go from his cross directly to Paradise. About three hours after he had said this, Jesus cried out:

Father, into thy hands I commend my spirit. *L 23:46*

Luke adds, ". . . and having said thus, he gave up the ghost."
L 23:46

Less than twenty-four hours before, at his Last Supper, Jesus had, with the greatest solemnity, instructed his disciples:

In my Father's house are many mansions; if it were not so, I would have told you. I go to prepare a place for you. *J 14:2*

The Greek word translated *mansions* is often translated as *rooms*, and that Greek word is also found in John 14:23 where the King James Version translates it as *abode*:

If a man loves me, he will keep my words; and my Father will love him, and we will come unto him, and make our *abode* with him.
J 14:23

In substance Jesus said that in his Father's house is an abode for each disciple. Jesus also said that he was going there to prepare those abodes.

The quotation continues:

And if I *go* and prepare a place for you, I will come again, and receive you unto myself, that where I am, there ye may be also.

. . . Ye have heard how I said unto you, "I go away, and come again unto you." If ye loved me, ye would rejoice, because I said, "*I go unto the Father*': for my Father is greater than I." *J 14:3, 28*

When Jesus said this to his disciples at his Last Supper he knew that he was about to die. Jesus described his coming journey in four different, but equivalent ways:

1. Going to "his Father's house." *J 14:2–4*
2. Going to "the Father." *J 14:28; J 16:16–17, 28*
3. Going to Paradise. *L 23:43*
4. Committing his spirit into the Father's hands. *L 23:46*

If, when Jesus said he committed his spirit to the Father, he was simply accepting his Father's will, and not describing his destination, it is clear from his statement quoted by Luke three verses earlier that he was going to "Paradise." *L 23:46, 43*

Jesus spoke Aramaic; and Luke wrote in Greek. We do not know which Aramaic word Jesus used that Luke translated into Greek as "Paradise." We do know that this word *Paradise* was of Persian origin and originally meant, literally, a walled garden, and by obvious extension, a royal garden.

The translators of the Greek Old Testament in use in Jesus' day had used this word *Paradise* a number of times to translate *garden*, including the Garden of Eden. *Genesis 2:8* Paul, writing in Greek, used the word to describe his "visions and revelation of the Lord." *2 Corinthians 12:1* He wrote that "he was caught up into Paradise, and heard unspeakable words, which it is not lawful for a man to utter." *2 Corinthians 12:4*

Finally, in the Book of The Revelation, John wrote:

To him that overcometh will I give to eat of the tree of life, which is in the midst of the Paradise of God. *Revelation 2:7*

The Gospels record many occasions when Jesus used the word *heaven*, but they record only one occasion when he used the word *Paradise*. This was when he said from the cross to the repentant criminal that "today thou shalt be with me in Paradise." L 23:43

The evening before, he had said to his disciples:

> I come forth from the Father, and am come into the world; again, I leave the world and go to the Father. *J 16:28*

Earlier that evening, he had said to his disciples:

> A little while, and ye shall not see me; and again, a little while, and ye shall see me, because I go to the Father. *J 16:16*

Reading his statements together, Jesus said that in a little while, on the day of crucifixion, he was going to the Father, to Paradise, the royal garden of God, where he would prepare an abiding place for his disciples.

Jesus claimed to have come down from heaven:

> I came down *from heaven*, not to do mine own will, but the will of him that sent me. *J 6:38*

Jesus also said:

> And no man hath ascended up to heaven, but he that came down *from heaven*, even the Son of man which is in heaven. *J 3:13*

Some manuscripts omit the words translated by the King James Version as "which is in heaven." Some modern translations follow those manuscripts and end Jesus' statement with "the Son of man."

It is embedded in the hearts and minds of Christians, not only that Jesus came down "from heaven", but that the Father is "in heaven." The most obvious example is the Lord's Prayer:

MATTHEW	LUKE
Our Father which art *in heaven*, . . . Mt 6:9	Our Father which art *in heaven*, . . . L 11:2

Jesus repeatedly used the phrase "your Father which is *in heaven*." *Mk 11:26; Mt 5:16, 45, 48; 7:11; 23:9* He also repeatedly used the phrase "my Father which is *in heaven*." *Mt 7:21; 10:32–33; 12:50; 16:17; 18:19*

In Jesus' familiar words the Father's will is done in heaven:

MATTHEW	LUKE
Thy will be done	Thy will be done,
in earth,	
as it is done *in heaven*.	as *in heaven*,
Mt 6:10	so in earth.
	L 11:2

This is because the Father is Lord of Heaven:

MATTHEW	LUKE
I thank thee, O Father,	I thank thee, O Father,
Lord of heaven	Lord of heaven
and earth, . . .	and earth, . . .
Mt 11:25	*L 10:21*

The Father is in heaven. He is Lord of that realm. Accordingly, his will is done there. Jesus recognized that angels are present there. *Mk 12:25; Mt 22:30; Mk 13:32; Mt 24:36*

Jesus remembered the Father in heaven and said:

For whosoever shall do the will of my Father which is *in heaven*, the same is my brother, and sister, and mother. *Mt 12:50*

Jesus exhorted his disciples:

Let your light so shine before men, that they may see your good works, and glorify your Father which is *in heaven*. *Mt 5:16*

Jesus claimed to have the ultimate power "in heaven":

All power if given unto me *in heaven* and in earth. *Mt 28:18*

Jesus taught that heaven is a place of both joy and judgment. He taught that heaven can be a place of joy when he said:

> I say unto you, that likewise *joy shall be in heaven* over one sinner that repenteth, more than over ninety and nine just persons, which need no repentance. *L 15:7*

Jesus taught that heaven was a place of judgment when he said:

> Whosoever therefore shall confess me before men, him will I confess also before my Father which is *in heaven*. But whosoever shall deny me before men, him will I also deny before my Father which is *in heaven*. *Mt 10:32–33*

Jesus told his followers to rejoice that "your names are written in heaven." *L 10:20* John calls this heavenly register "the Lamb's book of life." *Revelation 21:27; 13:8* ("Book of Life of the Lamb") Sometimes he calls it, simply, "the Book of Life." *Revelation 3:5; 17:8; 20:12, 15*

Not only are Christians registered in heaven, but great rewards await them there:

MATTHEW	LUKE
Blessed are ye,	Blessed are ye
when men shall revile you	when men shall hate you,
and persecute you,	and when they shall
and shall say all manner of	separate you
	from their company,
	and shall reproach you,
	and cast out your name as
evil	evil,
against you falsely	
for my sake.	for the Son of man's sake.
Rejoice,	Rejoice ye in that day,
and be exceeding glad: for	and leap for joy: for, behold,
great is your reward	your reward is great
in heaven. . .	*in heaven . . .*
Mt 5:11–12	*L 6:22–23*

Christians have great rewards in heaven. In fact, Jesus instructed them to lay up treasure or treasures in heaven, like deposits in a treasure house:

MATTHEW	LUKE
But lay up for yourselves	Provide yourselves bags which wax not old,
treasures *in heaven*,	a treasure *in the heavens* that faileth not,
where neither moth nor rust doth corrupt, and where thieves do not break through nor steal. Mt 6:20	[neither moth corrupteth]*

where no thief approacheth. L 12:33 * Conformed to Matthew's order |

This general instruction was also included in a specific prescription for a particular young man who happened to be rich. Jesus told him:

One thing thou lackest: go thy way, sell whatsoever thou hast, and give to the poor, and thou shalt have treasure *in heaven* . . . Mk 10:21 (Mt 19:21; L 18:22)

"Treasure in Heaven" is not a popular idea today, but it runs like a litany through Jesus' own words. Do we strike out his words, or do we change our ideas?

The modern mind has two objections: what evidence is there for the existence of heaven; and, if there is such a place, how could God be so crude as to allow men to accumulate treasure there?

The evidence, of course, is Jesus' own words as recorded in the Gospels. Jesus taught:

If ye continue in my word, then are ye my disciples indeed; and ye shall know the truth . . . J 8:31

It is true that Jesus did not give space-time coordinates for heaven. Jesus was content to describe that realm as simply the state of being with the Father. Ought Jesus' followers add to his brief description? Is it enough to know that Jesus has prepared a place there for each of us with his Father in heaven?

Jesus taught that "the pure in heart . . . shall see God." *Mt 5:8* He also taught that the angels of these little ones do "always behold the face of my Father which is in heaven." *Mt 18:10* Accordingly, Christians will see God in heaven.

In the heavenly city where John saw the Throne of God, he wrote that those who "are written in the Lamb's Book of Life" shall serve him:

> And they shall *see his face*, and his name shall be in their foreheads. And there shall be no night there; and they need no candle, neither light of the sun: for the Lord God giveth them light, and they shall reign for ever and ever. *Revelation 22:4–5*

JESUS ON DEATH

Jesus recognized that all men will "taste of death." He said:

MARK	MATTHEW	LUKE
Verily I say	Verily I say	But I tell
unto you,	unto you,	you
		of a truth,
that there be	there be	there be
some of them	some	some
that stand here	standing here	standing here
which shall not	which shall not	which shall not
taste of death,	taste of death,	taste of death,
till they	till they	till they
have seen the	see the	see the
Kingdom of God	Son of man	Kingdom of God.
come with power.	coming	*L 9:27*
Mk 9:1	in his Kingdom.	
	Mt 16:28	

Jesus did not dispute the reality of death. He told Mary and Martha that their brother, Lazarus, was dead:

Then said Jesus unto them plainly, "Lazarus is dead." *J 11:14*

Yet shortly thereafter Jesus told Martha:

And whosoever liveth and believeth in me shall never die. *J 11:26*

On another occasion, Jesus, after describing himself as the "bread of life", said that this is bread "that a man may eat thereof, and not die", and that "if any man eat of this bread, he shall live for ever." *J 6:48, 50, 51*

For Jesus, the contrast between his teaching and the old was stark:

Your fathers did eat manna in the wilderness, and *are dead*. This is the bread which cometh down from Heaven, that a man may eat thereof, and *not die*. *J 6:49–50*

Jesus taught:

Verily, verily, I say unto you, if a man keep my saying, he shall never see death. J 8:51

Verily, verily, I say unto you, he that believeth on me hath everlasting life. J 6:47

These sayings are very clear that death is a nonevent for the followers of Jesus:

... not die . . . J 6:50
... shall never die . . . J 11:26
... never see death . . . J 8:51
... live for ever . . . J 6:51
... hath everlasting life . . . J 6:47

Why is it then that Christians continue to die and be buried? Jesus did not deny death and decay; he did affirm that once the Christian life begins, it continues beyond the grave:

I am the resurrection and the life; he that believeth in me, though he were dead, yet shall he live. J 11:25

Though a Christian dies physically, he continues to live spiritually. Once Jesus' claims and teachings are accepted, the Christian life, which continues beyond the grave, begins:

Verily, verily, I say unto you, he that heareth my word, and believeth on him that sent me, hath everlasting life and shall not come into condemnation, but is passed from death unto life. J 5:24

ETERNAL LIFE

What is eternal life?
Jesus defined it:

And this is life eternal, that they may know thee the only true God, and Jesus Christ, whom thou hast sent. *J 17:3*

Jesus considered "eternal life" to be equivalent to "never perishing":

My sheep hear my voice, and I know them, and they follow me. And I give unto them *eternal life; and they shall never perish* . . . *J 10:27–28*

The question of eternal life concerned Jesus' contemporaries. On two occasions he was asked how to inherit eternal life: Once by a rich young ruler, and once by an ecclesiastical lawyer.
    We have three accounts of the rich young ruler's question:

MARK	MATTHEW	LUKE
R: Good Master, what shall I do that I may inherit eternal life?	R: Good Master, what good thing shall I do, that I may have eternal life?	R: Good Master, what shall I do to inherit eternal life?
J: . . . Thou knowest the commandments:	J: . . . If thou wilt enter into life, keep the commandments.	J: . . . Thou knowest the commandments:
	R: Which?	
Do not	J: [Thou shalt not	Do not

Mark (cont.)	**Matthew** (cont.)	**Luke** (cont.)
commit adultery.	commit adultery.]*	commit adultery.
Do not kill.	Thou shalt do no murder.	Do not kill.
Do not steal.	Thou shalt not steal.	Do not steal.
Do not bear false witness.	Thou shalt not bear false witness.	Do not bear false witness.
Honor thy father and mother.	Honor thy father and thy mother; and, thou shalt love thy neighbor as thyself.	Honor thy father and thy mother.
R: Master, all these have I observed from my youth.	R: All these things have I kept from my youth up. What lack I yet?	R: All these have I kept from my youth up.
J: One thing thou lackest: go thy way, sell whatsoever thou hast, and give to the poor; and thou shalt have treasure in heaven, and come, take up the cross, and follow me.	J: If thou wilt be perfect, go and sell that thou hast, and give to the poor; and thou shalt have treasure in heaven, and come	J: Yet lackest thou one thing: sell all that thou hast, and distribute unto the poor; and thou shalt have treasure in heaven, and come,
Mk 10:17–21	and follow me. *Mt 19:16–21* * Conformed to Mark's order]	follow me. *L 18:18, 20–22*

We have only one account of the ecclesiastical lawyer's question:

LAWYER: Master, what shall I do to inherit eternal life?
JESUS: What is written in the Law? How readest thou?
LAWYER: Thou shalt love the Lord thy God with all thy heart, and
    with all thy soul, and with all thy strength, and with all thy
    mind; [*Deuteronomy 6:5*] and thy neighbor as thyself [*Leviticus 19:18*].
JESUS: Thou hast answered right; this do, and thou shalt live.
    L 10:25–28

The first question to decide is whether Jesus' answer to the lawyer and the ruler are timeless universal theological answers, or only answers to the spiritual needs of each questioner. They were only answers to the spiritual needs of each questioner, because Jesus gave different answers to the identical question: What shall I do to inherit eternal life?

He told the lawyer to keep the Law; he told the ruler to keep the Law *and* to sell his possessions *and* to follow Jesus.

The ruler's problem was his "great possessions" and he "went away grieved." *Mk 10:22* The lawyer's problem was his pride, and to show his prideful expertise, he quibbled:

And who is my neighbor? *L 10:29*

The pride of the lawyer is evident in the first line of the story:

And behold, a certain lawyer stood up, and *tempted* him, saying, "Master, what shall I do to inherit eternal life?" *L 10:25*

The King James' word *tempted* is archaic here and accordingly, is misleading. Modern translations use variants of *test* instead of *tempt*. This was a test question put by a specialist in the Law to see what this unauthorized lay teacher knew.

The lawyer's intent was not to get information about eternal life. Jesus sensed this and proceeded to simply agree with the lawyer's expertise about his own specialty, not to give timeless truth about eternal life.

Jesus' disciples also thought in terms of eternal life. Peter acknowledged to Jesus:

Thou hast the words of eternal life. And we believe and are sure that thou art that Christ, the Son of the living God. *J 6:68–69*

Jesus, with the greatest solemnity, assured some Jewish listeners:

Verily, verily, I say unto you, if a man keep my saying, he shall never see death. *J 8:51*

The same idea of never dying was more fully stated when Jesus said to Martha, the sister of Lazarus:

I am the resurrection and the life. He that believeth in me though he were dead, yet shall he live. And whosoever liveth and believeth in me *shall never die.* Believest thou this? *J 11:25–26*

"Shall never die" is equivalent to saying "shall never perish." According to Jesus, "eternal life" is "never perishing." He said:

And I give unto them eternal life; and they shall never perish . . . *J 10:28*

Jesus' statement continued:

Neither shall any man pluck them out of my hand. My Father, which gave them me, is greater than all; and no man is able to pluck them out of my Father's hand. *J 10:28–29*

Jesus thus stated that he controlled eternal life for those his Father had given him. This power of Jesus is confirmed by another statement of his which was as follows:

> As thou [the Father] hast given him [thy Son] power over all flesh, that he should give eternal life to as many as thou hast given him. *J 17:2*

The equivalence of "never perishing" and "eternal life" is shown by Jesus' famous statement of his mission:

> And as Moses lifted up the serpent in the wilderness, even so must the Son of Man be lifted up: that whosoever believeth in him *should not perish, but have eternal life.* For God so loved the world, that he gave his only begotten Son, that whosoever believeth in him *should not perish, but have eternal life. J 3:14–16*

It is obvious that in this quotation from the King James Version that "eternal life" and "everlasting life" are used interchangeably. There are other examples:

He that believeth on me	Whoso eateth my flesh, and drinketh my blood,
hath everlasting life.	hath eternal life.
I am that bread of life.	*J 6:54*
J 6:47–48	

In English, *everlasting* and *eternal* are often used interchangeably, even though strictly speaking *eternal* means without beginning or end, while *everlasting* applies to the endless future. Behind the English translations are the Greek words of the Gospel manuscripts, but we do not have the Aramaic words that Jesus actually used. Modern versions often standardize on the phrase "eternal life."

The subtle interplay of the words and phrases Jesus used to explain eternal life is shown by the following extended quotation from the 6th Chapter of John:

And this is the will of him that sent me, that everyone which seeth the Son, and believeth on him, may have *everlasting life*; and I will raise him up at the last day.

. . . Verily, verily, I say unto you, he that believeth on me hath *everlasting life*. I am that bread of life. Your fathers did eat manna in the wilderness, and are dead. This is the bread which cometh down from heaven, that a man may eat thereof, and *not die*. I am the living bread which came down from heaven. If any man eat of this bread, he *shall live forever*; . . .

Whoso eateth my flesh, and drinketh my blood, *hath eternal life*; and I will raise him up at the last day.

. . . This is that bread which came down from heaven; not as your fathers did eat manna and are dead. He that eateth of this bread *shall live forever. J 6:40, 47–51, 54, 58*

In this quotation Jesus moves from the simple words of *not die* to the phrase "shall live forever." It seems obvious that Jesus was talking about a single idea, an idea we call eternal life. When he talked about this idea, he used a number of different phrases which were equivalent so far as he was concerned. As translated into English, these phrases were eternal life—never perish—never see death—shall never die—should not perish—not die—live forever. *J 10:28, 8:51, 11:26, 3:16, 6:50, 6:51* Nothing is gained by adding this collage of phrases. Jesus' general meaning is clear.

Jesus also laid down the conditions for obtaining eternal life. These conditions are stated in various ways. The formulation everyone knows is John 3:16 where the condition is stated as belief: "whosoever believeth in him." In John 3:18 it becomes belief "in the name of the only begotten Son of God."

Almost as well known is Jesus' statement:

He that loveth his life shall lose it, and he that hateth his life in this world shall keep it unto *life eternal. J 12:25*

More obscure is Jesus' conversation with the Samaritan woman at the well in Sychar. Jesus told her:

> If thou knewest the gift of God, and who it is that saith to thee, "Give me to drink," thou wouldest have asked of him, and he would have given thee *living water*.

> . . . Whosoever drinketh of this water shall thirst again, but whosoever drinketh of the water that I shall give him shall never thirst; but the water that I shall give him shall be in him a well of water springing up into *everlasting life. J 4:10, 13–14*

Jesus used other metaphors of eating and drinking to explain the conditions of eternal life:

> Eat [or eateth] of this bread. *J 6:51 (58)*

> Eateth my flesh, and drinketh my blood. *J 6:54*

For those offended by such metaphors, it should be pointed out that in the same discourse in which they were used, Jesus made the same point with these words:

> And this is the will of him that sent me, that every one *that seeth the Son, and believeth on him*, may have everlasting life . . .

> . . . Verily, verily, I say unto you, he that *believeth on me* hath everlasting life. *J 6:40, 47*

Later on Jesus made the same point in still different words:

> Verily, verily, I say unto you, if a man keep my saying, he shall never see death. *J 8:51*

Jesus' ultimate explanation of the conditions of eternal life is his statement:

And whosoever *liveth and believeth in me* shall never die. Believeth thou this? *J 11:26*

Jesus' statement that "he that hateth his life in this world shall keep it unto life eternal" was a call to commitment of one's life. *J 12:25* As such, it is related to commitment to discipleship. This is made express in another statement of Jesus:

If any man come to me, and *hate not* his father, and mother, and wife, and children, and brethren, and sisters, yea, *and his own life also*, he cannot be my disciple. *L 14:26*

When Jesus makes hate of one's own life a condition of eternal life, he is really saying nothing different than be a disciple of Jesus, believe on him. This commitment will involve a rejection of one's life "in this world." *J 12:25*

Jesus also promised "eternal life" as a reward for this commitment:

MARK	MATTHEW	LUKE
Verily I say unto you,	And	Verily I say unto you,
there is no man	every one	there is no man
that hath left	that hath forsaken	that hath left
house,	houses,	house,
or brethren,	or brethren,	or parents,
or sisters,	or sisters,	
or father, or mother,	or father, or mother,	or brethren,
or wife, or children,	or wife, or children,	or wife, or children,
or lands,	or lands,	
for my sake,	for my name's sake,	for the Kingdom of
and the gospel's,		God's sake,
but he shall receive	shall receive	who shall not receive
an hundredfold	an hundredfold,	manifold more
now in this time,		in this present time,
houses, and brethren,		
and sisters,		
and mothers,		
and children,		

MARK (cont.)	MATTHEW (cont.)	LUKE (cont.)
and lands,		
with persecutions;		
and in the	and shall	and in the
world to come	inherit	world to come
eternal life.	*everlasting life.*	*life everlasting.*
Mk 10:29–30	Mt 19:29	L 18:29–30

A more accurate translation of "the world to come" is "the age to come", which is the Kingdom age which was then about to begin and still continues.

The group of statements relating to eating and drinking relate to partaking of Jesus' person or drinking his living water, and as such are figurative statements equivalent to believing in him. This equivalency is clear from one sustained discourse in which Jesus said:

> Verily, verily, I say unto you, he that *believeth on me* hath everlasting life. I am that bread of life. . . . I am the living bread which came down from heaven. If any man *eat of this bread*, he shall live for ever; and the bread that I will give is my flesh, which I will give for the life of the world.
>
> . . .*Whosoever eateth my flesh, and drinketh my blood, hath eternal life*; and I will raise him up at the last day. J 6:47–48, 51, 54

So far as Jesus was concerned, each of the phrases emphasized in the foregoing quotations stated the same idea: believeth on me = eat of me, the living bread = eateth my flesh, including drinketh my blood. It follows that the explicit phrases "eateth my flesh and drinketh my blood" are not meant sacramentally but as equivalent of "believeth on me."

It is obvious that when Jesus spoke of himself as being "the living bread" he is speaking figuratively just as he was when he spoke of giving "living water." He was not "bread", but he was, figuratively, the bread giving life in contrast to the manna given in the wilderness, which left its eaters dead at the end of their natural lives.

In Jesus' mind and speech there is no break between saying I am, figuratively speaking, "the living bread" and this "living bread" is "my flesh", which if you eat thereof, you have eternal life. Jesus' statement begins by saying, "He that believeth on me hath everlasting life" and ends saying "he that eateth of this bread shall live for ever." *J 6:47, 58* Eating "the living bread" was meant by Jesus to be the same as believing on him.

In a sense it is irrelevant how a person can claim eternal life, since it is a *gift* from Jesus, and through him, from his Father:

> My sheep hear my voice, and I know them, and they follow me.
> And I *give* unto them eternal life . . . My Father, which *gave* them
> me, is greater than all . . . *J 10:27–29*

Paul echoes Jesus' teaching that eternal life is a *gift* from his Father when he writes in Romans that "the gift of God is eternal life through Jesus Christ our Lord." *Romans 6:23*

Jesus said that his Father sent him and told him "what I should say, and what I should speak." And he continued:

> And I know that his commandment is life everlasting: whatsoever
> I speak therefore, even as the Father said unto me, so I speak.
> *J 12:49–50*

Jesus summed up the whole matter of eternal life in one terse and solemn statement:

> Verily, verily, I say unto you, he that heareth my word, and believeth
> on him that sent me, hath everlasting life, and shall not come into
> condemnation, but is passed from death unto life. *J 5:24*

The phrase "shall not come into condemnation" has been so stressed that Jesus' statement is distorted and his meaning lost. Jesus was talking about everlasting life, and he simply said in substance, "If you hear my word and believe upon my Father who sent me, you have everlasting life."

Jesus' phrase about escaping condemnation is secondary and incidental to Jesus' main point: The condition of everlasting life is simple, listen to my word and believe upon my Father who sent me.

Paul wrote of "our Saviour Jesus Christ, who hath abolished death and brought life and immortality to light through the Gospel." *2 Timothy 1:10*

For Christians, death has been abolished. Christians bypass death since they have already passed into eternal life:

> Verily, verily, I say unto you, he that heareth my word, and believeth on him that sent me, hath everlasting life, and . . . is passed from death unto life. *J 5:24*

CHAPTER 22

THE LAST THINGS

JESUS AND THE END OF THE WORLD

Jesus' own statements about the end of the world are seldom considered as a whole. Instead, his statements are used as fragmented bits to fit someone else's apocalyptic schema. If it is Jesus who is to return a second time, it is crucial to consider fully and fairly what he said about his return.

In the last week of his life, Jesus was in Jerusalem and was in and about the Temple, the great Jewish national shrine. As Jesus left the Temple probably on the Tuesday before the Friday on which he was crucified, one of his disciples said to him:

> Master, see what manner of stones and what buildings are here!
> *Mk 13:1*

Jesus looked beyond the building to its fate and replied:

MARK	MATTHEW	LUKE
Seest thou these great buildings?	See ye not all these things?	As for these things which ye behold, the days will come in which
	Verily I say unto you,	

MARK (cont.)	MATTHEW (cont.)	LUKE (cont.)
There shall not	there shall not	there shall not
be left	be left here	be left
one stone	one stone	one stone
upon another,	upon another,	upon another,
that shall not be	that shall not be	that shall not be
thrown down.	thrown down.	thrown down.
Mk 13:2	*Mt 24:2*	*L 21:6*

Josephus, a first-century Jewish historian, described the Temple as follows:

> Now the Temple was built of stones that were white and strong, and each of their length was twenty-five cubits, their height was eight, and their breadth about twelve; . . . *Josephus, Antiquities Of The Jews, Book XV, Ch. XI, Sec. 3*

Converting these cubit measurements into feet, each stone was about thirty-seven and a half feet long, twelve feet high and eighteen feet wide. Not only were the stones immense, they were finely polished. *Josephus, op. cit. Book XV, Ch XI, Sec. 5*

The Temple was surrounded by several courtyards, and the outer courtyard, the Court of the Gentiles, had a perimeter of about 4140 feet. This enormous Temple complex had taken forty-six years to build and "was adorned with goodly stones and gifts." *J 2:20; L 21:5*

Jesus' prediction that this great national shrine would be razed stuck in his disciples' minds, and, as soon as they got their chance, they asked him about it. Their chance came when, apparently later the same day, he sat with them on the Mount of Olives, a ridge near Jerusalem, and they could talk privately. *Mk 13:3; Mt 24:3*

The question they put was:

MARK	MATTHEW	LUKE
Tell us	Tell us	Master,
when shall	when shall	but when shall
these things be?	*these things* be?	*these things* be?
And what shall be	And what shall be	And what sign

MARK (cont.)	**MATTHEW** (cont.)	**LUKE** (cont.)
the sign	the sign	will there be
when all *these things*		when *these things*
shall be fulfilled?	of thy coming,	shall come to pass?
Mk 13:4	and of the end	*L 21:7*
	of the world?	
	Mt 24:3	

Before Jesus' answer is analyzed, the variations in the question as recorded in the three gospels should be noted. All three gospels record the question as being, "When shall *these things* be?"

The crucial issue is, are "these things" simply the destruction of the Temple, or was it a broader question? *Mk 13:1–3; Mt 24:1–3; L 21:5–6*

Only Matthew adds a second question which may be simply an elaboration of the "these things" question:

And what shall be the sign of thy coming and of the end of the world? *Mt 24:3*

Jesus apparently answered this Gentile question first, and then turned to the specific question of the destruction of the Temple and said:

MARK	**MATTHEW**	**LUKE**
But when ye	When ye therefore	And when ye
shall see	shall see	shall see
the abomination	the abomination	Jerusalem
of desolation,	of desolation,	
spoken of by Daniel	spoken of by Daniel	
the prophet, standing	the prophet, stand in	compassed
where it ought not,	the holy place,	with armies,
(let him that	(whoso readeth,	then know
readeth understand)	let him understand)	that the desolation
		thereof is nigh.
then let	then let	Then let
them that	them which	them which
be in Judea	be in Judea	are in Judea

MARK (cont.)	**MATTHEW** (cont.)	**LUKE** (cont.)
flee to	flee into	flee to
the mountains,	the mountains;	the mountains,
and let him that is	let him which is	and let them which are
on the housetop	on the housetop	in the midst of it
not go down	not come down	depart out:
into the house,		
neither enter therein,		
to take	to take	
any thing	any thing	
out of his house;	out of his house;	and
and let him	neither let him	let not them
that is	which is	which are
in the field	in the field	in the countries
not turn back again	return back	enter thereinto.
for to take up	to take	
his garment.	his clothes.	
		For these be
		the days of vengeance,
		that all things
		which are written
		may be fulfilled.
But woe to them	And woe unto them	But woe unto them
that are with child,	that are with child,	that are with child,
and to them	and to them	and to them
that give suck	that give suck	that give suck
in those days!	in those days!	in those days!
		L 21:20–23
And pray ye	But pray ye	
that your flight	that your flight	
be not	be not	
in the winter.	in the winter,	
Mk 13:14–18	neither	
	on the Sabbath day.	
	Mt 24:15–20	

At this point Luke has material that is not found in either Matthew or Mark. Luke writes:

> For there shall be great distress in the land, and wrath upon this people. And they shall fall by the edge of the sword, and shall be led away captive into all nations; and Jerusalem shall be trodden down of the Gentiles, until the times of the Gentiles be fulfilled. *L 21:23–24*

When the three gospel accounts of Jesus' answer are compared, it is clear that Luke has material that neither Matthew nor Mark have. The problem is compounded by the further question whether the sentence in each of the three gospels referring to "desolation" are in fact parallel sentences and refer to the same event:

MARK	MATTHEW	LUKE
But when ye	When ye therefore	And when ye
shall see	shall see	shall see
the abomination	*the abomination*	Jerusalem
of desolation,	*of desolation,*	compassed
spoken of	spoken of	with armies,
by Daniel the prophet,	by Daniel the prophet,	
standing where	stand in the	
it ought not,	holy place,	then know that
		the desolation thereof
		is nigh.
(let him that readeth	(whoso readeth	
understand),	let him understand),	
then let them	then let them	Then let them
that be in Judea	which be in Judea	which are in Judea
flee to	flee into	flee to
the mountains.	the mountains.	the mountains.
Mk 13:14	*Mt 24:15–16*	*L 21:20–21*

In the first place, the use of the English word *desolation* in all three accounts creates a false identity: "abomination of desolation" is not the same as "desolation thereof", i.e., the desolation of Jerusalem. Matthew and Mark expressly refer to the prophet Daniel as the source of the phrase they use, "the abomination of desolation", which will stand "where it ought not", or "in the holy place." *Mk 13:14; Mt 24:15* This means the Temple in Jerusalem.

In fact this event prophesied by Daniel had already happened once before in 167 B.C. when Antiochus IV Epiphanes, a Hellenistic conqueror of Jerusalem, had erected a statue of Zeus in the Temple and built an idol altar upon its altar and offered swine sacrifices upon it. Josephus, the Jewish historian, describes the incident in detail:

> And when the king had built *an idol altar upon God's altar, he slew swine upon it, and so offered a sacrifice neither according to the law, nor the Jewish religious worship in that country.* He also compelled them to forsake the worship which they paid their own God, and to adore those whom he took to be gods: and made them build temples and raise idol altars, in every city and village, and offer swine upon them every day. He also commanded them not to circumcise their sons, and threatened to punish any that should be found to have transgressed his injunction. He also appointed overseers, who should compel them to do what he commanded. And indeed many Jews there were who complied with the king's commands, either voluntarily, or out of fear of the penalty that was denounced: but the best men, and those of the noblest souls, did not regard him, but did pay a greater respect to the customs of their country than concern as to the punishment which he threatened to the disobedient; on which account they every day underwent great miseries and bitter torments; for they were whipped with rods, and their bodies were torn to pieces, and were crucified while they were still alive and breathed: they also strangled those women and their sons whom they had circumcised, as the king had appointed, hanging their sons about their necks as they were upon the crosses. And if there were any sacred book of the law found, it was destroyed; and those with whom they were found, miserably perished also. *Josephus, Antiquities Of The Jews, Book XII, Ch. V, Sec. 4*

Matthew and Mark agree that such a sacrilege will be repeated; that is a different thing than "Jerusalem compassed with armies" to which Luke refers. *L 21:20* Such a sacrilege could occur without

Jerusalem being besieged, and Jerusalem could be besieged without such a sacrilege taking place.

If we combine Luke's statement as to the desolation or destruction of Jerusalem with his unique statement as to "the times of then Gentiles", we have a composite statement that mentions Jerusalem in both its parts, while Matthew and Mark do not mention Jerusalem in their parallel sections at all, and it leaves Matthew's and Mark's accounts, and the rest of Luke's accounts essentially parallel. *Mk 13:5–27; Mt 24:4–31; L 21:8–19, 21–23, 25–28* Luke's composite statement then reads as follows:

> And when ye shall see Jerusalem compassed with armies, then know that the desolation thereof is nigh.
>
> . . . And they shall fall by the edge of the sword, and shall be led away captive into all nations; and Jerusalem shall be trodden down of the Gentiles, until the times of the Gentiles be fulfilled. *L 21:20, 24*

After all the centuries since Luke was written, it is futile to speculate why or how these two verses got separated and why or how they got interspersed in Luke's version of Jesus' general statement as to the end of the world.

This composite section of Luke deals with the fate of Jerusalem and does not expressly mention the destruction of the Temple. But if Jerusalem was to be desolated, it would be expected that the Temple, the heart of the city, would also be desolated.

This composite section from Luke is Jesus' prophecy as to the fate of Jerusalem and the Temple and fits well with certain indisputable historical facts. *L 21:20, 24* About forty years after his prophecy, in A.D. 66, the Jews revolted and in the course of the revolt, the Romans, led by Titus, besieged Jerusalem. The city fell in A.D. 70, and both the city and the Temple were razed.

This event is described by Josephus, the Jewish historian and a participant in that revolt, as follows:

> Now, as soon as the army had no more people to slay or to plunder, because there remained none to be the objects of their fury, (for they would not have spared any, had there remained any other such

work to be done), Caesar gave orders that they should now demolish the *entire city and temple*, but should leave as many of the towers standing as were of the greatest eminecy; that is, Phasaelus, and Hippicus, and Mariamne, and so much of the wall as enclosed the city on the west side. This wall was spared, in order to afford a camp for men as were to lie in garrison; as were the towers also spared, in order to demonstrate to posterity what kind of city it was, and how well fortified which the Roman valour had subdued; but for all the rest of the wall, it was so thoroughly laid even with the ground by those that dug it up to the foundations, that there was nothing left to make those that came thither believe it had ever been inhabited. *Josephus, Wars Of The Jews, Book VII, Ch. I, Sec. 1*

The Roman army "compassed" Jerusalem. L 21:20 When the city fell, Jews did "fall by the edge of the sword" and were "led away captive into all nations." L 21:24 The Roman Tenth Legion "with certain troops of horsemen, and companies of footmen" was left to garrison the site. *Josephus, Wars Of The Jews, Book VII, Ch. I, Sec. 2*

Josephus describes how the captivity began:

2. And now, since his soldiers were already quite tired with killing men, and yet there appeared to be a vast multitude still remaining alive, Caesar gave orders that they should kill none but those that were in arms, and opposed them, but should take the rest alive. But, together with those whom they had orders to slay, they slew the aged and the infirm; but for those that were in their flourishing age, and who might be useful to them, they drove them together into the temple, and shut them up within the walls of the court of the women; over which Caesar set one of his freedmen, as also Fronto, one of his own friends; which last was to determine every one's fate, according to his merits. So this Fronto slew all those had been seditious and robbers, who were impeached one by another; but of the young men, he chose out the tallest and most beautiful, and reserved them for *the triumph*; and as for the rest of the multitude that were above seventeen years old, he put them into bonds, and sent them to the Egyptian mines. Titus also sent a great number into the provinces, as a present to them, that they might be destroyed upon their theatres, by the sword and by the wild beasts;

but those that were under seventeen years of age were sold for slaves.
Josephus, Wars Of The Jews, Book VI, Ch. IX, Sec. 2

Titus earned a Roman triumph for crushing this Jewish revolt. On the Arch of Titus which still stands in Rome the Jewish captives are depicted.

In A.D.132 the Jews again revolted against the Romans and Jerusalem fell again in A.D.135. This time the Romans plowed the site and built on it a new Roman city, Aelia Capitolina. A pagan shrine to Jupiter Capitolinus was erected on the site of the Temple and Jews were prohibited from living in Jerusalem. From that time forward the Jews never again controlled Jerusalem until 1950 when the Israeli government took over one part of the then divided city.

Jesus said:

And they shall fall by the edge of the sword, and shall be led away captive into all nations; and Jerusalem shall be trodden down of the Gentiles, until the time of the Gentiles be fulfilled. *L 21:24*

THE TIMES OF THE GENTILES

Jesus' prophecy as to Jerusalem has already been fulfilled. The question remaining is when are "the times of the Gentile" fulfilled?

This Gentile era is probably the gospel-preaching era that precedes the end of the world referred to in Matthew and Mark as follows:

MARK	MATTHEW
And the gospel	And this gospel of the Kingdom
must first be published among all nations. *Mk 13:10*	shall be preached in all the world for a witness unto all nations, and then shall the end come. *Mt 24:14*

After his resurrection Jesus told the eleven disciples:

Go ye therefore, and teach all nations, baptizing them in the name of the Father, and of the Son, and of the Holy Spirit: teaching them to observe all things whatsoever I have commanded you; and lo, I am with you always, even unto the end of the world. *Mt 28:19–20*

Paul referred to this Gentile gospel era as follows:

For I would not, brethren, that you should be ignorant of this mystery, lest ye should be wise in your own conceits; that blindness in part is happened to Israel, until the fulness of the Gentiles be come. *Romans 11:25*

Paul is referring to Israel's partial failure to accept Jesus. The Christian church at the time he wrote still had a substantial Jewish membership. It became a Gentile church thereafter and so continues until this day.

Perhaps it is a sign of the end of the Gentile era that a few Jews are now beginning to accept Jesus and his claims. What is certain is that the gospel has been "preached in all the world for a witness to all nations" and that this was substantially accomplished only in the nineteenth and twentieth centuries. *Mt 24:14* The process continues as attempts are made to reach the last few peoples and tribes. This is not to say that the world has been converted, only that the gospel has been "preached in all the world."

During this gospel-preaching era and before the fearsome signs of the end of the world such as, nation rising against nation, kingdom rising against kingdom, earthquakes, famines, and pestilences, believers will be persecuted, flogged in synagogues, imprisoned and brought before kings and rulers for Jesus' sake.

This will be their opportunity to testify to their faith. Jesus therefore gave directions as to how they should then testify:

MARK	LUKE
But take heed	But *before* all these,
to yourselves:	[signs of the end]
for they shall	they shall
	lay their hands on you,
	and persecute you,
deliver you up	delivering you up
to councils, and	
in the synagogues	to the synagogues,
ye shall be beaten;	and into prisons,
and ye shall be brought	being brought
before rulers and kings	before kings and rulers
for my sake,	for my name's sake.
	And it shall turn to you
for a testimony	for a testimony.
against them.	
. . . But when they	
shall lead you,	
and deliver you up,	Settle it therefore
take no thought	in your hearts,
beforehand	

MARK (cont.)	LUKE (cont.)
what ye shall speak,	
neither do ye	not
premeditate;	to meditate before
	what ye shall answer:
but whatsoever	for I will
shall be given you	give you
in that hour,	a mouth
that speak ye:	and wisdom,
for it is not ye	which all your adversaries
that speak,	shall not be able
but the Holy Spirit.	to gainsay nor resist.
Mk 13:9, 11	*L 21:12–15*

Mark 13:10 is omitted from the foregoing comparison of the gospel accounts because it is an aside that interrupts Mark's statement about testimony before authorities, civil and religious, and because it is parallel to Matthew 24:14 dealing with the preaching of the gospel to all nations. These two statements have already been quoted and compared when Jesus' statements about the gospel-preaching era were analyzed.

The gospel-preaching era has been full of persecutions of Christians by authorities, both civil and religious. Christian persecution by the Roman authorities in the first three centuries after Jesus' death is an undisputable fact of history. Jesus' reference to Christians being beaten in synagogues was fulfilled in the days of the early church when Christians were considered heretics by synagogue Jews. The book of Acts is the prime evidence.

Acts quotes Paul as saying:

Lord, they know that I imprisoned and beat in every synagogue them that believed on thee. *Acts 22:19*

And I punished them oft in every synagogue, and compelled them to blaspheme. *Acts 26:11*

In Second Corinthians, Paul wrote:

Of the Jews five times received I forty stripes save one. *2 Corinthians 11:24*

Jesus described this period of persecution and betrayal as ending with his followers being "hated of all men for my name's sake":

MARK	MATTHEW	LUKE
Now the brother shall betray the brother to death, and the father the son;	Then shall they deliver you up to be afflicted, and shall kill you . . .	And ye shall be betrayed both by parents, and brethren, and kinsfolks and friends;
and children shall rise up against their parents and shall cause them to be put to death.	And then shall many be offended, and shall betray one another, and shall hate one another. And many false prophets shall rise, and shall deceive many. And because iniquity shall abound, the love of many shall wax cold.	and some of you shall they cause to be put to death.
And ye shall be hated of all men for my name's sake;	[And ye shall be hated of all nations for my name's sake.]*	And ye shall be hated of all men for my name's sake.
but he that shall endure unto the end,	But he that shall endure unto the end,	But there shall not an hair of your head perish.

Mark (cont.)	**Matthew** (cont.)	**Luke** (cont.)
the same	the same	In your patience
shall be saved.	shall be saved.	possess ye
Mk 13:12–13	*Mt 24:9–13*	your souls.
	* Conformed to	*L 21:16–19*
	Mark's order	

The times of the Gentiles end with Christians being hated of all men for Jesus' name sake.

After the End of the Gentile Era
The End-Time Signs Begin

The end–time signs begin after the end of the Gentile era. The first sign to appear is the abomination of desolation spoken of by the prophet Daniel standing "in the holy place." *Mt 24:15 (Mk 13:14)* This is apparently a sacrilege of the Temple such as occurred in 167 B.C. For this to happen it would seem necessary for the Temple, which was finally destroyed in A.D.132, to be rebuilt first.

Those then in Judea should flee to the mountains without even waiting to get a coat since the great tribulation is about to begin:

MARK	MATTHEW
For in those days	For then
shall be affliction,	shall be great tribulation,
such as was not	such as was not
from the beginning	since the beginning
of the creation	of the world
which God created	
unto this time,	to this time,
neither shall be.	no, nor ever shall be.
And except	And except
that the Lord	those days
had shortened	should be shortened,
those days,	there should
no flesh	no flesh
should be saved;	be saved;
but for the elect's sake,	but for the elect's sake
whom he hath chosen,	
he hath shortened	those days
the days.	shall be shortened.
Mk 13:19–20	*Mt 24:21–22*

At this time of tribulation Christ will not yet have returned. The passages from Mark and Matthew just quoted, continue thus:

MARK	MATTHEW
And *then*	*Then*

Mark (cont.)	Matthew (cont.)
if any man	if any man
shall say	shall say
to you,	unto you,
lo, here is Christ,	lo, here is Christ,
or, lo, he is there,	or there,
believe him not:	believe it not.
for	For there shall
false Christs	arise false Christs,
and false prophets	and false prophets,
shall rise,	
and shall shew	and shall shew
signs and wonders,	great signs and wonders;
to seduce,	insomuch that,
if it were possible,	if it were possible,
	they shall deceive
even the elect.	the very elect.
But take ye heed:	
behold,	Behold,
I have foretold you	I have told you before.
all things.	*Mt 24:23–25*
Mk 13:21–23	

Jesus had begun his answer to the end–time question "When shall these things be?" with a general caution against false Christs and here he repeats it more specifically and also puts this phenomena in its appropriate time frame. Jesus' initial general caution about false Christs was combined with a list of end–time signs which will follow the persecutions of the gospel-preaching age. His disciples asked privately, "Tell us, when shall these things be?" *Mk 13:3–4; Mt 24:3 (L 21:7)* Jesus answered:

Mark	Matthew	Luke
Take heed	Take heed	Take heed
lest any man	that no man	that ye be
deceive you:	deceive you:	not deceived:
for many	for many	for many
shall come	shall come	shall come

MARK (cont.)	MATTHEW (cont.)	LUKE (cont.)
in my name,	in my name,	in my name,
saying,	saying,	saying,
"I am Christ,"	"I am Christ,"	"I am Christ,"
		and the time
		draweth near;
and shall deceive	and shall deceive	go ye not therefore
many.	many.	after them.
And when ye	And ye	But when ye
shall hear of	shall hear of	shall hear of
wars	wars	wars
and rumors of war,	and rumors of wars;	and commotions,
	see that	
be ye not troubled:	ye be not troubled:	be not terrified:
for such things	for all these things	for these things
must	must	must
needs be;	come to pass,	first come to pass;
but the end	but the end	but the end
shall not be yet.	is not yet.	is not by and by.
For nation shall rise	For nation shall rise	Nation shall rise
against nation,	against nation,	against nation,
and kingdom	and kingdom	and kingdom
against kingdom;	against kingdom;	against kingdom;
and there shall be	and there shall be	and
earthquakes	famines,	great earthquakes
		shall be
in diverse places,	and	in diverse places,
and there shall be	pestilences,	and famines,
famines and troubles.	and earthquakes,	and pestilences;
	in diverse places.	
These are	All these are	and fearful sights
the beginnings	the beginnings	and great signs
of sorrows.	of sorrows.	shall there be
Mk 13:5–8	*Mt 24:4–8*	from heaven.
		L 21:8–11

Jesus pointed out the false Christs will come and that there will be "wars and rumors of wars" but the end is not yet. Nor does the struggle of nation against nation, kingdom against kingdom, earthquakes, famines, pestilences signify the end. They are only the beginning of the end, the beginning of sorrows.

Jesus' concern was that his followers would be deceived by the false Christs and not only warned against them, but stressed that his second coming will be an unmistakable event. He told his disciples:

> The days will come, when ye shall desire to see one of the days of the Son of man, and ye shall not see it. And they shall say to you, "See here," or, "See there;" go not after them, nor follow them. For as the lightning, that lighteneth out of the one part under heaven, shineth unto the other part under heaven, so shall also the Son of man be in his day. But first must he suffer many things, and be rejected of this generation. *L 17:22–25*

Despite Jesus' caution he had first to suffer many things, and be rejected of *this generation*, his disciples still wanted to know, "Where, Lord?" *L 17:25, 37*

Jesus answered:

> Wheresoever the body is, thither will the eagles be gathered together. *L 17:37 (Mt 24:28)*

Modern translations substitute *vultures* for "eagles." That is more accurate. "Body" means a carcass. *Mt 24:28* Jesus' image was of a cloud of vultures circling high in a clear desert sky above a rotting carcass stinking in the shimmering heat.

Basically Jesus' answer to the question of "Where?" was, "Don't worry, it will be so obvious, so unmistakably obvious", like circling vultures visible for miles, like lightening lighting up the whole sky. Don't worry about the "Lo here" and "Lo there" fellows. You won't need to be told when Jesus comes as the Son of man. His appearance will surge over the whole sky like a tremendous flash of lightning:

MATTHEW	LUKE
Wherefore if they	And they
shall say unto you,	shall say to you,
"Behold,	"See here,"
he is in the desert,"	or,
go not forth;	"See there;"
"Behold,	go not after them,
he is in the secret chambers,"	nor follow them.
believe it not.	
For as the lightning	For as the lightning,
cometh out of	that lighteneth out of
the east,	the one part under heaven,
and shineth	shineth
even unto	unto
the west,	the other part under heaven;
so shall also	so shall
the coming of	also the
the Son of man	Son of man
be.	be in his day.
Mt 24:26–27	L 17:23–24

Although Jesus' second coming will be unmistakable, he also gave a list of the final signs that will appear in the heavens after the persecutions and betrayals and after the false Christs, the wars and rumors of war, the famines, earthquakes, and pestilences. Jesus said:

MARK	MATTHEW	LUKE
But in those days,	Immediately	And there
after that tribulation,	*after* the tribulation	shall be signs
	of those days	
the sun	shall the sun	in the sun,
shall be darkened,	be darkened,	
and the moon	and the moon	and in the moon,

MARK (cont.)	MATTHEW (cont.)	LUKE (cont.)
shall not give	shall not give	
her light,	her light,	
and the stars	and the stars	and in the stars,
of heaven shall fall,	shall fall from heaven,	and upon the earth
		distress of nations,
		with perplexity;
		and the sea
		and the waves roaring;
		men's hearts
		failing them
		for fear,
		and for looking after
		those things
		which are coming
		on the earth:
and	and	for
the powers that are	the powers	the powers
in heaven	of the heavens	of heaven
shall be shaken.	shall be shaken.	shall be shaken.
And then	And then	And then
shall they see	shall appear	shall they see
	the sign of	
	the Son of man	
	in heaven,	
	and then shall	
	all the tribes	
	of the earth	
	mourn;	
	and they shall see	
the Son of man	the Son of man	the Son of man
coming	coming	coming
in the clouds	in the clouds	in a cloud
	of heaven	
with great power	with power	with power
and glory.	and great glory.	and great glory.
And then	And	L 21:25–27
shall he send	he shall send	
his angels,	his angels	

MARK (cont.)

and shall
gather together
his elect
from the four winds,
from the uttermost
part
of the earth
to the uttermost part
of heaven.
Mk 13:24–27

MATTHEW (cont.)
with a great sound
of a trumpet,
and they shall
gather together
his elect
from the four winds,
from one end
of heaven
to the other.
Mt 24:29–31

LUKE (cont.)

Luke adds a note of jubilant exultation:

And when these things begin to come to pass, then look up, and lift
up your heads; for your redemption draweth nigh. *L 21.28*

The end of the days of woe and vengeance and false Christs is
shown by the darkening sun, a moon not giving light and by stars
falling from heaven. *Mk 13:24–25; Mt 24:29–30; L 21.25–26*

After this awesome flourish, the Son of man will appear in the
clouds with great power and glory, and will gather his elect from
the uttermost parts of both earth and heaven.

The Taken and the Left

Despite the fact that Jesus second coming will be preceded by awesome signs in the sky, life on earth will be continuing its ordinary round. Then in an instant, all will be changed, changed forever. We have two accounts of Jesus' statement on this:

MATTHEW	LUKE
But as the days of Noah were,	And as it was in the days of Noah,
so shall also	so shall it be also
the coming of	in the days of
the Son of man be.	the Son of man.
For as in the days	
that were before the flood,	
they were eating and drinking,	They did eat, they drank,
marrying	they married wives,
and giving in marriage,	they were given in marriage,
until the day	until the day
that Noah entered into the ark,	that Noah entered into the ark,
and knew not	
until the flood came,	and the flood came,
and took them all away.	and destroyed them all.
	Likewise also as it was
	in the days of Lot;
	they did eat, they drank,
	they bought, they sold,
	they planted, they builded.
	But the same day
	that Lot went out of Sodom,
	it rained
	fire and brimstone from heaven,
	and destroyed them all.
So shall also	Even thus shall it be
the coming of	in the day when
the Son of man be.	the Son of man is revealed.
Mt 24:37–39	In that day,

MATTHEW (cont.)	LUKE (cont.)
	he which shall be upon the housetop, and his stuff in the house, let him not come down to take it away; and he that is in the field, let him likewise not return back.
	Remember Lot's wife.
	Whosoever shall seek to save his life shall lose it; and whosoever shall lose his life shall preserve it.
	I tell you, *in that night* there shall be two men in one bed; the one shall be taken, the other shall be left.
Two women shall be grinding at the mill; the one shall be taken, and the other left. *Mt 24:41*	Two women shall be grinding together; the one shall be taken, and the other left.
Then shall two be in the field: the one shall be taken and the other left. *Mt 24:40*	Two men shall be in the field: one shall be taken, the other left. *L 17:26–36*

These accounts show that Jesus' second coming could be either in the daytime when men are in the fields and women are grinding grain, or at night when people are in bed. In substance Jesus said that if it is night and two shall be in one bed, one may be taken; if it is day and two shall be working together, one may be taken.

On the day when Jesus comes, life, as in the days of Noah and Lot, will be continuing its ordinary round, oblivious of the cataclysm which is about to happen with stunning swiftness, dividing all mankind into two classes: Those taken and those left.

Jesus Taught That No One Knows the Day and Hour of His Second Coming

Jesus taught that no one, absolutely no one, not even radio preachers, knows the day and hour of his second coming. He did teach that there will be signs that will be obvious like the seasonal greening of fig trees:

MARK	MATTHEW	LUKE
Now learn a parable of the fig tree. When her branch is yet tender, and putteth forth leaves, ye know	Now learn a parable of the fig tree. When his branch is yet tender, and putteth forth leaves, ye know	Behold the fig tree, and all the trees. When they now shoot forth, ye see and know of your own selves
that summer is near.	that summer is nigh.	that summer is now nigh at hand.
So ye in like manner, when ye shall see these things come to pass, know that it is nigh, even at the doors.	So likewise ye, when ye shall see all these things, know that it is near, even at the doors.	So likewise ye, when ye see these things come to pass, know ye that *the Kingdom of God* is nigh at hand.
Verily I say unto you, that *this generation* shall not pass, till all these things be done. Heaven and earth shall pass away, but my words shall not pass away.	Verily I say unto you, *this generation* shall not pass, till all these things be fulfilled. Heaven and earth shall pass away, but my words shall not pass away.	Verily I say unto you, *this generation* shall not pass away, till all be fulfilled. Heaven and earth shall pass away. L 21:29–33
But of *that day*	But of *that day*	

MARK (cont.)	MATTHEW (cont.)	LUKE (cont.)
and that hour	*and hour*	
knoweth no man,	knoweth no man,	
no, not the angels	no, not the angels	
which are in heaven,	of heaven,	
neither the Son,		
but the Father.	but my Father only.	
Mk 13:28–32	*Mt 24:32–36*	

Luke expressly says that it is the Kingdom of God that is near. *L 21:31* Both Matthew and Mark simply say "it" is near. *Mk 13:29; Mt 24:33* Some modern translations of Matthew and Mark have, "he is near" for "it is near." From the general context of these passages the "it" probably refers to Jesus' second coming at the end of the world and not to the initial coming of the Kingdom of God. See "Jesus' Timetable For The Coming Of The Kingdom Of God", pp. 491–496. Luke simply does not make the clear distinction we now make between the coming of the Kingdom of God and Jesus' second coming, just as Matthew in another context wrote of some persons standing there not tasting of death till they see "the Son of man coming" while Mark and Luke wrote of seeing "the Kingdom of God":

MARK	MATTHEW	LUKE
Till they have seen	Till they see	Till they see
the Kingdom of God	the Son of man	the Kingdom of God.
come with	coming in	*L 9:27*
power.	his Kingdom.	
Mk 9:1	*Mt 16:28*	

Since not even Jesus himself knew the day and the hour, it is impossible to be precise when he will return as the apocalyptic Son of man. Jesus' phrase translated "this generation" is vague. An alternative translation of that phrase is "this race", which avoids the question of "how long." Jesus' phrase can also be translated as "this era", which avoids the implication of a relatively short period of time implied in the phrase "this generation." If Jesus' phrase means "this era", it fits well into the other things which Jesus said as to the Gentile era since then Jesus simply reiterates that this Gentile era will not end until all the events he had outlined occur.

The point is to be ready when Jesus returns as the apocalyptic Son of man:

MARK	MATTHEW	LUKE
Take ye head, watch and pray: *for ye know not when the time is.*	Watch therefore: *for ye know not what hour your Lord doth come.*	
For the Son of man is as a man taking a far journey, who left his house, and gave authority to his servants, and to every man his work, and commanded the porter to watch.	But know this, that if the goodman of the house had known in what watch the thief would come, he would have watched, and would not have suffered his house to be broken up.	And take heed to yourselves, lest at any time your hearts be overcharged with surfeiting, and drunkenness, and cares of this life, and so *that day* come upon you unawares.
		For as a snare shall it come on all them that dwell on the face of the whole earth.
Watch ye therefore: for ye know not when the master of the house cometh, at even or at midnight, or at	Therefore, be ye also ready: for in such an hour as ye think not the Son of man cometh. *Mt 24:42–44*	Watch ye therefore, and pray always, that ye may be accounted worthy to escape all these things that shall come to pass

MARK (cont.)	MATTHEW (cont.)	LUKE (cont.)
the cock-crowing,		and to stand before
or in the morning.		the Son of man.
Lest coming suddenly		*L 21:34–36*
he find you sleeping.		

And what I say
unto *you*,
I say unto *all*,
"Watch."
Mk 13:33–37

Luke alone has another long exhortation to readiness:

Let your loins be girded about, and your lights burning. And ye yourselves like unto men that wait for their lord, when he will return from the wedding; that when he cometh and knocketh, they may open unto him immediately.

Blessed are those servants, whom the lord when he cometh shall find watching. Verily I say unto you, that he shall gird himself, and make them to sit down to meat, and will come forth and serve them. And if he shall come in the second watch, or come in the third watch, and find them so, blessed are those servants.

And this know, that if the goodman of the house had known what hour the thief would come, he would have watched, and not have suffered his house to be broken through. Be ye therefore ready also: for the Son of man cometh at an hour when ye think not. *L 12:35–40*

Peter asked, "Lord, speakest thou this parable unto us, or even to all? *L 12:41*

Jesus' answer as given in Luke is paralleled by a statement in Matthew:

LUKE	MATTHEW
Who then is	Who then is
that faithful and wise steward,	a faithful and wise servant,

LUKE (cont.)	MATTHEW (cont.)
whom his lord	whom his lord
shall make ruler	hath made ruler
over his household,	over his household,
to give them	to give them
their portion	
of meat in due season?	meat in due season?
Blessed is that servant	Blessed is that servant
whom his lord	whom his lord
when *he cometh*	when *he cometh*
shall find so doing.	shall find so doing.
Of a truth I say unto you,	Verily I say unto you,
that he will make him	that he shall make him
ruler over all	ruler over all
that he hath.	his goods.
But and if	But and if
that servant say	that evil servant shall say
in his heart,	in his heart,
"My lord delayeth *his coming,*"	"My lord delayeth *his coming,*"
and shall begin to beat	and shall begin to smite
the manservants and maidens,	his fellowservants,
and to eat and drink	and to eat and drink
and to be drunken,	with the drunken,
the lord of that servant	the lord of that servant
will come in a day	shall come in a day
when he looketh not for him,	when he looketh not for him,
and at an hour	and in an hour
when he is not aware,	that he is not aware of,
and will cut him in sunder,	and shall cut him asunder,
and will appoint him	and appoint him
his portion	his portion
with the unbelievers.	with the hypocrites.
	There shall be
	weeping and gnashing of teeth.
And that servant,	*Mt 24:45–51*

LUKE (cont.)
which know his lord's will,
and prepared not himself,
neither did
according to his will,
shall be beaten
with many stripes.

But he that knew not,
and did commit things
worthy of stripes,
shall be beaten
with few stripes.
For unto whomsoever
much is given,
of him
shall be much required;
and to whom
men have committed much,
of him
they will ask the more.
L 12:42–48

MATTHEW (cont.)

Jesus' coming may be delayed, but his servants are not, at their peril, to be unready. Jesus also told the parable of the ten virgins to make his point:

Then shall the Kingdom of Heaven be likened unto ten virgins, which took their lamps and went forth to meet the bridegroom. And five of them were wise, and five were foolish. They that were foolish took their lamps, *and took no oil with them*, but the wise took oil in their vessels with their lamps.

"While the bridegroom tarried, they all slumbered and slept. And at midnight there was a cry made, "Behold, the bridegroom cometh; go ye out to meet him.""

Then all those virgins arose, and trimmed their lamps.

And the foolish said unto the wise, "Give us of your oil, for our lamps are gone out."

But the wise answered, saying, "Not so, lest there be not enough for us and you; but go ye rather to them that sell, and buy for your-selves."

And while they went to buy, the bridegroom came; and they that were ready went in with him to the marriage, and the door was shut.

Afterwards came also the other virgins, saying, "Lord, Lord, open to us."

But he answered and said, "Verily I say unto you, I know you not."

Watch therefore, for ye know neither the day nor the hour wherein the Son of Man cometh. *Mt 25:1–13*

The phrase, "wherein the Son of man cometh", is omitted in modern translations on the basis of the manuscript evidence. The implication of the parable, however, is that those in the Kingdom await the bridegroom, who is Christ. The point of the parable is that those in the Kingdom had better be ready for Christ's com-ing—it is not enough to be on the alert. After all, the five foolish virgins were on the alert, but they were not ready. They were un-prepared.

Both the parable of the pounds found in Luke and the parable of the talents found in Matthew have an undercurrent of warning to employ your talents well until Jesus returns. Luke opens with the sentence: "A certain nobleman went into a far country to re-ceive for himself a kingdom, and to return." *L 19:12* Matthew de-scribes the nobleman as "a man traveling into a far country, who called his own servants, and delivered unto them his goods" and states that "after a long time the lord of those servants cometh, and reckoneth with them." *Mt 25:14, 19*

Jesus is that nobleman who is to return and those two parables add to the warnings contained in the parable of the ten virgins and the to warnings about the good man of the house who would have watched if he had known when the thief would come.

The point of all these parables is simple: Watch! You do not know when the Lord will come.

The Lord will come with glory and majesty:

When the Son of man shall come in his glory, and all the holy angels with him, then shall he sit upon the throne of his glory. And before him shall be gathered all nations, and he shall separate them one from another, as a shepherd divideth his sheep from the goats. And he shall set the sheep on the right hand, but the goats on the left.

Then shall the King say unto them on his right hand, "Come, ye blessed of my Father, inherit the Kingdom prepared for you from the foundation of the world: for I was an hungred, and ye gave me meat; I was thirsty, and ye gave me drink; I was a stranger, and ye took me in; naked, and ye clothed me; I was sick, and ye visited me; I was in prison, and ye came unto me."

Then shall the righteous answer him, saying, "Lord, when saw we thee an hungred, and fed thee? Or thirsty, and gave thee drink? When saw we thee a stranger, and took thee in? Or naked, and clothed thee? Or when saw we thee sick, or in prison, and came unto thee?"

And the King shall answer and say unto them, "Verily I say unto you, inasmuch as ye have done it unto one of the least of these my brethren, ye have done it unto me."

Then shall he say also unto them on the left hand, "Depart from me, ye cursed, into everlasting fire, prepared for the devil and his angels: for I was an hungred, and ye gave me no meat; I was thirsty, and ye gave me no drink; I was a stranger, and ye took me not in; naked, and ye clothed me not; sick, and in prison, and ye visited me not."

Then shall they also answer him, saying, "Lord, when saw we thee an hungred, or athirst, or a stranger, or naked, or sick, or in prison, and did not minister unto thee?"

Then shall he answer them, saying, "Verily I say unto you, inasmuch as ye did it not to one of the least of these, ye did it not to me."

And these shall go away into everlasting punishment, but the righteous into life eternal. *Mt 25:31–46*

The preachers of judgment and righteousness preach the verses of repentance and salvation; but the sheep who shall inherit the Kingdom of God are those who fed the hungry, clothed the naked, and visited the sick and imprisoned. The shouters of the Lord's imminent return are usually not much interested in the hungry, naked, sick and imprisoned; those who remember the hungry, naked, sick and imprisoned do not believe that the world will ever end or that the Lord would be so gross as to send anyone into everlasting fire. The world does not believe that the Son of man will come in his glory and sit in judgment upon all nations for it believes that there is no God, or, in any case, that the eternal laws of God have been suspended due to lack of interest.

A CATECHISM:
JESUS' ANSWERS

Who is God?

Jesus said that "God is . . . Spirit." *J 4:24*

How is God to be worshipped?

Jesus said that they that worship God "must worship him in spirit and in truth." *J 4:24*

Is there more than one god?

Jesus said that "the Lord our God is one Lord" and that the Father is "the only true God." *Mk 12:29; J 17:3*

Has anyone ever seen God?

Jesus said that no man "hath seen the Father, save he which is of God, he hath seen the Father" and that "Ye have neither heard his voice at any time, nor seen his shape." *J 6:46; 5:37*

Jesus also said:

He that hath seen me hath seen the Father. *J 14:9*

He that seeth me seeth him that sent me. *J 12:45*

How then can I know God?
Jesus said:

If ye had known me, ye should have known my Father also. *J 8:19, 14:7*

How did Jesus describe his relationship to God?
Jesus said that "my Father is greater than I" and that "I and my Father are one." *J 14:28, 10:30*

What did his statement that "I and my Father are one" mean to Jesus?
Jesus meant:

The Father is in me, and I in him. *J 10:38*

I am in the Father, and the Father in me. *J 14:10–11*

Thou, Father, art in me, and I in thee. *J 17:21*

Didn't Jesus describe himself in other ways than being one with the Father?
Yes. He said that I am "a man that hath told you the truth, which I have heard of God", and that "I am the Son of God." *J 8:40, 10:36; Mt 27:32. (J 9:35–37)*

Why did Jesus come into the world?
Jesus repeatedly said that the Father sent him. *Mk 9:37; Mt 10:40; L 9:48, 10:16; J 4:34, 5:23, 6:38–40, 44, 57, 7:28–29, 8:29, 42, 10:36, 12:49, 13:20, 14:24, 17:3, 18, 21, 23, 20:21*
Jesus also phrased it this way:

I am coming in my Father's name. *J 5:43*

I came forth from the Father and am come into the world. *J 16:28*

I proceeded forth and came from God; neither came I of myself, but he sent me. *J 8:42*

Did Jesus claim to preexist with God before he came in his Father's name?

Jesus said:

Before Abraham was, I AM. *J 8:58*

O Father, glorify thou me with thine own self with the glory which I had with thee before the world was. *J 17:5*

What was the source of Jesus' teaching?

Jesus said:

For I have not spoken of myself; but the Father which sent me, he gave me a commandment, what I should say, and what I should speak. *J 12:49*

As my Father hath taught me, I speak these things. *J 8:28*

My doctrine is not mine, but his that sent me." *J 7:16*

The word which ye hear is not mine, but the Father's which sent me. *J 14:24*

What proof did Jesus offer for his claim that he taught what God had given him?

Jesus said:

My doctrine is not mine, but his that sent me. If any man will do his will, he shall know of the doctrine, whether it be of God, or whether I speak of myself. *J 7:16–17*

If I do not the works of my Father, believe me not. But if I do, though ye believe me not, believe the works. *J 10:37–38*

What does it mean to believe on Jesus?
Jesus said:

He that believeth on me, believeth not on me, but on him that sent me. *J 12:44*

He that receiveth me receiveth him that sent me. *Mt 10:40*

Whosoever shall receive me, receiveth not me, but him that sent me. *Mk 9:37*

Whosoever shall receive me receiveth him that sent me. *L 9:48*

He that receiveth me receiveth him that sent me. *J 13:20*

He that despiseth me despiseth him that sent me. *L 10:16*

How shall we do the work of God?
Jesus said:

This is the work of God, that ye believe on him whom he hath sent. *J 6:29*

Are there many paths to God?
Jesus said:

I am the way, the truth, and the life; no man cometh unto the Father but by me. *J 14:6*

Verily, verily, I say unto you, I am the door of the sheep. All that ever came before me are thieves and robbers, but the sheep did not hear them. I am the door; by me if any man enter in, he shall be saved, and shall go in and out, and find pasture. *J 10:7–9*

Who has eternal life?

Jesus said:

Verily, verily, I say unto you, he that heareth my word, and believeth on him that sent me, hath everlasting life. *J 5:24*
Verily, verily, I say unto you, he that believeth on me hath everlasting life. *J 6:47*

Verily, verily, I say unto you, if a man keep my saying, he shall never see death. *J 8:51*

Whosoever liveth and believeth in me shall never die. *J 11:26*

Jesus also said that he was the bread of life "which cometh down from heaven, that a man may eat thereof and not die" and "he shall live forever." *J 6:48, 50–51*

What is eternal life?

Jesus said:

This is life eternal, that they might know thee the only true God, and Jesus Christ, whom thou hast sent. *J 17:3*

Who are Jesus' true disciples?

Jesus said:

If ye continue in my word, then are ye my disciples indeed. *J 8:31*

Where two or three are gathered together in my name, there am I in the midst of them. *Mt 18:20*

By this shall all men know that ye are my disciples, if ye have love one to another. *J 13:35*

How did Jesus characterize his true disciples?

Jesus said:

Ye are my friends, if ye do whatsoever I command you. Henceforth I call you not servants: for the servant knoweth not what his lord doeth; but I have called you friends, for all things that I have heard of my Father I have made known unto you. *J 15:14–15*

What did Jesus teach about being born again?

Jesus said:

Except a man be born of water and of the Spirit, he cannot enter into the Kingdom of God. That which is born of the flesh is flesh; and that which is born of the Spirit is spirit. Marvel not that I said unto thee, "Ye must be born again." *J 3:5–7*

How is one born of the Spirit?

Jesus said:

The wind bloweth where it listeth, and thou hearest the sound thereof, but canst not tell whence it cometh, and whither it goeth: so is every one that is born of the Spirit. *J 3:8*

What does the Spirit do after you are born of the Spirit?

Jesus said that "he dwelleth with you, and shall be in you." *J 14:17*

What else does the Holy Spirit do?

Jesus said:

These things have I spoken unto you, being yet present with you. But the Comforter, which is the Holy Spirit, whom the Father will send in my name, he shall teach you all things, and bring all things to your remembrance, whatsoever I have said unto you. *J 14:25–26*

What was Jesus' mission?

Jesus said:

As long as I am in the world, I am the light of the world. *J 9:5*

I am come a light into the world, that whosoever believeth on me should not abide in darkness. *J 12:46*

I am the light of the world; he that followeth me shall not walk in darkness, but shall have the light of life. *J 8:12*

Was Jesus' mission judgment?

No. Jesus said:

If any man hear my words, and believe not, I judge him not: for I come not to judge the world, but to save the world. *J 12:47*

What is the conclusion of the whole matter?

Jesus said:

Verily, verily, I say unto you, he that heareth my word, and believeth on him that sent me, hath everlasting life, and shall not come into condemnation, but is passed from death unto life. *J 5:24*

INDEX

MATTHEW

MATTHEW

Matthew

MATTHEW

Matthew

Matthew

MATTHEW

MATTHEW

MATTHEW

MATTHEW

Matthew

MATTHEW

Matthew

Matthew

MATTHEW

MATTHEW

Matthew

MATTHEW — MARK

MARK

Mark

MARK

Mark

MARK

Mark

MARK

Mark

Mark

MARK

Mark

Mark — Luke

LUKE

LUKE

LUKE

LUKE

LUKE

LUKE

LUKE

Luke

LUKE

LUKE

LUKE

LUKE

Luke

LUKE

John

John

John

John

JOHN

John

JOHN

9:11	155, 939, 947, 950, 995	9:35	157, 733, 939, 950, 996, 1057, 1128
9:12	155, 939	9:36	157, 733, 939, 950, 996, 1057, 1128
9:13	156, 939, 947		
9:14	155, 702, 939, 947, 975	9:37	157, 733, 939, 950, 1057, 1128
9:15	156, 702, 939, 947, 950	9:38	733, 939, 950, 1057
		9:39	157, 450, 1057
9:16	156, 453, 702, 939, 947, 948, 950, 975, 993	9:40	450, 1057
		9:41	158, 450, 867, 1057
		10:1	158
9:17	156, 939, 948, 950	10:2	158
9:18	156, 939, 948, 950	10:3	158
9:19	156, 939, 946, 950	10:4	158
9:20	156, 939, 946, 948, 949, 950	10:5	158
		10:6	475, 476
9:21	156, 939, 948, 950	10:7	159, 765, 860, 1130
9:22	154, 939, 948, 950	10:8	159, 860, 1130
9:23	939, 948, 950	10:9	159, 781, 850, 860, 1130
9:24	157, 939, 948, 950, 993		
		10:10	159
9:25	157, 939, 949, 950	10:11	159, 361, 765
9:26	157, 939, 949, 950	10:12	159
9:27	157, 939, 949, 950	10:13	159
9:28	157, 939, 949, 950, 993	10:14	159, 361, 433, 486, 587, 765
9:29	157, 939, 949, 950	10:15	159, 361, 433, 587, 765
9:30	157, 939, 949, 950		
9:31	157, 939, 949, 950	10:16	159, 361, 433
9:32	157, 939, 946, 949, 950	10:17	159, 739
		10:18	159, 568, 739
9:33	157, 939, 949, 950, 995	10:19	159, 568
		10:20	159, 568, 825
9:34	157, 939, 949, 950, 993	10:21	159, 825
		10:22	159, 160, 486
		10:23	160, 486

John

JOHN

JOHN

JOHN

John

John

John

JOHN — ACTS

Acts

ACTS

Acts

ACTS — 1 CORINTHIANS

1 Corinthians — Ephesians

PHILIPPIANS — 1 PETER

1 Peter — The Revelation

LEVITICUS — DEUTERONOMY

1 SAMUEL — PROVERBS

Isaiah — Malachi

Isaiah

Jeremiah

Ezekiel

Daniel

Hosea

Jonah

Micah

Zechariah

Malachi

Ancient Histories and Other Sources

To order additional copies of

A LAWYER
LOOKS AT THE
GOSPELS

send $44.95 plus shipping and handling to

Books Etc.
PO Box 1888
Seattle, WA 98104

or have your credit card ready and call

(800) 917-BOOK